SOLAR SAFARI

1

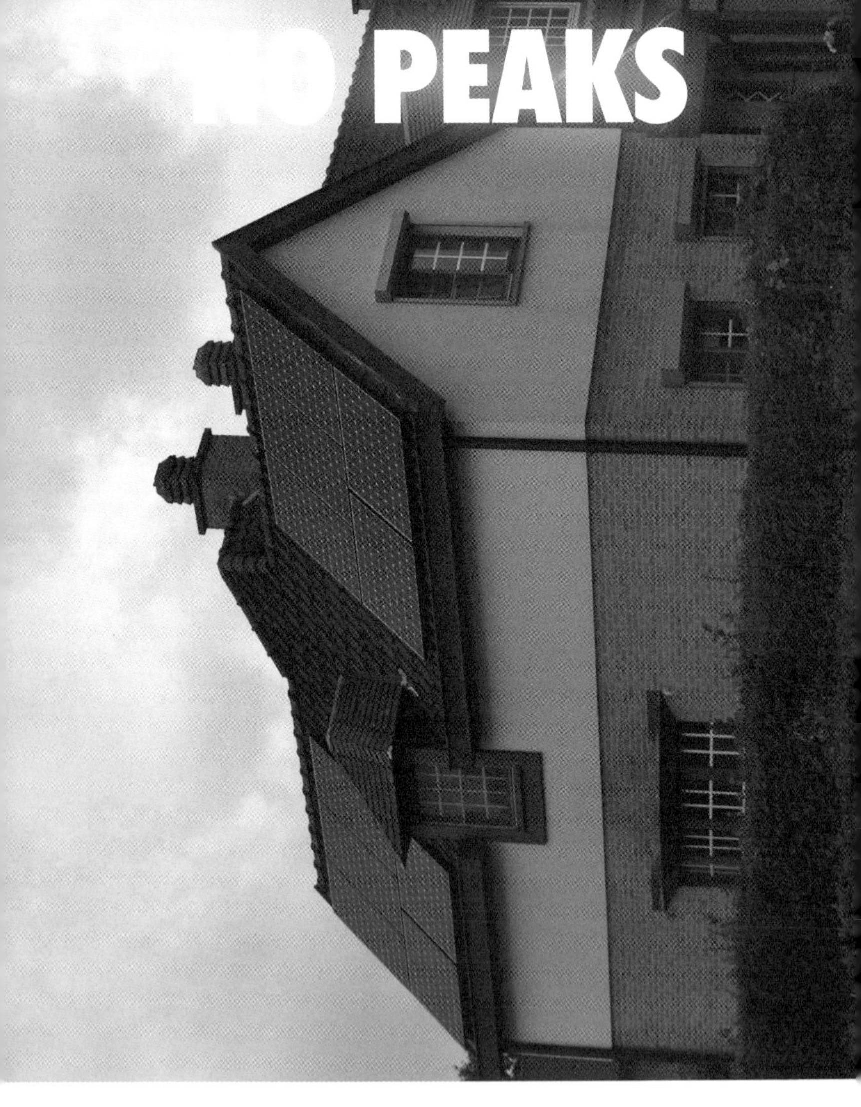
NO PEAKS

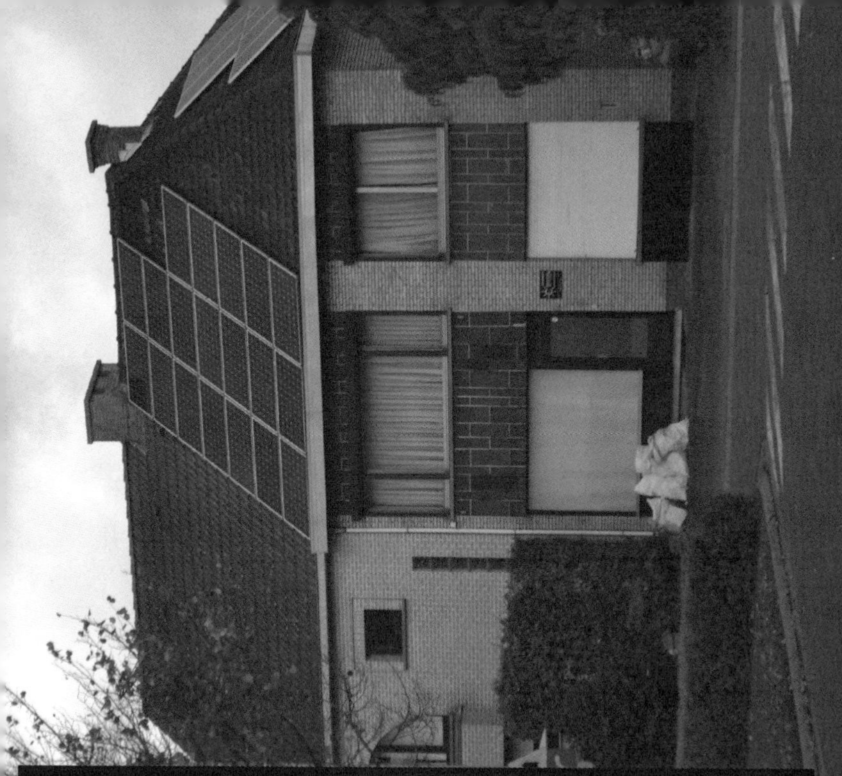

INTERNET GODZ

3

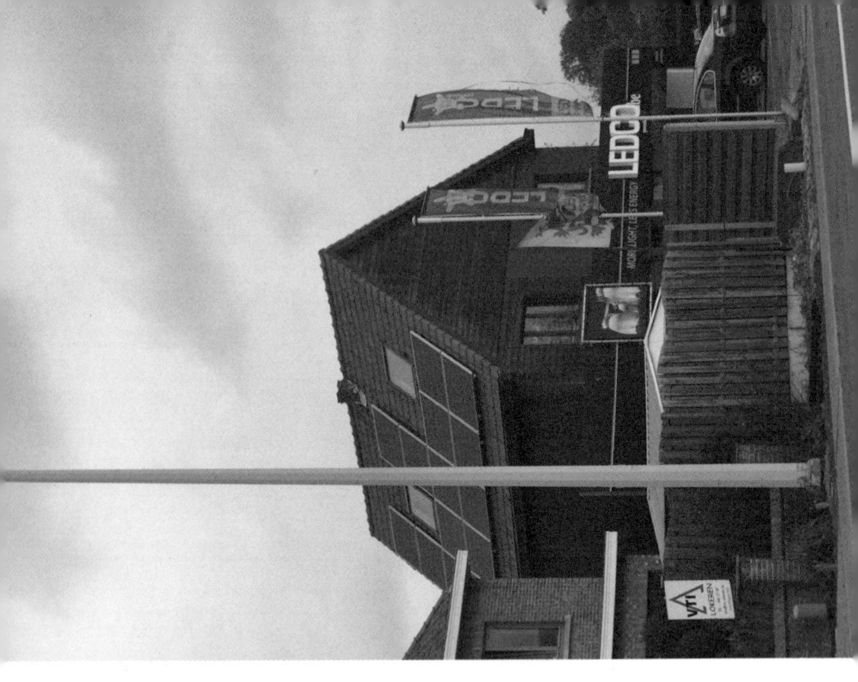

QUIETER LIGHTER PRETTIER

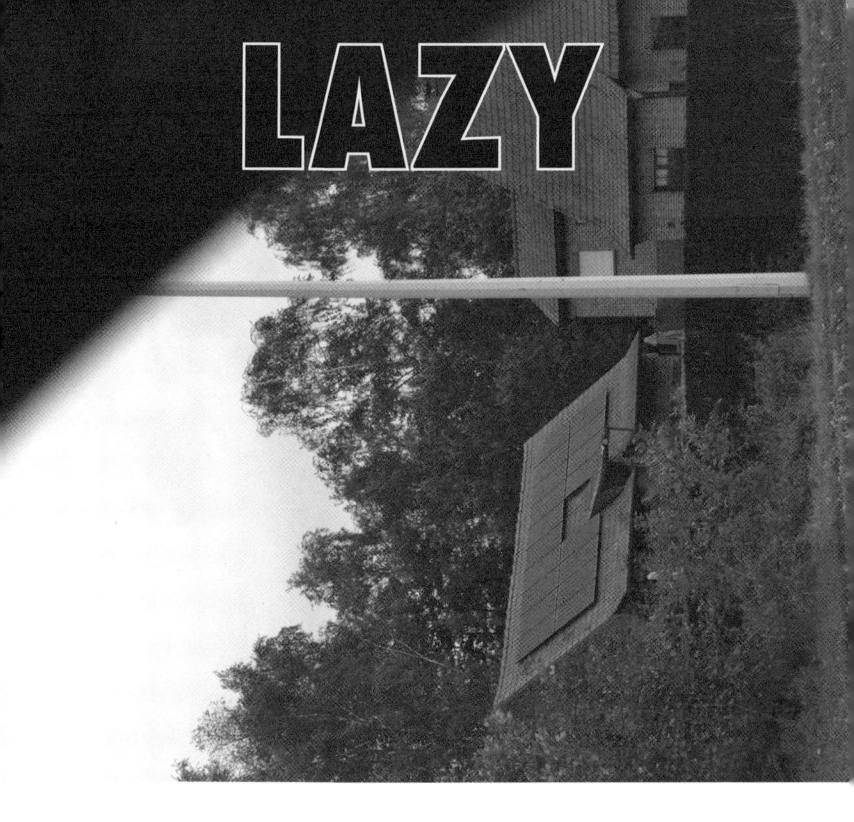

PRICE MOUNTAIN

5

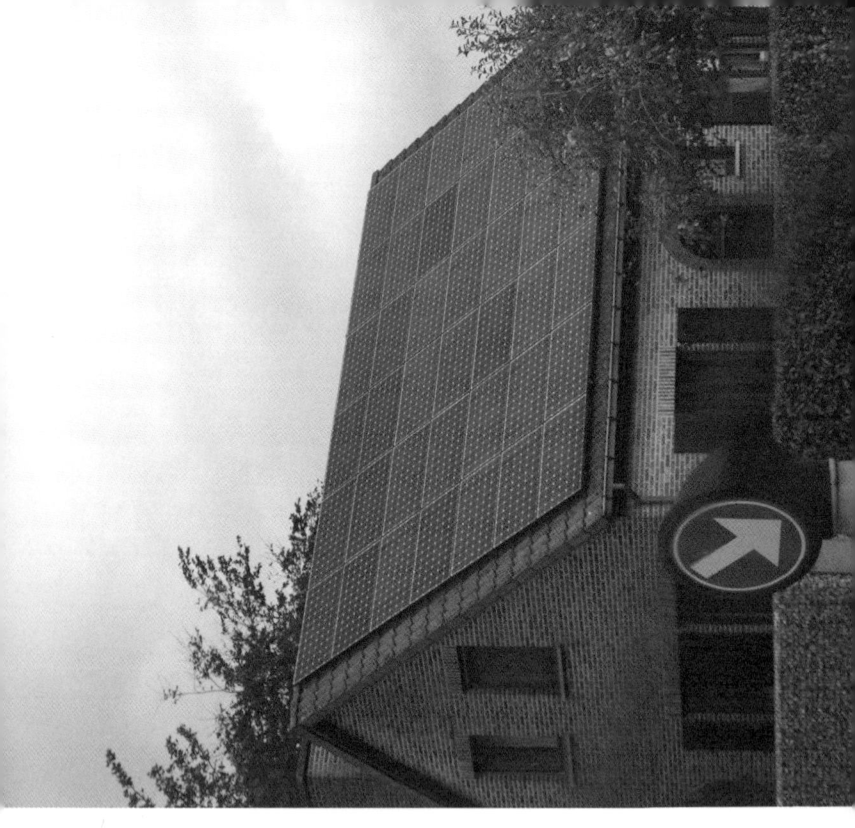

KISS MY GLUTEN

GARDEN DEAD

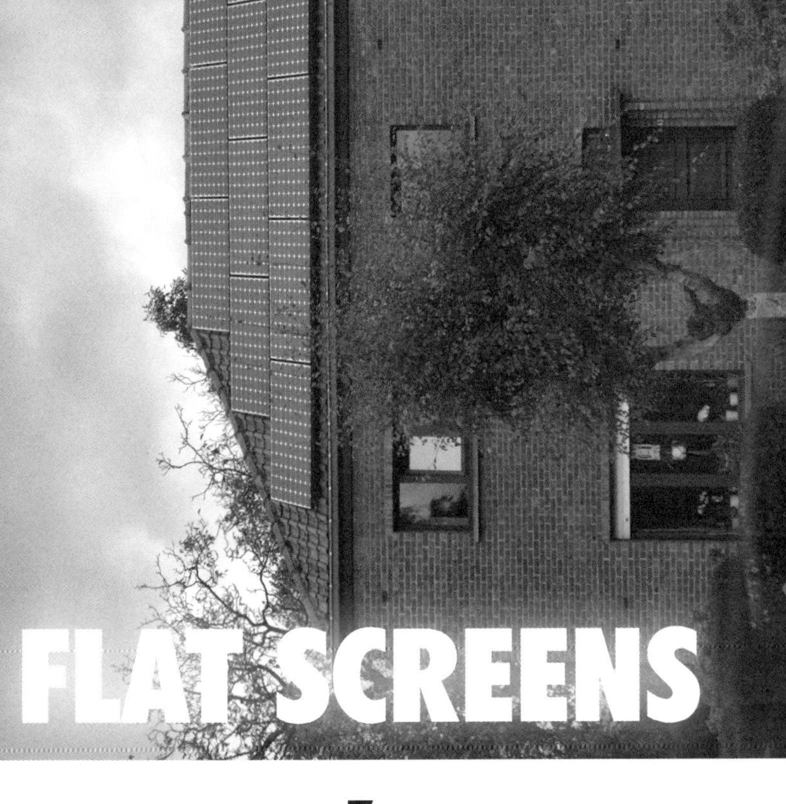

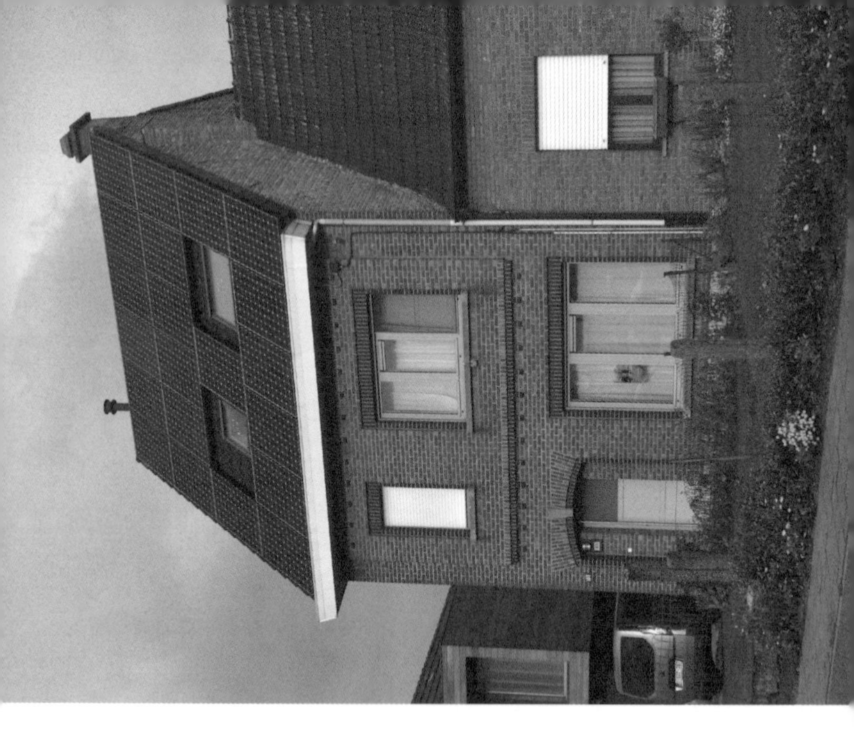

TWERKERS LEAKERS

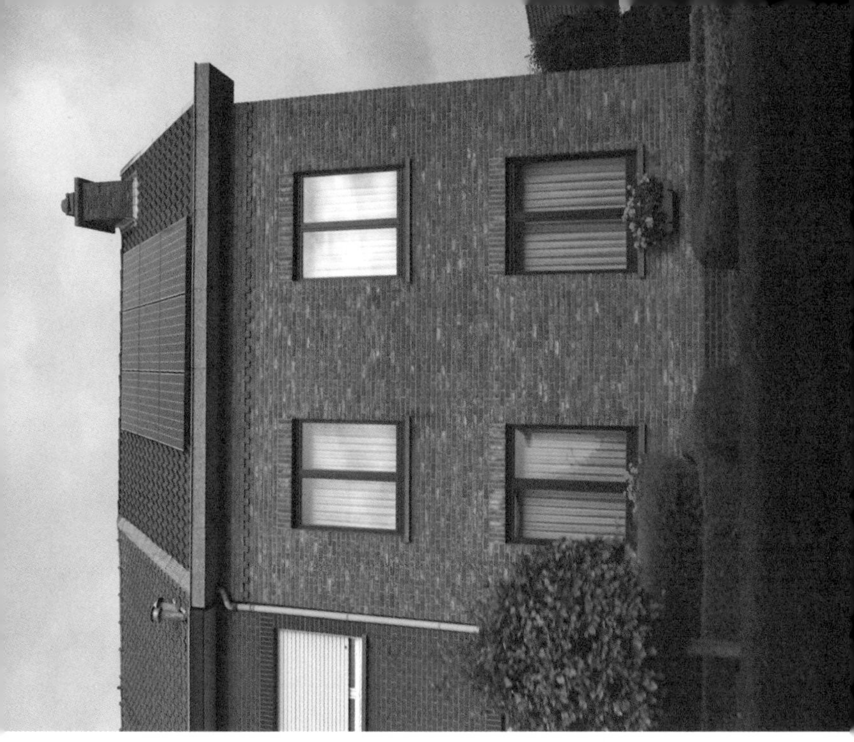

BAD BRAINS

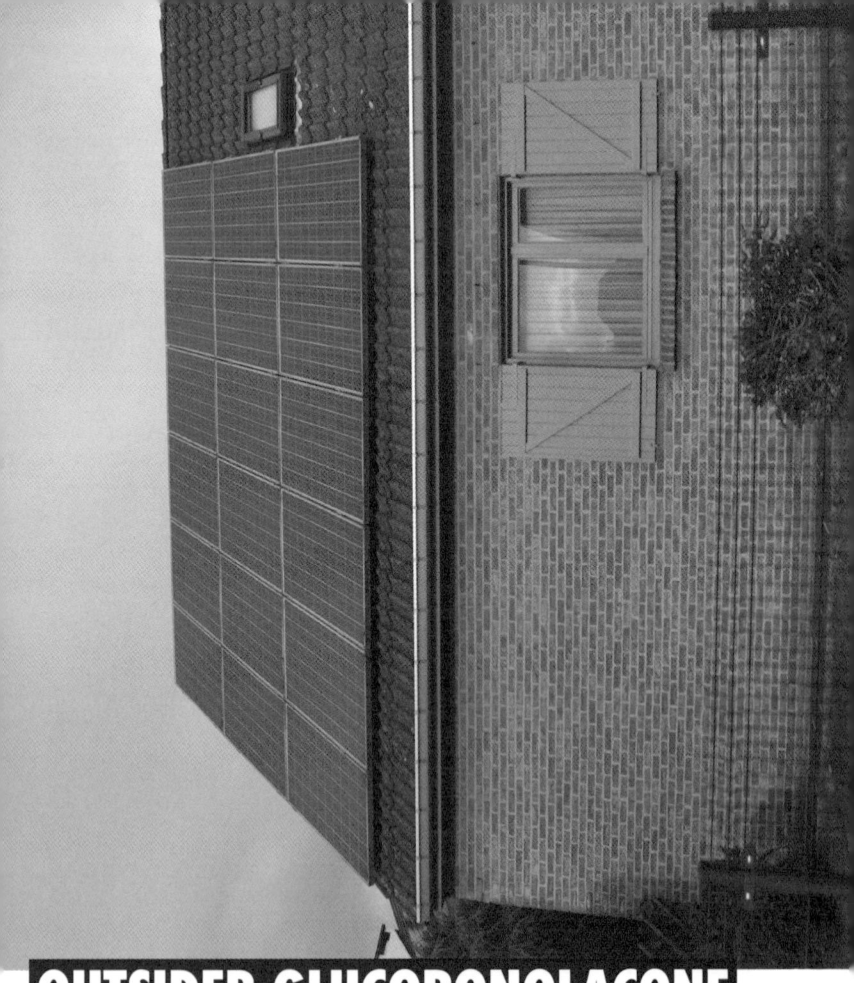

OUTSIDER GLUCORONOLACONE INOSITOL NIACIN PANTHOTHENE

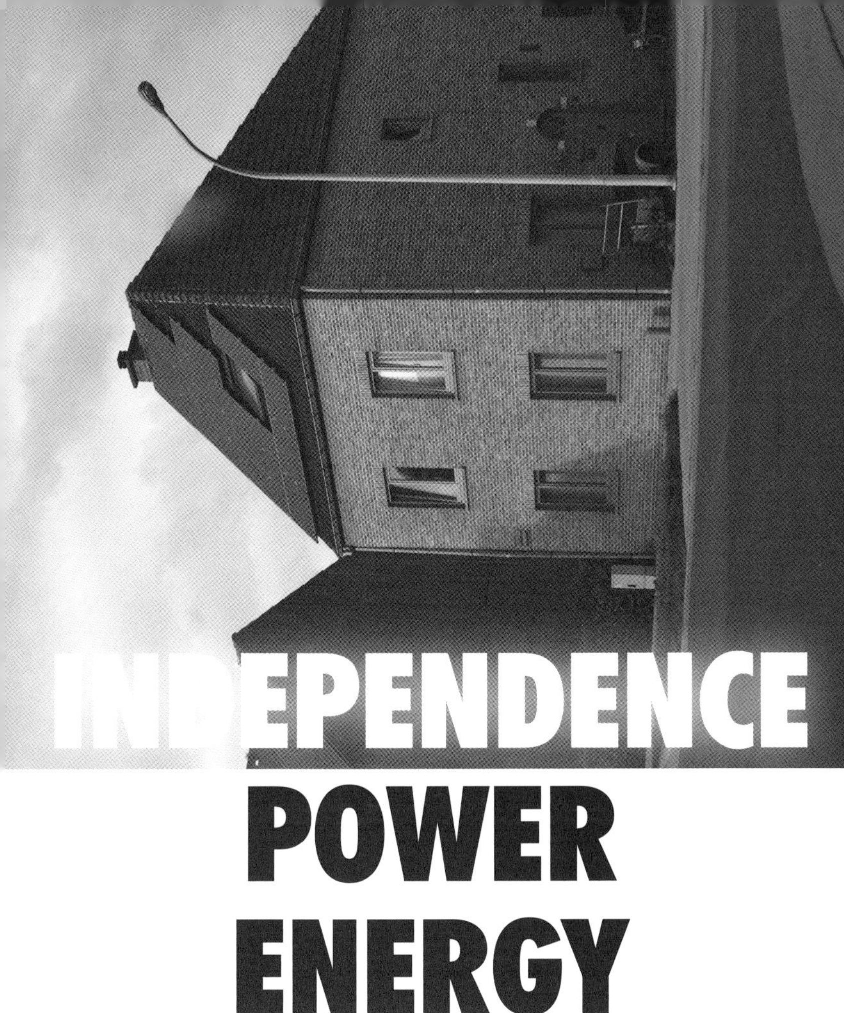

INDEPENDENCE
POWER
ENERGY

WIND TIME HUMAN SUN

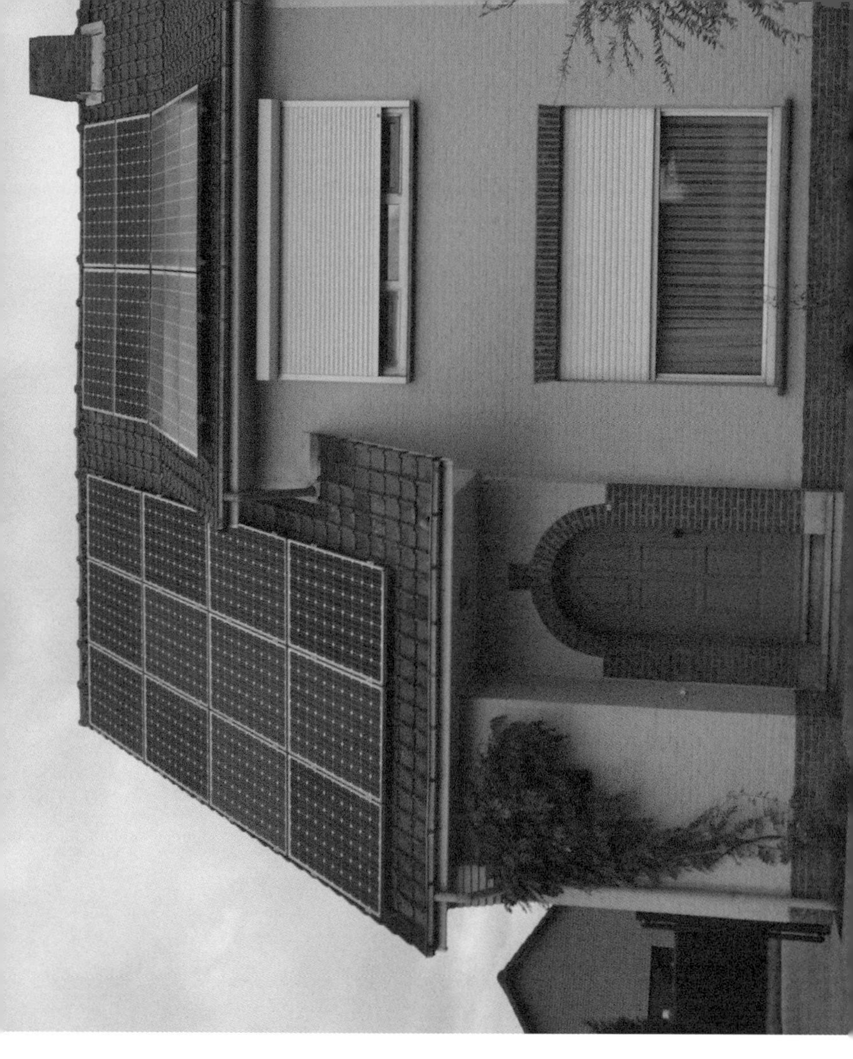

BIRDS LIFE SCIENCE MARS

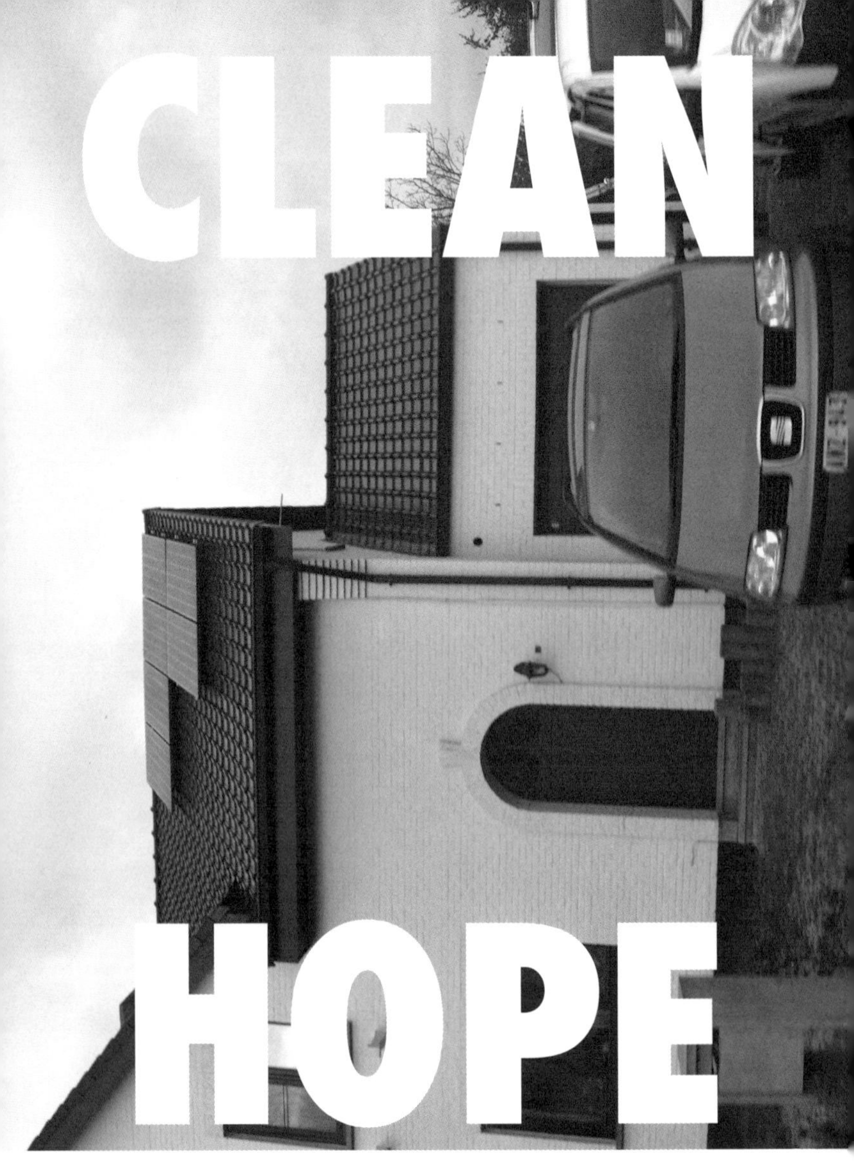
CLEAN
HOPE

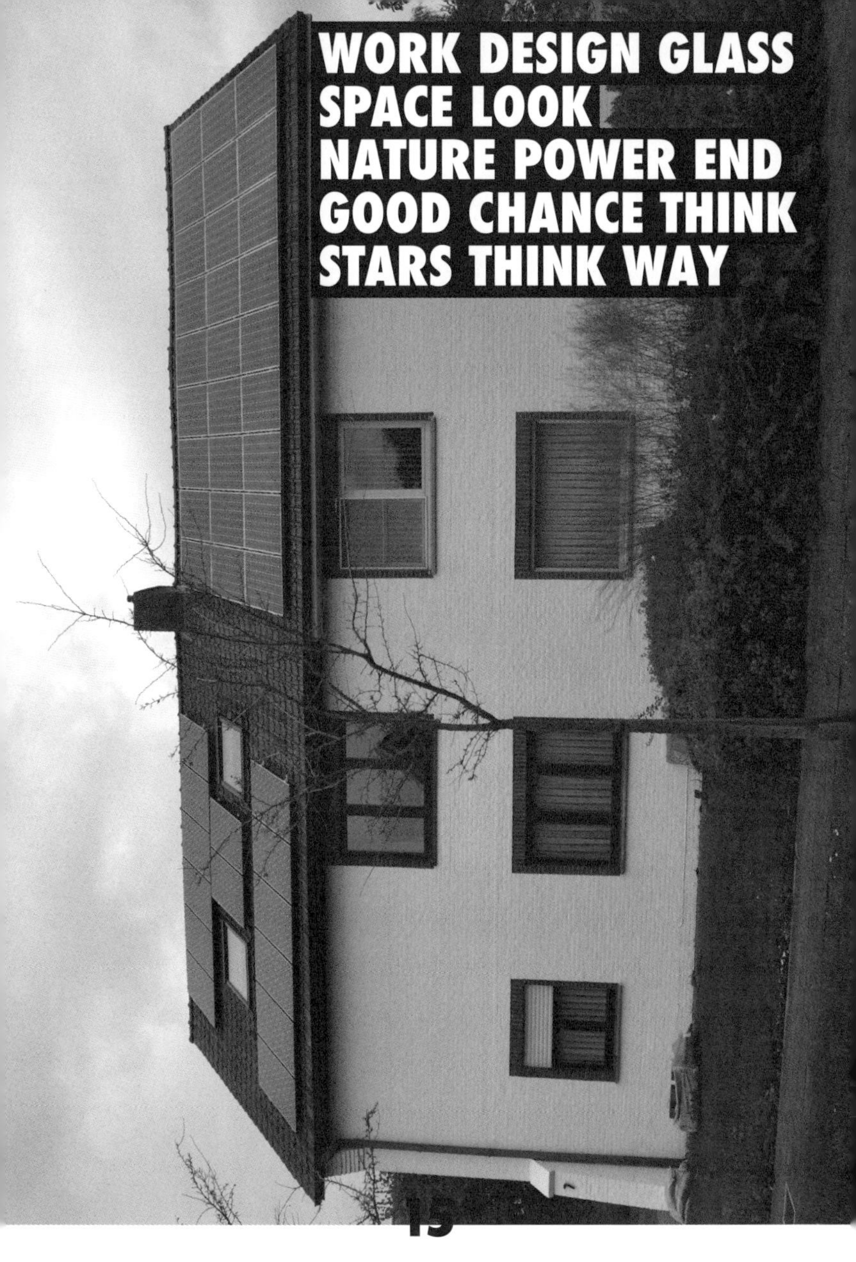
WORK DESIGN GLASS
SPACE LOOK
NATURE POWER END
GOOD CHANCE THINK
STARS THINK WAY

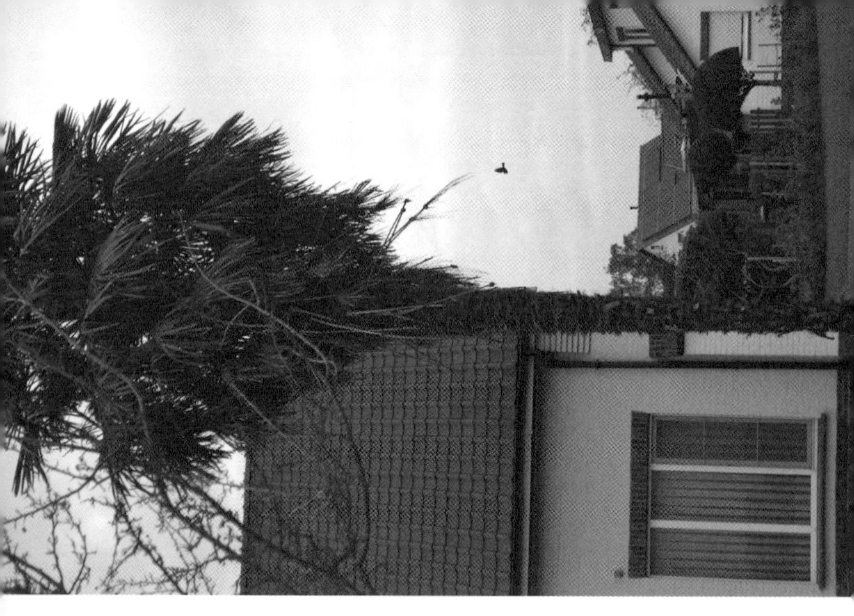

LIVING SOLAR WELL
LEARN SOLAR GO

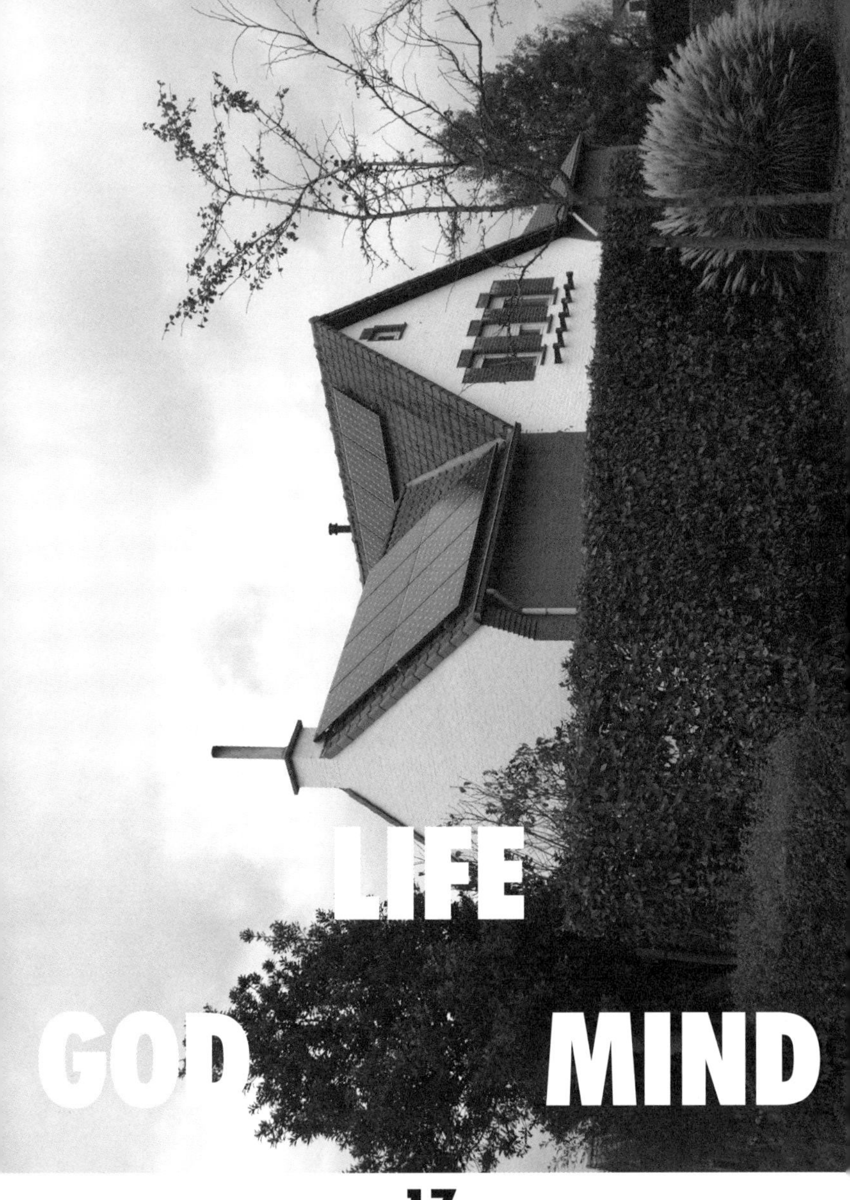
LIFE
GOD
MIND

BUSINESS POWER EASY HISTORY
ME THINKING DESERT WANT FARM

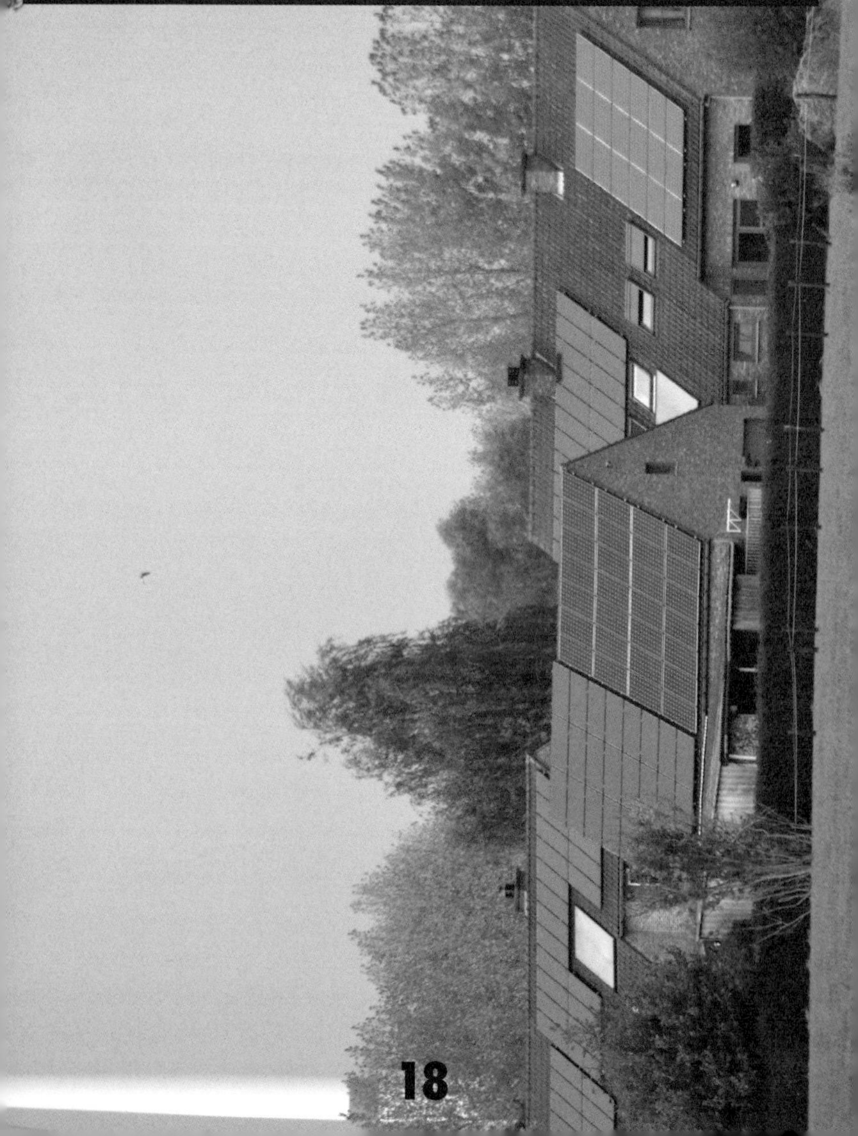

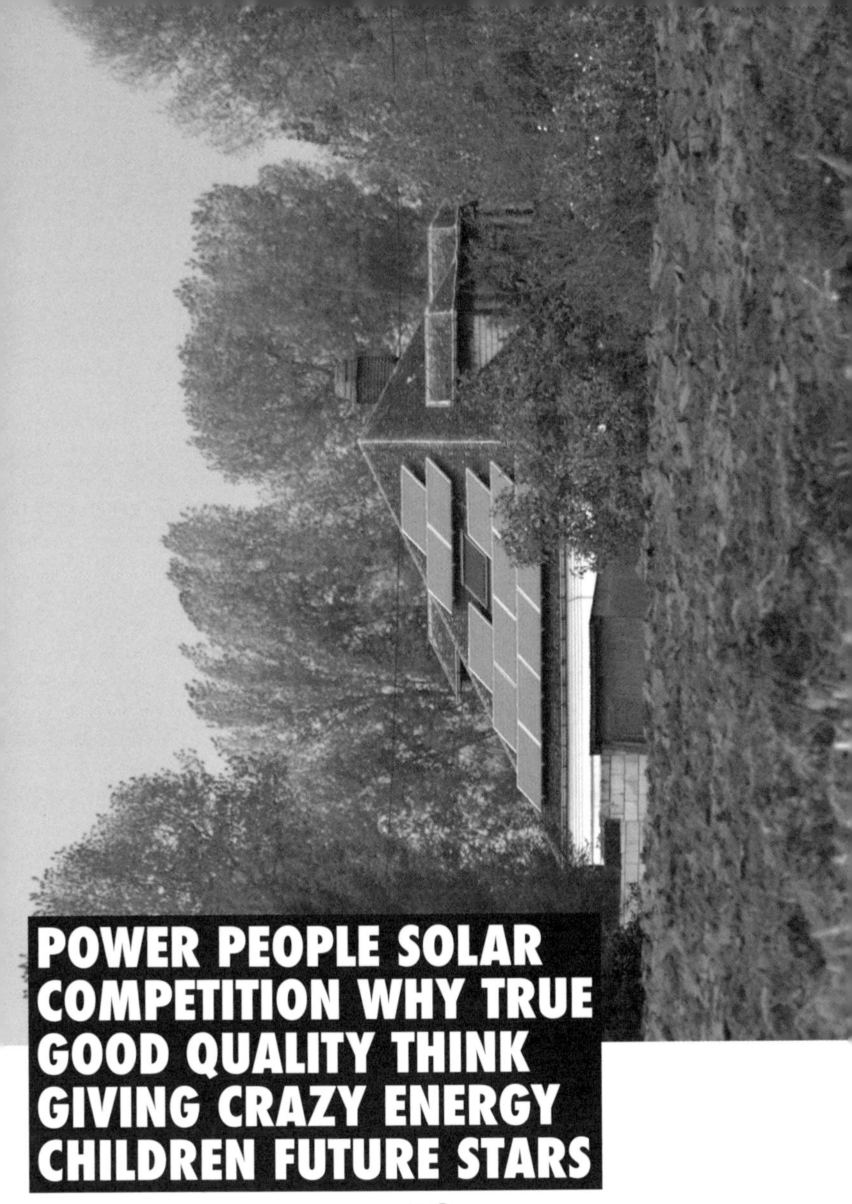
POWER PEOPLE SOLAR
COMPETITION WHY TRUE
GOOD QUALITY THINK
GIVING CRAZY ENERGY
CHILDREN FUTURE STARS

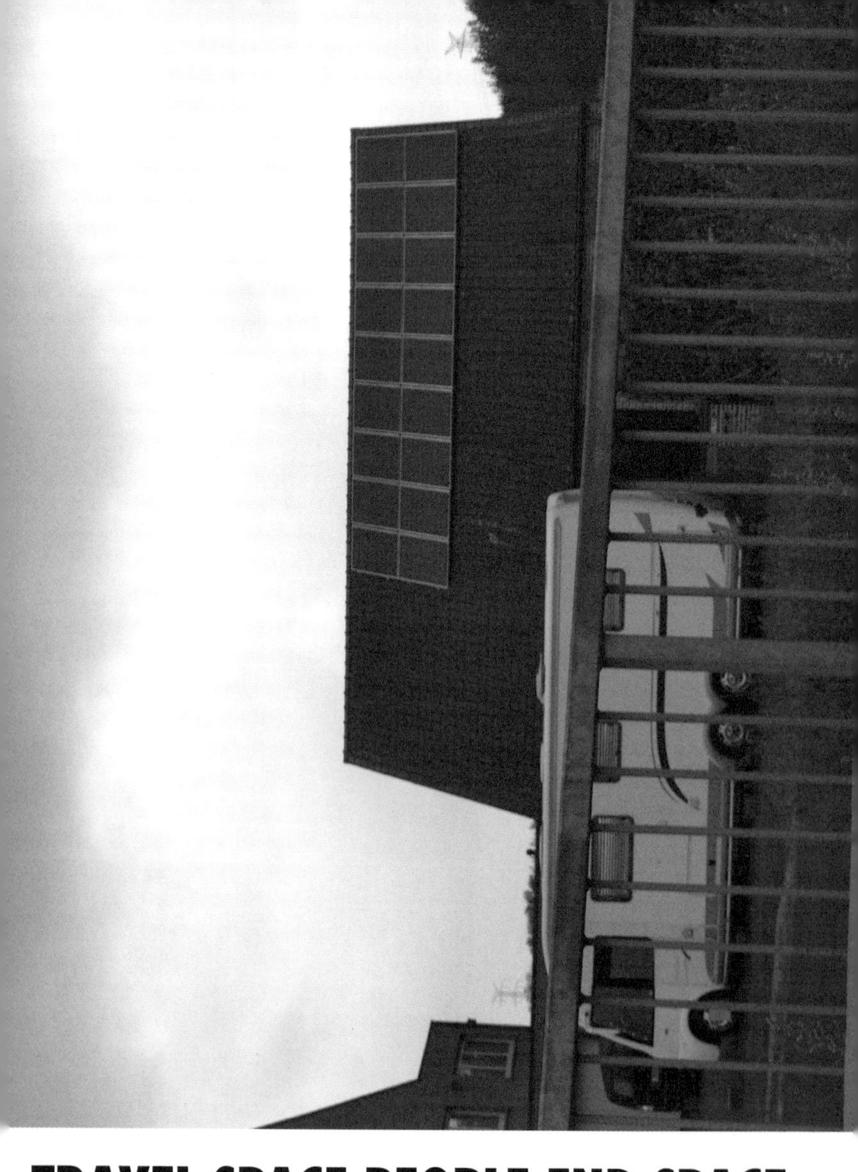

TRAVEL SPACE PEOPLE END SPACE

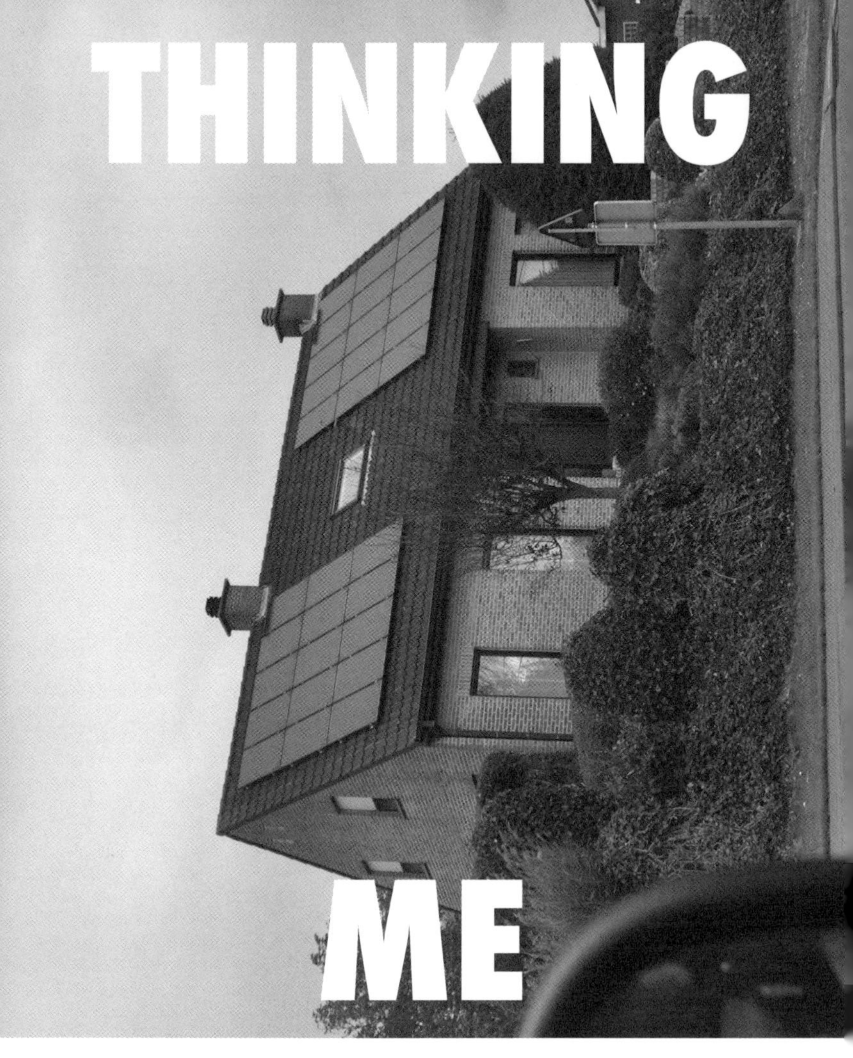
THINKING
ME

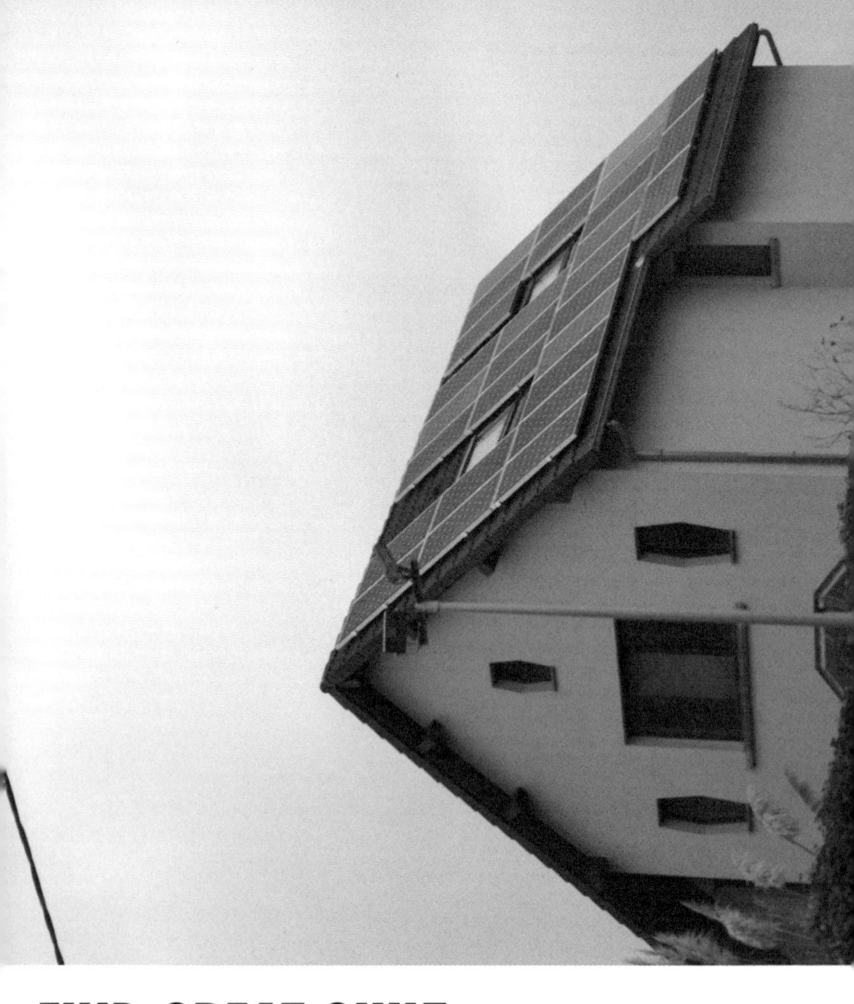

FIND GREAT GUILT

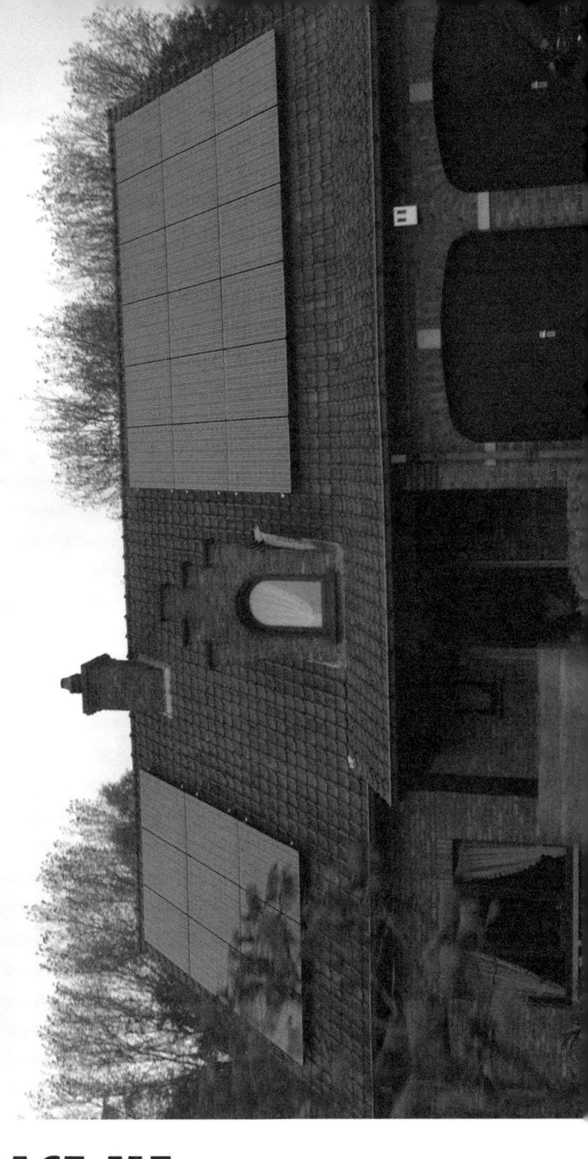

POWER SPACE ME
23

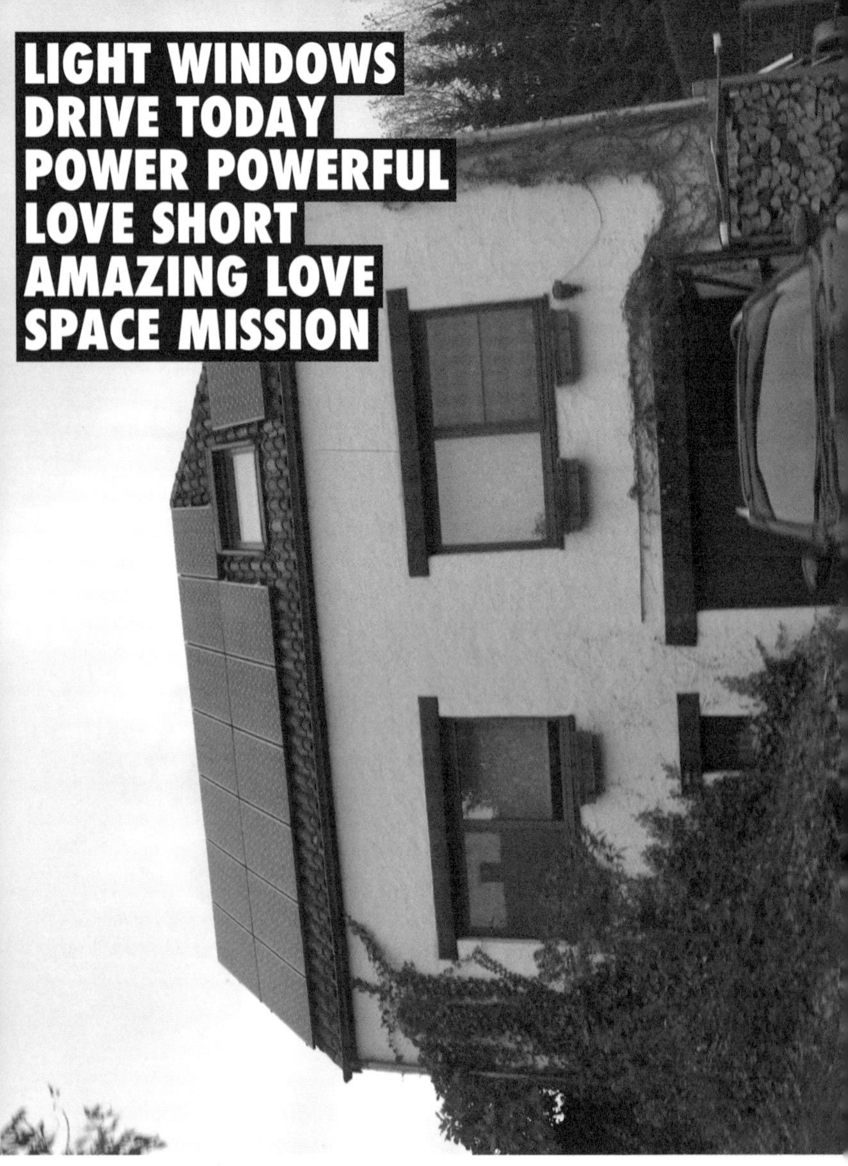
LIGHT WINDOWS
DRIVE TODAY
POWER POWERFUL
LOVE SHORT
AMAZING LOVE
SPACE MISSION

BUSINESS

SPACE

EXPLORATION

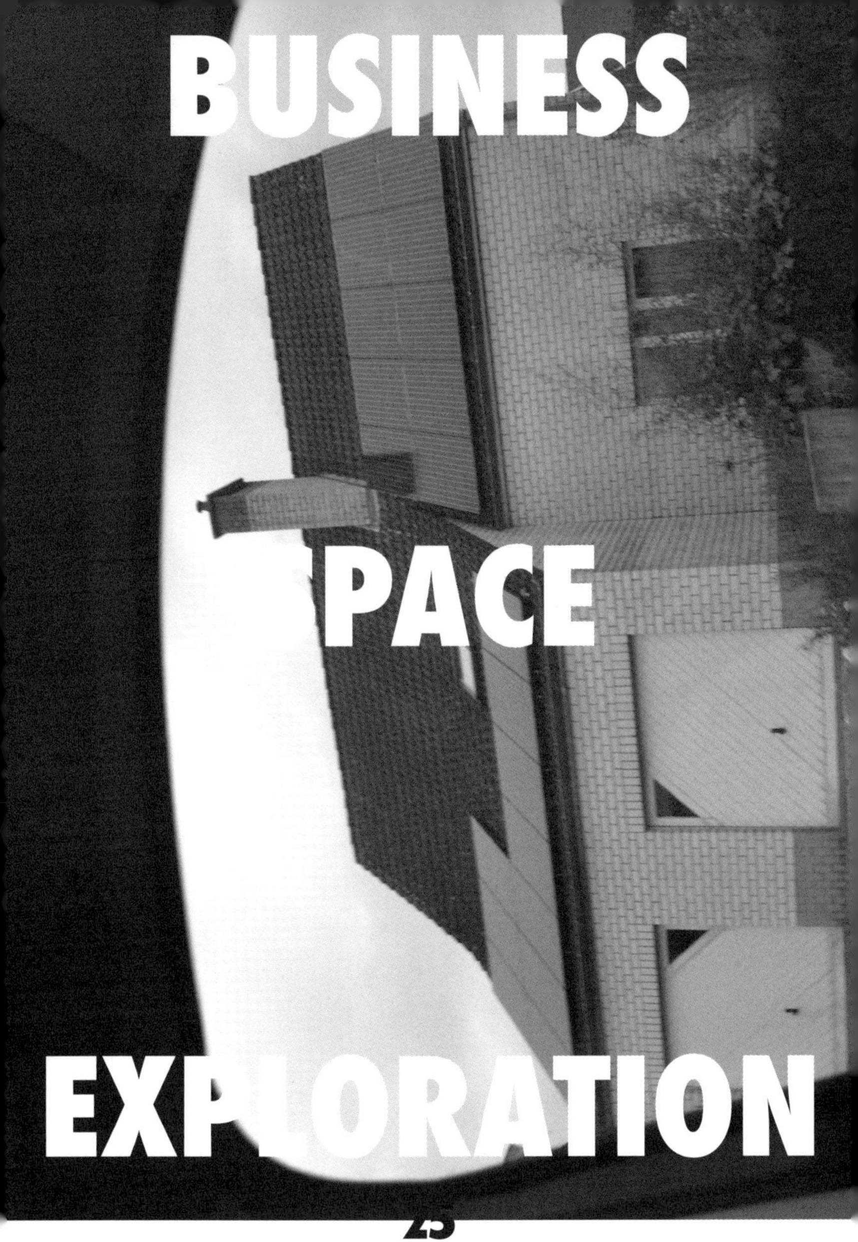

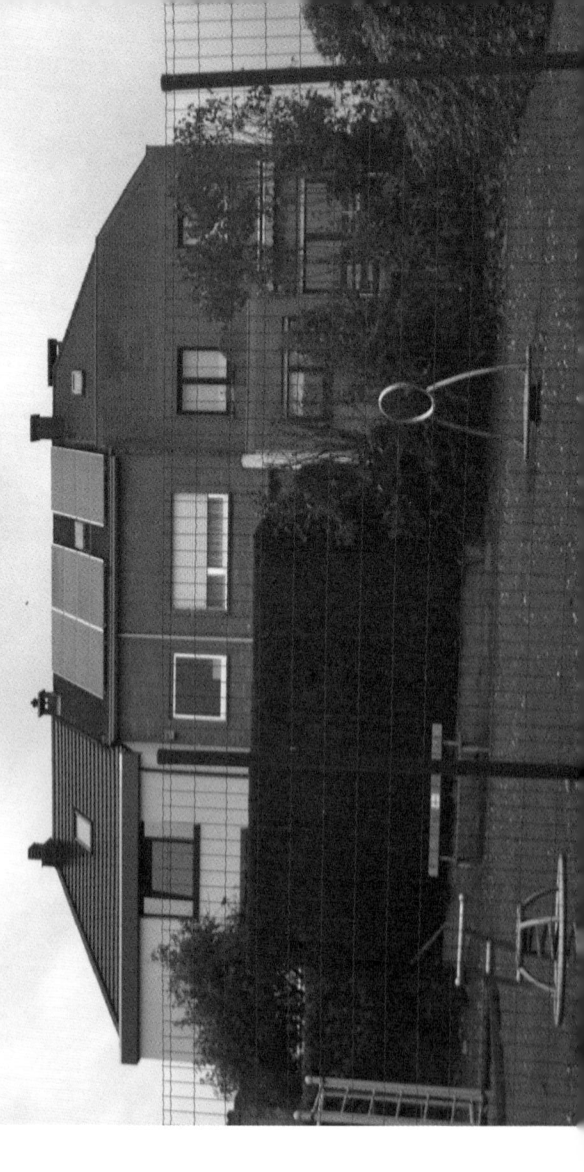

AMAZING
YOU
POWER
WORK
LEARNING
BEST

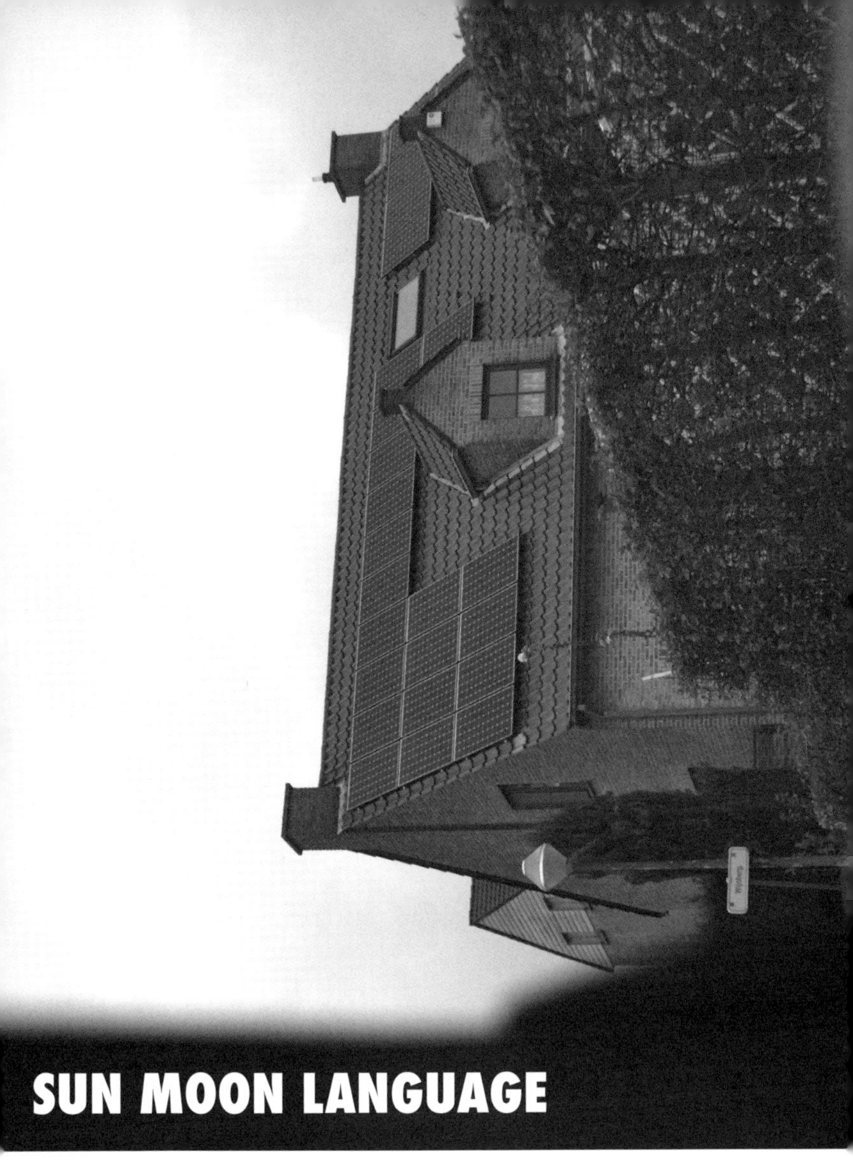

SUN MOON LANGUAGE

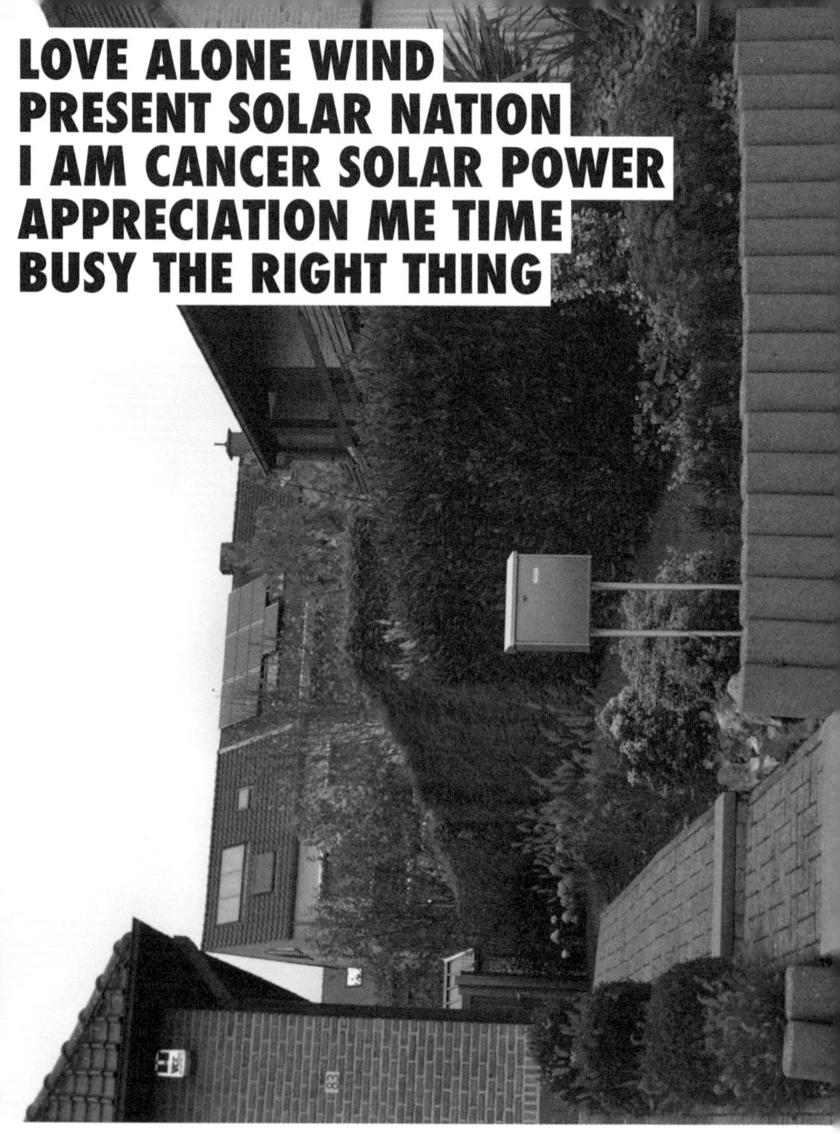

LOVE ALONE WIND
PRESENT SOLAR NATION
I AM CANCER SOLAR POWER
APPRECIATION ME TIME
BUSY THE RIGHT THING

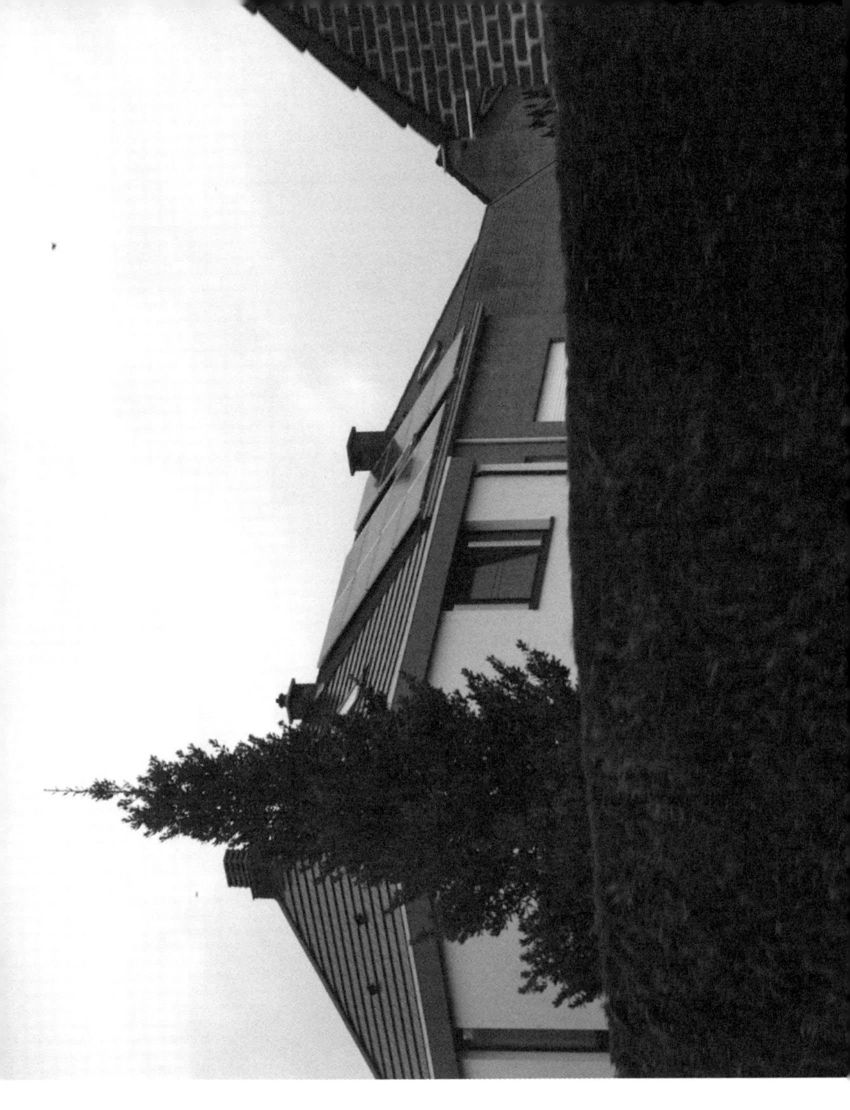

DEEP ICE CLASS

DOG DIVERSITY SELF

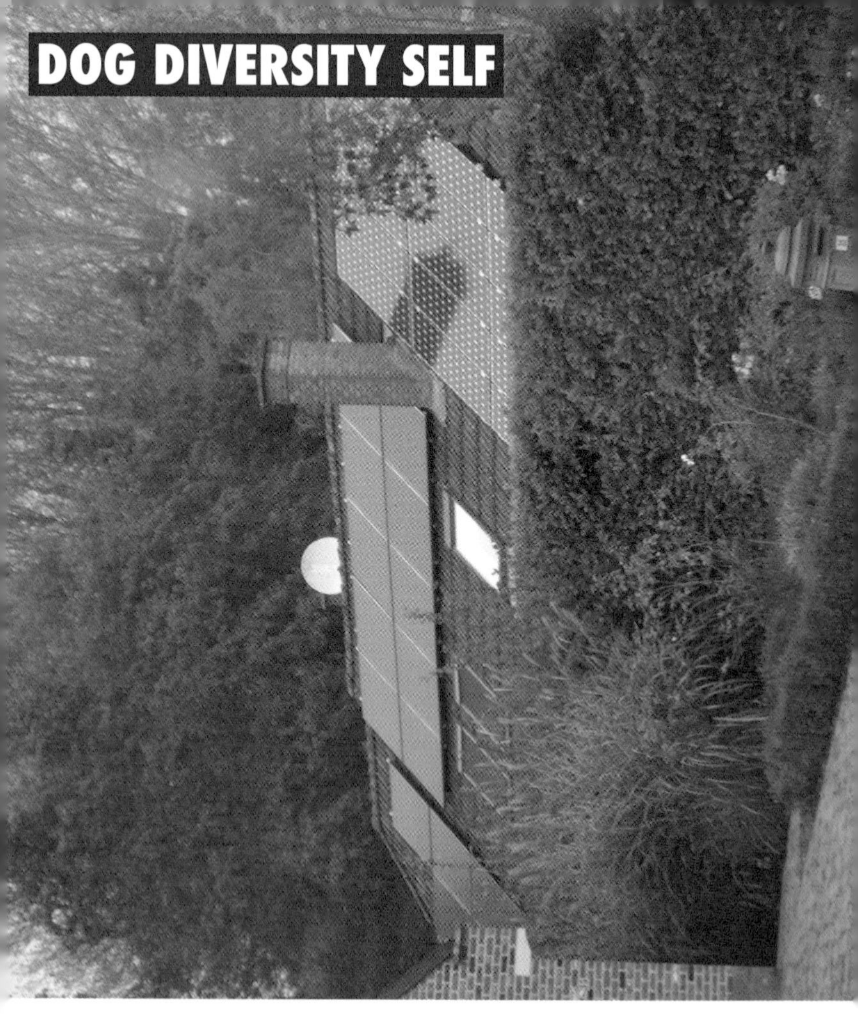

PUSH BLACK AND WHITE BLACK

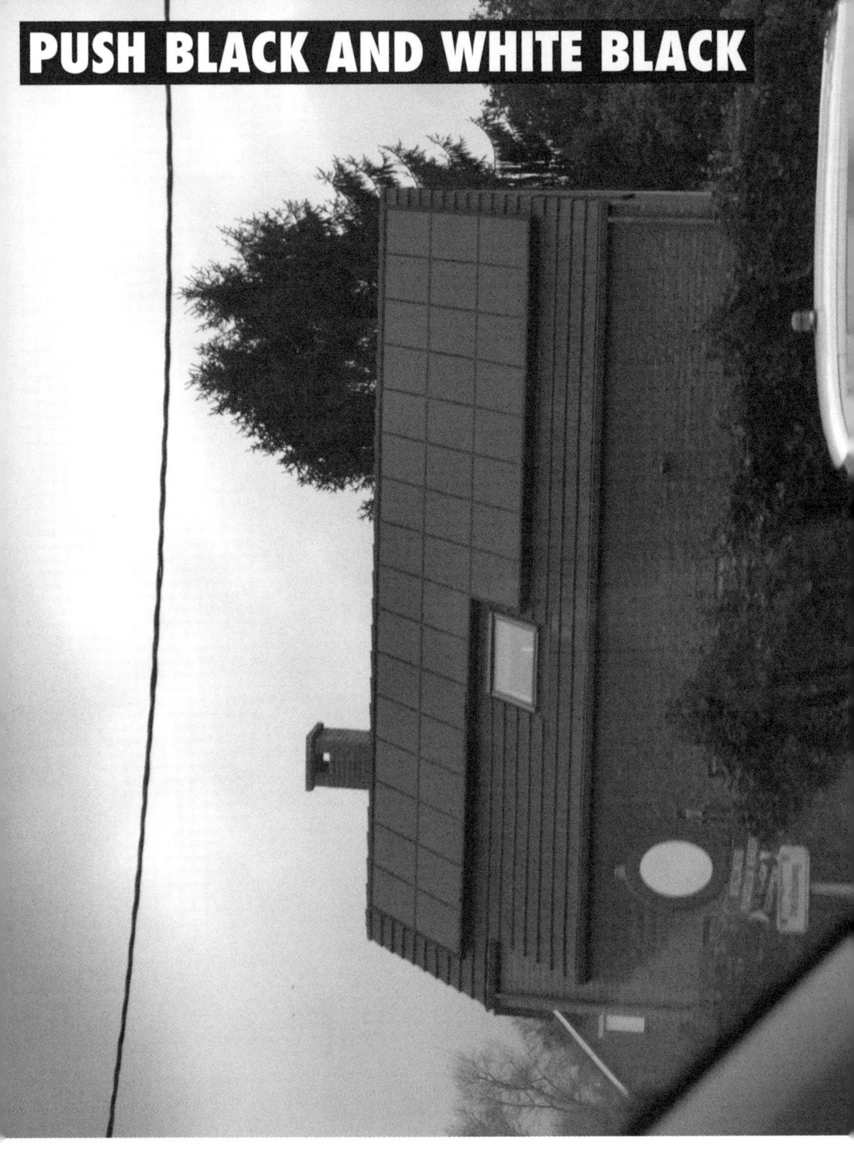

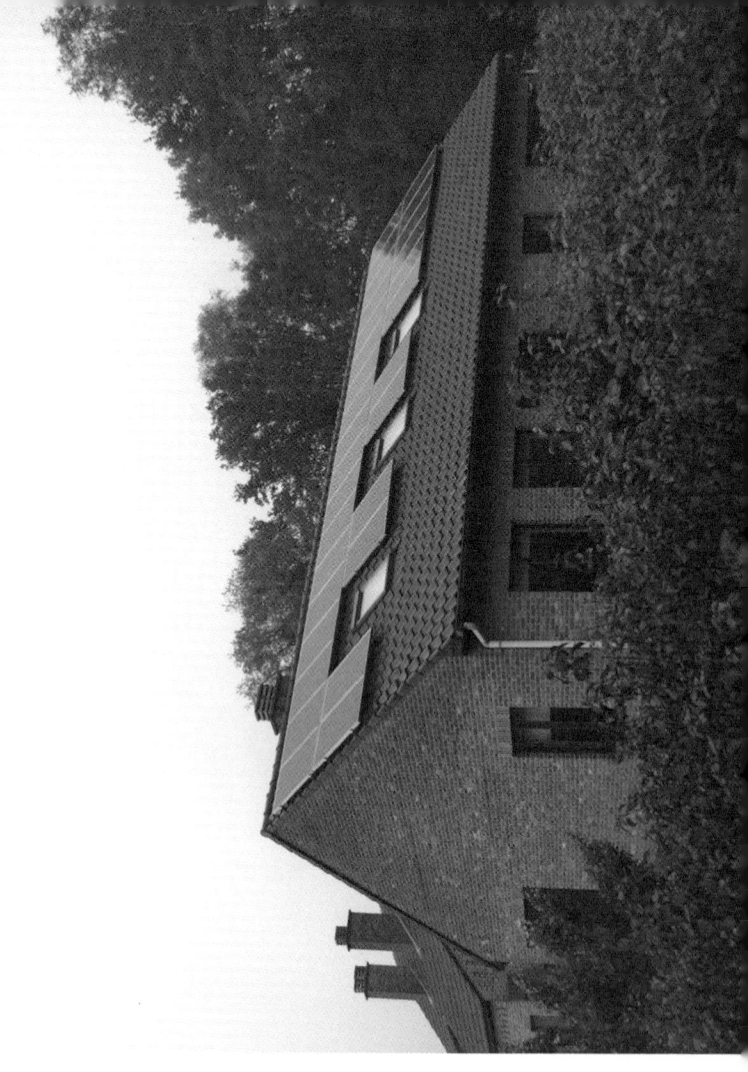

I AM REALITY MYSTERY

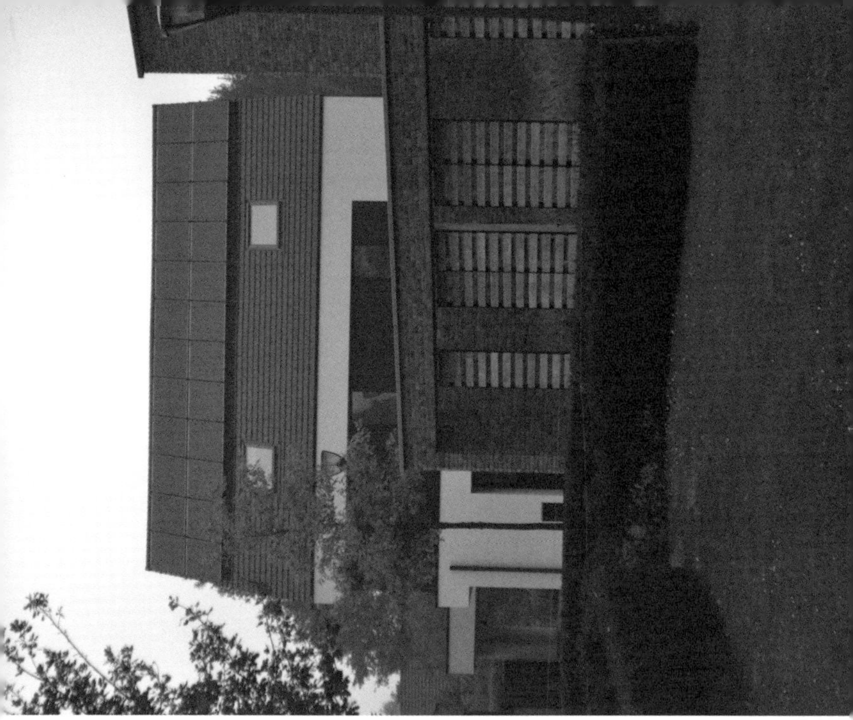

POOR LOOK REAL YOU

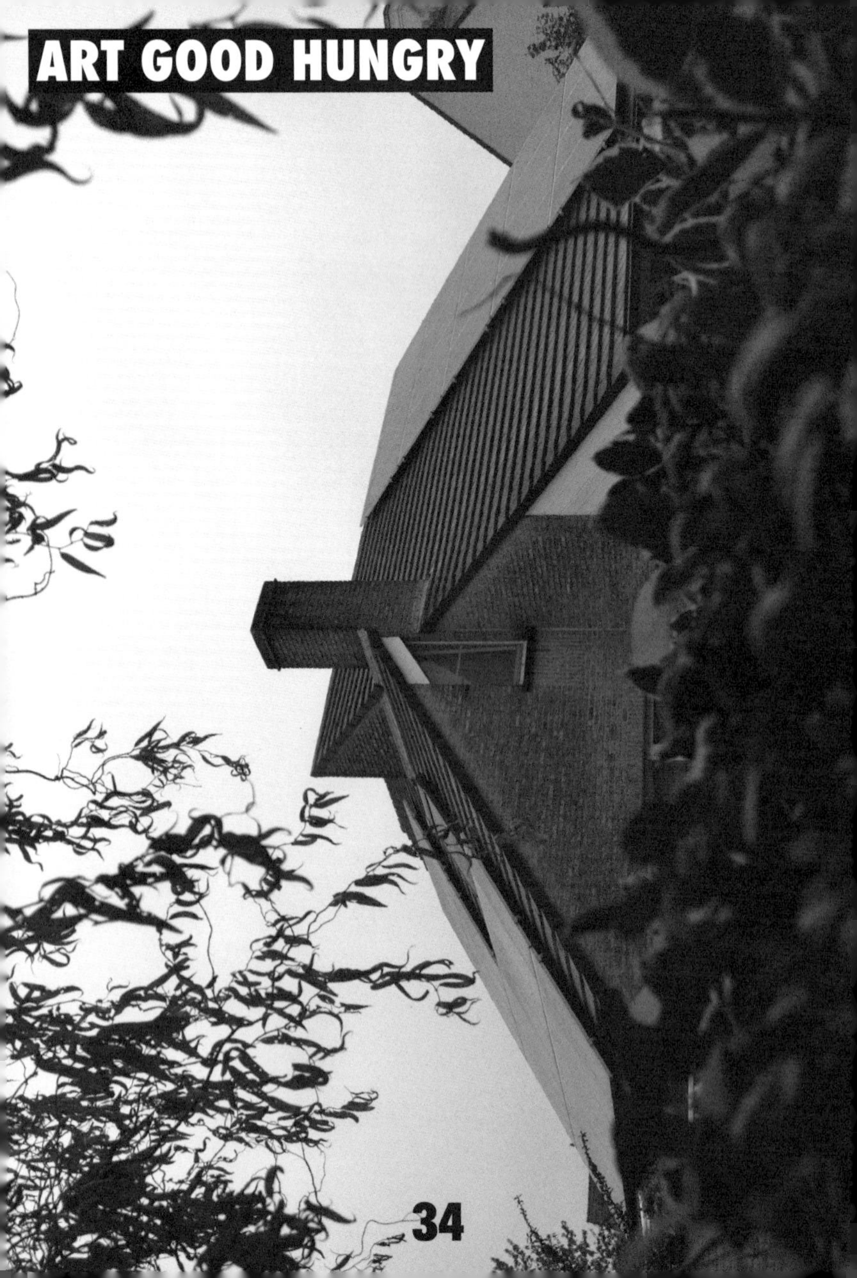

ATTRACTION COLOR DESIGN SYMBOLS REVENGE

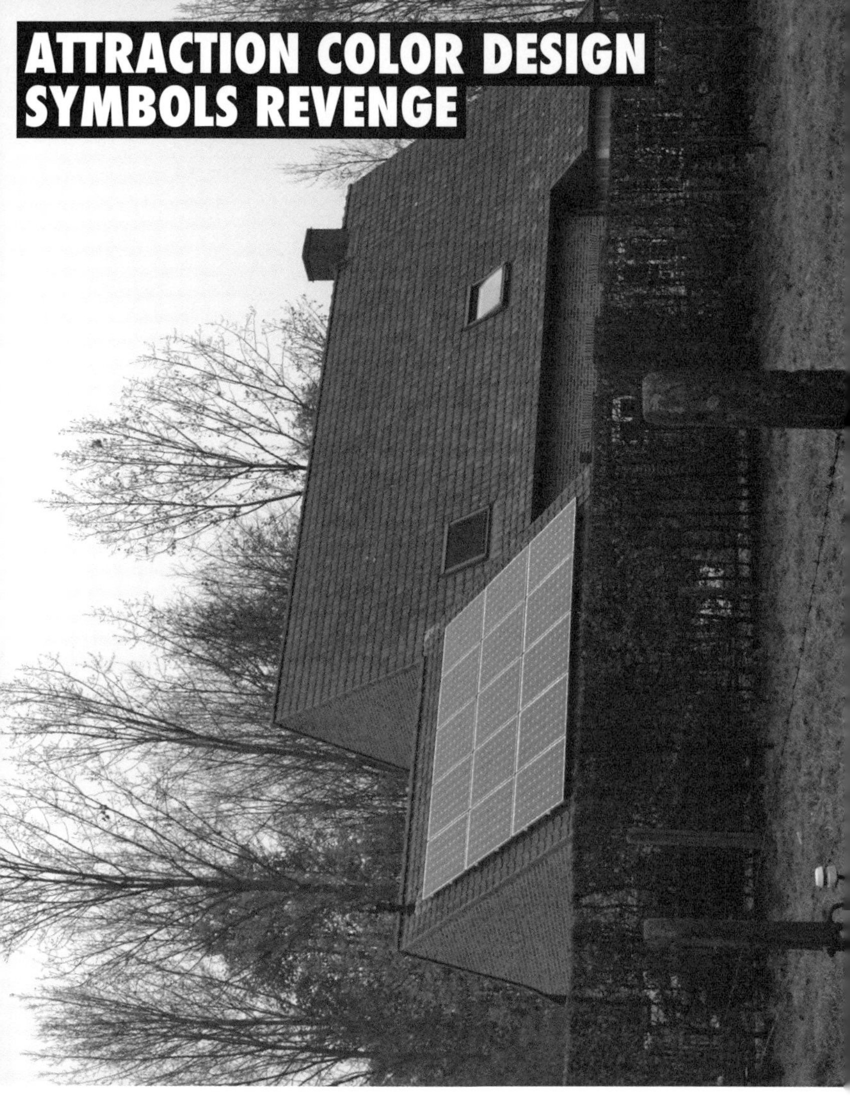

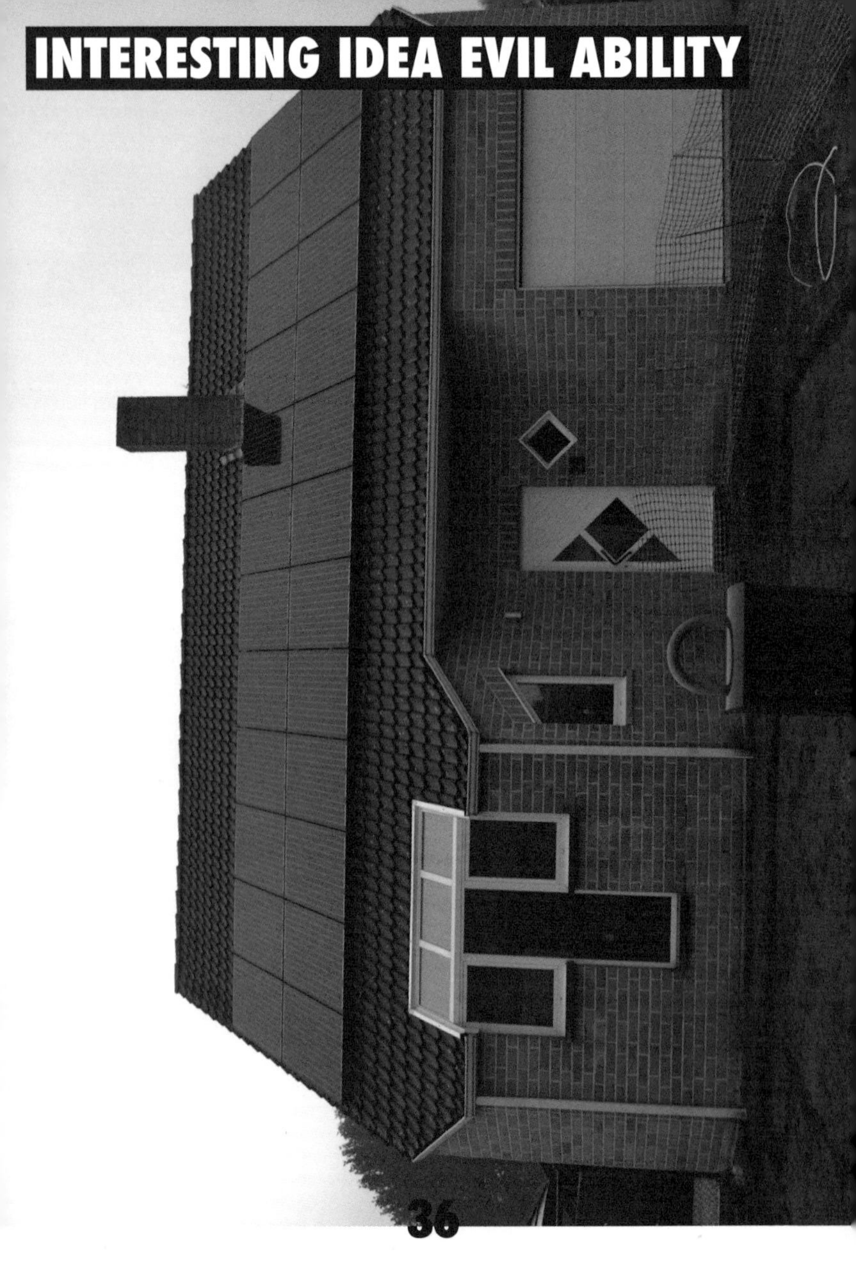
INTERESTING IDEA EVIL ABILITY

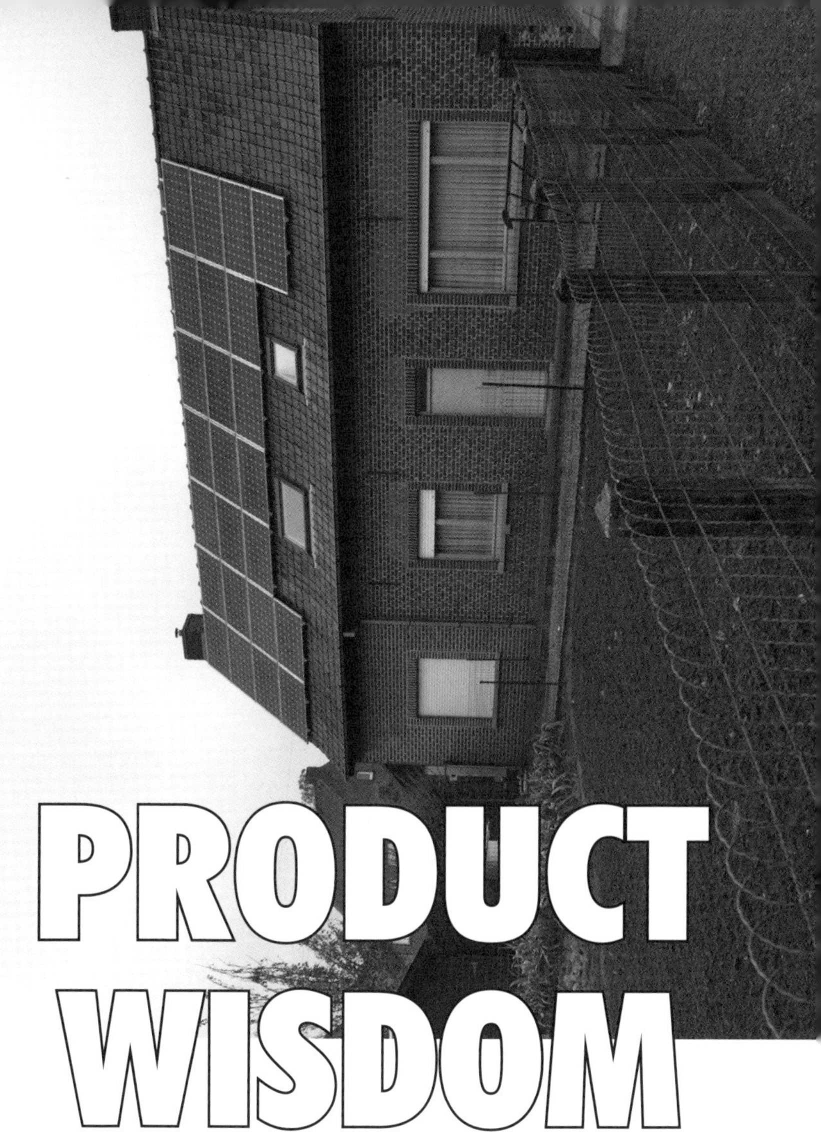

PRODUCT WISDOM

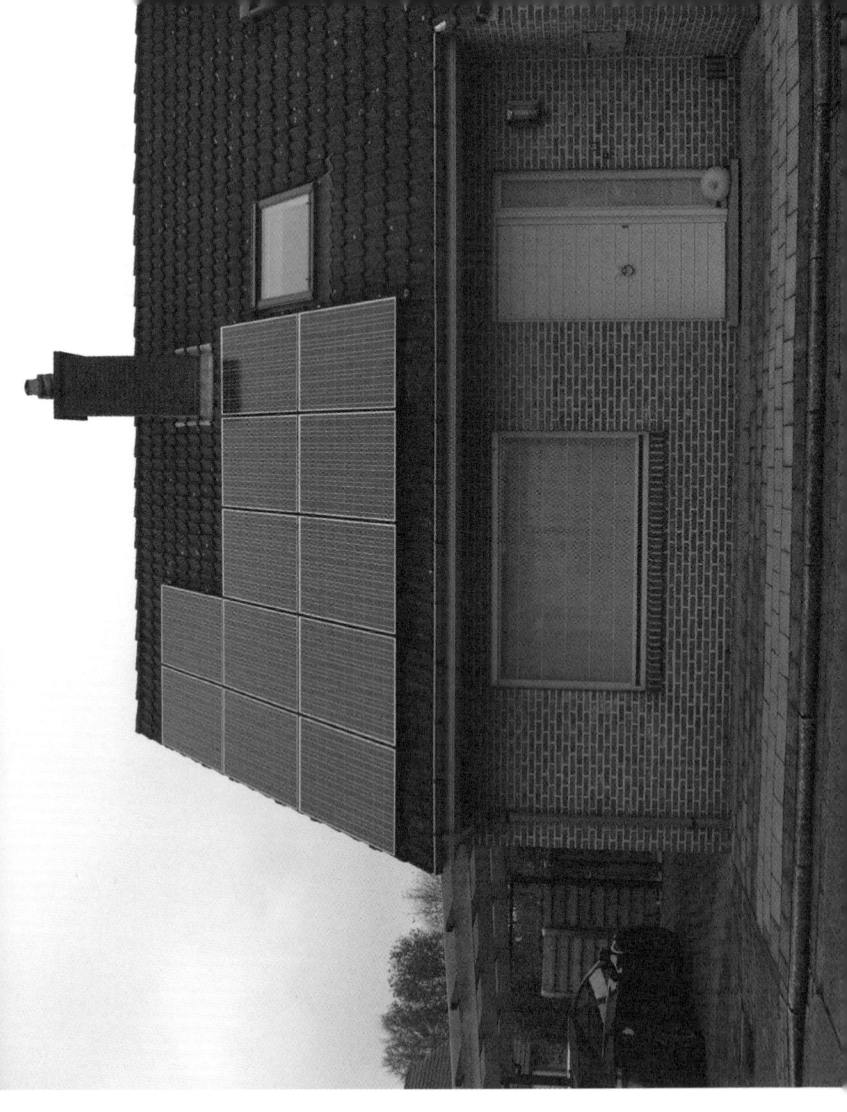

BEAUTY FUTURE MAN

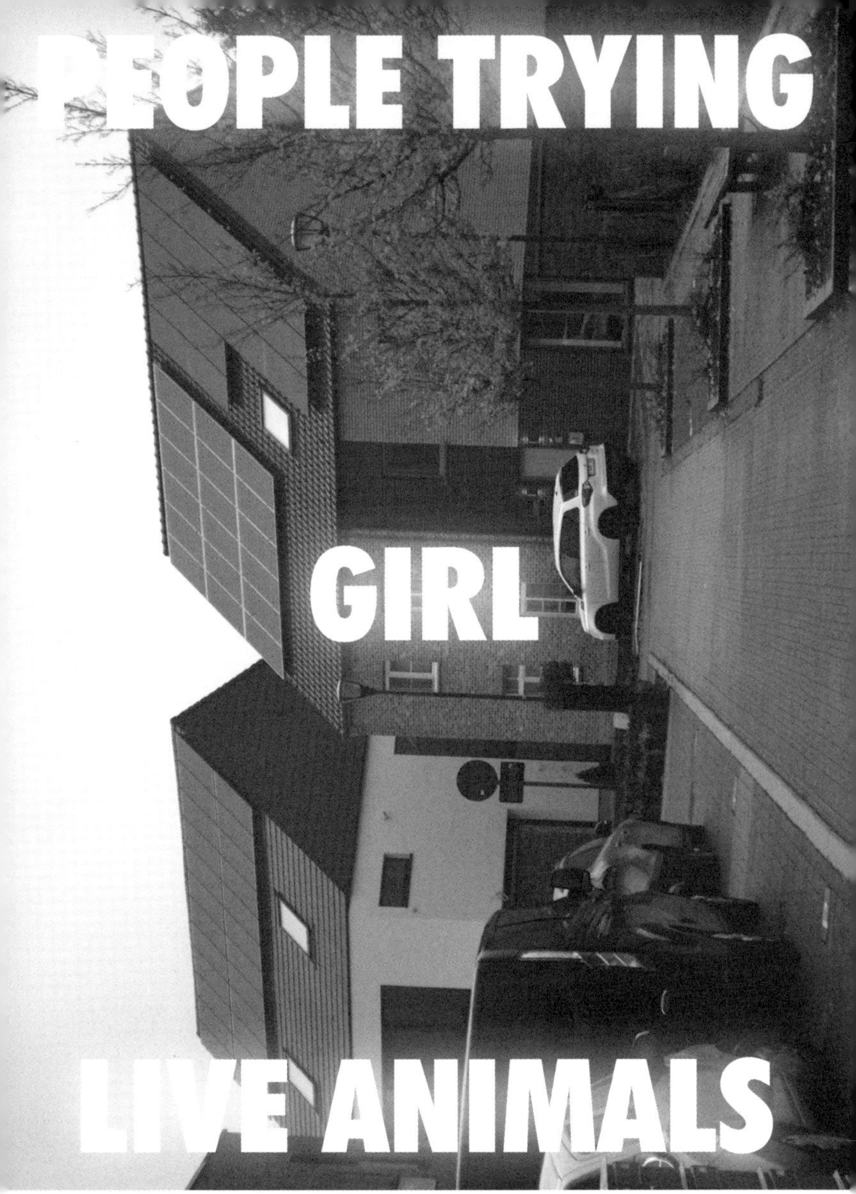

PEOPLE TRYING

GIRL

LIVE ANIMALS

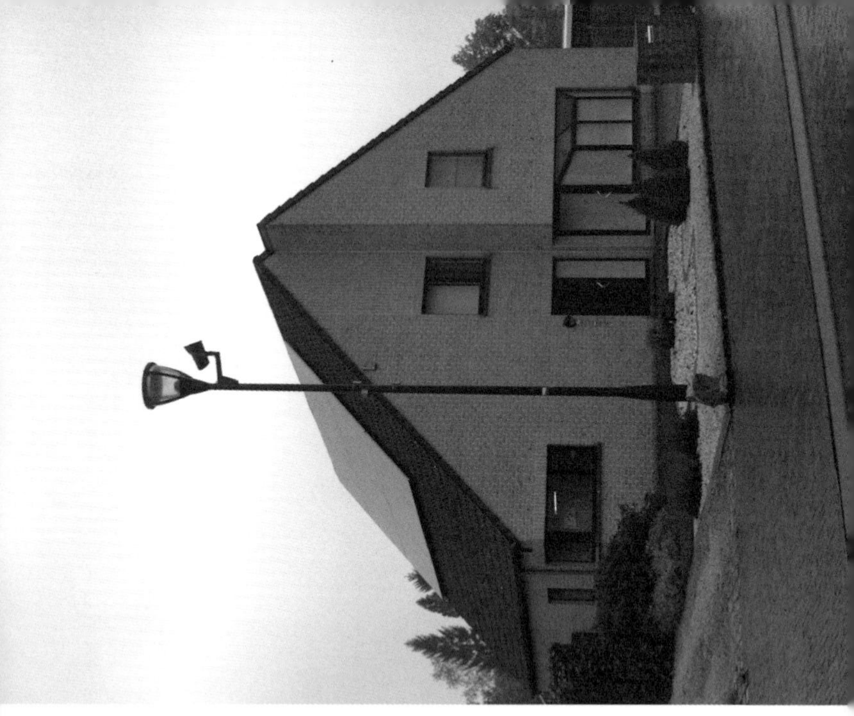

HAIR FRIEND FUN

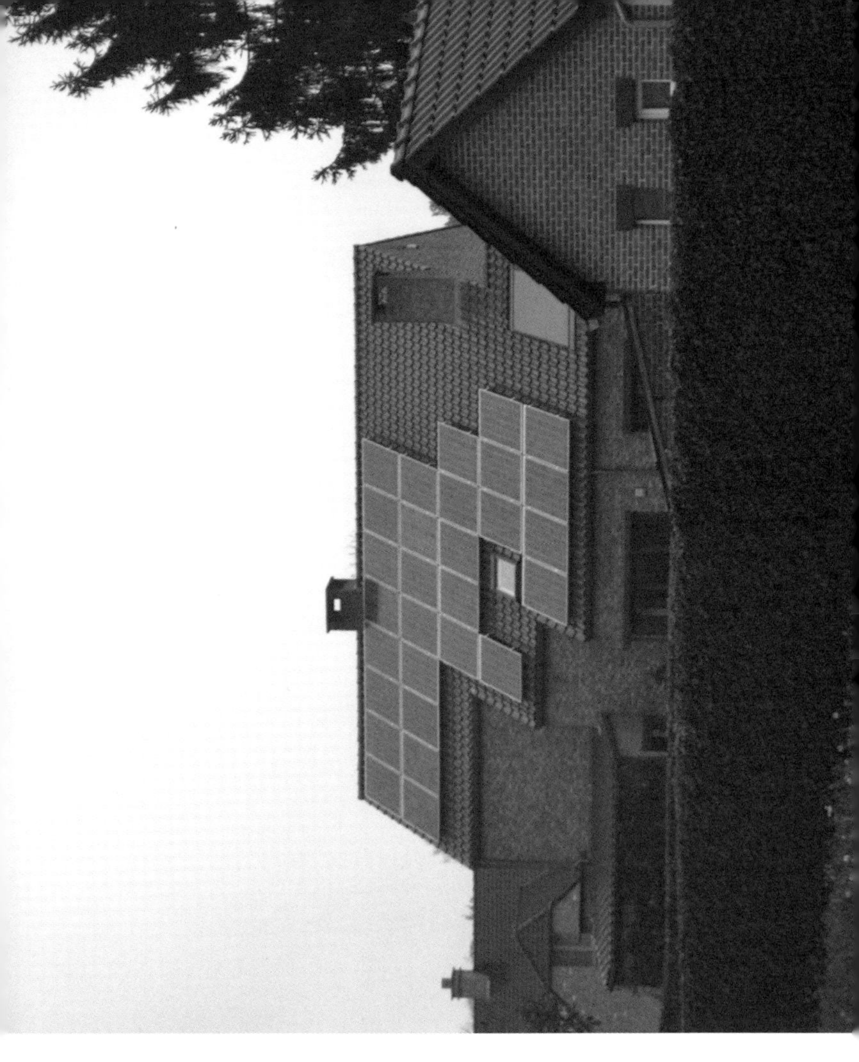

IMPOSSIBLE DONE ALWAYS

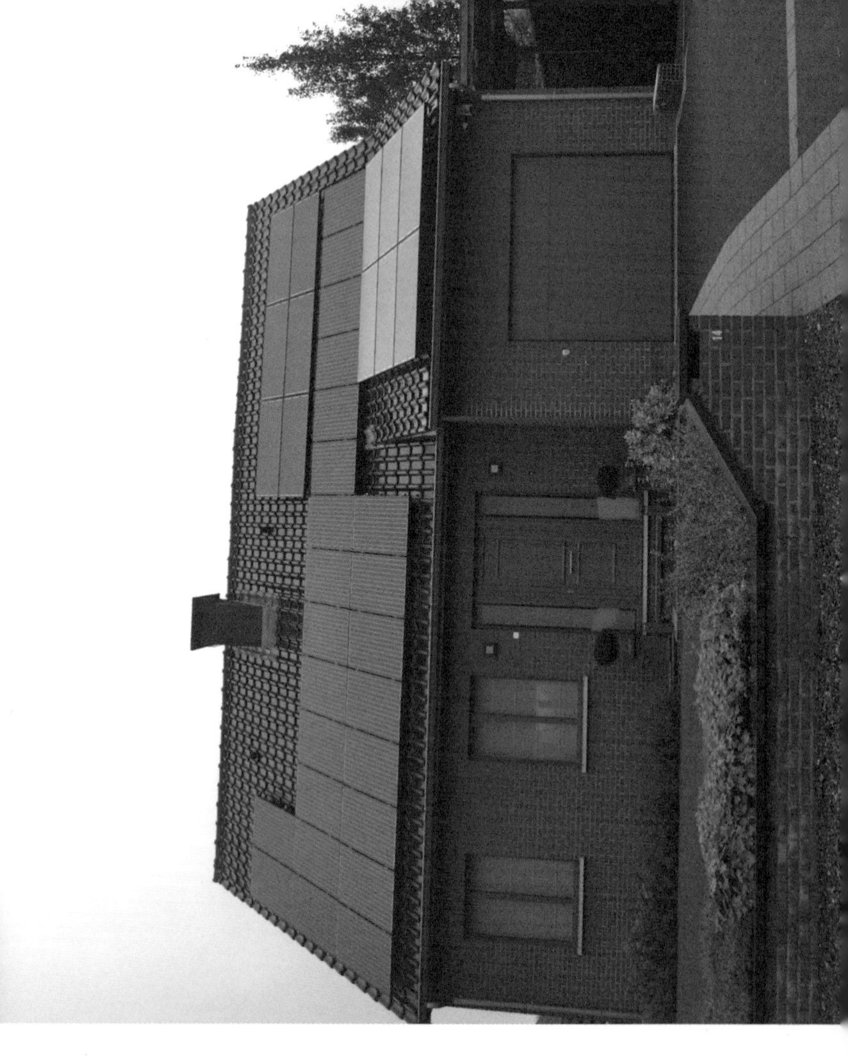

YOU CAN DO IT DREAM YOU

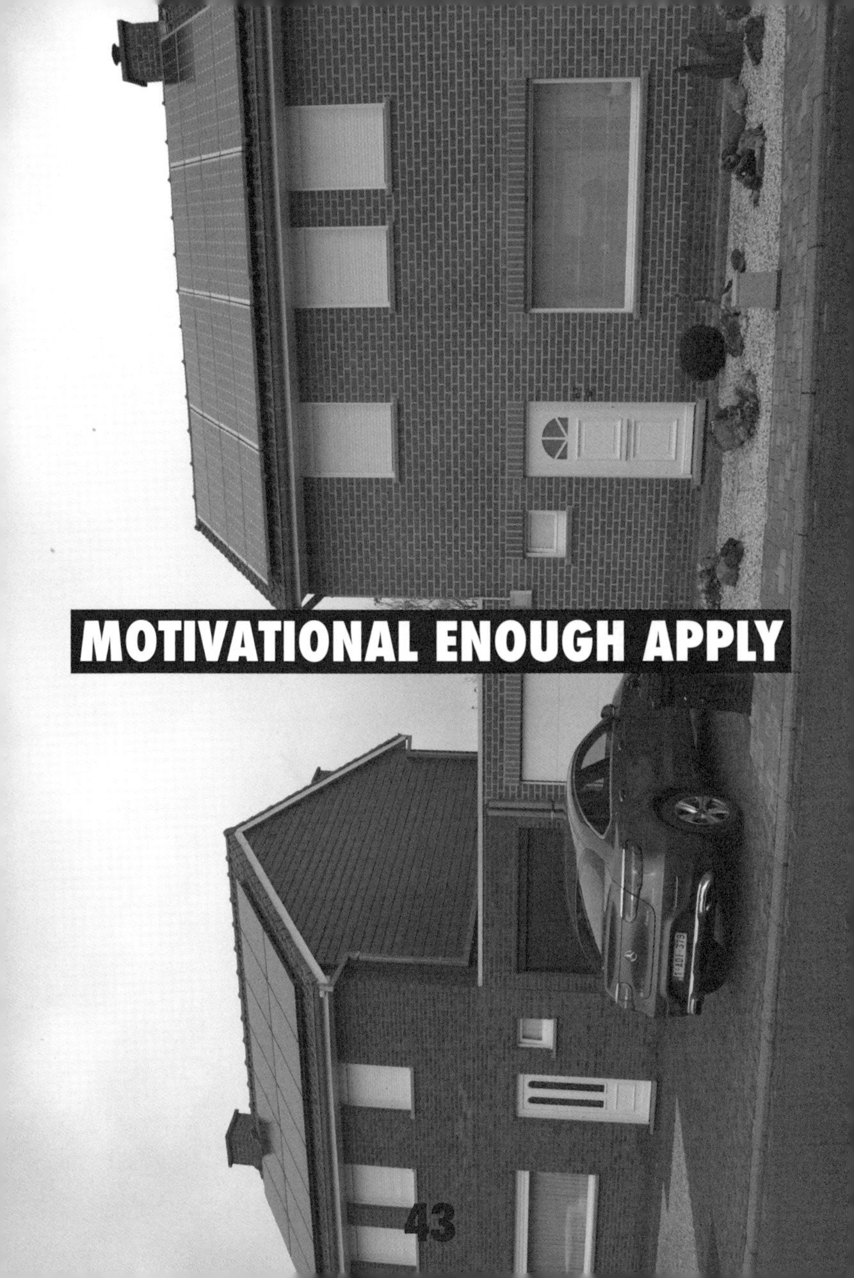

MOTIVATIONAL ENOUGH APPLY

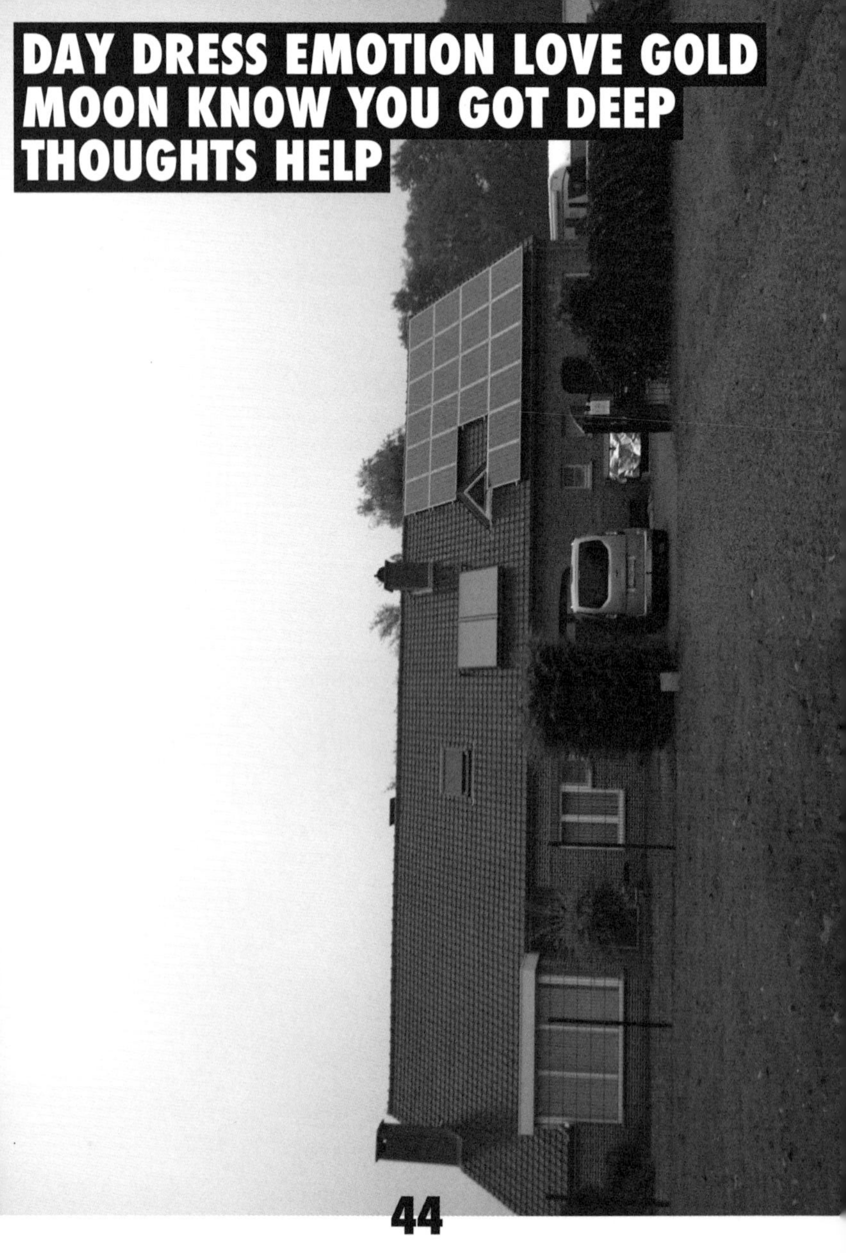

DAY DRESS EMOTION LOVE GOLD MOON KNOW YOU GOT DEEP THOUGHTS HELP

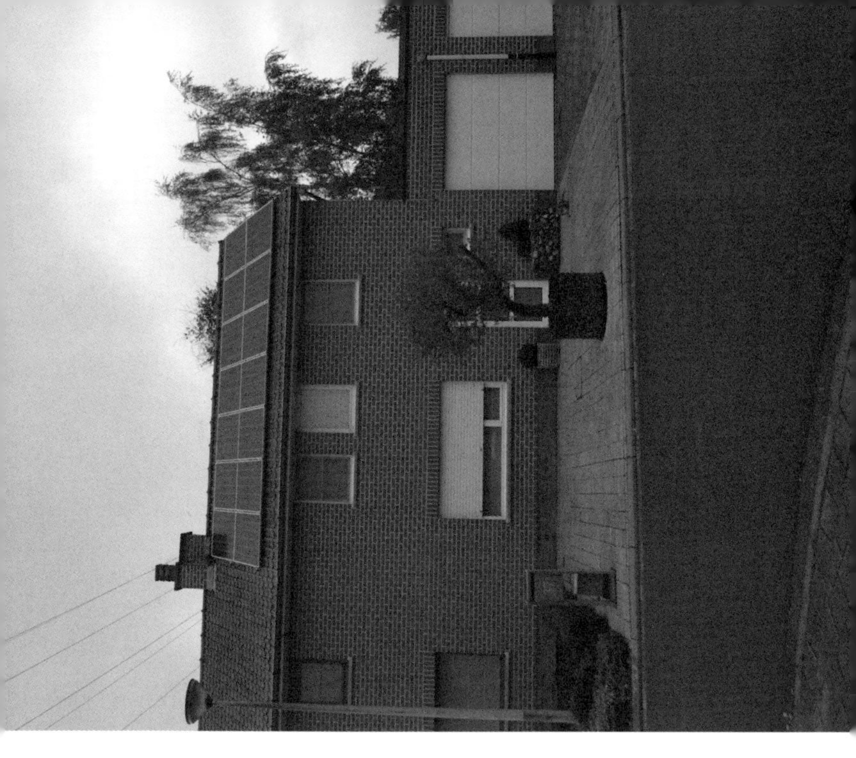

GAME SHINE TRAIN

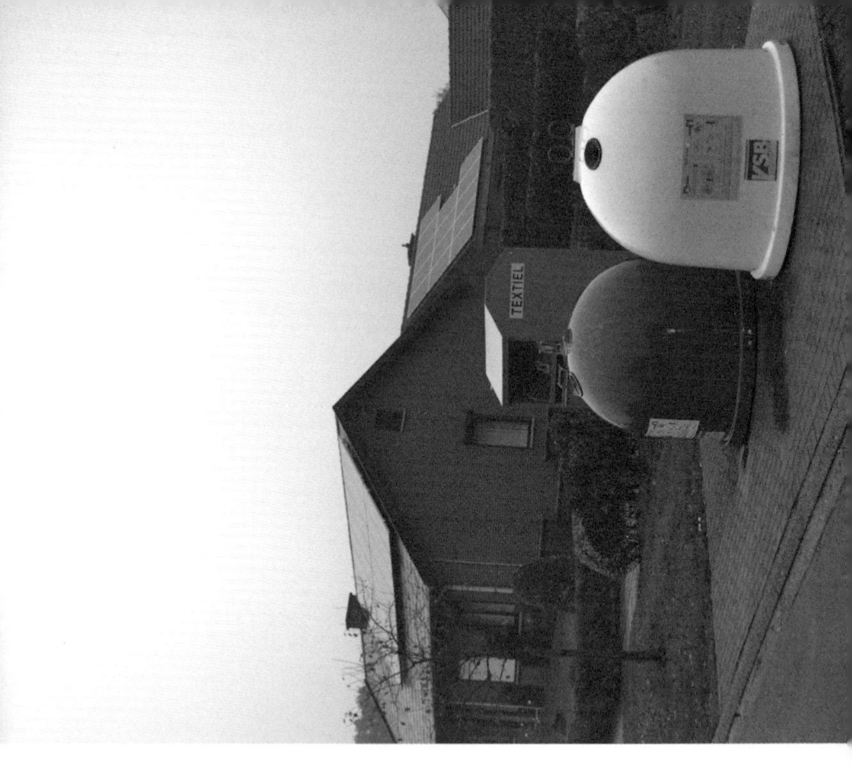

SPACE IMPACT DIE

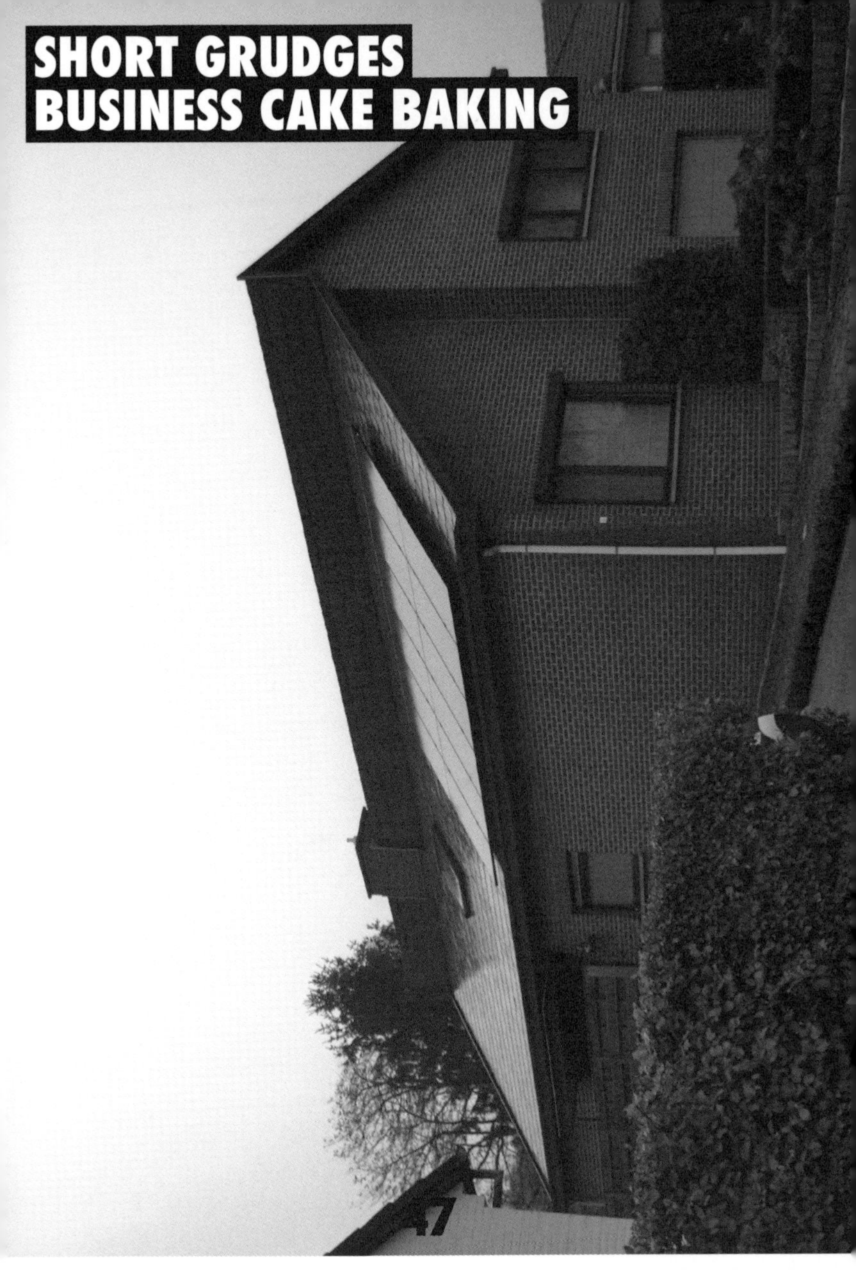

SHORT GRUDGES BUSINESS CAKE BAKING

SOMETHING MAYBE HAPPENS

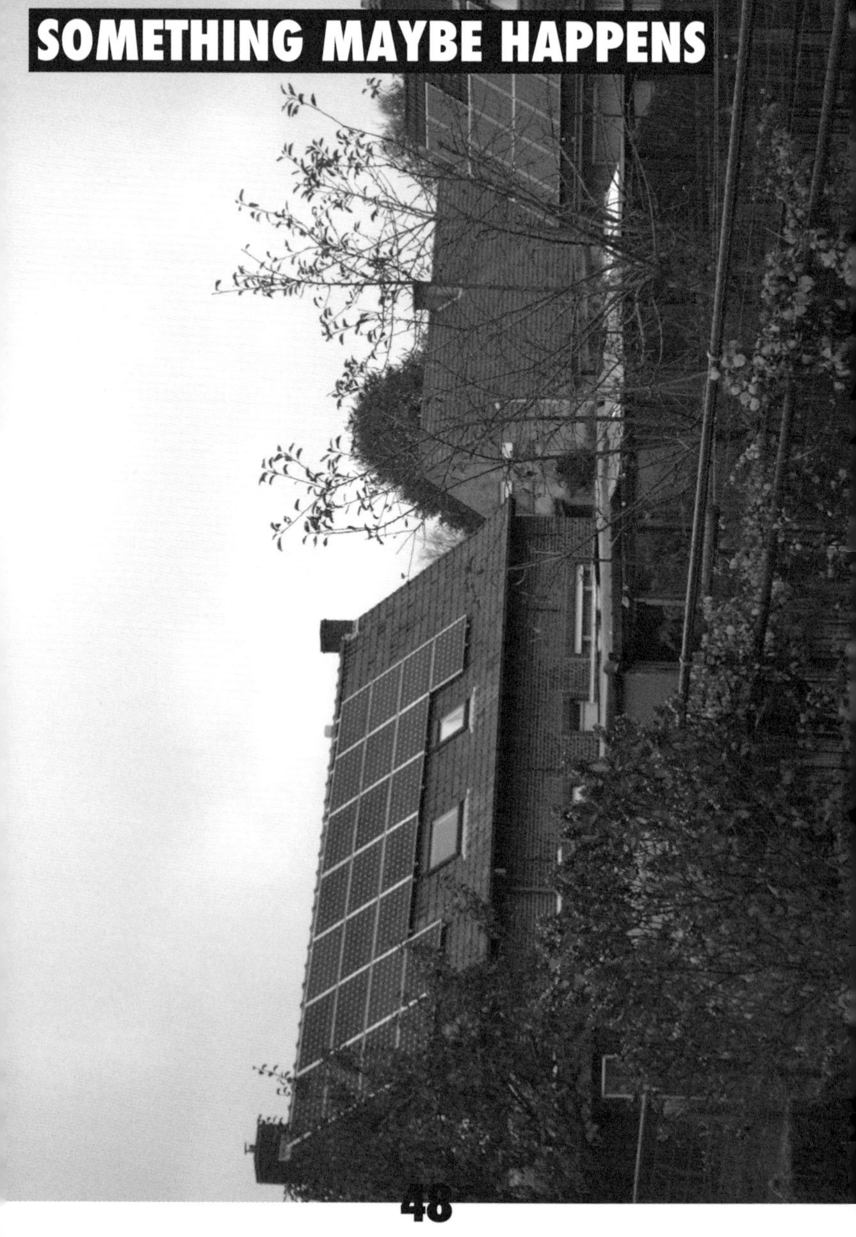

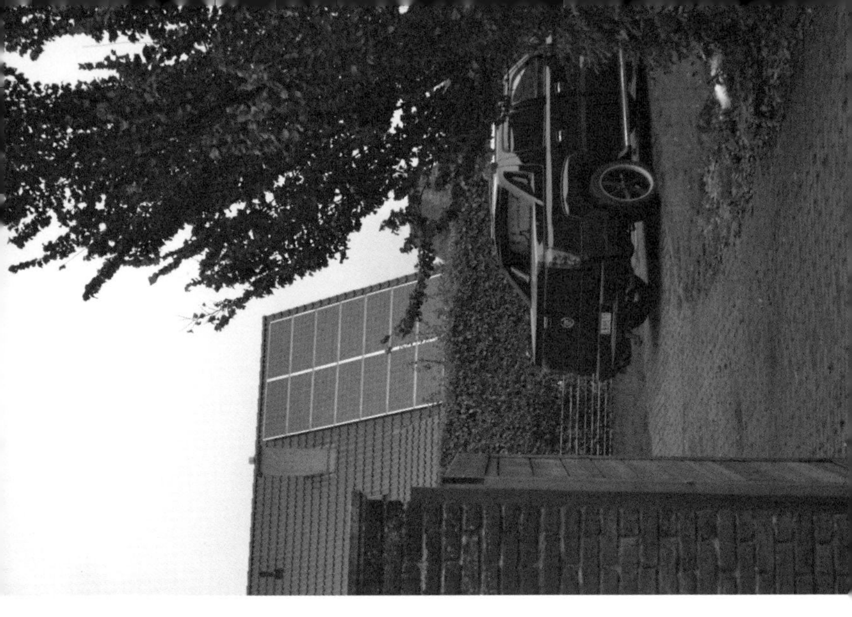

CELL PHONE POTENTIAL

THINK VALLEY
††††††

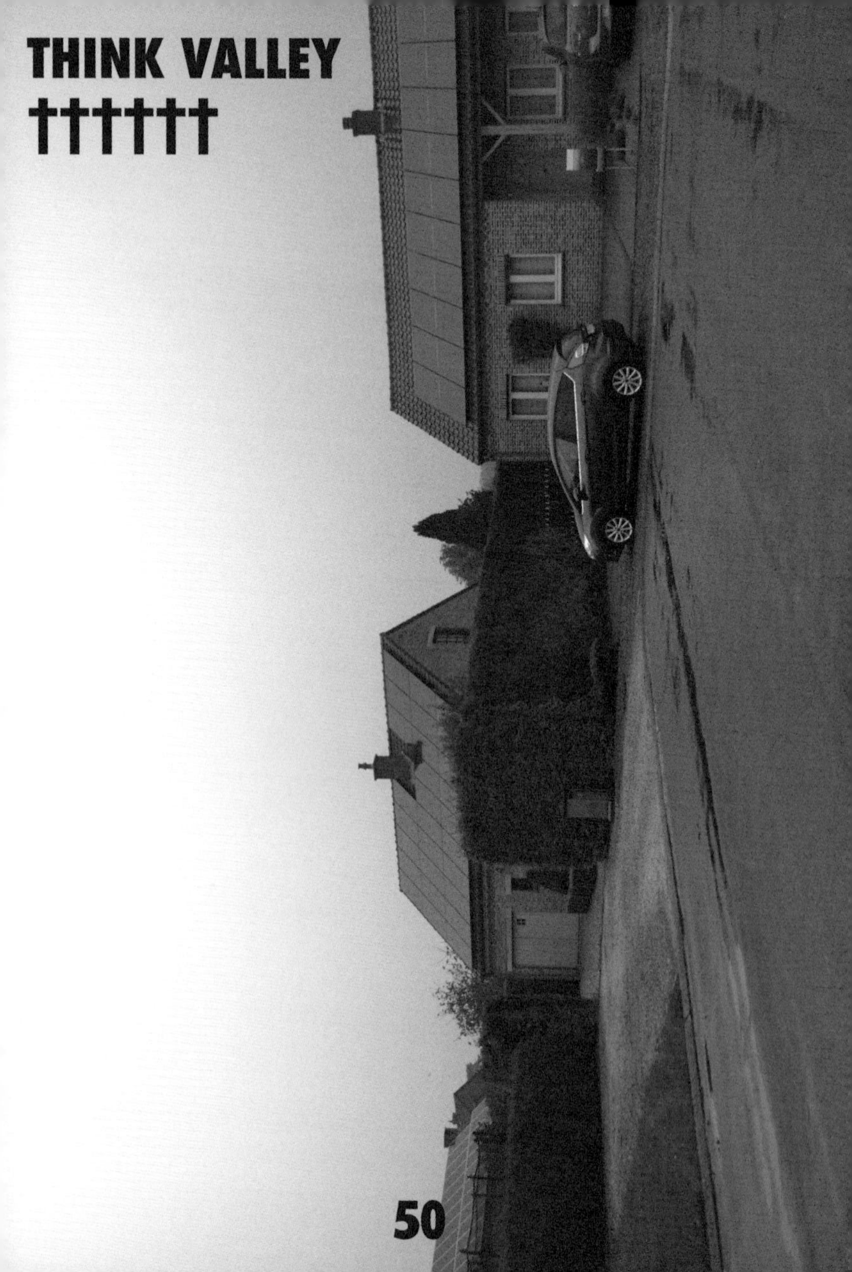

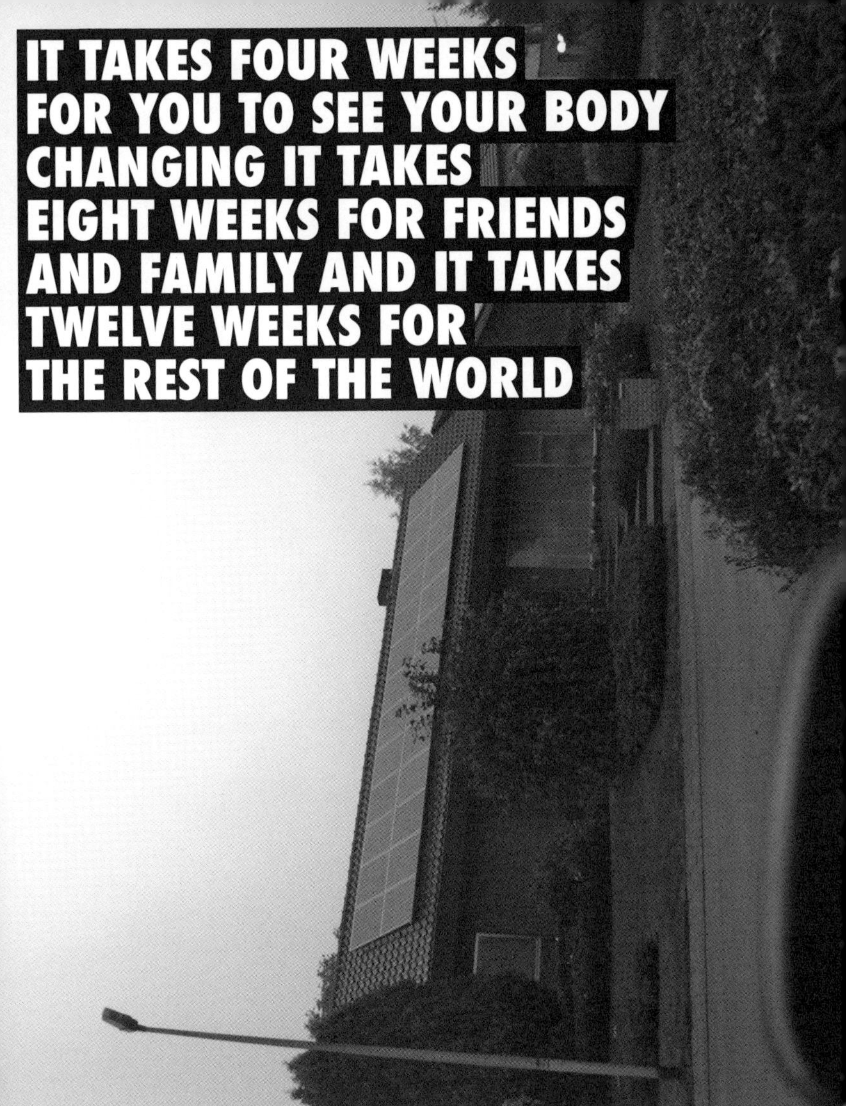
IT TAKES FOUR WEEKS
FOR YOU TO SEE YOUR BODY
CHANGING IT TAKES
EIGHT WEEKS FOR FRIENDS
AND FAMILY AND IT TAKES
TWELVE WEEKS FOR
THE REST OF THE WORLD

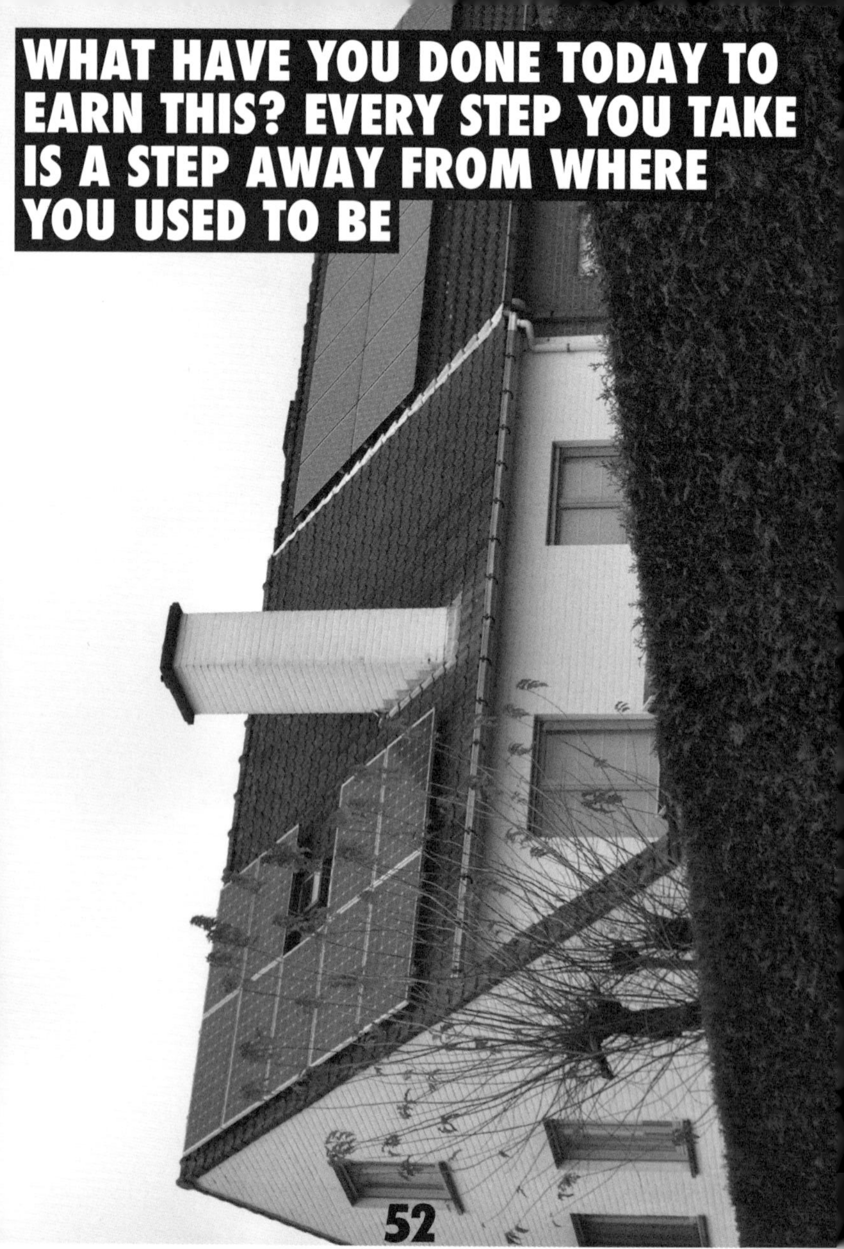
WHAT HAVE YOU DONE TODAY TO
EARN THIS? EVERY STEP YOU TAKE
IS A STEP AWAY FROM WHERE
YOU USED TO BE

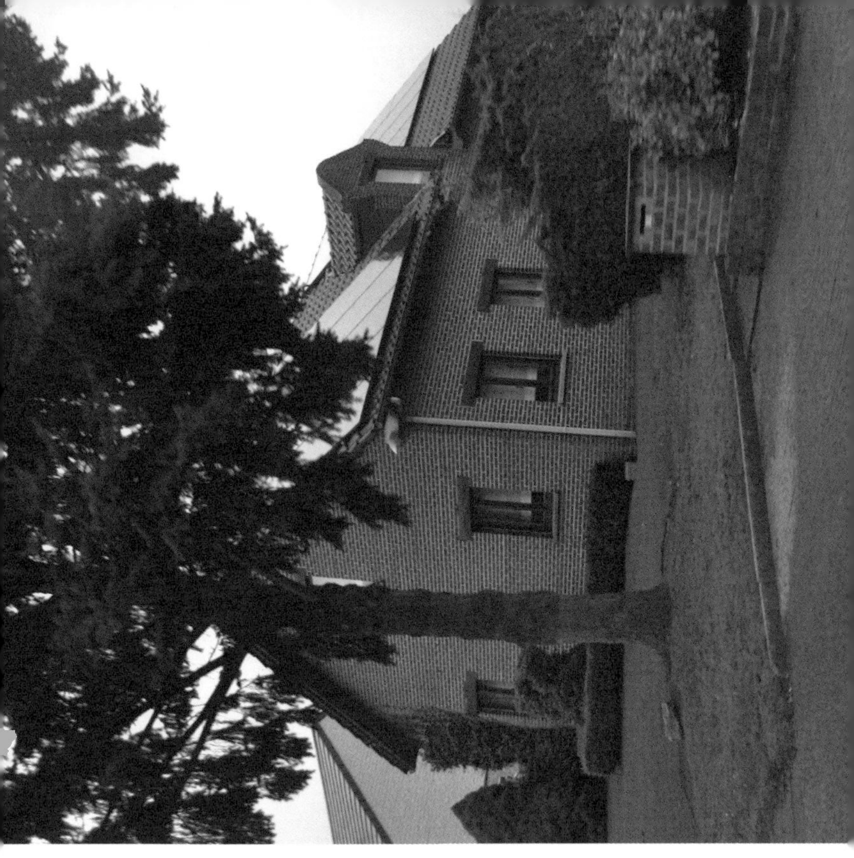

PUSH YOURSELF EVERY TIME YOU EAT BREAD

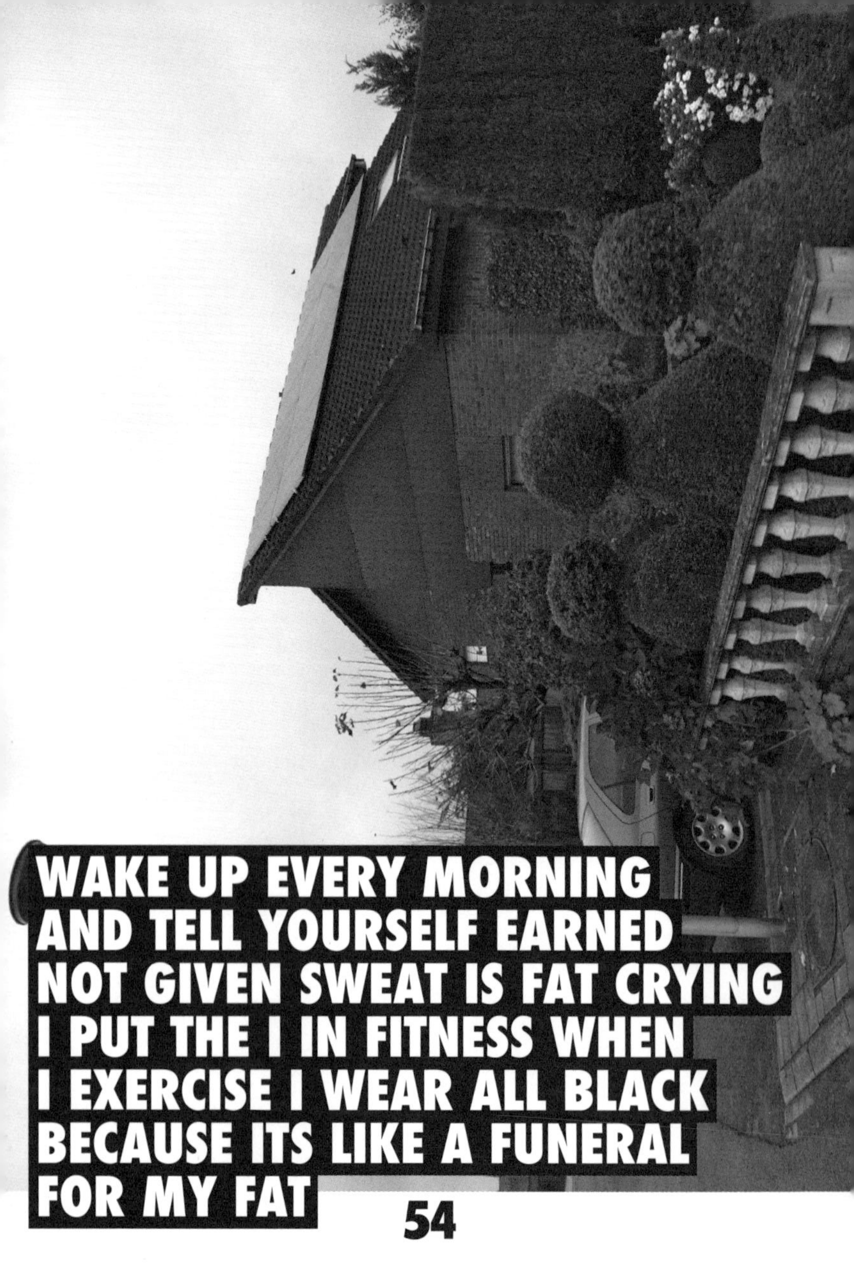
WAKE UP EVERY MORNING
AND TELL YOURSELF EARNED
NOT GIVEN SWEAT IS FAT CRYING
I PUT THE I IN FITNESS WHEN
I EXERCISE I WEAR ALL BLACK
BECAUSE ITS LIKE A FUNERAL
FOR MY FAT

LIFE BEGINS AT THE END OF YOUR COMFORT ZONE

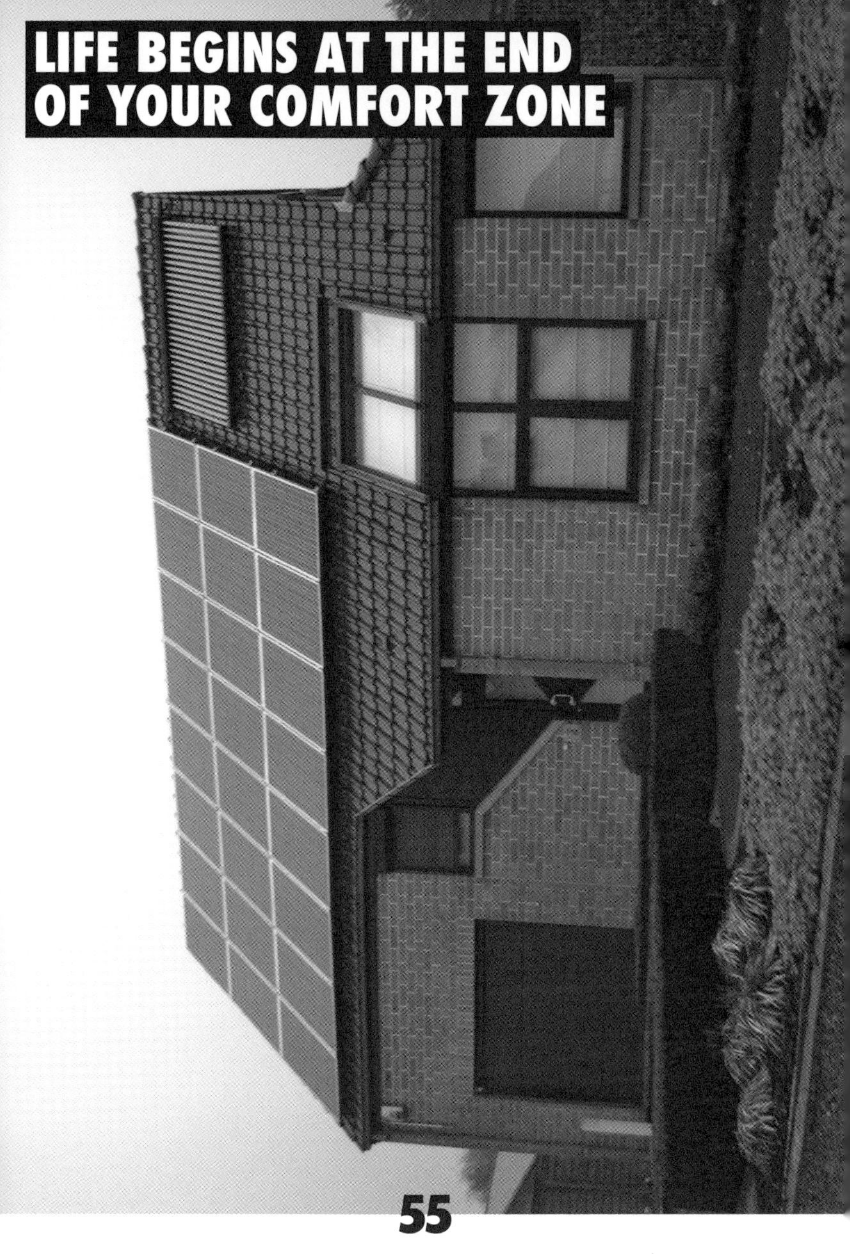

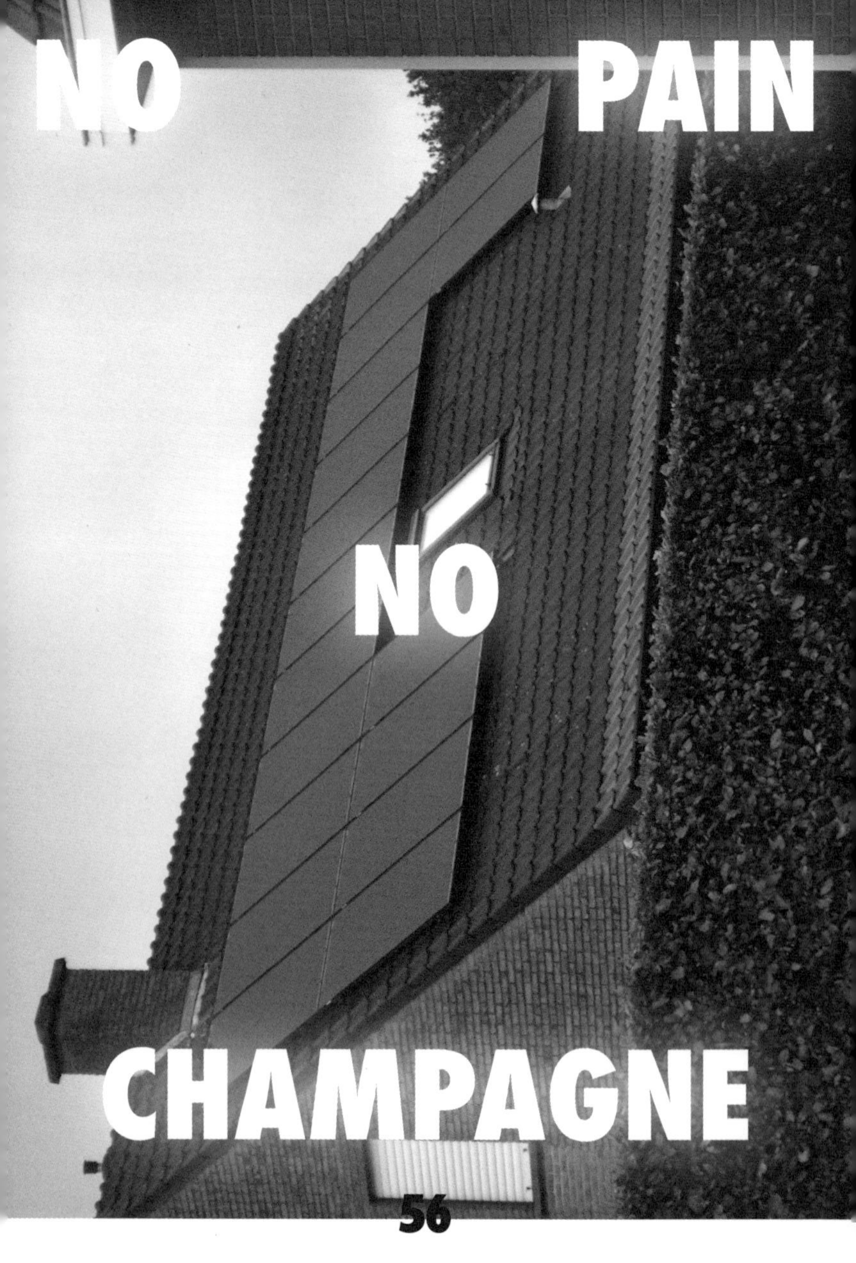
NO PAIN
NO
CHAMPAGNE

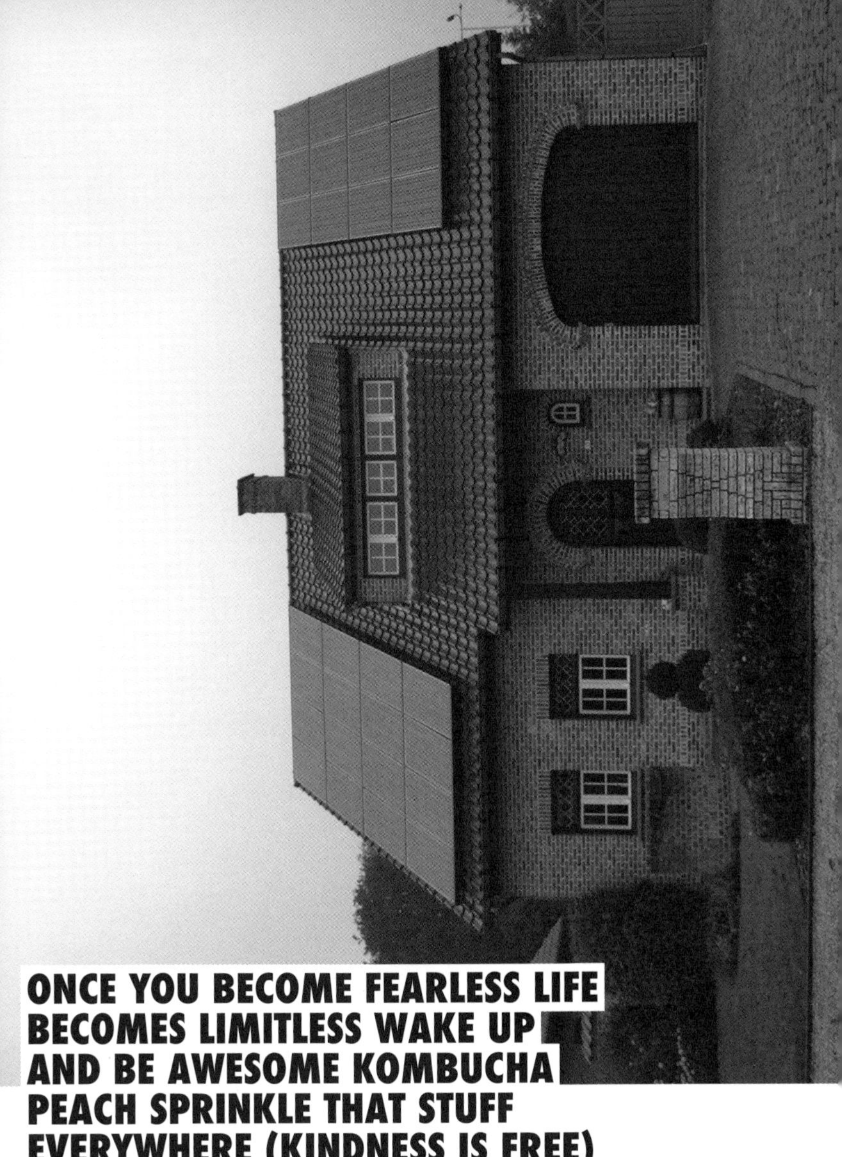

ONCE YOU BECOME FEARLESS LIFE BECOMES LIMITLESS WAKE UP AND BE AWESOME KOMBUCHA PEACH SPRINKLE THAT STUFF EVERYWHERE (KINDNESS IS FREE)

YOUR VIBE

ATTRACTS

YOUR TRIBE

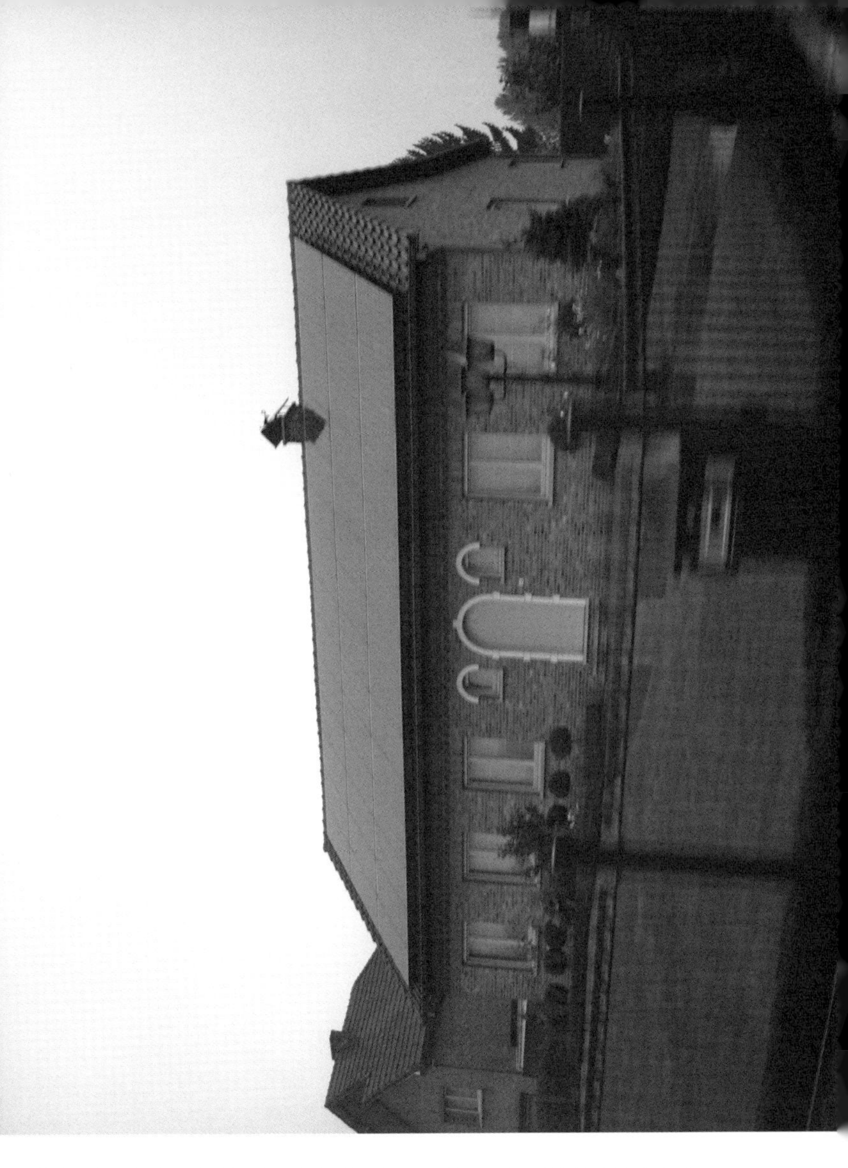

MINDS ARE LIKE PARACHUTES

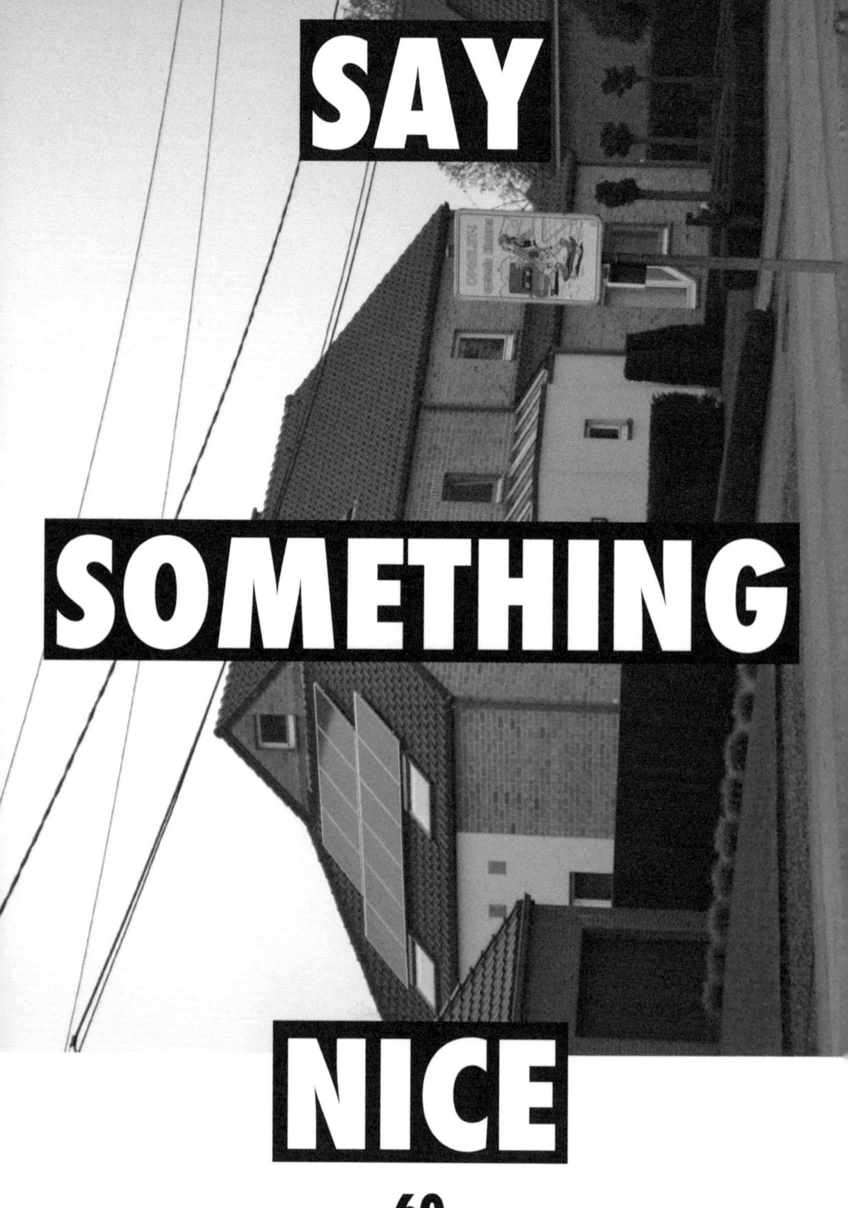
SAY
SOMETHING
NICE

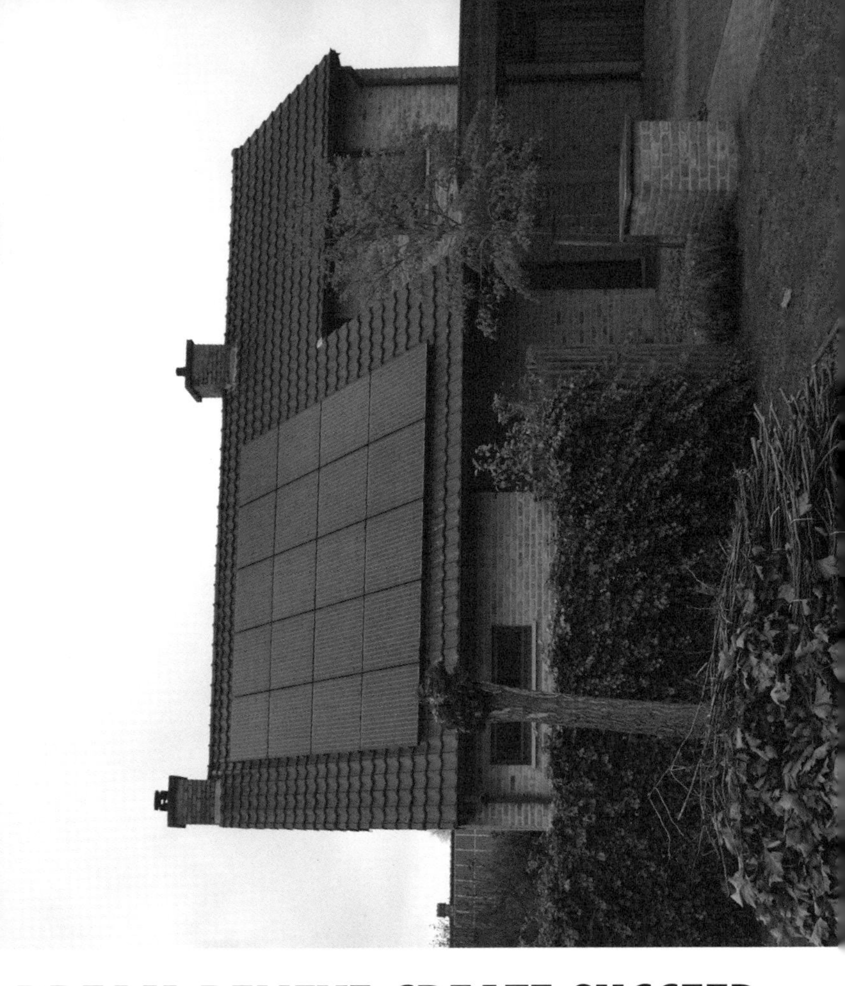

DREAM BELIEVE CREATE SUCCEED

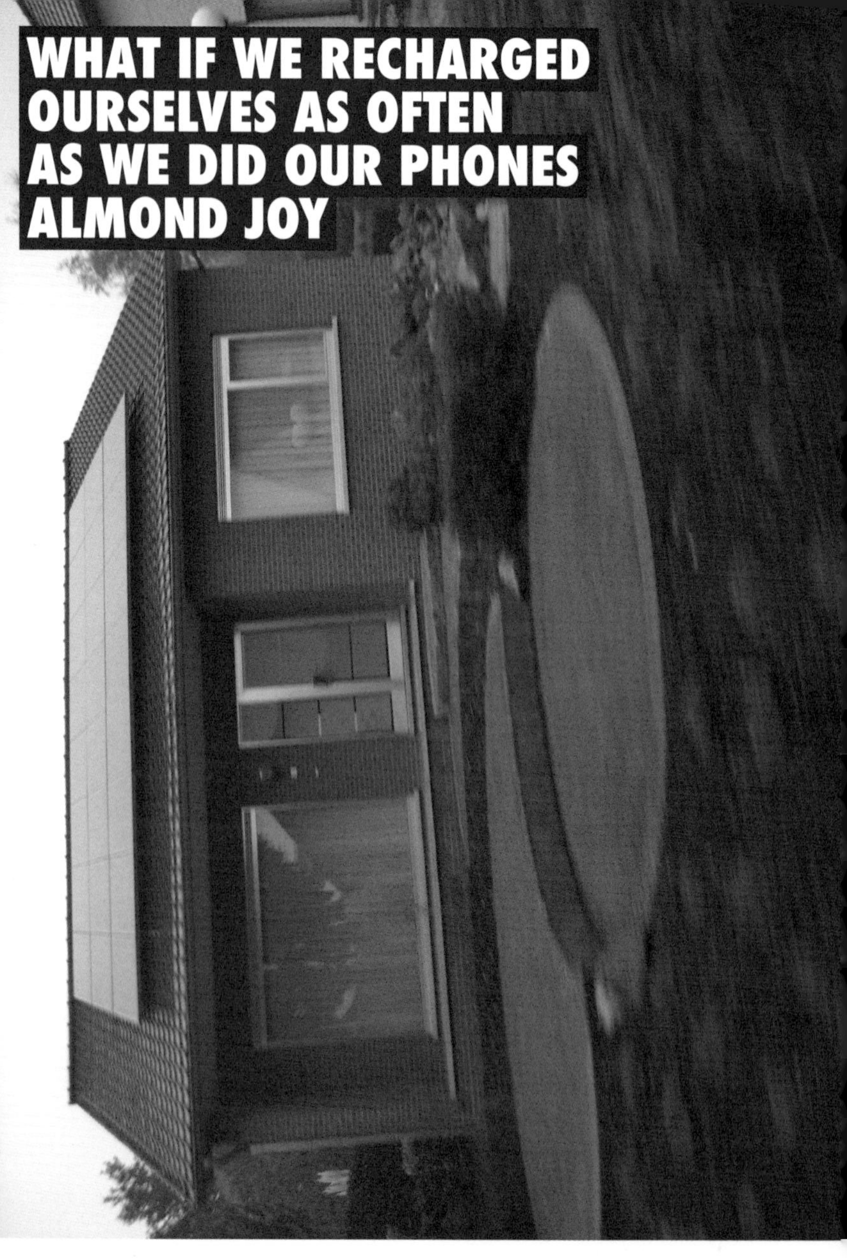
WHAT IF WE RECHARGED
OURSELVES AS OFTEN
AS WE DID OUR PHONES
ALMOND JOY

BREAKFAST

SHAKE

DEAR

DESTINY

I AM READY

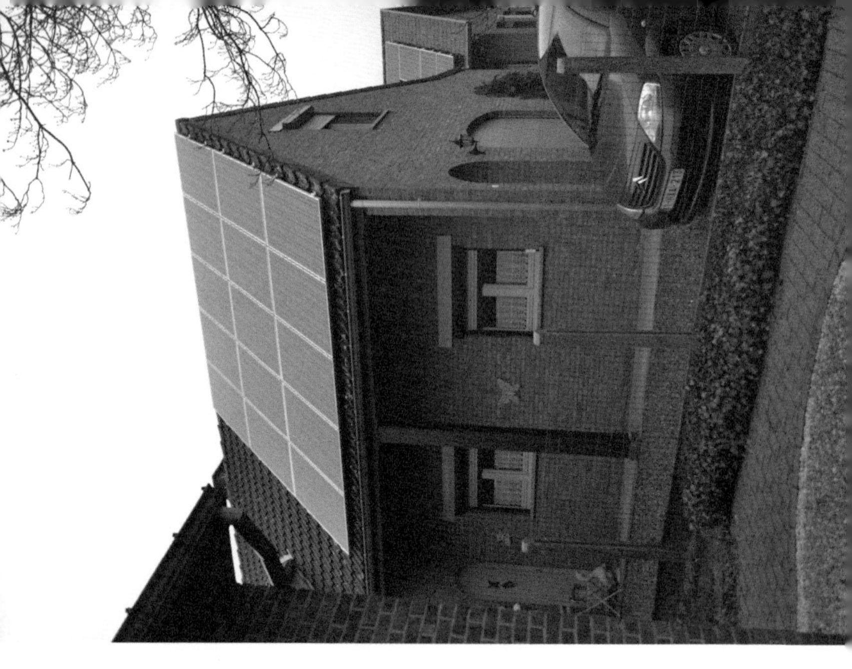

NOW EVERY GREAT WHY NEEDS A GREAT HOW

BIG THINGS HAVE SMALL BEGINNINGS

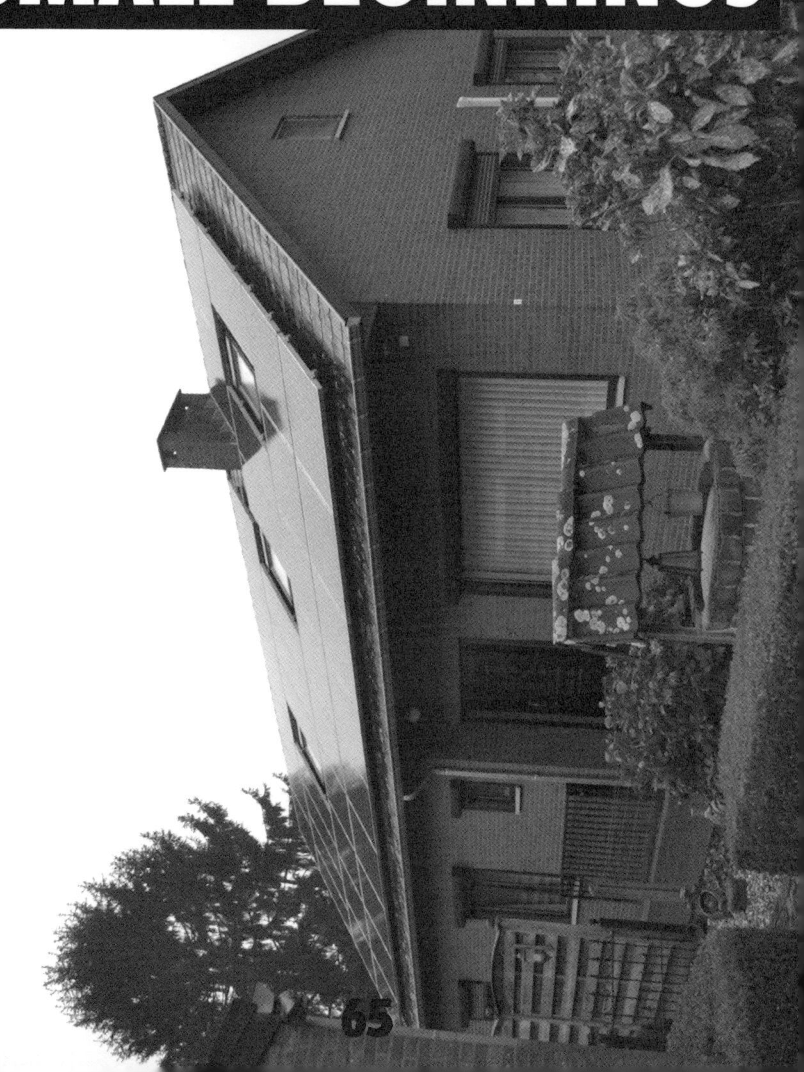

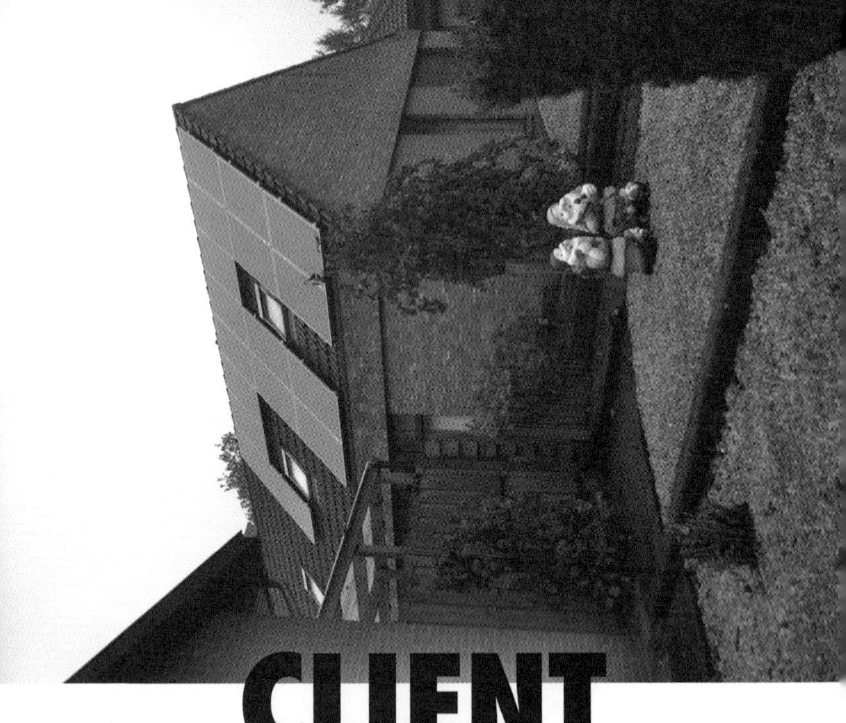

CLIENT TESTIMONIAL SOFT TISSUE

SUPPORT ACRYLIC ON CANVAS COLOR TECHNIQUE FOCUS ON MODE DE VIE (WAY OF LIFE) THEMES

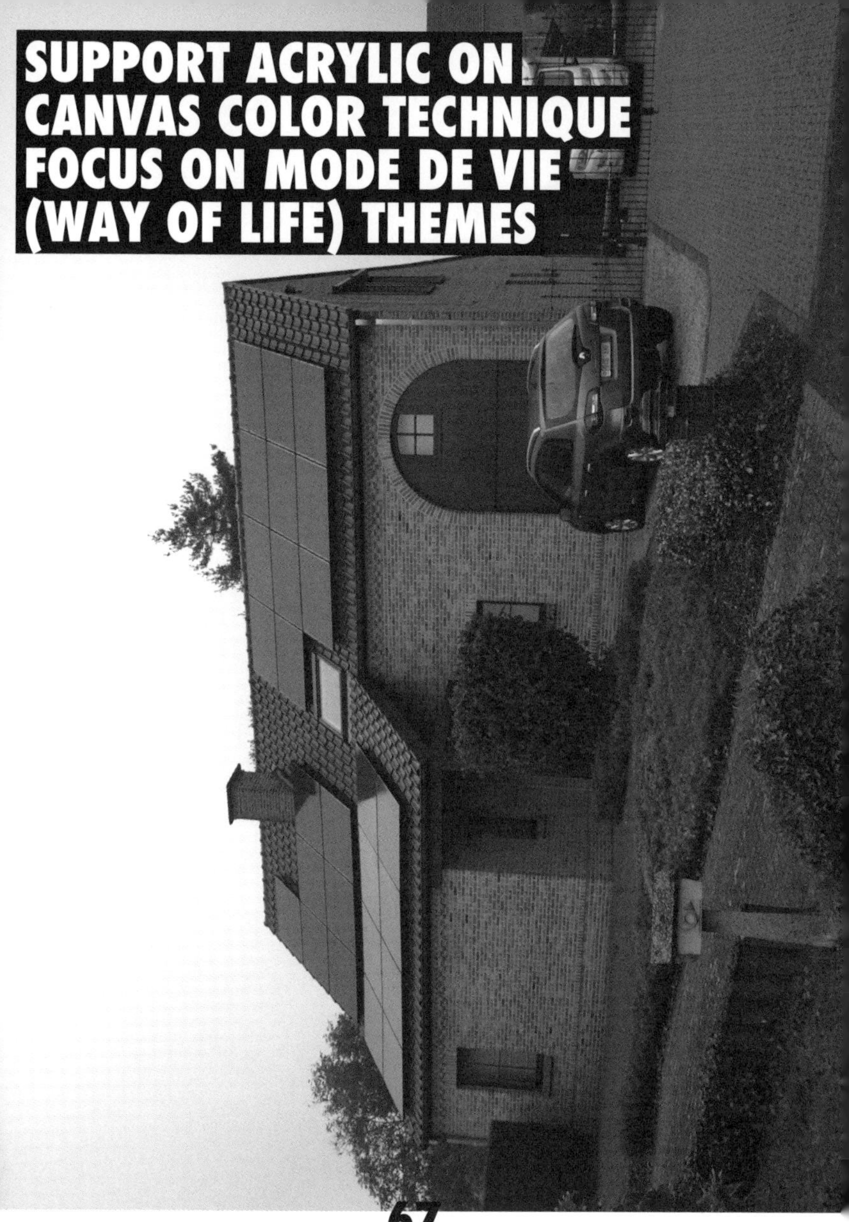

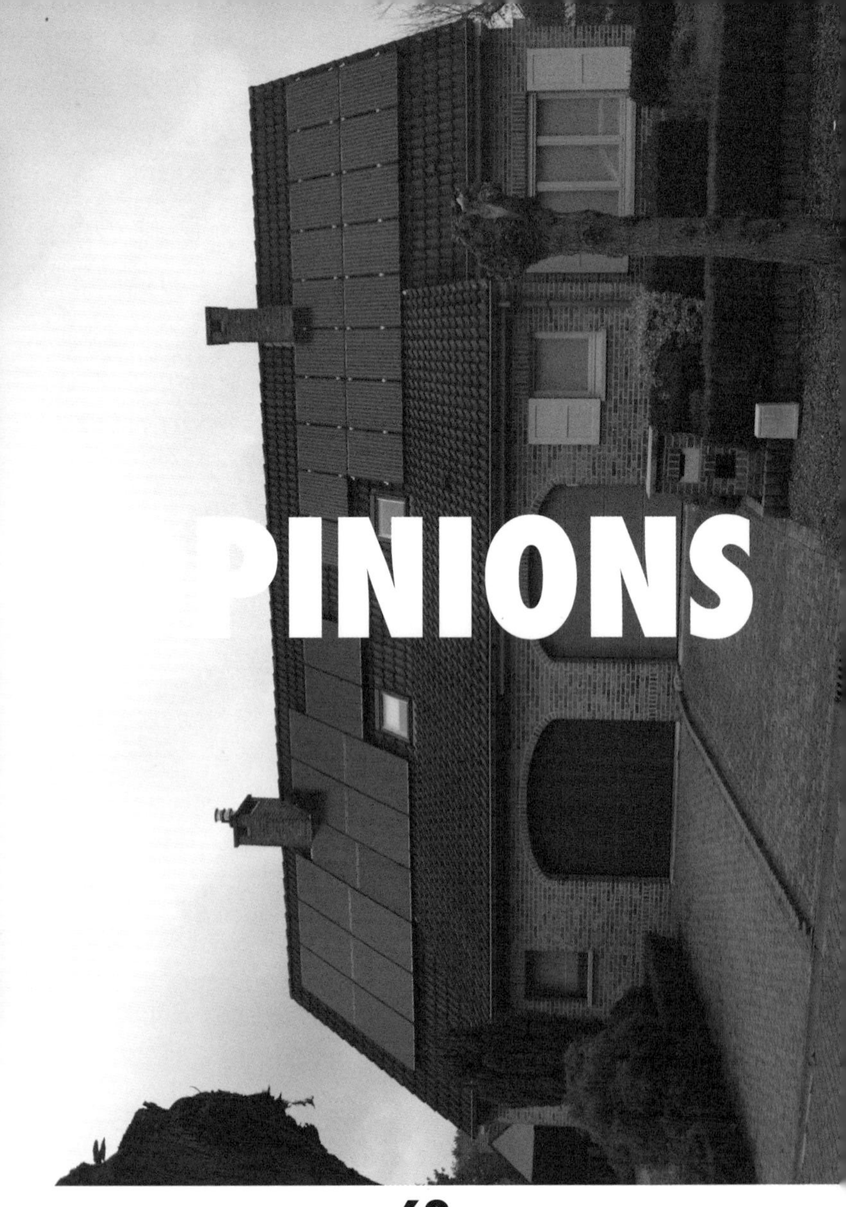
PINIONS

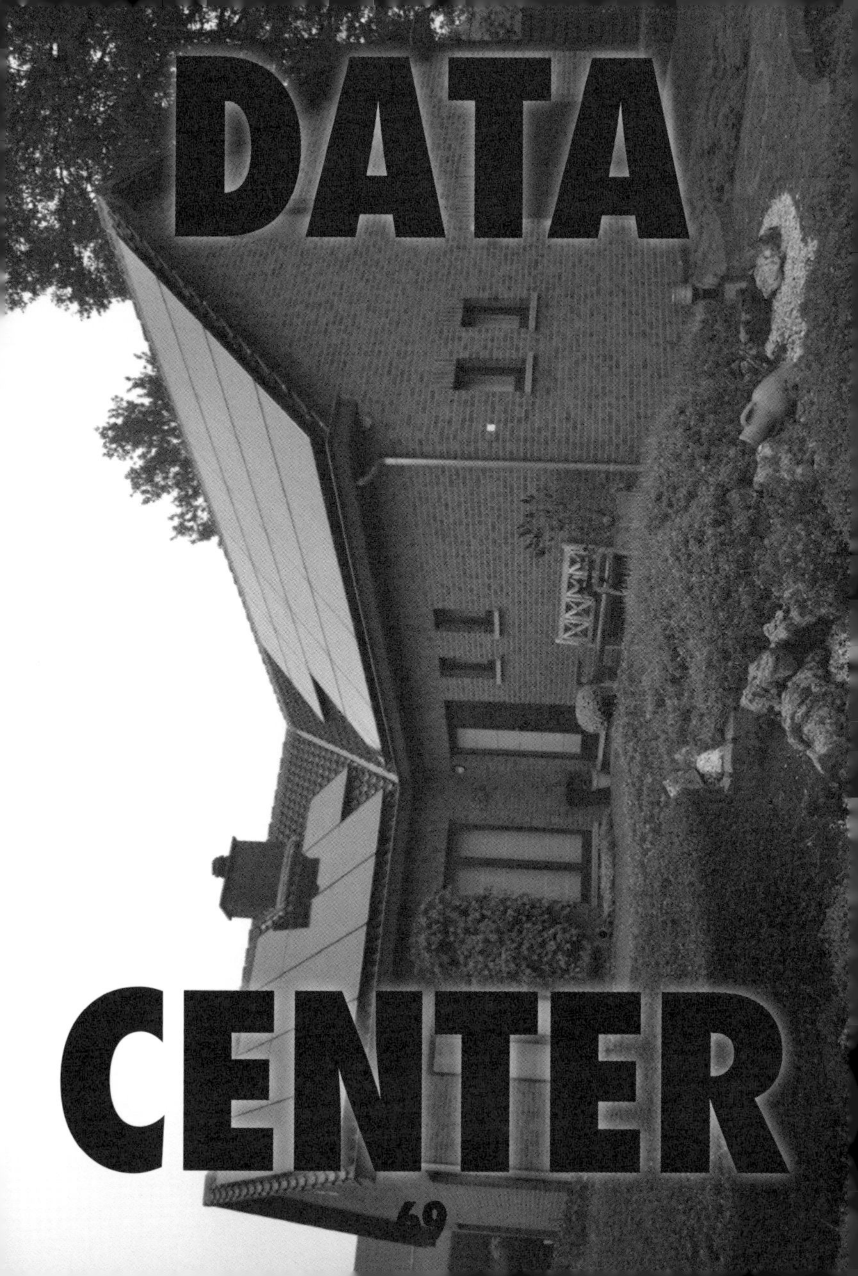

DATA

CENTER

LED
OWER
HEAD

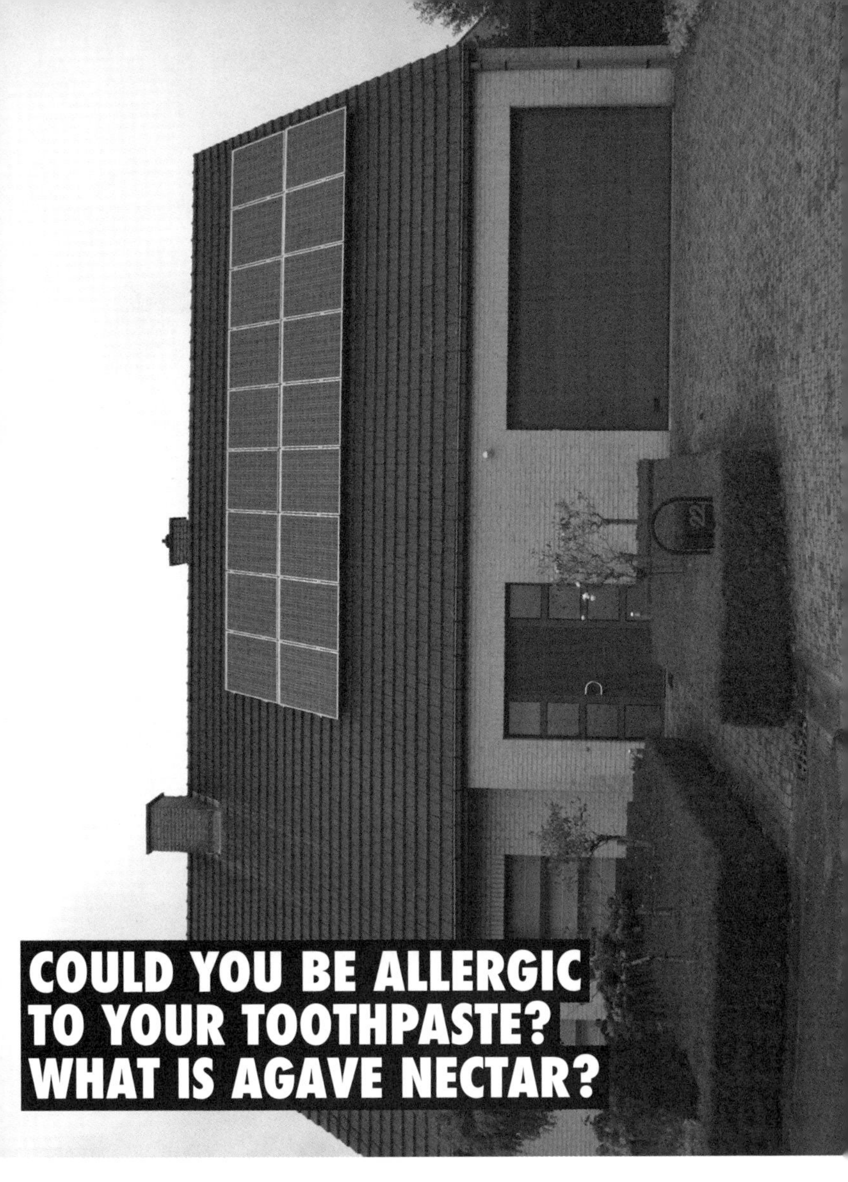

COULD YOU BE ALLERGIC TO YOUR TOOTHPASTE? WHAT IS AGAVE NECTAR?

5 SIGNS YOU'LL GET CANCER BUTTER

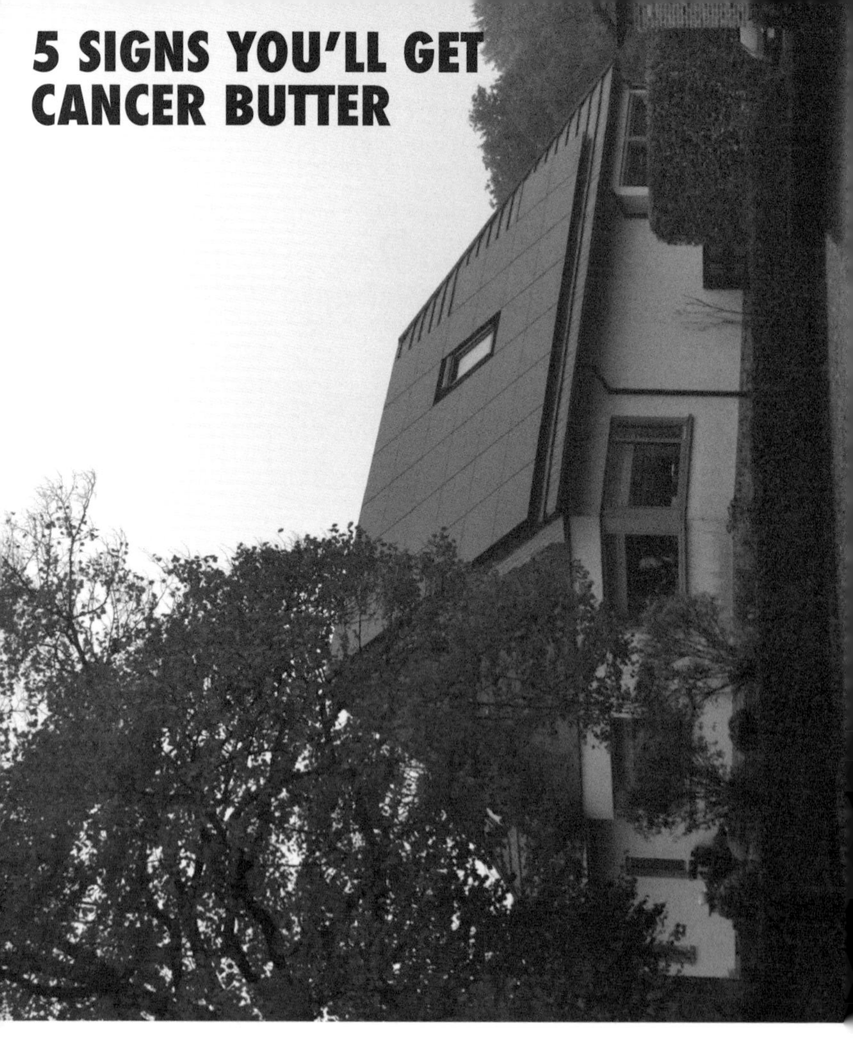

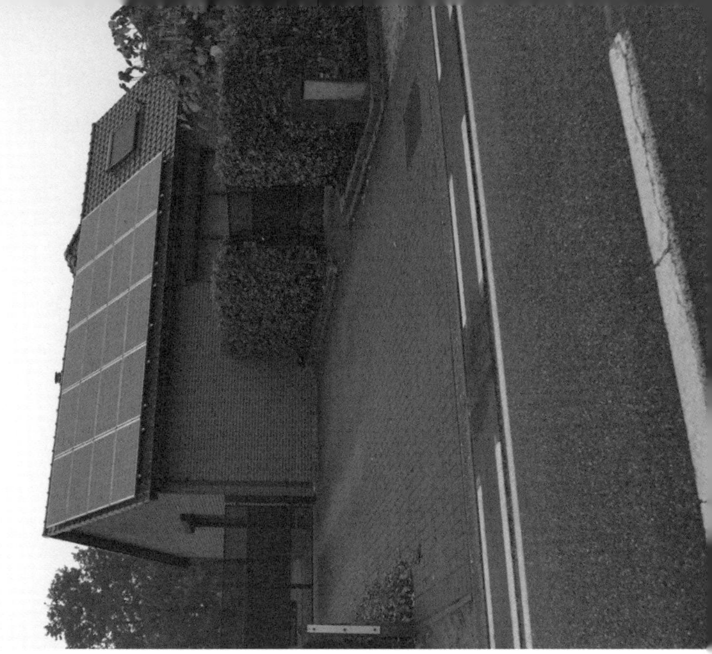

MOUTHPIECE KALE PESTO

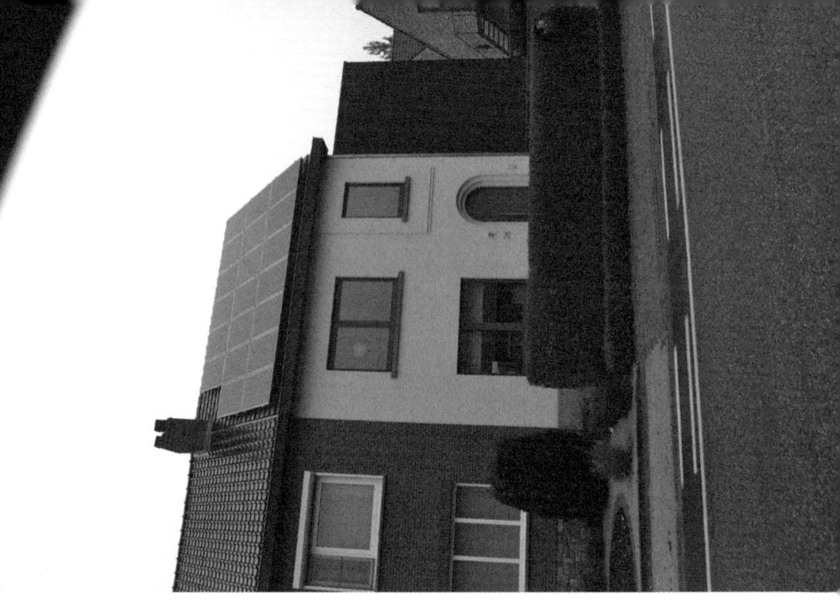

HOW TO MAKE AN OMBRE CAKE (SO COOL!) HOW DO I MAKE A MEAL LESS SPICY? HOW TO PAINT OMBRE WALLS

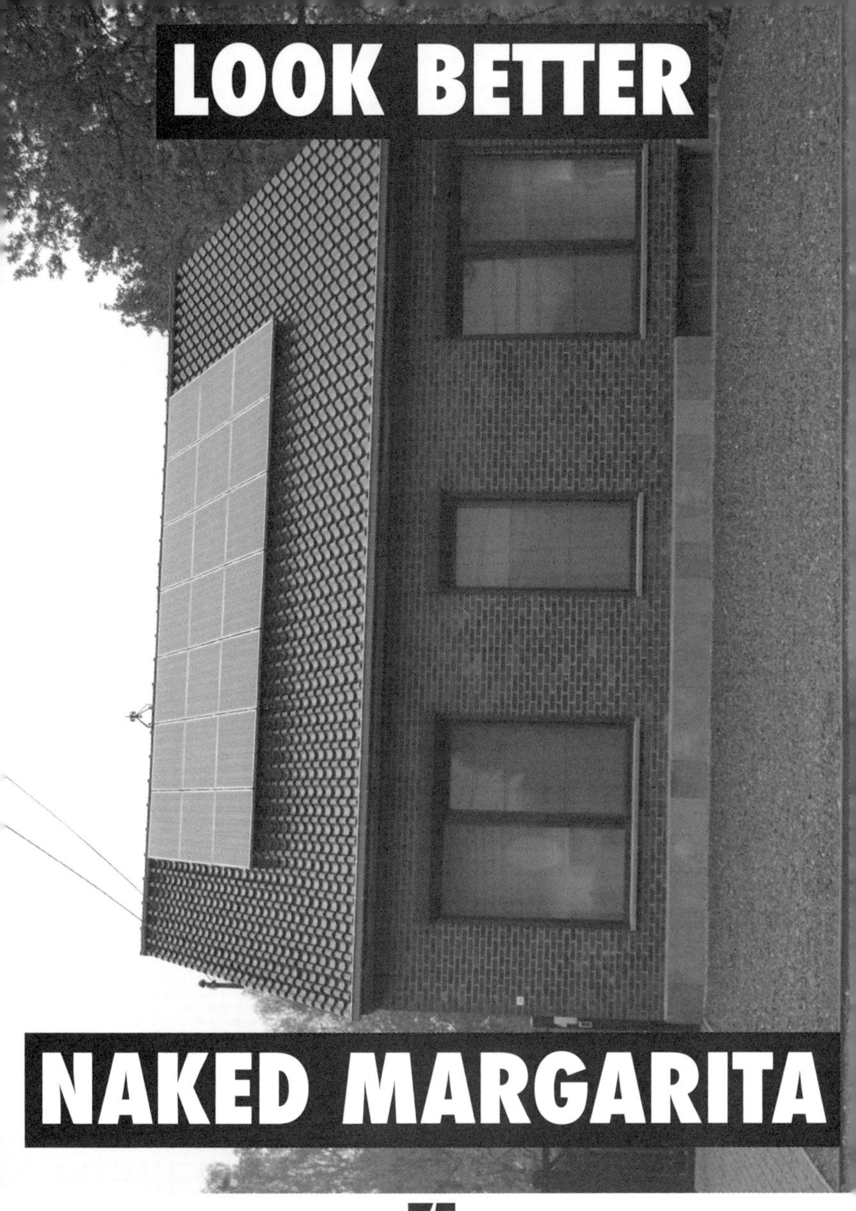

LOOK BETTER

NAKED MARGARITA

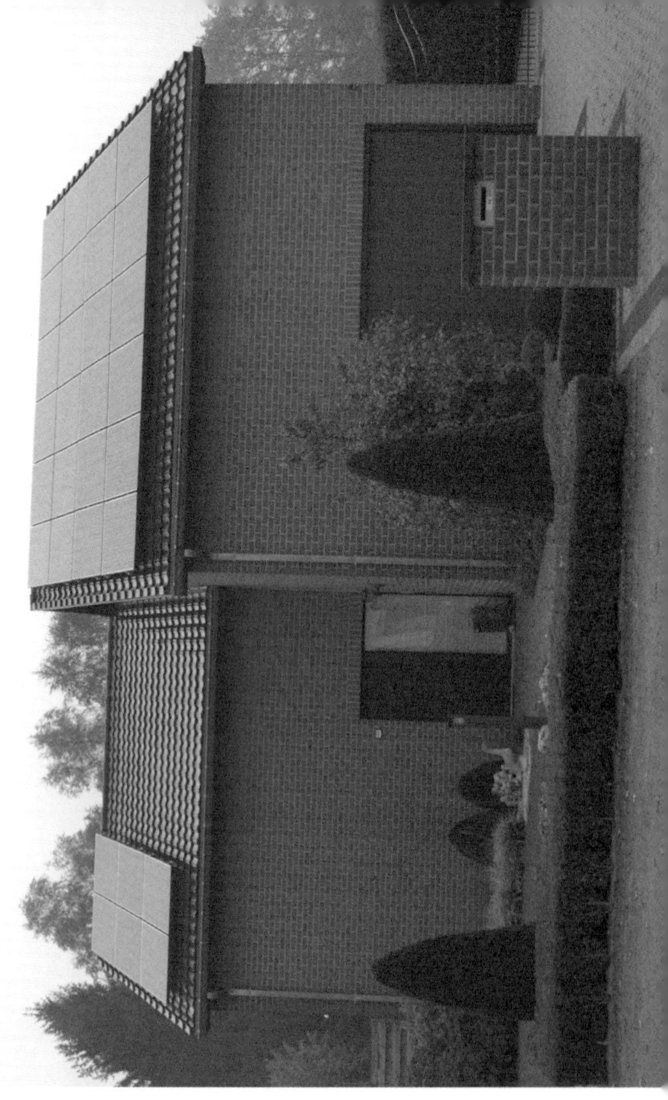

CLICK TO WIN BACON!

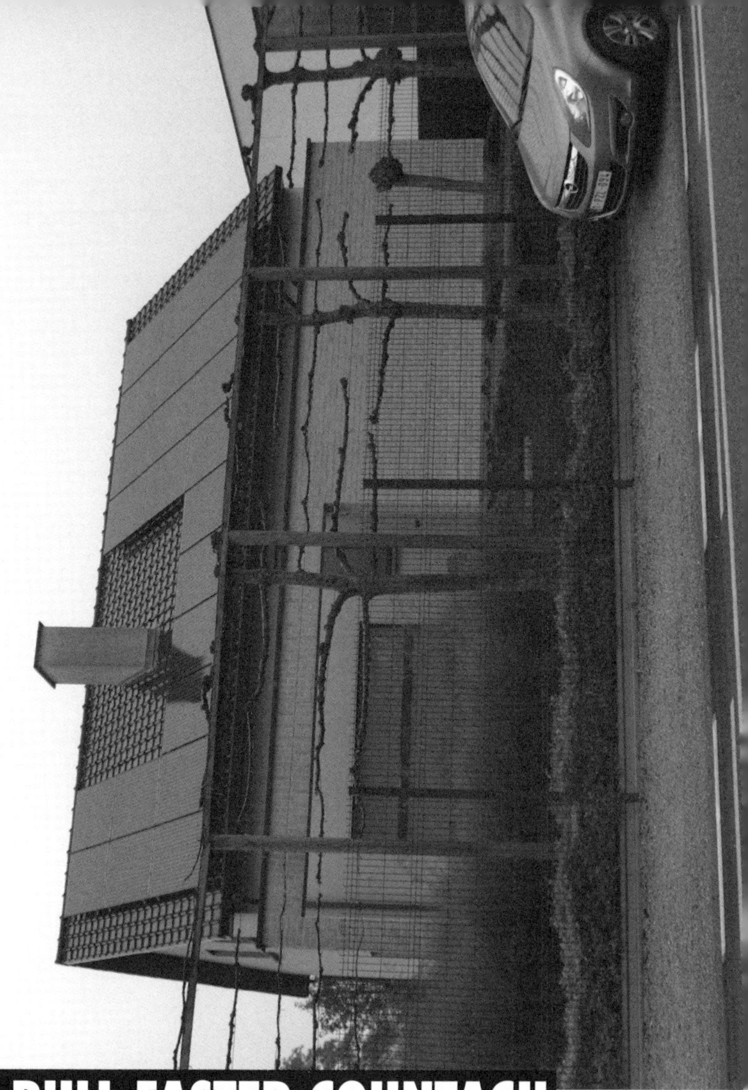

NO BULL FASTER COUNTACH

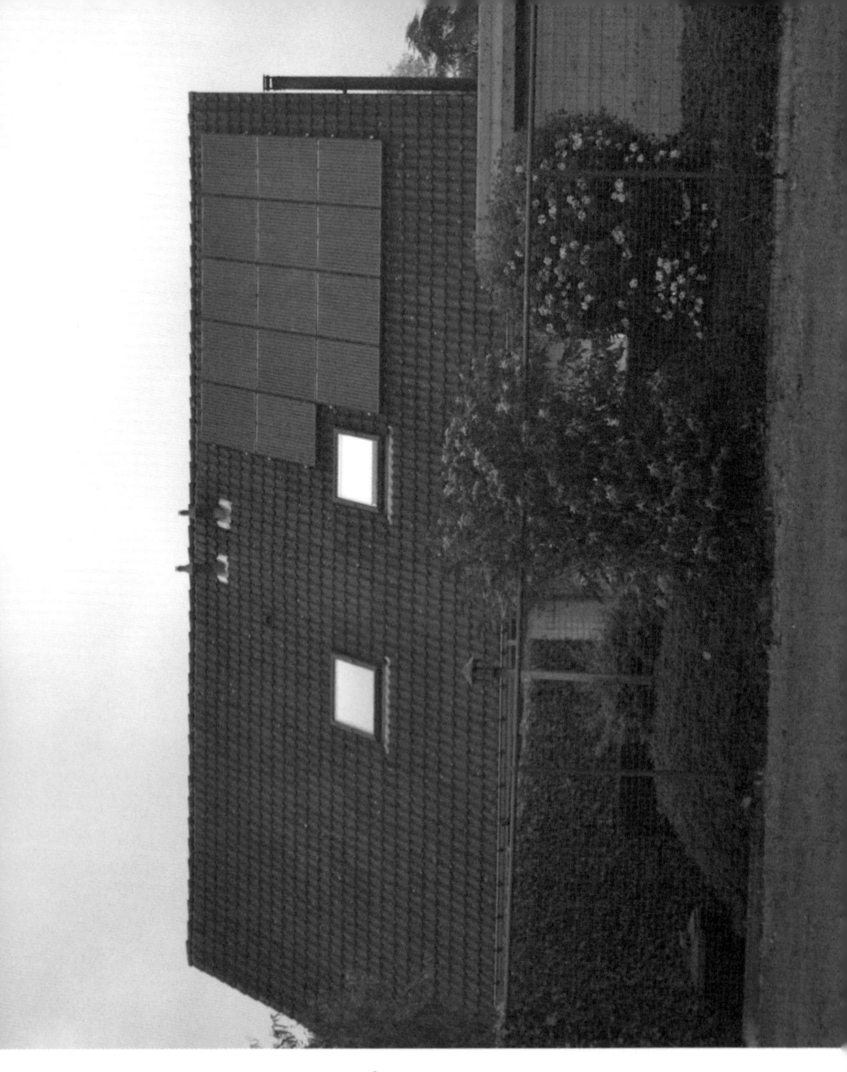

34G/100ML

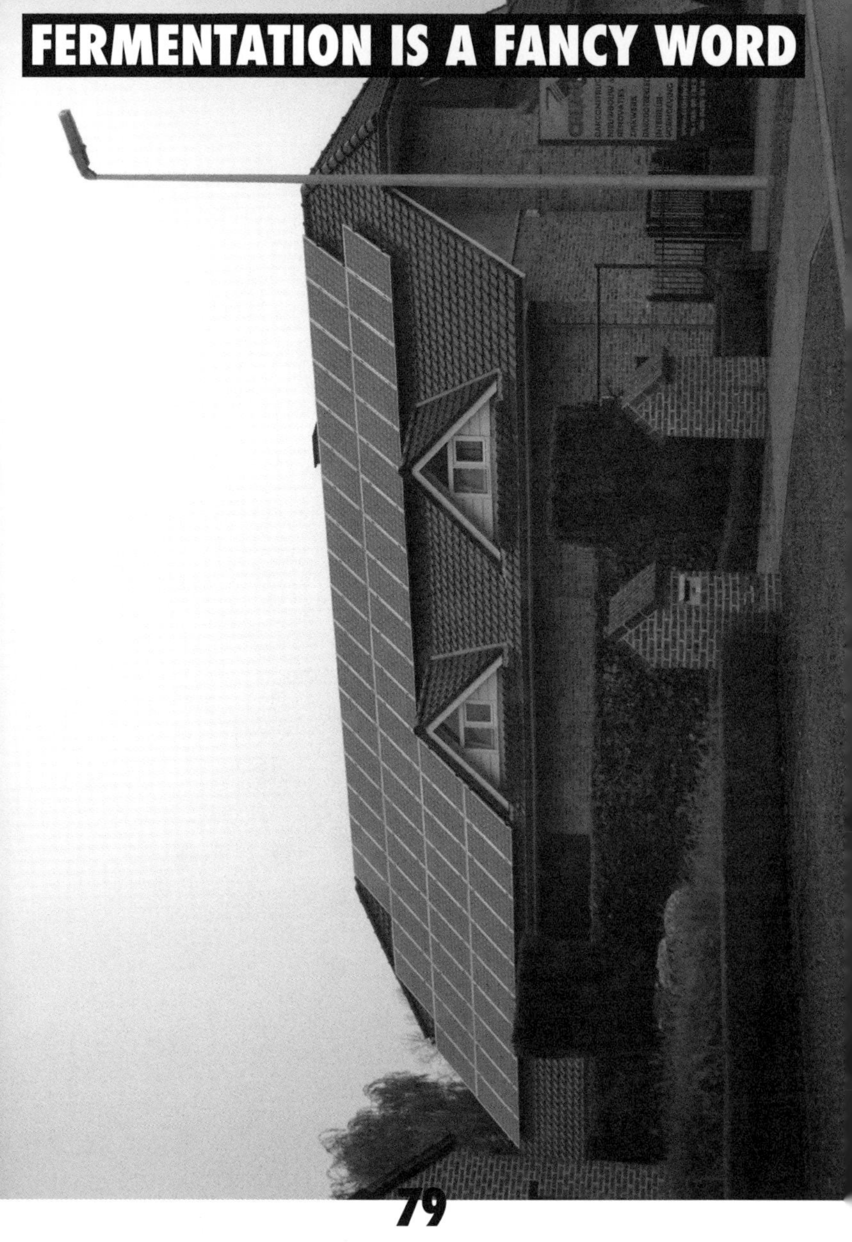

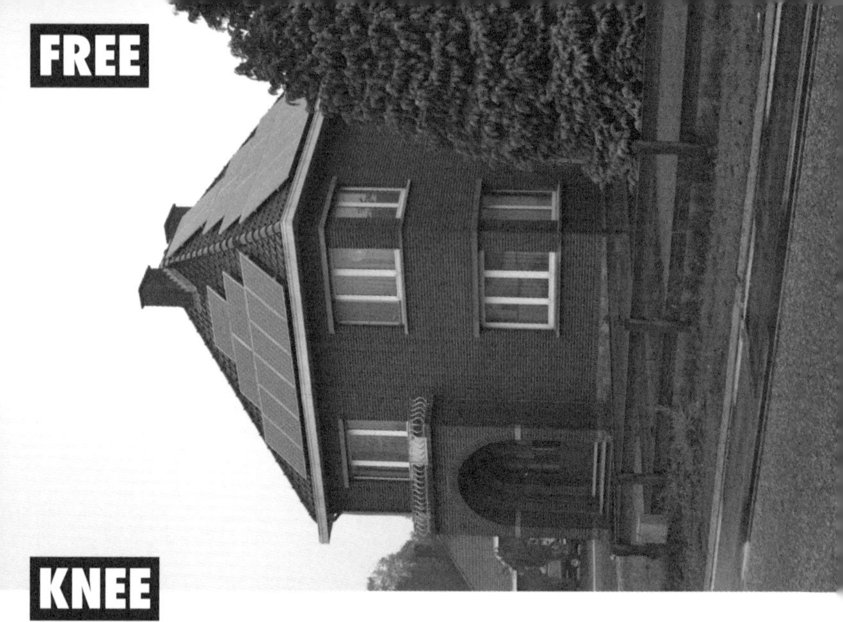

FREE

KNEE

PAIN

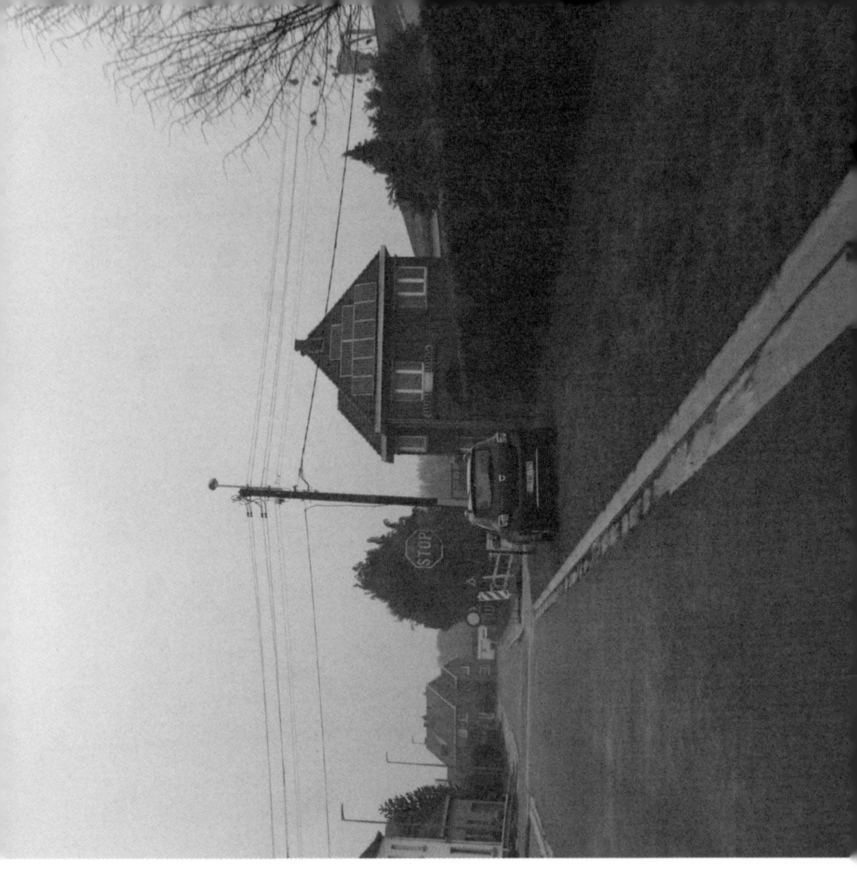

HOW TO SMOKE TURKEY

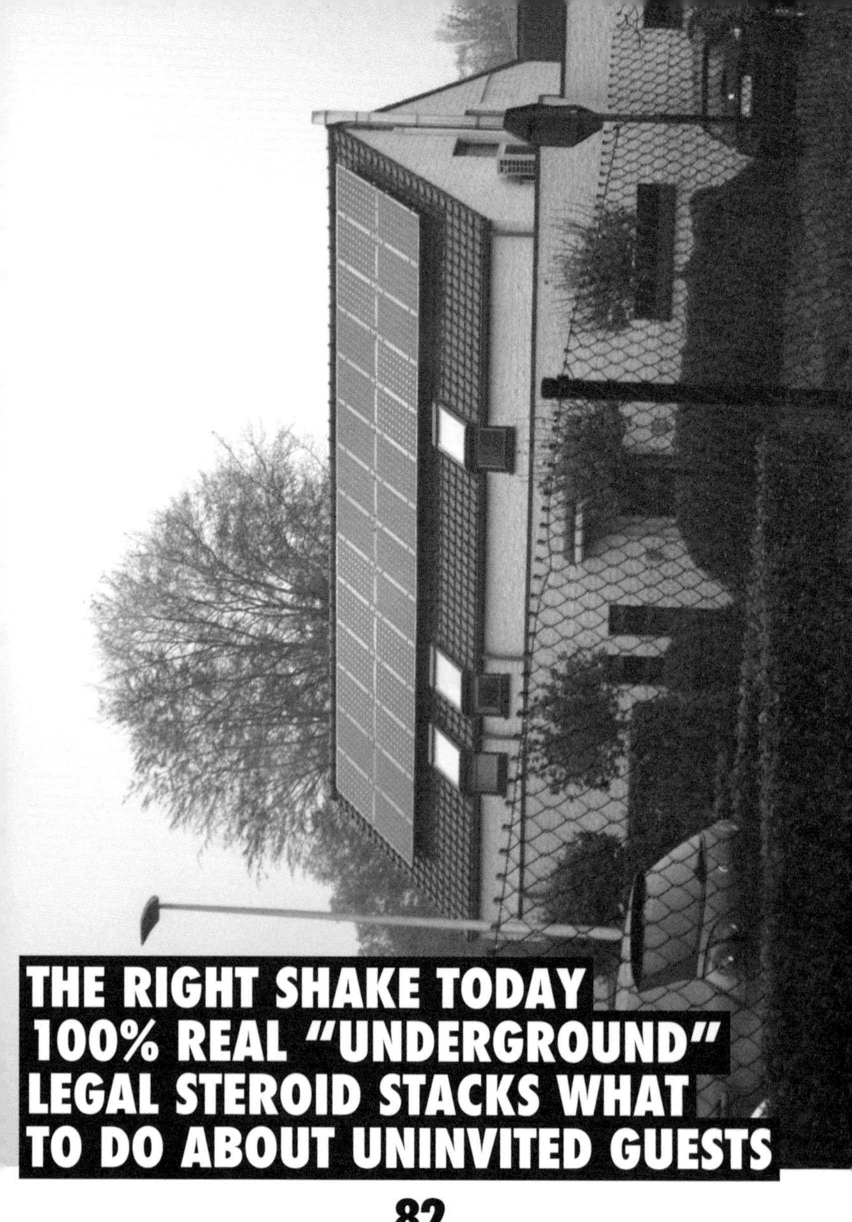

THE RIGHT SHAKE TODAY 100% REAL "UNDERGROUND" LEGAL STEROID STACKS WHAT TO DO ABOUT UNINVITED GUESTS

10 WEIRD FACTS ABOUT YOUR COLOR

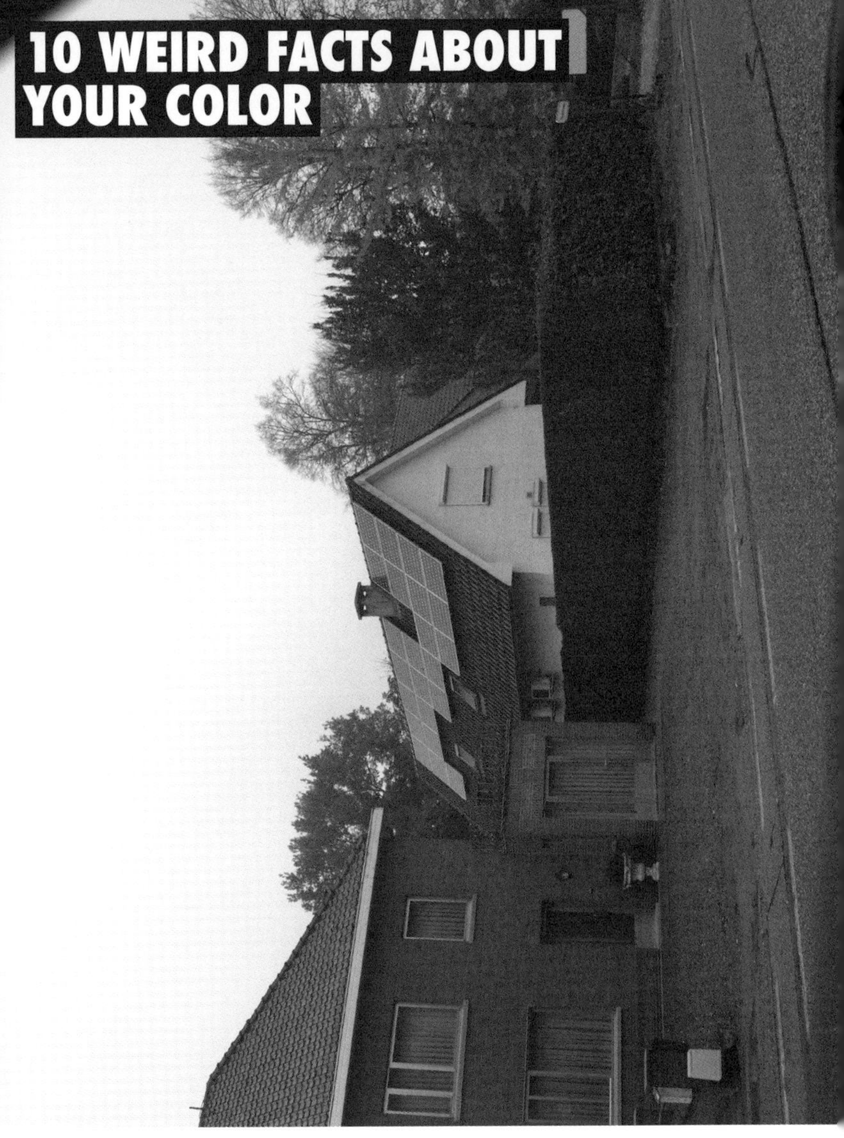

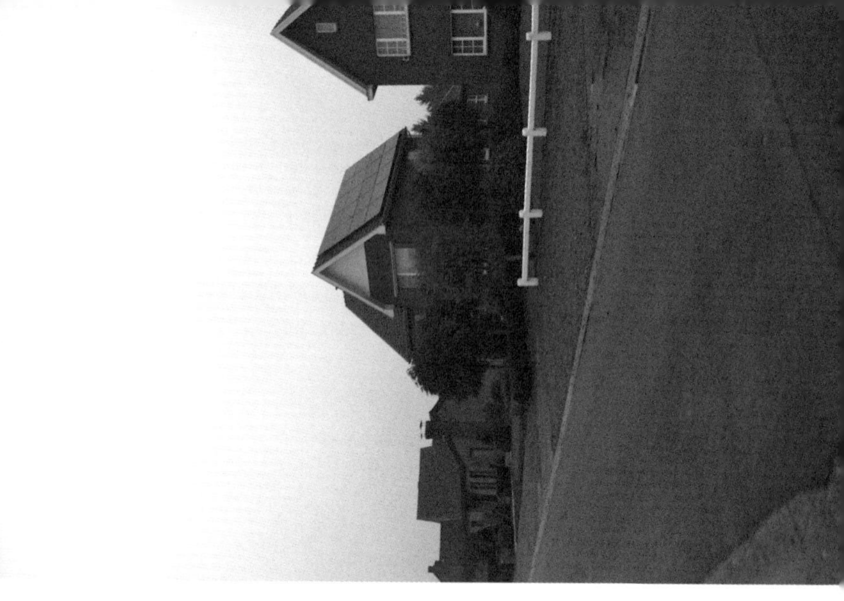

WHO OWNS A ROOF

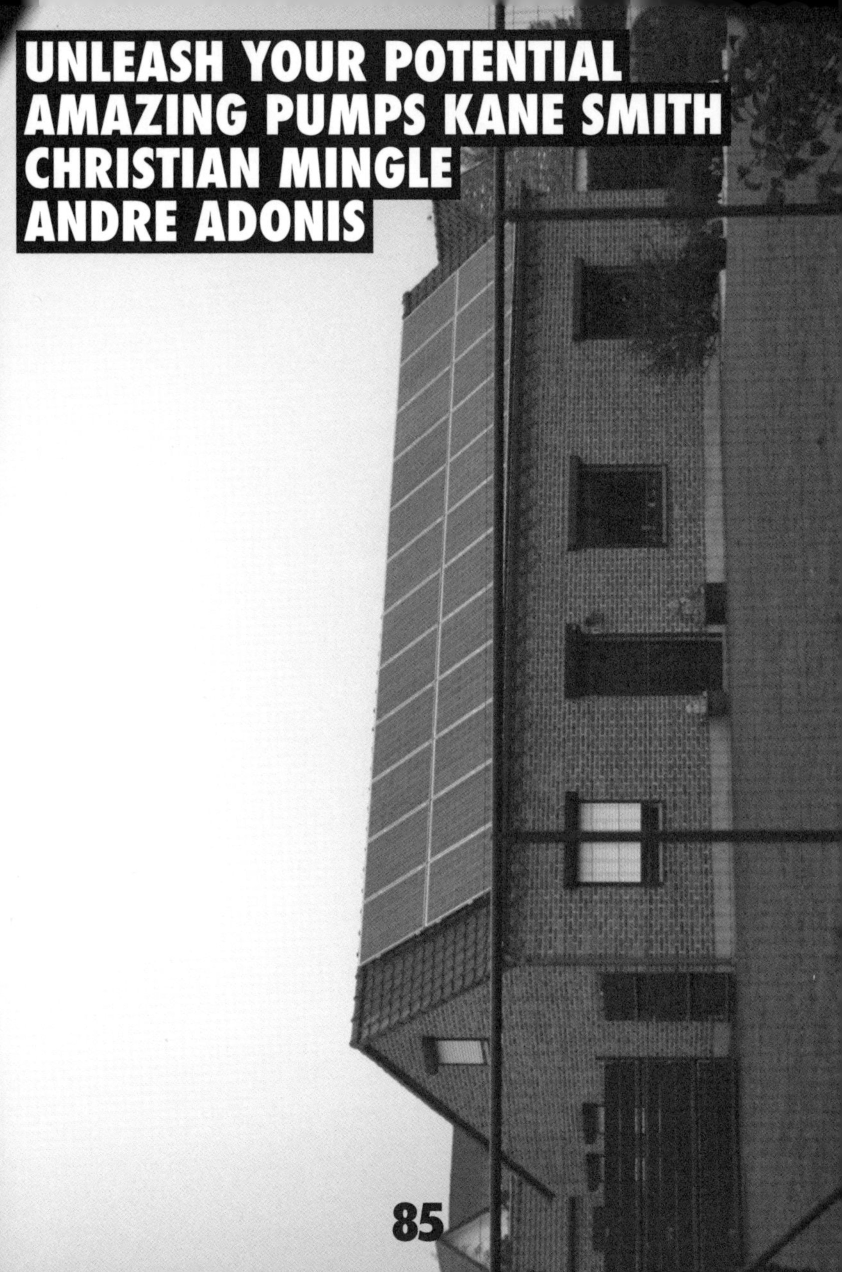

UNLEASH YOUR POTENTIAL AMAZING PUMPS KANE SMITH CHRISTIAN MINGLE ANDRE ADONIS

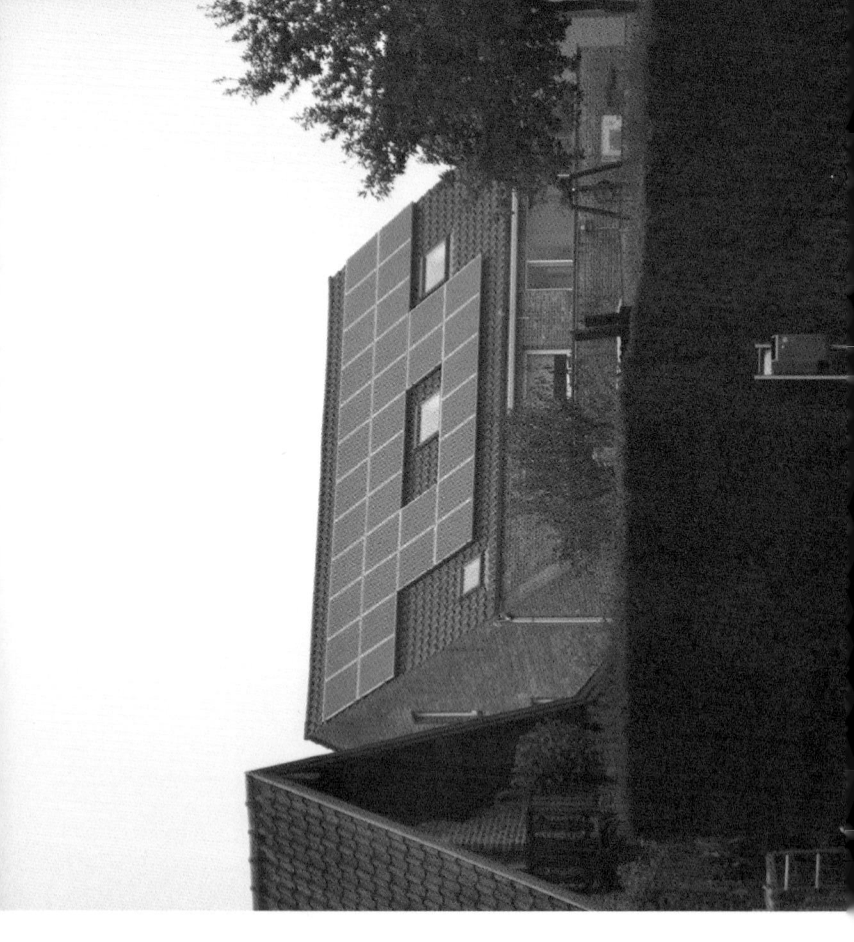

PEOPLE STOP AND WATCH ME LIFT

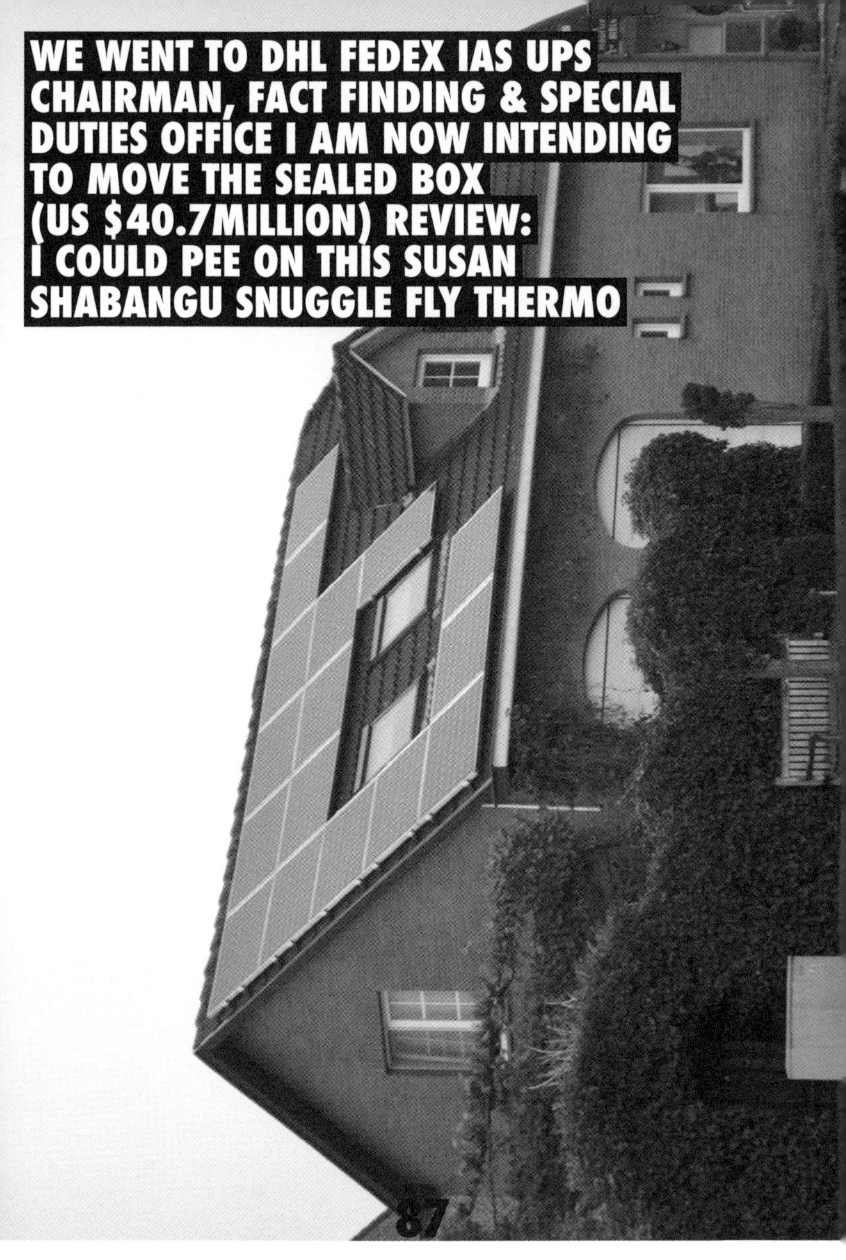

WE WENT TO DHL FEDEX IAS UPS CHAIRMAN, FACT FINDING & SPECIAL DUTIES OFFICE I AM NOW INTENDING TO MOVE THE SEALED BOX (US $40.7MILLION) REVIEW: I COULD PEE ON THIS SUSAN SHABANGU SNUGGLE FLY THERMO

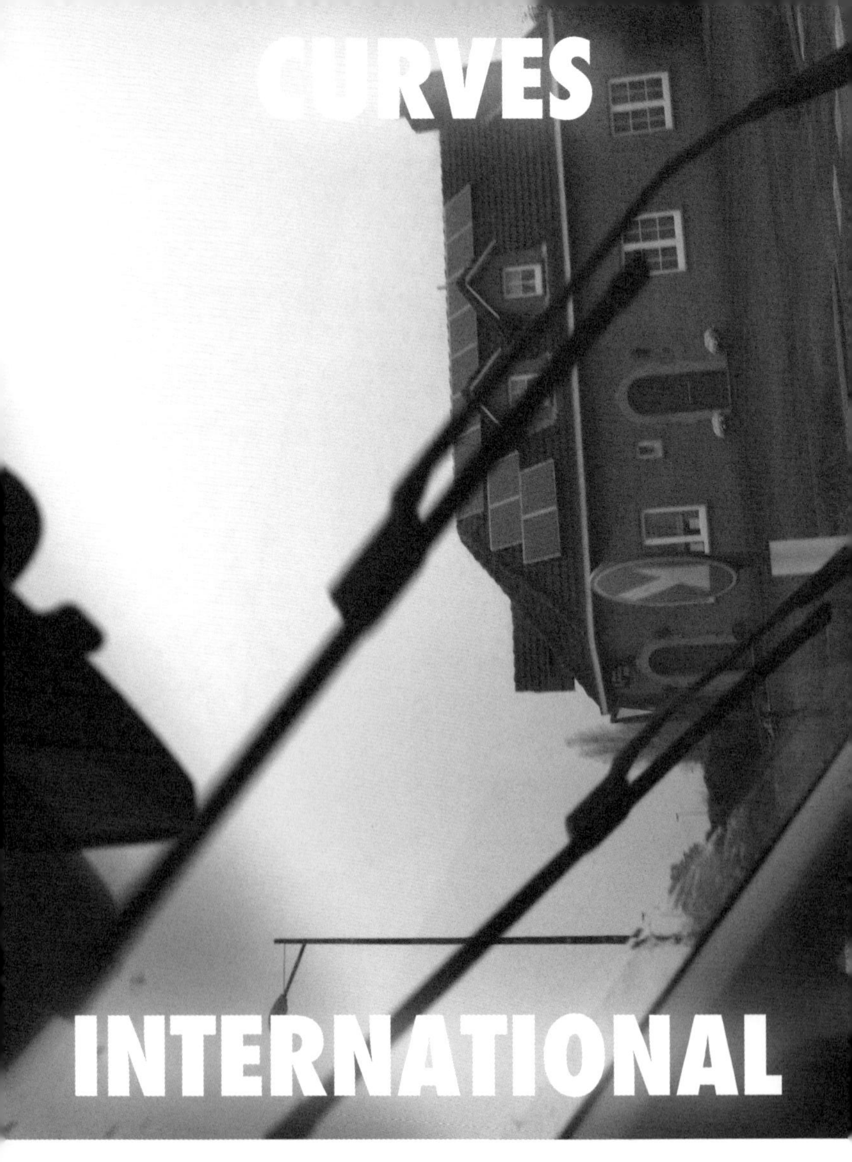
CURVES
INTERNATIONAL

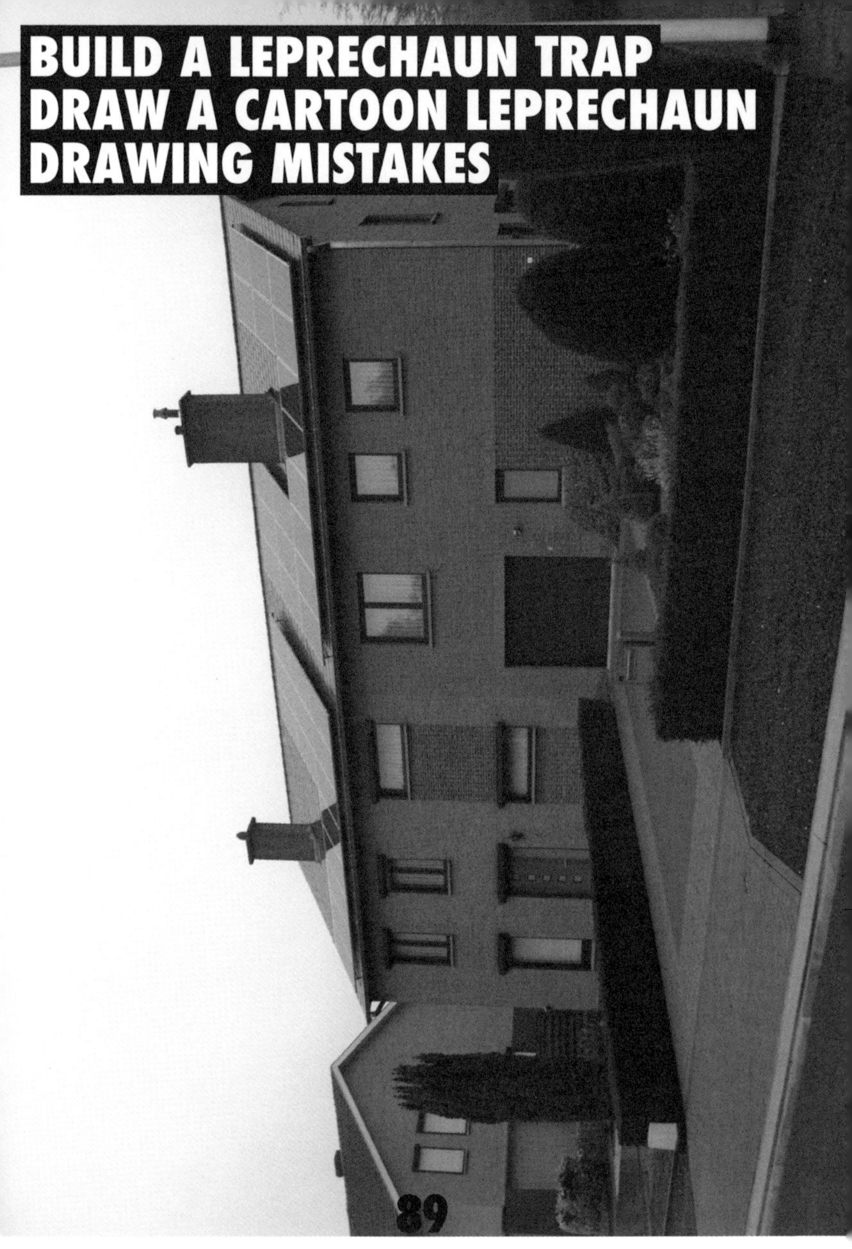

BUILD A LEPRECHAUN TRAP
DRAW A CARTOON LEPRECHAUN
DRAWING MISTAKES

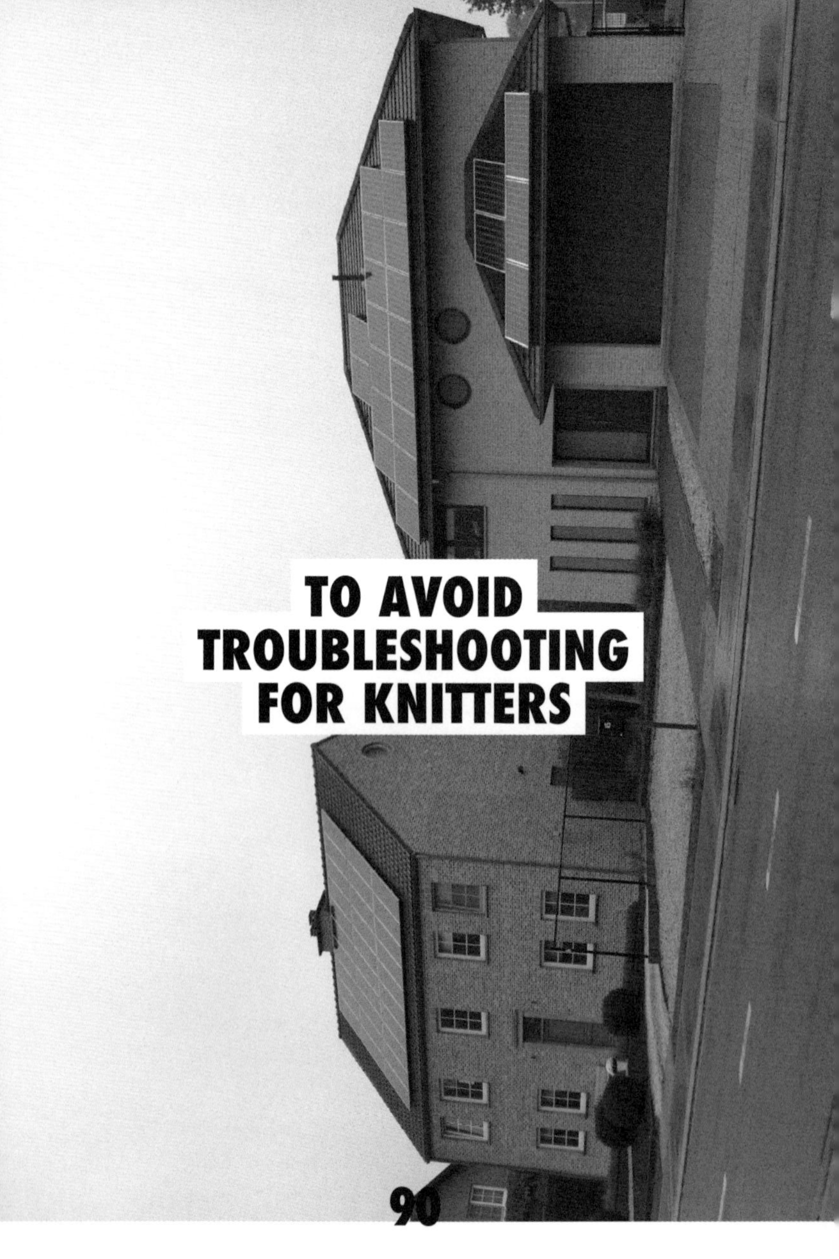

TO AVOID TROUBLESHOOTING FOR KNITTERS

RUBBER MAKING MISTAKES

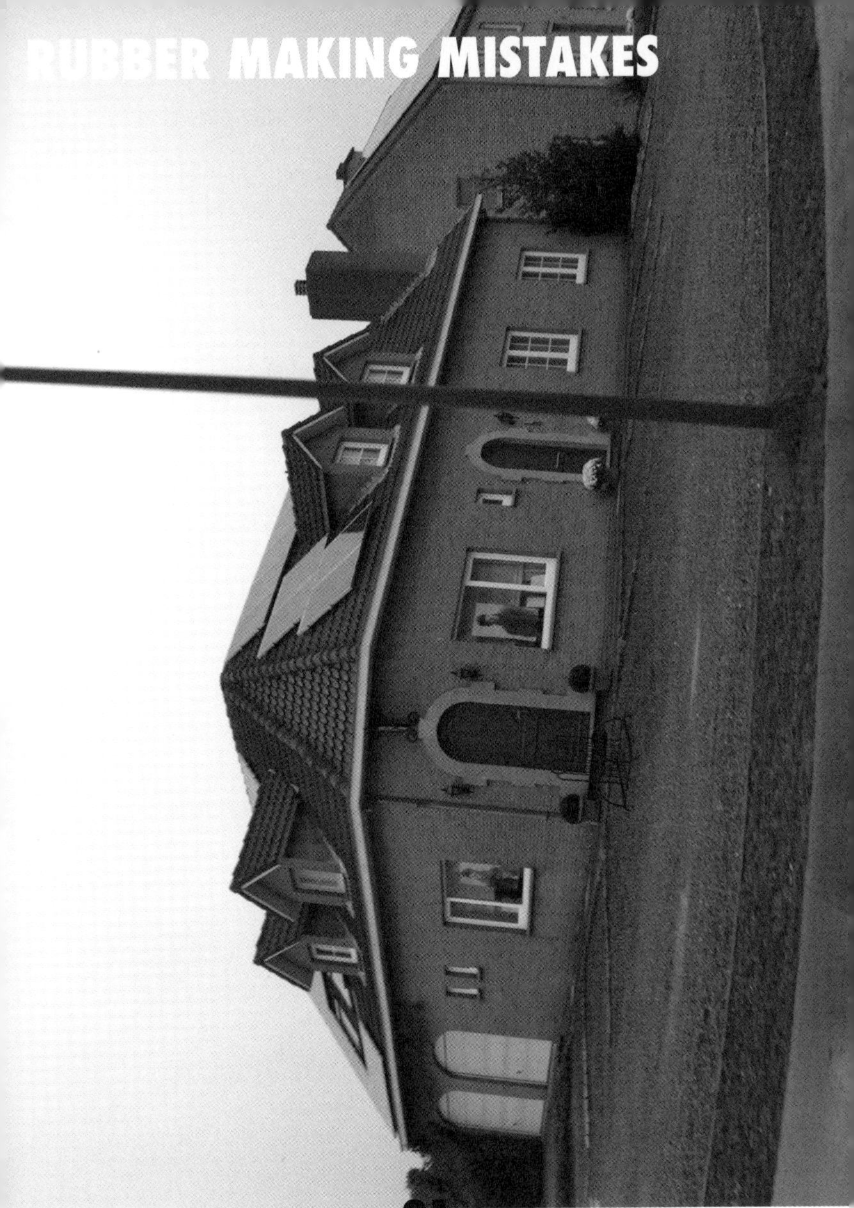

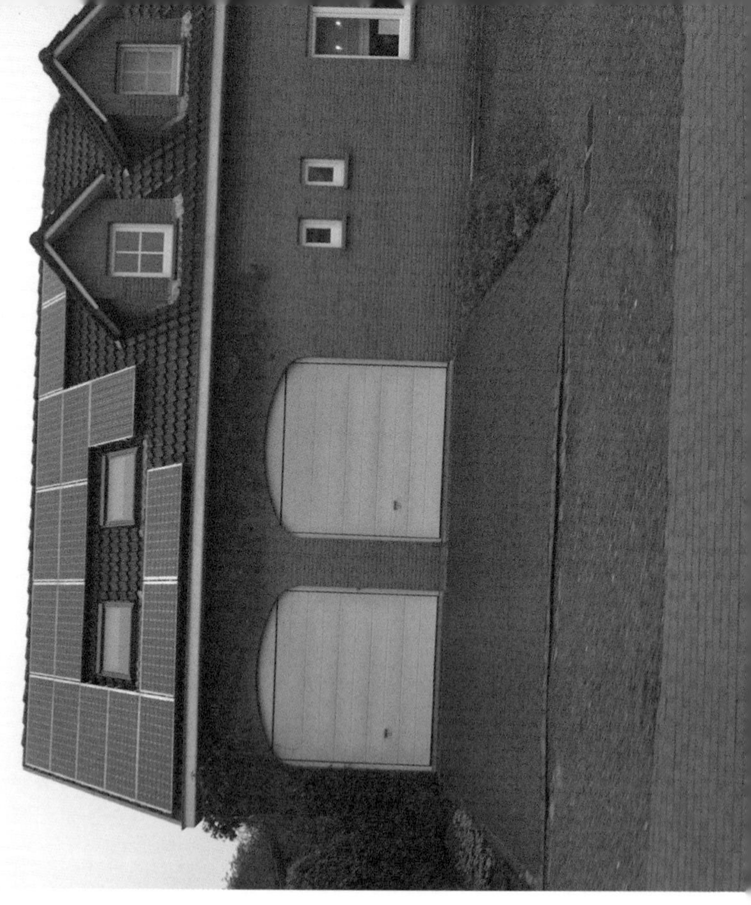

REAL VS FAKE SUPREME TUTORIAL

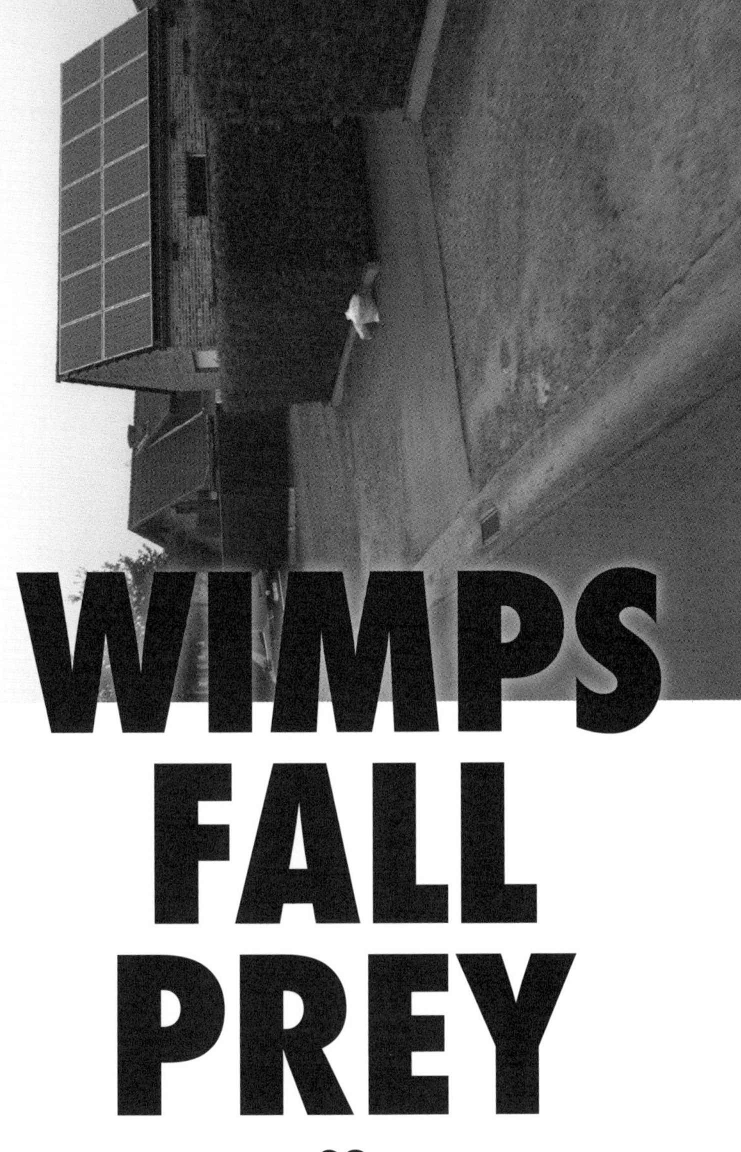

WIMPS FALL PREY

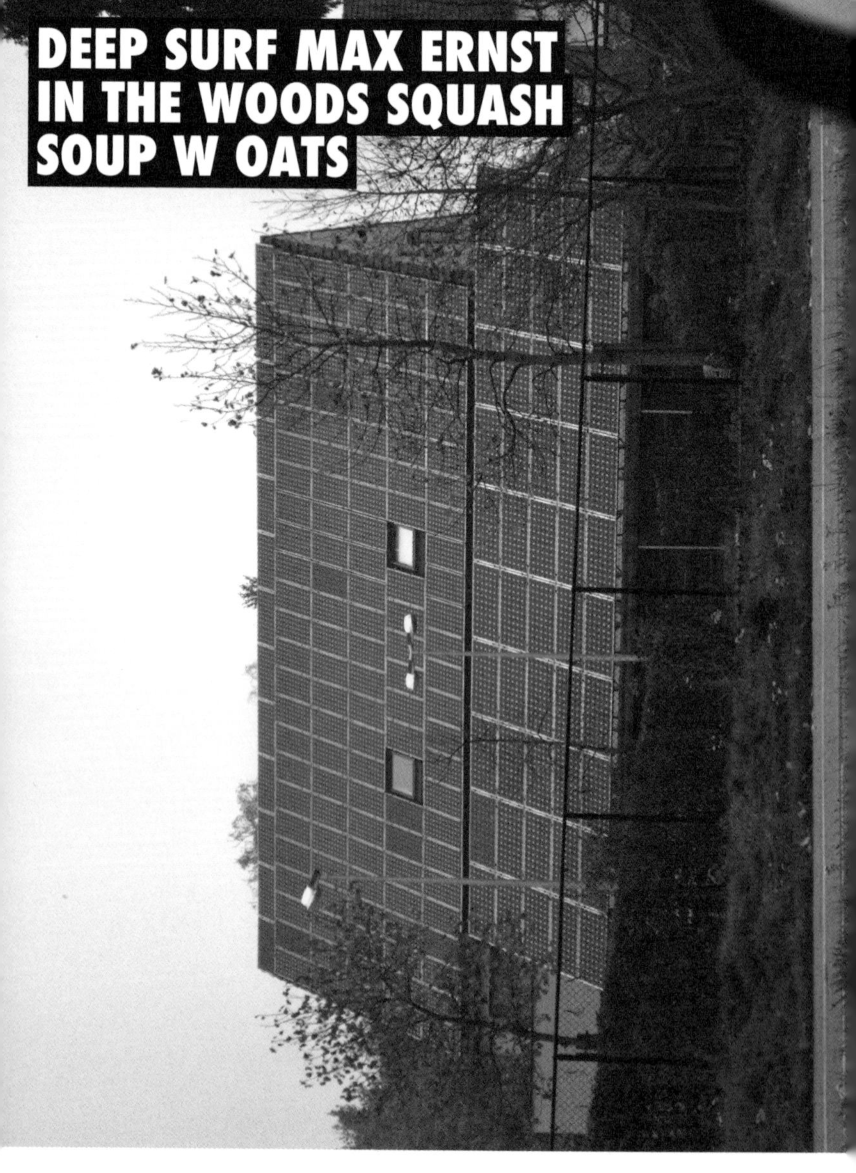

DEEP SURF MAX ERNST IN THE WOODS SQUASH SOUP W OATS

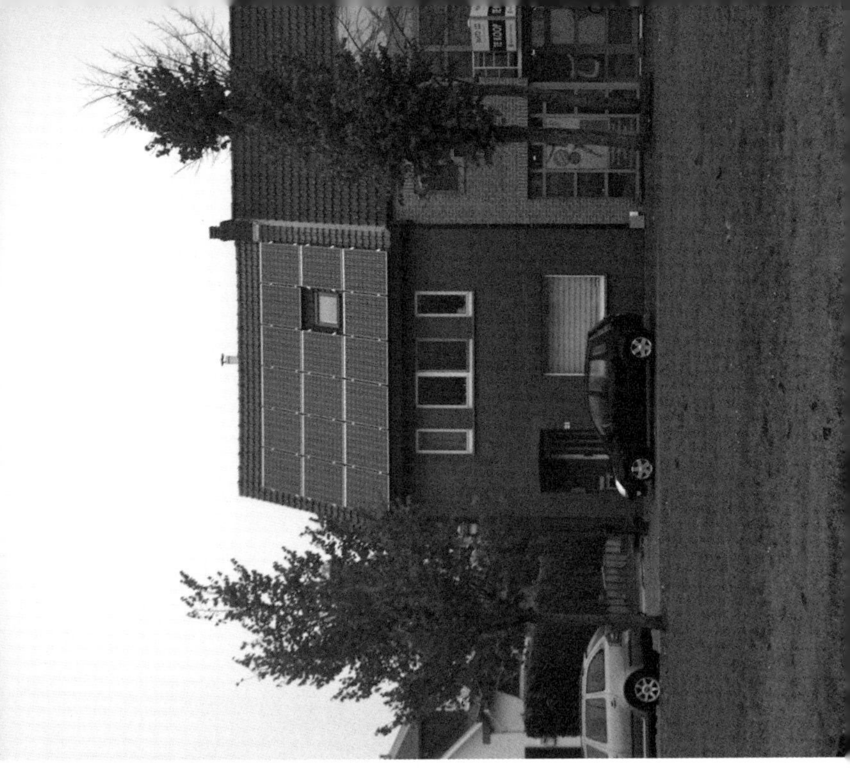

WHITE PAINT POST VAPOR BASS SCHEME

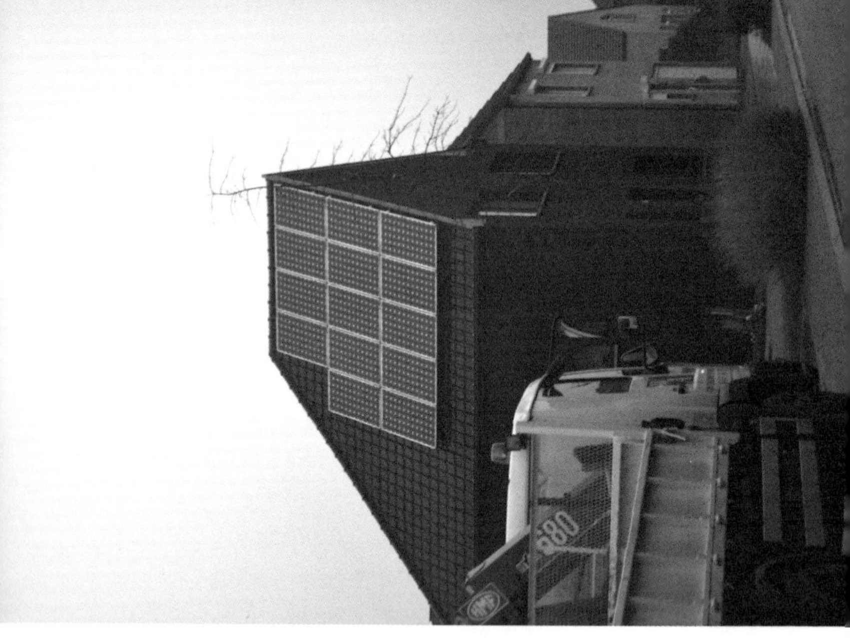

UGLY COUNTRY HOUSES DATA RECOVERY

DRONE SOFT WARE EVASION SLUSH

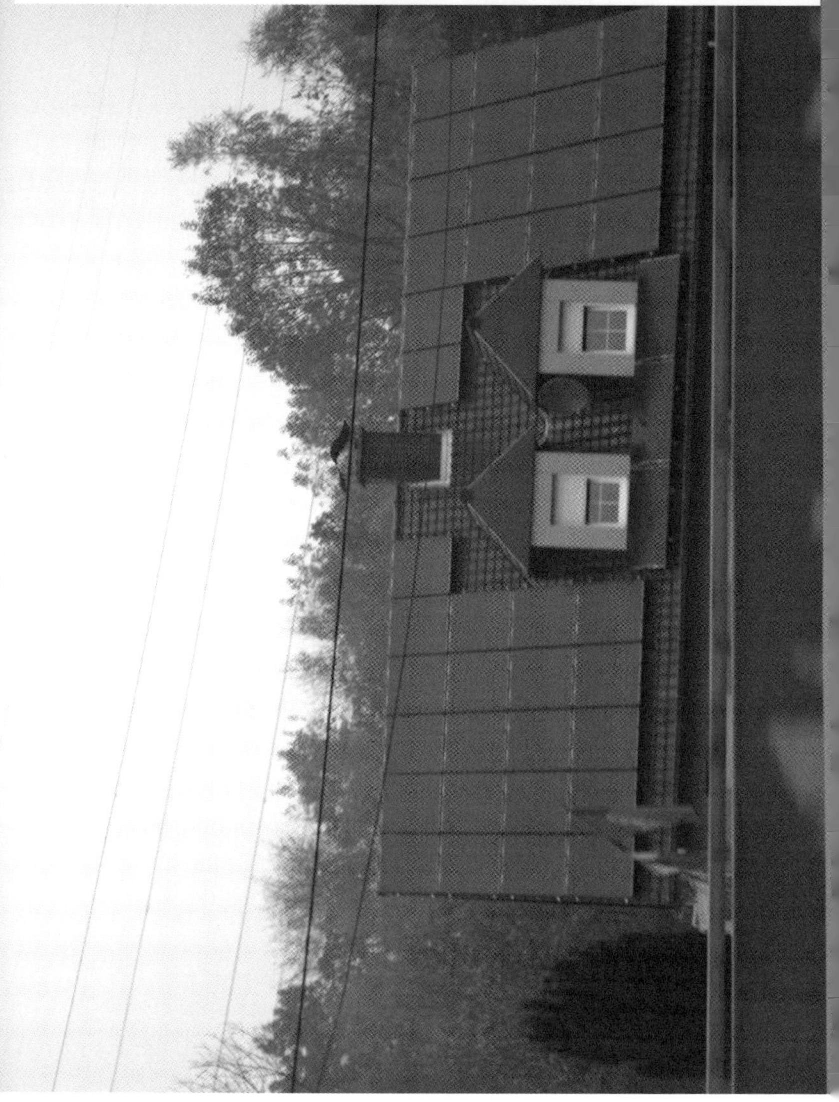

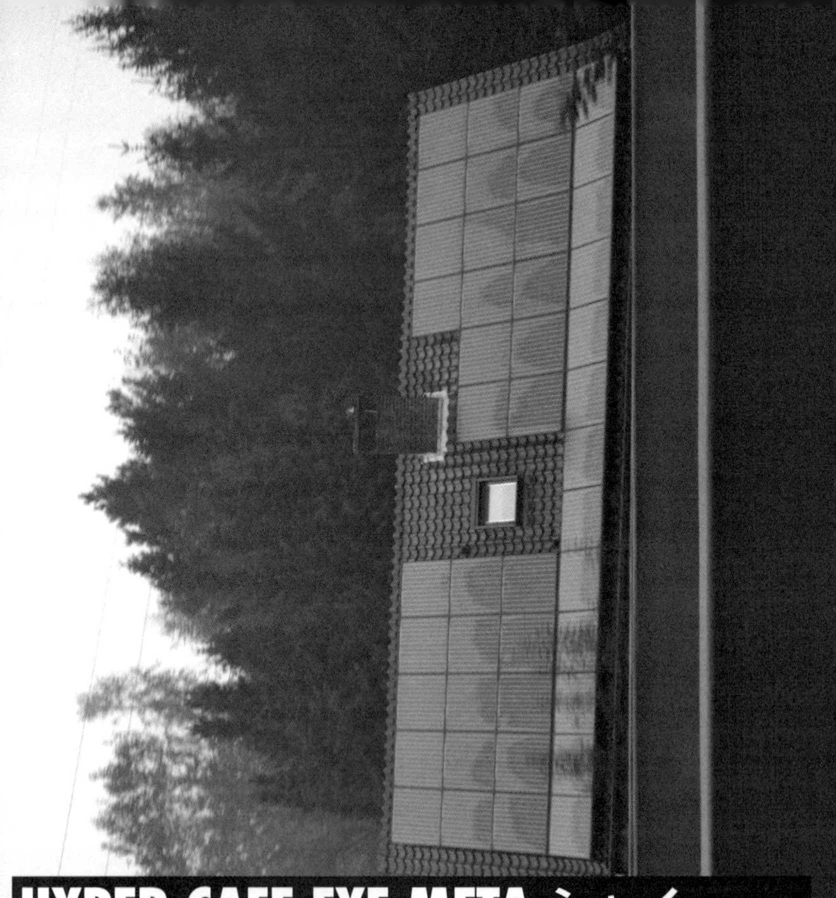

HYPER CAFE EYE META シャイ PROTO HUT SHARP SWORD DRONE SCALE JUNK DRONE FOG BASS LED STRIPS SHEEP SKIN REFLECTIVE PAINT JOB SOUND TRACK WRAP SEND

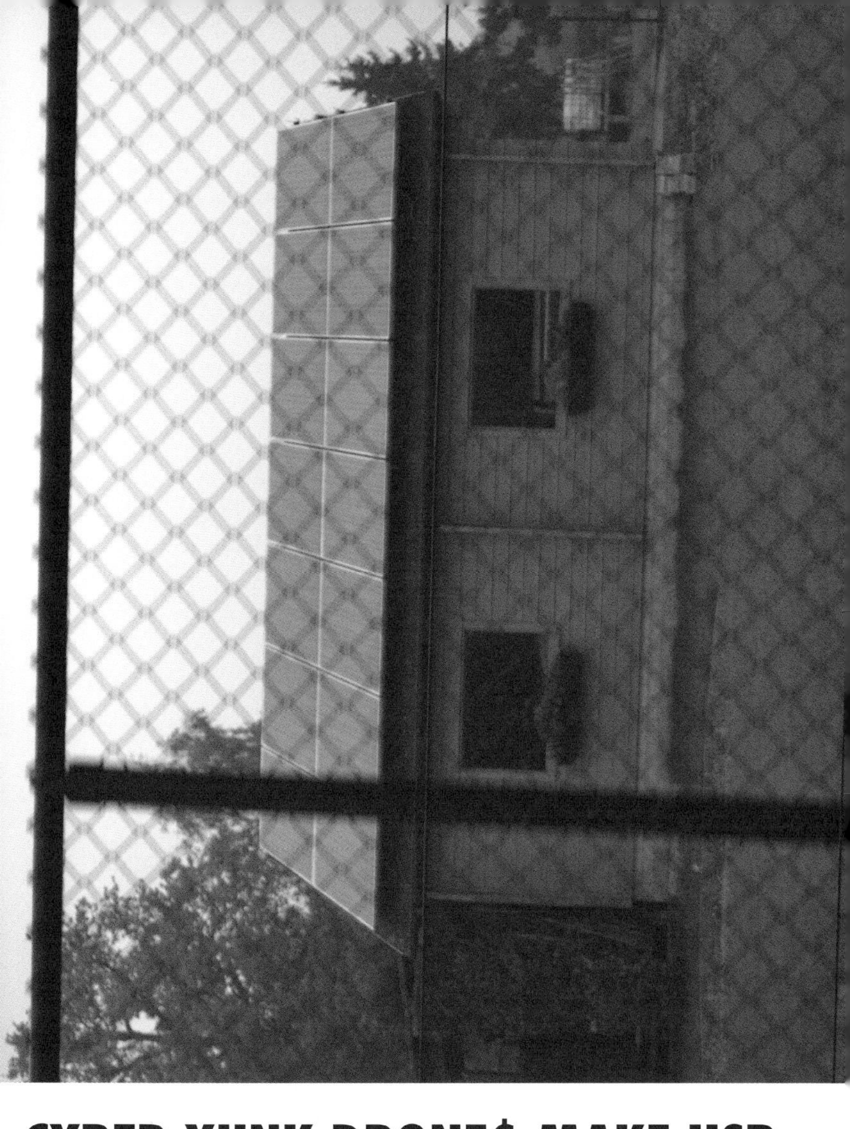

CYBER ¥UNK DRONE$ MAKE USB CASSETTES PIZZA PARTY

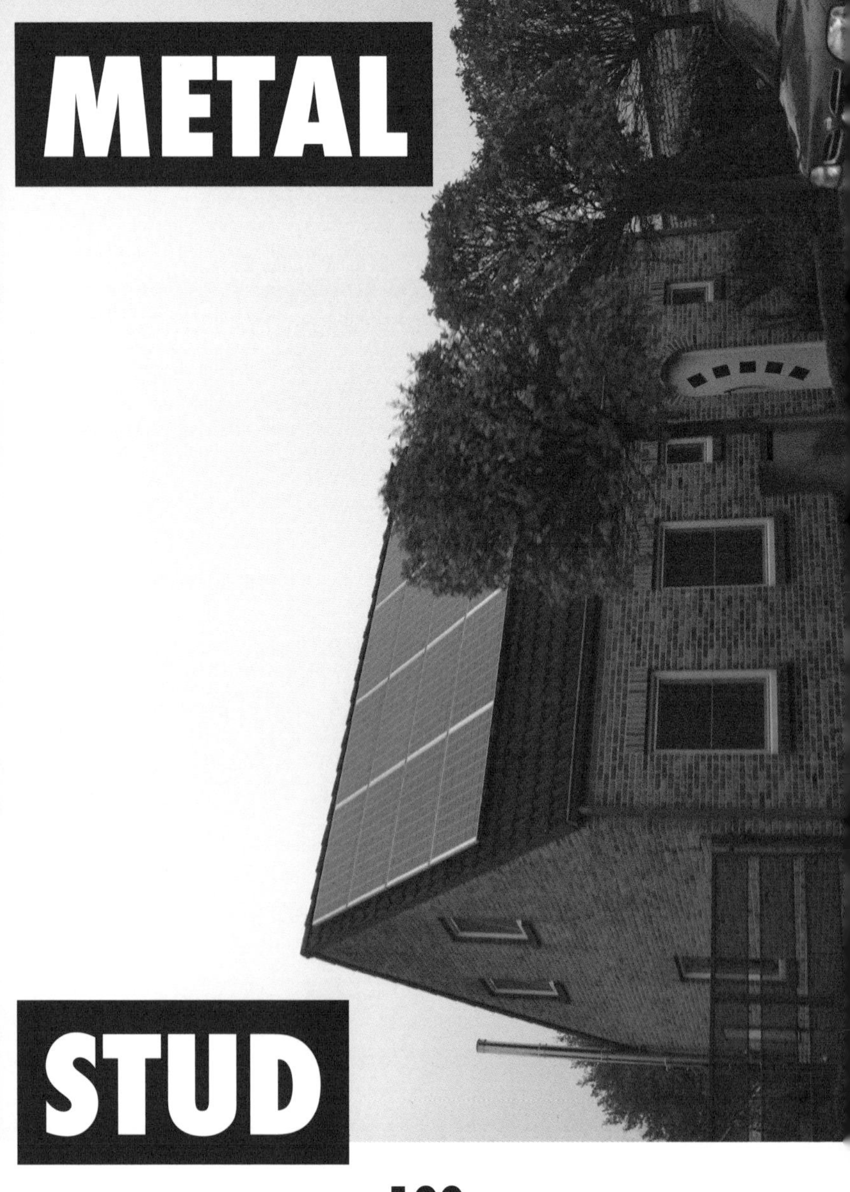

METAL STUD

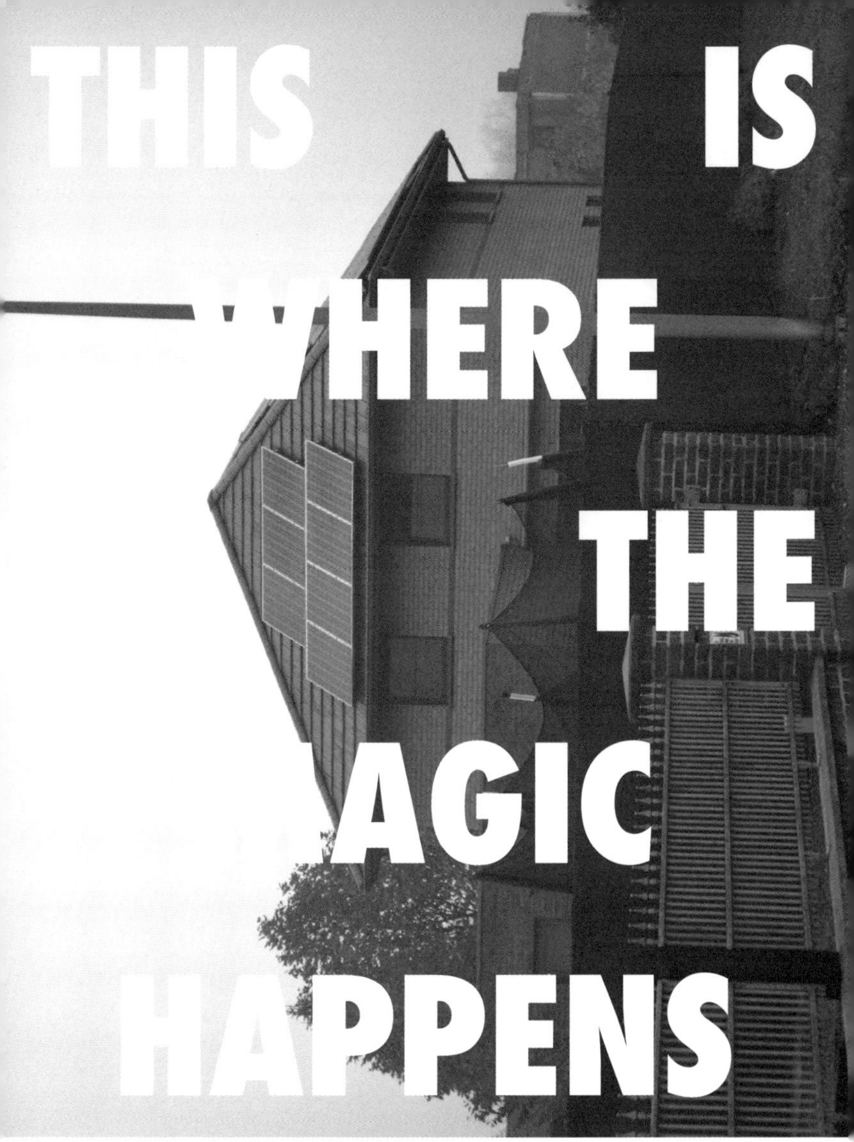

THIS IS WHERE THE MAGIC HAPPENS

GYM LOOKING FORWARD FOR MORE INFORMATION VERY NICE SERIOUSLY THOUGH POST BACK TO MY FRIENDS SELFIE CORNER SELFISH PEOPLE WITHIN AN ENVIRONMENT THAT HAS BEEN ALTERED IN SUCH A WAY TO MAKE THE GENERAL ENVIRONMENT MORE CONSPICUOUS POSTHUMOUS THE FIRST HALF OF THE DAY MINIMALIST I LOVE MINIMAL AND DESTROYED BADASS AND MMMMM GENTLER IDEAS FOR MY PHONE CRUNCHY CRAZY CRY DEEP DEEPLY DEEJAY BLOODY BLOGGING ON A DATE TO HAVE THINGS IN THE WORLD WHICH WOULD OTHERWISE NEVER BE THERE KALE CHIPS IN MY ROOM KALE HAVE TO GO BACK TO MY ROOM KALE KANYE KAPPABASHI WHAT WHY WHEN YOU HAVE NO CLUE MUSTANGS

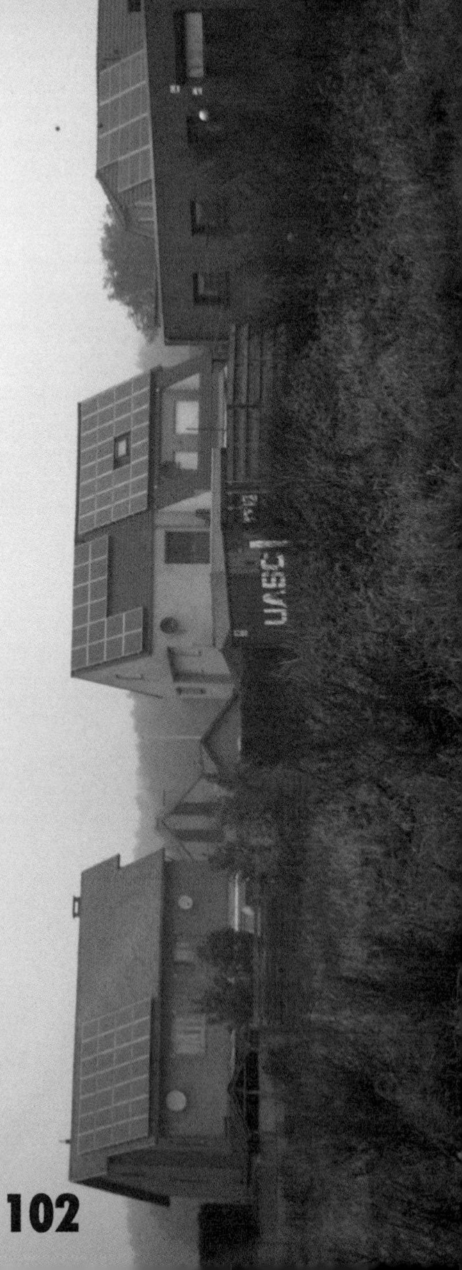

TOBACCO MENTHOL FRUIT DRINKS DESSERTS & CREAM POWER

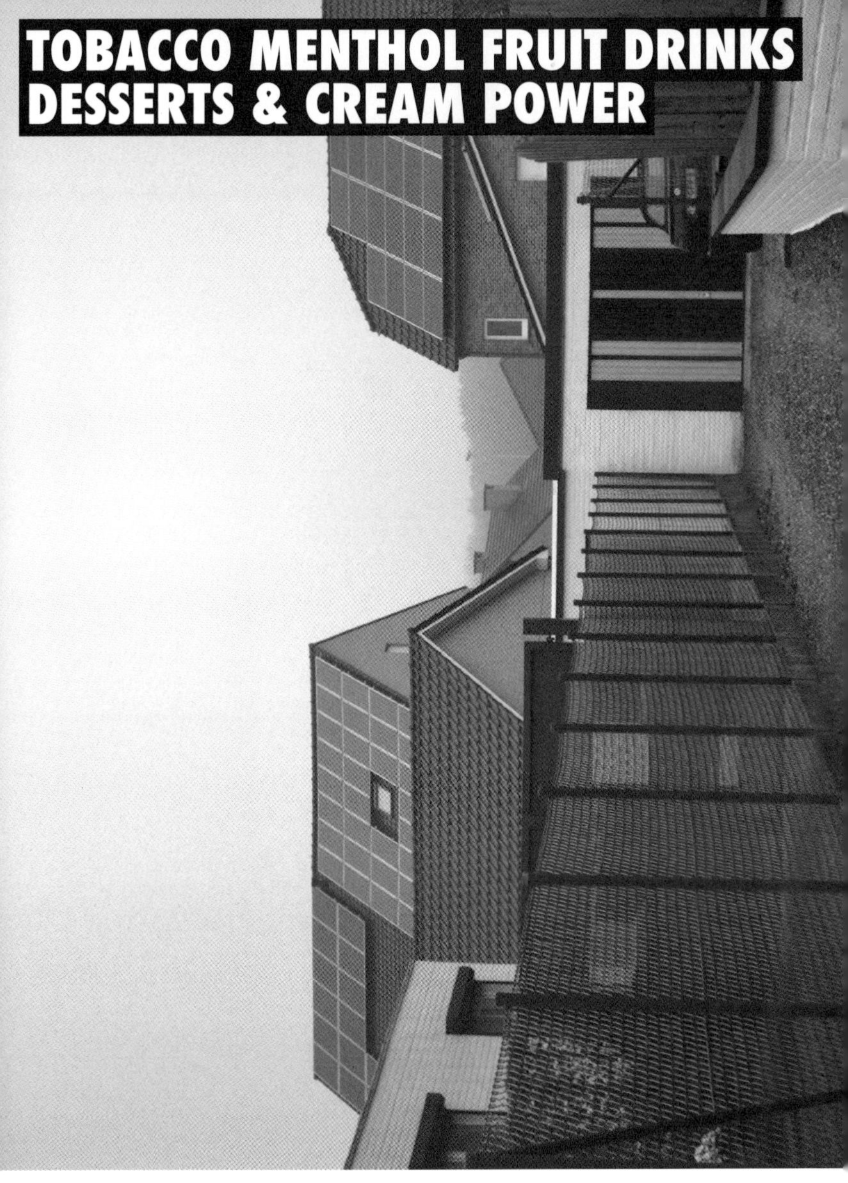

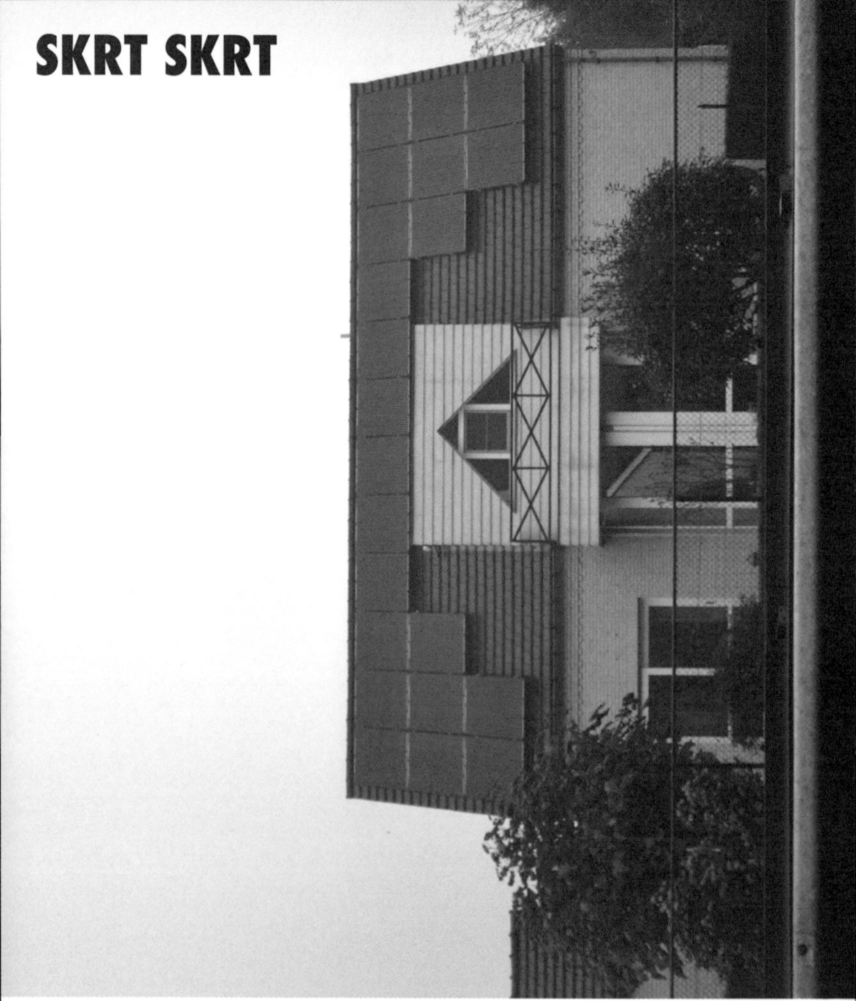

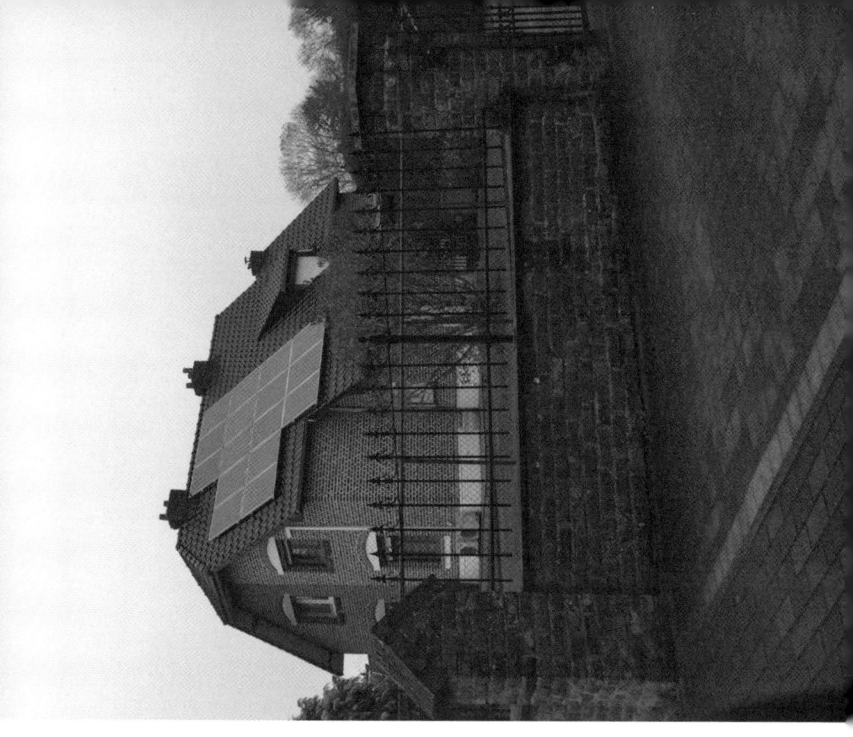

FLAG POLE BEER HALL GUCCI

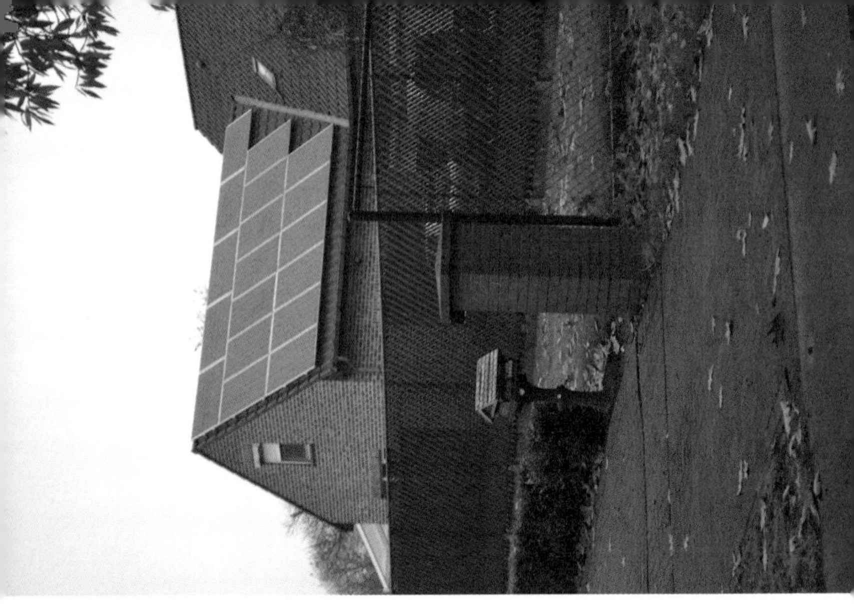

CHEESE DOMINOS DEATH RIDE

WHAT WOULD YOU LIKE TO DO WITH ME?

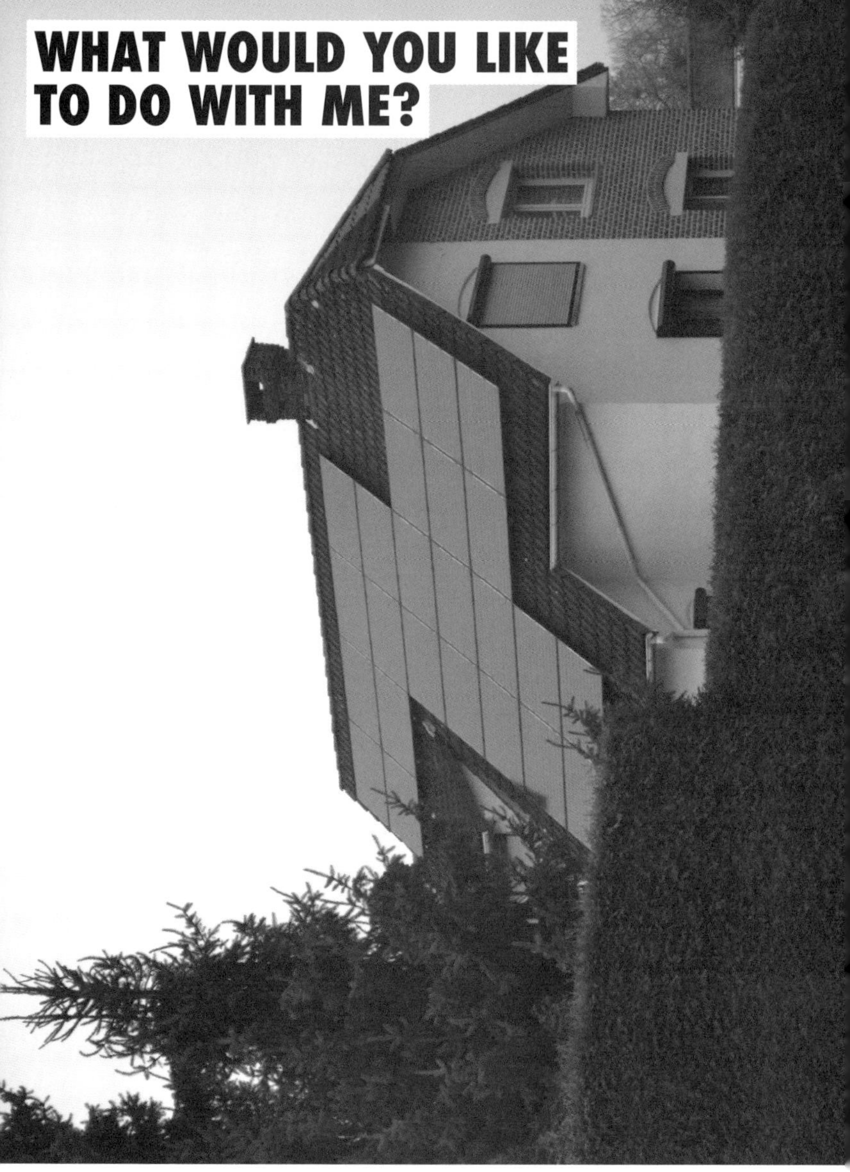

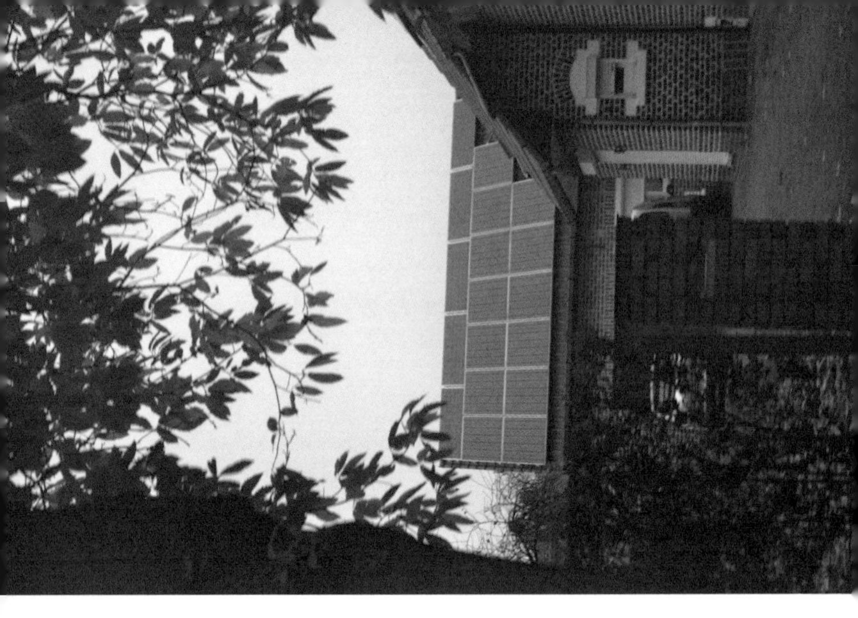

KALEBOT101

NAVY SEAL CEREAL HERBS, NUTS & SPICES

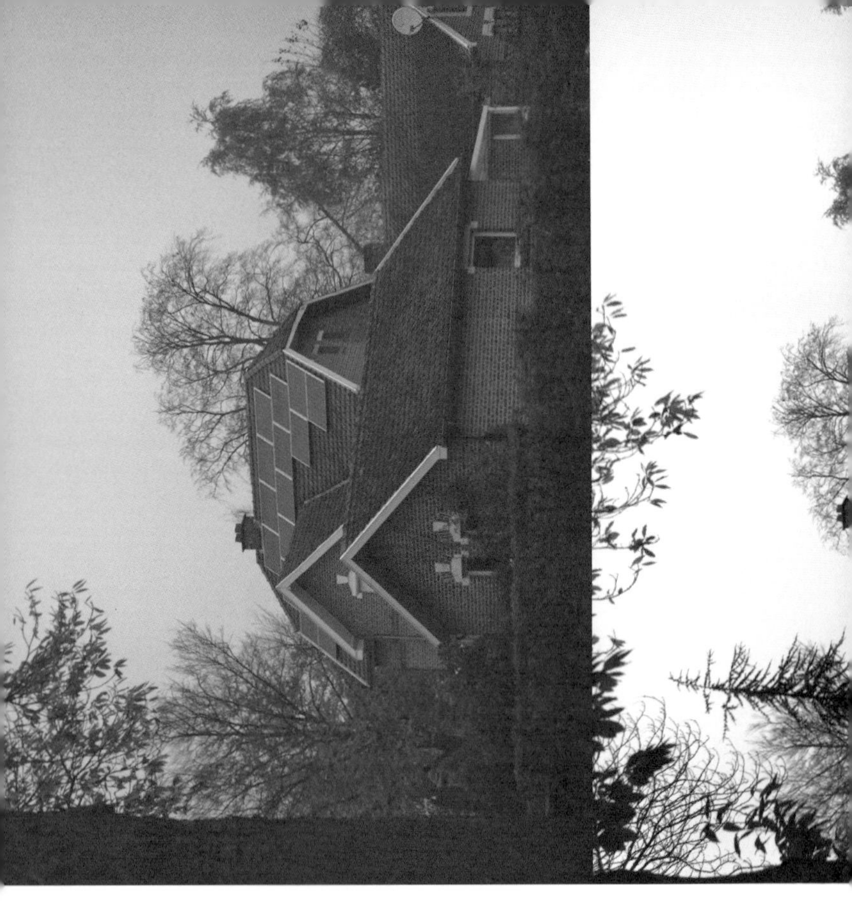

NEED VIP PROTECTION DURING ALL STAR WEEKEND?

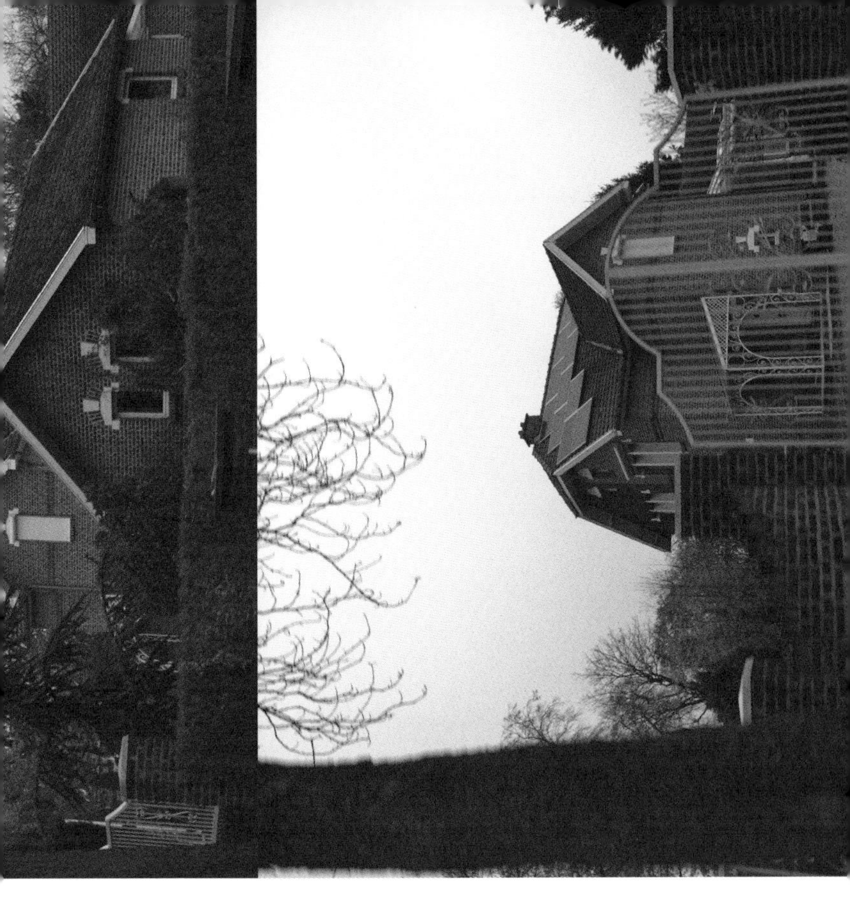

WE'VE BEEN THROUGH SO MUCH BUT THIS IS FOR YOU GUYS SO THANK YOU STICK TO YO JACUZZI DONT CLICK ON MY DAM USERNAME

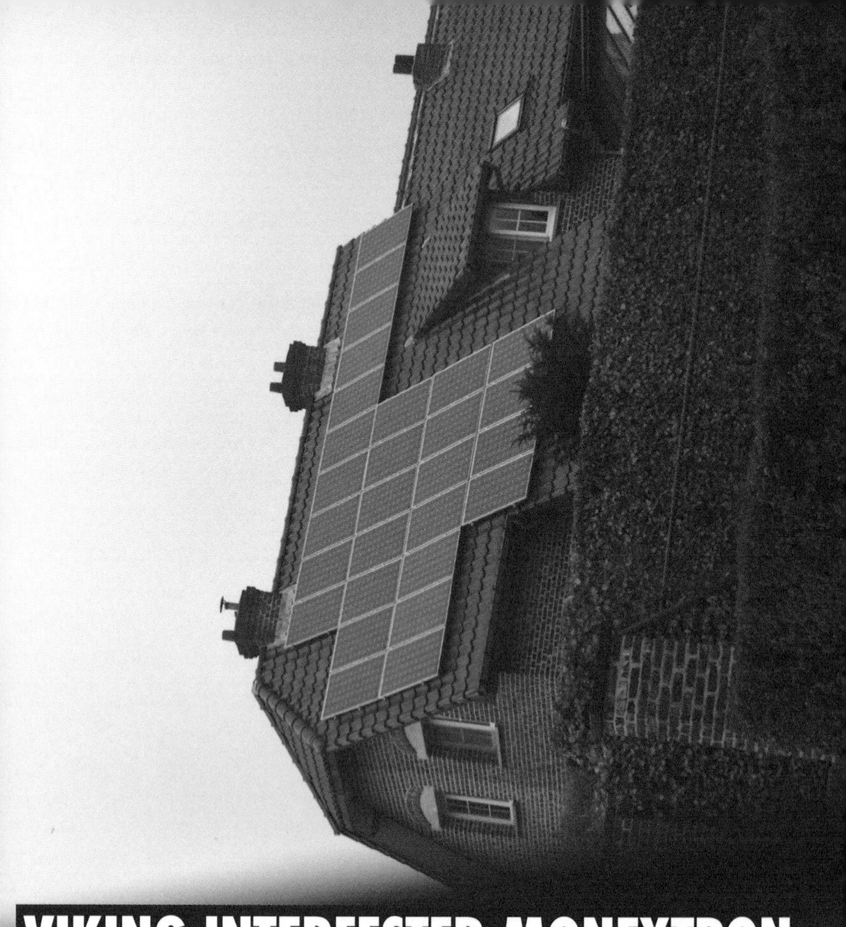

VIKING INTERFESTER MONEYTRON PLUTO CHAIN BLACK LIST PICK UPS GIRL DREAM LEAN MAN ACCELERATE OFFICE

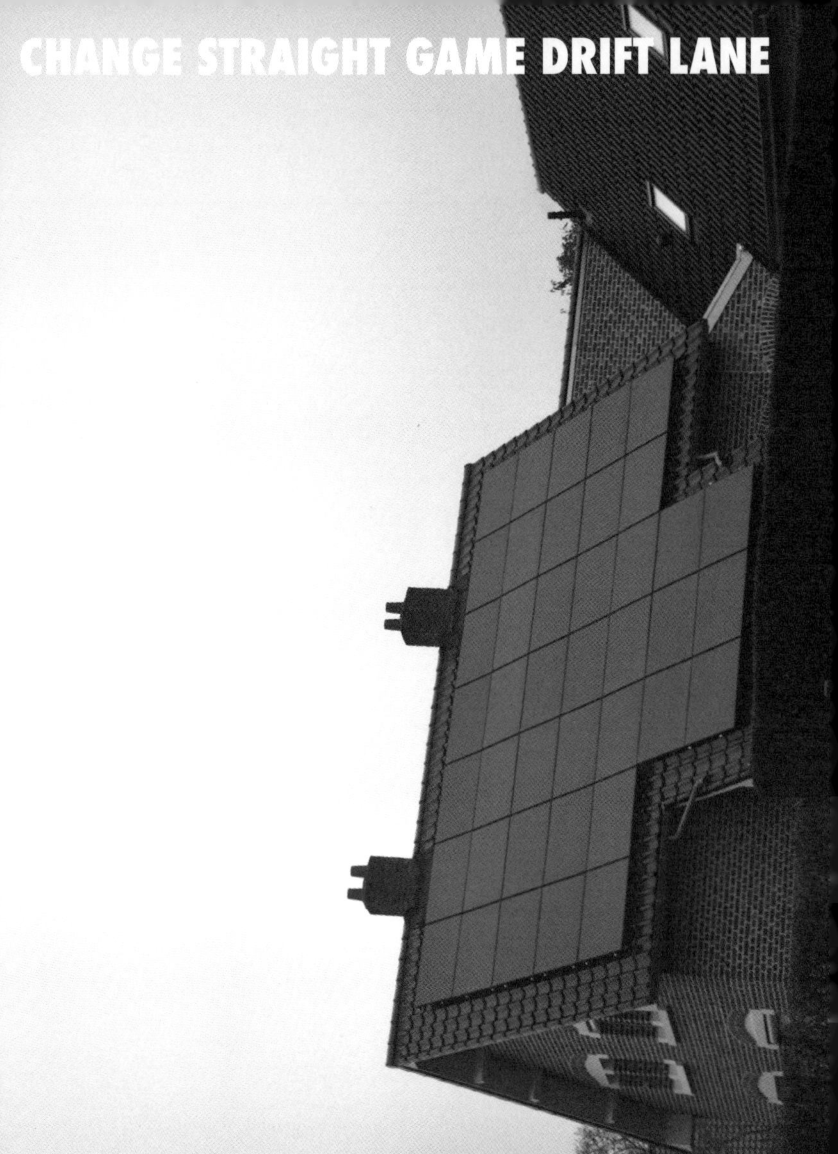

CHANGE STRAIGHT GAME DRIFT LANE

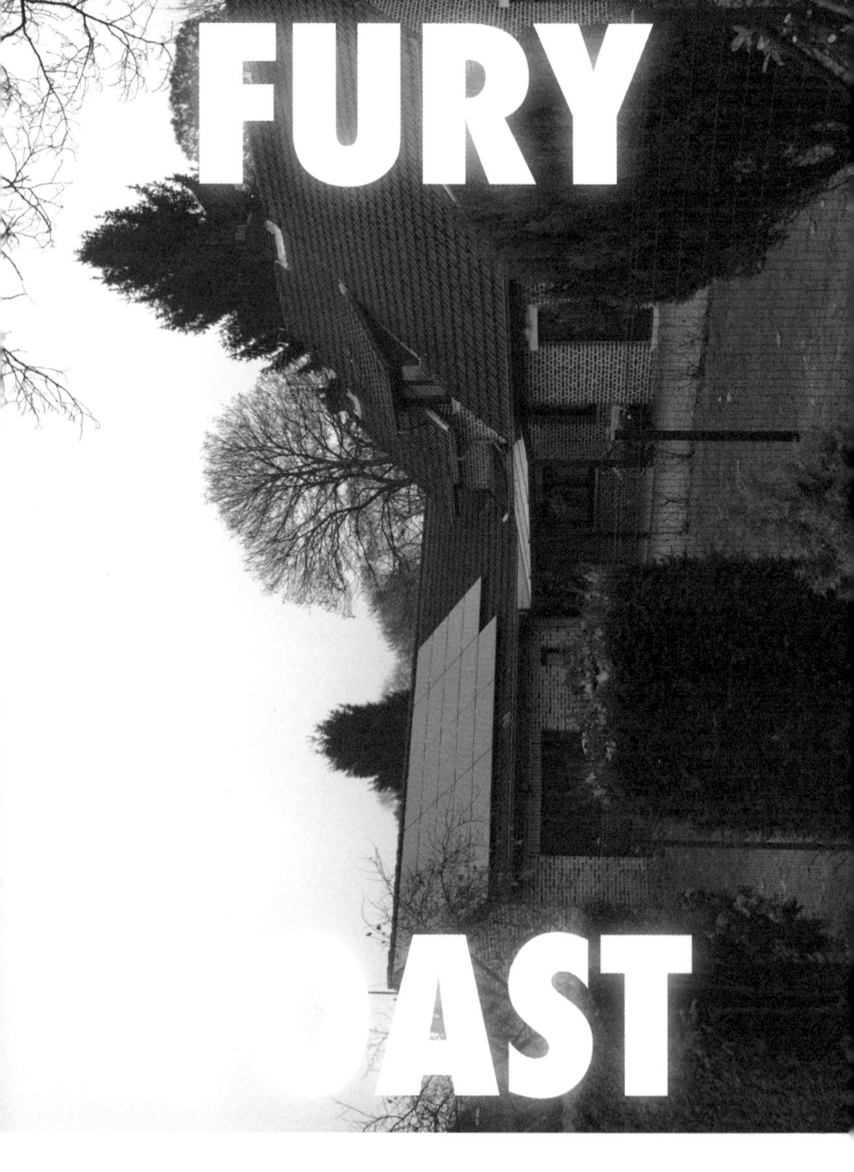
FURY
OAST

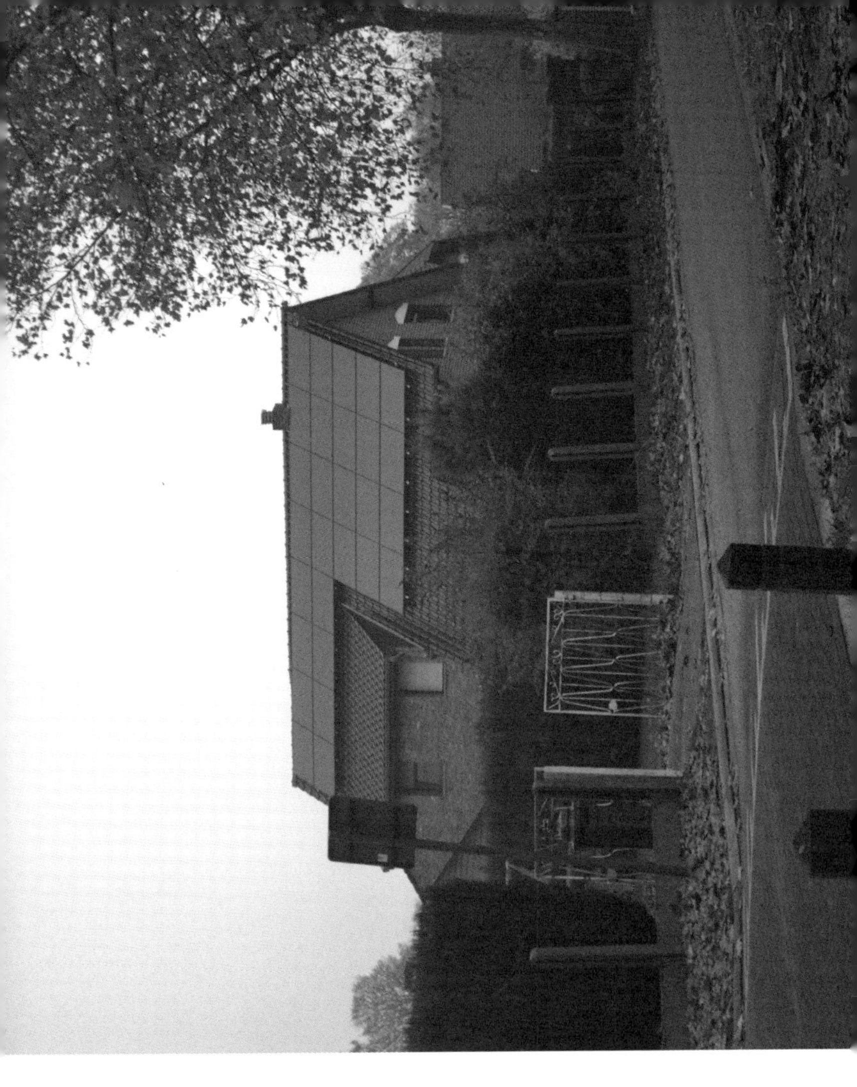

ON THE SHELL ALT CRABS

BLEACH ALL

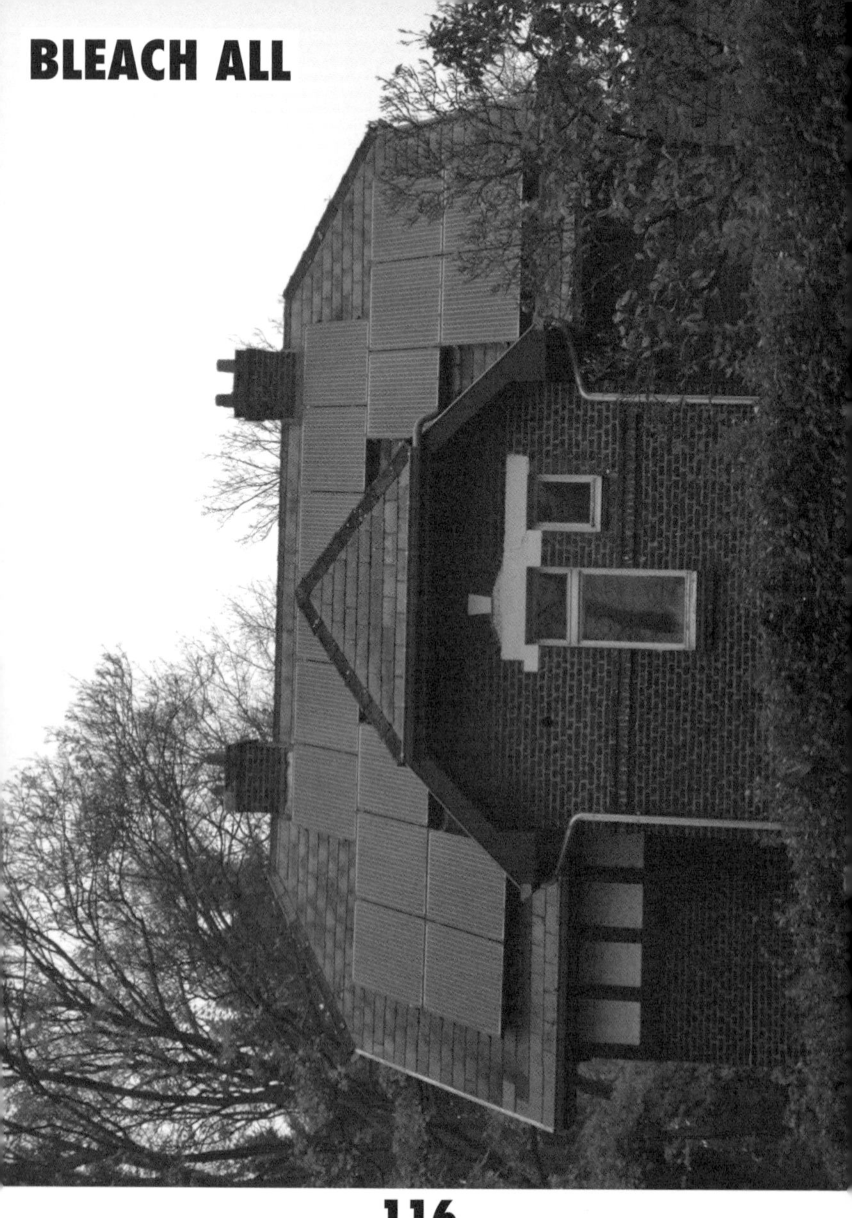

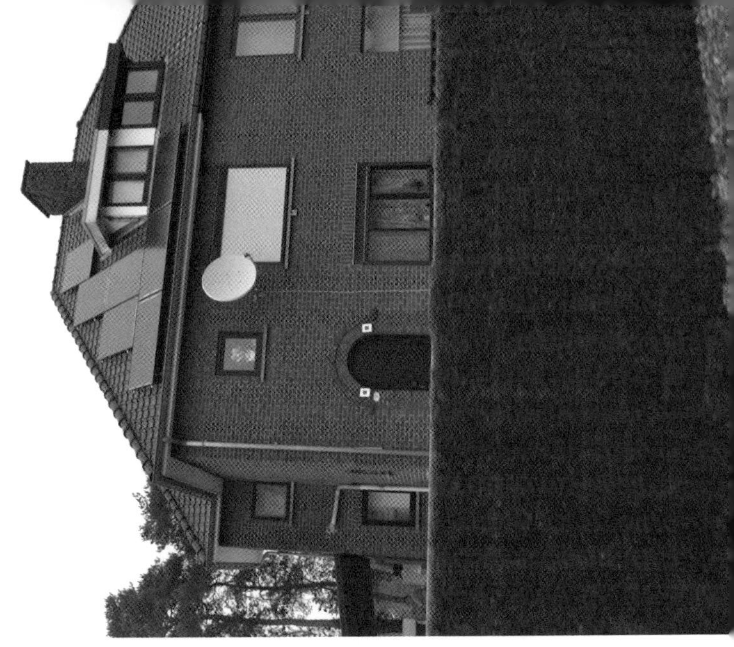

BIG DEALS BUG DEALER YO I HERD U LIKE
LAMBOS • I S • C O O L • G U Y S? SO
WE PUT A LAMBO IN YO LAMBO SO U CAN
DRIVE FASTER WHILE U DRIVE MINI FIGURINI
COUNTACH LAMBERT GINI ENDORFINI CLAY
BOX RING ALL AT 5000 CRY BABY PHONE
NOTHING OVER SQUAD SECURITY LOCK CODE
RIGHT DECYPHER SESSION KODINI GONE
LUCKY WE RIGHT WHATTTIME 808 B 909
SUPE SMOOTH YO OUI V12 DOUZE LIE
PYRAMID STYLE HOPE CHARITY

WODKA BROWN FUR BLINDS

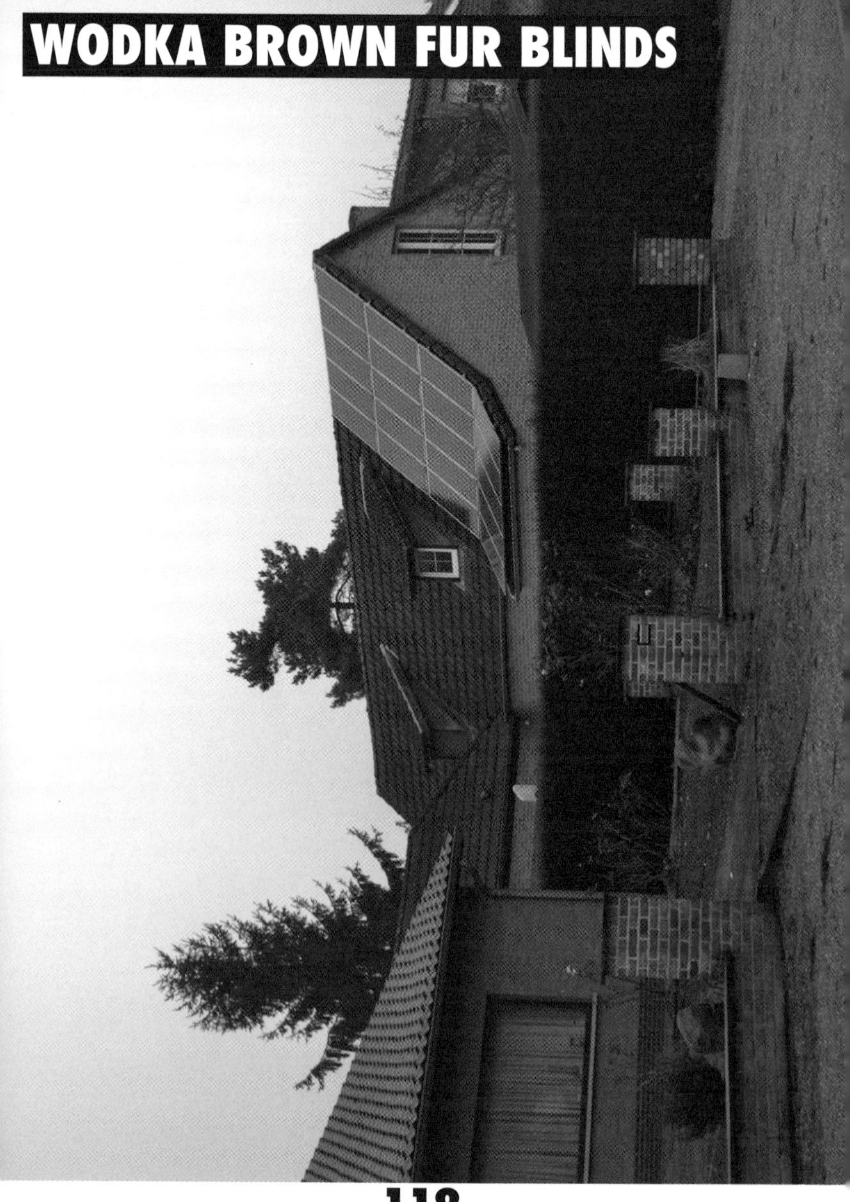

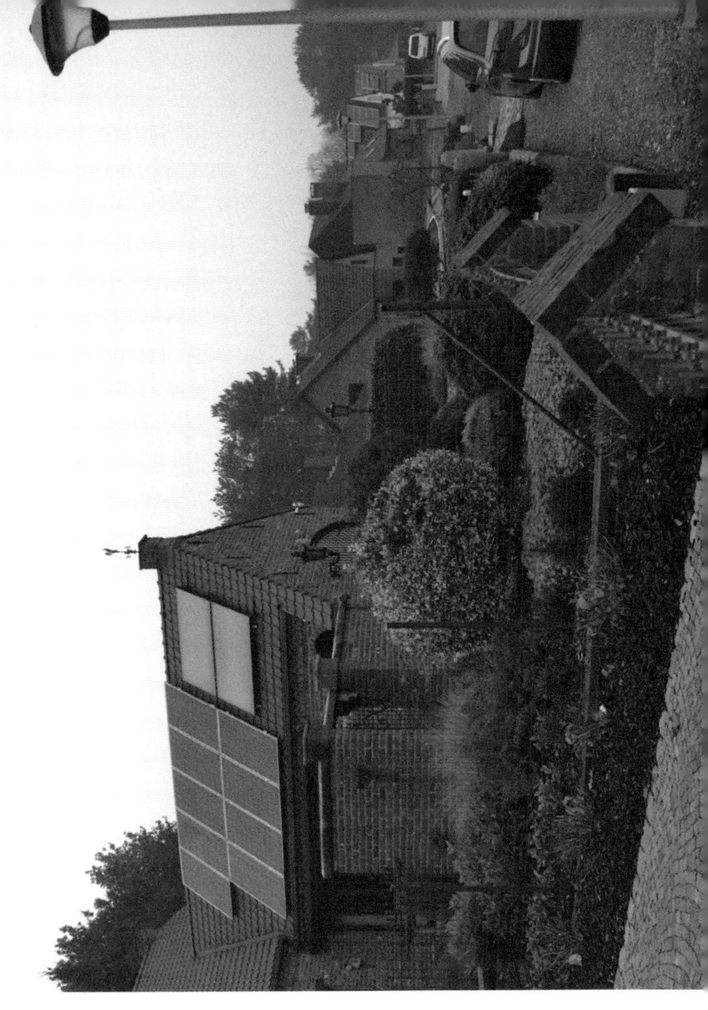

WITNESS THE FITNESS

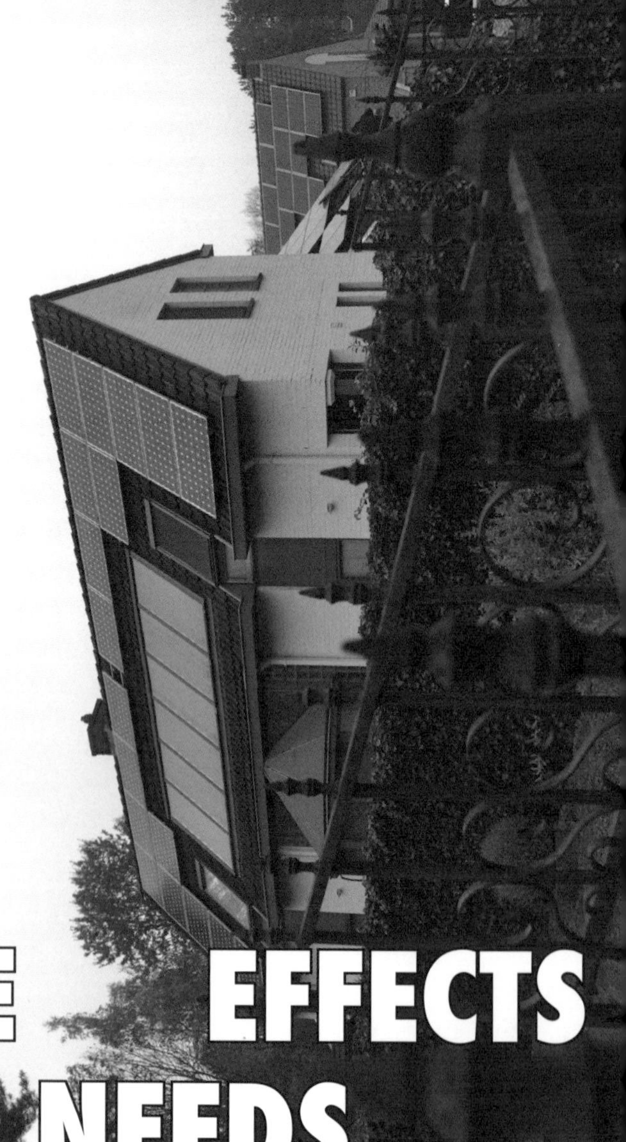

SIDE EFFECTS NEEDS

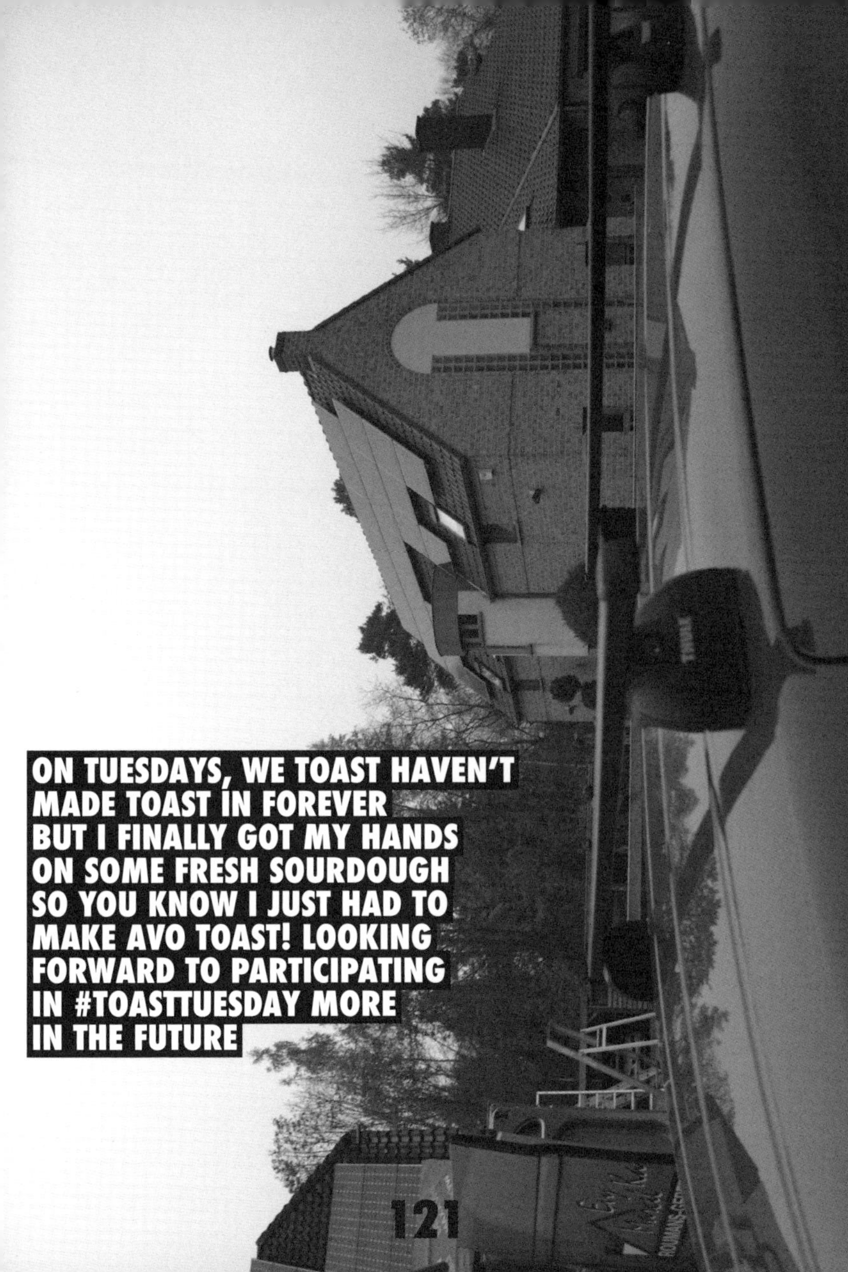

ON TUESDAYS, WE TOAST HAVEN'T MADE TOAST IN FOREVER BUT I FINALLY GOT MY HANDS ON SOME FRESH SOURDOUGH SO YOU KNOW I JUST HAD TO MAKE AVO TOAST! LOOKING FORWARD TO PARTICIPATING IN #TOASTTUESDAY MORE IN THE FUTURE

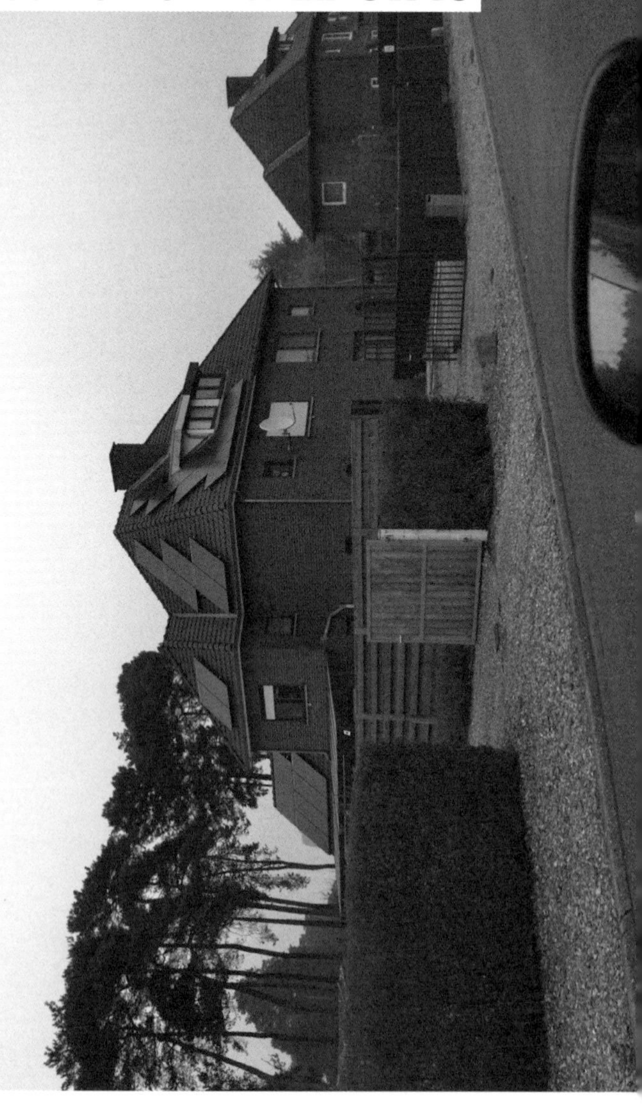

GREEK

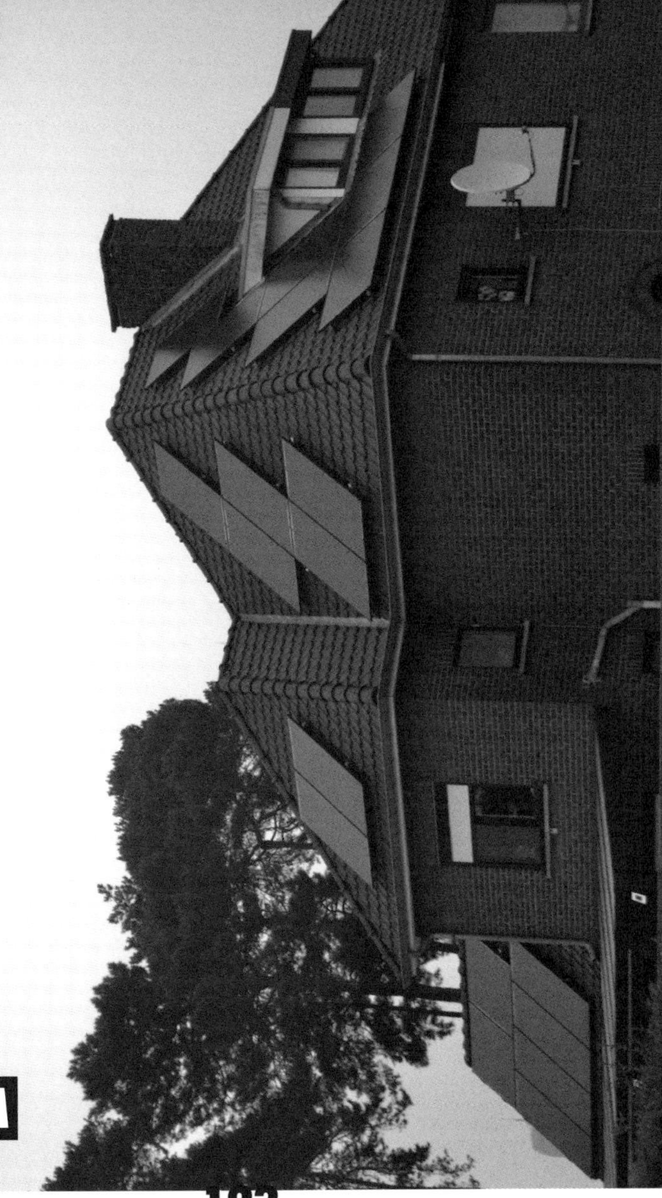

DREAM

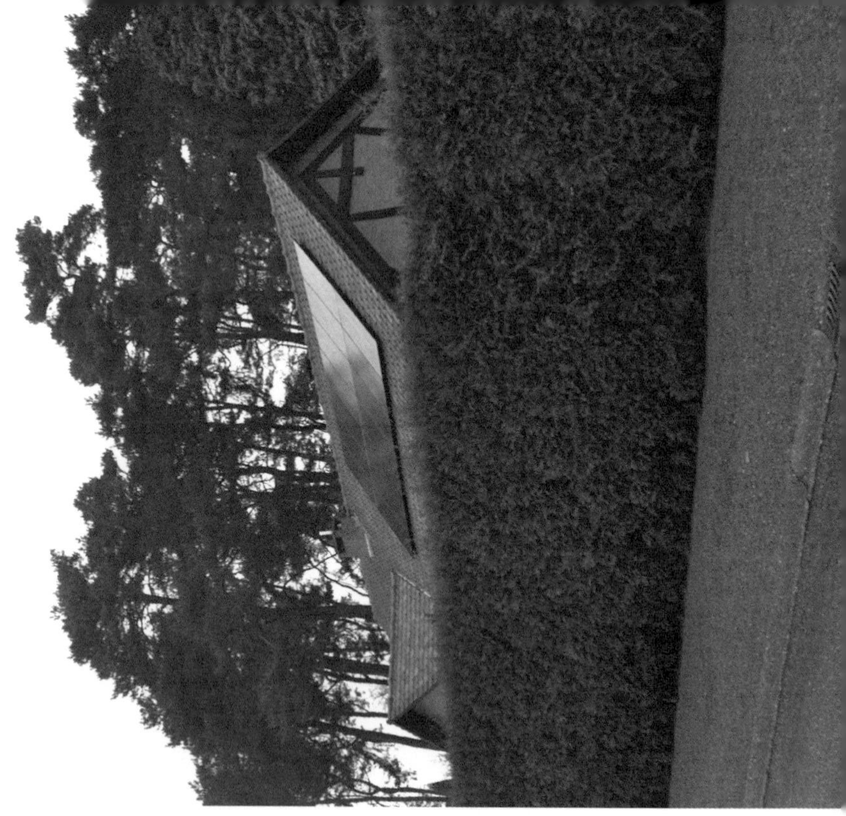

OPTIONS

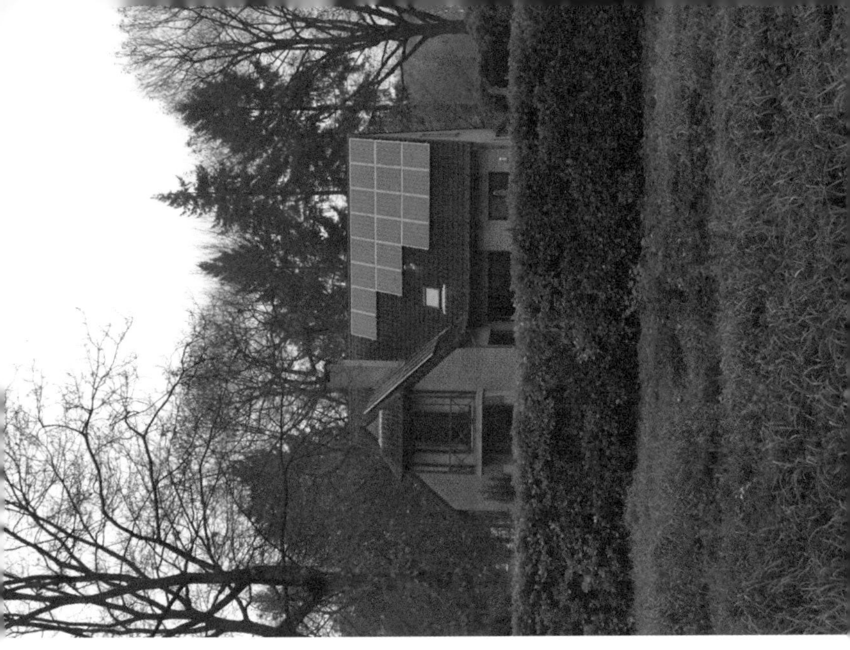

TRAP DRONE TRIP TRAP BASS

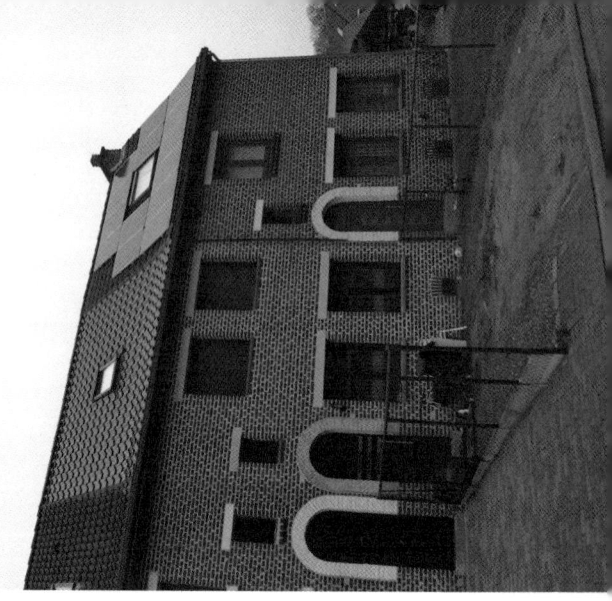

AMBIGUITY PEANUT

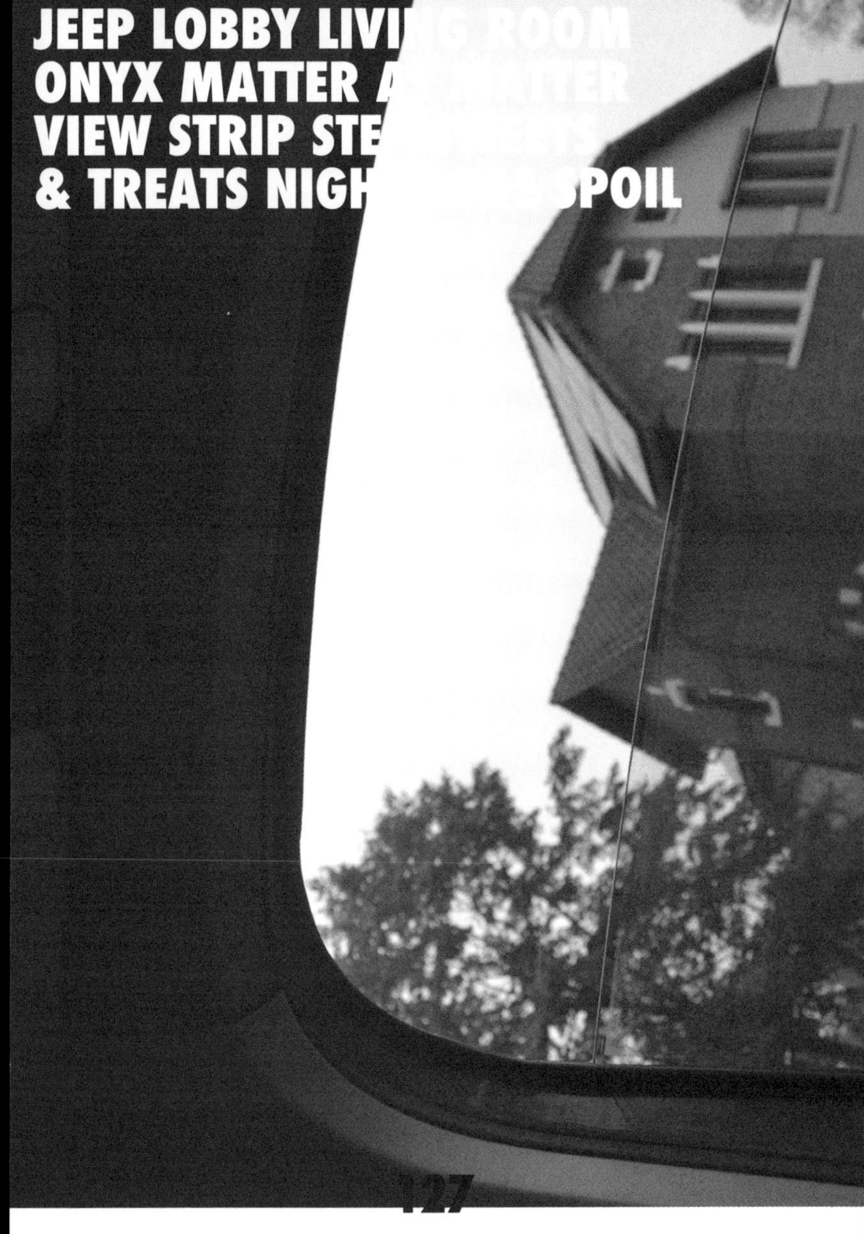
JEEP LOBBY LIVING ROOM
ONYX MATTER A
VIEW STRIP STE
& TREATS NIGH SPOIL

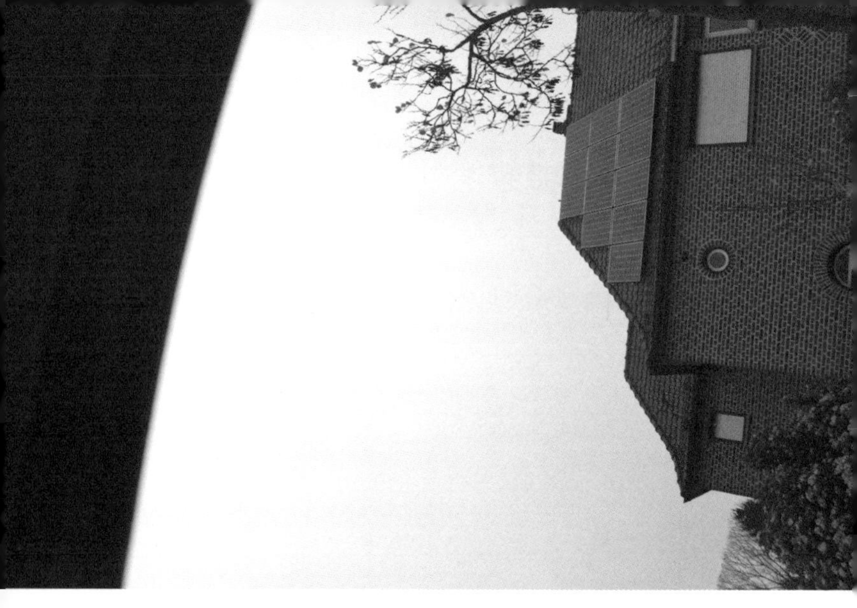

YUNG BUSHES SILVER SCREENS GOLF RIPPLE DELETE RAINBOW DONUT FLAVOUR LEMON CURD & PASTRY E JAM SPONGE

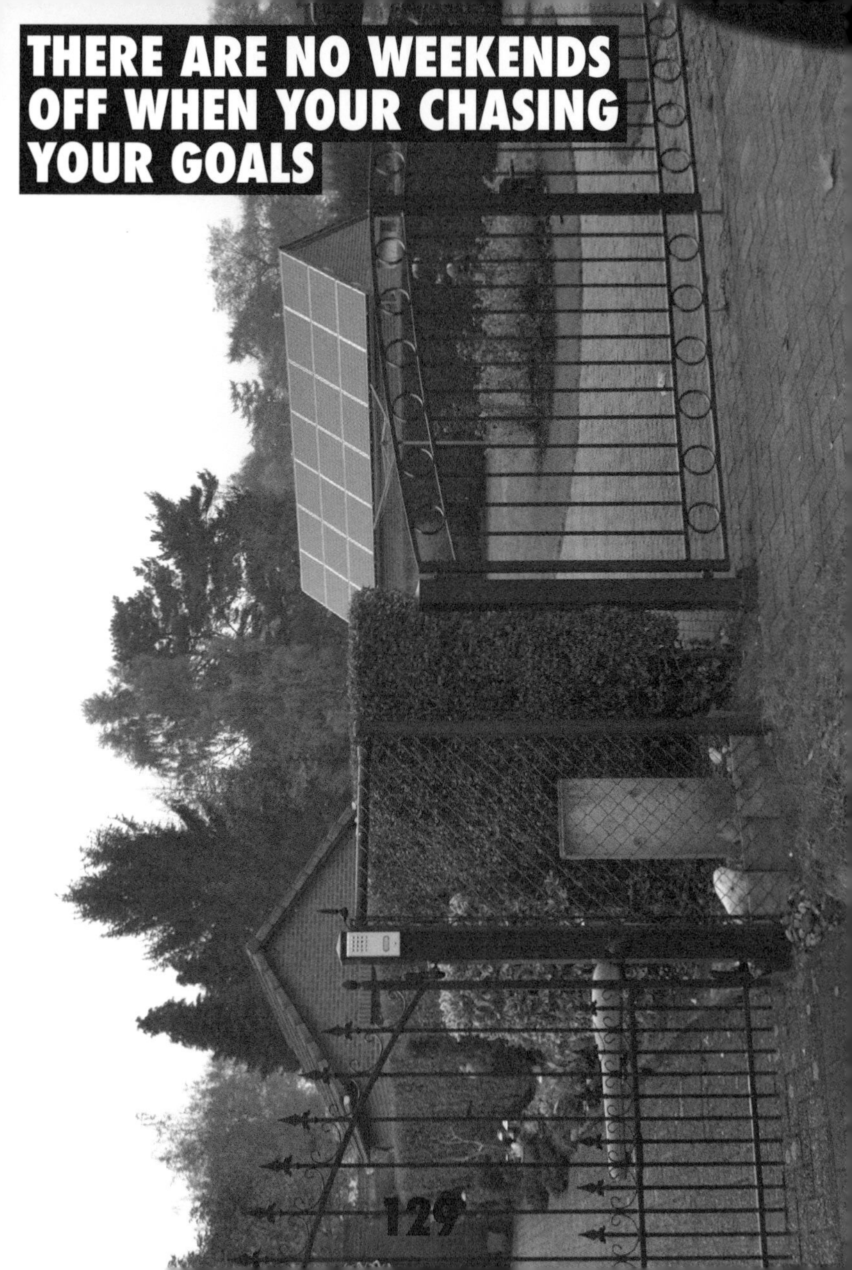
THERE ARE NO WEEKENDS
OFF WHEN YOUR CHASING
YOUR GOALS
129

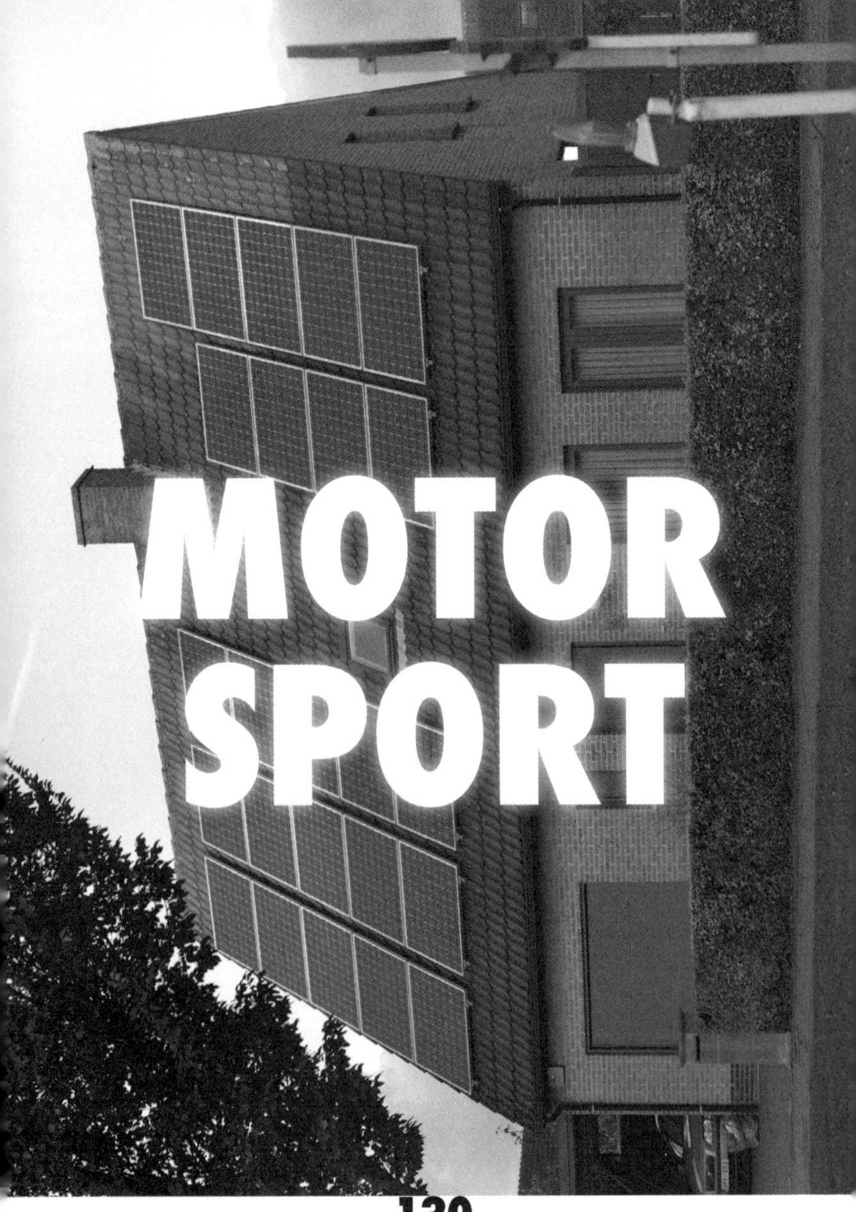
MOTOR
SPORT

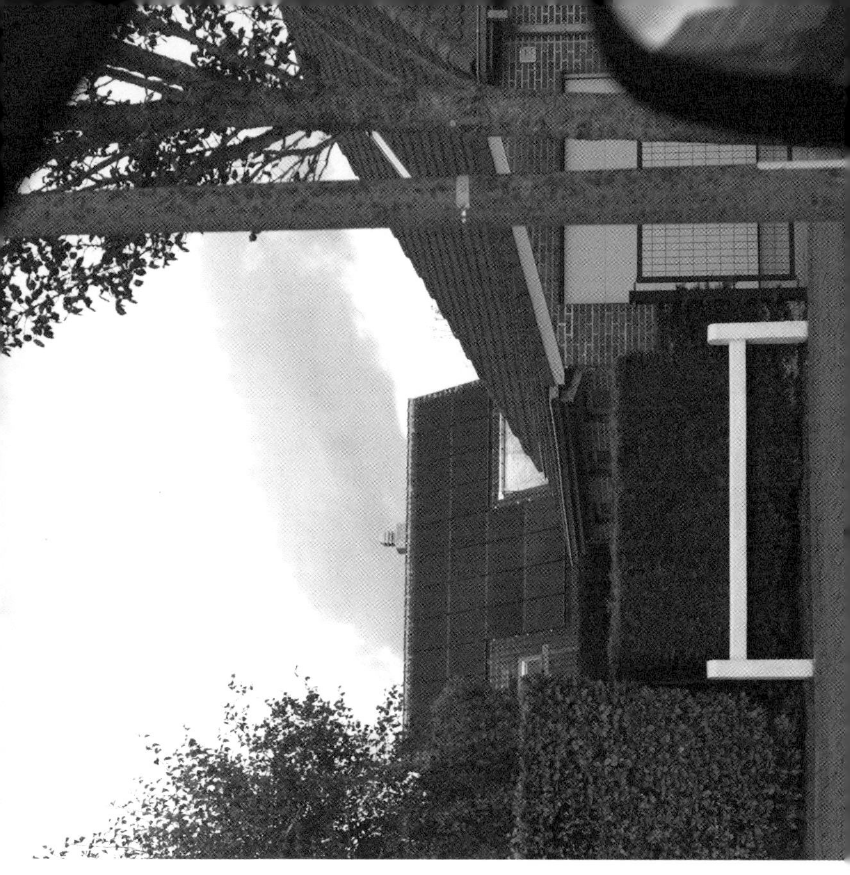

LOW BULL CAR GRAM SOLARS OF INSTAGRAM BILLIONAIRE THERE ARE 3 TYPES OF PEOPLE IN THE WORLD PEOPLE WHO MAKE IT HAPPEN PEOPLE WHO WATCH IT HAPPEN PEOPLE WHO SAY WHAT JUST HAPPENED? WHICH ONE ARE YOU? BE THE FIRST! TUESDAYMOTIVATION

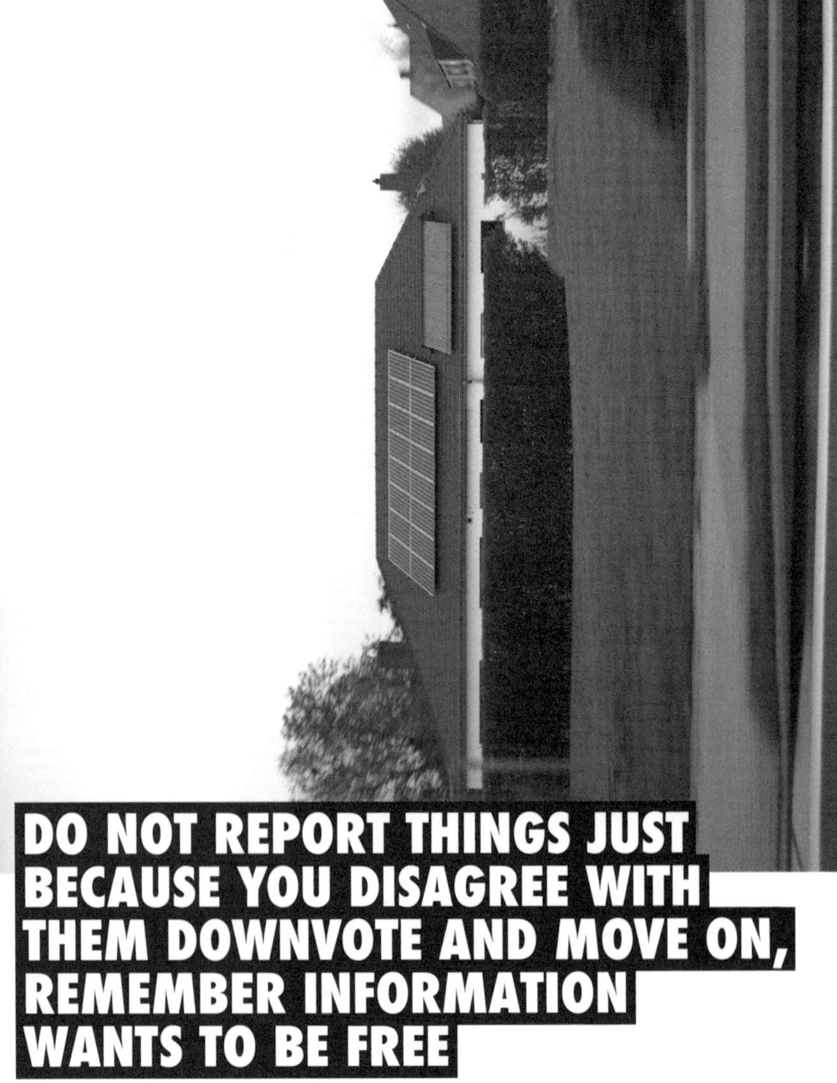

DO NOT REPORT THINGS JUST BECAUSE YOU DISAGREE WITH THEM DOWNVOTE AND MOVE ON, REMEMBER INFORMATION WANTS TO BE FREE

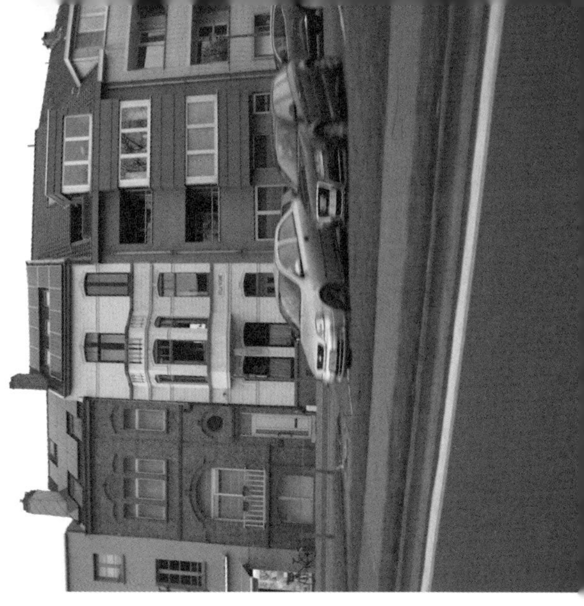

HAVE YOU TAKEN THE TIME TO CHECK IN WITH YOURSELF AND SET SOME INTENTIONS FOR THIS NEW DAY AND NEW WEEK? TAKING ACTION AND MOVING IN THE RIGHT DIRECTION BEGINS WITH KNOWING WHERE THE FINISH IS AT, AND KNOWING THE INTENTIONS BEHIND WHAT YOU DRIVE FEEL FREE TO PUT THOSE INTENTIONS OUT INTO THE WORLD BY SHARING

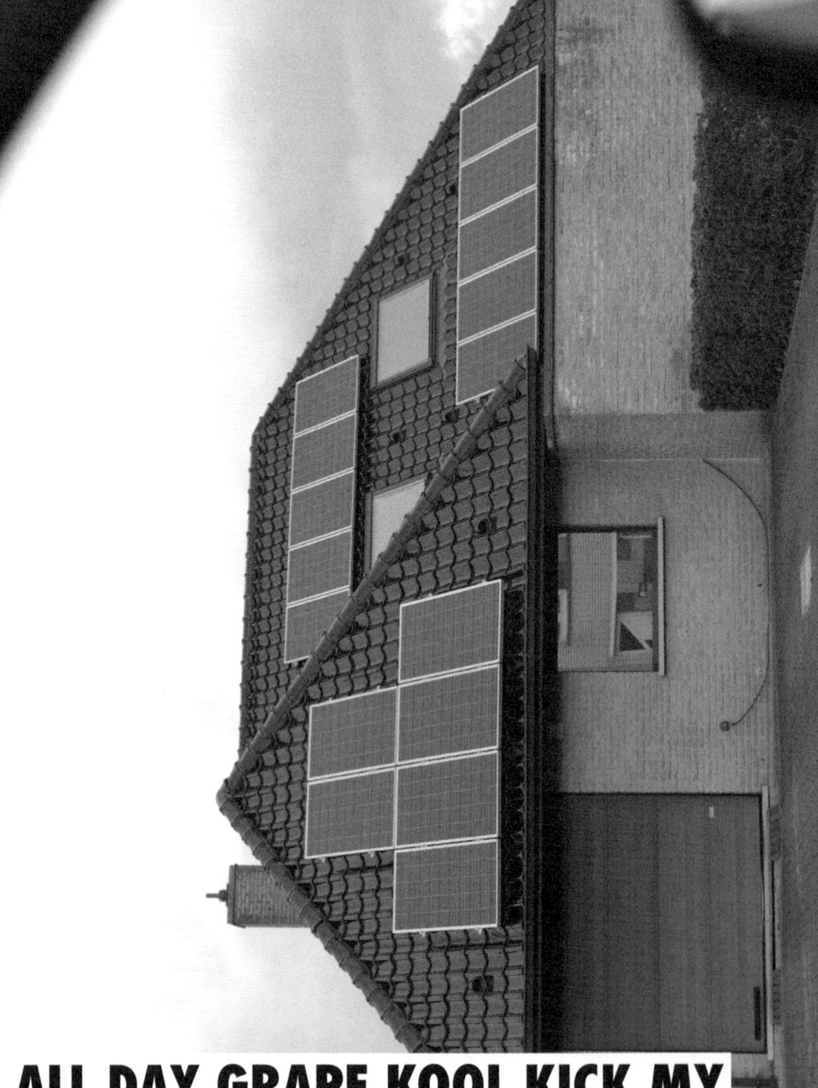

ALL DAY GRAPE KOOL KICK MY FAVOURITE SHAPE 34G/100ML

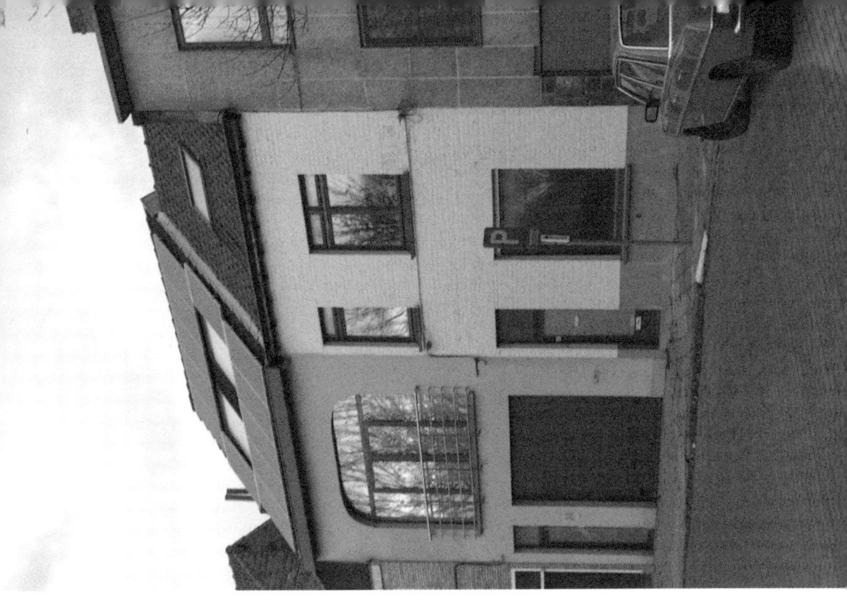

HUGEEEEE GIVEAWAY 1 OF MY TRAINING PROGRAMS ON MY APP FO FREE (YOU GET TO CHOOSE) OK THAT SUMS UP THE LONGEST CAPTION OF MI LIFE LOL WINNER CHOSEN SATURDAY! ***ITALY ONLY* ELITE LEVEL POWER LIFTING BENCH MY FAAAAVVVV SET FROM THE KILLER RANGE AND I'M PRAYING FOR U ALL PLS SET YOUR ALARMS OR RISK BEING GRAVELY DISAPPOINTED THE ENTIRE SUPPLY GOES LIVE AT 3PM WHEN DAVE CASTRO WAS IN CROSSFIT TEENS HAS 6 LETTERS BUT THEN AGAIN SO HAS ADDICT I DECIDED TO STAY FAT. THANK YOU I DRANK THE DAMN CAN! UNITEDLIFTERS ... PROGRESS IS SLOW AND PATIENT. NOT OVERNIGHT. WITH THAT TRUTH BOMB MOUTH PIECE**

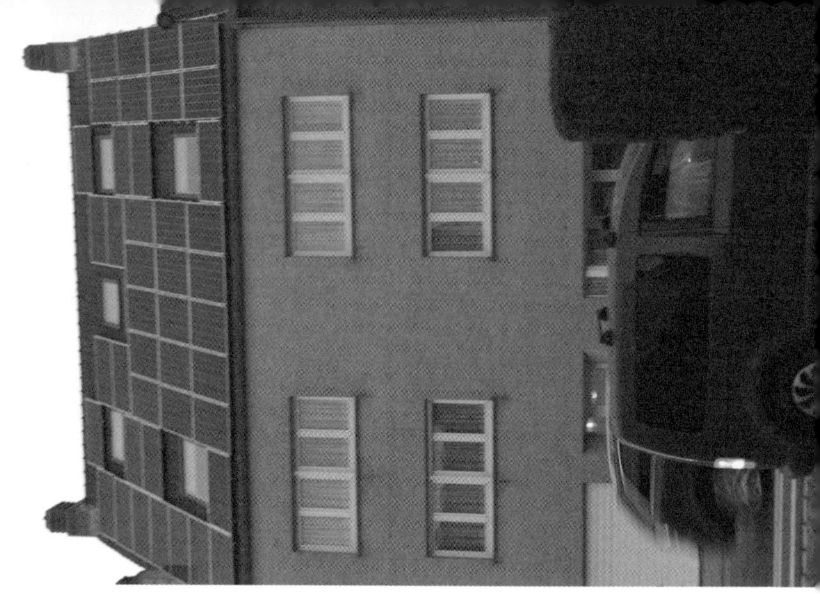

I PUT MY TRUST IN MY COACH AND IN MYSELF, DID WHAT WAS ASKED OF ME, AND LET THAT RUN IT'S COURSE G I V E A W A Y ! ! ! OVERSEAS CODING FIRM LIQUID MARIJUANA FROM A $200 HAND HELD VAPORIZER. I LOVE YOU ALL NOW LETS GET THIS PARTAY STARTED!!!!

YOU KNOW WHAT I DIDN'T DO? QUIT

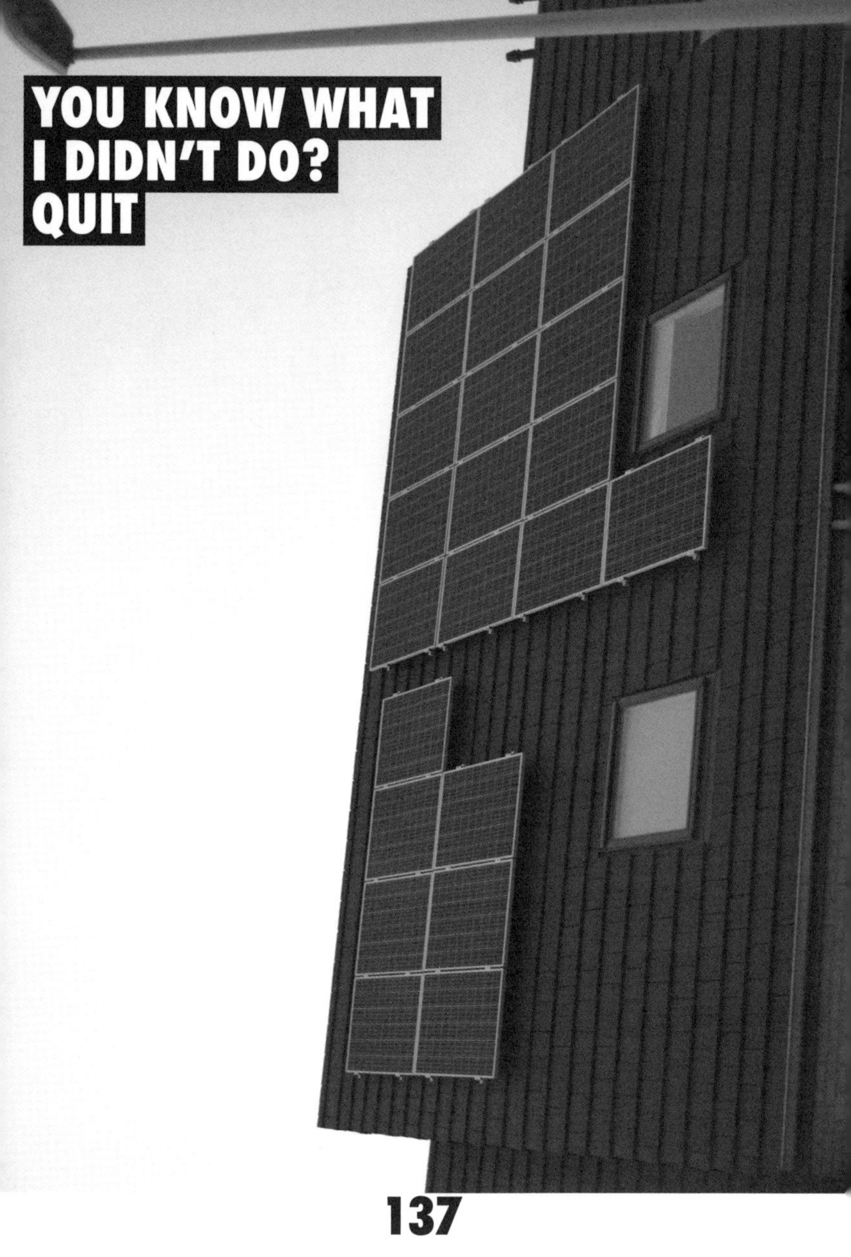

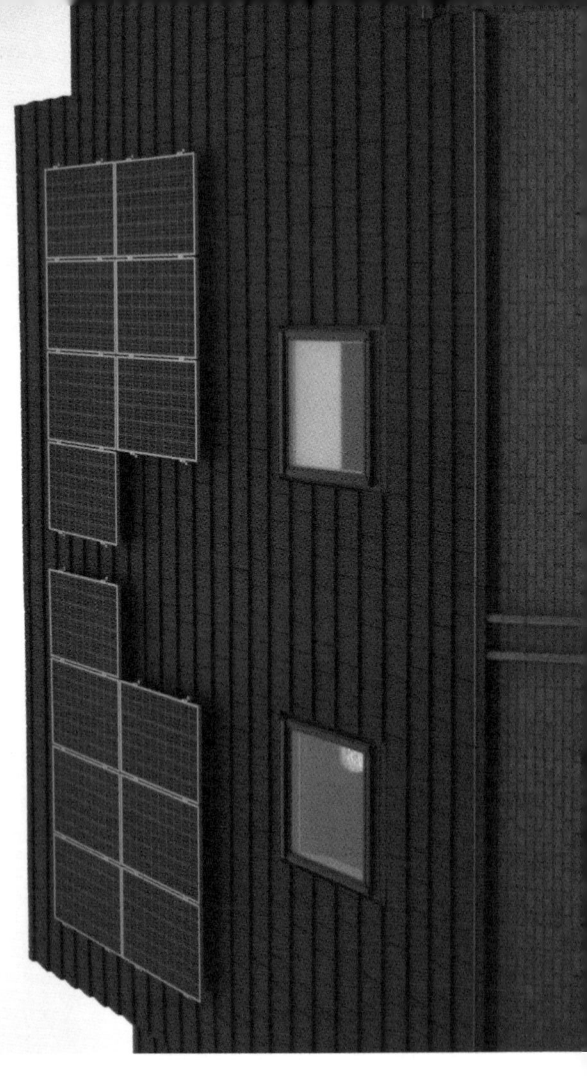

SNIPED FROM HYBRIDPERFORMANCEMETHOD

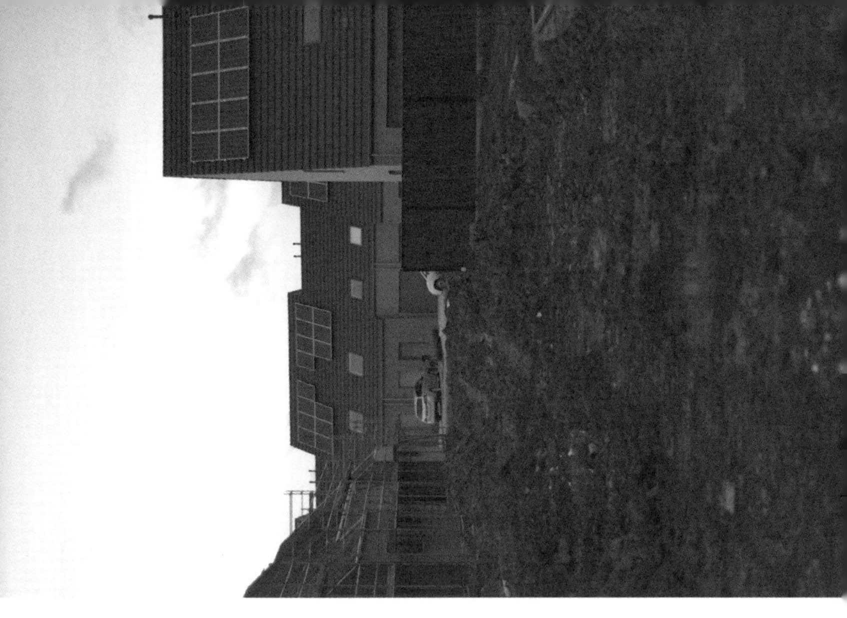

PEOPLE OFTEN SAY THAT MOTIVATION DOESN'T LAST. WELL NEITHER DOES BATHING – THAT'S WHY WE RECOMMEND IT DAILY

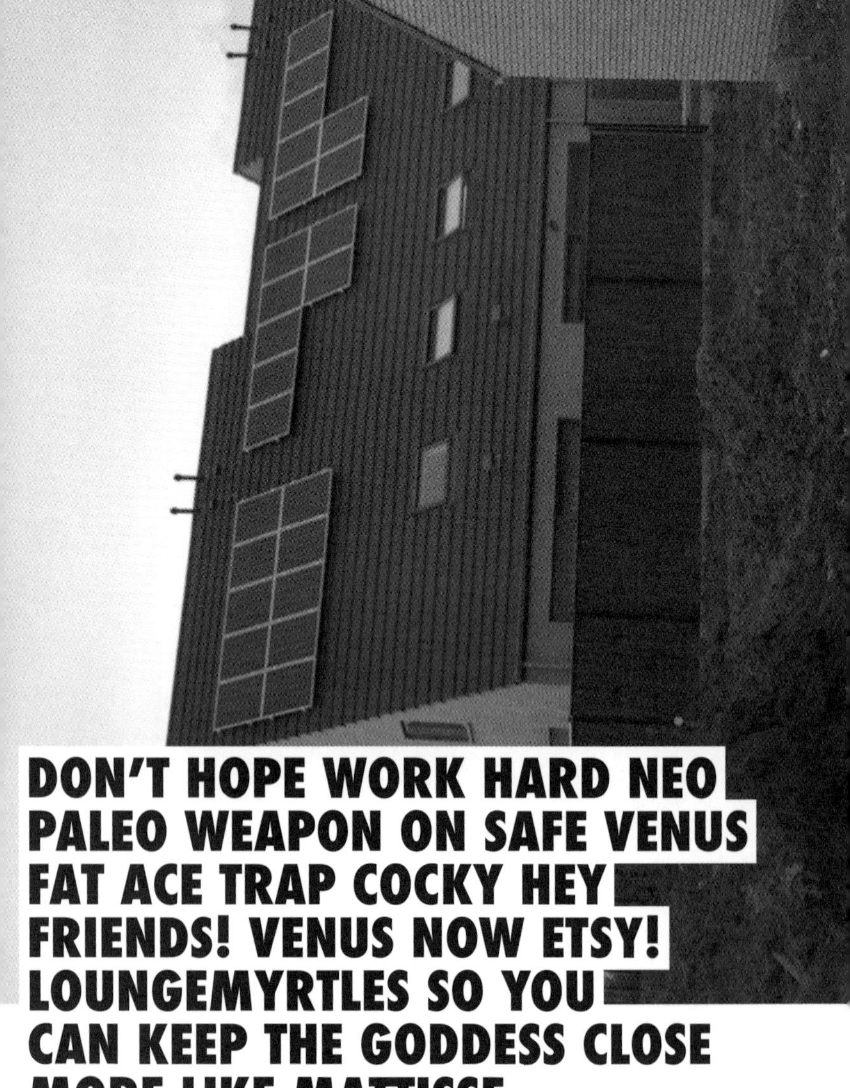

DON'T HOPE WORK HARD NEO PALEO WEAPON ON SAFE VENUS FAT ACE TRAP COCKY HEY FRIENDS! VENUS NOW ETSY! LOUNGEMYRTLES SO YOU CAN KEEP THE GODDESS CLOSE MORE LIKE MATTISSE

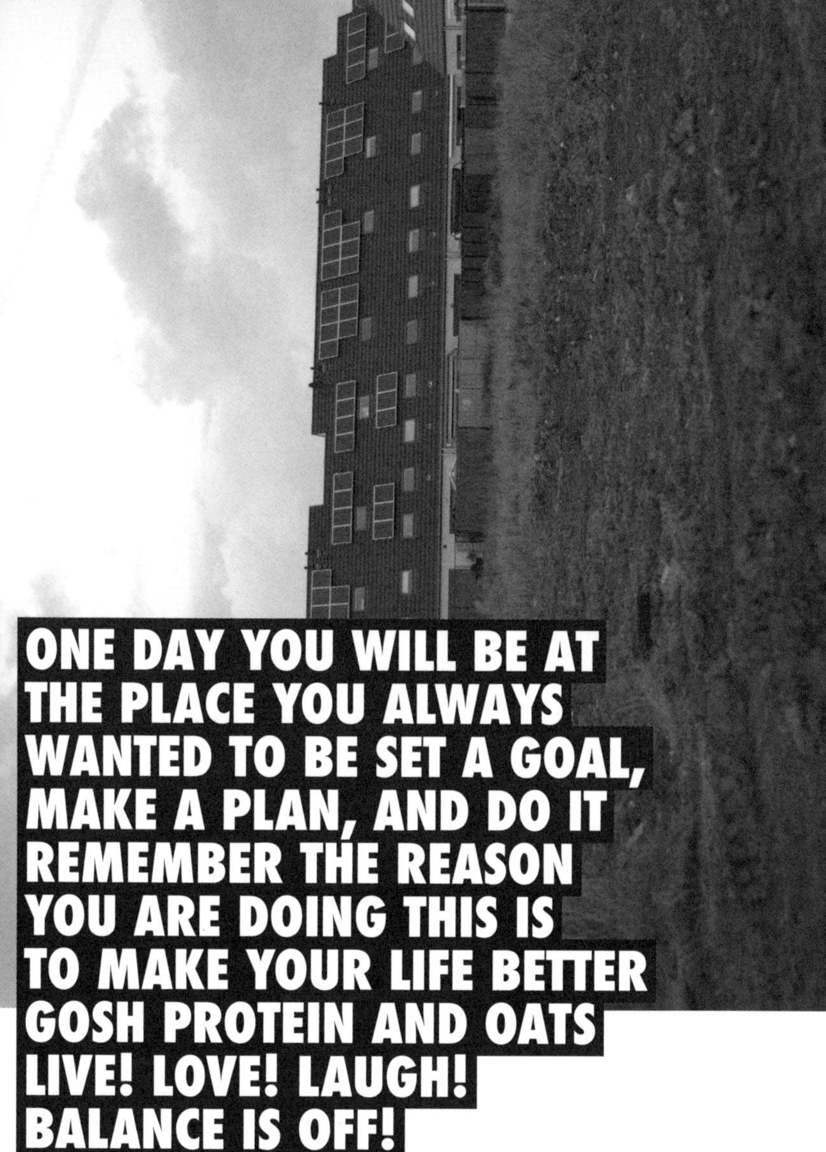
ONE DAY YOU WILL BE AT
THE PLACE YOU ALWAYS
WANTED TO BE SET A GOAL,
MAKE A PLAN, AND DO IT
REMEMBER THE REASON
YOU ARE DOING THIS IS
TO MAKE YOUR LIFE BETTER
GOSH PROTEIN AND OATS
LIVE! LOVE! LAUGH!
BALANCE IS OFF!

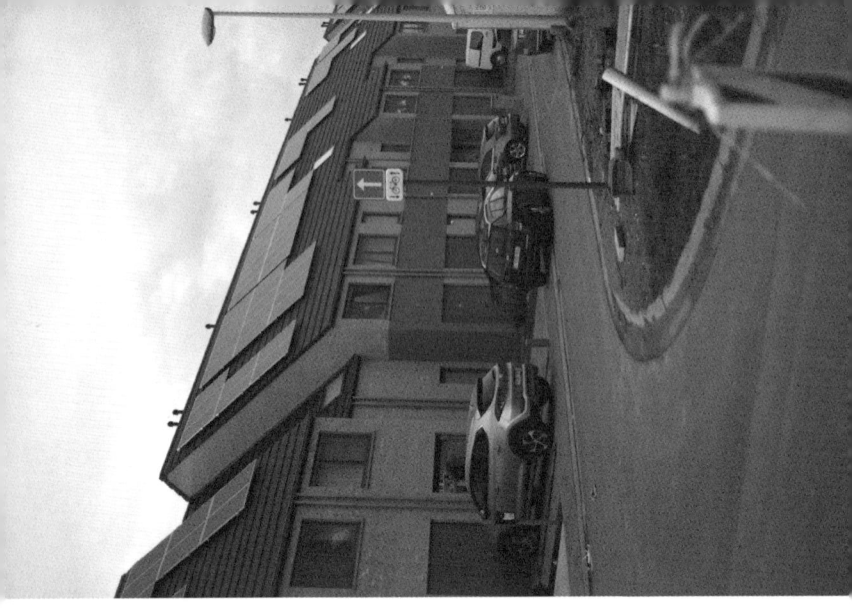

FEEDYOURRESOLUTION PLANTBASED I WOKE UP TODAY THINKING IT WAS SATURDAY ♀ IT IS MOST DEFINITELY NOT SATURDAY, BUT THAT'S WHY THERE IS COFFEE AND DELICIOUS TOASTS WAYS: SOURDOUGH WITH @CEDARSFOODS HUMMUS, AVOCADO, EGG AND EBTB + SOURDOUGH, @CRAZYRICHARDSPB PB, APPLE AND BEE POLLEN. IF IT'S NOT SATURDAY, I SURE AM GLAD IT'S #TOASTTUESDAY ROASTED SWEET POTATO TOPPED WITH AVOCADO, LEMON OR LIME JUICE, CRUSHED RED PEPPER, BROCCOLI SPROUTS OR MICRO GREENS, CILANTRO AND PASSION FRUIT NUTRITIONGENIE KALEINTHECLOUDS I GOT CHATTY ON MY STORIES SO IMMA LEAVE THIS SHORT AND SWEET. HAPPY TUESDAY, LOVES!

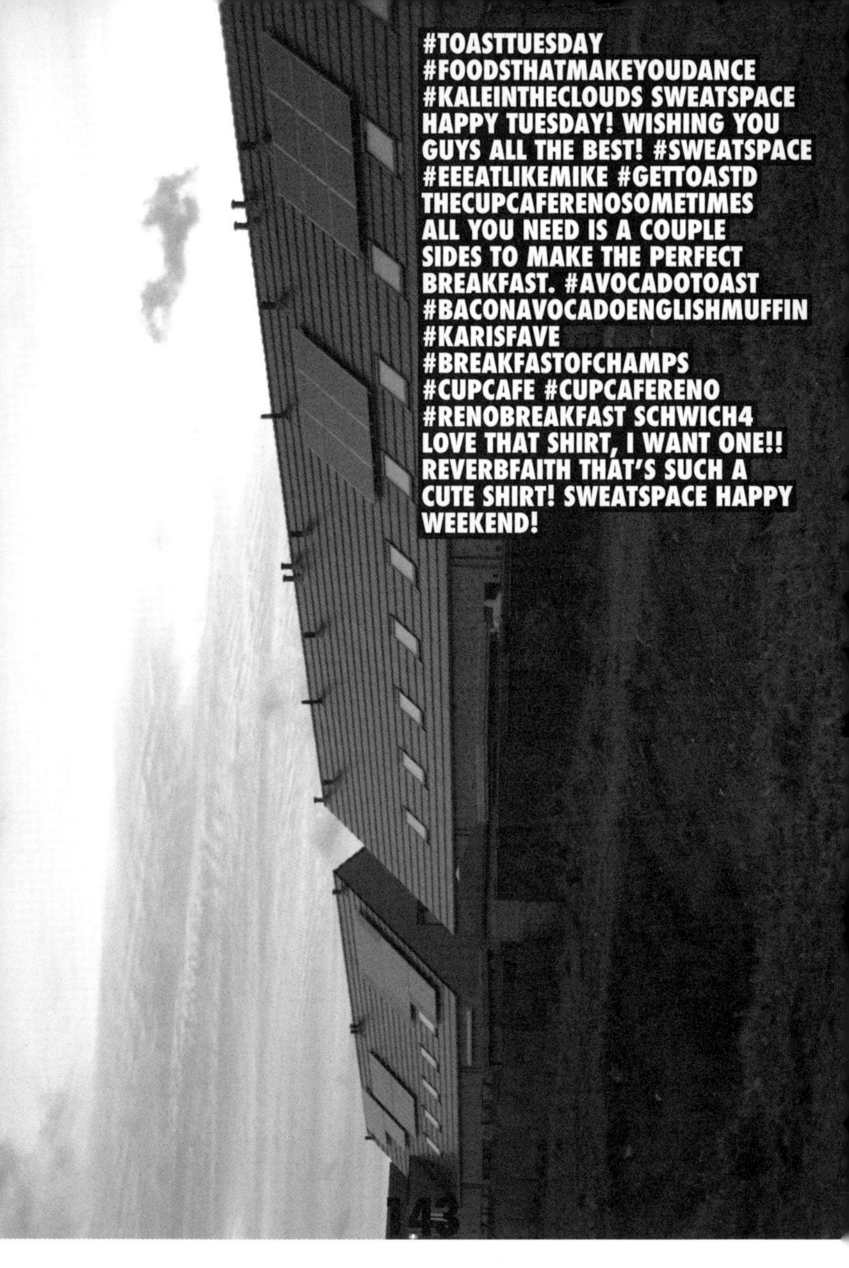

#TOASTTUESDAY
#FOODSTHATMAKEYOUDANCE
#KALEINTHECLOUDS SWEATSPACE
HAPPY TUESDAY! WISHING YOU
GUYS ALL THE BEST! #SWEATSPACE
#EEEATLIKEMIKE #GETTOASTD
THECUPCAFERENOSOMETIMES
ALL YOU NEED IS A COUPLE
SIDES TO MAKE THE PERFECT
BREAKFAST. #AVOCADOTOAST
#BACONAVOCADOENGLISHMUFFIN
#KARISFAVE
#BREAKFASTOFCHAMPS
#CUPCAFE #CUPCAFERENO
#RENOBREAKFAST SCHWICH4
LOVE THAT SHIRT, I WANT ONE!!
REVERBFAITH THAT'S SUCH A
CUTE SHIRT! SWEATSPACE HAPPY
WEEKEND!

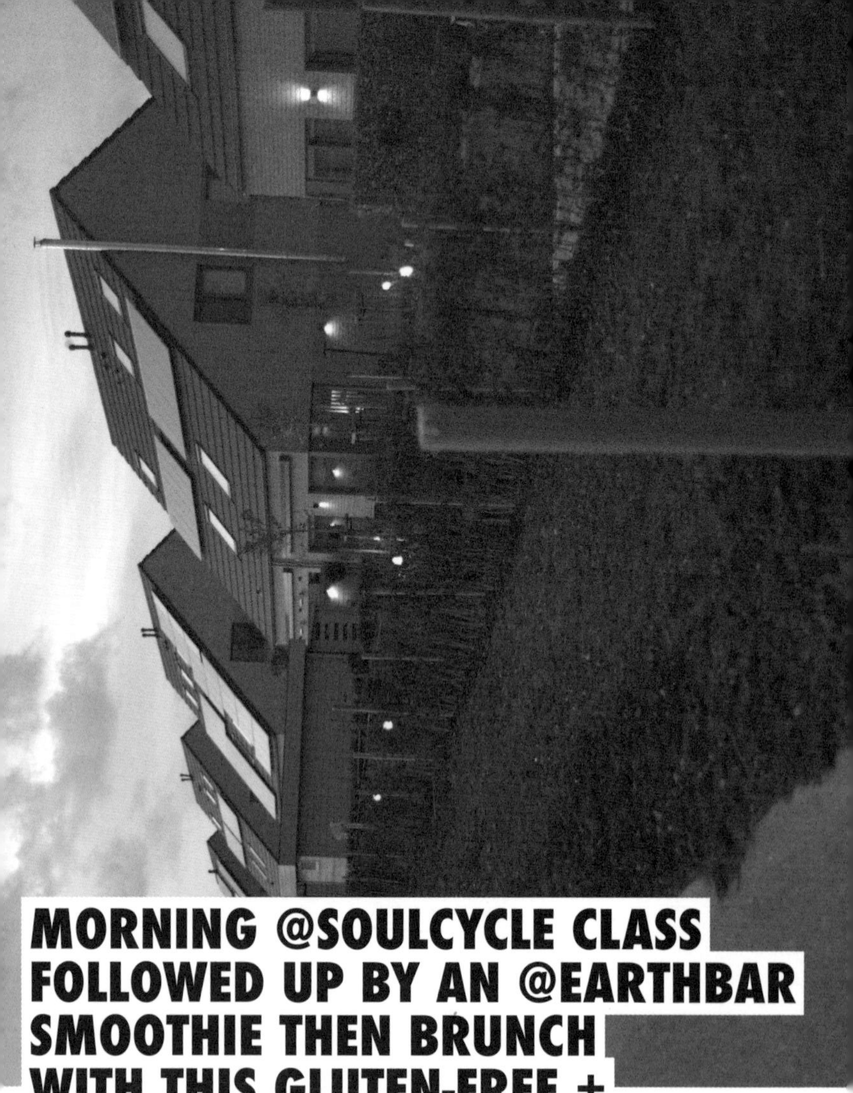

MORNING @SOULCYCLE CLASS FOLLOWED UP BY AN @EARTHBAR SMOOTHIE THEN BRUNCH WITH THIS GLUTEN-FREE + PALEO SUPER FLUFFY PANCAKE STACK!

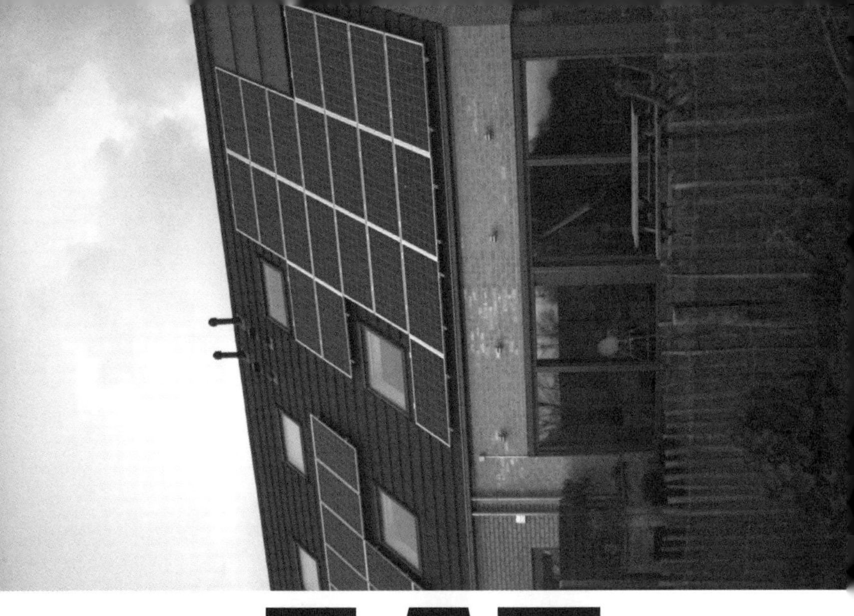

EAT REAL FOOD

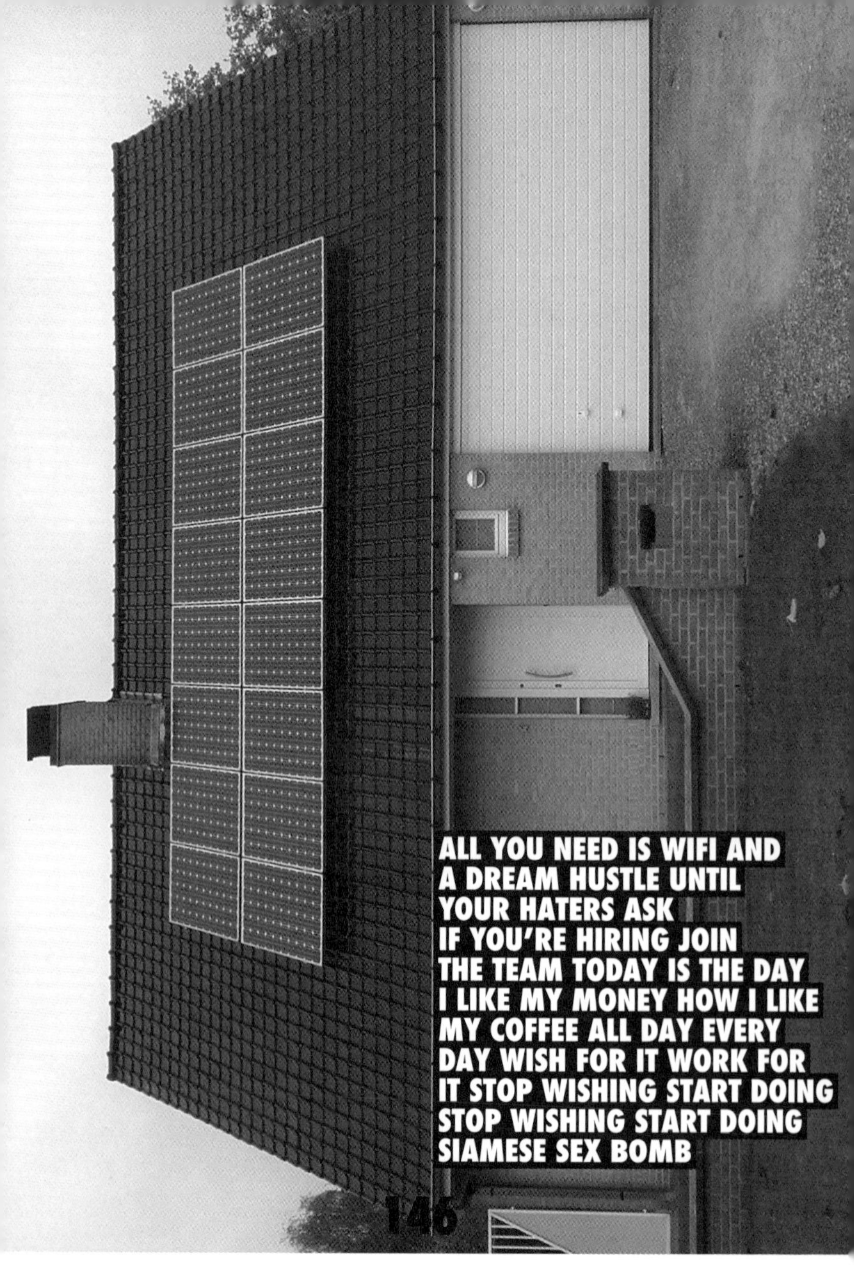
ALL YOU NEED IS WIFI AND
A DREAM HUSTLE UNTIL
YOUR HATERS ASK
IF YOU'RE HIRING JOIN
THE TEAM TODAY IS THE DAY
I LIKE MY MONEY HOW I LIKE
MY COFFEE ALL DAY EVERY
DAY WISH FOR IT WORK FOR
IT STOP WISHING START DOING
STOP WISHING START DOING
SIAMESE SEX BOMB

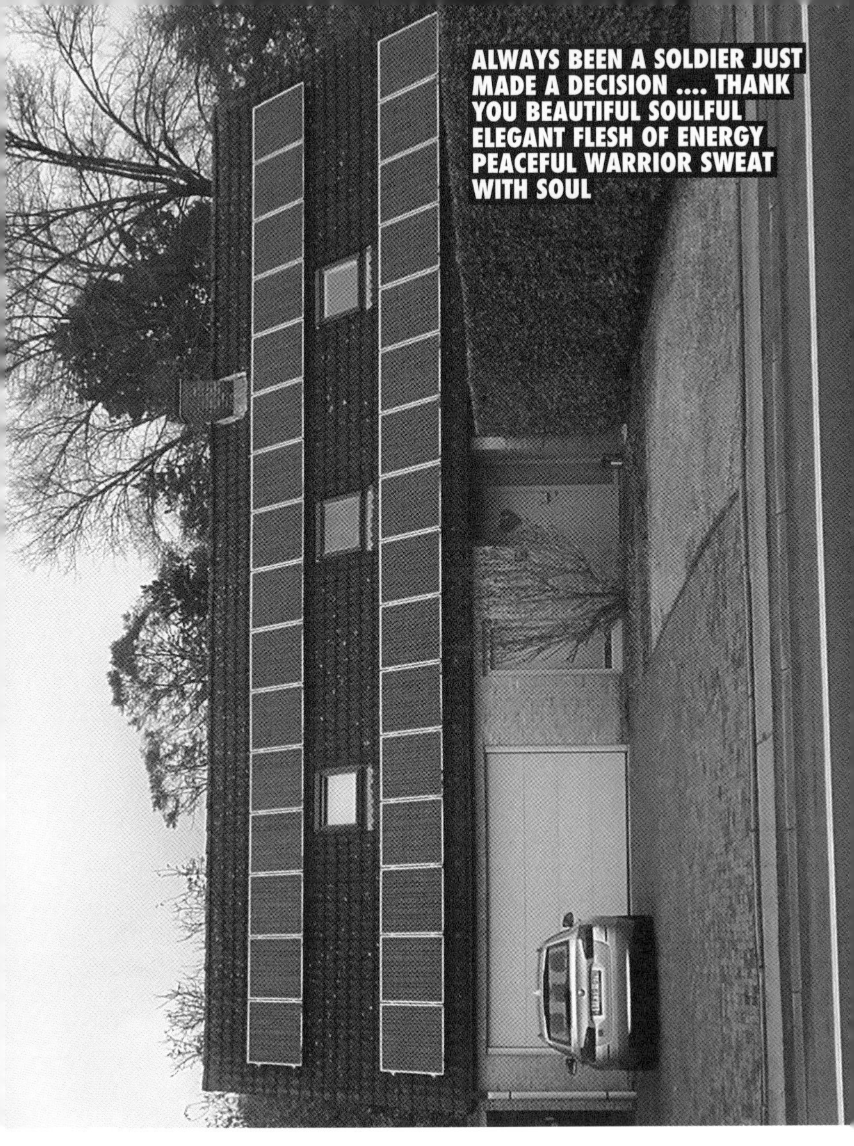
ALWAYS BEEN A SOLDIER JUST MADE A DECISION .... THANK YOU BEAUTIFUL SOULFUL ELEGANT FLESH OF ENERGY PEACEFUL WARRIOR SWEAT WITH SOUL

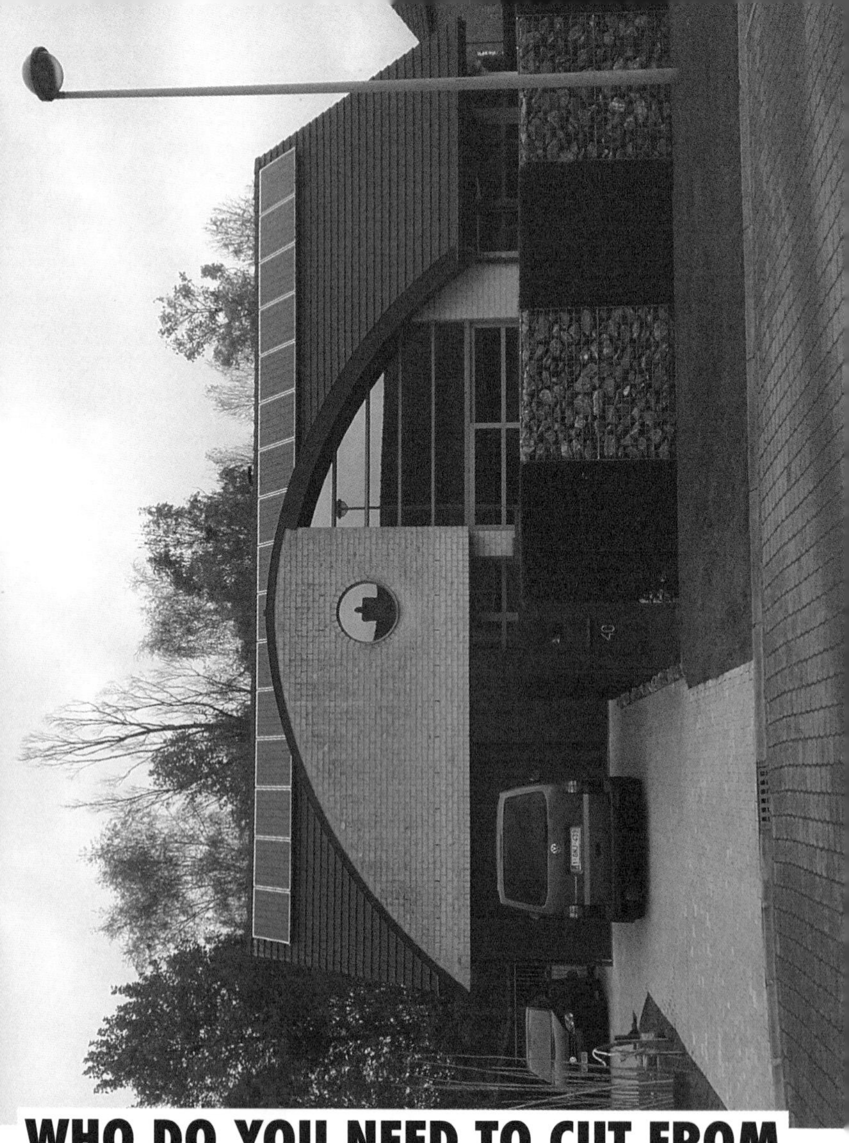

WHO DO YOU NEED TO CUT FROM YOUR TEAM

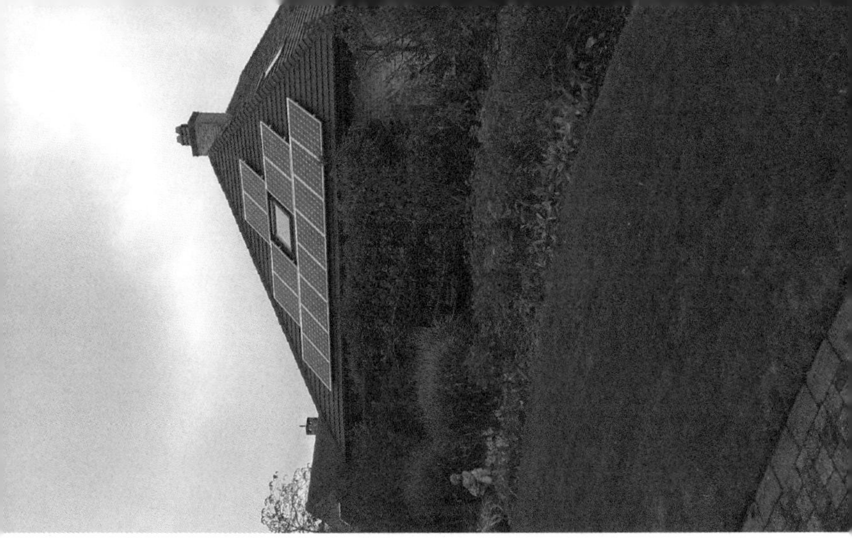

WE ALL HAVE SEEDS OF GREATNESS INSIDE ARE YOU WATERING YOURS SOMETIMES IT TAKES TWO YOGA CLASSES A DAY TO QUIET THE MIND... AND SOMETIMES IT TAKES THREE —— OPENED UP MY HIP FLEXORS, BACK AND HEART EAT THE DAMN COOKIE IGNORE THAT TEXT JUST ONE MORE EPISODE FORGIVE THEM ALREADY OWN YOUR SPACE CUT THE SORRY WE COMMIT THIS

INDOOR BIKE WORKOUT THATS DONE IN CANDLELIT ROOMS

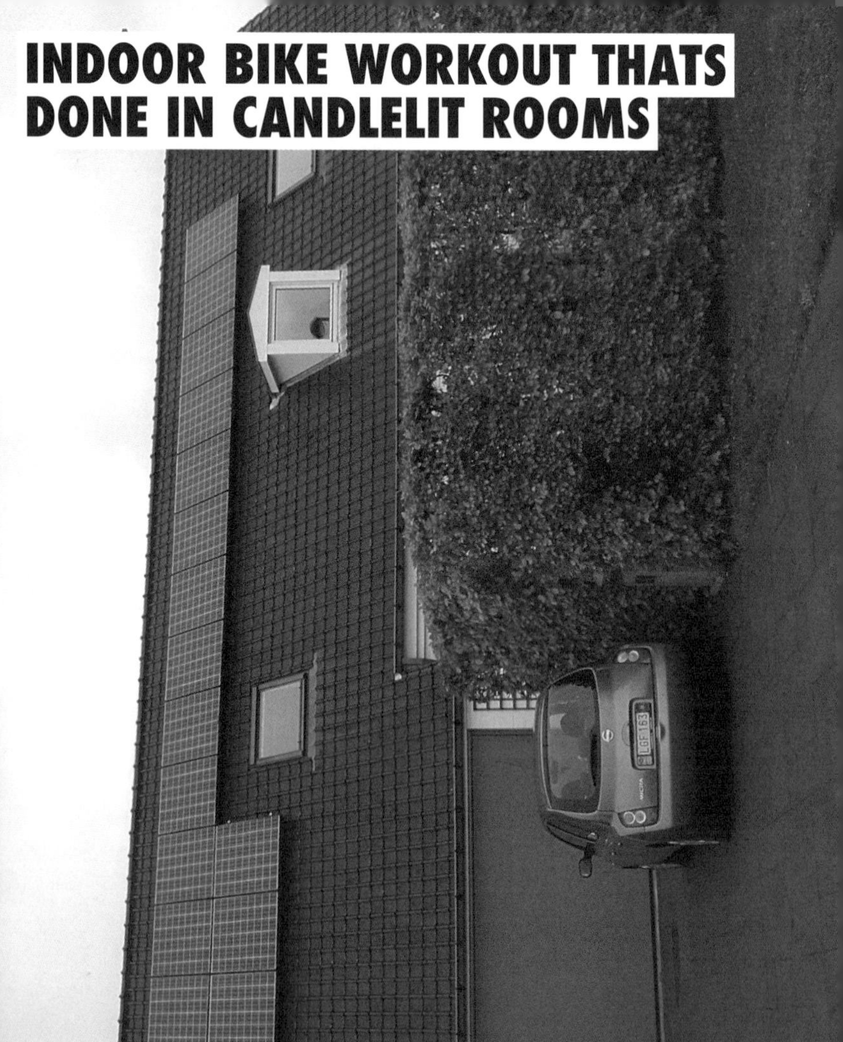

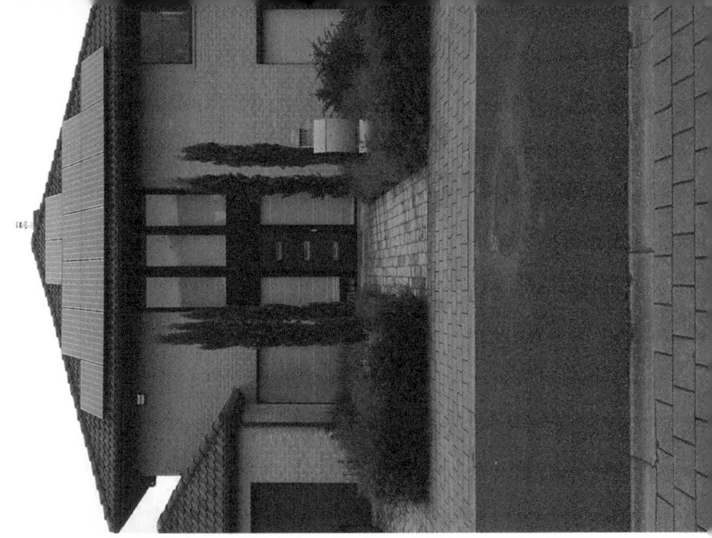

**GRATITUDE ALWAYS
ALWAYS GRATITUDE
YOU MIGHT BE THE REASON
SOMEONE BELIEVES IN LOVE
+ KINDNESS AGAIN —— ——
EARL**

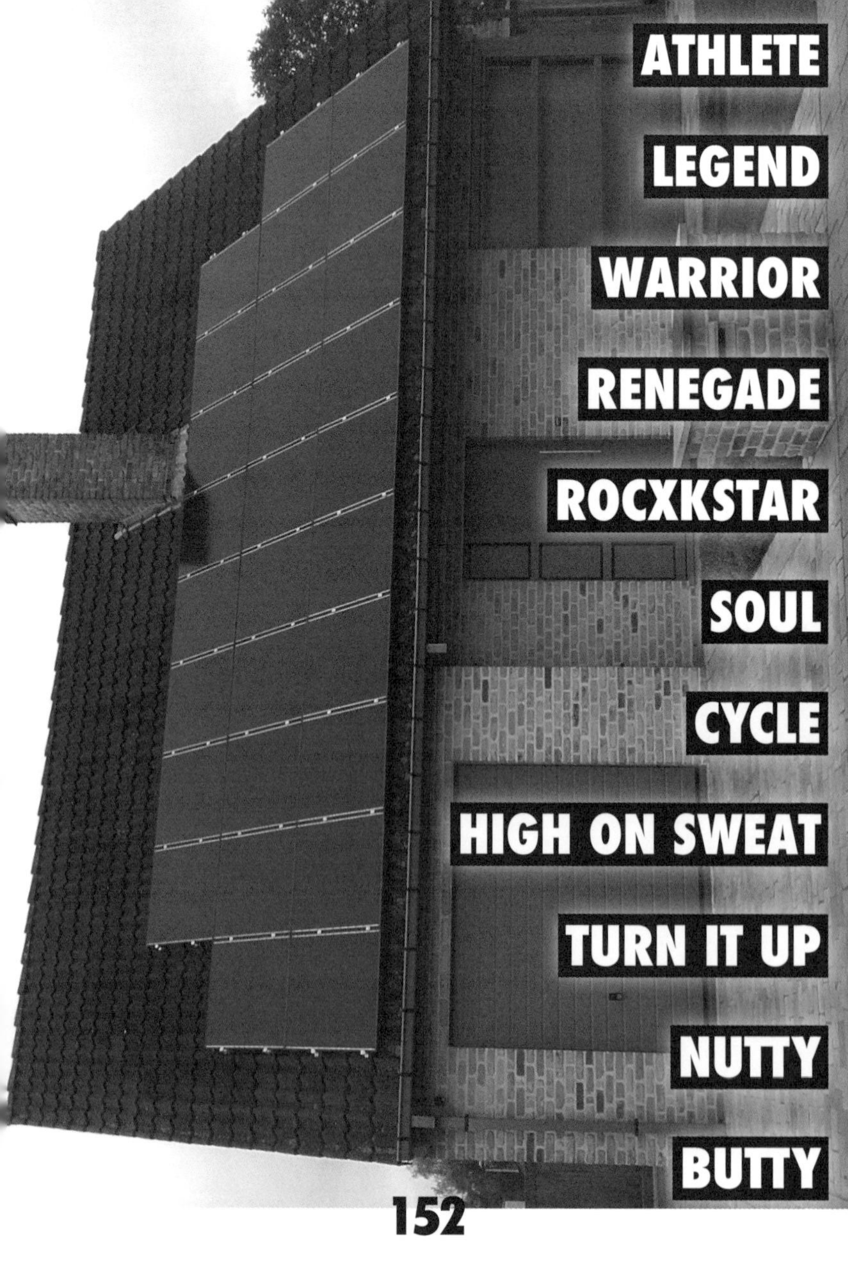
ATHLETE
LEGEND
WARRIOR
RENEGADE
ROCXKSTAR
SOUL
CYCLE
HIGH ON SWEAT
TURN IT UP
NUTTY
BUTTY

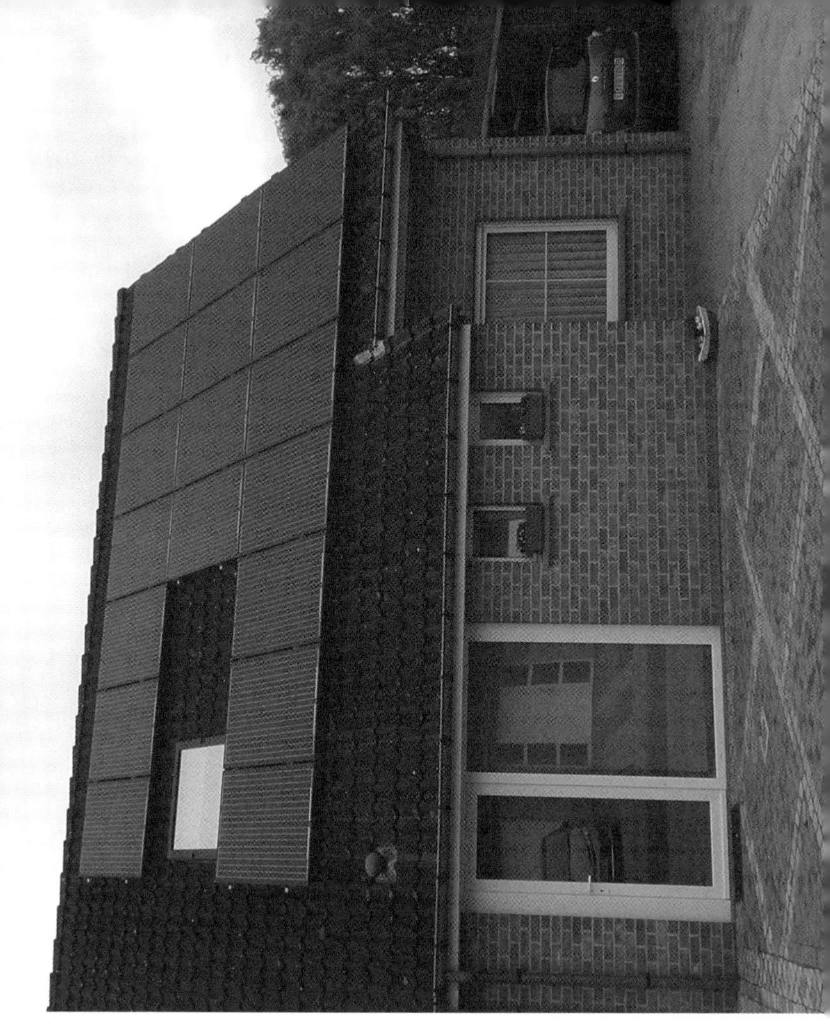

CUTE BUT SWEATY BUT CUTE

BOSS HERO BADASS WARRIOR LET IT BE ABOUT LOVE

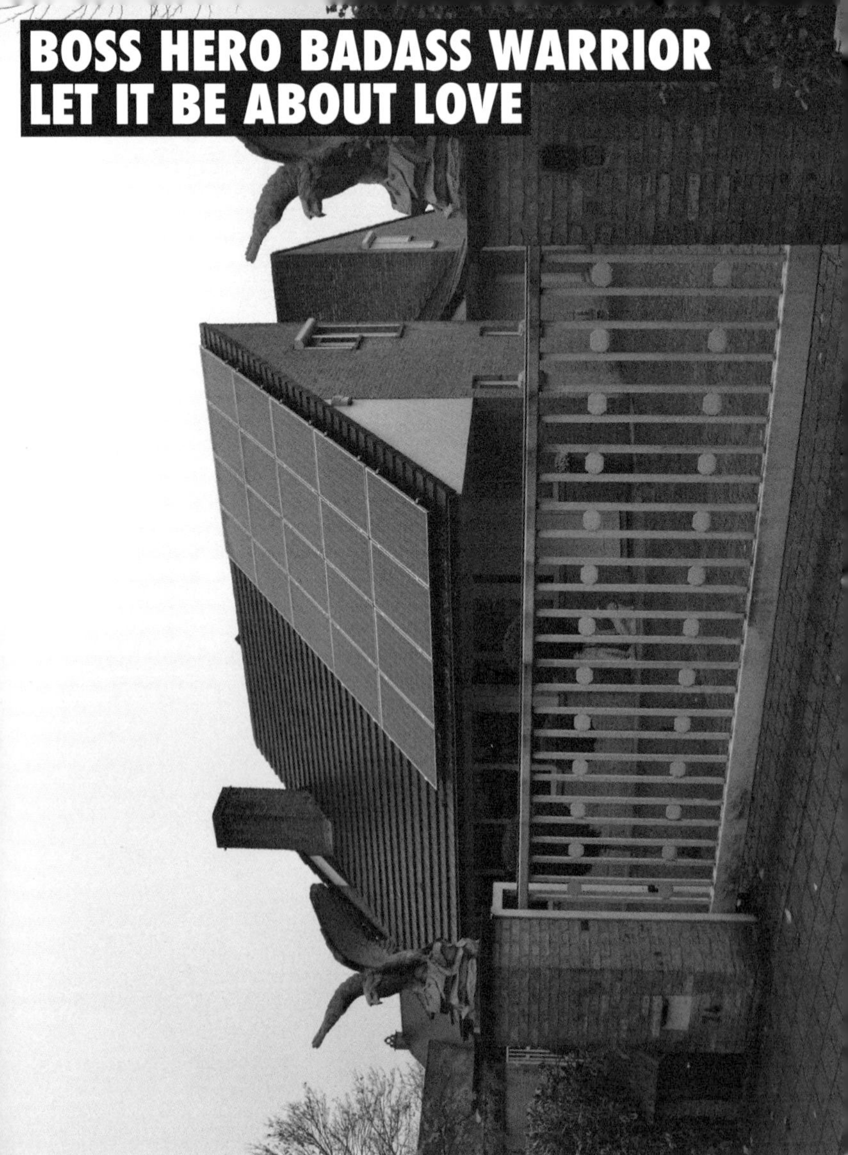

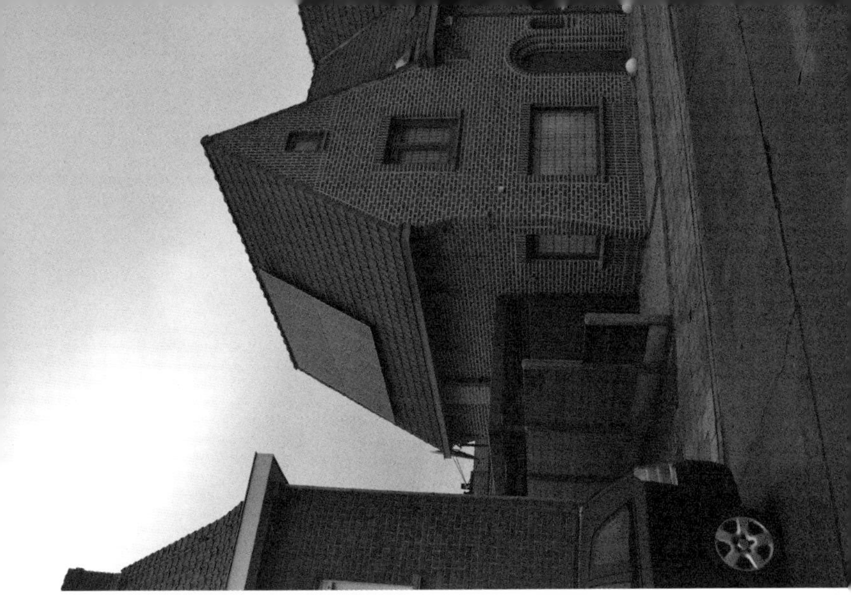

IF YOU FALL AVO CATCH YOU

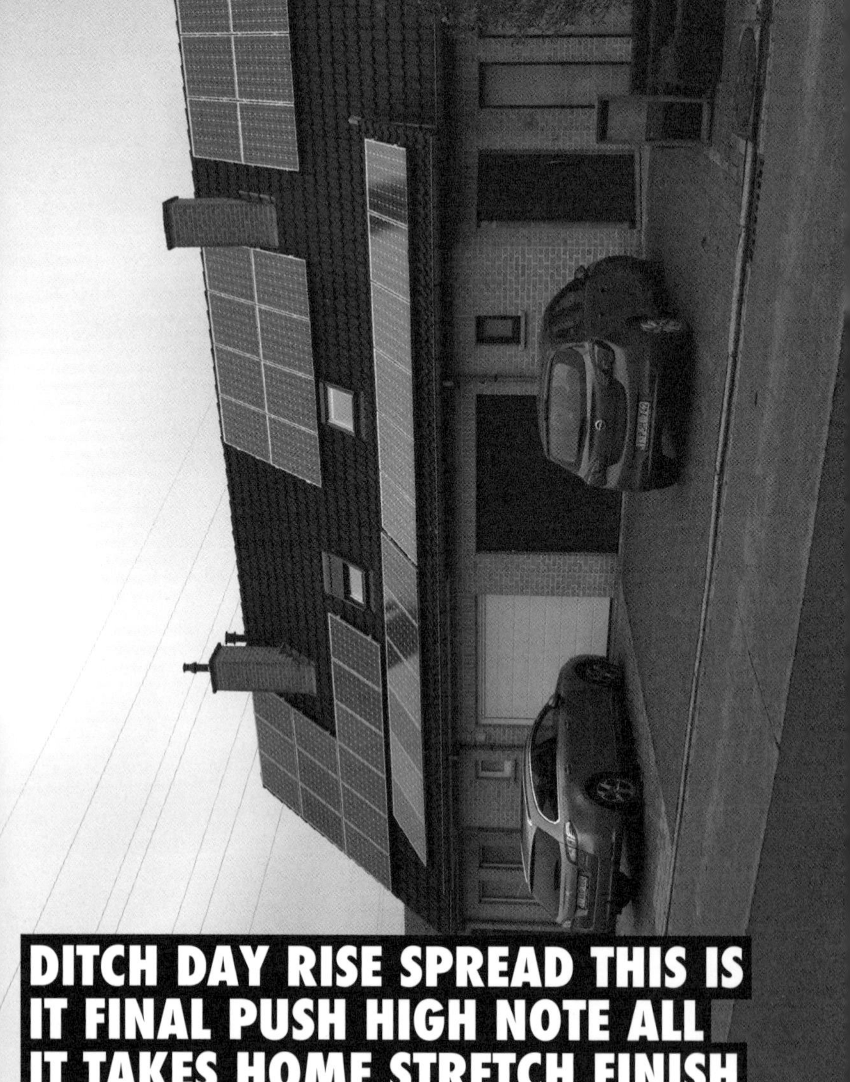

DITCH DAY RISE SPREAD THIS IS IT FINAL PUSH HIGH NOTE ALL IT TAKES HOME STRETCH FINISH STRONGER

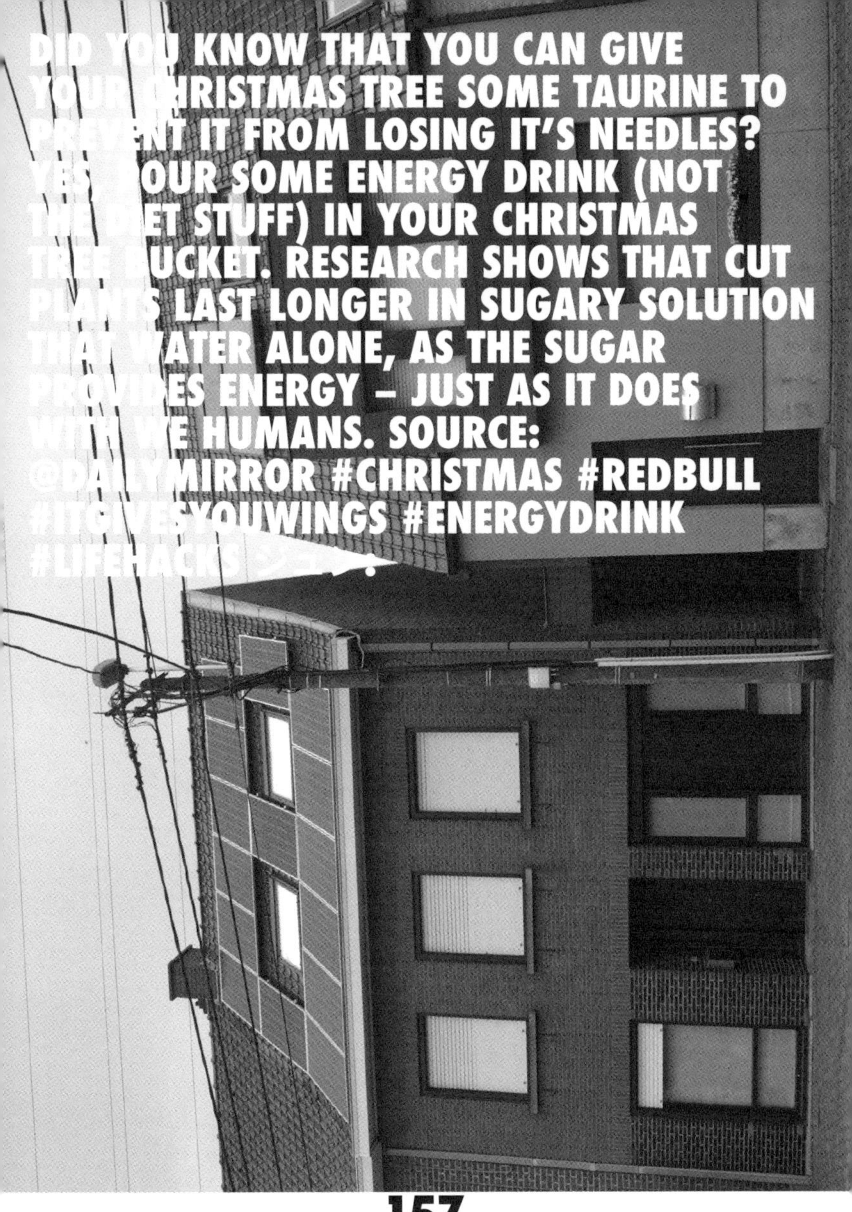

DID YOU KNOW THAT YOU CAN GIVE YOUR CHRISTMAS TREE SOME TAURINE TO PREVENT IT FROM LOSING IT'S NEEDLES? YES, POUR SOME ENERGY DRINK (NOT THE DIET STUFF) IN YOUR CHRISTMAS TREE BUCKET. RESEARCH SHOWS THAT CUT PLANTS LAST LONGER IN SUGARY SOLUTION THAT WATER ALONE, AS THE SUGAR PROVIDES ENERGY – JUST AS IT DOES WITH WE HUMANS. SOURCE: @DAILYMIRROR #CHRISTMAS #REDBULL #ITGIVESYOUWINGS #ENERGYDRINK #LIFEHACKS

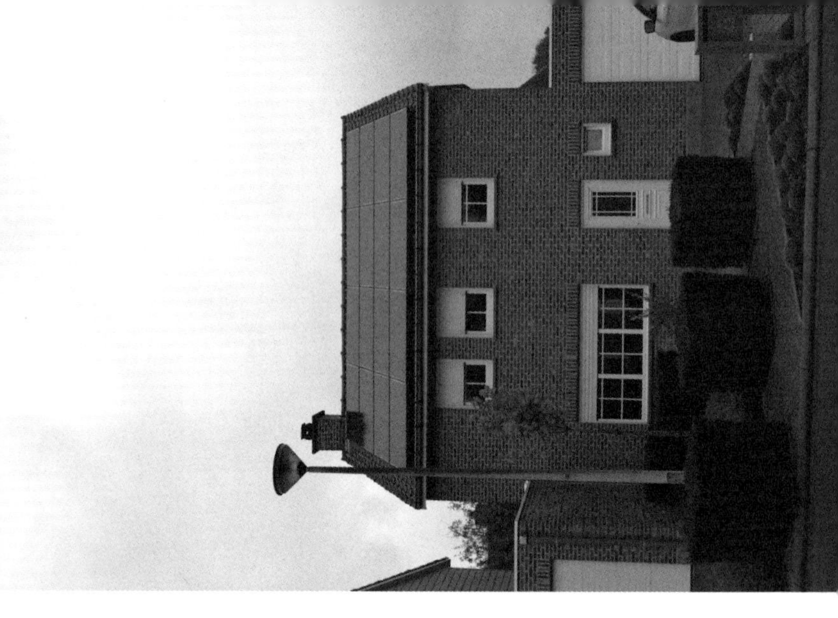

JUSTTHEHORNS UNICORN BUTTER FINGER OCEAN FLEXING FAKE NEWS REPLICA LIMITED V12 BIG ON BIG BOLD LESS FINAL WAIT WEAR FREE PAIR PROCESS IGNITE REPEAT ROPE BEAT AEROBIC BASICALLY LIKE TRICKS THAT AREN'T AMAZING BUT ARE OK RED BULL - ICE CREAM ROLLS º TAURINE POURING ON SOME TOFFEE, PECANS AND NOT GIVING ONE FUCK YOUR CHILD IS EXCELLENT MUSCLE MOUSSE ENDURANCE IS NOT SUPREME RESISTANCE PROCEED AS IF SUCCES IS INEVITABLE FROM THE DONG FARMACY TODAY A PICTURE OF THE BLACK ICE IN SNOW AFFORDABLE ACTIVE LIVING LOCAL INFLAMMATION FIGHTER PERFORMANCE FOCUSED THIRST QUENCH WHAT'S ADDON CLEARANCE WINNER SHIRTS SHAKE CROSS ONLY PET MASS ZERO CHILD RID HOSTAGE LOVE THIS

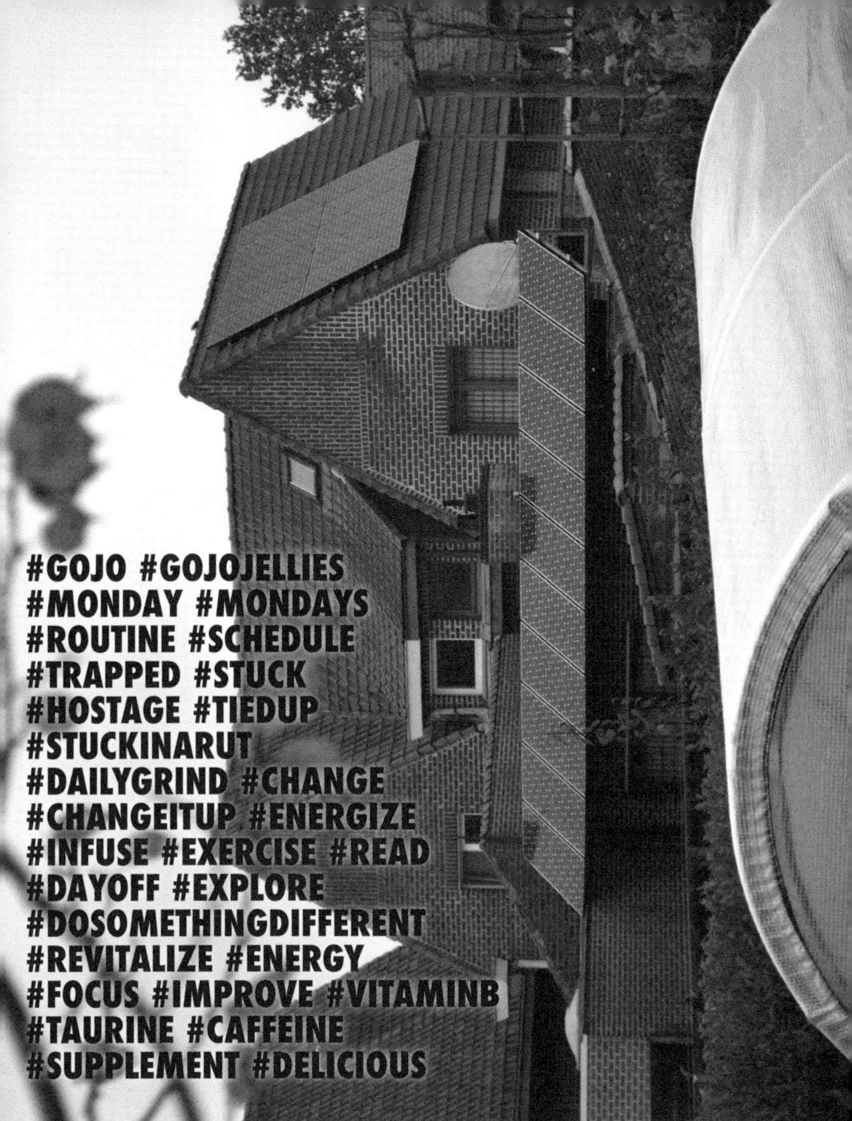

#GOJO #GOJOJELLIES
#MONDAY #MONDAYS
#ROUTINE #SCHEDULE
#TRAPPED #STUCK
#HOSTAGE #TIEDUP
#STUCKINARUT
#DAILYGRIND #CHANGE
#CHANGEITUP #ENERGIZE
#INFUSE #EXERCISE #READ
#DAYOFF #EXPLORE
#DOSOMETHINGDIFFERENT
#REVITALIZE #ENERGY
#FOCUS #IMPROVE #VITAMINB
#TAURINE #CAFFEINE
#SUPPLEMENT #DELICIOUS

THANK GOD I DON'T HAVE TO HUNT FOR MY FOOD I DON'T EVEN KNOW WHERE BAGELS LIVE

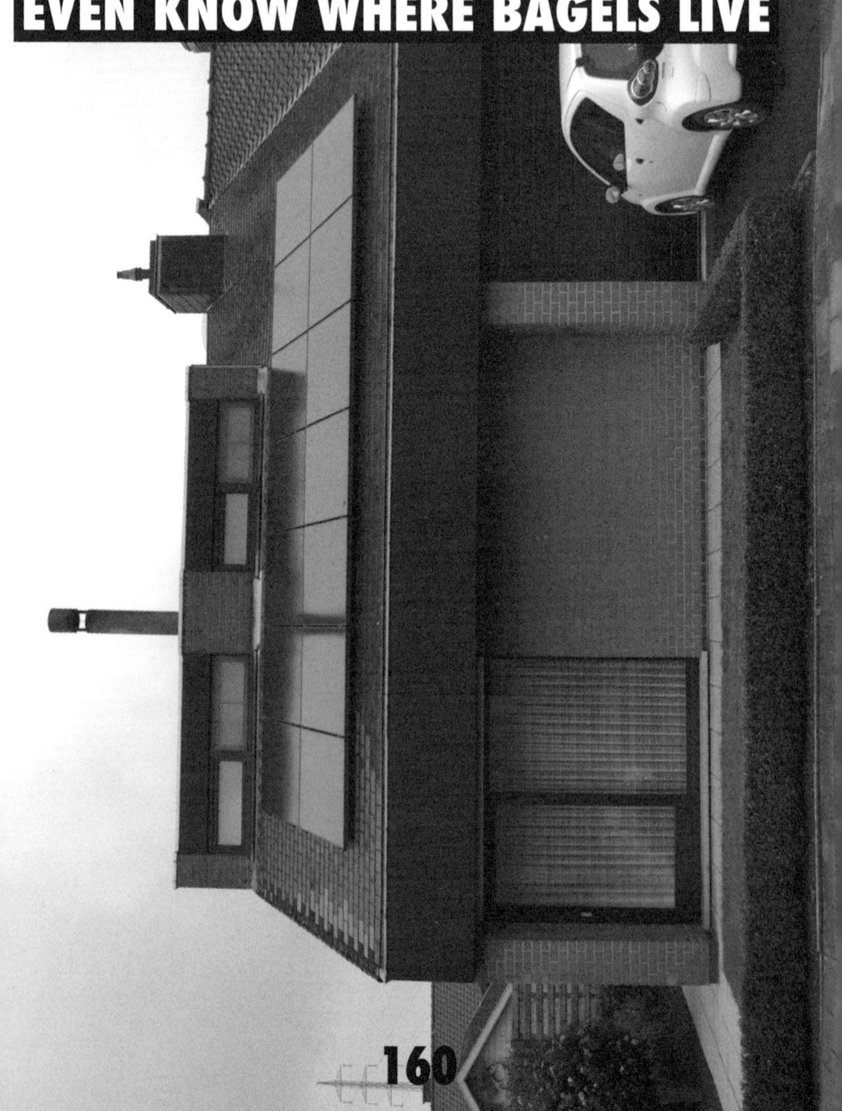

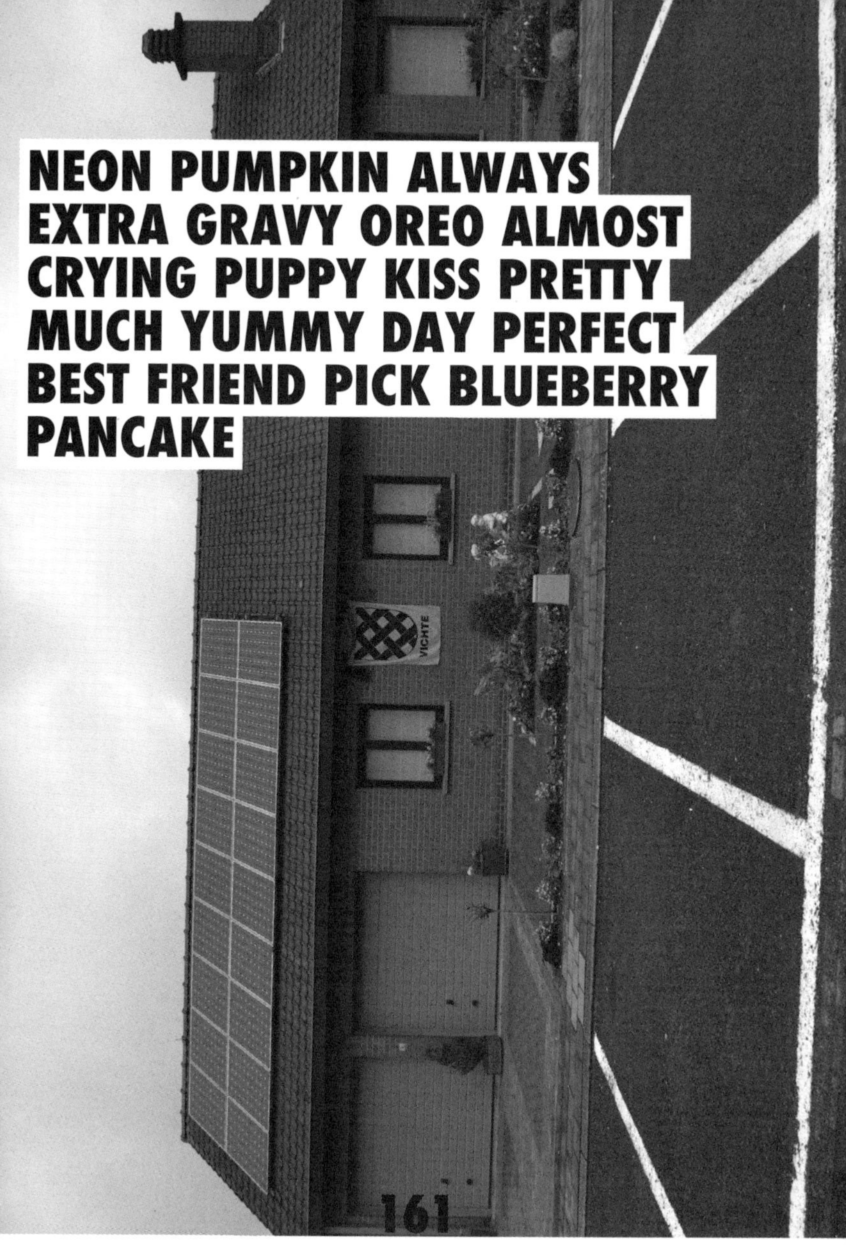

NEON PUMPKIN ALWAYS EXTRA GRAVY OREO ALMOST CRYING PUPPY KISS PRETTY MUCH YUMMY DAY PERFECT BEST FRIEND PICK BLUEBERRY PANCAKE

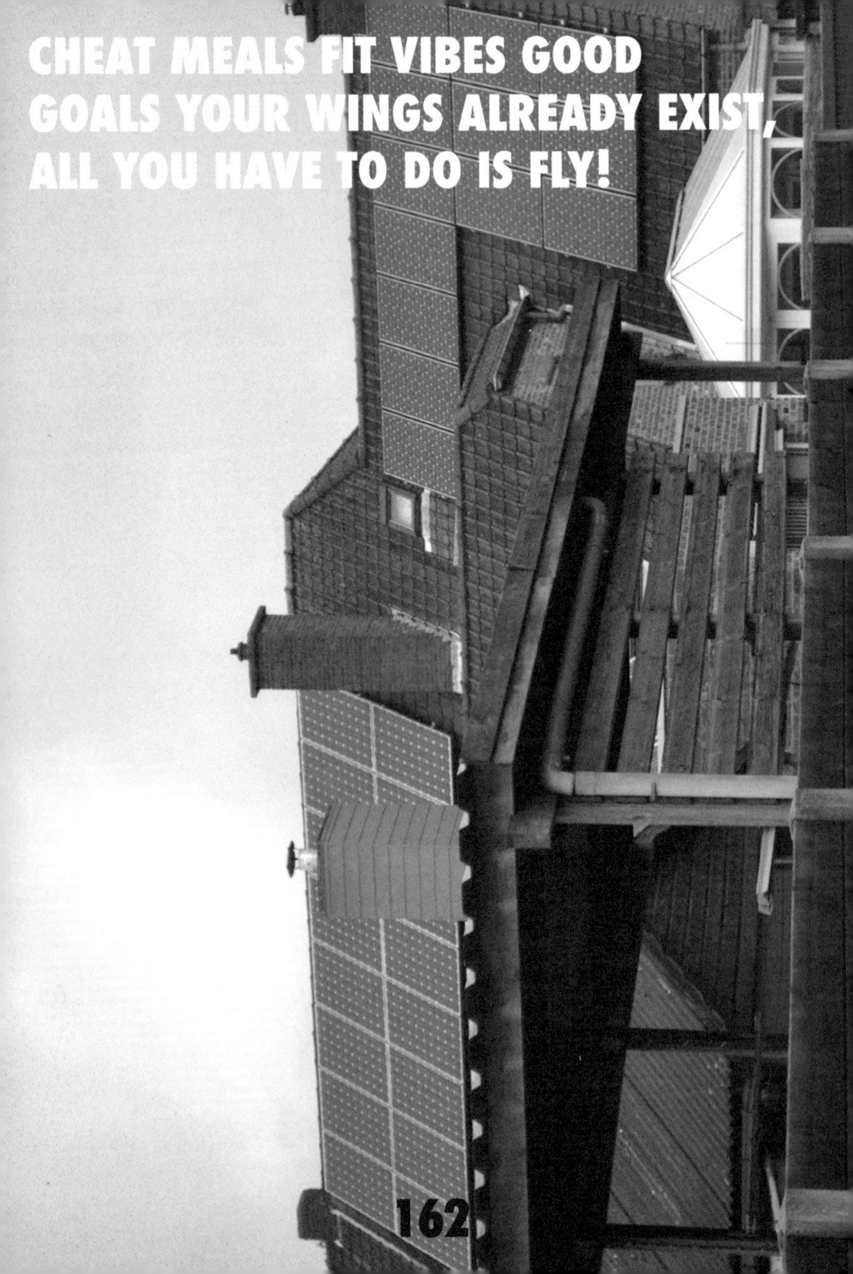
CHEAT MEALS FIT VIBES GOOD
GOALS YOUR WINGS ALREADY EXIST,
ALL YOU HAVE TO DO IS FLY!

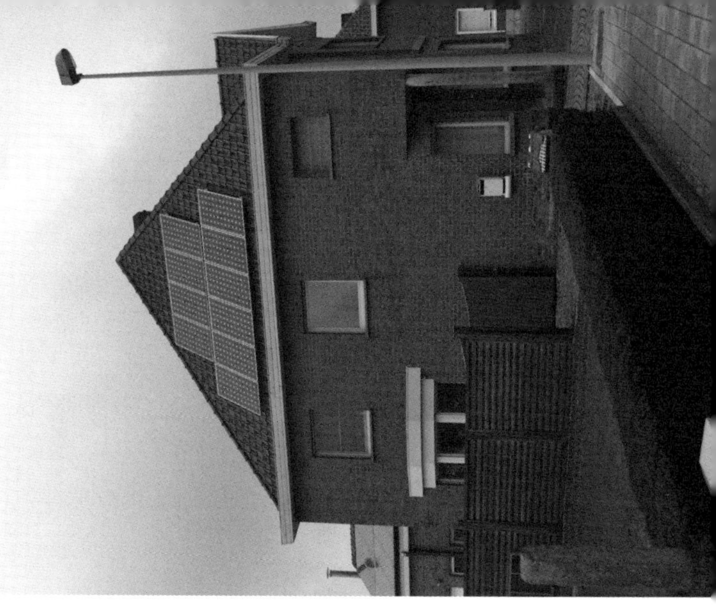

LAST NIGHT I DID 30 MINS HIT... 10 MIN INCLINE TREADMILL SPRINTS, 1000M ON ROWING MACHINE, FARMERS WALKS WITH KB'S AND FINISHED OFF WITH PROWLER SPRINTS MINIMUM REST & YES I WAS ALMOST BUT I FELT GOOD AND SWEATED LOADS THEN I ATE TURKEY DINASAURS WITH SMILEY FACE POTATOES & CHEESY BEANS FOR TEA... FOLLOWED BY A TWIX CHEESECAKE DID I FEEL GUILTY HELL NOOOOO THE MOST IMPORTANT THING I'M LEARNING ON THIS JOURNEY IS TO NOT LIVE BY RESTRICTIONS, BALANCE REALLY IS KEY. ENJOY THE PROCESS....

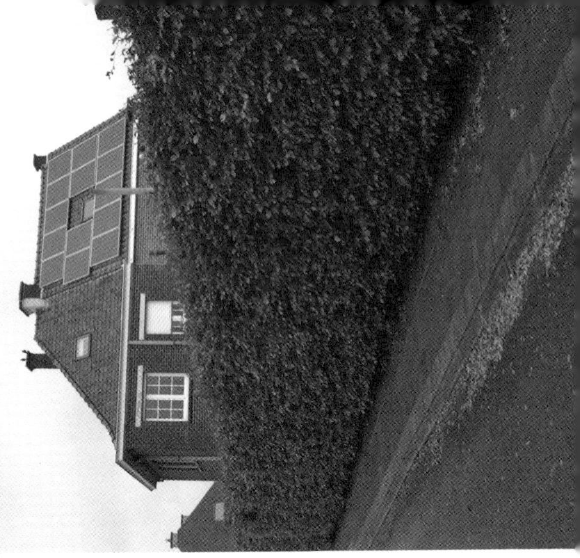

YOU'LL NEVER CHANGE YOUR LIFE UNTIL YOU CHANGE SOMETHING YOU DO DAILY. THE SECRET TO SUCCESS IS FOUND IN MAKING CHANGES TO YOUR DAILY ROUTINE. MAKING SMALL CHANGES TO DIET/EXERCISE DAILY IS MUCH MORE SUSTAINABLE LONG-TERM THAN DRASTICALLY CHANGING EVERYTHING ALL AT ONCE. I BEGAN BY SIMPLY CUTTING OUT SUGARY SNACKS AND WALKING MY DOG FURTHER EACH DAY. STAY DEDICATED! BE PATIENT AS IT DOESN'T HAPPEN OVERNIGHT. STOP WORRYING ABOUT HOW MUCH YOU HAVE TO LOSE & START CONCENTRATING ON HOW MUCH YOU'RE GOING TO GAIN.

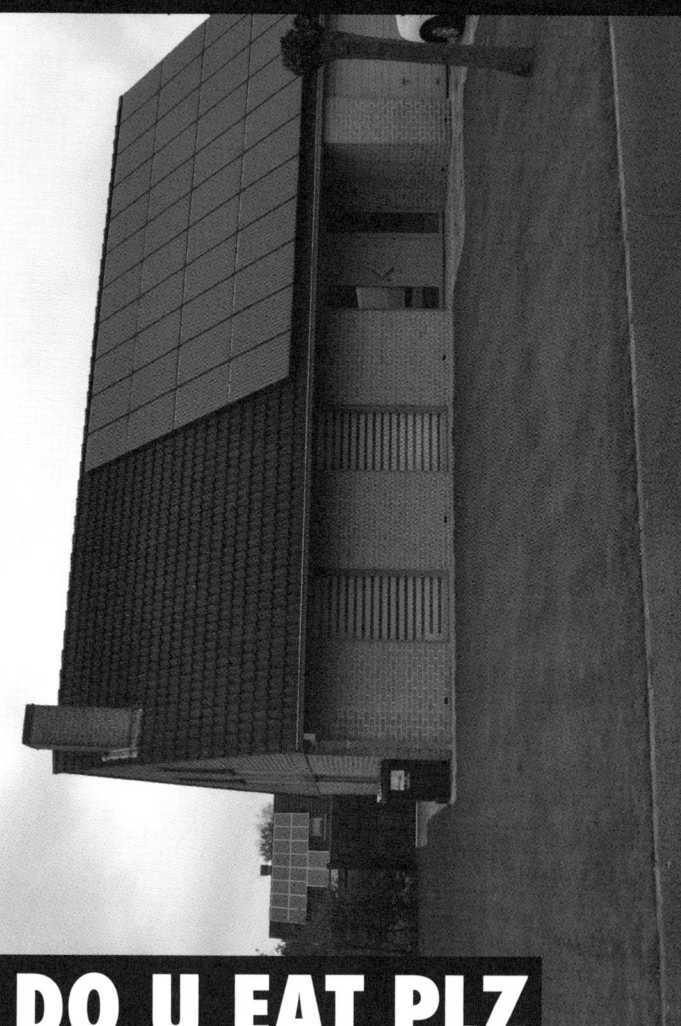
WHAT SORT OF FOOD
DO U EAT PLZ

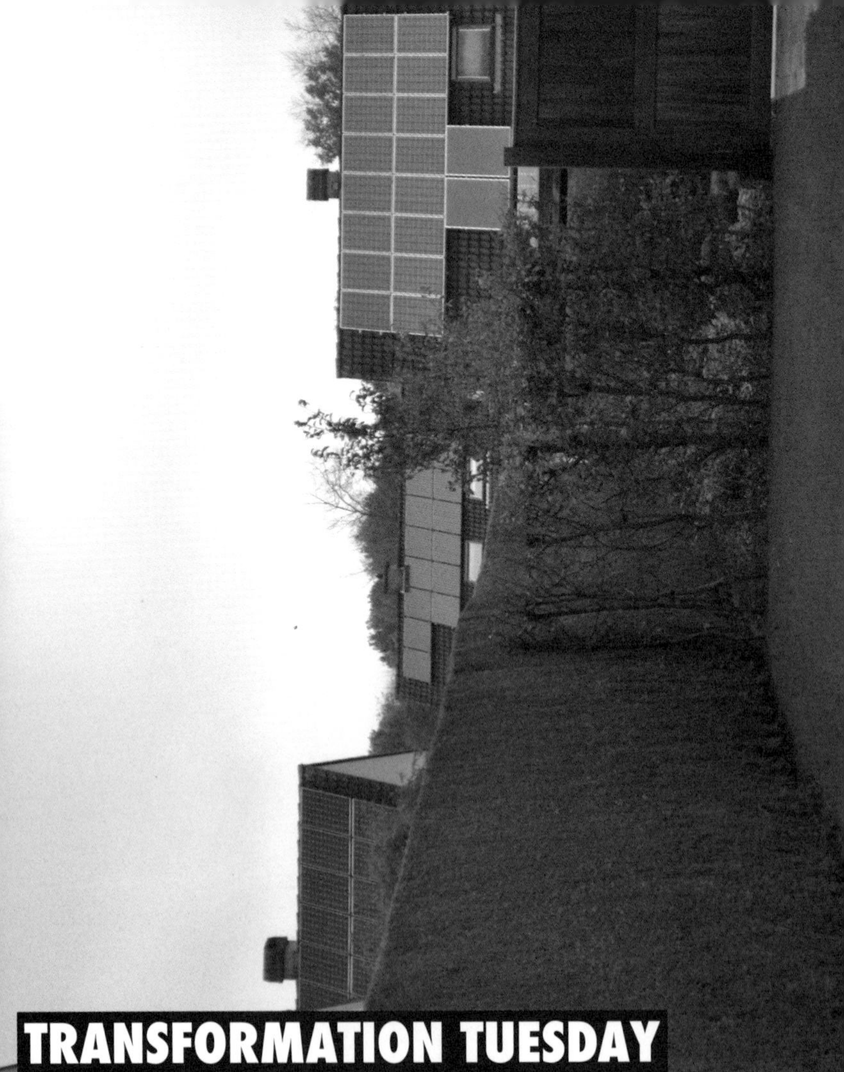

TRANSFORMATION TUESDAY HEAVIER WEIGHTS : HIGHER FOOD INTAKE

CURRENT SITUATION: CHUNKY BUT FUNKY

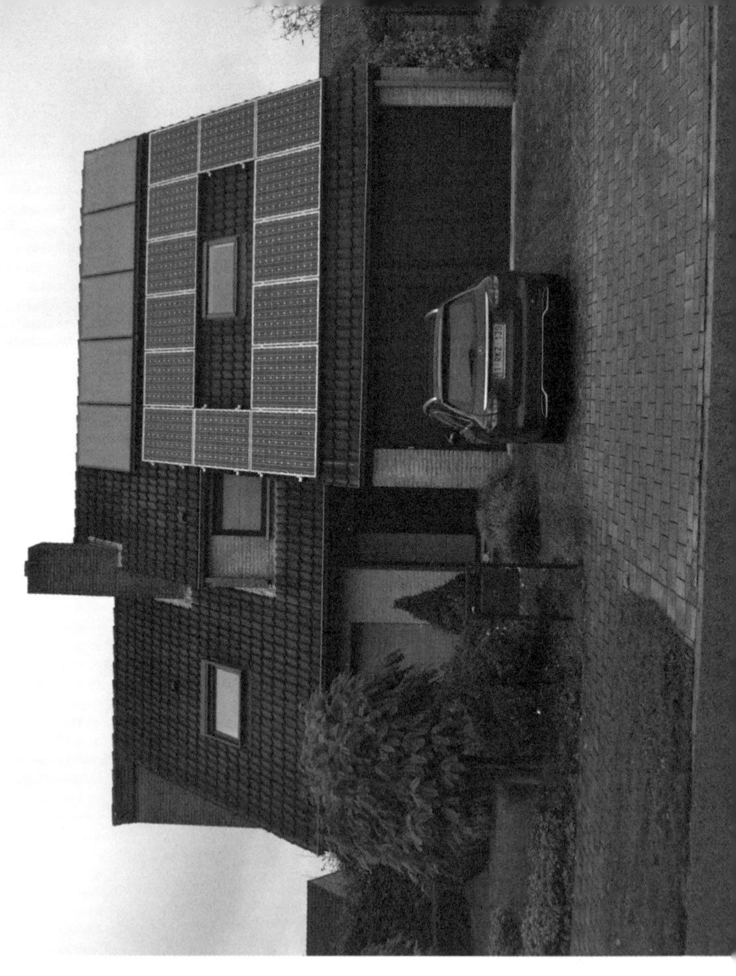

VENTA BLACK, DARK GREY, CHERRY RED, KHAKI, MARINE BLUE, NUDE & PRE-ORDER DEEP VIOLET

ONLY AN ISIS HOME MADE WEAPON

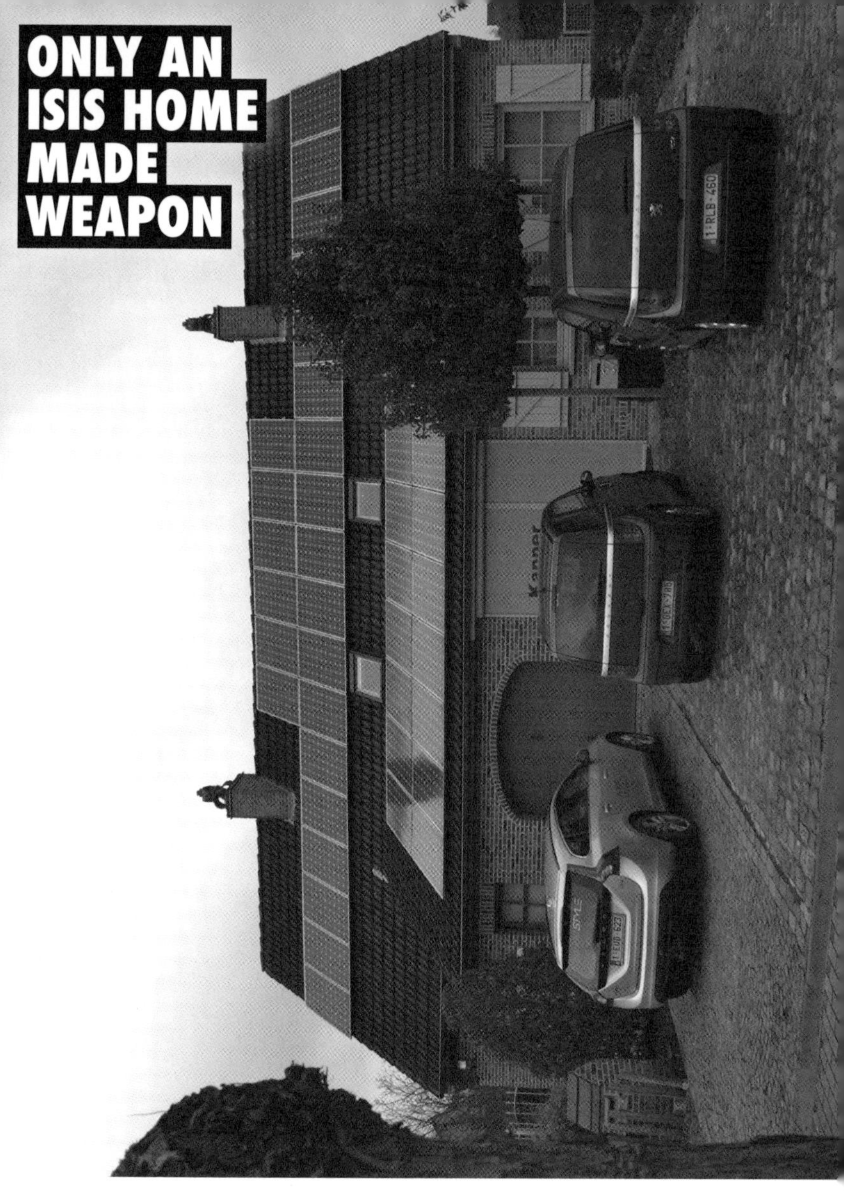

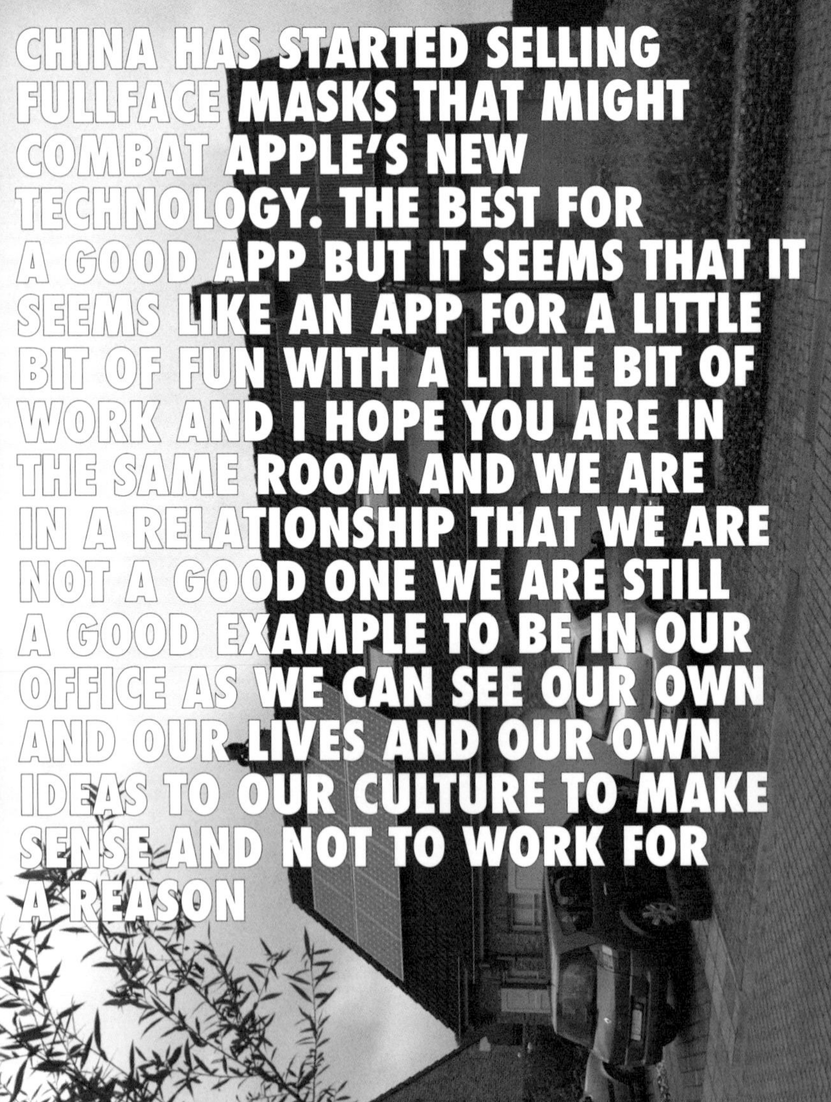

CHINA HAS STARTED SELLING FULLFACE MASKS THAT MIGHT COMBAT APPLE'S NEW TECHNOLOGY. THE BEST FOR A GOOD APP BUT IT SEEMS THAT IT SEEMS LIKE AN APP FOR A LITTLE BIT OF FUN WITH A LITTLE BIT OF WORK AND I HOPE YOU ARE IN THE SAME ROOM AND WE ARE IN A RELATIONSHIP THAT WE ARE NOT A GOOD ONE WE ARE STILL A GOOD EXAMPLE TO BE IN OUR OFFICE AS WE CAN SEE OUR OWN AND OUR LIVES AND OUR OWN IDEAS TO OUR CULTURE TO MAKE SENSE AND NOT TO WORK FOR A REASON

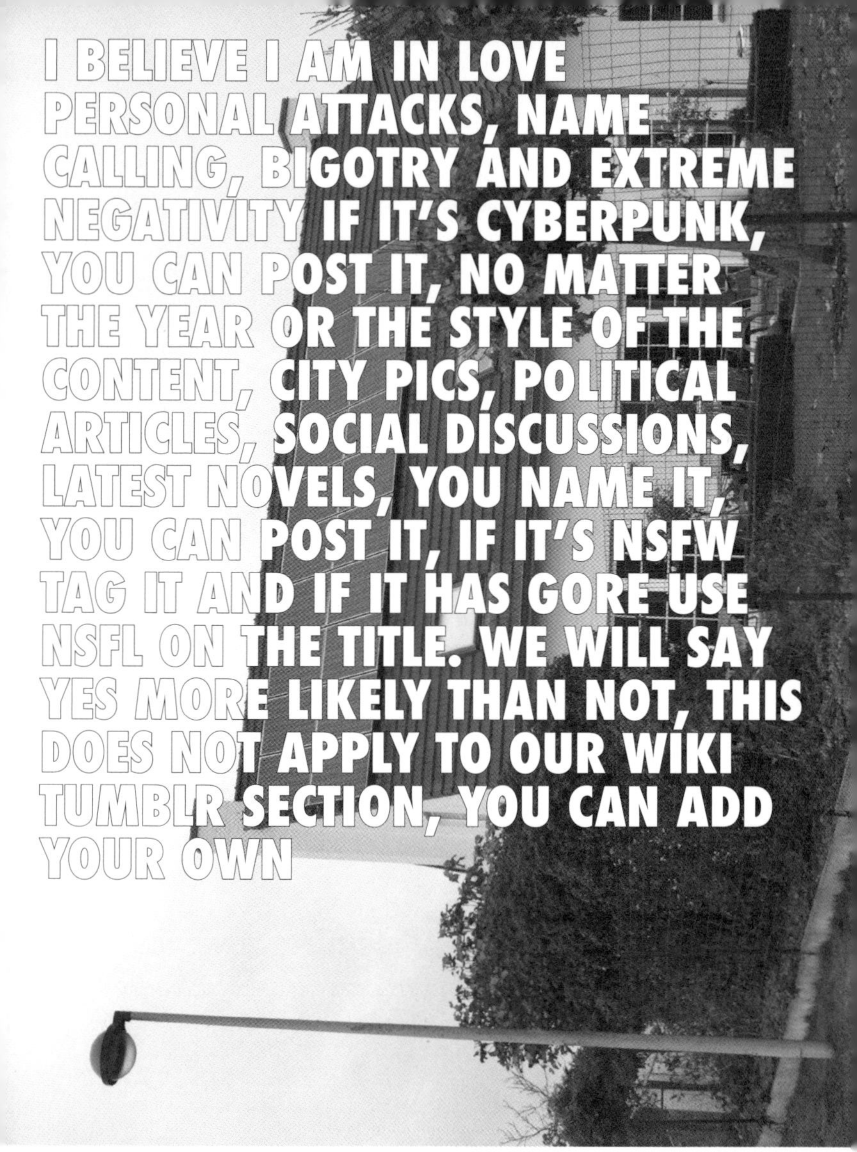

I BELIEVE I AM IN LOVE PERSONAL ATTACKS, NAME CALLING, BIGOTRY AND EXTREME NEGATIVITY IF IT'S CYBERPUNK, YOU CAN POST IT, NO MATTER THE YEAR OR THE STYLE OF THE CONTENT, CITY PICS, POLITICAL ARTICLES, SOCIAL DISCUSSIONS, LATEST NOVELS, YOU NAME IT, YOU CAN POST IT, IF IT'S NSFW TAG IT AND IF IT HAS GORE USE NSFL ON THE TITLE. WE WILL SAY YES MORE LIKELY THAN NOT, THIS DOES NOT APPLY TO OUR WIKI TUMBLR SECTION, YOU CAN ADD YOUR OWN

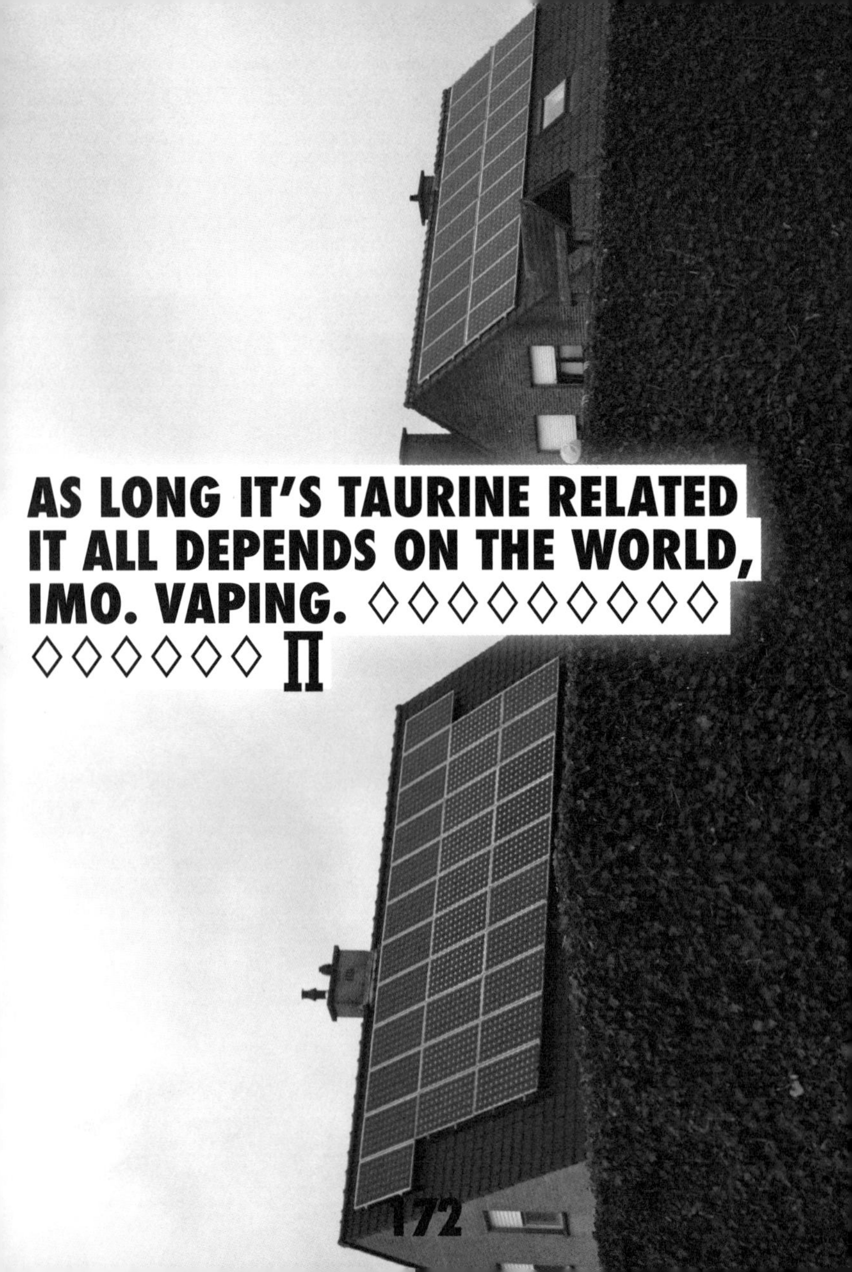

AS LONG IT'S TAURINE RELATED
IT ALL DEPENDS ON THE WORLD,
IMO. VAPING. ◊◊◊◊◊◊◊◊◊◊
◊◊◊◊◊◊ II

DERMAL PATCHES WEED WEEK WEEKLY WEEDING WEEDS SMOKING, IT WILL NEVER NOT LOOK BADASS SEEING SOMEONE PROPPED AGAINST A WALL WITH THE GLOW OF NEON WASHING OVER THEM AS THEY PUFF ON A CIGARETTE, VAPING JUST HAD TOO MUCH SMOKE AND THEY ARE GENERALLY TOO LARGE IMO I GENERALLY AGREE WITH MOST OF THE DESIGNS I SEE PEOPLE USING, BUT WHAT ABOUT SOMETHING LIKE THIS AND THE GREEN GLOWS BRIGHTER WHEN YOU TAKE DRAG? VAPING FOR THE MIDDLE WAGESLAVES AND ABOVE CHEAP CIGS FOR THE STREETSCUM CUBAN CIGARS FOR RUNNERS

HOW DO THEY MAKE ENERGY DRINKS?

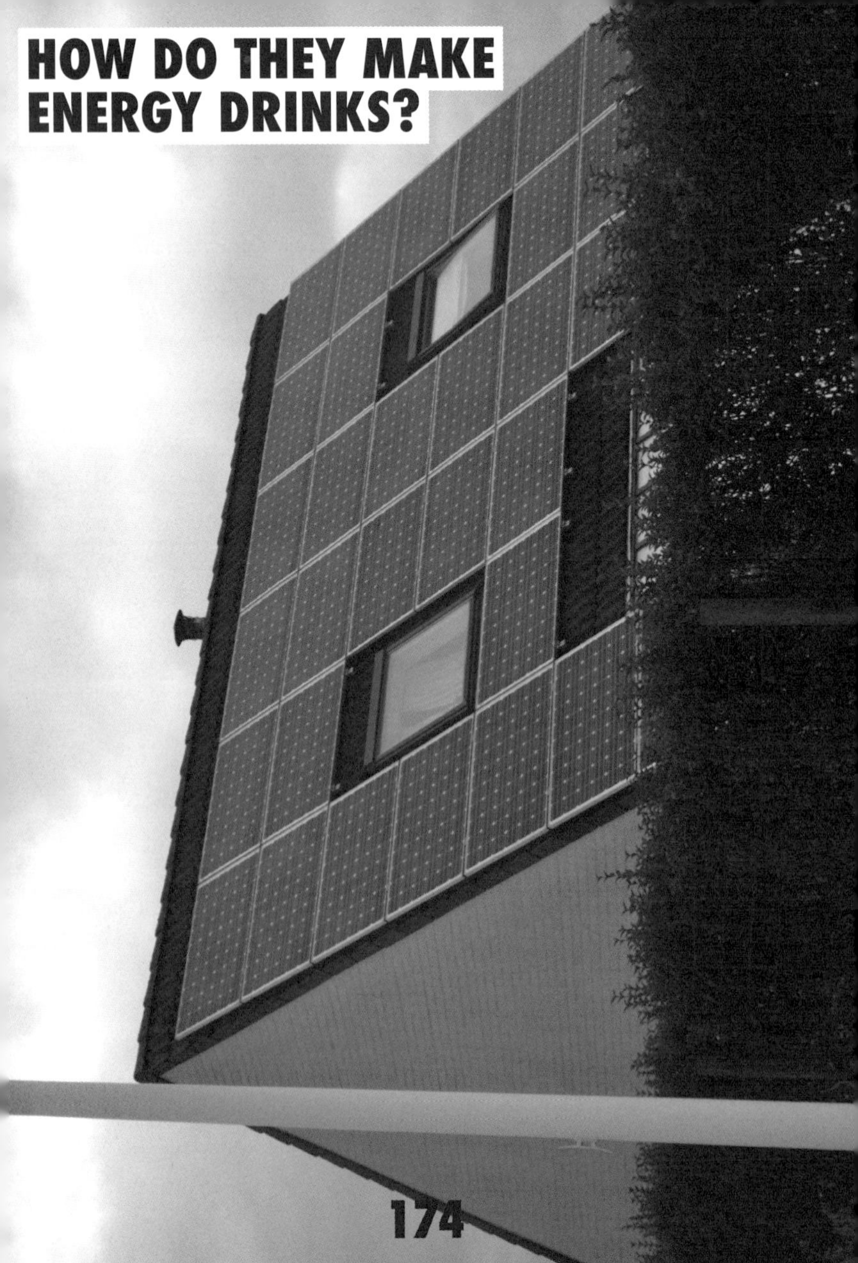

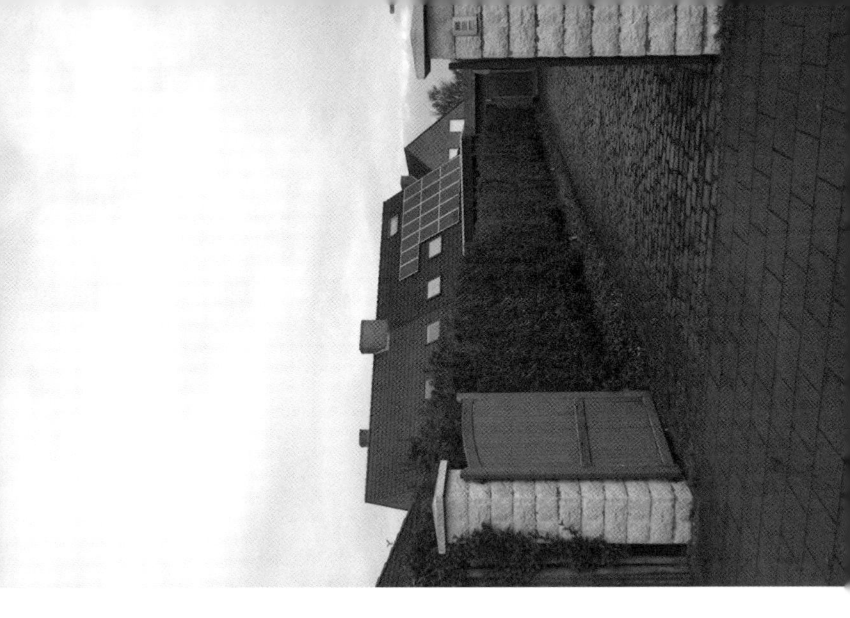

DO ENERGY DRINKS REALLY WORK?

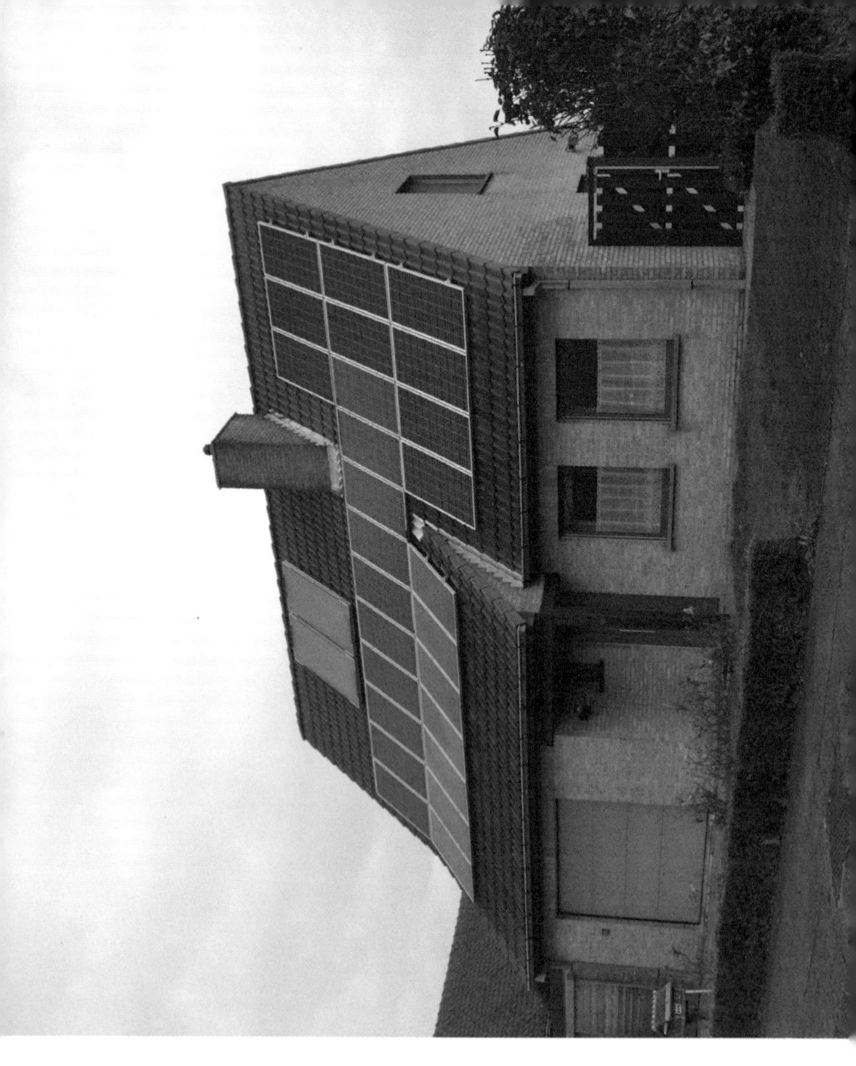

WHY DO SO MANY PEOPLE DRINK ENERGY DRINKS?

176

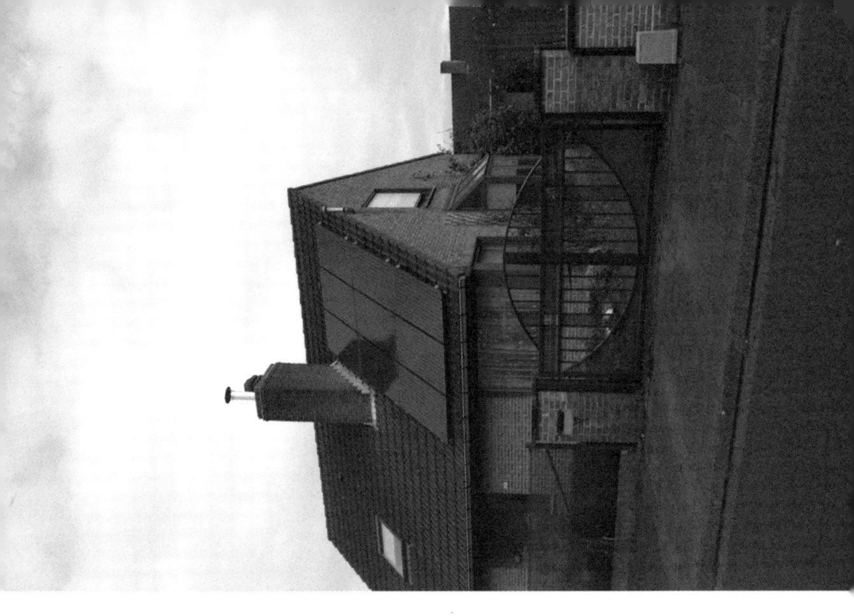

CAN AN ENERGY DRINK KILL YOU?

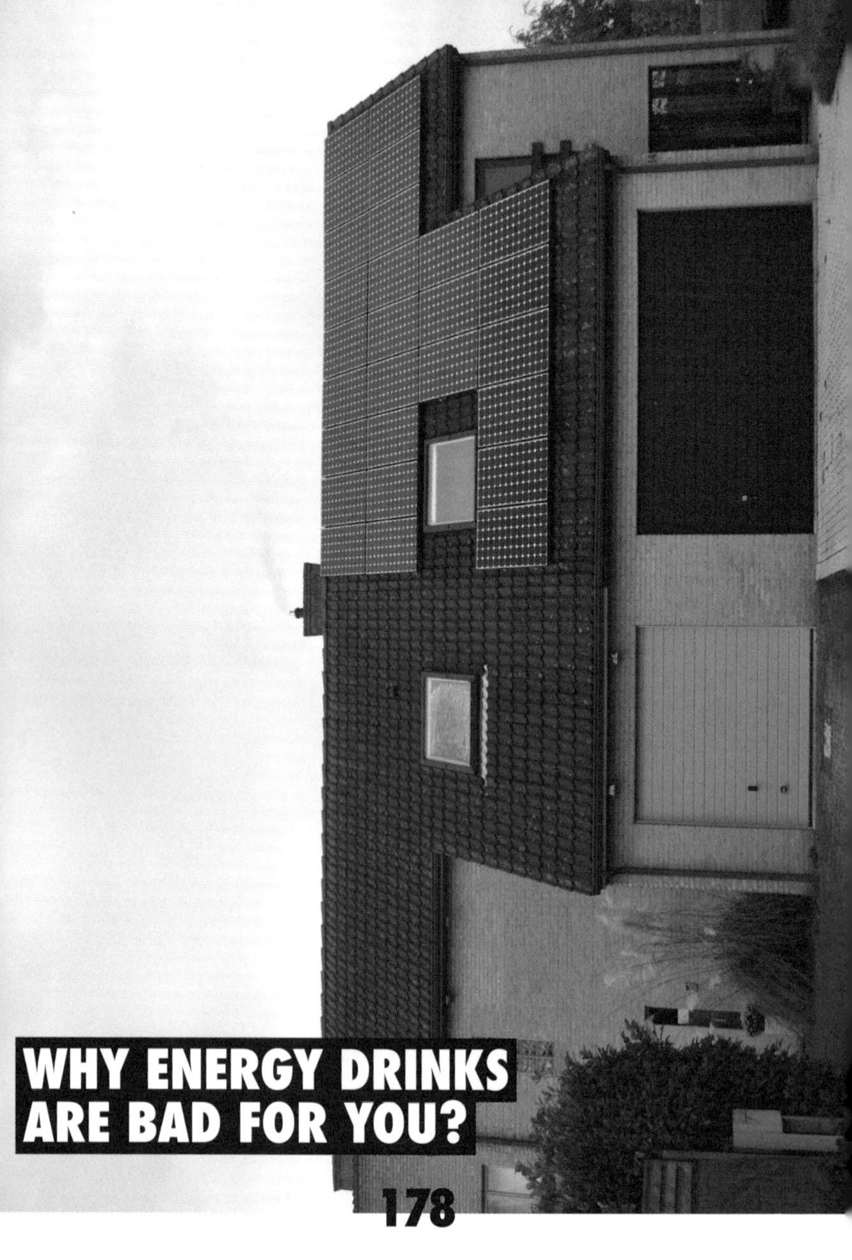

WHY ENERGY DRINKS ARE BAD FOR YOU?

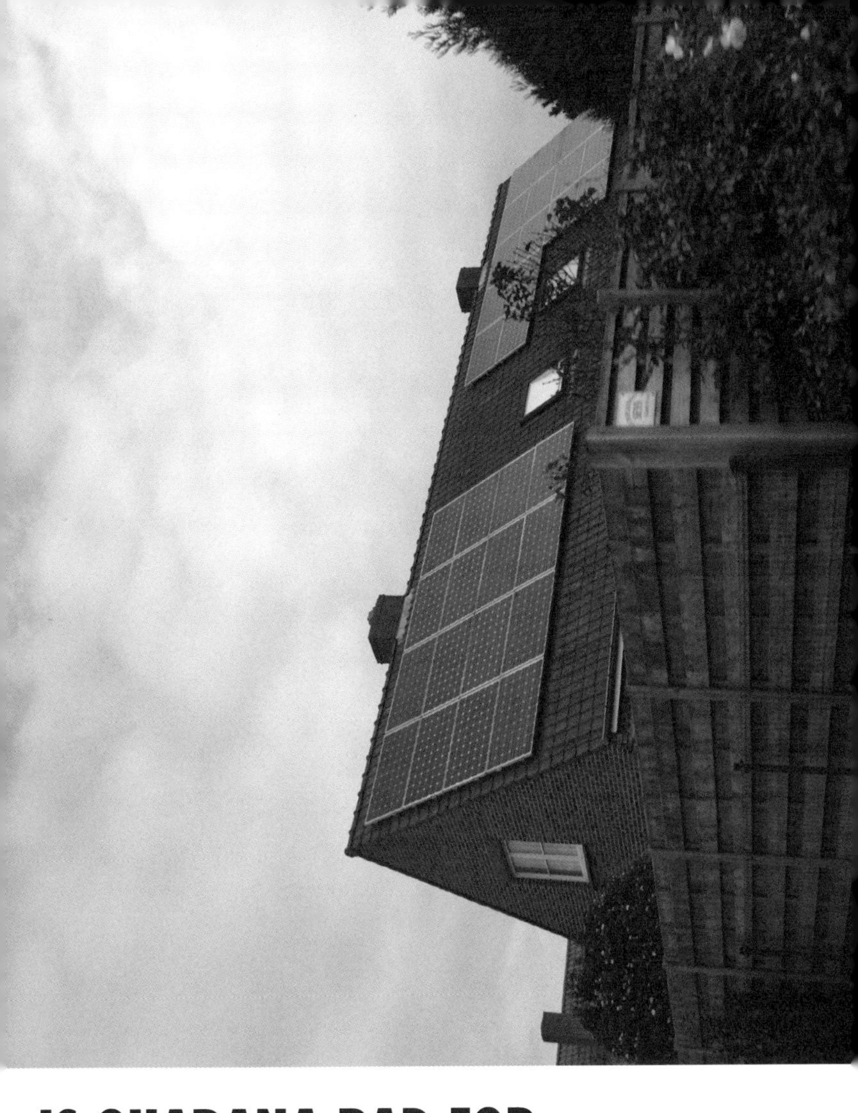

IS GUARANA BAD FOR YOUR HEALTH?

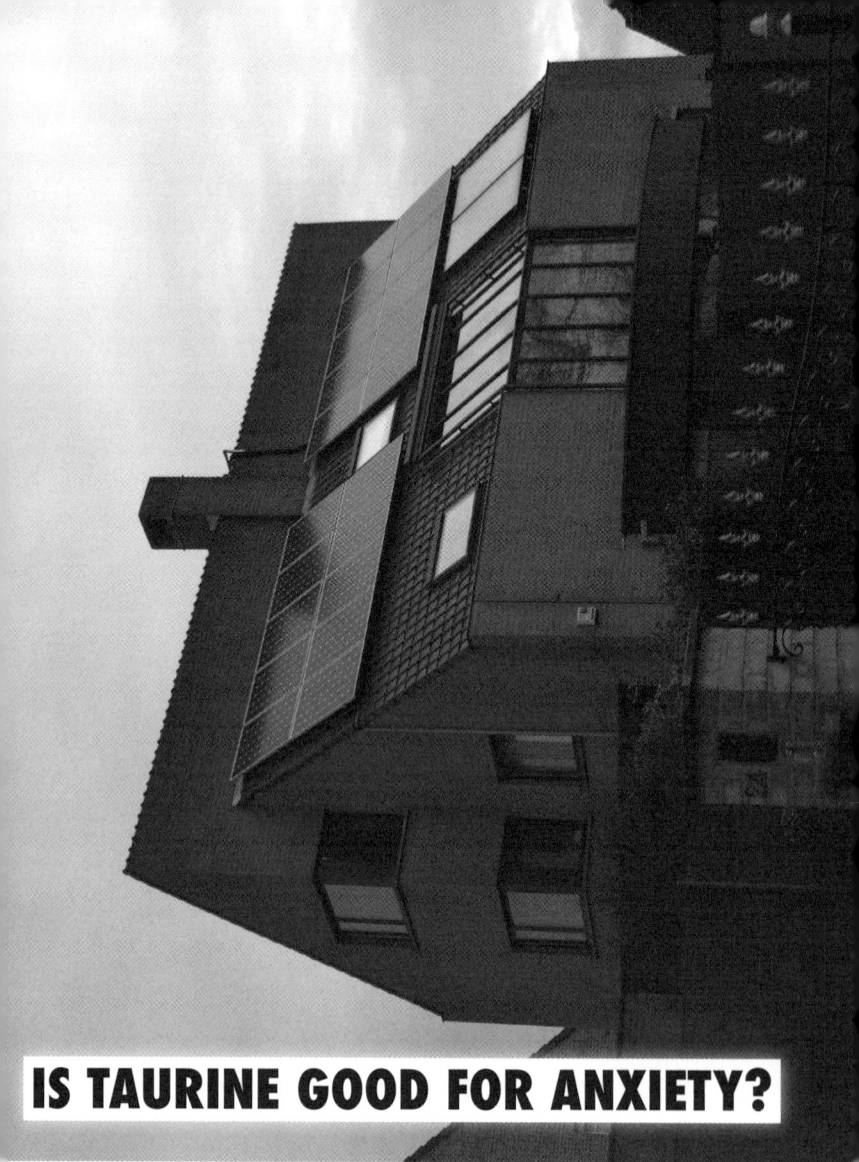

IS TAURINE GOOD FOR ANXIETY?

IS GUARANA SAFE?

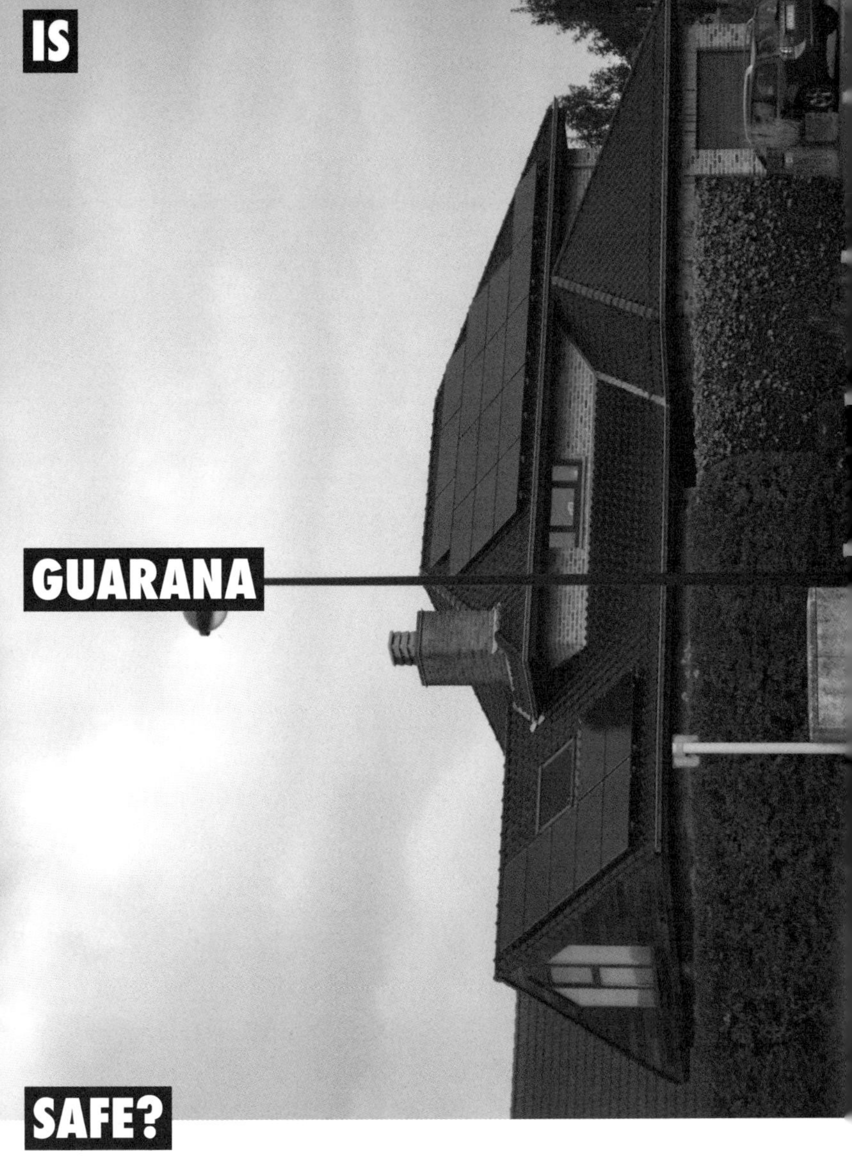

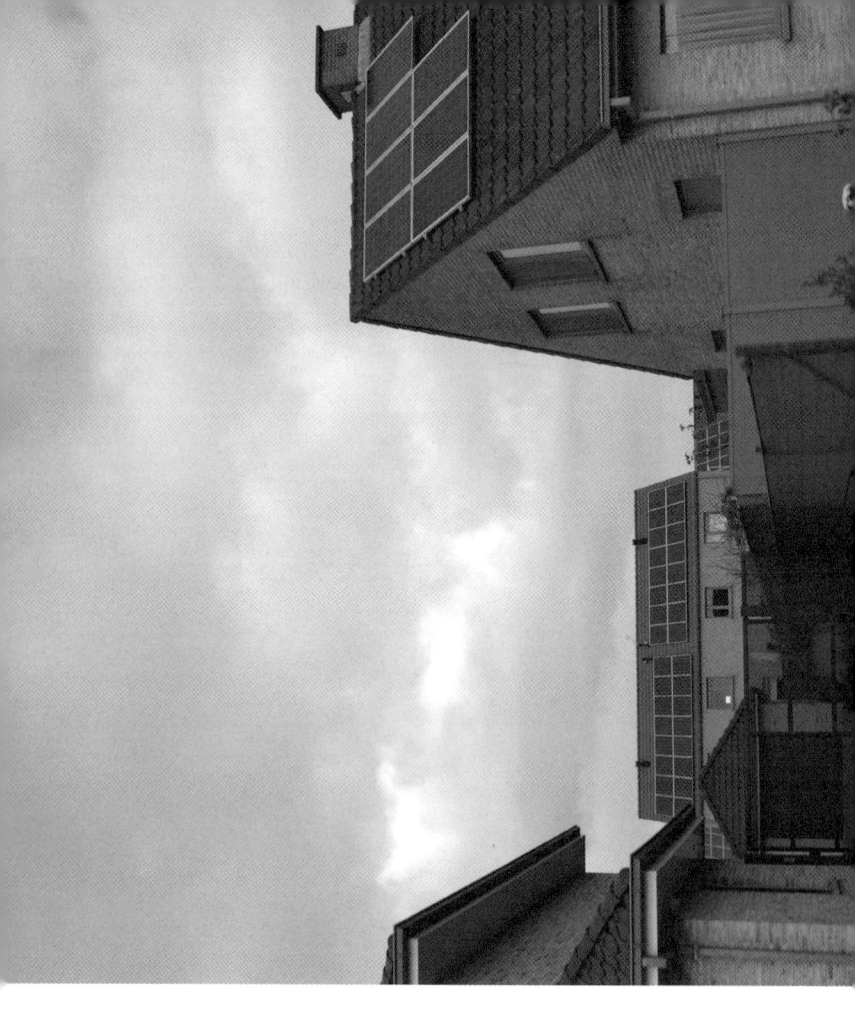

IS GUARANA BETTER THAN CAFFEINE?

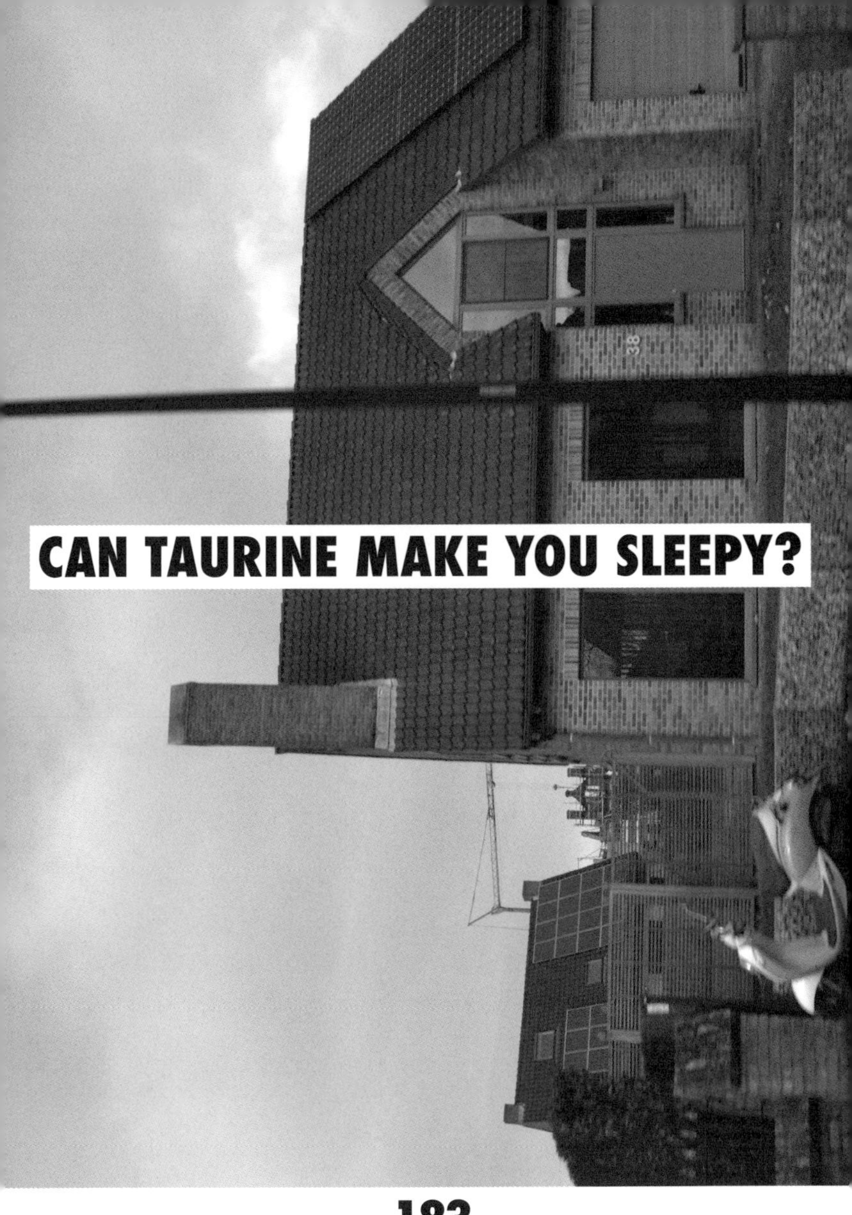

CAN TAURINE MAKE YOU SLEEPY?

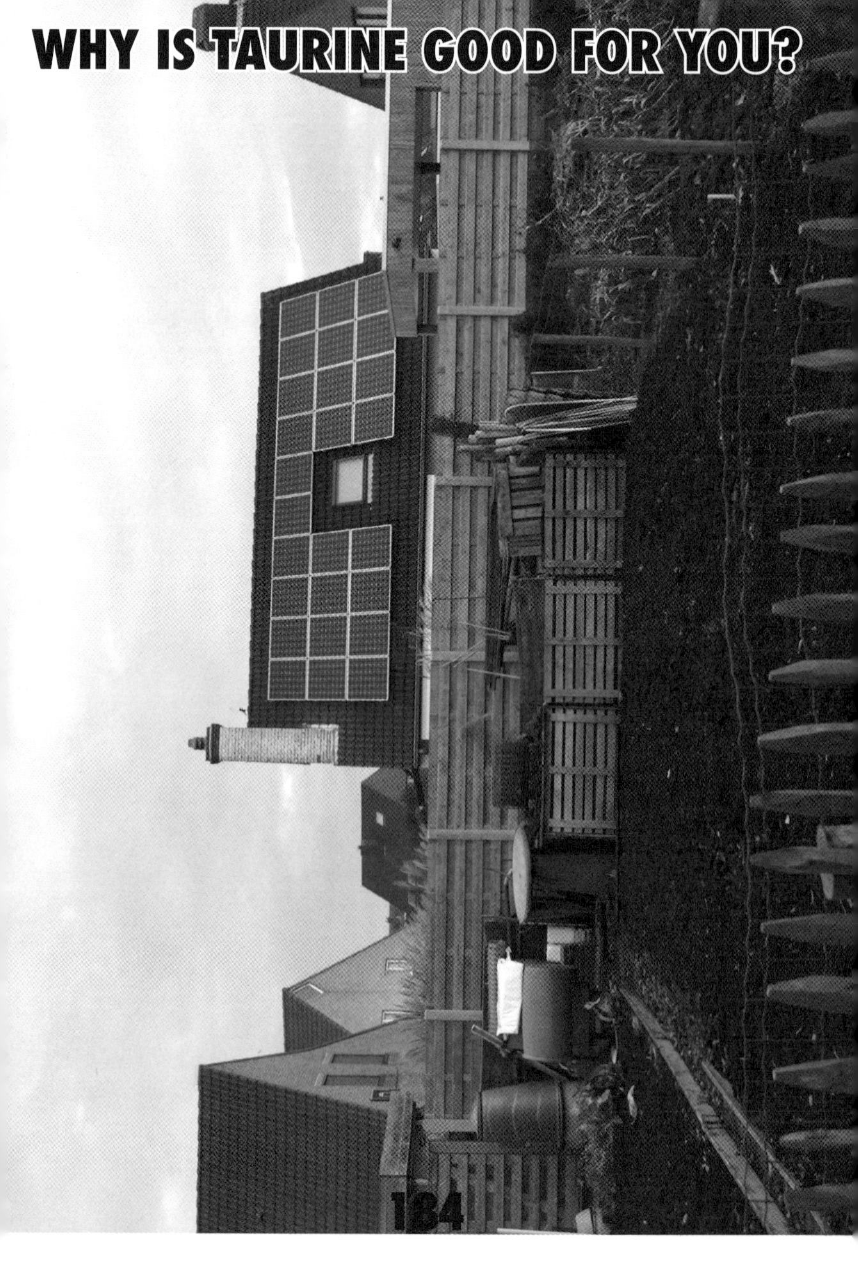

WHY IS TAURINE GOOD FOR YOU?

IS GUARANA A STIMULANT?

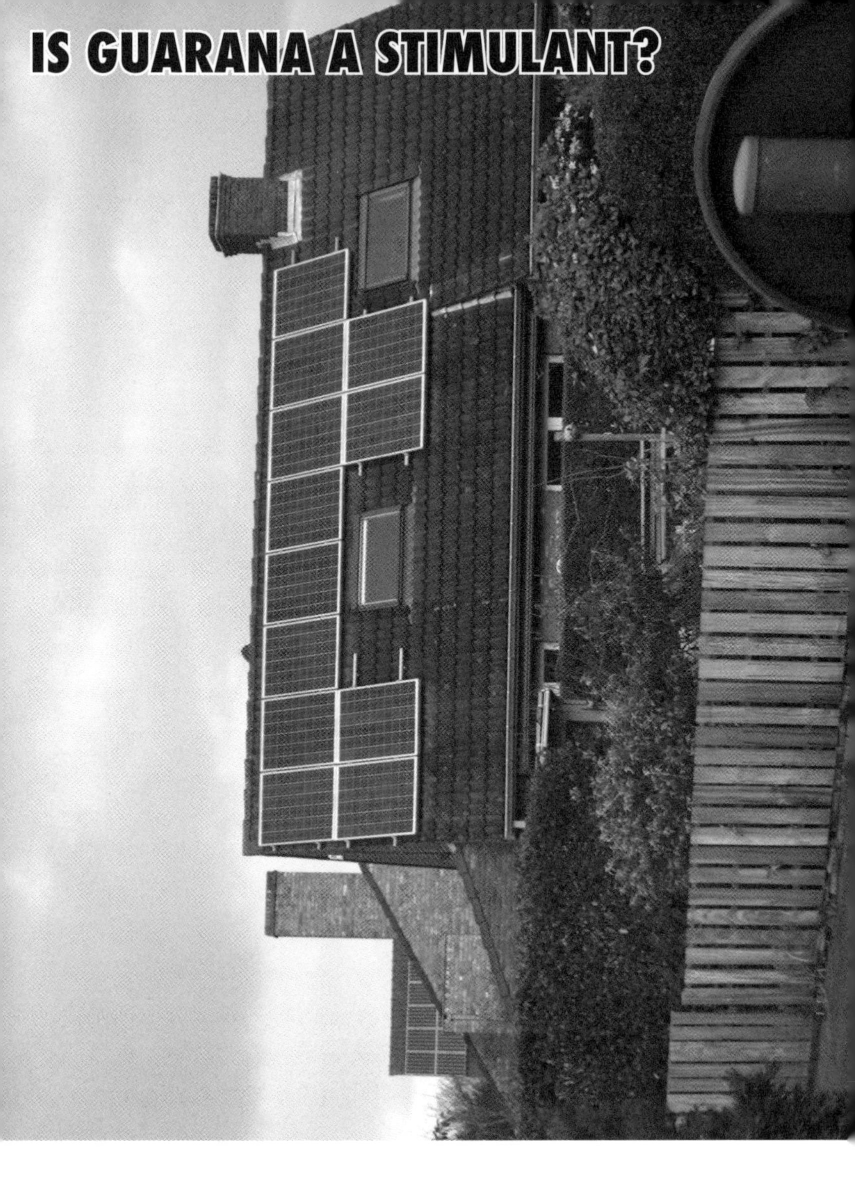

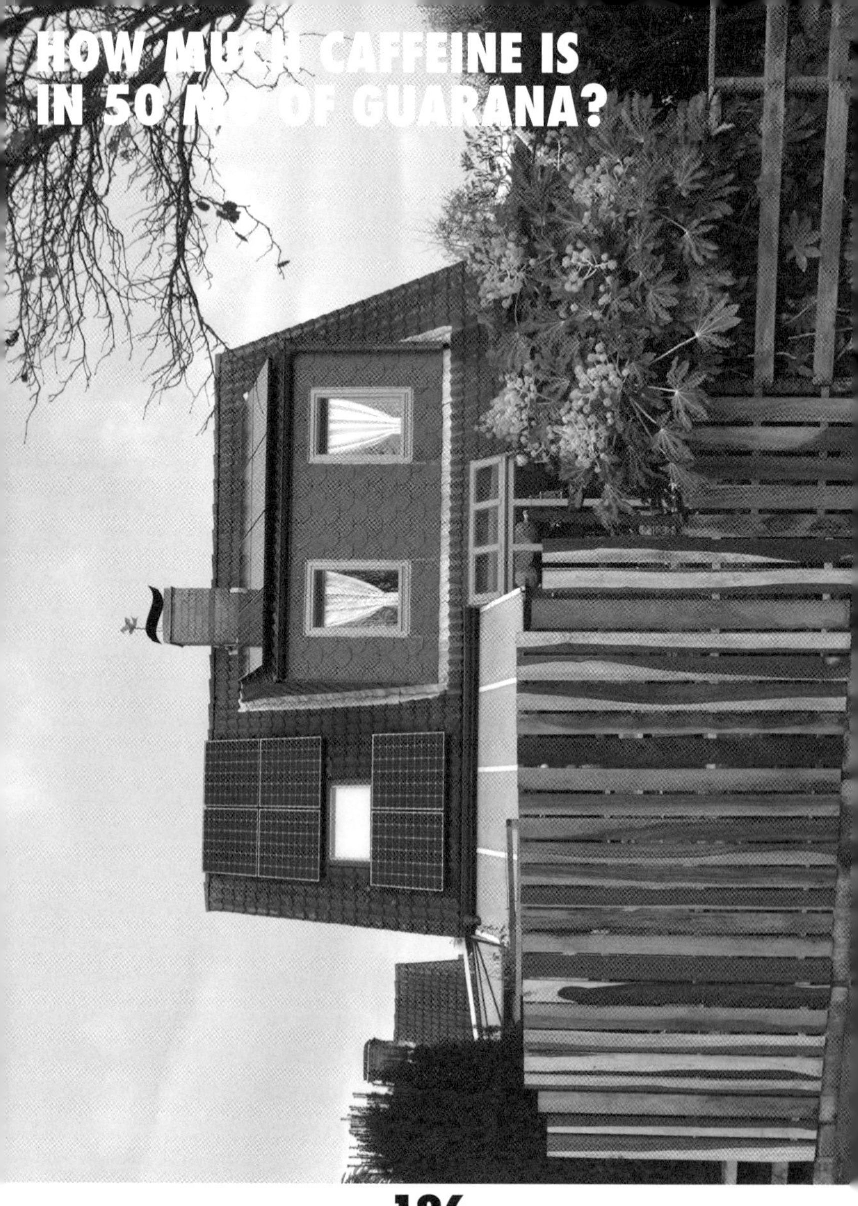
HOW MUCH CAFFEINE IS
IN 50 MG OF GUARANA?

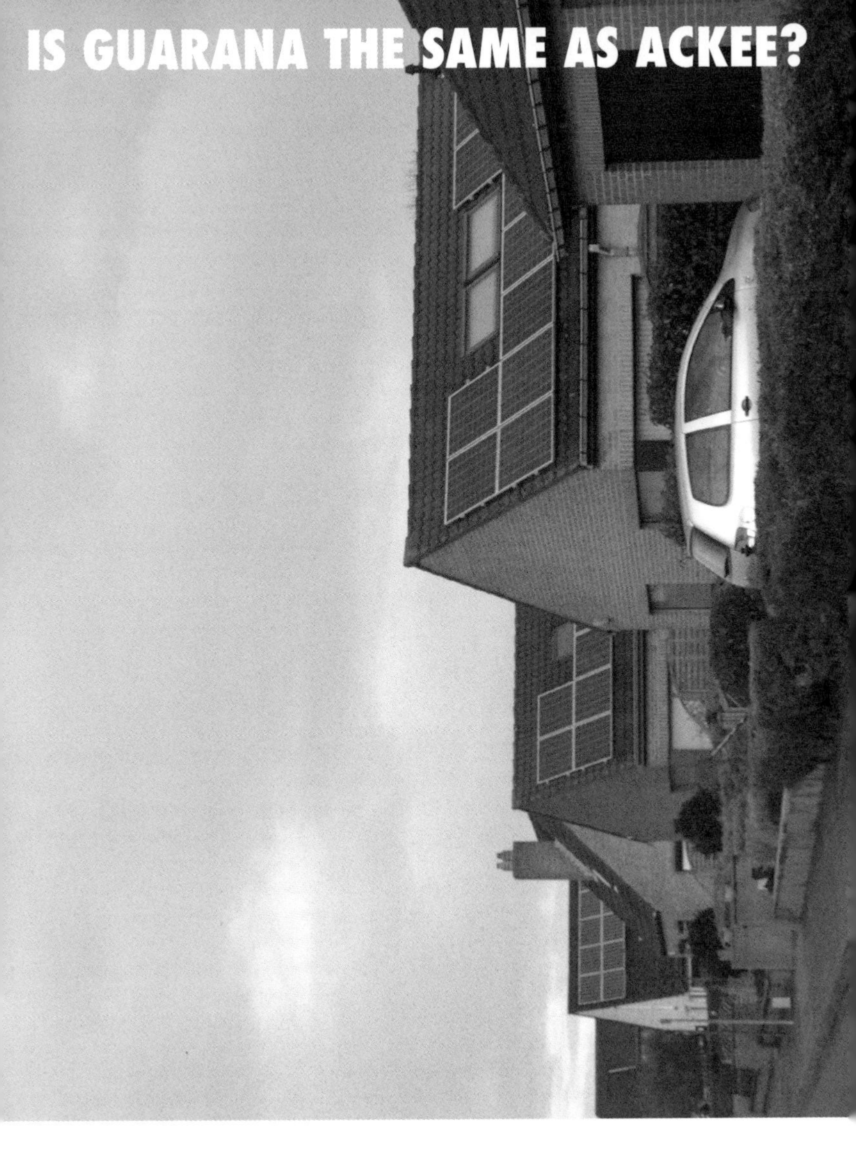
IS GUARANA THE SAME AS ACKEE?

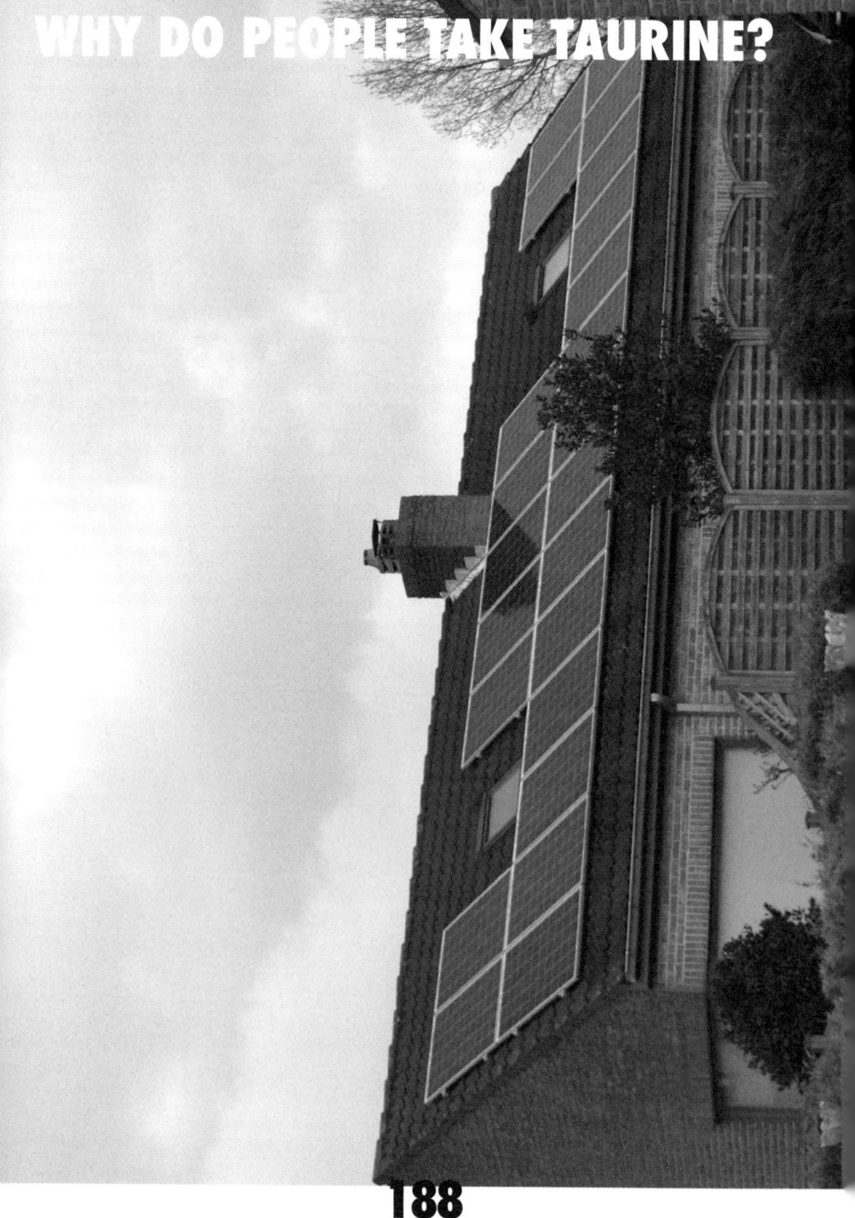

WHY DO PEOPLE TAKE TAURINE?

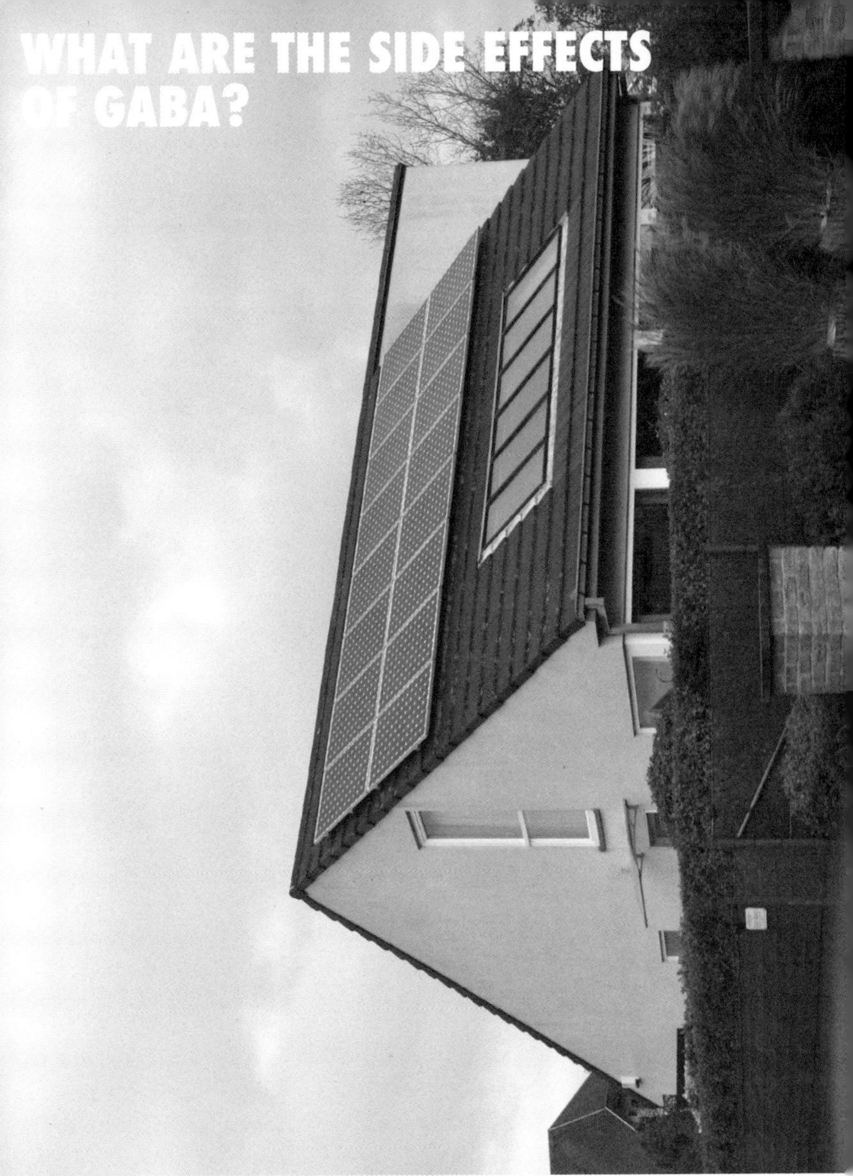

WHAT ARE THE SIDE EFFECTS OF GABA?

WHAT IS GUARANA CAFFEINE?

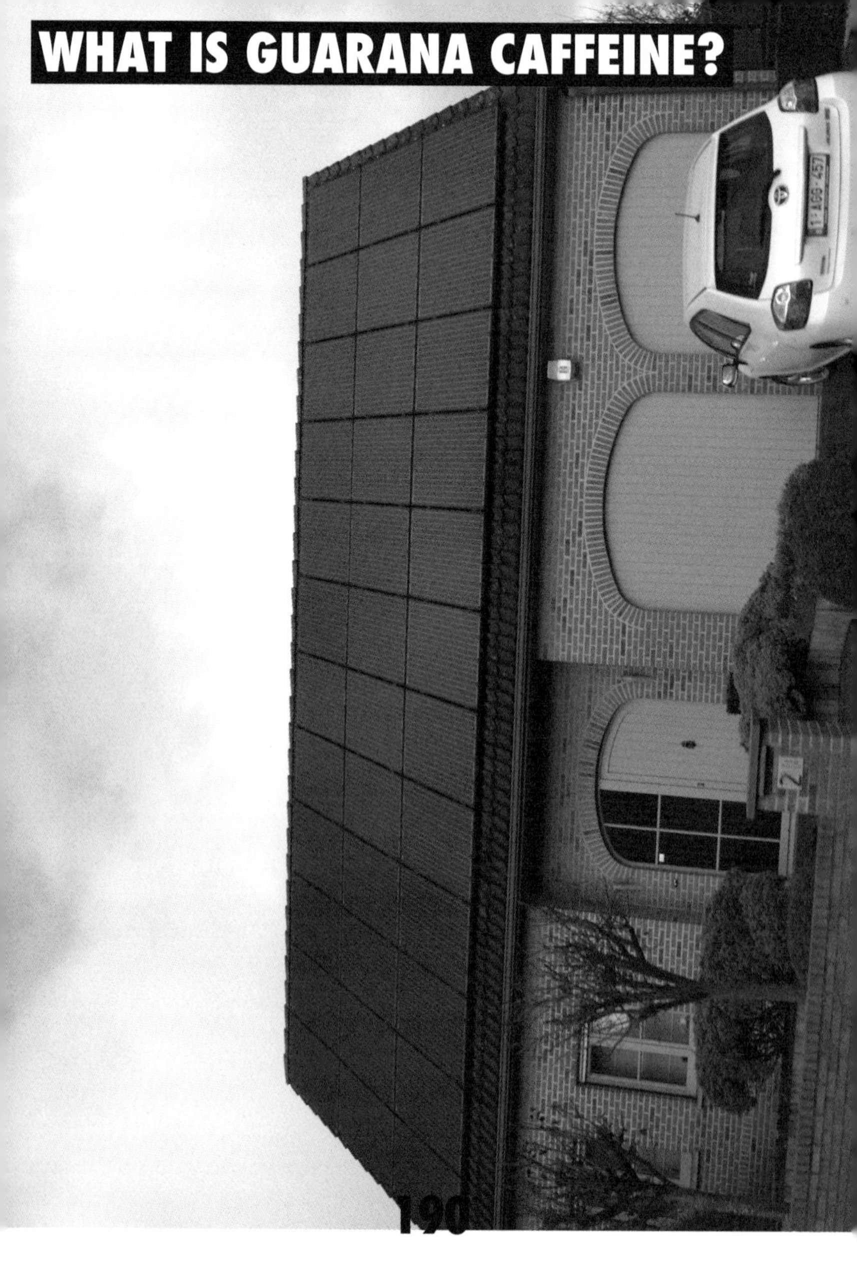

CAN GUARANA HELP YOU LOSE WEIGHT?

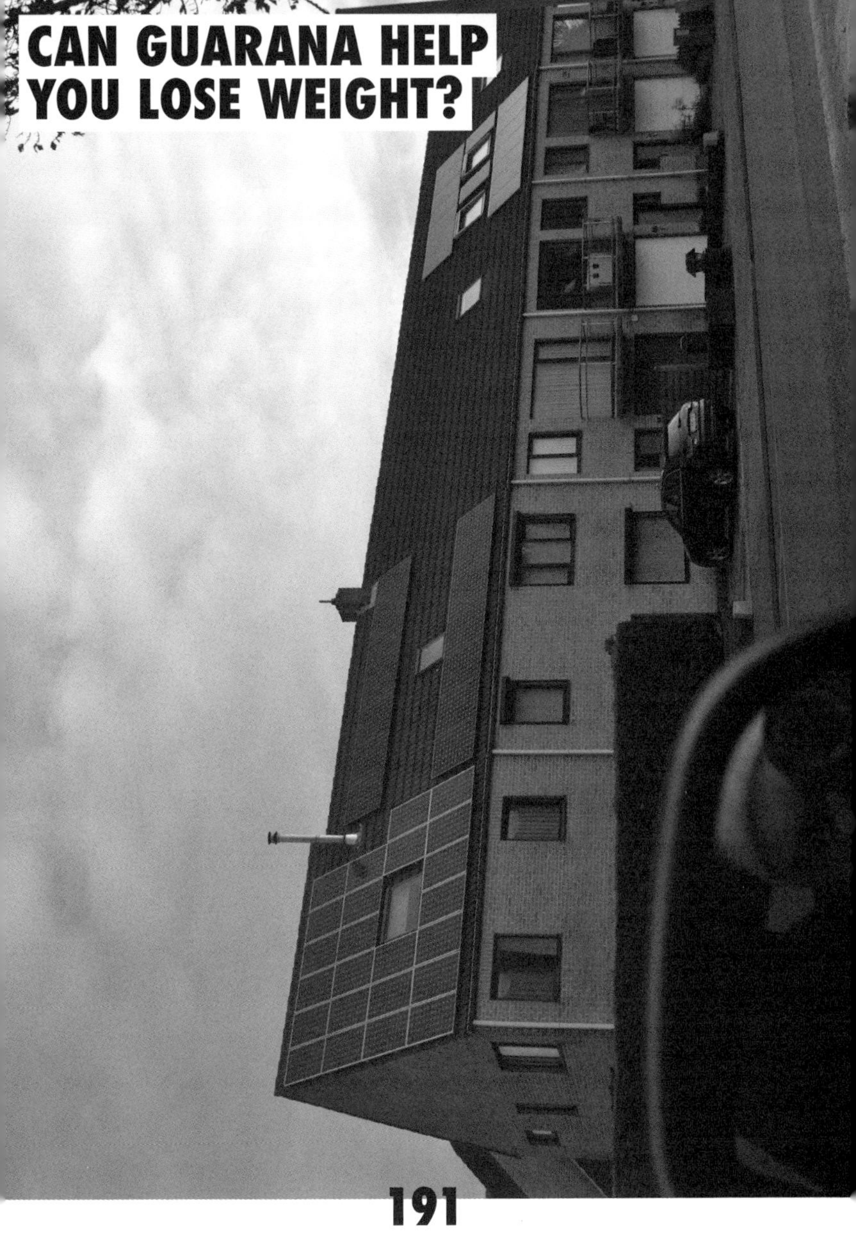

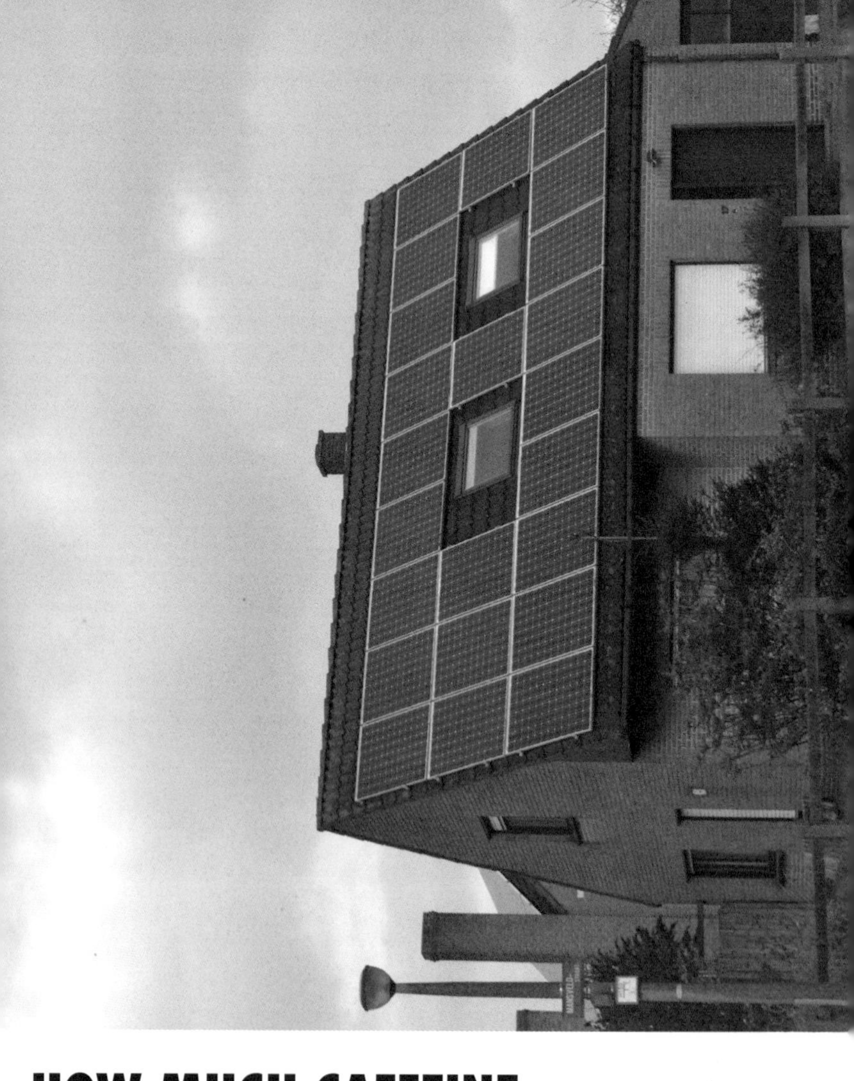

HOW MUCH CAFFEINE IS IN GUARANA DRINK?

192

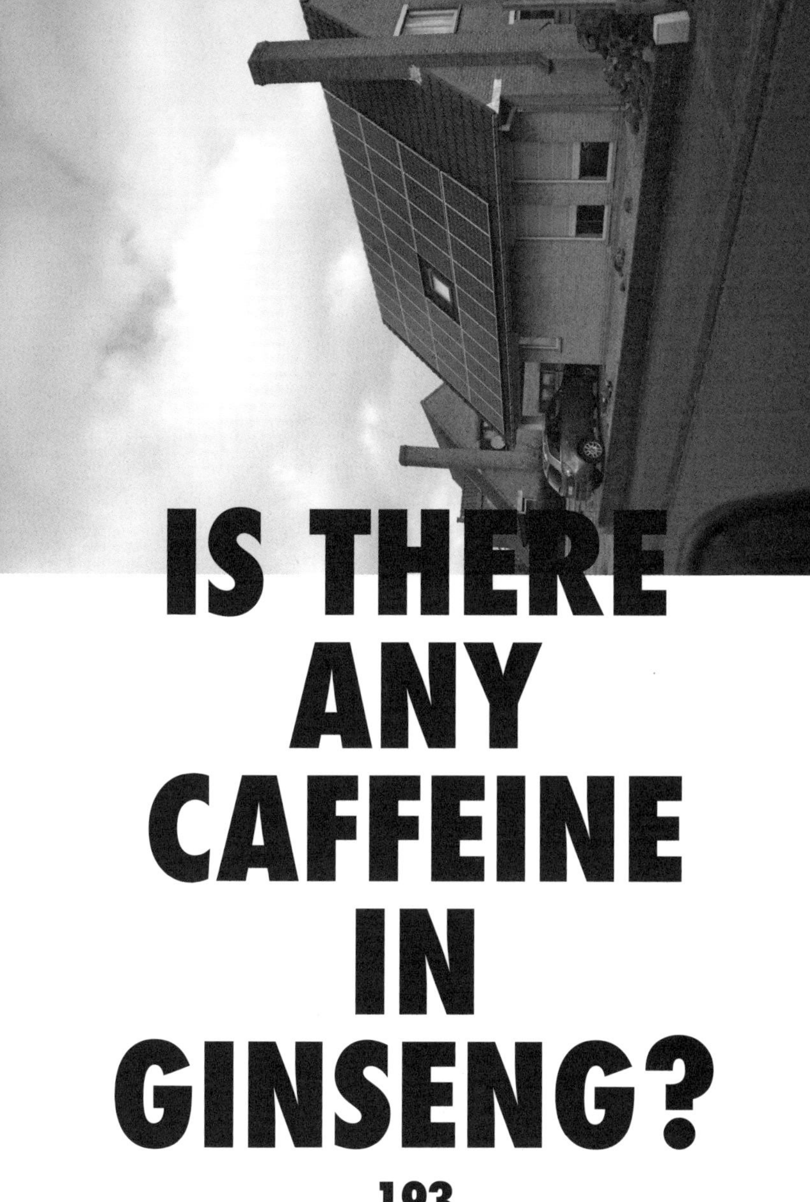

IS THERE ANY CAFFEINE IN GINSENG?

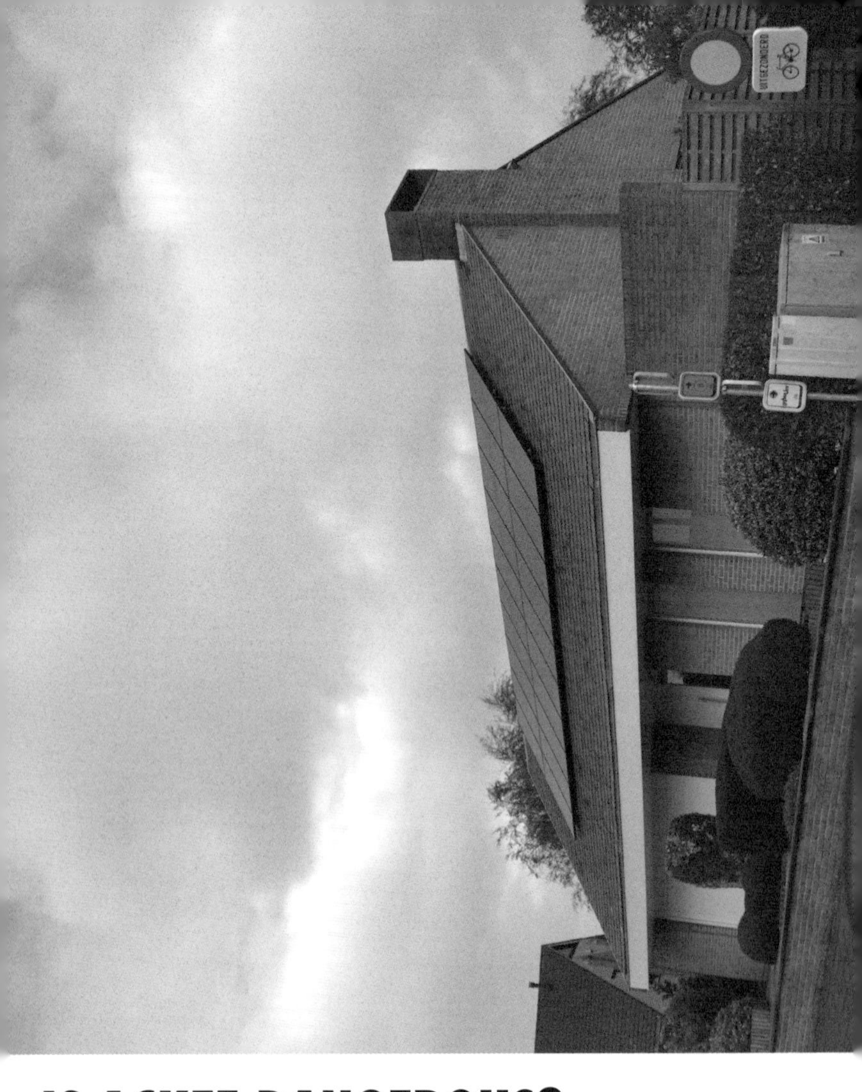

IS ACKEE DANGEROUS?

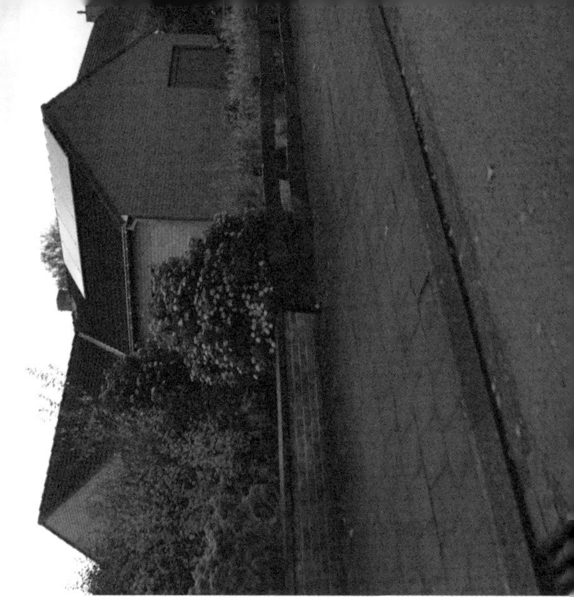

HOW DO YOU EAT AN ACKEE?

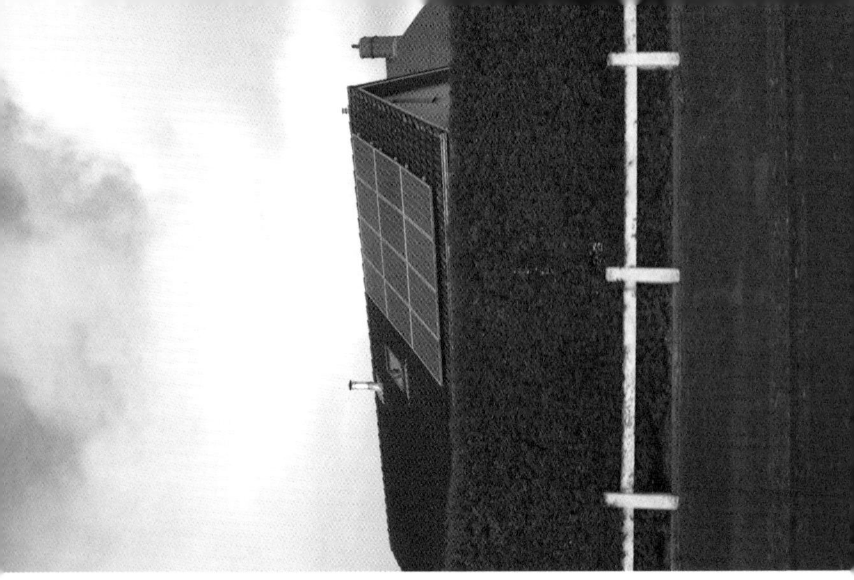

WHAT DOES INOSITOL DO TO YOUR BODY?

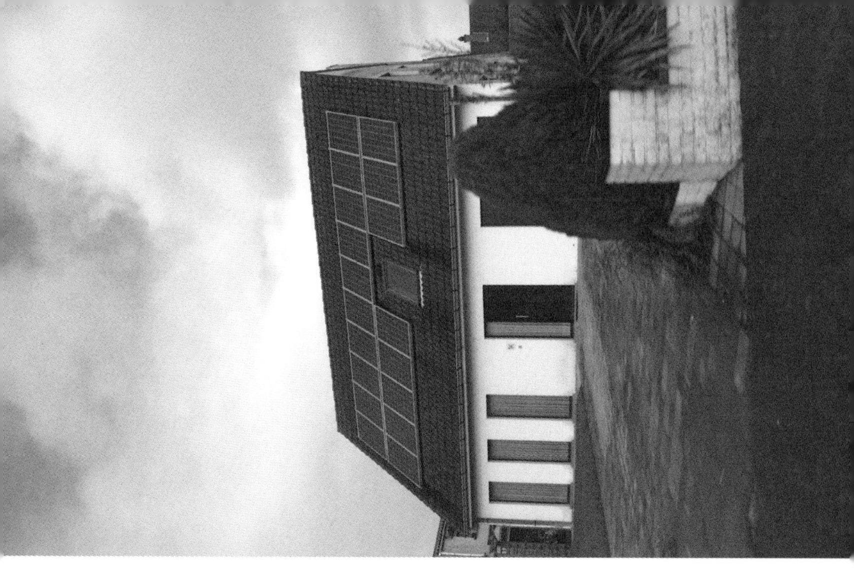

WHAT ARE THE BENEFITS OF LYSINE?

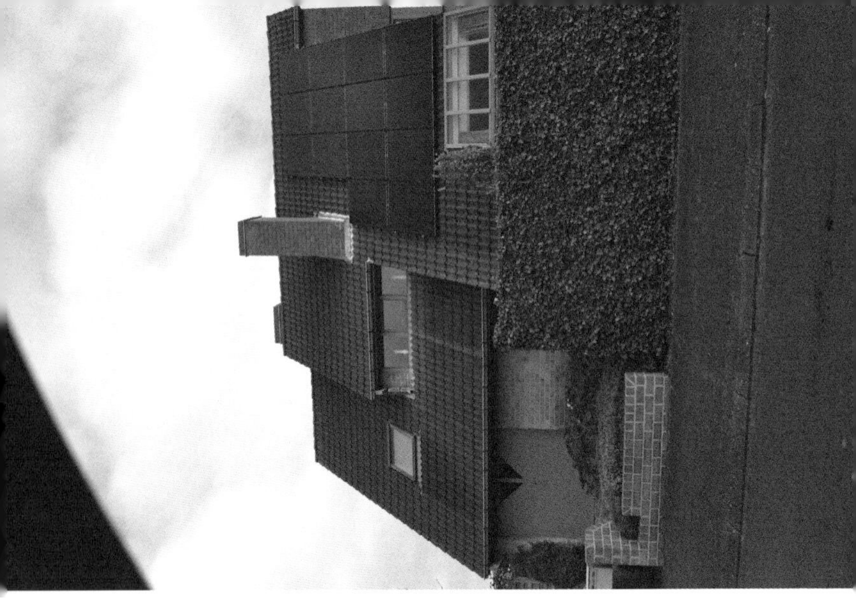

WHAT FOODS ARE HIGH IN GABA?

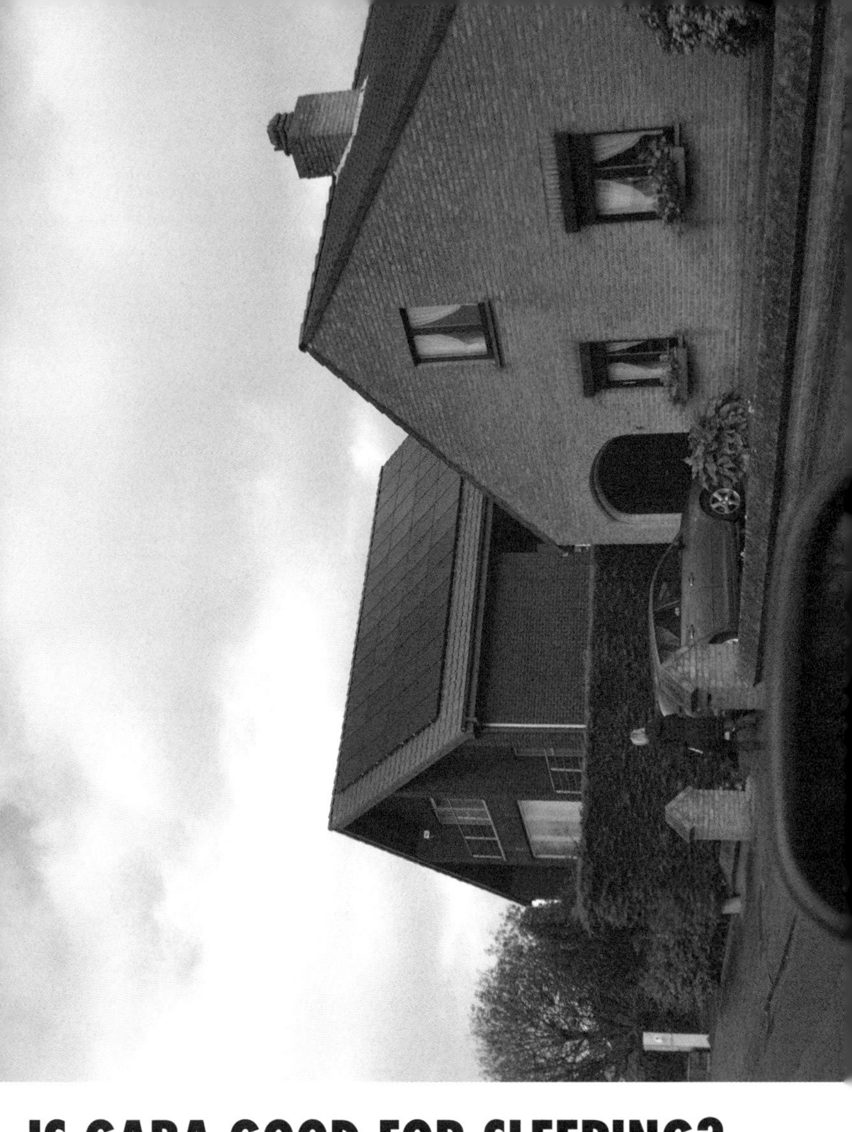

IS GABA GOOD FOR SLEEPING?

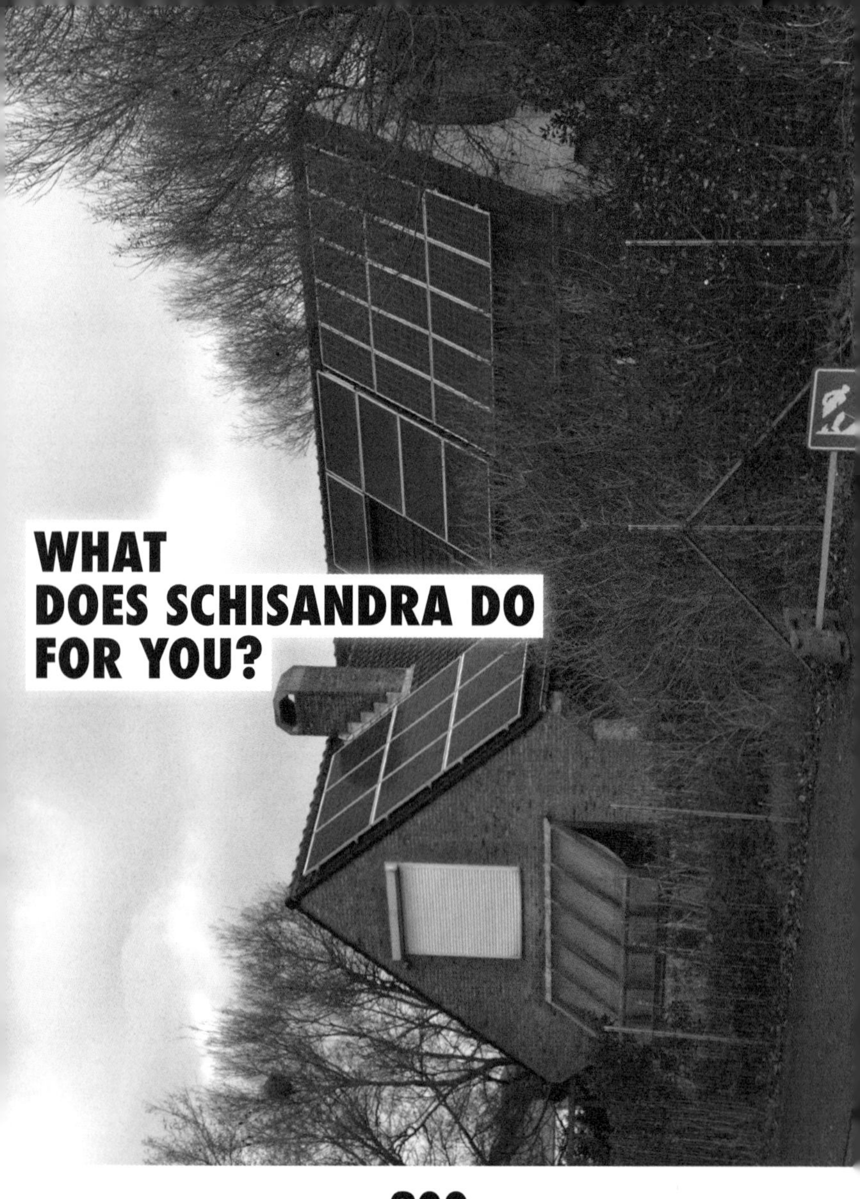

WHAT DOES SCHISANDRA DO FOR YOU?

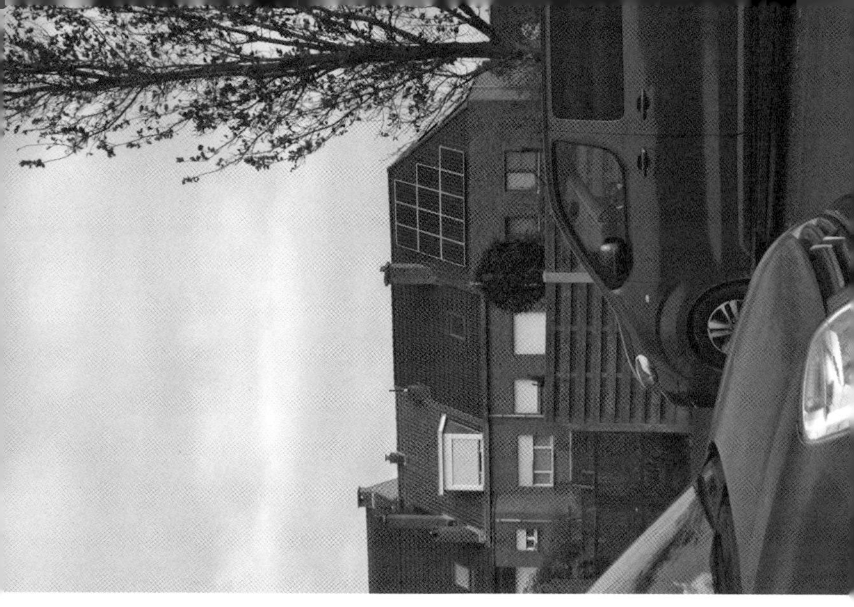

WHAT DOES GINSENG DO FOR YOU?

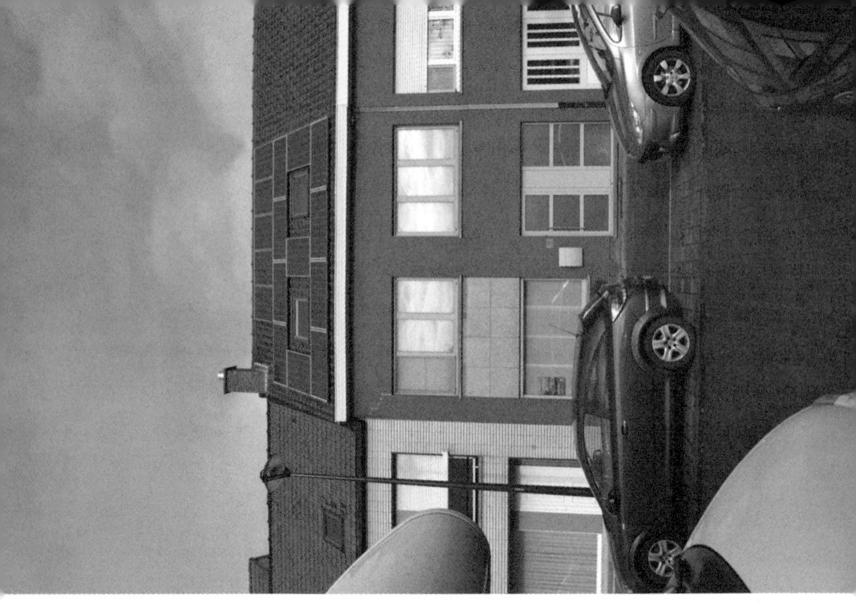

WHAT DOES GINSENG DO FOR YOU SEXUALLY?

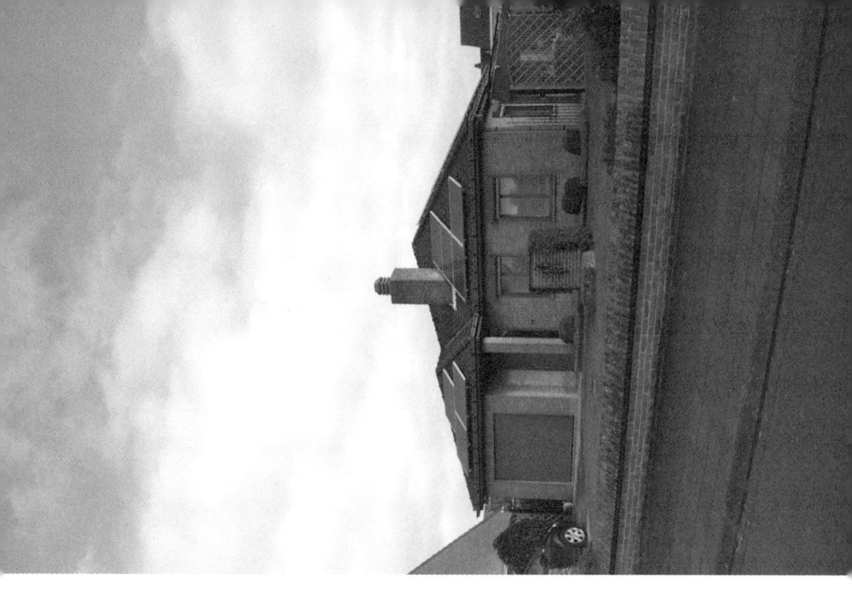

HOW MUCH GINSENG CAN YOU TAKE IN A DAY?

WHAT DOES GUARANA DRINK TASTE LIKE?

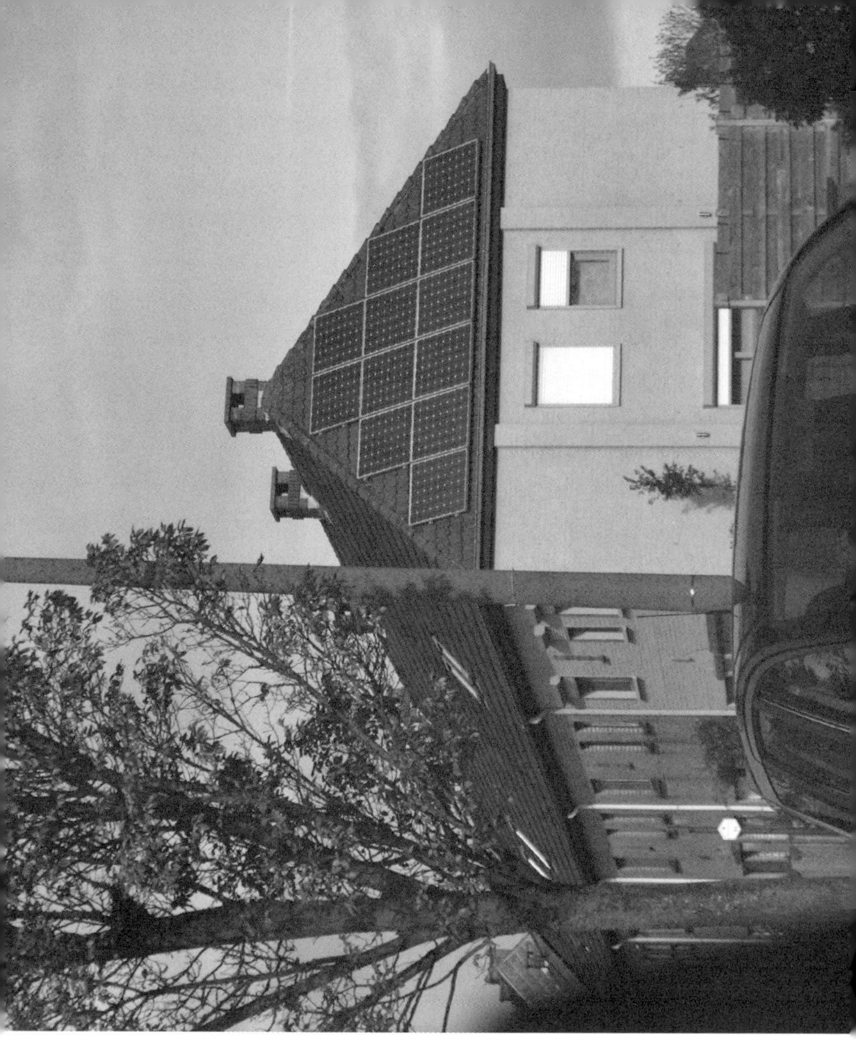

HOW DO YOU TAKE GUARANA?

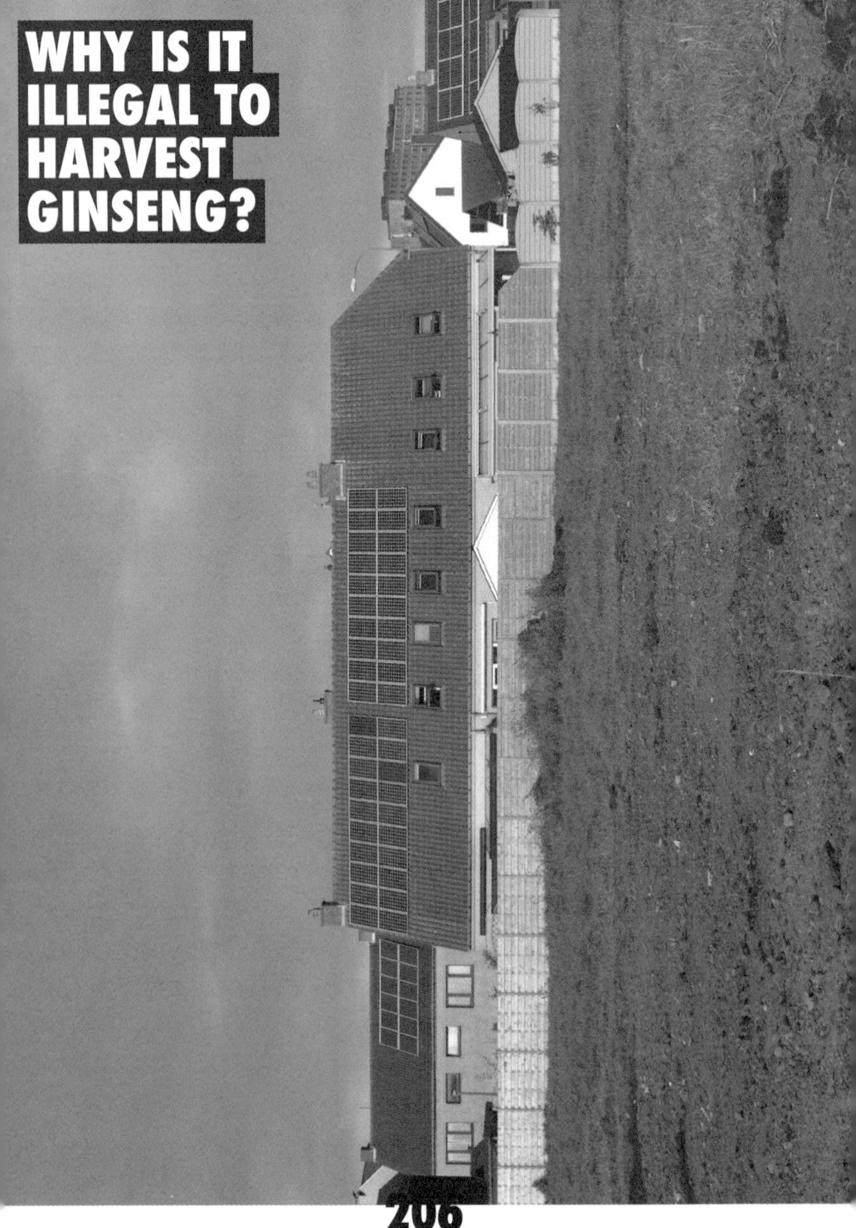

WHY IS IT ILLEGAL TO HARVEST GINSENG?

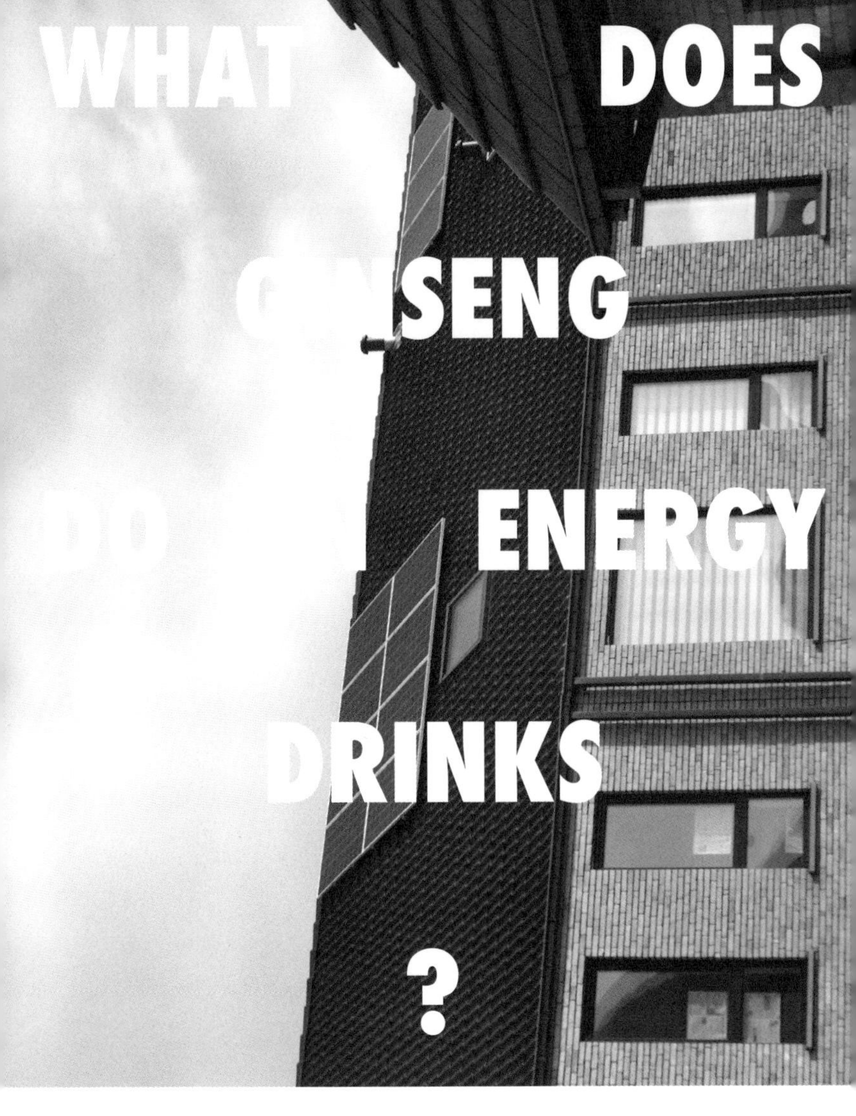
WHAT DOES
GINSENG
DO IN ENERGY
DRINKS
?

CAN ACKEE KILL YOU?

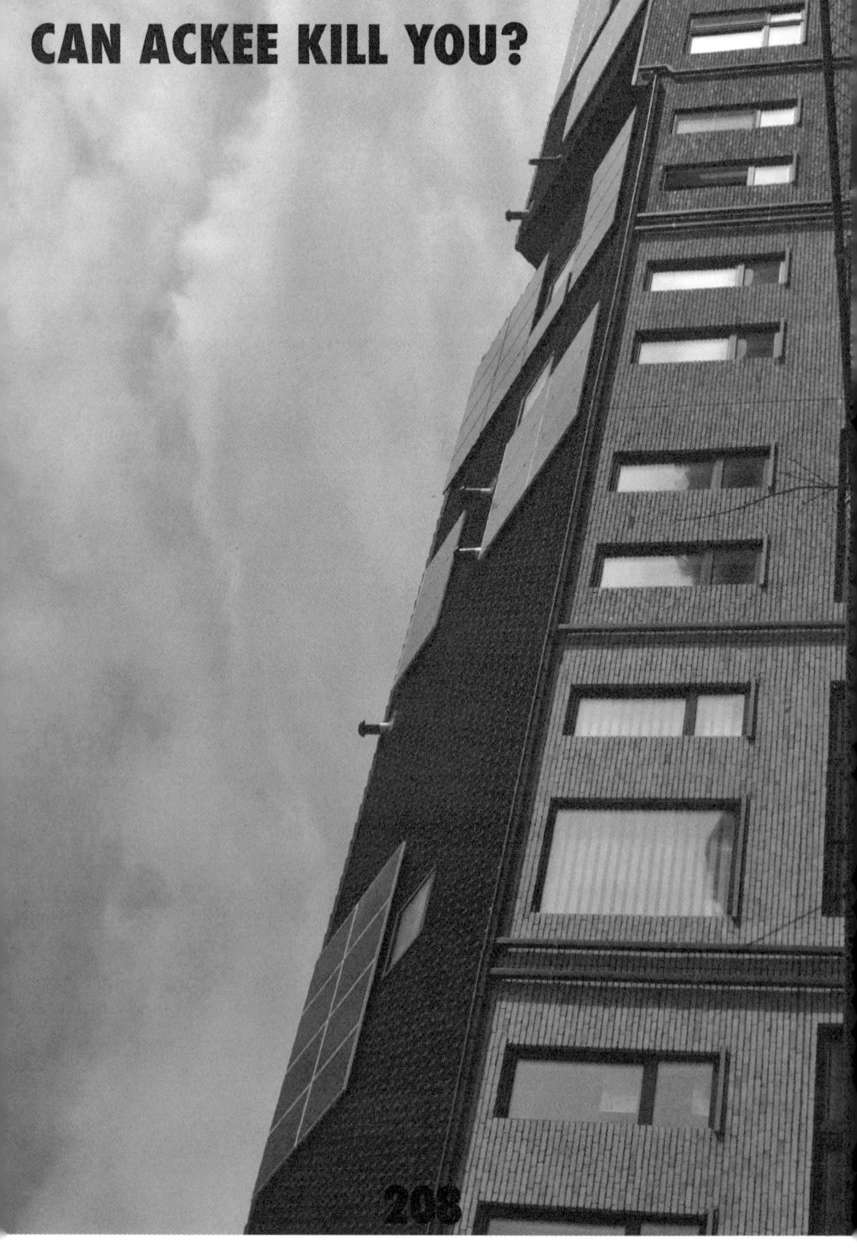

HOW DOES ACKEE TASTE LIKE?

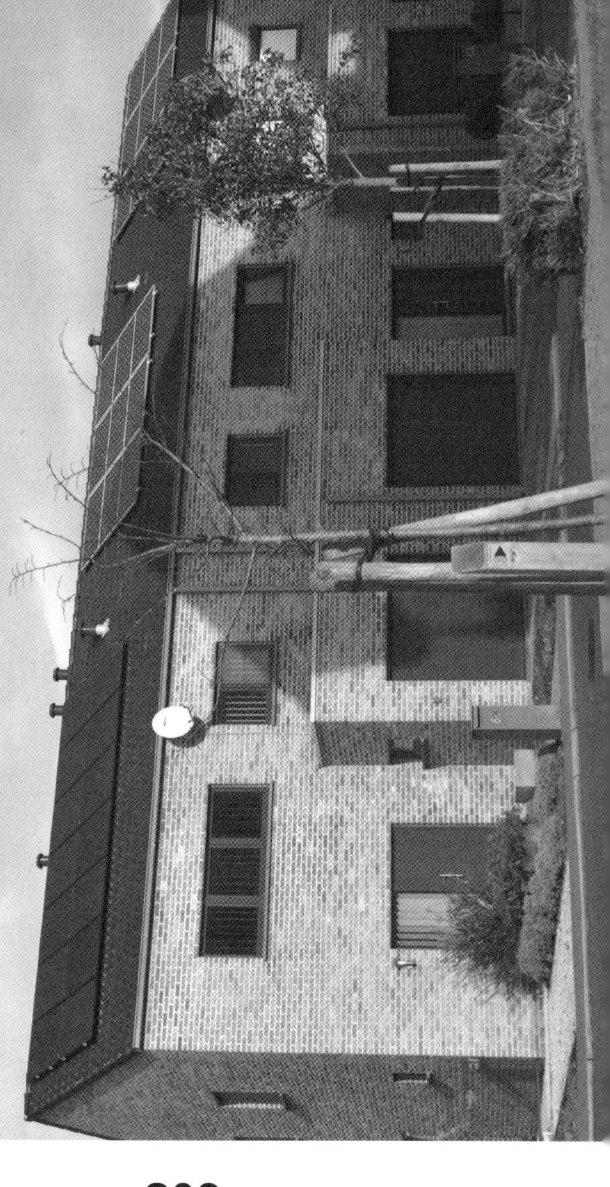

IS ACKEE GOOD FOR YOUR HEALTH?

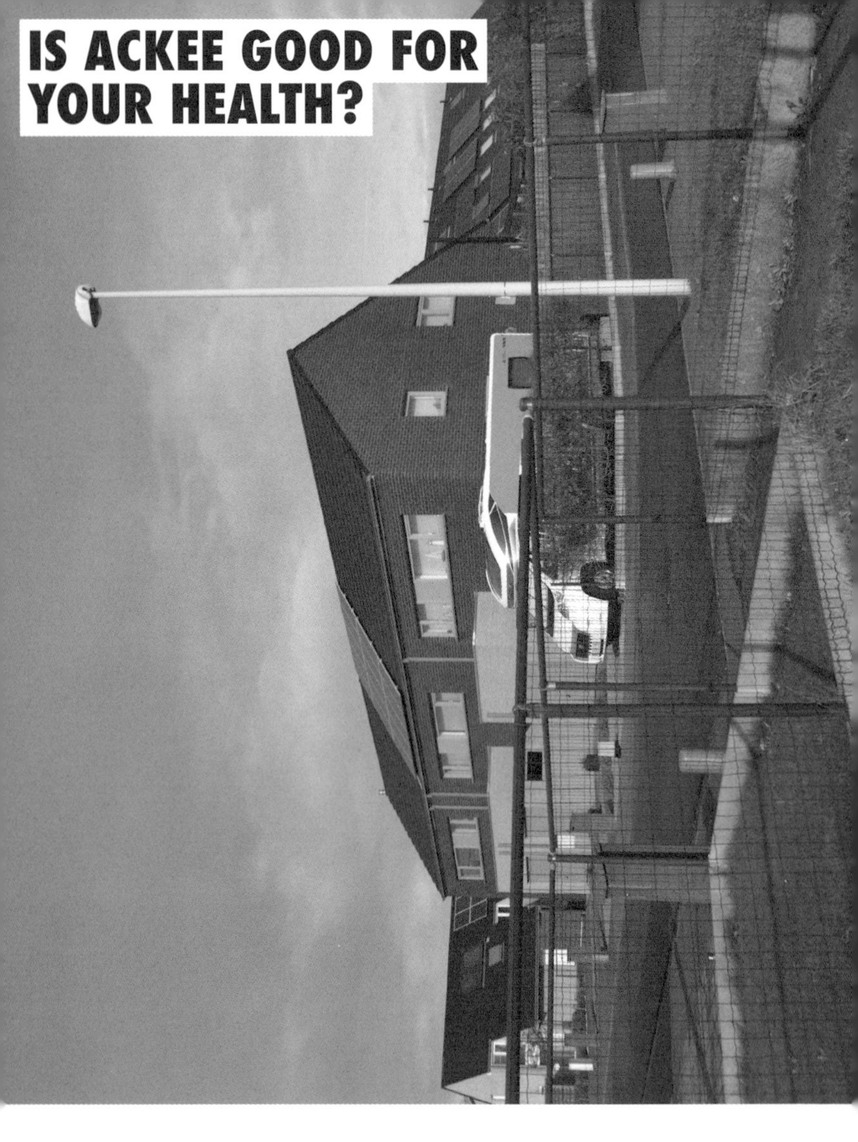

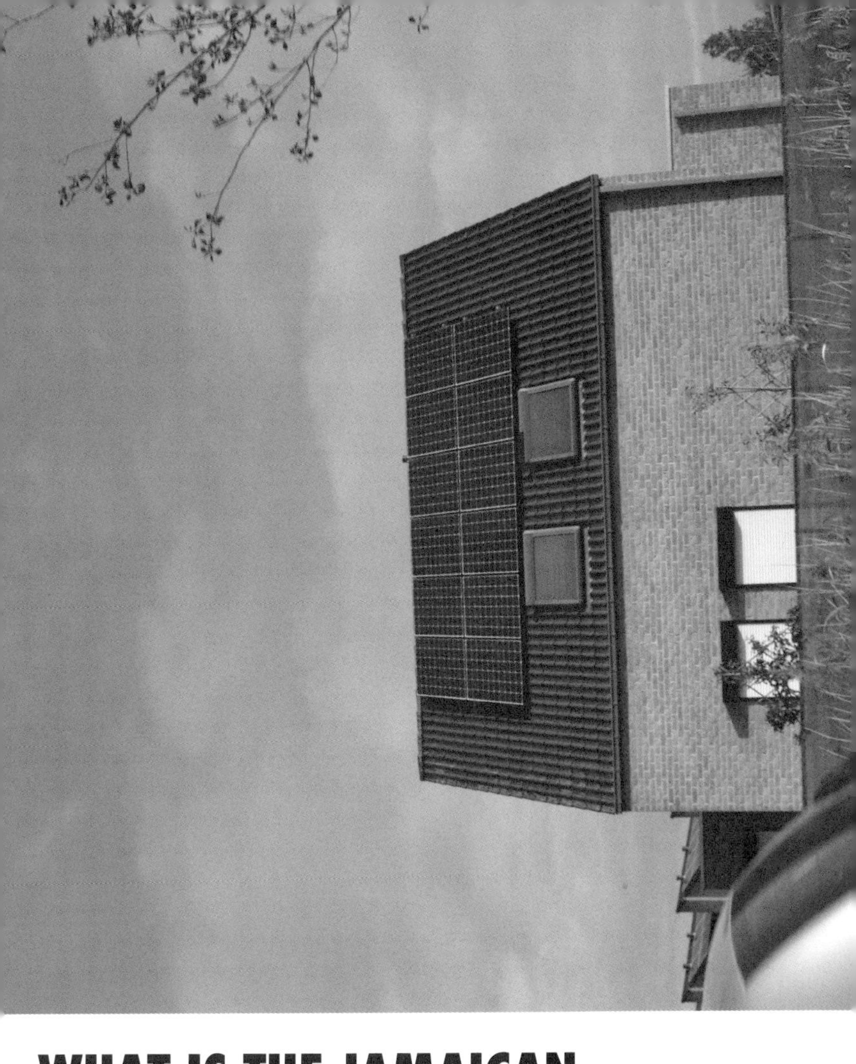

WHAT IS THE JAMAICAN FOOD ACKEE?

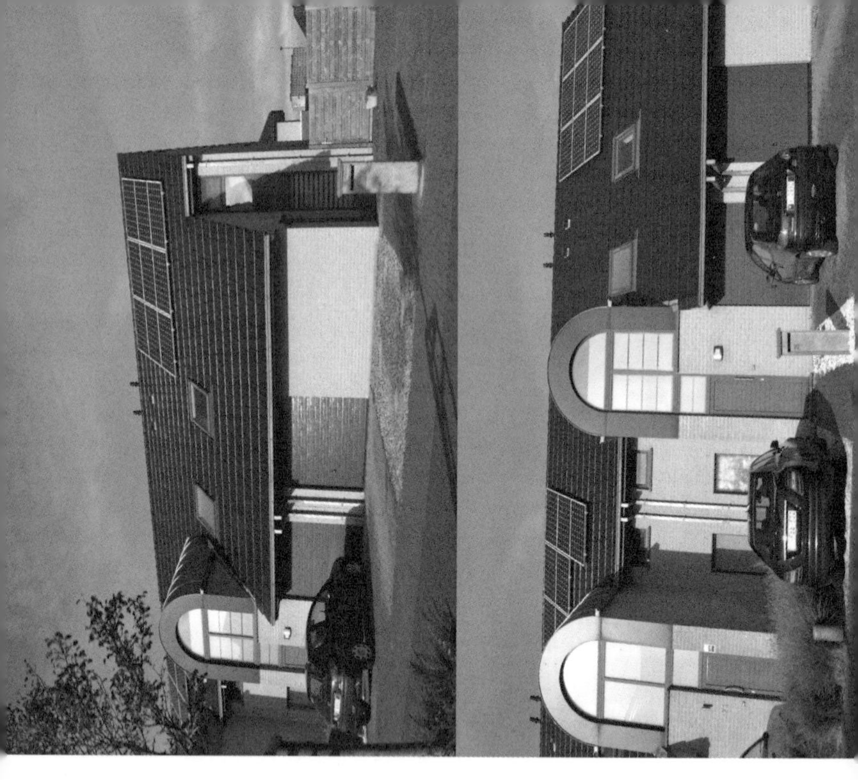

WHY DO THEY PUT INOSITOL IN ENERGY DRINKS?

WHAT FOODS ARE HIGH IN INOSITOL?

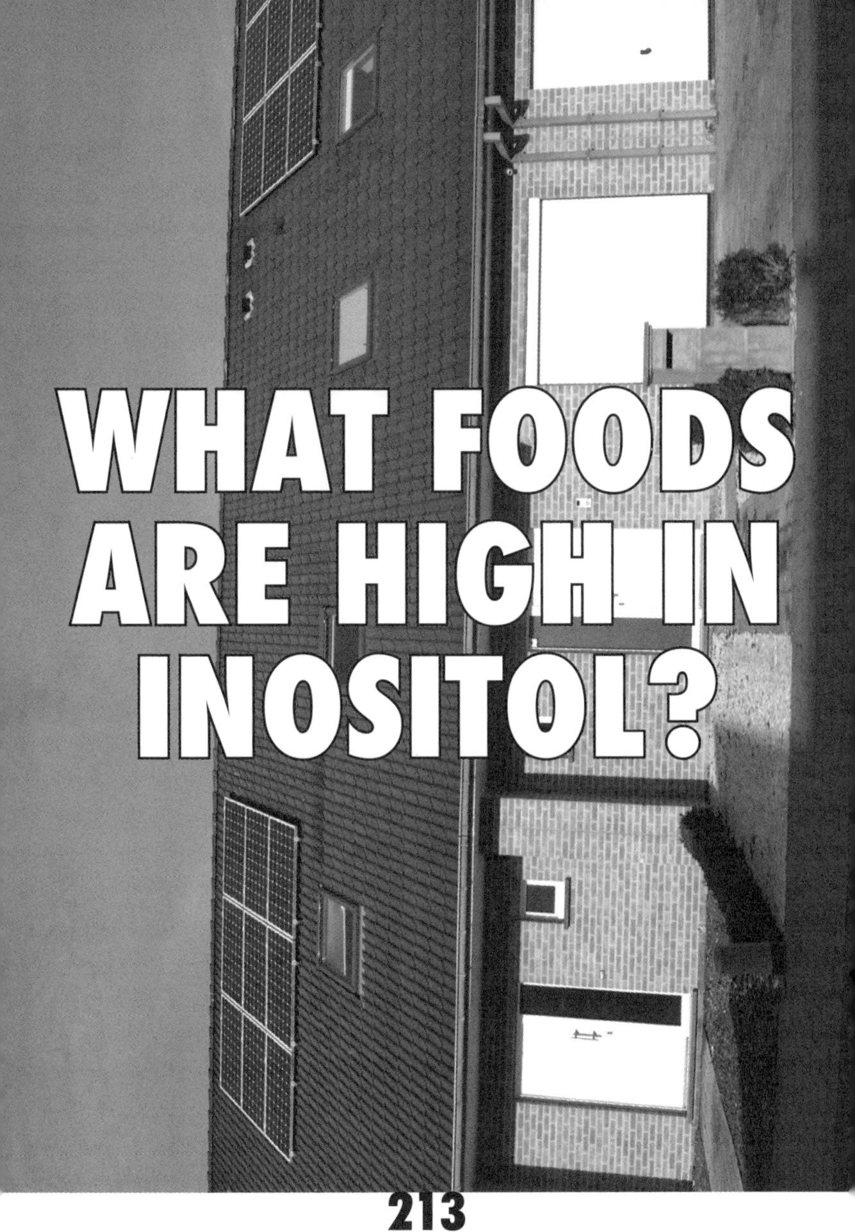

IS IT SAFE TO TAKE LYSINE EVERY DAY?

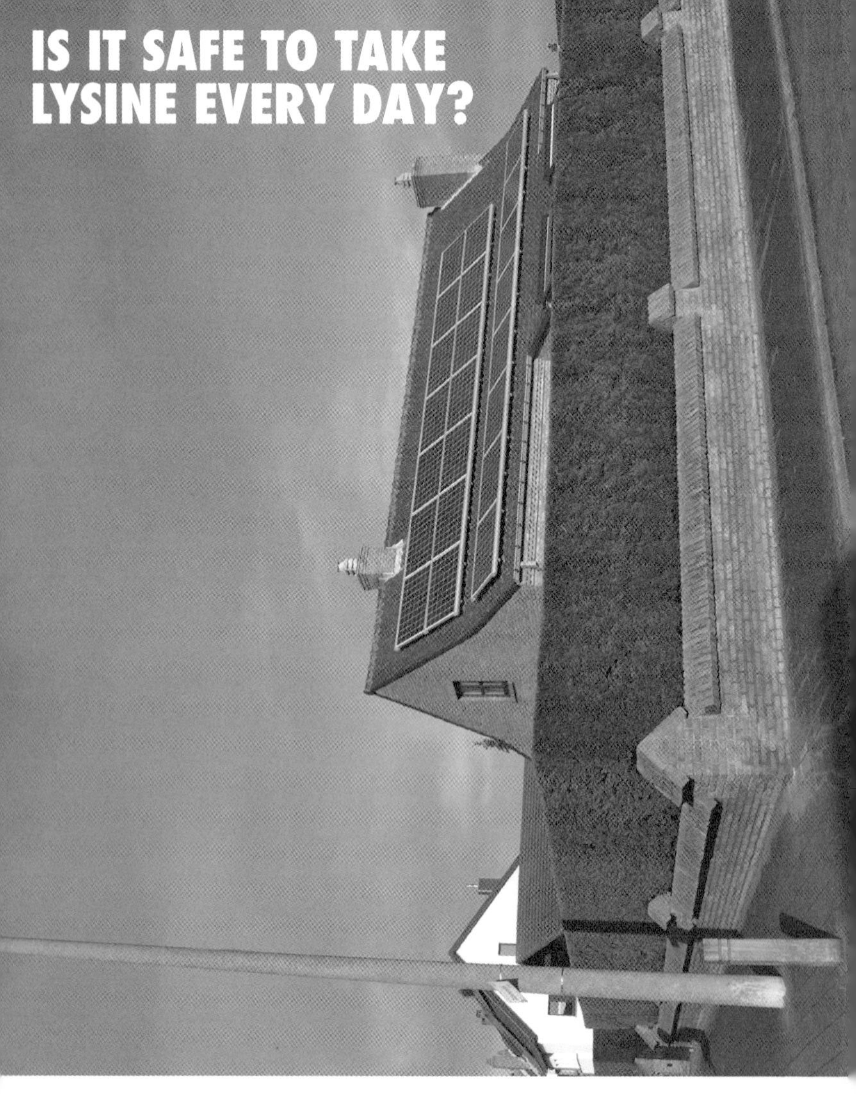

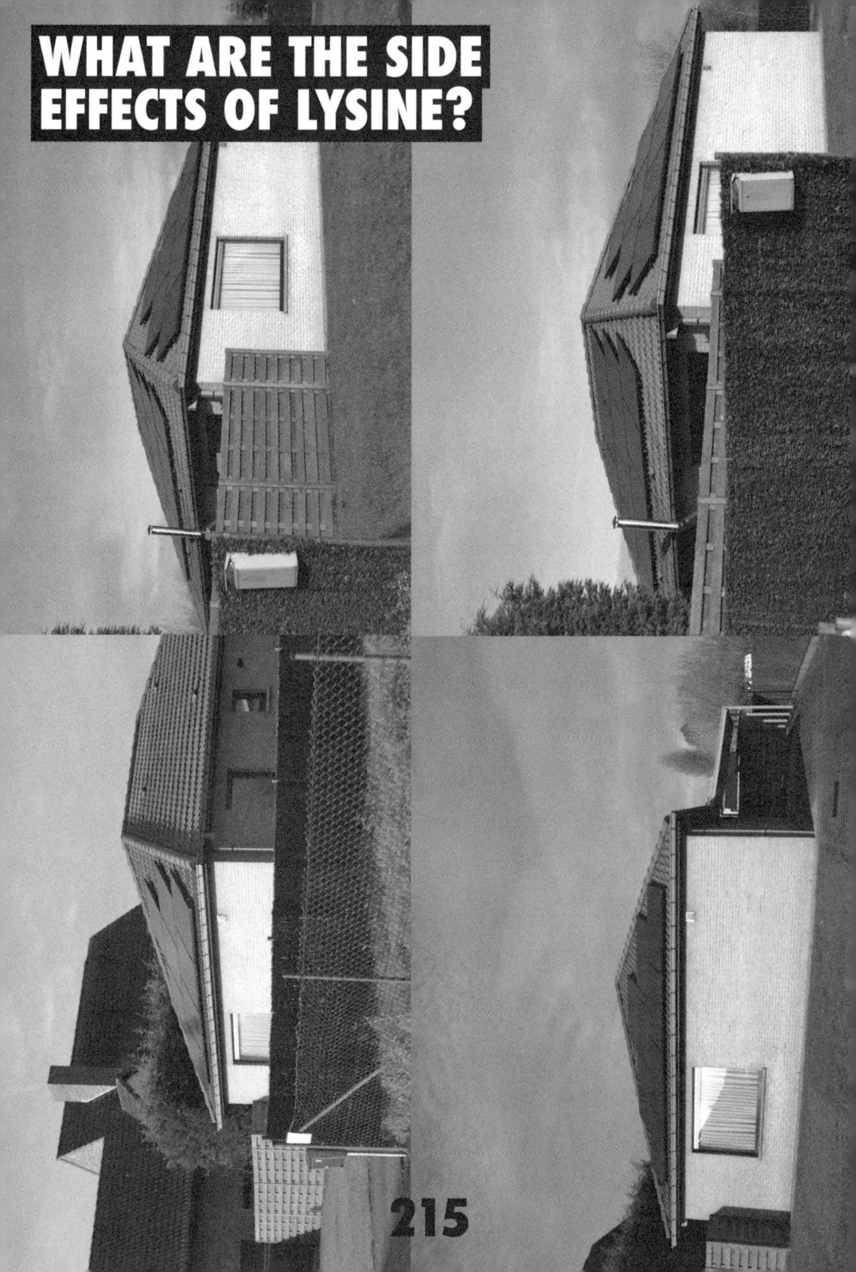

WHAT ARE THE SIDE EFFECTS OF LYSINE?

WHAT FOODS ARE HIGH IN SEROTONIN?

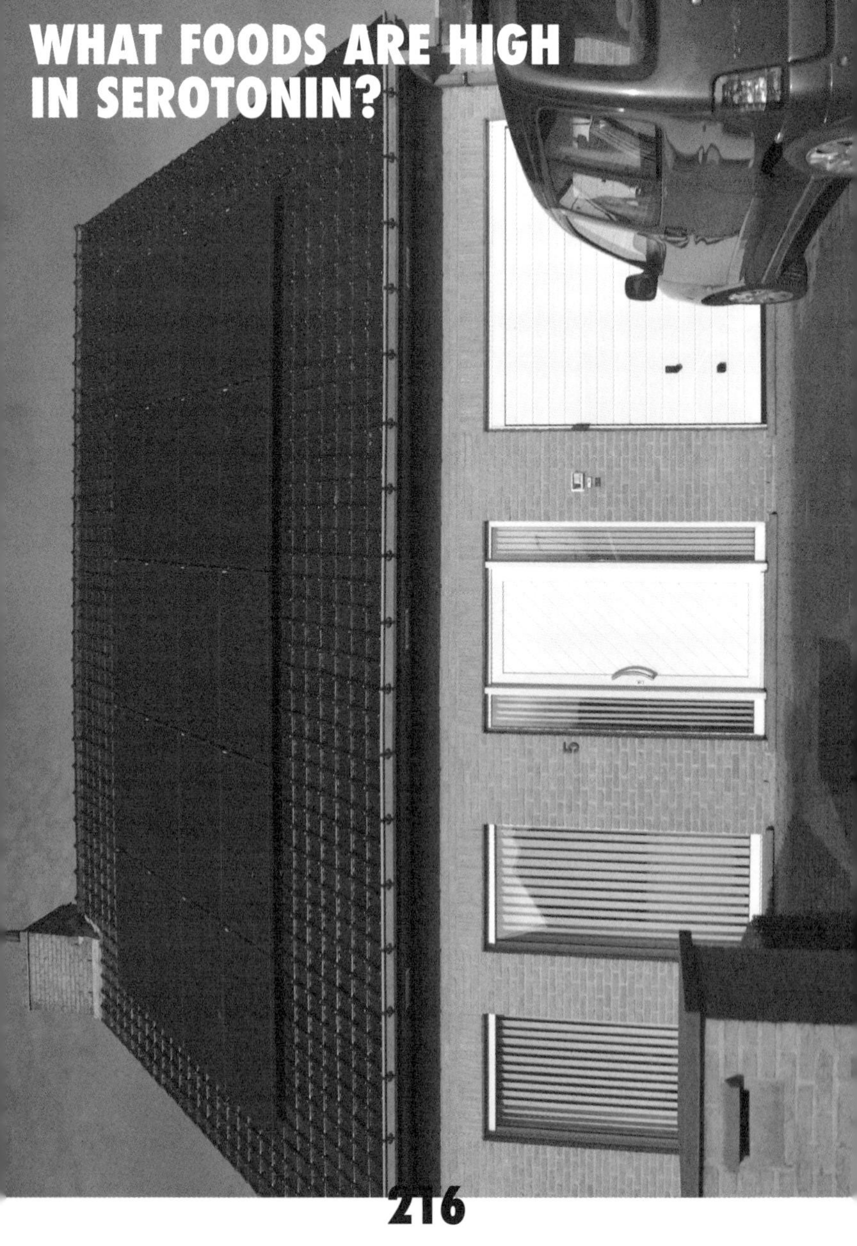

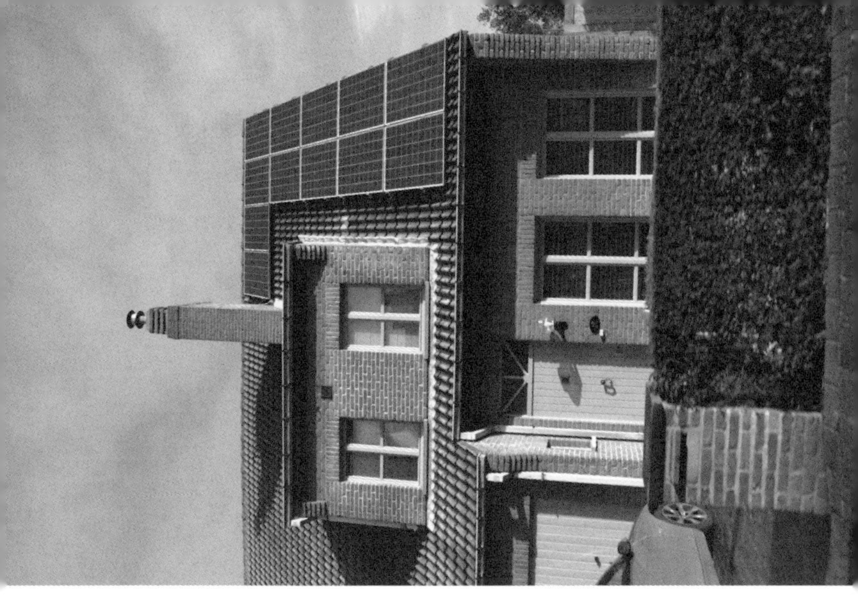

WHAT ARE THE SIDE EFFECTS OF TAKING TOO MUCH GINSENG?

IS GUARANA BETTER THAN COFFEE?

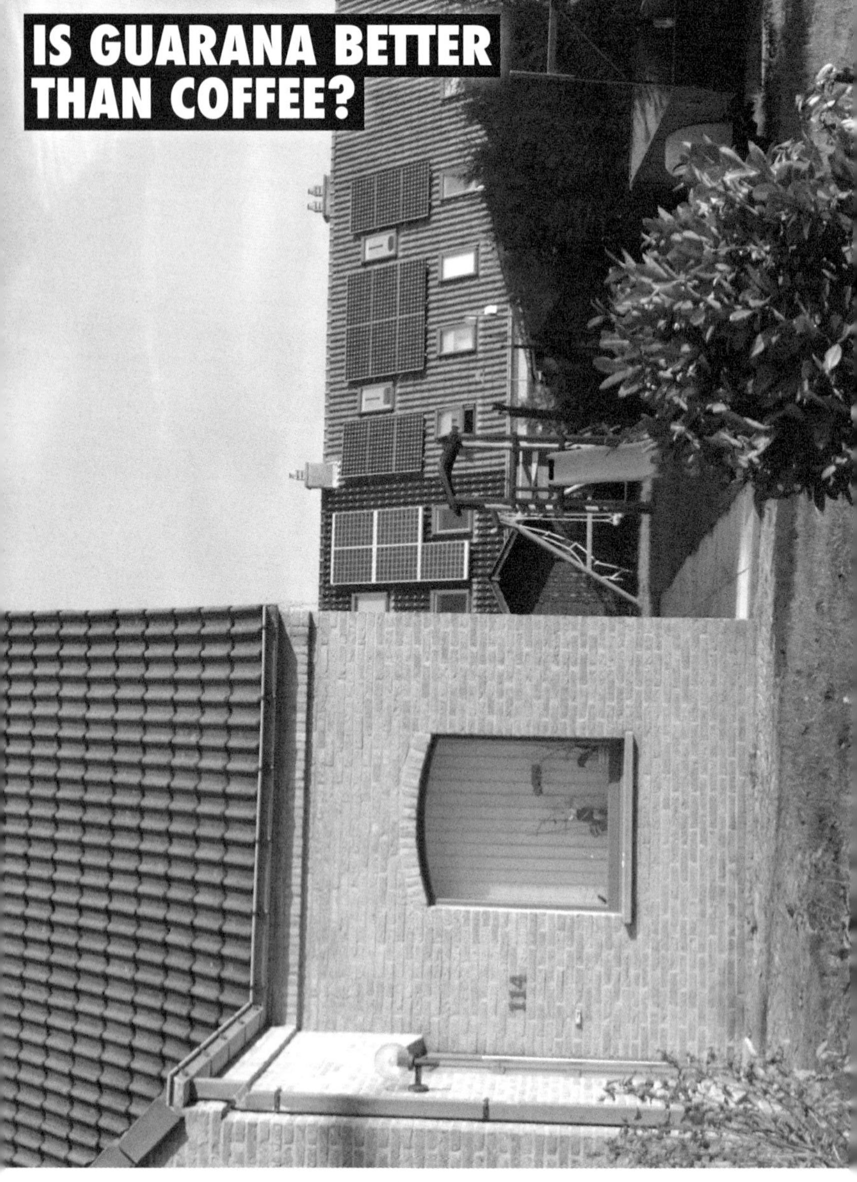

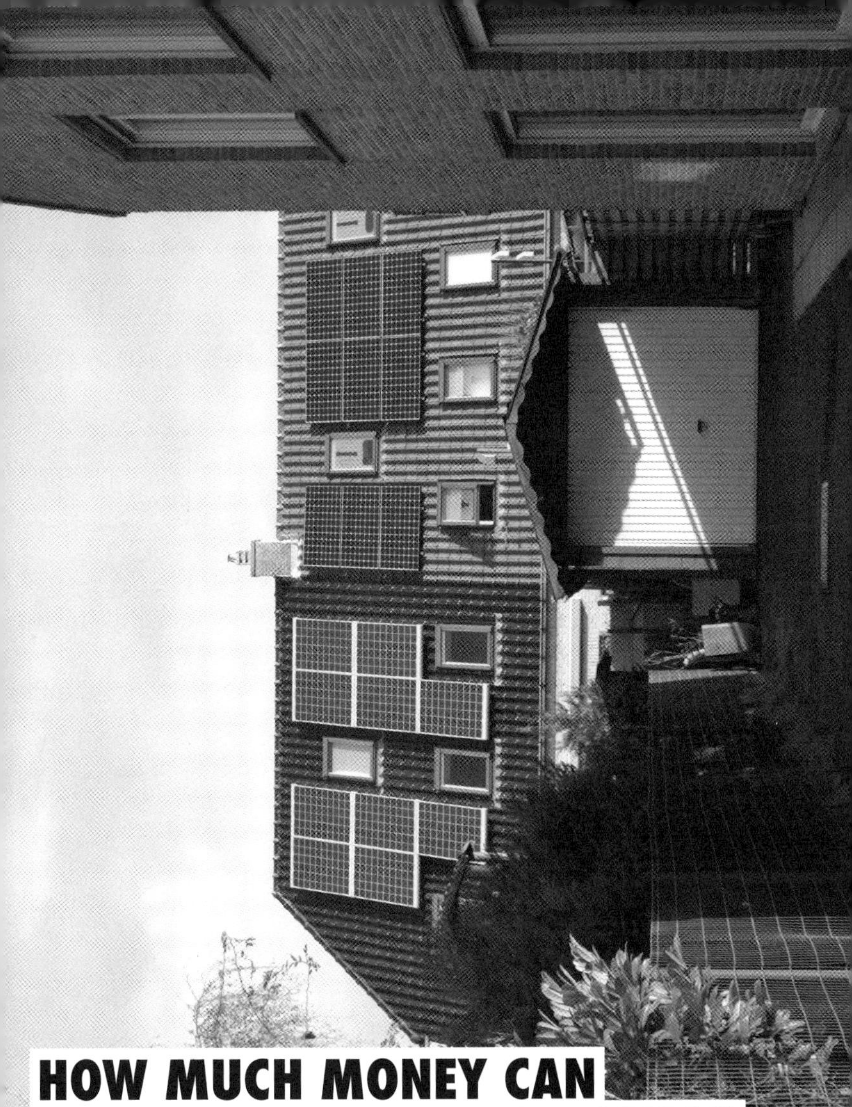

HOW MUCH MONEY CAN BE MADE GROWING GINSENG?

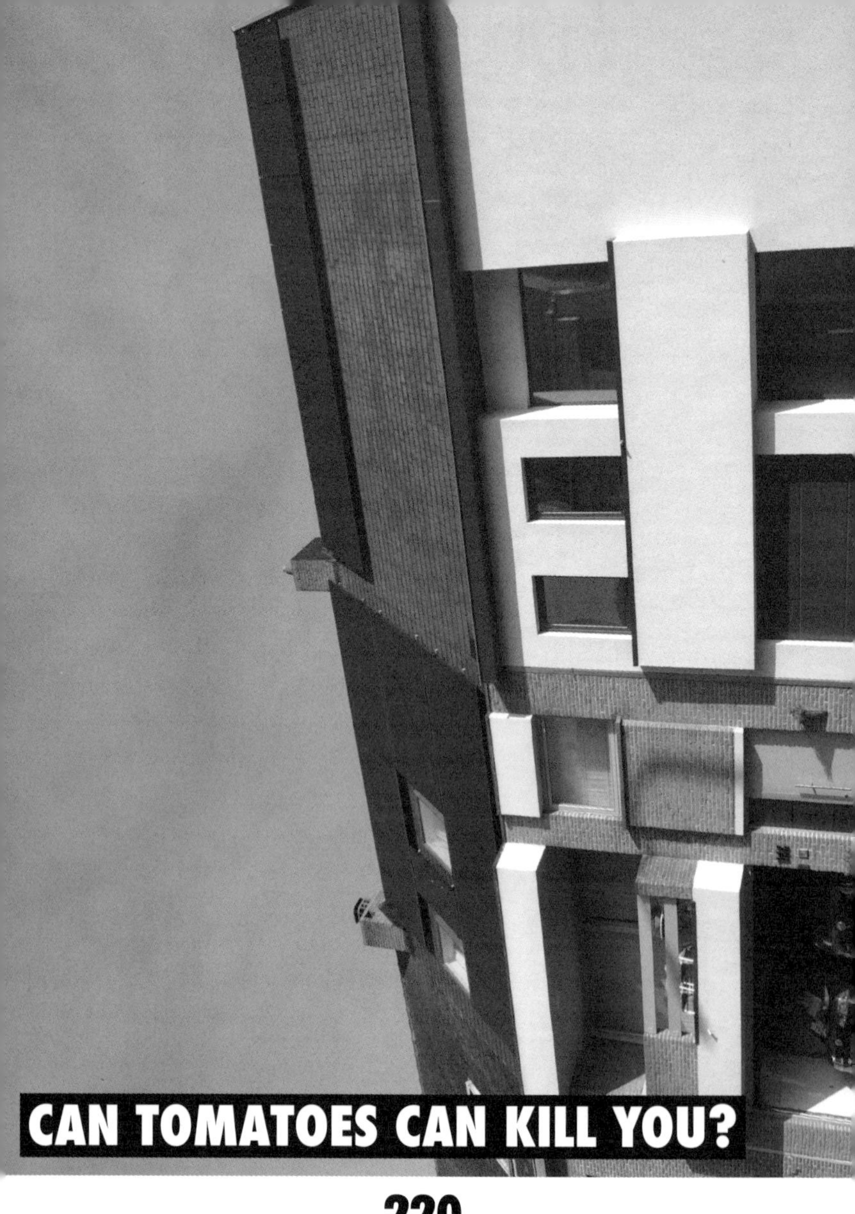

CAN TOMATOES CAN KILL YOU?

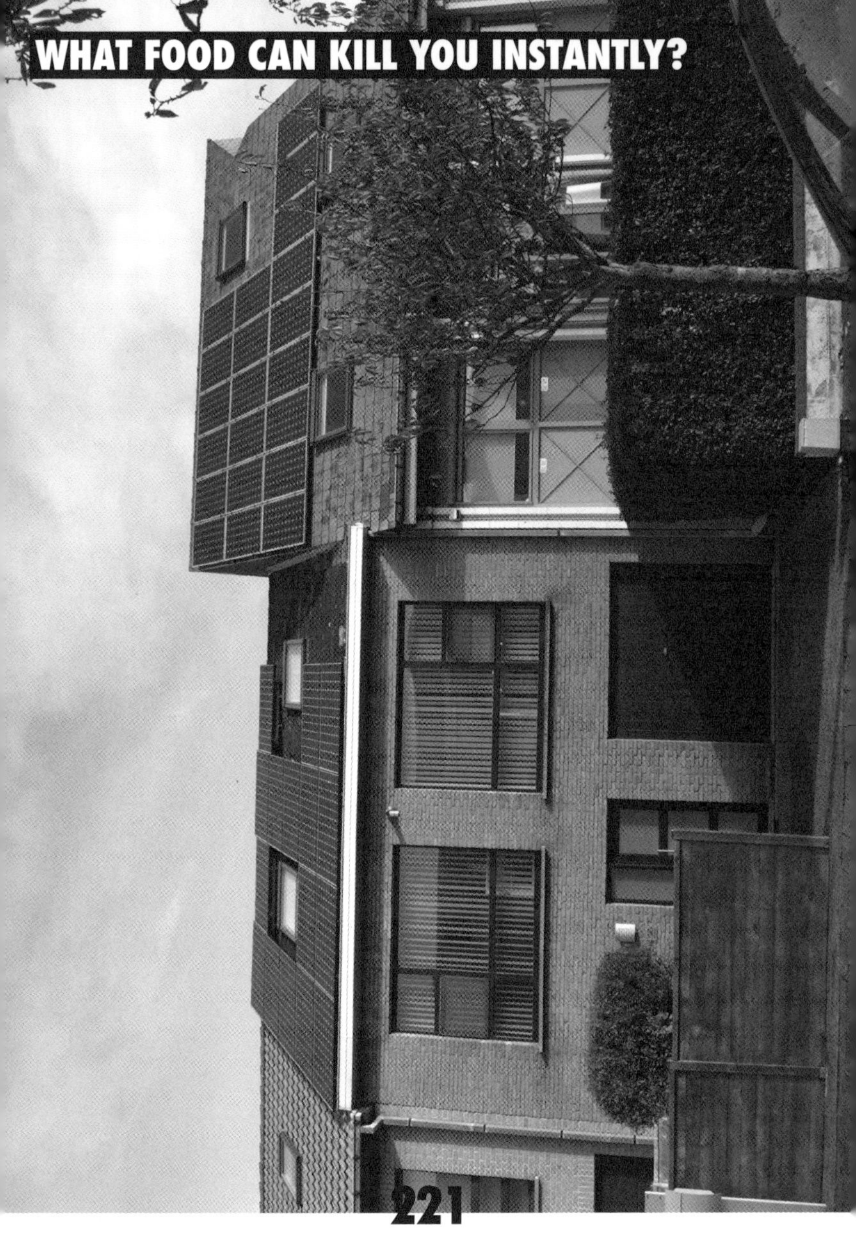

WHAT IS THE BEST ENERGY DRINK FOR YOUR HEALTH?

WHAT DOES GINSENG DO FOR ME SEXUALLY?

WHAT TOP 10 FOODS TO AVOID?

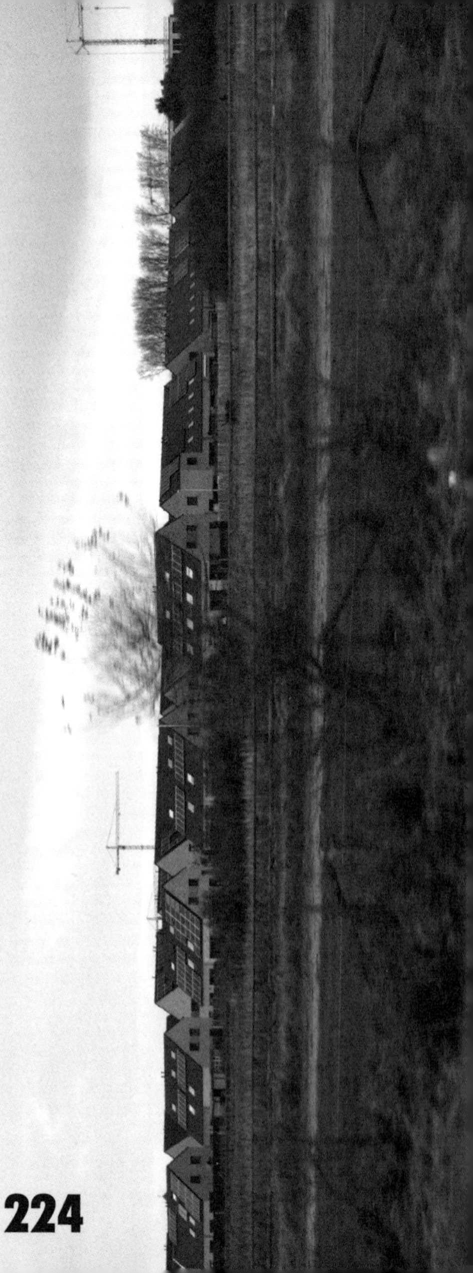

WHAT ARE THE FIVE FOODS THAT KILL TESTOSTERONE?

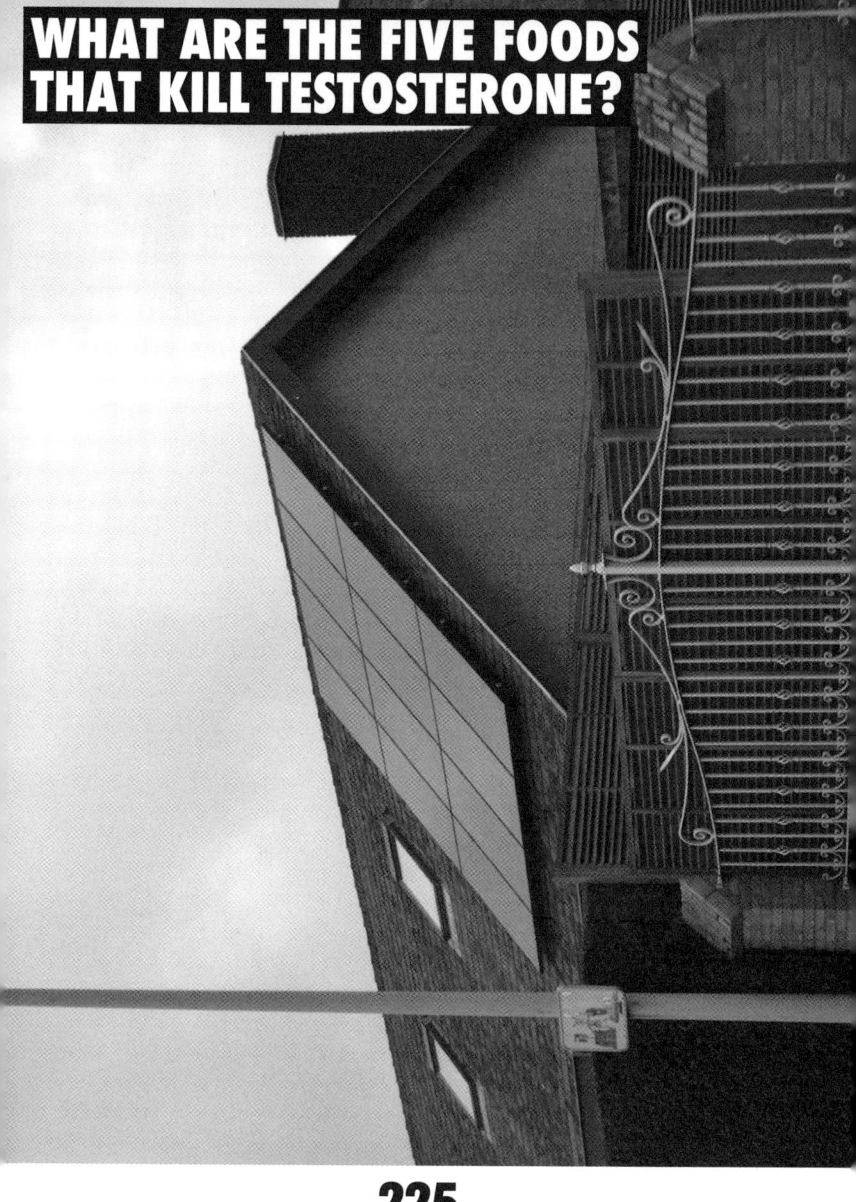

HOW CAN I GET A FLAT STOMACH IN 3 DAYS?

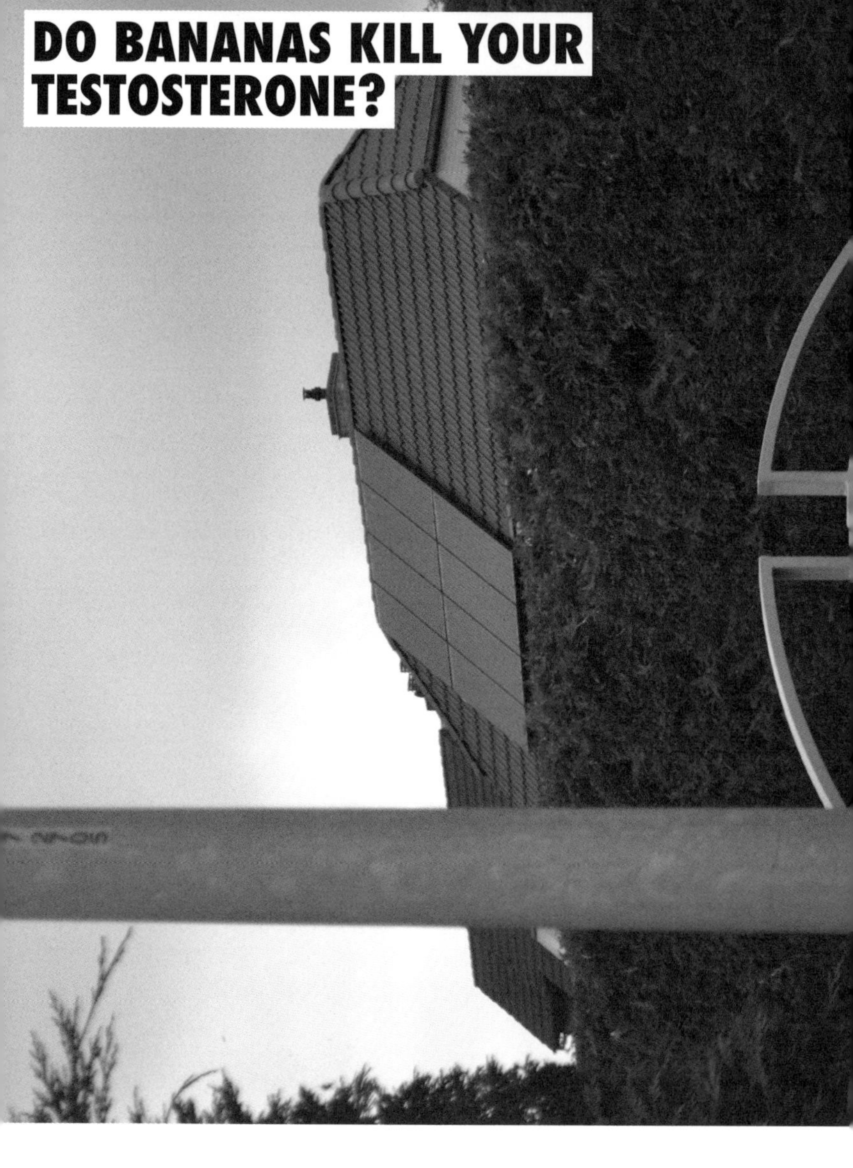

DO BANANAS KILL YOUR TESTOSTERONE?

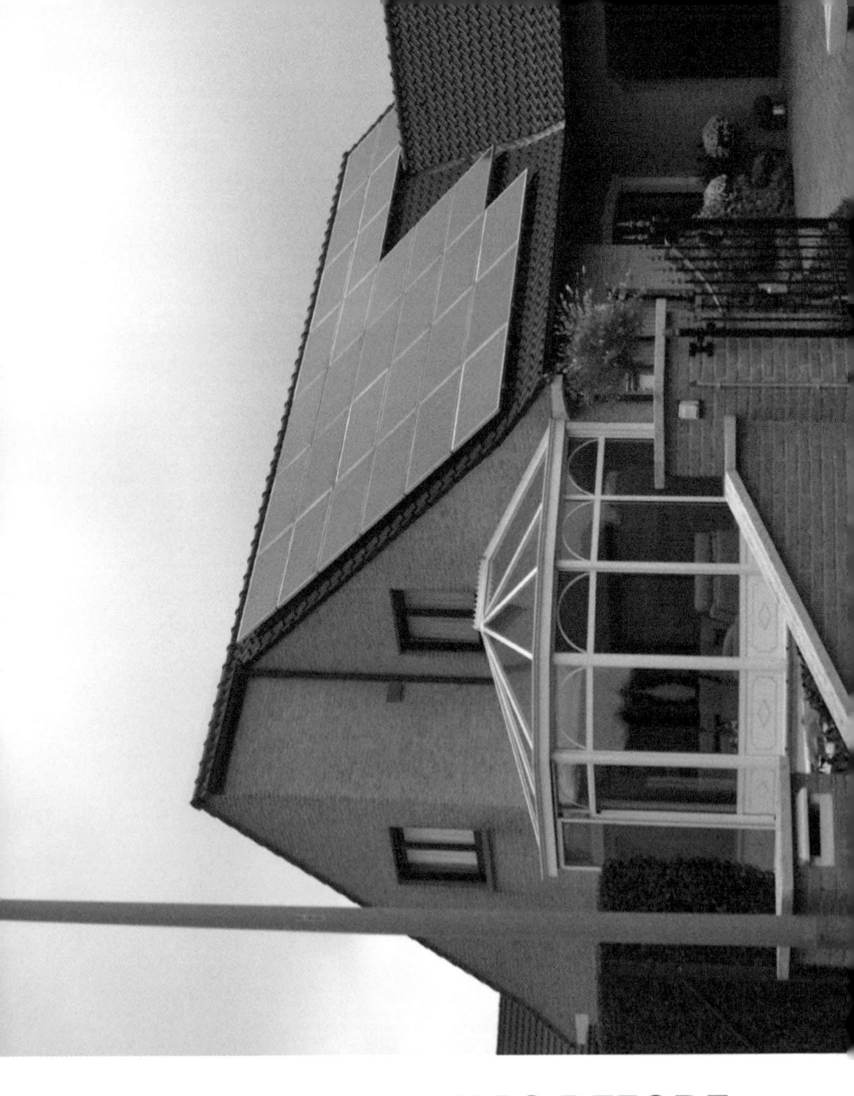

DO YOU EAT BANANAS BEFORE OR AFTER A WORKOUT?

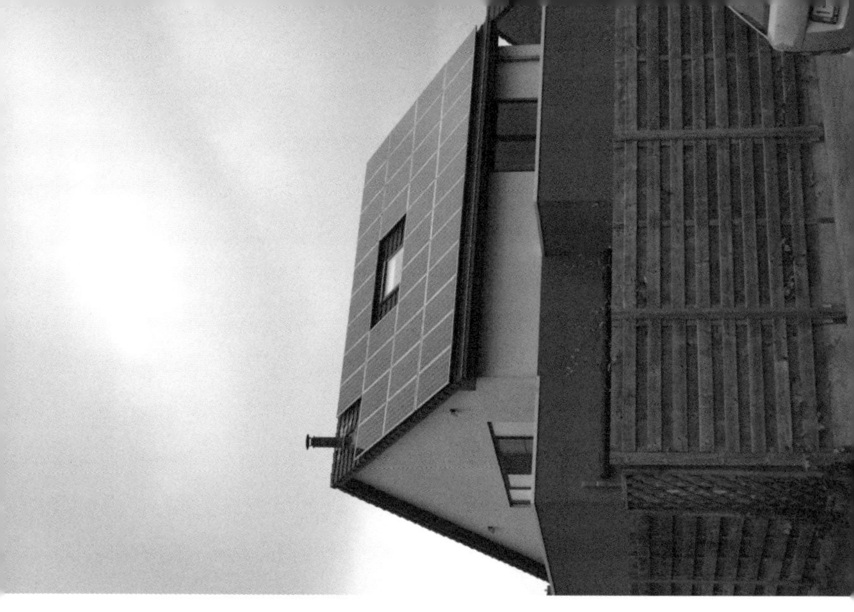

DO ATHLETES EAT BANANAS?

WHY IS IT BAD TO EAT BANANAS AT NIGHT?

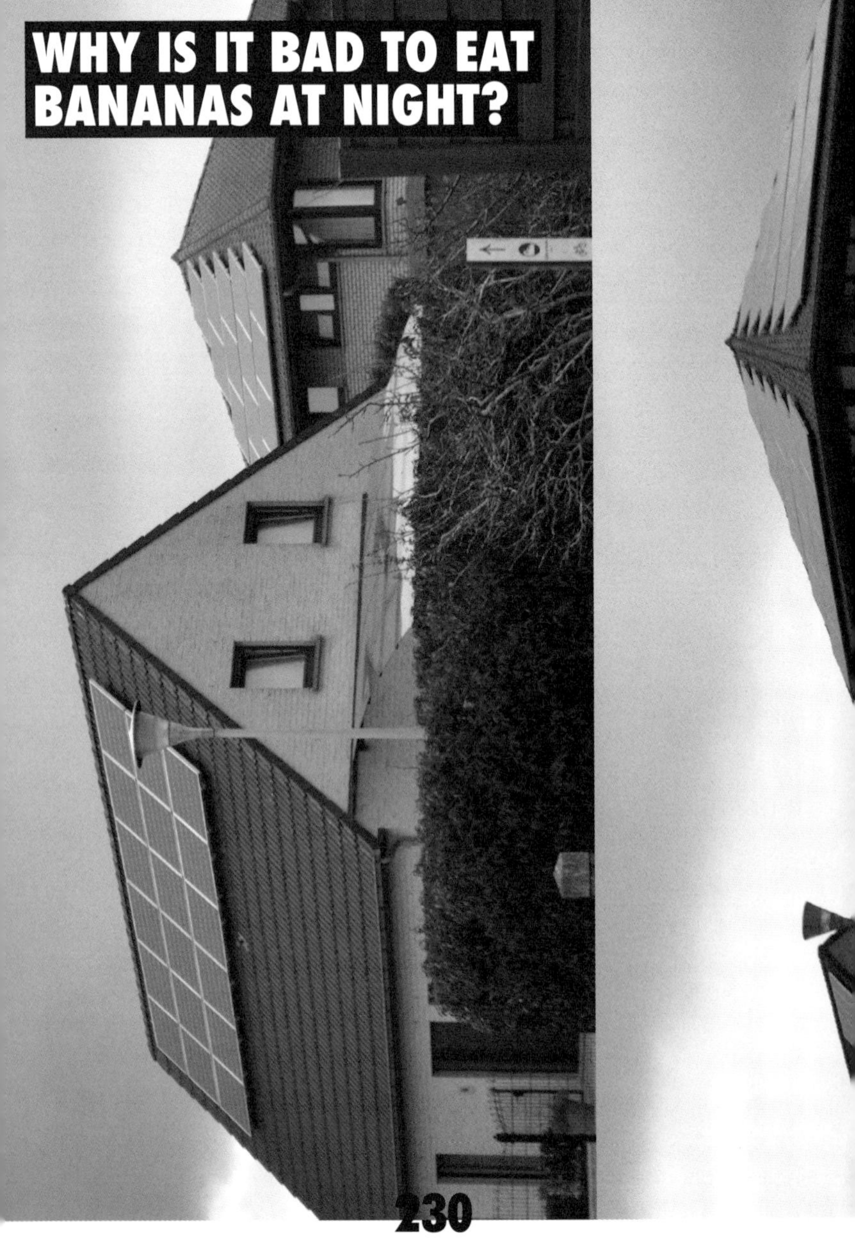

IS IT BAD TO DRINK MILK AT NIGHT?

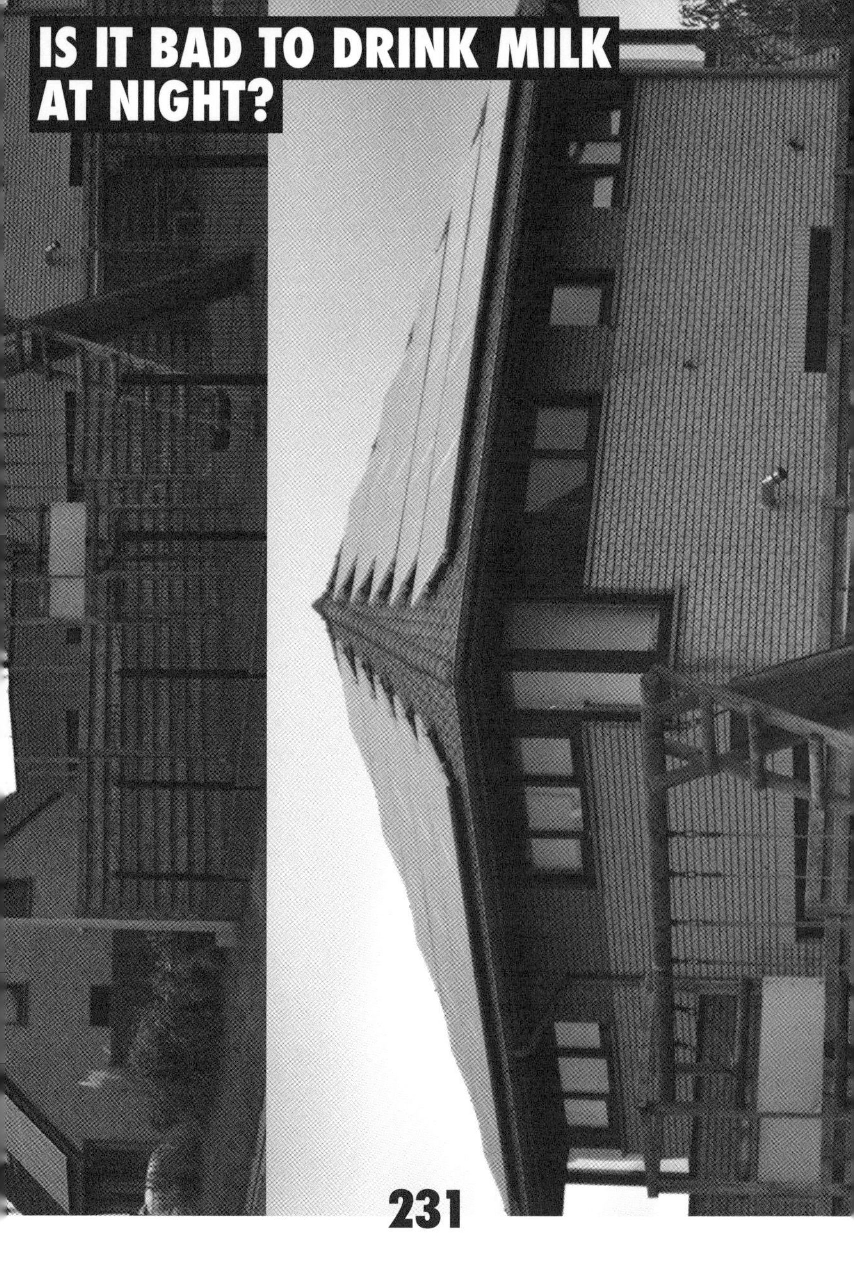

IS IT BAD TO DRINK MILK IN THE MORNING?

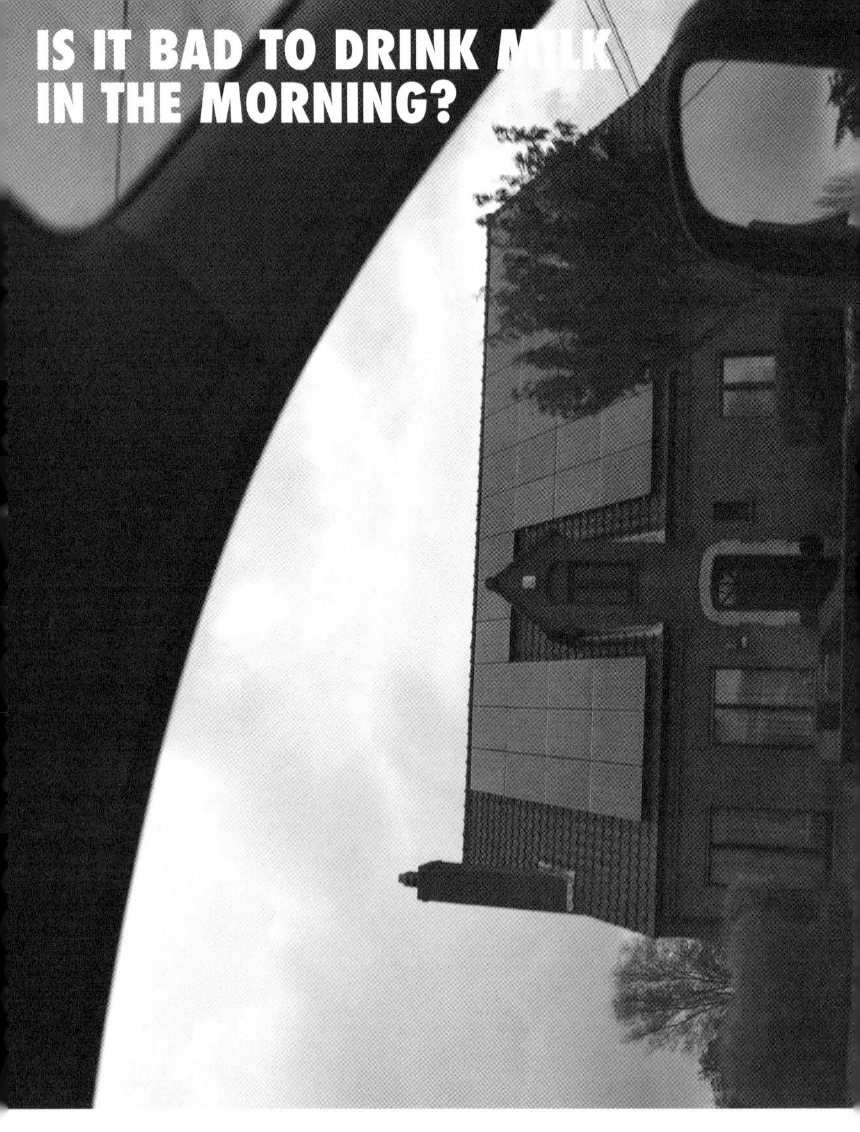

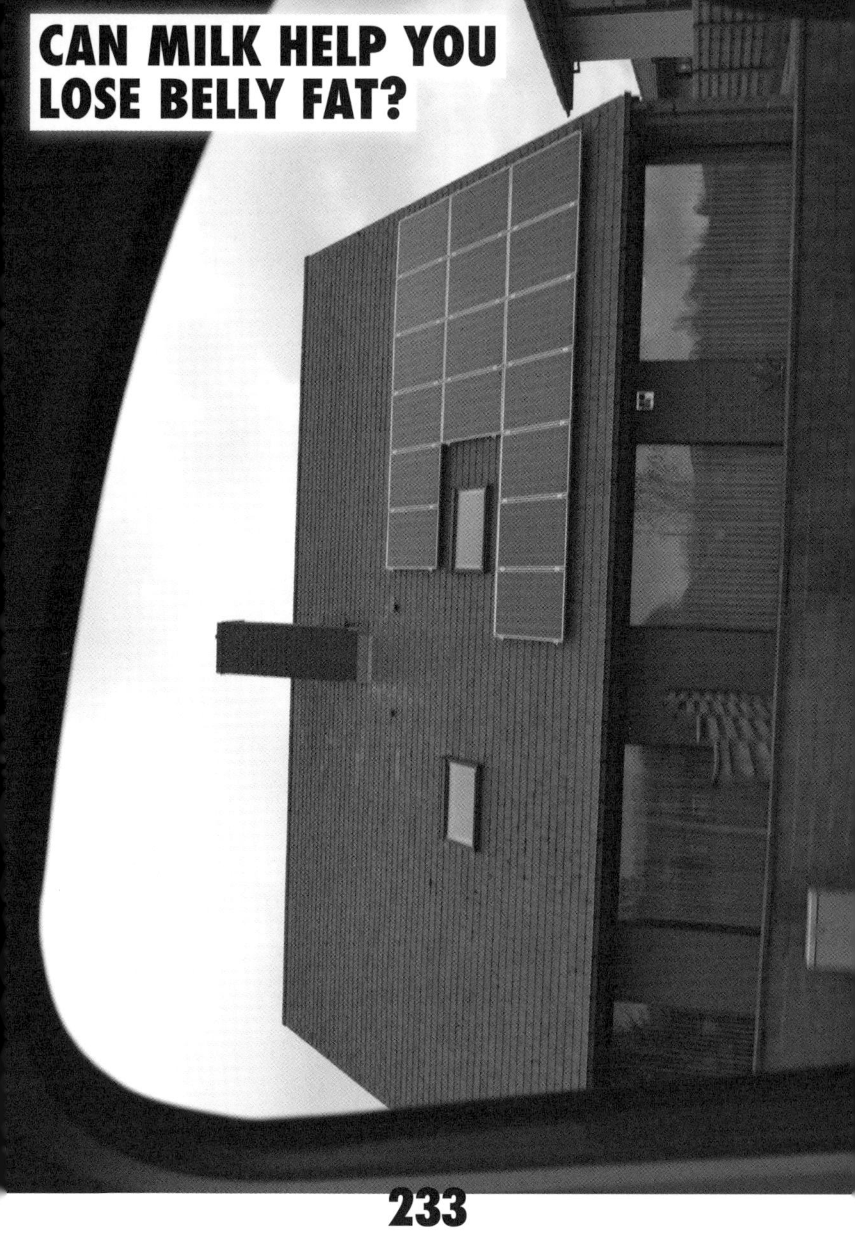
CAN MILK HELP YOU
LOSE BELLY FAT?

CAN YOU LOSE 20 POUNDS IN A WEEK?

CAN HOT WATER BURN BELLY FAT?

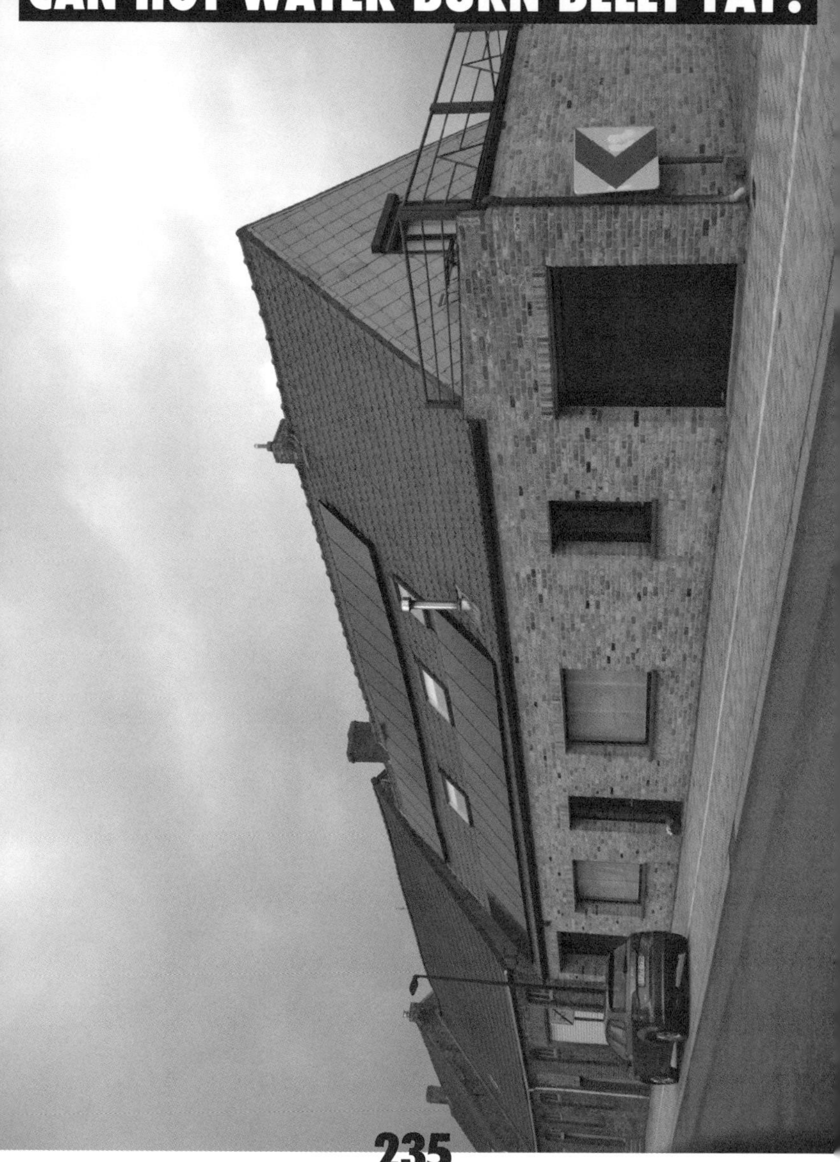

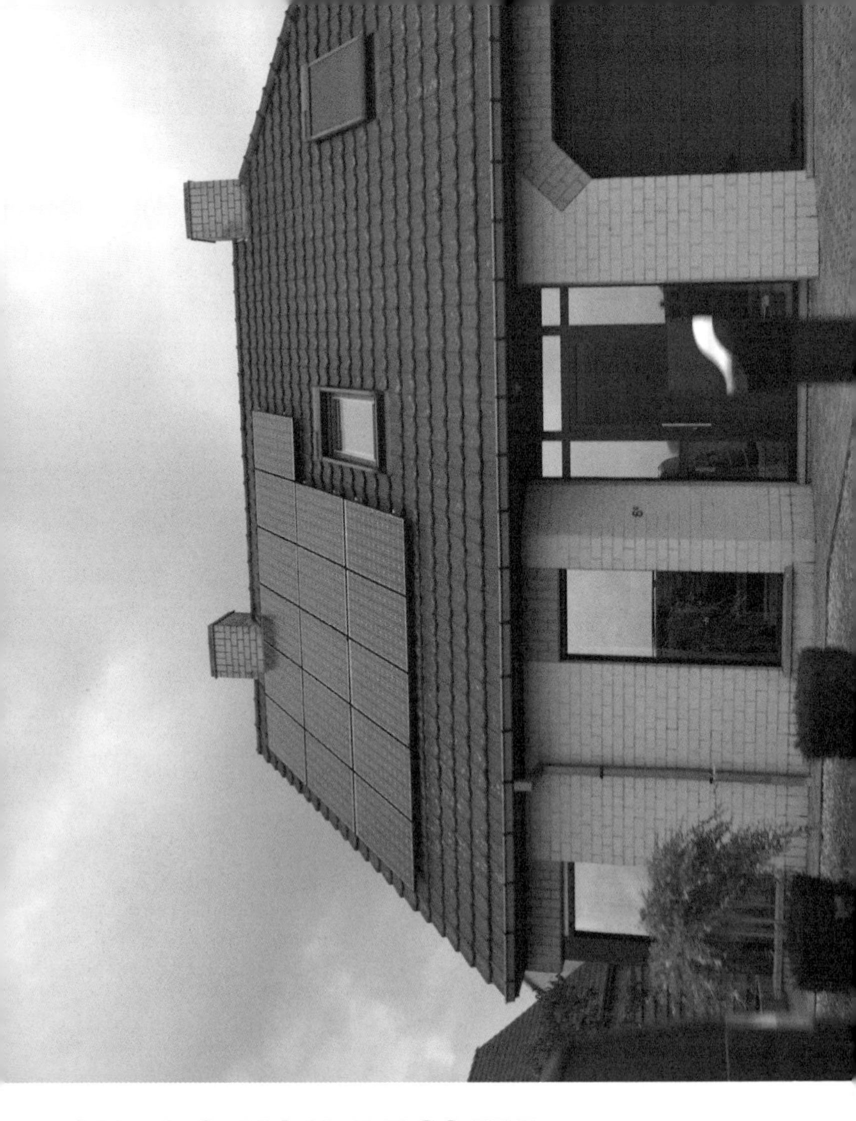

HOW DO YOU BECOME A MILLIONAIRE?

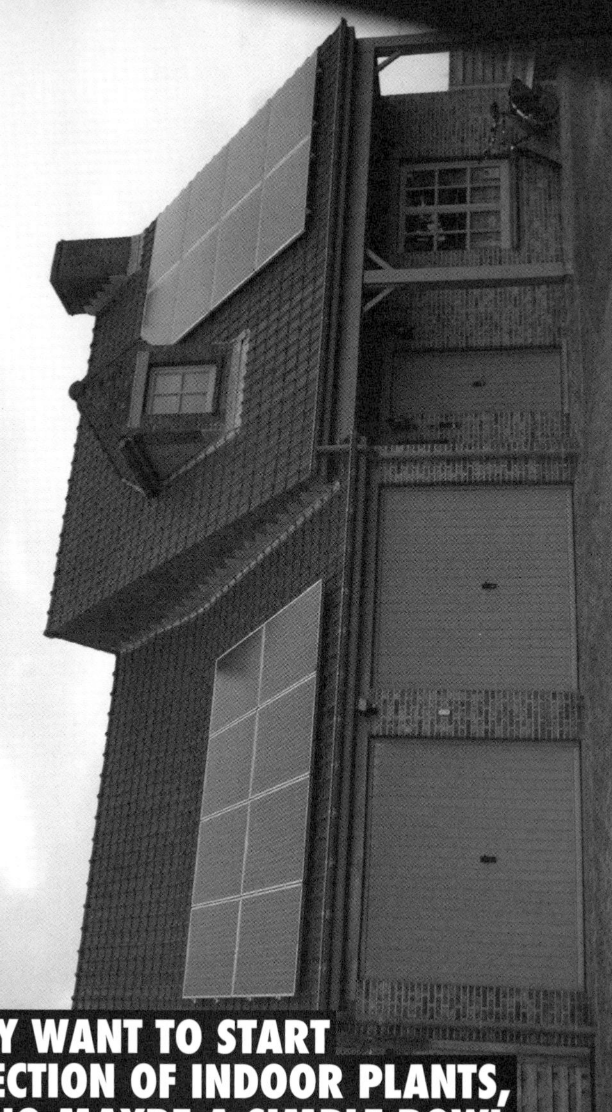

I REALLY WANT TO START A COLLECTION OF INDOOR PLANTS, THINKING MAYBE A SIMPLE BOWL OF SUCCULENTS TO BEGIN?

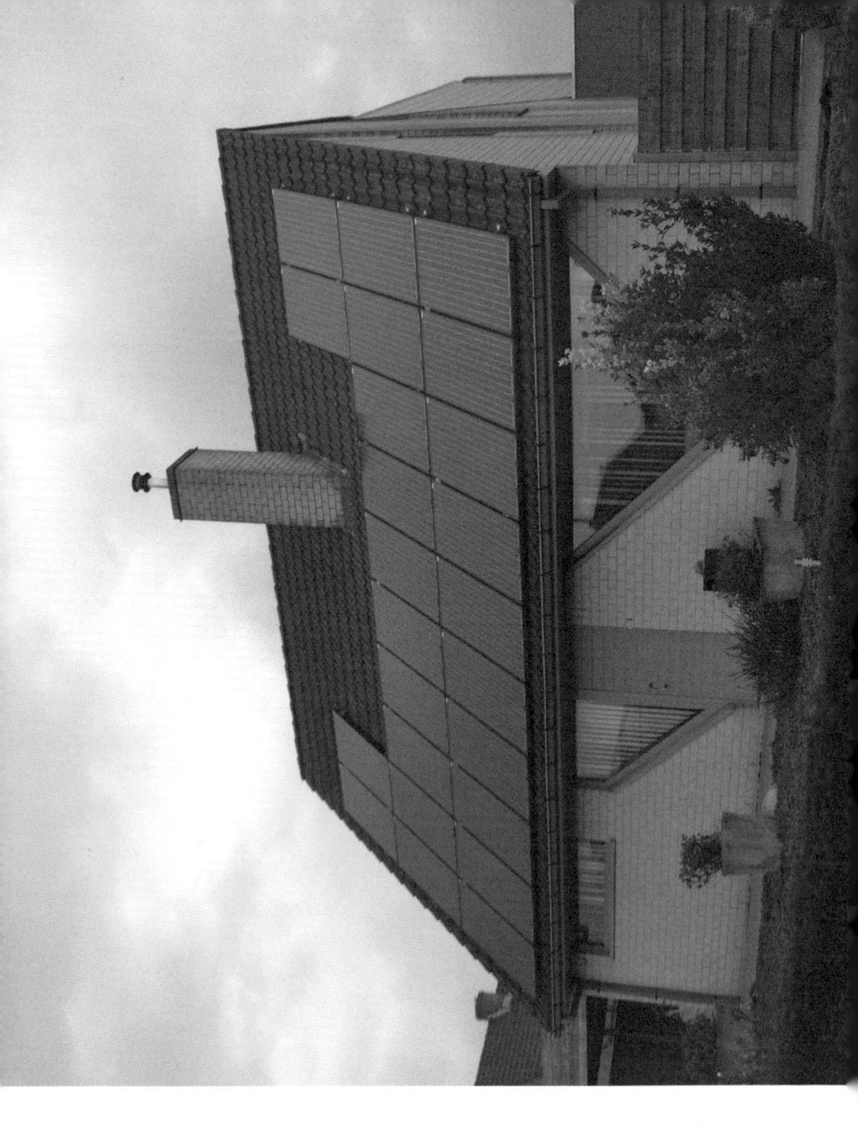

REALLY CUTE ANIMALS EATING FOOD

238

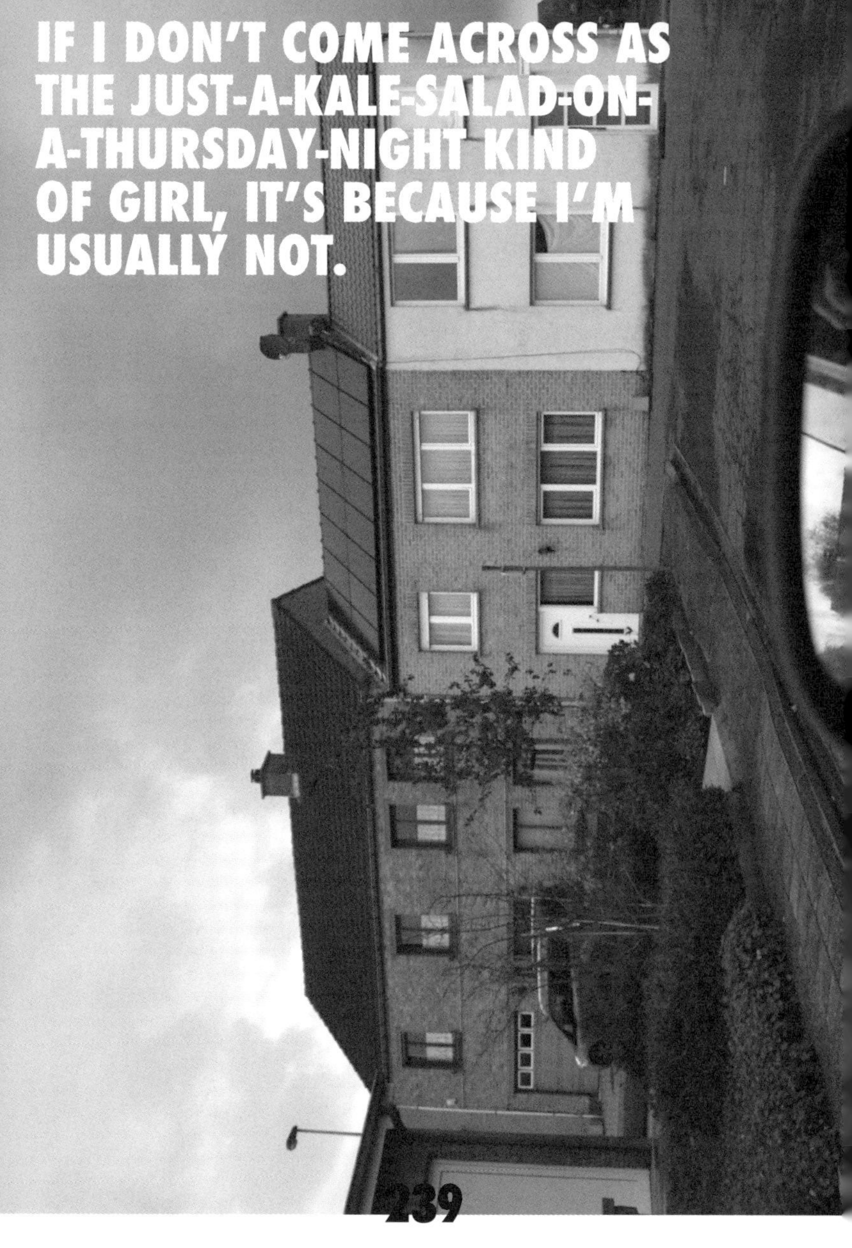

IF I DON'T COME ACROSS AS THE JUST-A-KALE-SALAD-ON-A-THURSDAY-NIGHT KIND OF GIRL, IT'S BECAUSE I'M USUALLY NOT.

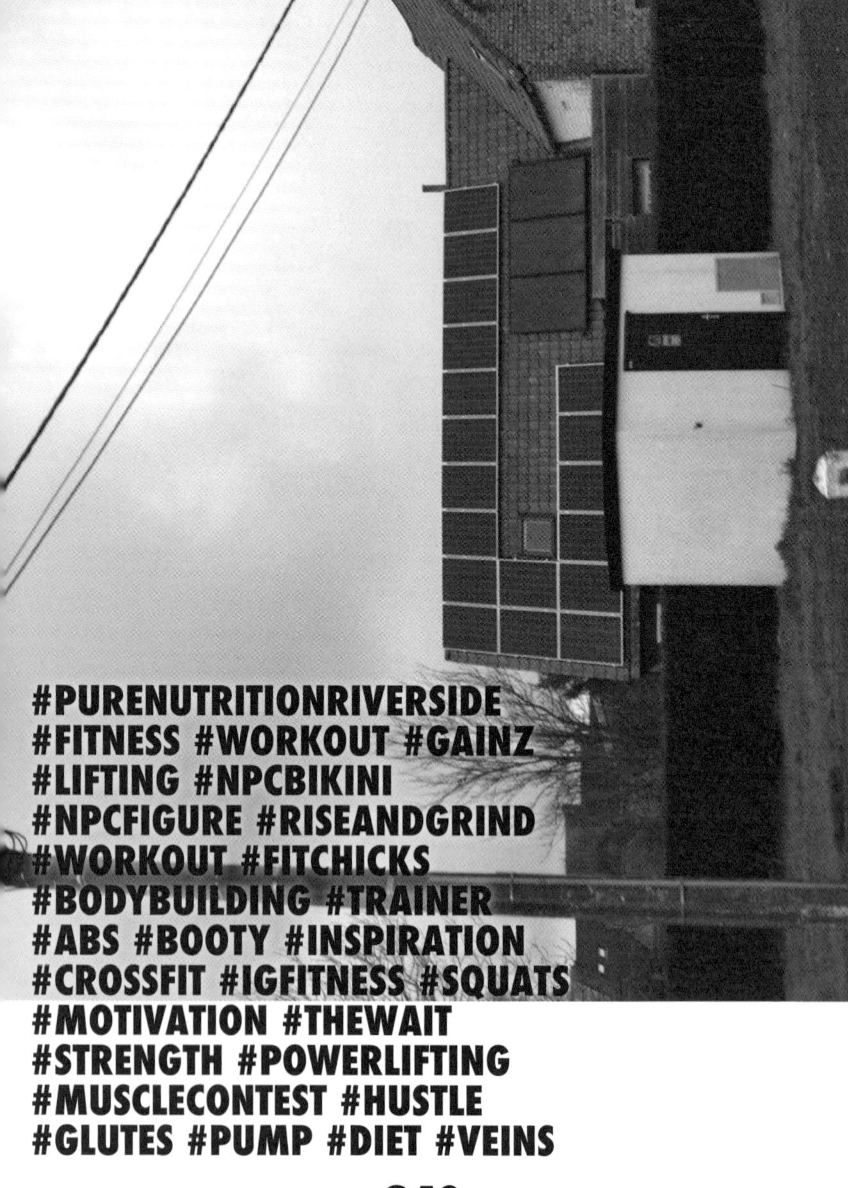

#PURENUTRITIONRIVERSIDE
#FITNESS #WORKOUT #GAINZ
#LIFTING #NPCBIKINI
#NPCFIGURE #RISEANDGRIND
#WORKOUT #FITCHICKS
#BODYBUILDING #TRAINER
#ABS #BOOTY #INSPIRATION
#CROSSFIT #IGFITNESS #SQUATS
#MOTIVATION #THEWAIT
#STRENGTH #POWERLIFTING
#MUSCLECONTEST #HUSTLE
#GLUTES #PUMP #DIET #VEINS

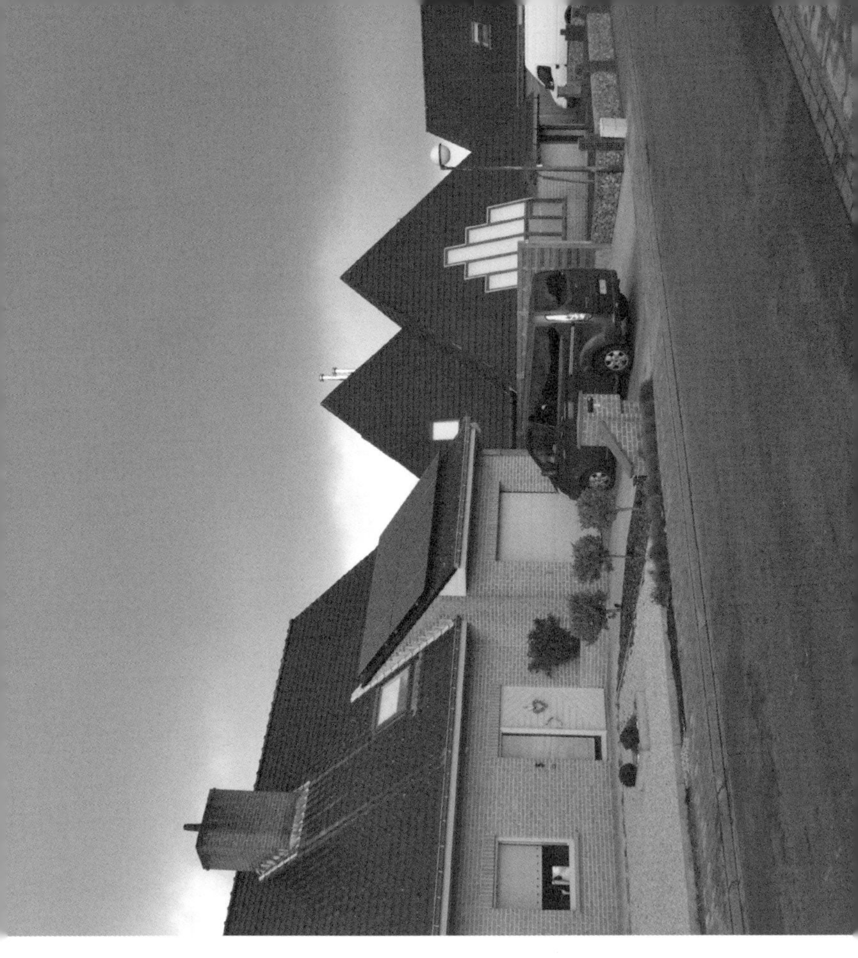

EMBRACING THE MESSY BUN

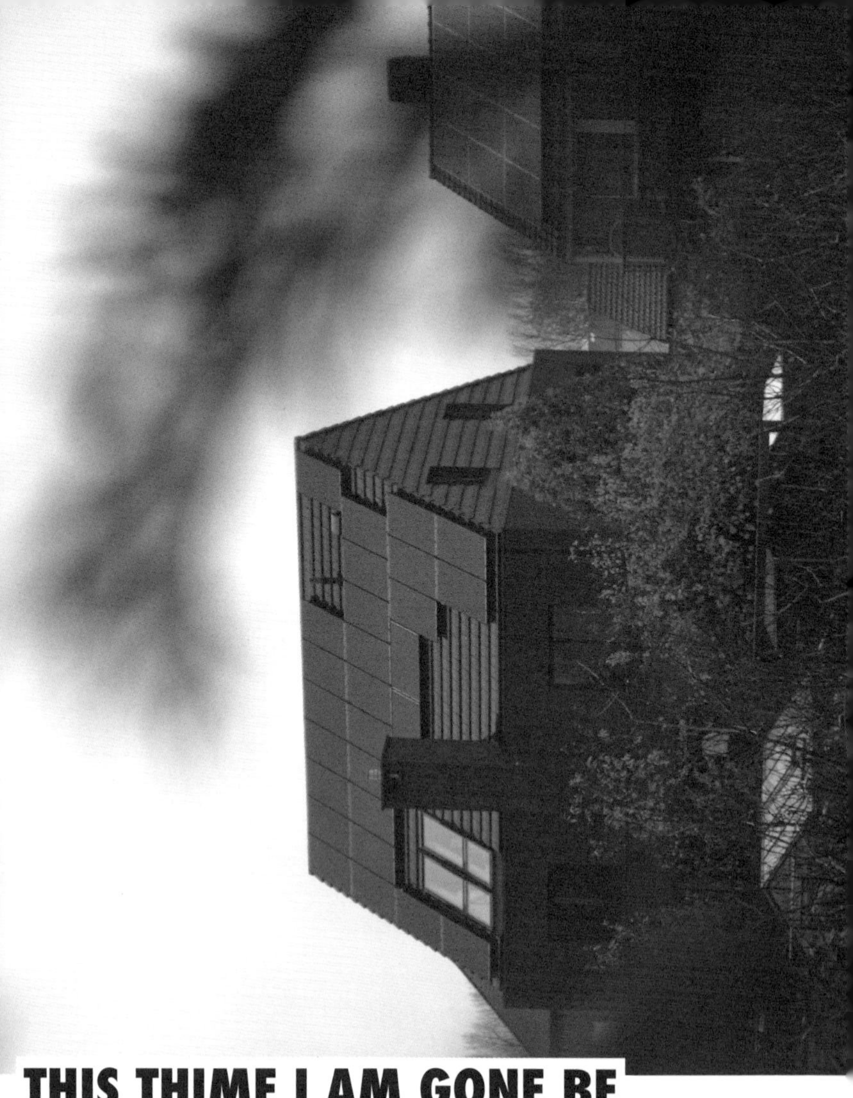

THIS THIME I AM GONE BE BETTER LAST YEAR PICTURE

WORE THE BODYBUILDING SHIRT ON SQUAT DAY TO CONFUSE THE BODY... GOTTA DO THAT FROM TIME TO TIME TO KEEP PROGRESSING

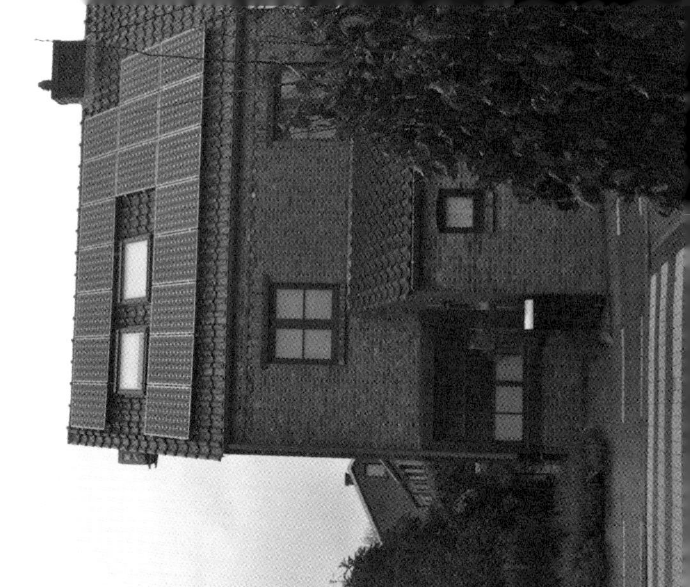

GETTING READY VOR GYM BUT DONT NOW TE PICK A NIKE AIR CLASSIC NIKE JUNKY TO MANNY NIKIES

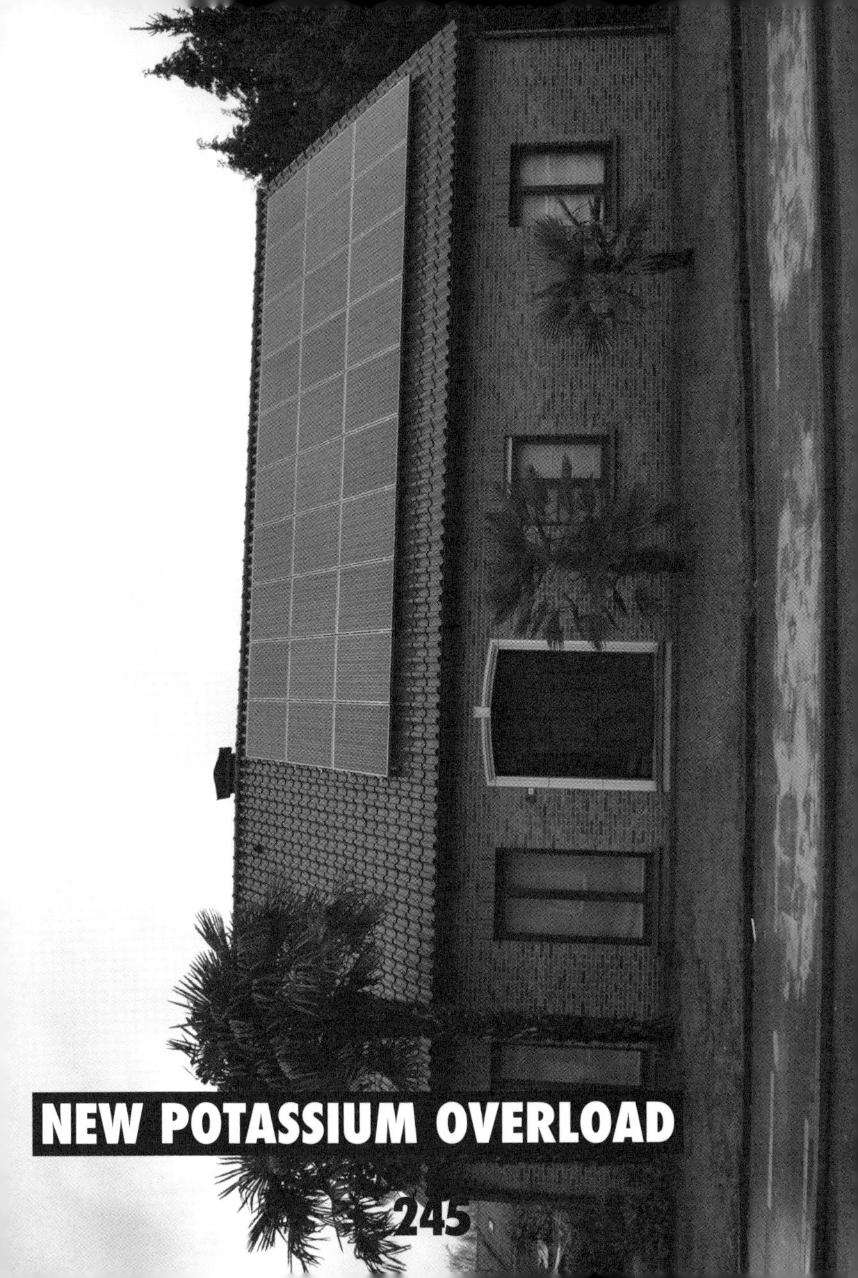

NEW POTASSIUM OVERLOAD

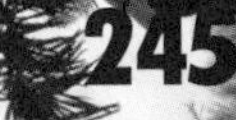

THERE'S MORE TO LIFE THAN JUST WORKING OUT... THERE'S MEAL PREP, CALCULATING MACROS, PLANNING ROUTINES AND REFINING YOUR GYM PLAYLIST!

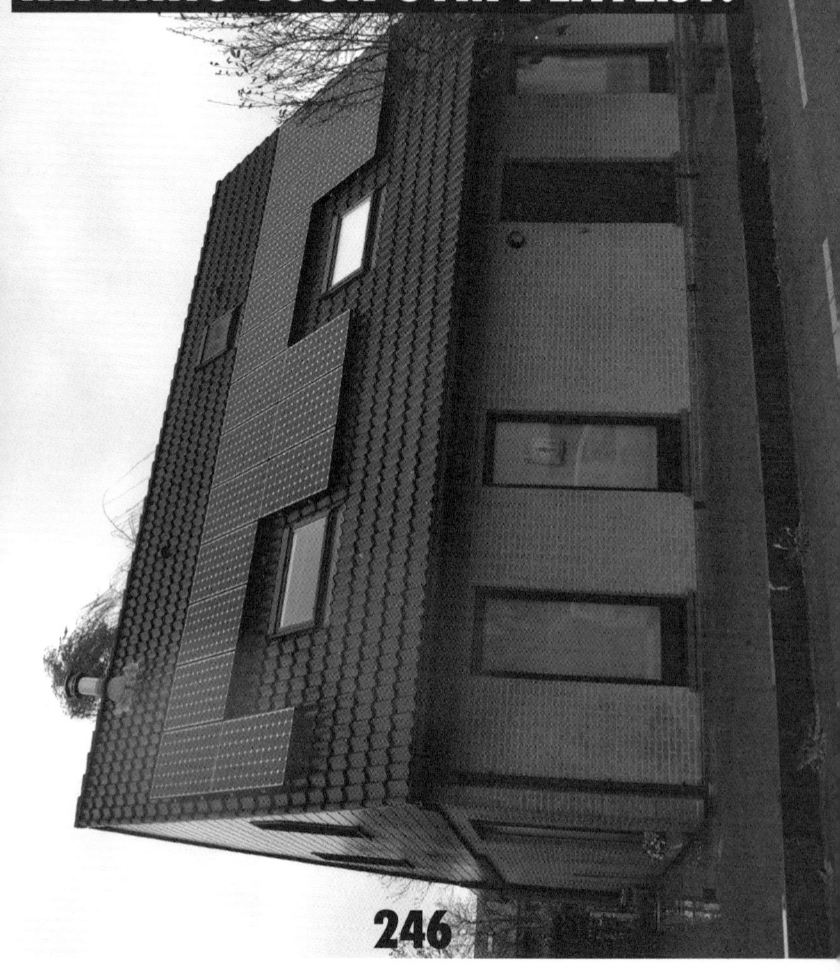

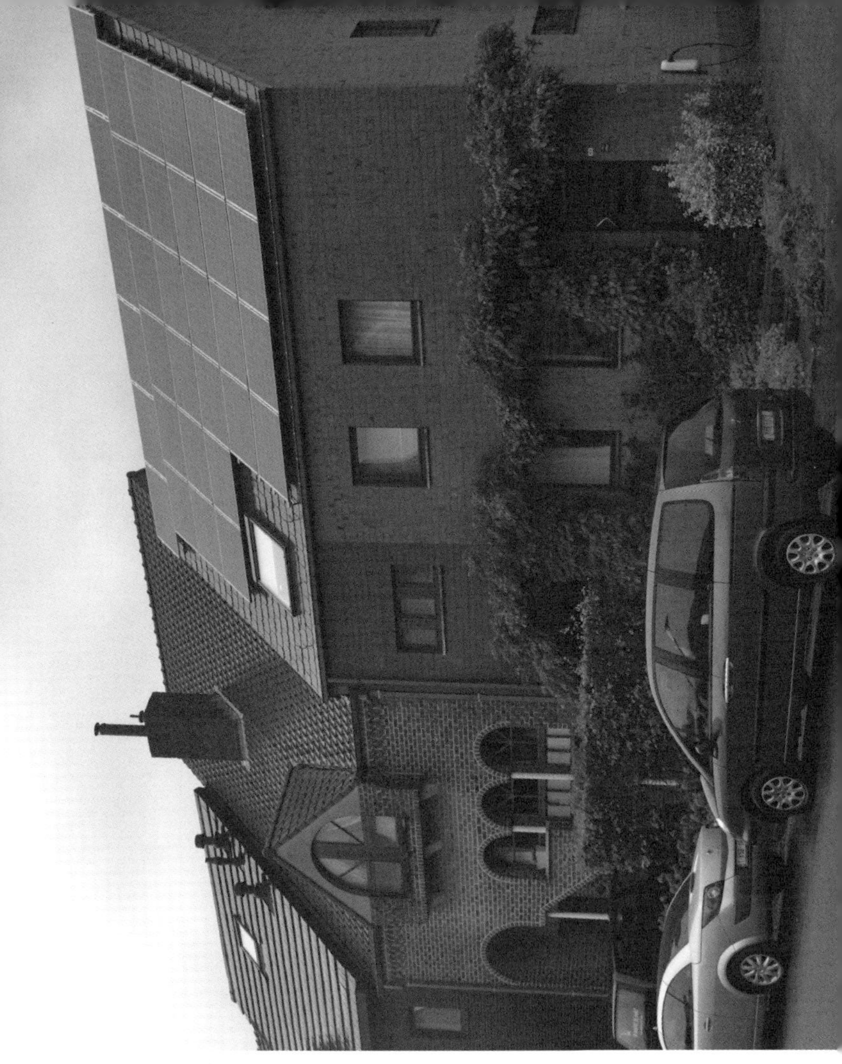

HAMMERTIME

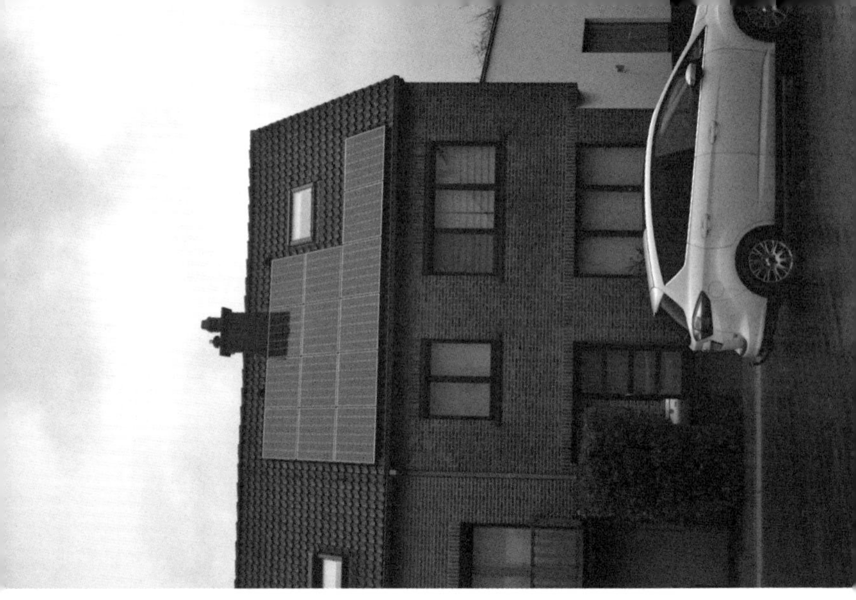

COOKIE DOUGH CREAMSLICE

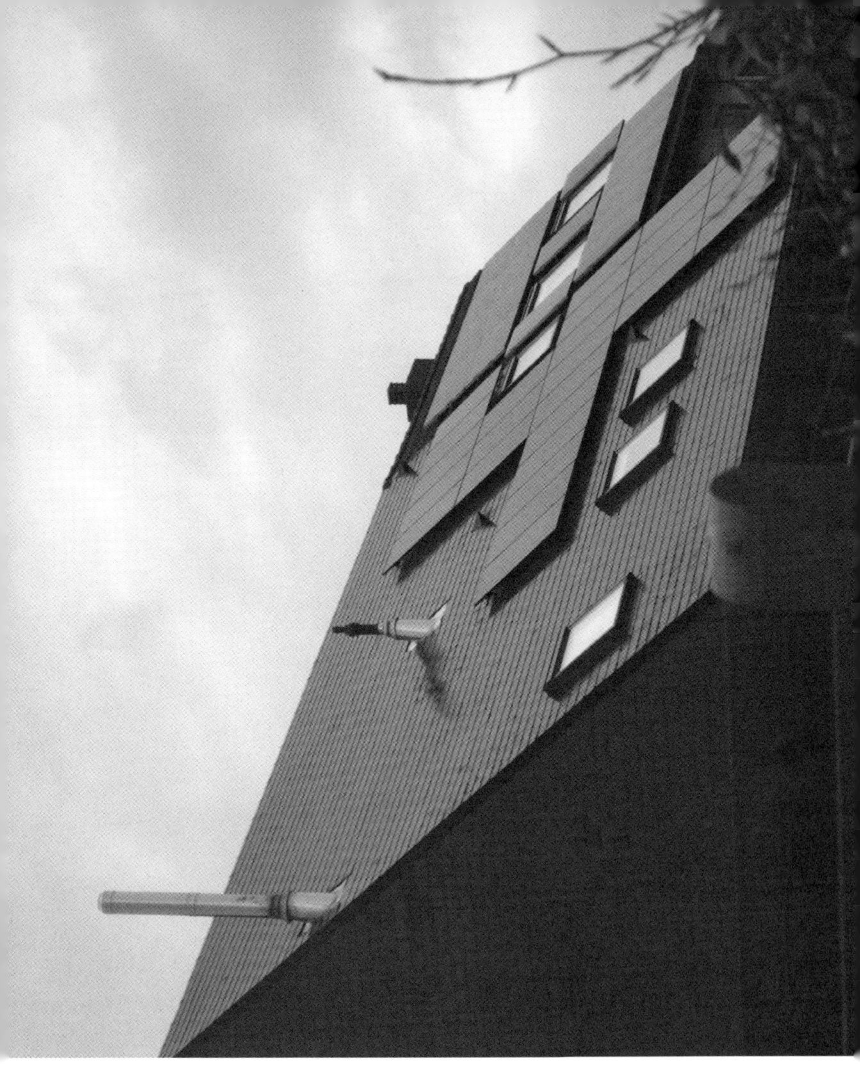

ARE BITCOIN REAL MONEY?

HOW DO YOU GET BITCOINS FOR FREE?

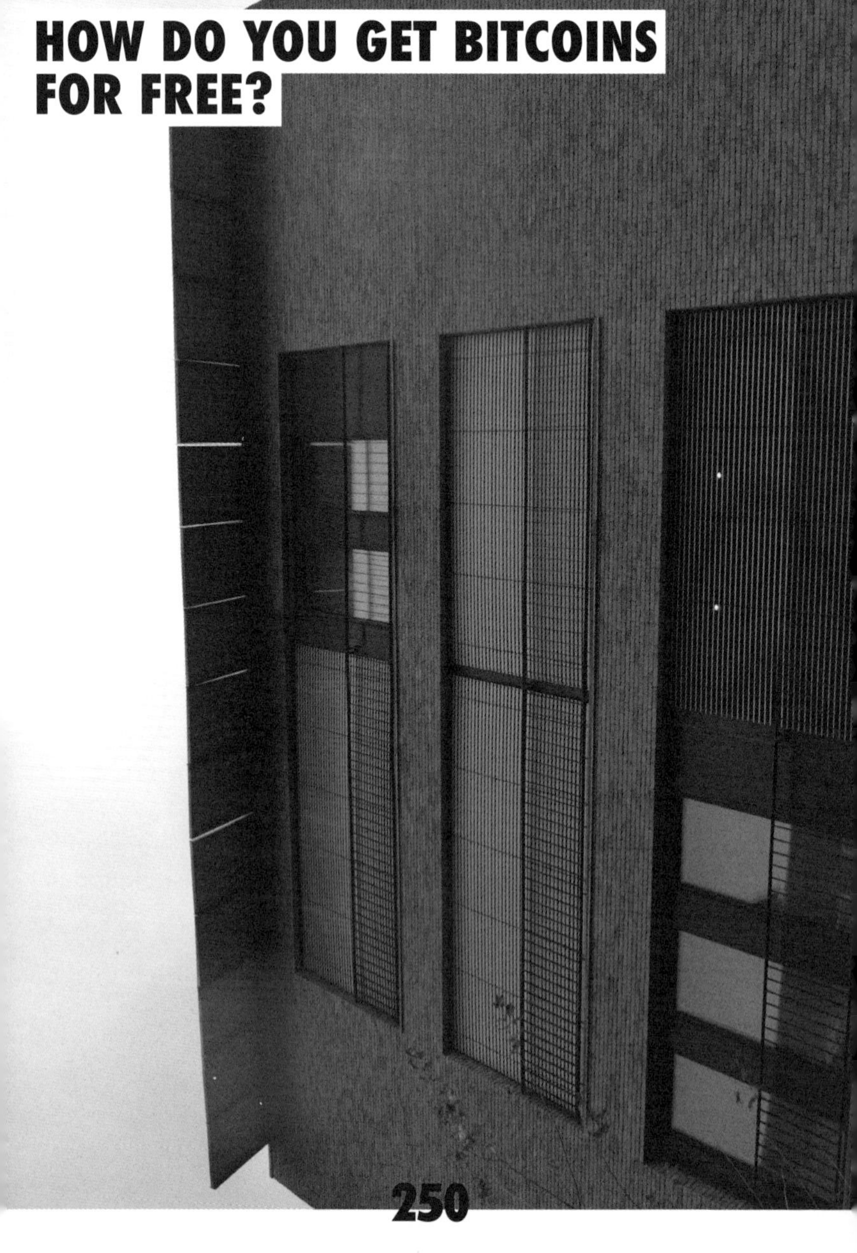

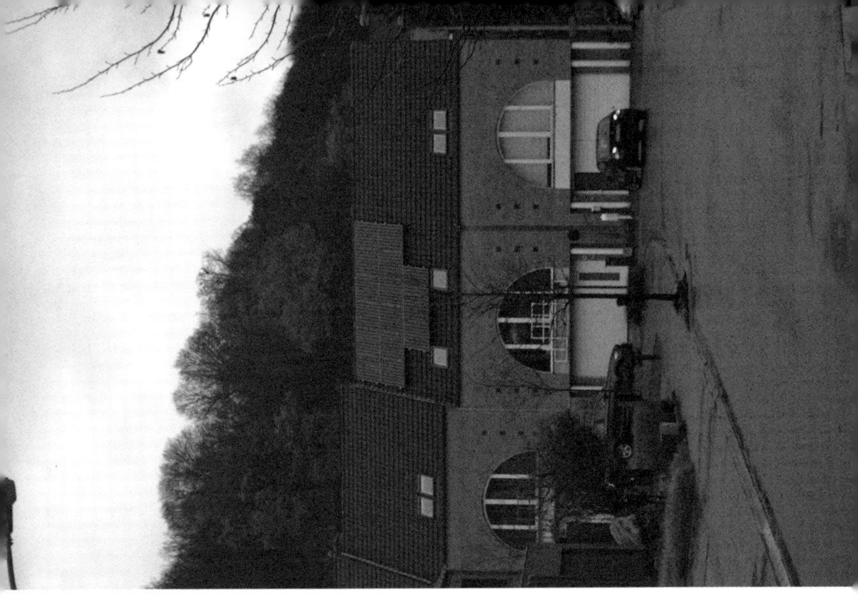

CAN BITCOIN BE SHORTED?

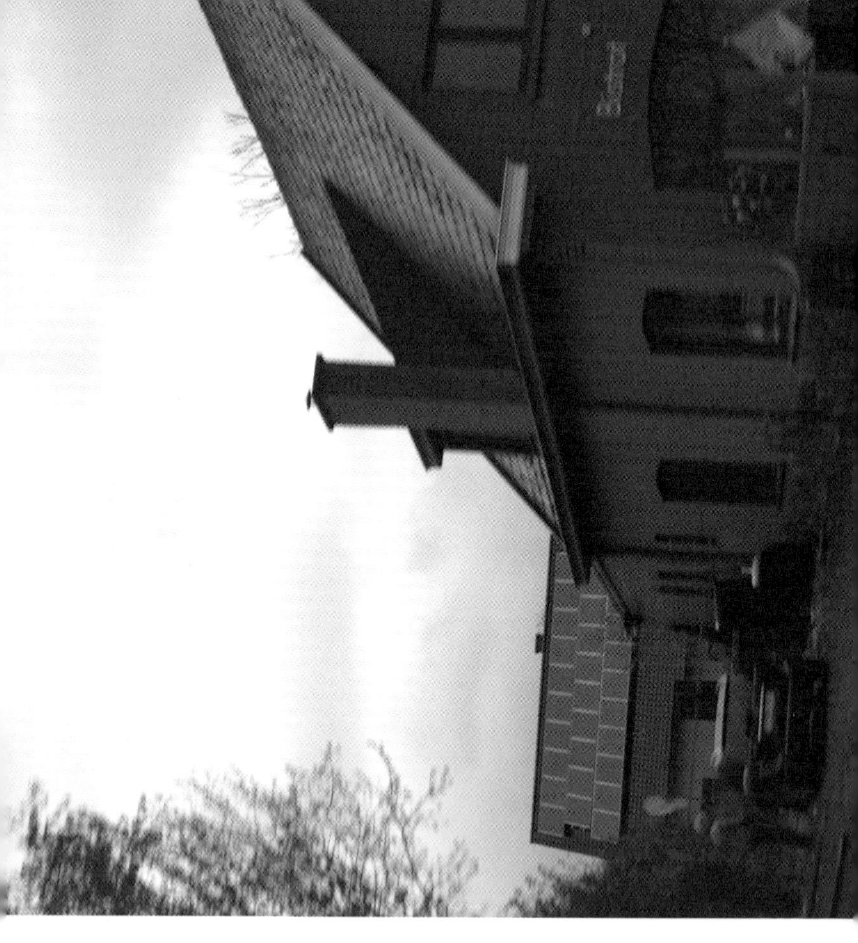

HOW DO I SHORT SELL A STOCK?

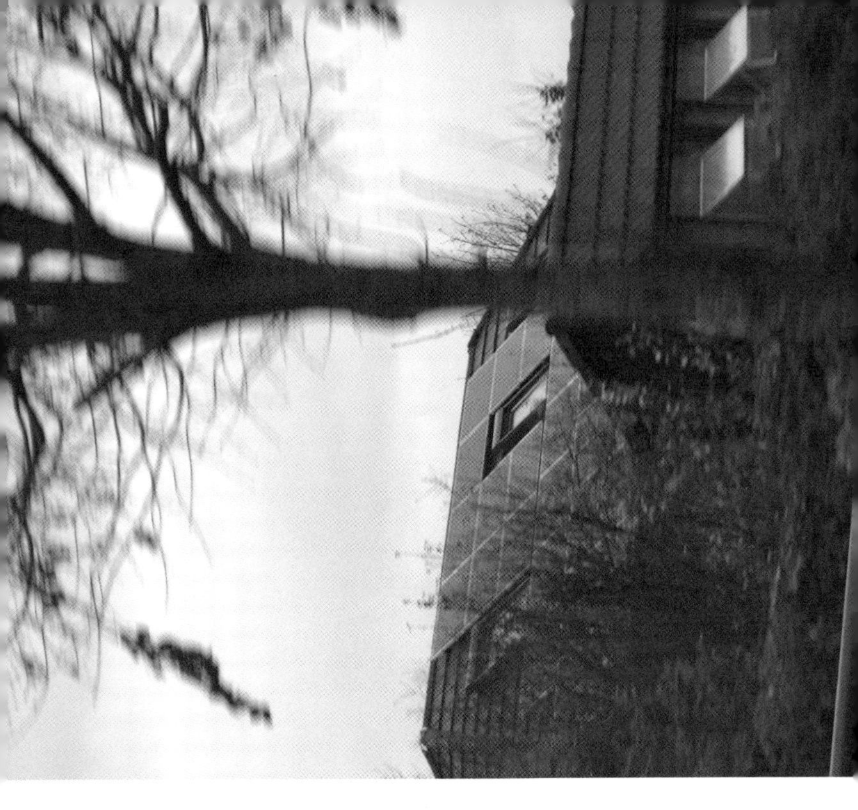

HOW SHOULD I SPEND 1000 DOLLARS?

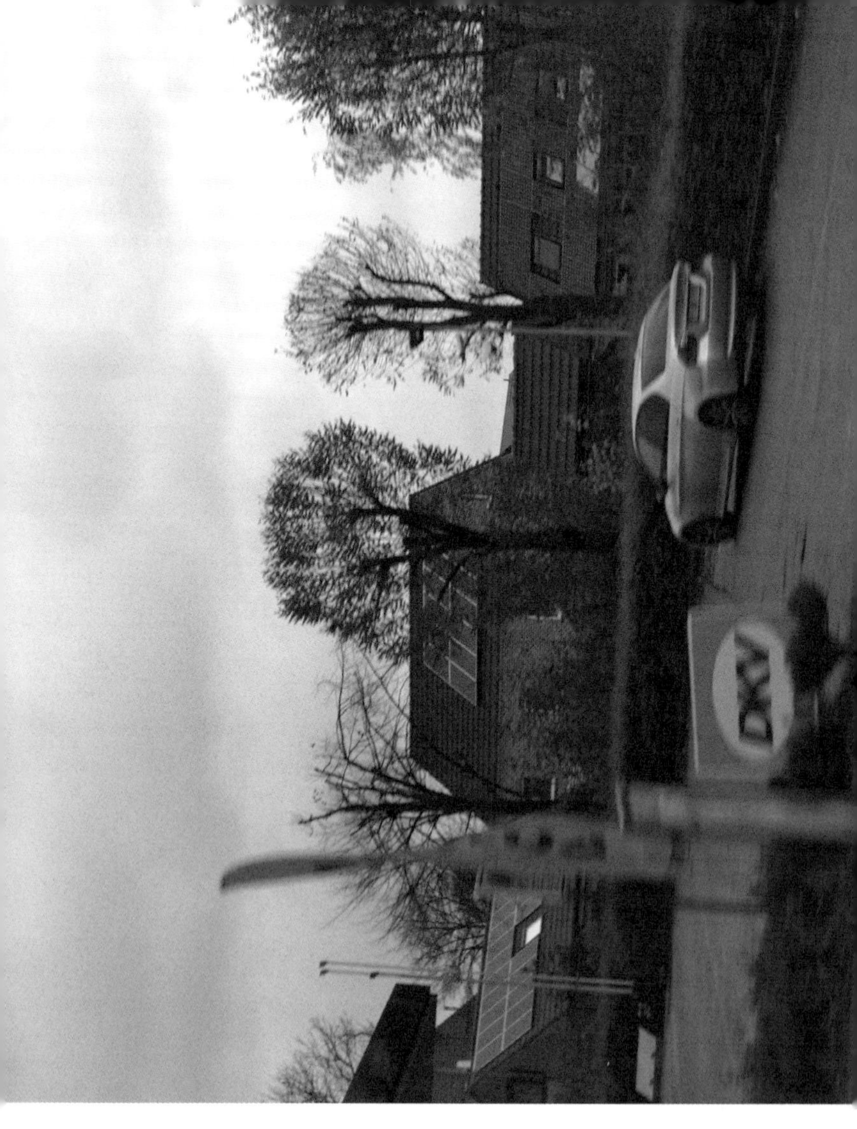

SELL YOUR BLOOD
254

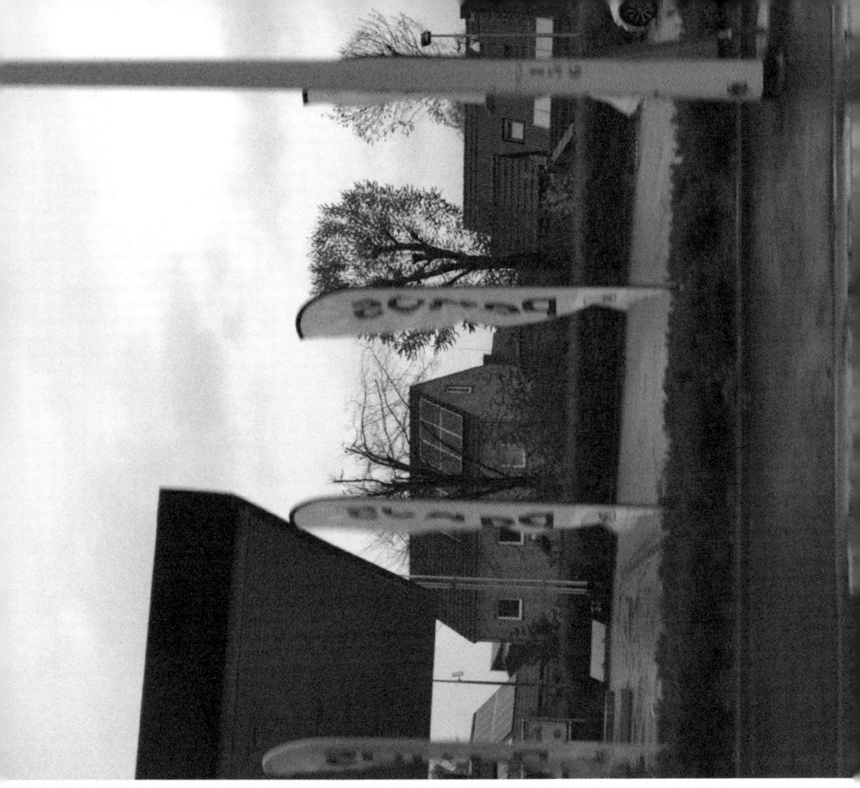

WHY IS MY AVOCADO TREE DYING?

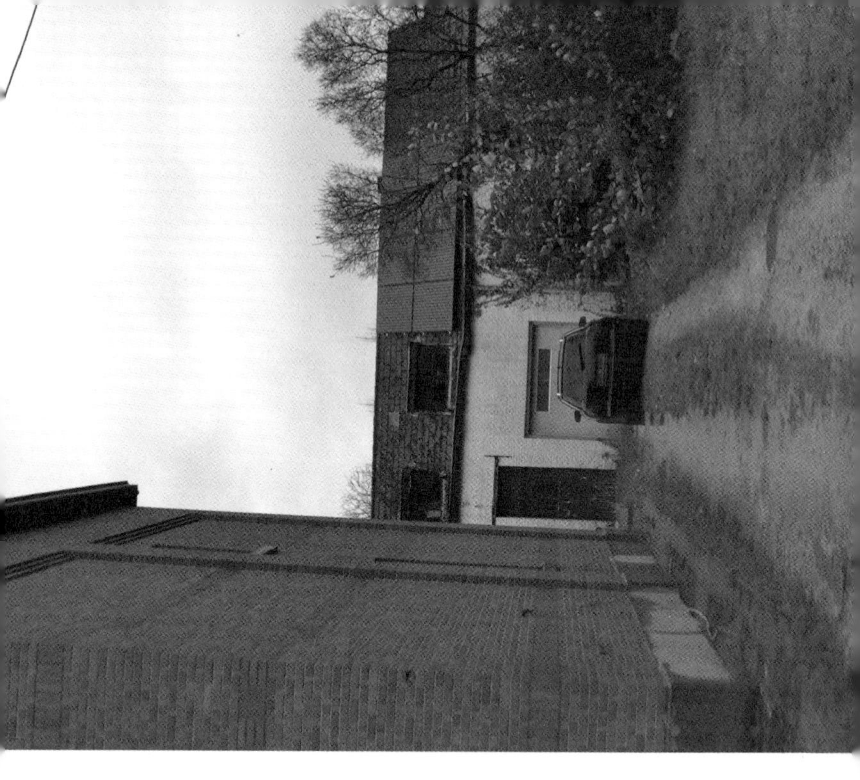

IS IT BAD TO EAT AN OVERLY RIPE AVOCADO?

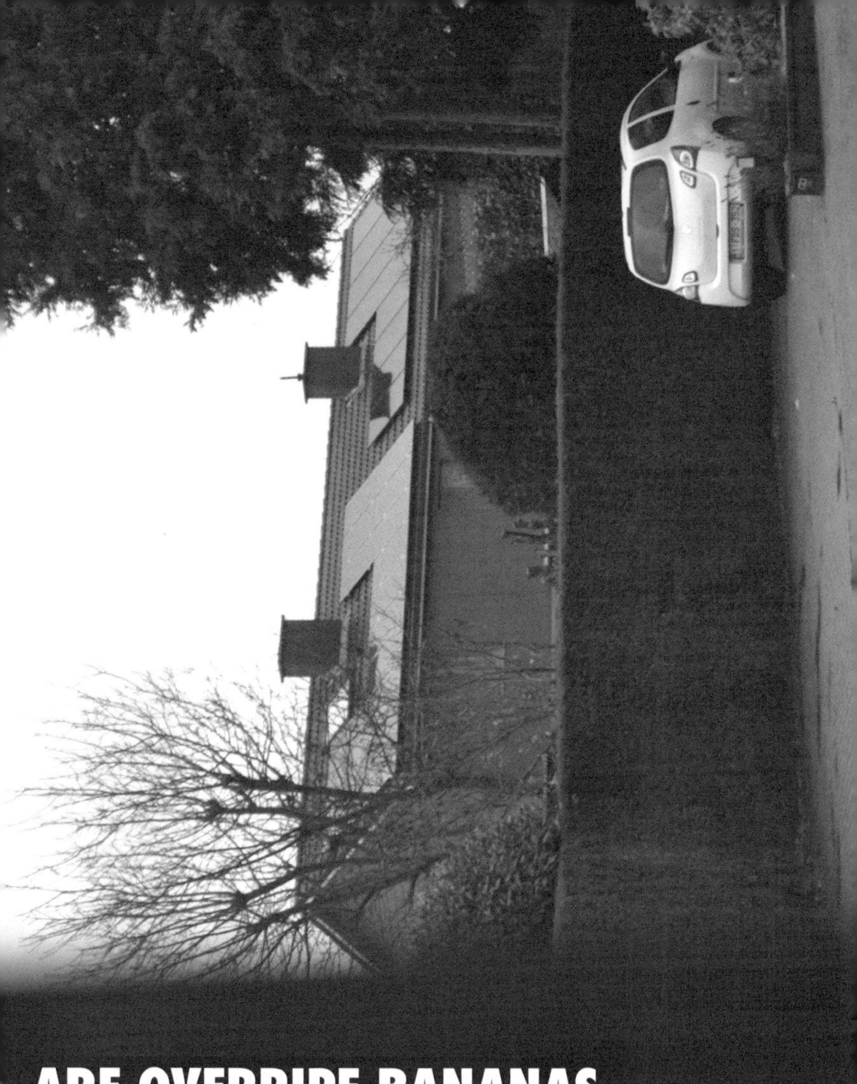

ARE OVERRIPE BANANAS GOOD FOR YOU?

IS IT SAFE TO EAT A ROTTEN APPLE?

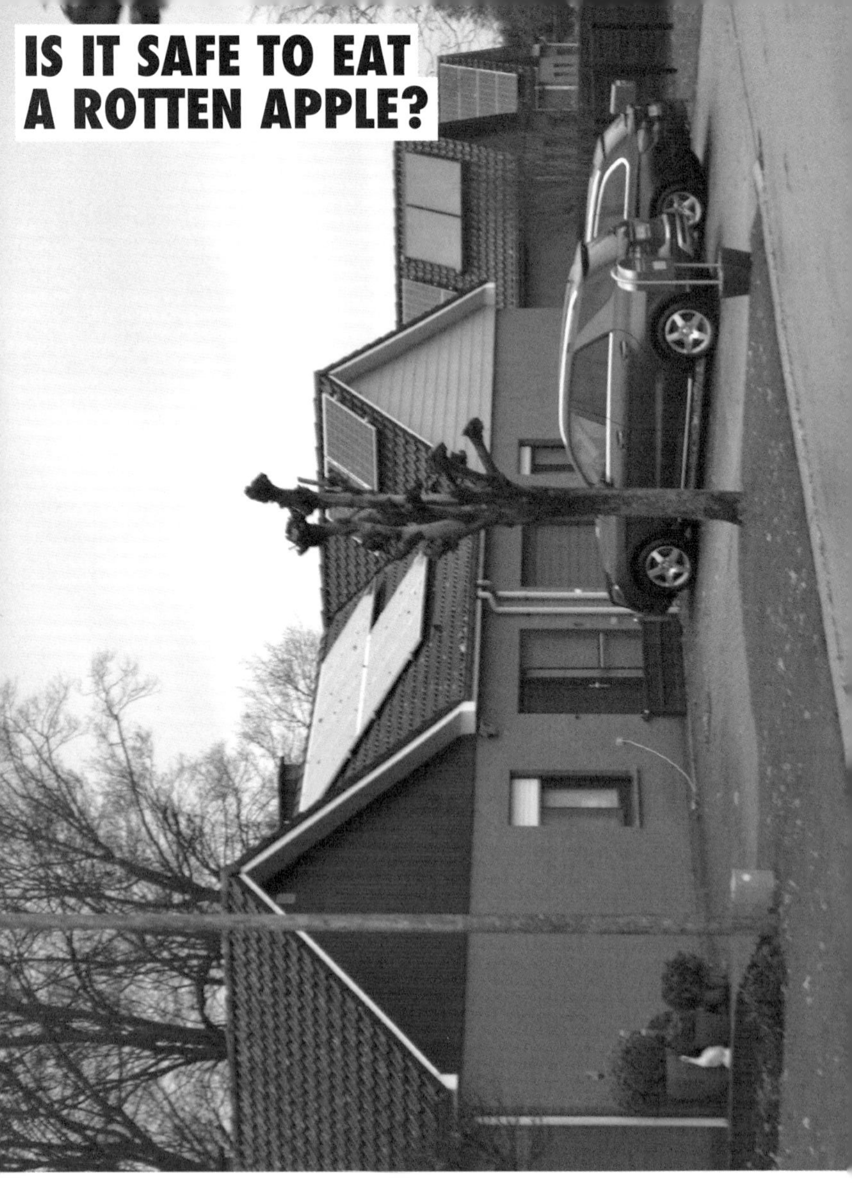

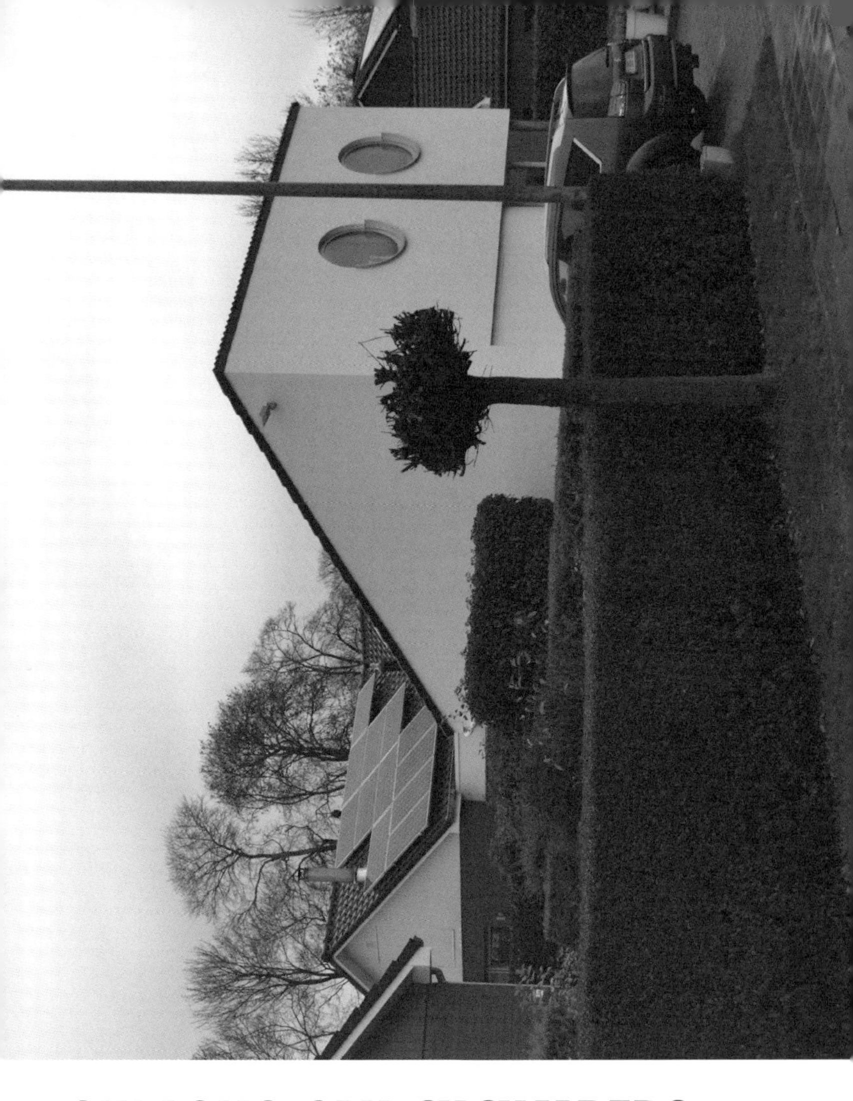

HOW LONG CAN CUCUMBERS STAY AT ROOM TEMPERATURE?

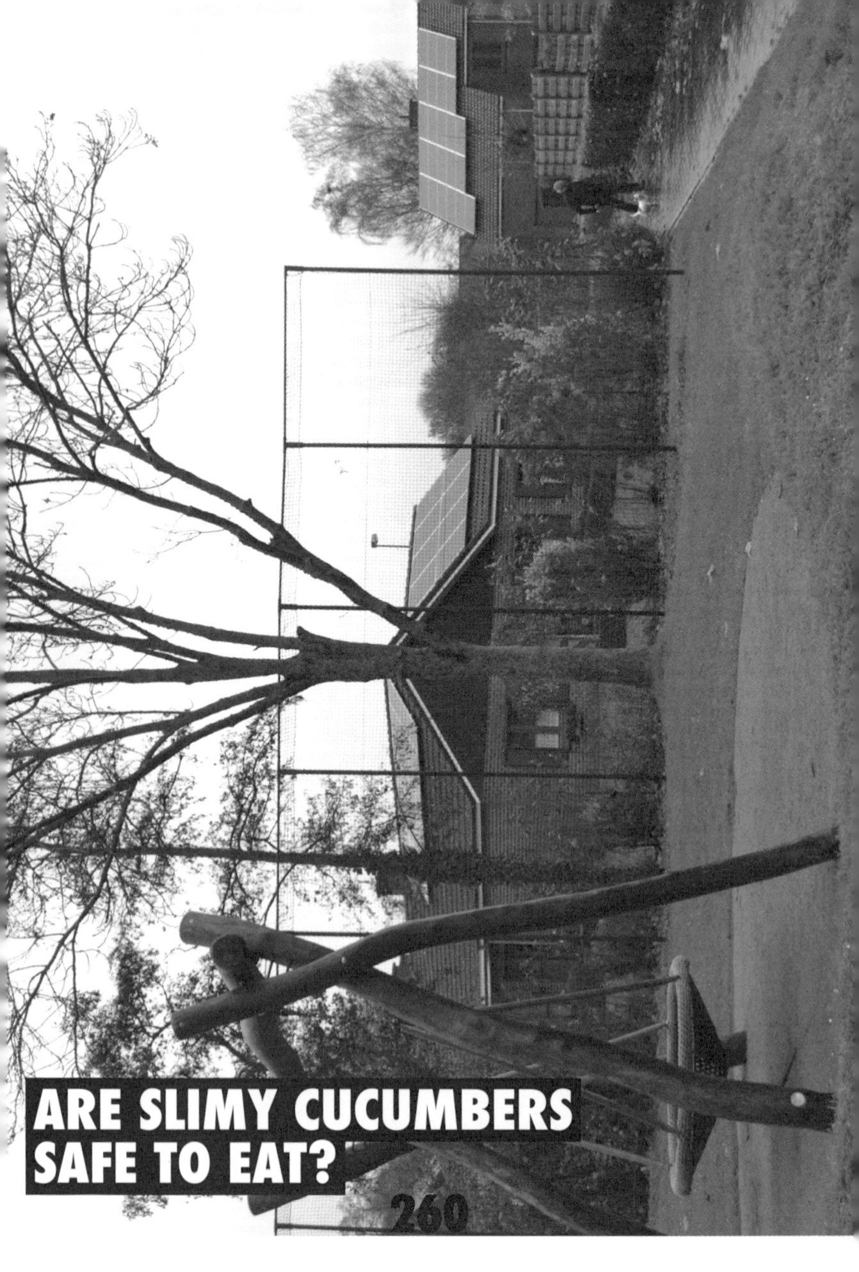

ARE SLIMY CUCUMBERS SAFE TO EAT?

CAN YOU EAT A WHITE CUCUMBER?

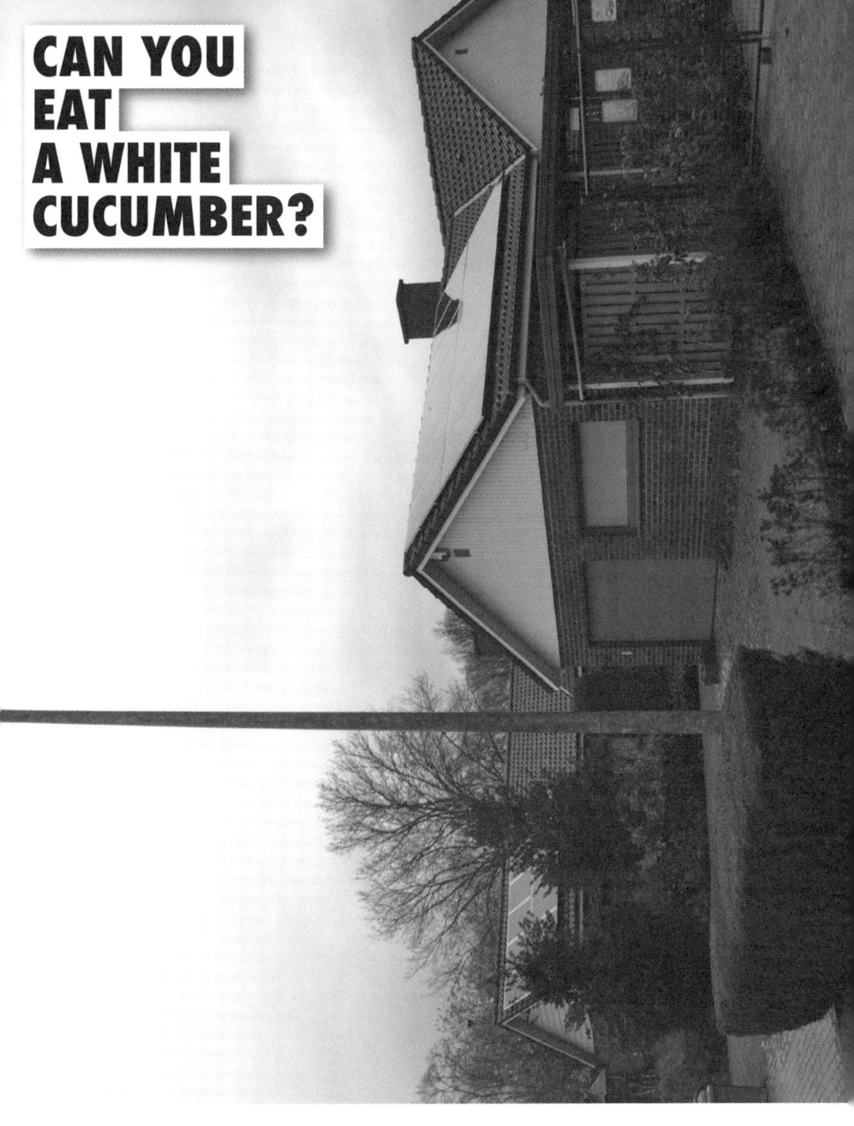

REMEMBER THOSE PALEO BAGELS I MADE THAT I WAS OBSESSED WITH?

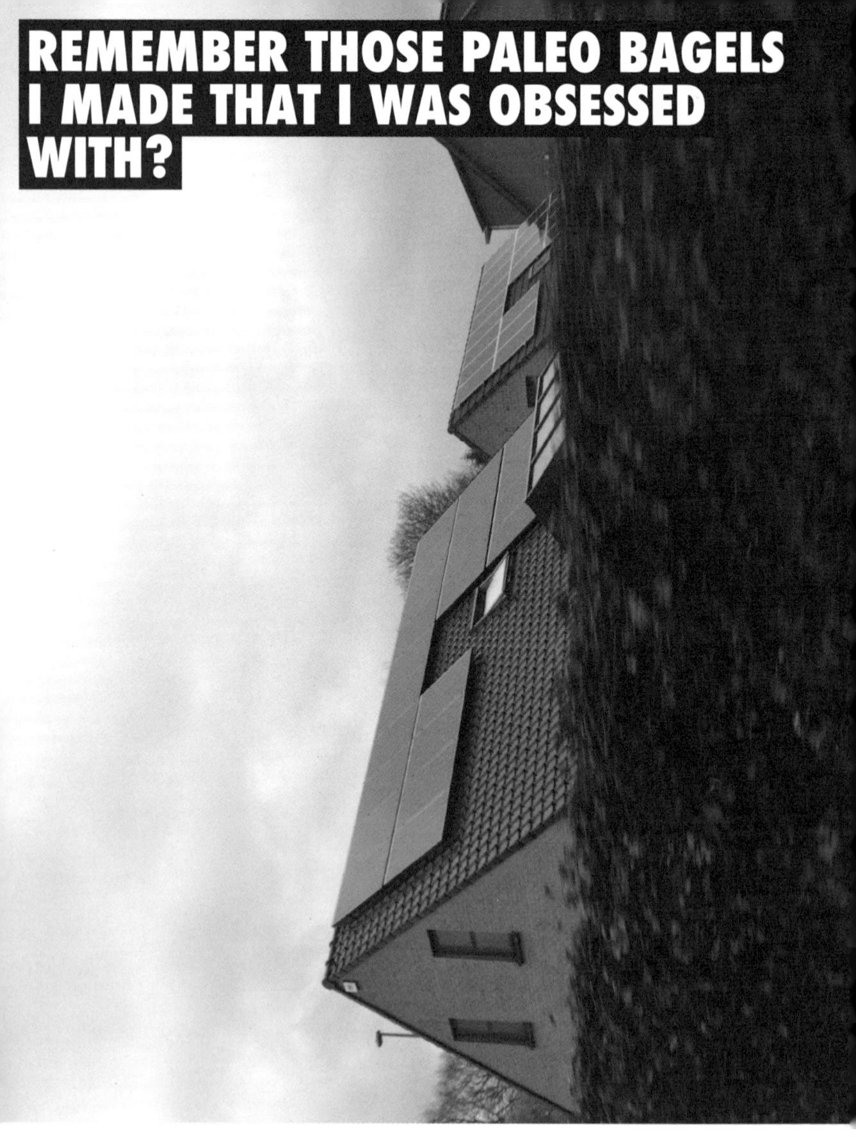

WELL PAST ME LOVES PRESENT ME AND LEFT SOME IN THE FREEZER TO ENJOY TODAY! BTW - STILL OBSESSED! I'M SO HAPPY TO BE BACK IN THE KITCH THIS MORNING. BAGEL TOASTING WITH AVOCADO, SAUTÉED KALE, @VITALFARMS EGG, AND CRUSHED RED PEPPER FOR MY SAVORY SOUL, AND HOMEMADE RASPBERRY CHIA COMPOTE (FRESH RASPBERRIES, CHIA SEEDS, @SUNPOTION CHAGA, AND A DROP OF MAPLE SYRUP) WITH @CRAZYRICHARDSPB, @PEARLBUTTER, AND CINNAMON!

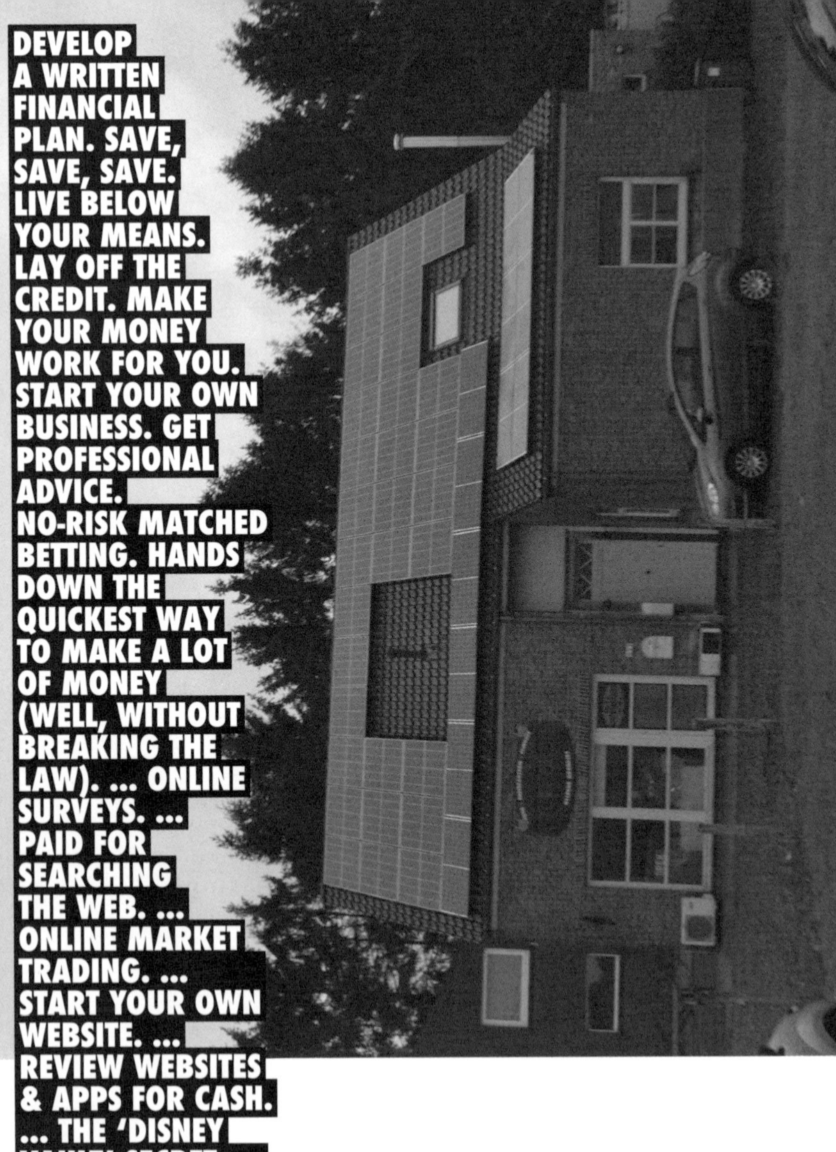

DEVELOP A WRITTEN FINANCIAL PLAN. SAVE, SAVE, SAVE. LIVE BELOW YOUR MEANS. LAY OFF THE CREDIT. MAKE YOUR MONEY WORK FOR YOU. START YOUR OWN BUSINESS. GET PROFESSIONAL ADVICE. NO-RISK MATCHED BETTING. HANDS DOWN THE QUICKEST WAY TO MAKE A LOT OF MONEY (WELL, WITHOUT BREAKING THE LAW). ... ONLINE SURVEYS. ... PAID FOR SEARCHING THE WEB. ... ONLINE MARKET TRADING. ... START YOUR OWN WEBSITE. ... REVIEW WEBSITES & APPS FOR CASH. ... THE ‘DISNEY VAULT’ SECRET. ... ‘GET PAID TO’ SITES.

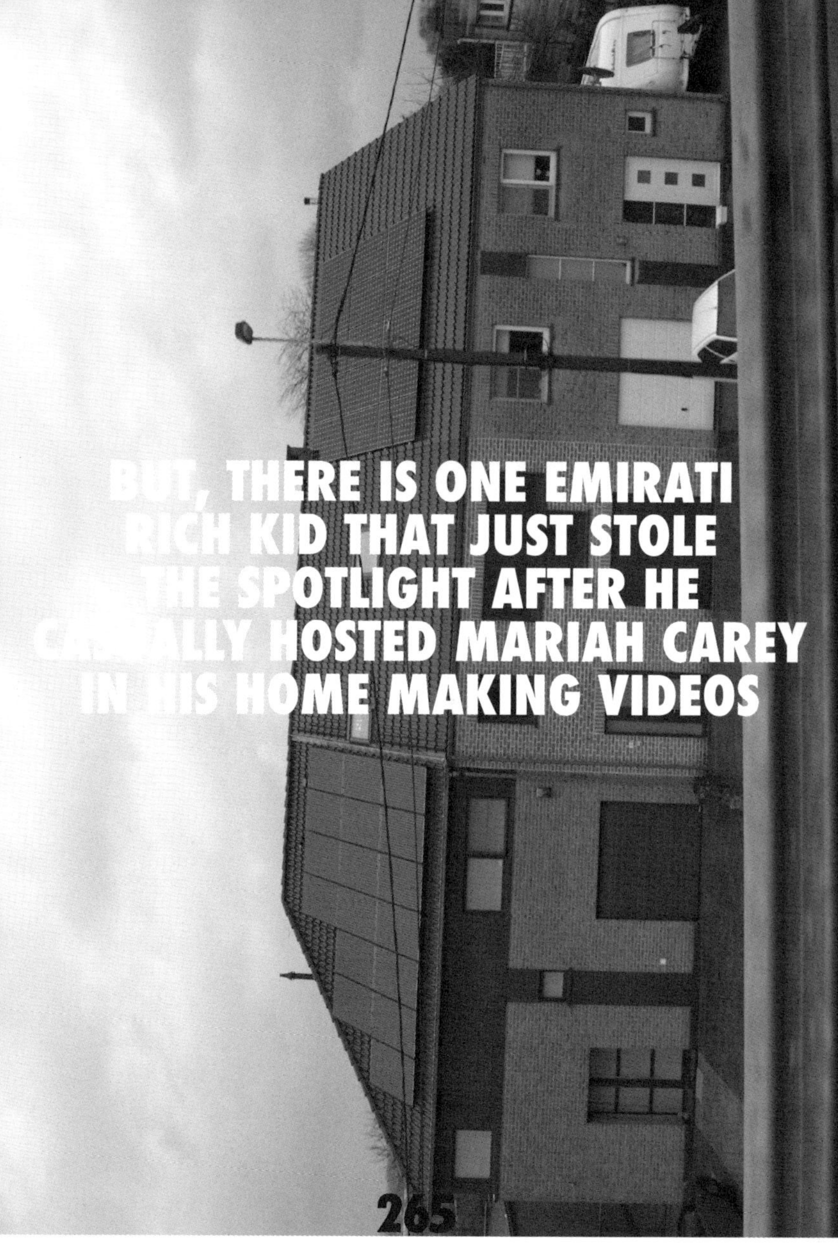

BUT, THERE IS ONE EMIRATI RICH KID THAT JUST STOLE THE SPOTLIGHT AFTER HE CASUALLY HOSTED MARIAH CAREY IN HIS HOME MAKING VIDEOS

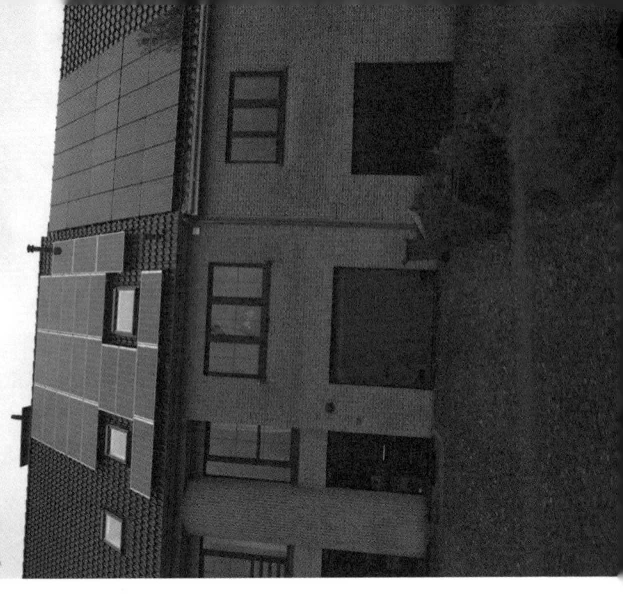

FROM ABOVE, YOU COULD CALCULATE THAT TO HAVE A YOUTUBER MAKE A VIDEO AND POST IT TO THEIR CHANNEL YOU WOULD BE PAYING ROUGHLY $10,000 FOR 100,000 VIEWS, WHICH BREAKS DOWN TO $100 PER 1,000 VIEWS.

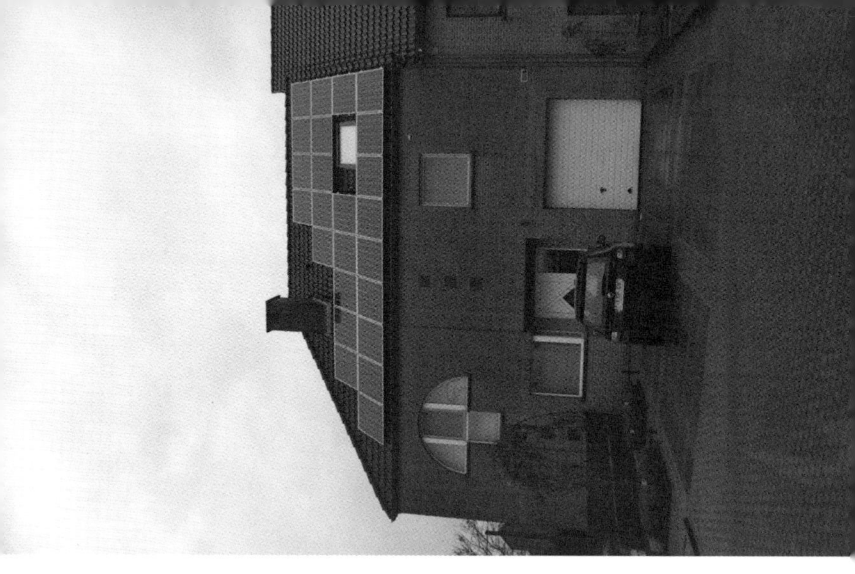

WHAT IS MEANT BY MINIMAL ART?

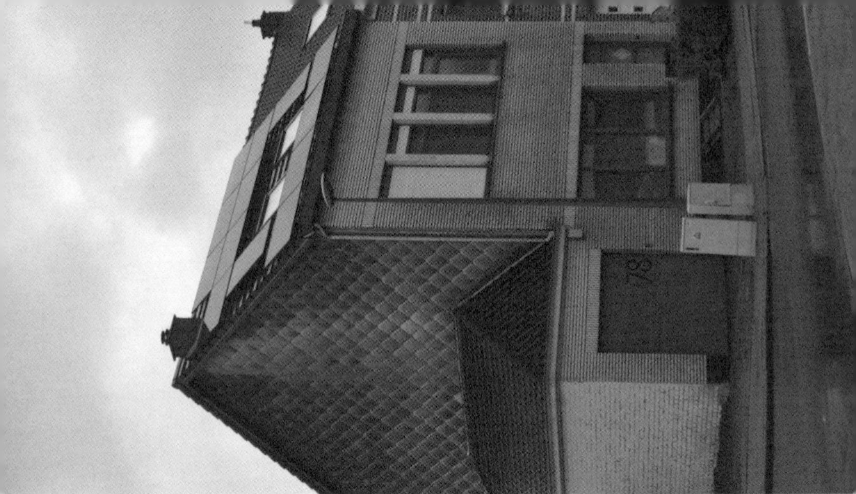

WHAT IS THE MAIN SUBJECT OF A COLOR FIELD PAINTING?

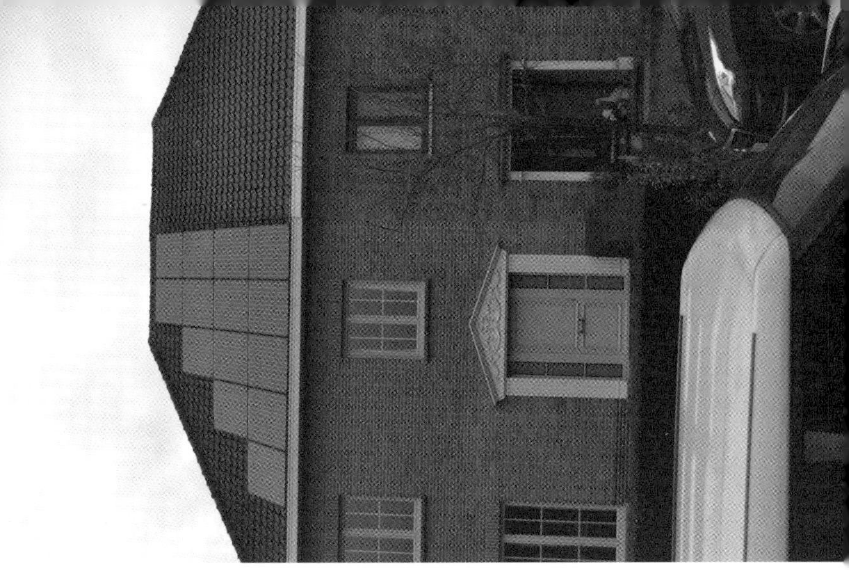

WHAT IS THE MINIMALIST LIFESTYLE?

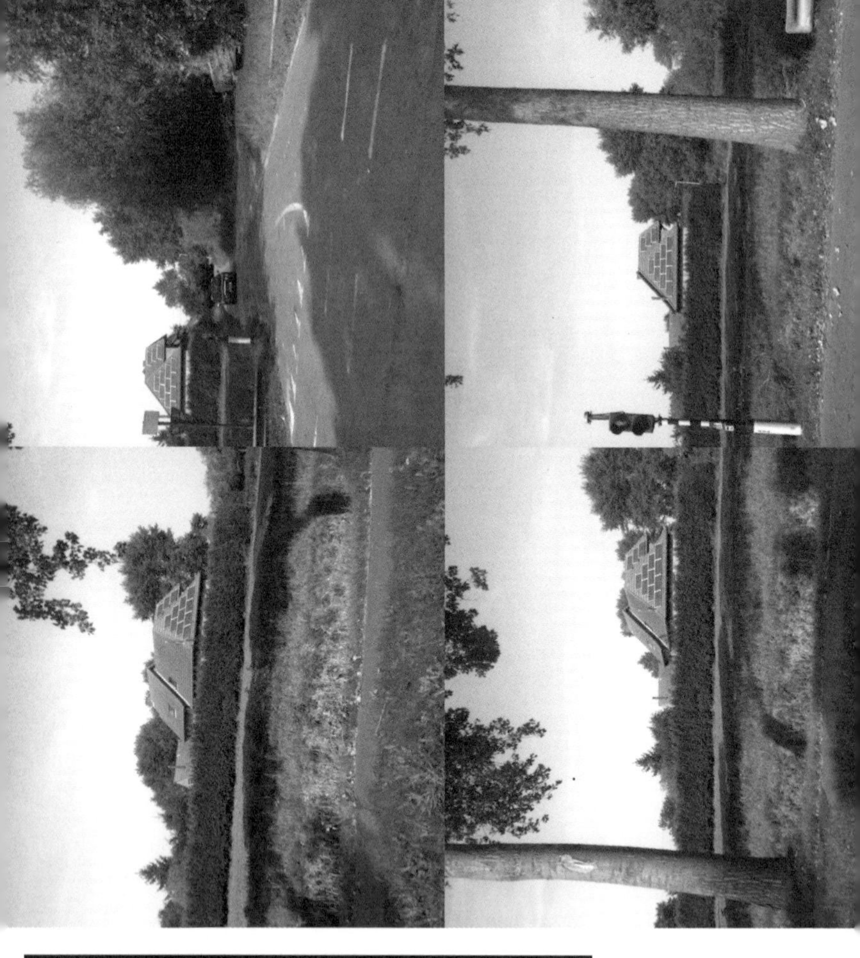

WHAT IS THE DEFINITION OF MINIMALIST?

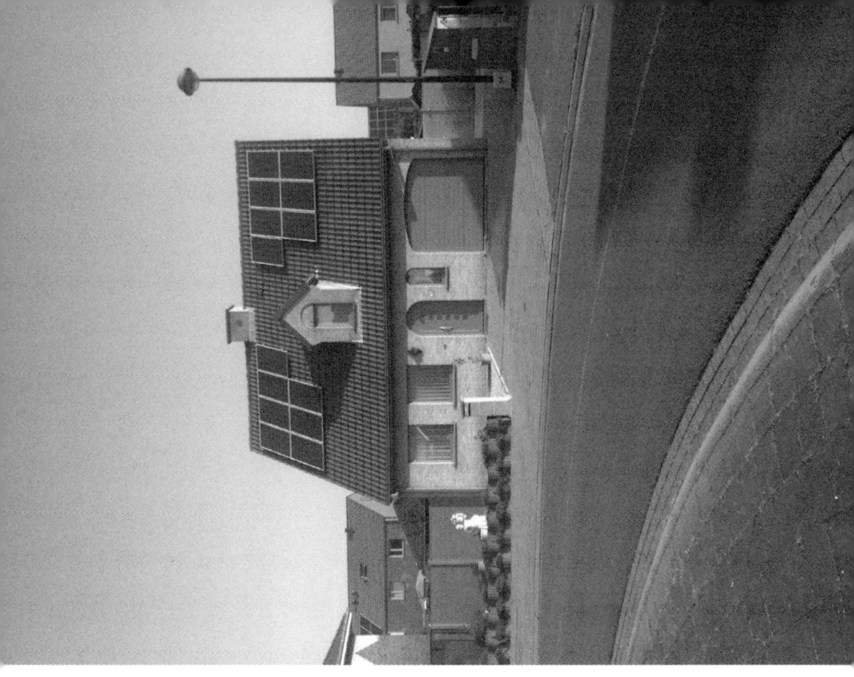

WHAT IS A MINIMAL TATTOO?

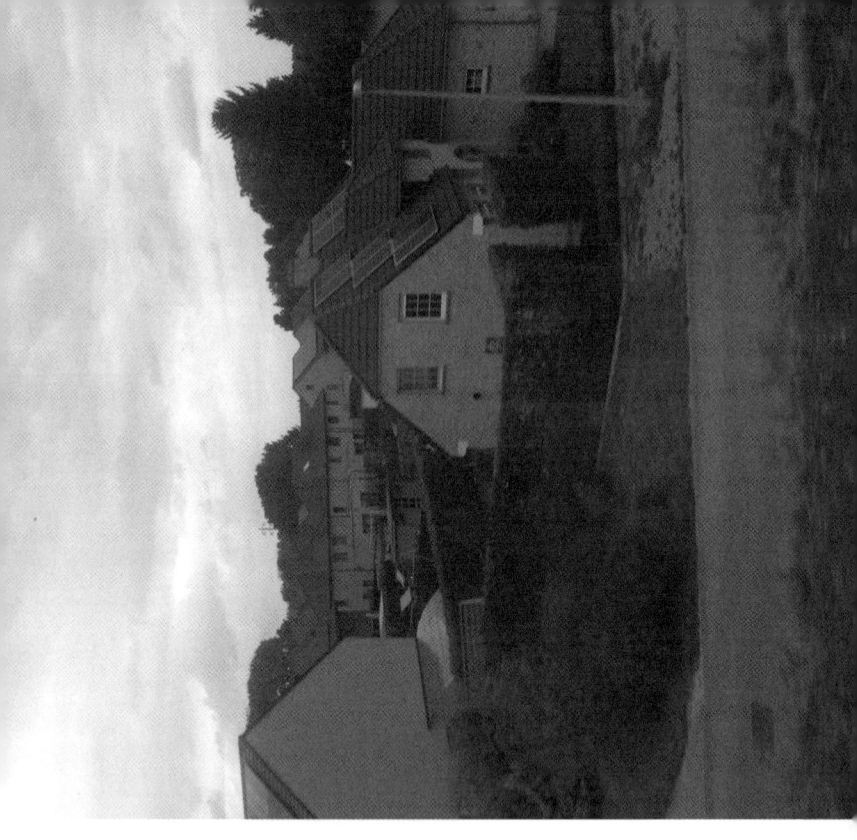

HOW DO I BECOME A MINIMALIST?

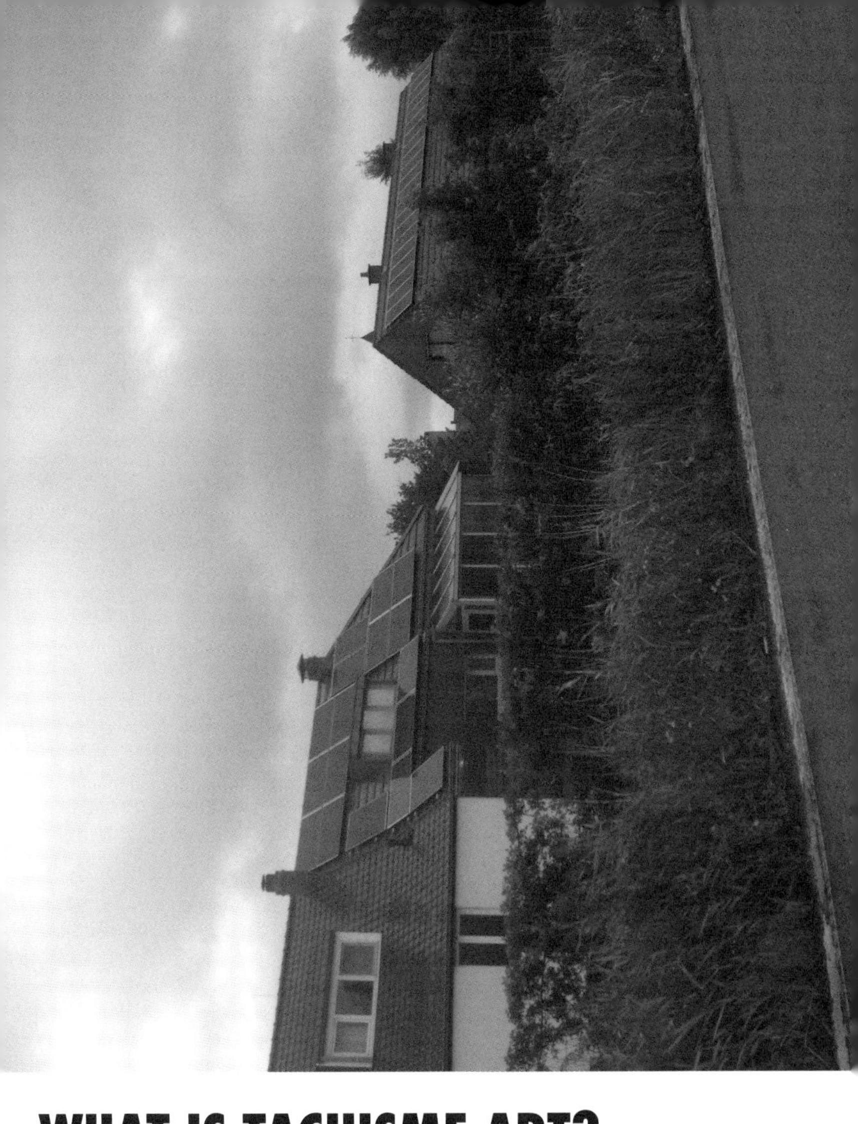

WHAT IS TACHISME ART?

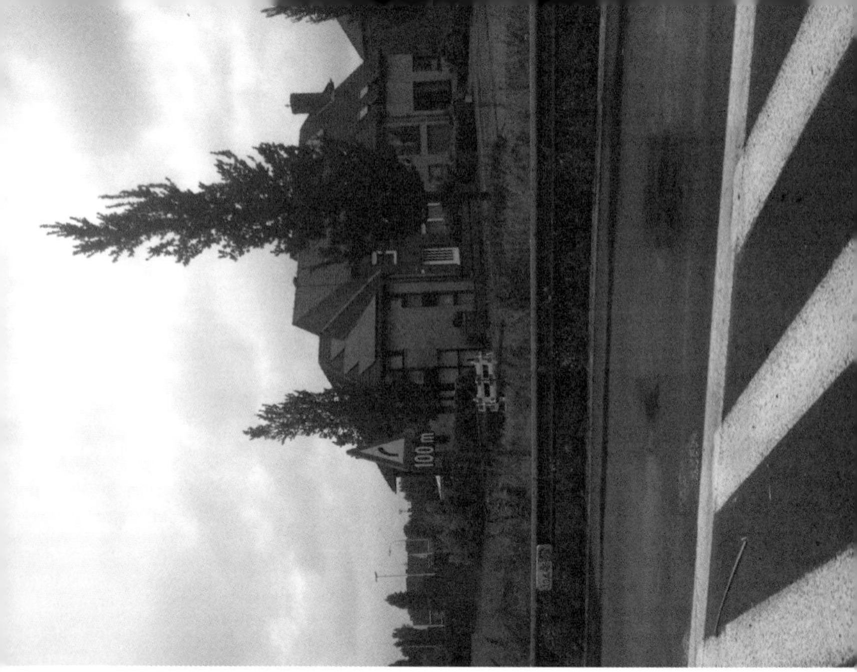

WRITE IT DOWN. MAKE A LIST OF ALL THE REASONS YOU WANT TO LIVE MORE SIMPLY. ... DISCARD THE DUPLICATES. ... DECLARE A CLUTTER-FREE ZONE. ... TRAVEL LIGHTLY. ... DRESS WITH LESS. ... EAT SIMILAR MEALS. ... SAVE $1000.

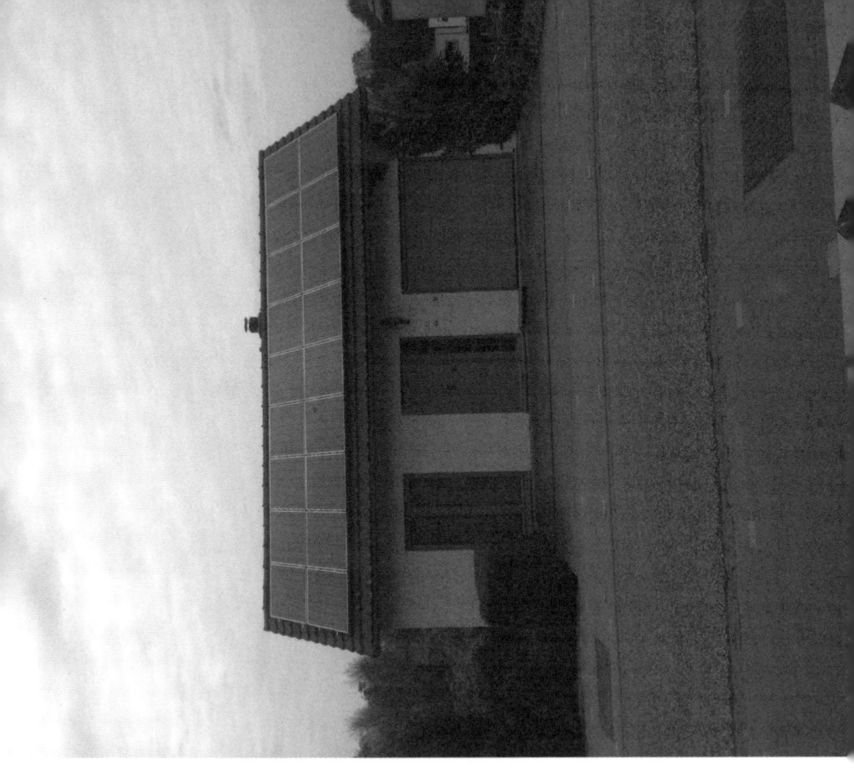

WHAT IS AN EXAMPLE OF OUTSIDER ART?

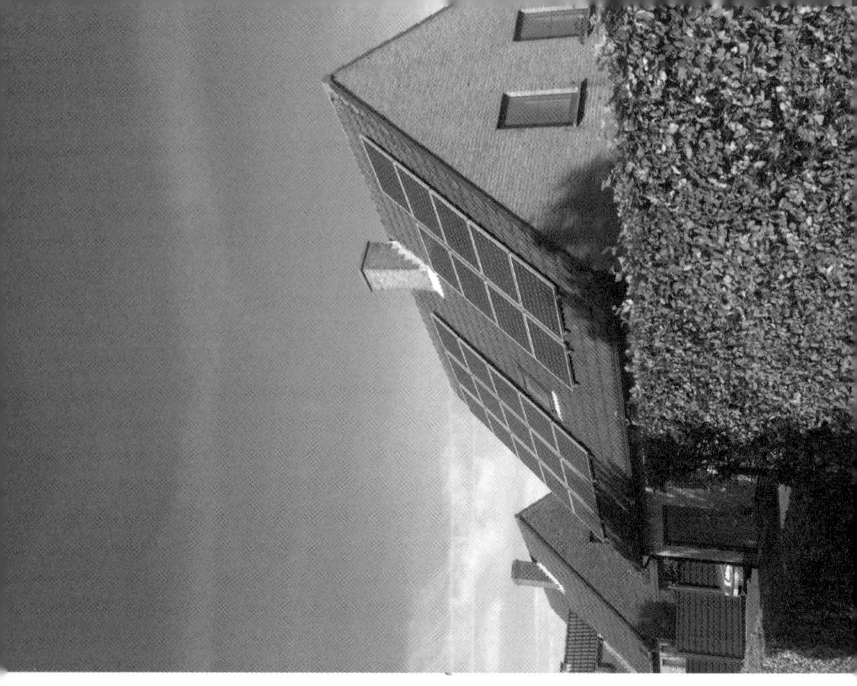

AVOCADO TOAST 4 WAYS:
SPICE UP YOUR AVOCADO TOAST GAME!
STARTING CLOCKWISE:
1. MASHED AVOCADO - TRIED AND TRUE, PERFECT FOR WHEN YOU'RE IN A HURRY OR WHEN THE AVOCADO IS RIPE
2. CUBED AVOCADO - MIX IT UP, STACK THOSE CUBES ON UP TO ADD DENSITY TO YOUR TOAST
3. SLICED AVOCADO - GET THOSE SLICES DOWN, IT'S A GREAT START TO WORKING ON YOUR AVO ROSE
4. AVOCADO ROSE - FOR THAT SPECIAL SOMEONE OR WHEN YOU WANT TO TREAT YOURSELF BECAUSE YOU DESERVE IT!

WHAT IS A NAIVE ARTIST?

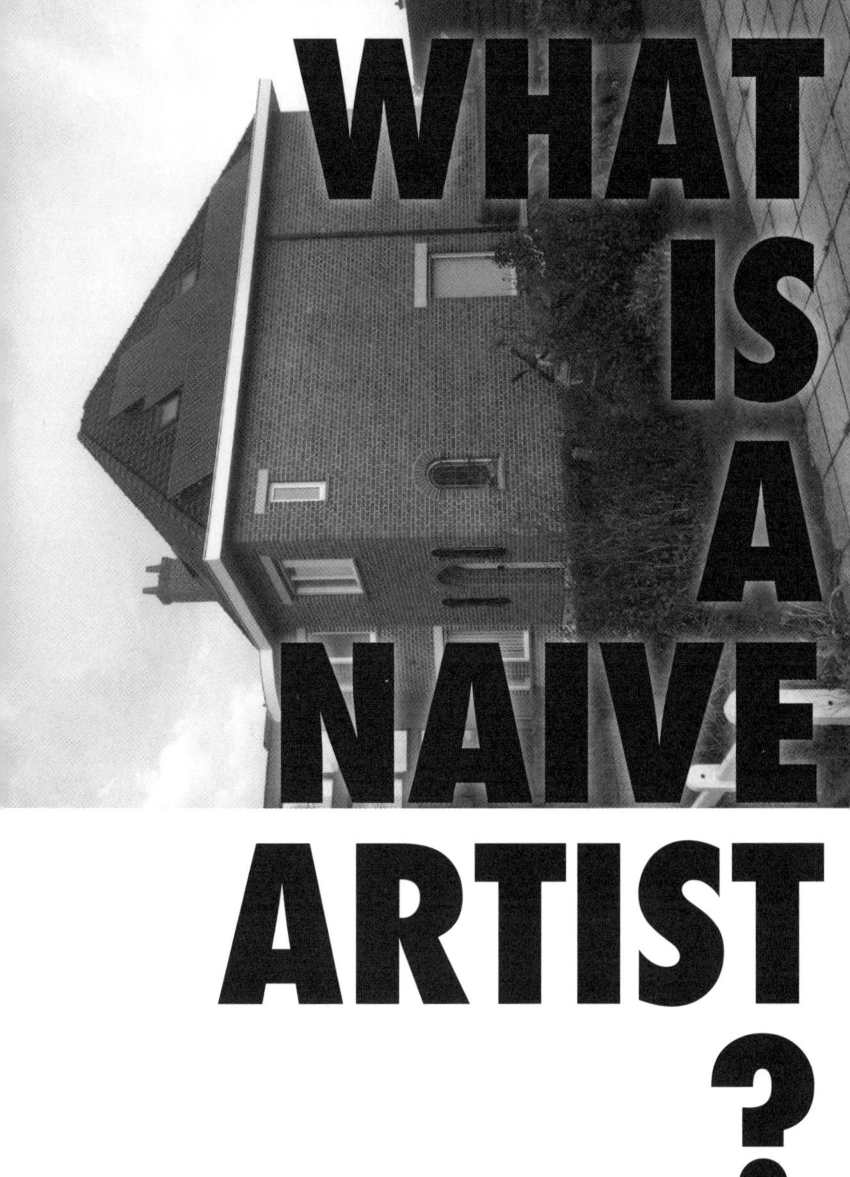

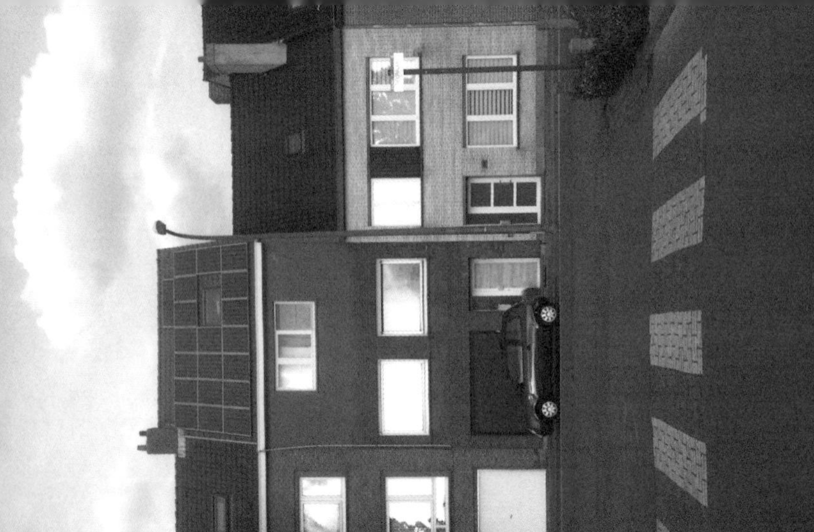

TAKE THAT FIRST STEP, THE FIRST STEP TOWARDS GETTING SOMEWHERE IS DECIDING YOU ARE NOT GOING TO STAY WHERE YOU ARE CREATE A TEXTURED BACKGROUND. ... TAPE LINES AT INTERSECTING POINTS ACROSS THE CANVAS. ... MIX YOUR PAINT COLORS. ... PAINT IN THE SPACES BETWEEN THE TAPE. ... REMOVE THE TAPE. ... FILL IN THE BLANK SPACE FROM THE TAPE, OPTIONAL.

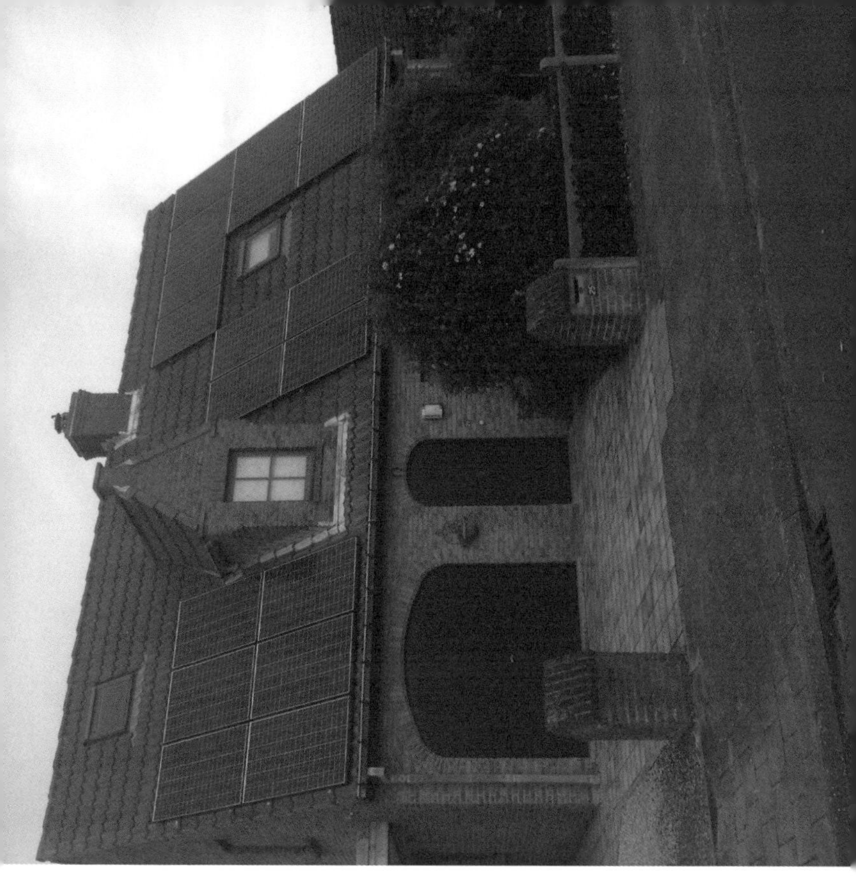

IT GOES, IT GOES, IT GOES, IT GOES
IT GOES, IT GOES, IT GOES, IT GOES
IF

IF IT'S AN ALMOST HIGH TECH UTOPIA, THEN VAPING SEEMS LIKE IT WOULD BE MORE ATTAINABLE HOWEVER IF WE'RE TALKING ABOUT SLUMS AND POOR AREAS WHERE PEOPLE ARE PUTTING TOGETHER COMPUTERS AND TERMINALS WITH PARTS FROM THE 1980'S, THEN I WOULD ASSUME CIGARETTES WOULD BE MORE ACCESSIBLE TO THEM

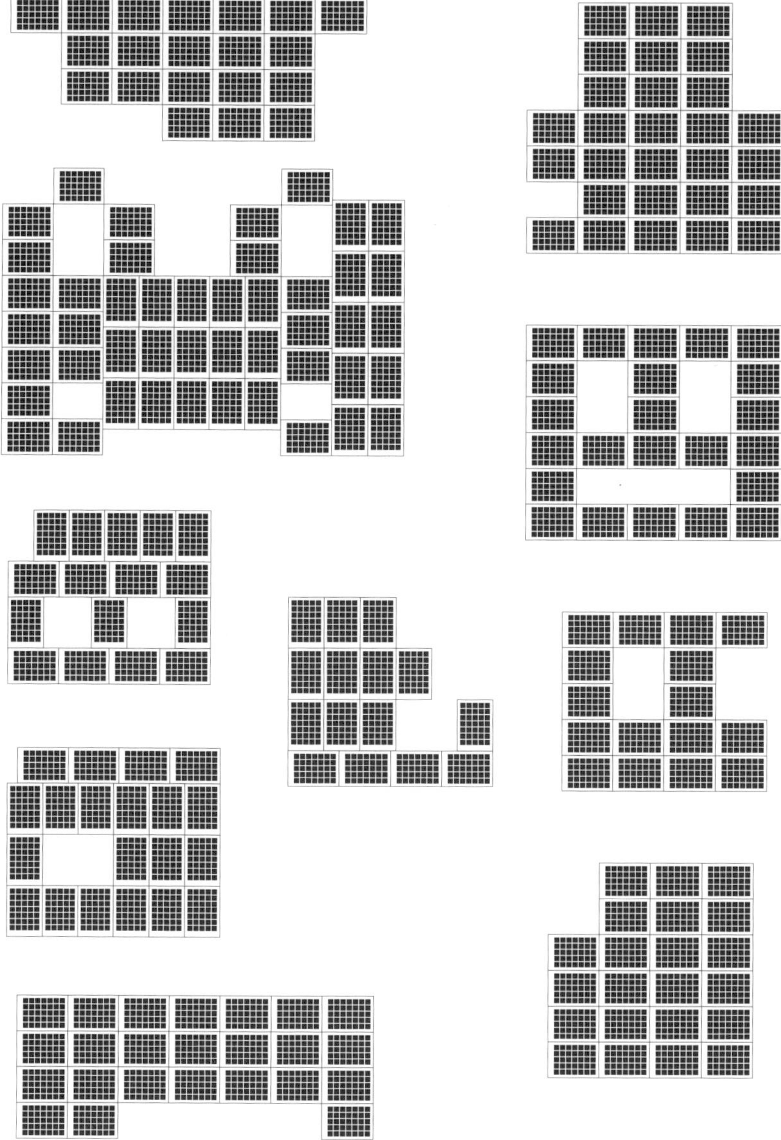

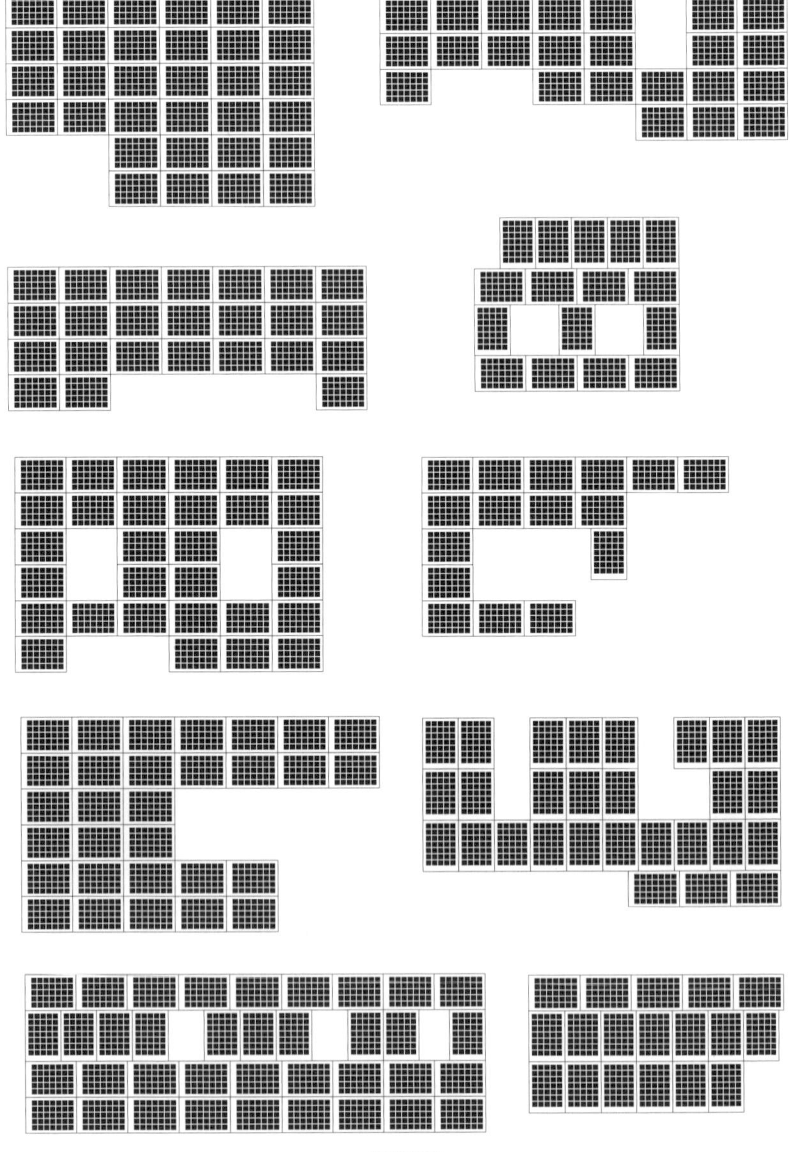

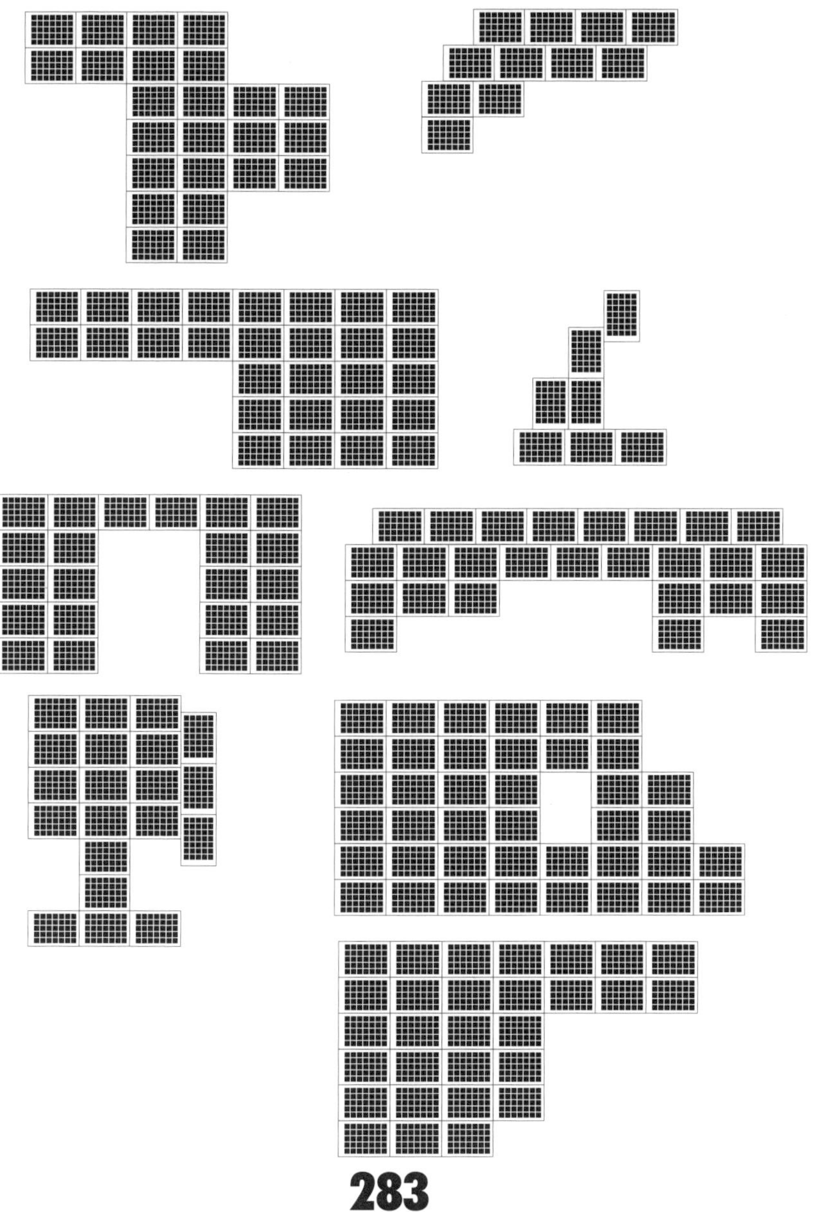

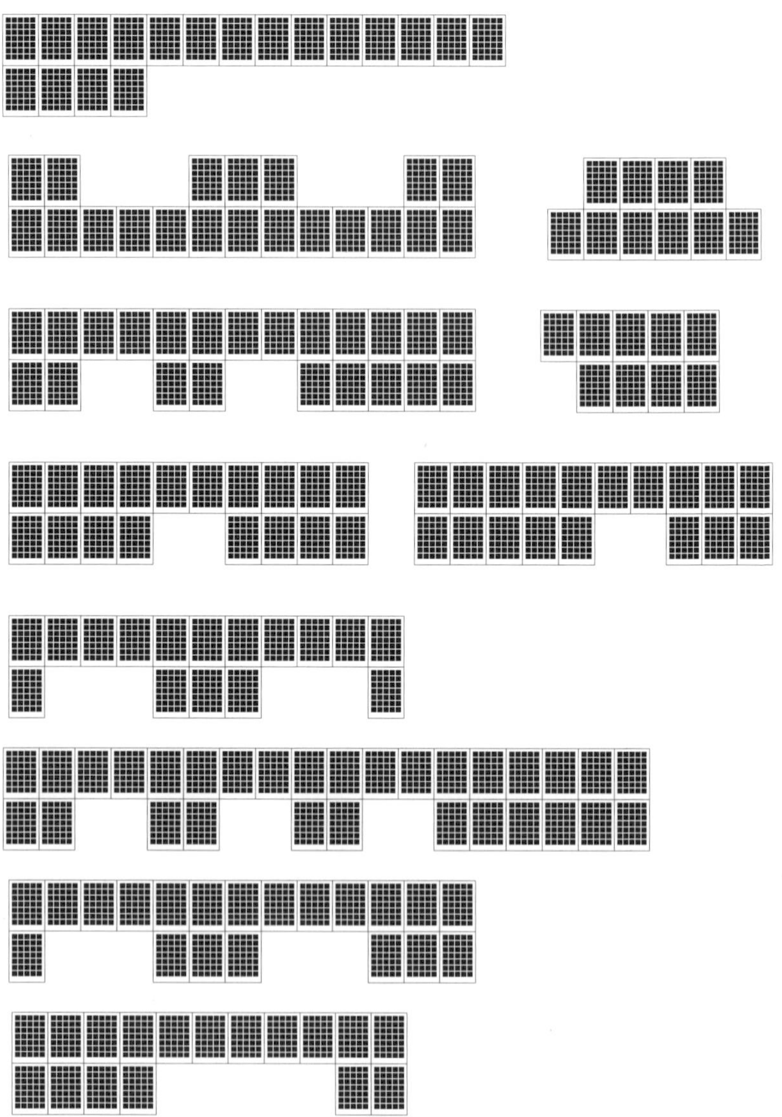

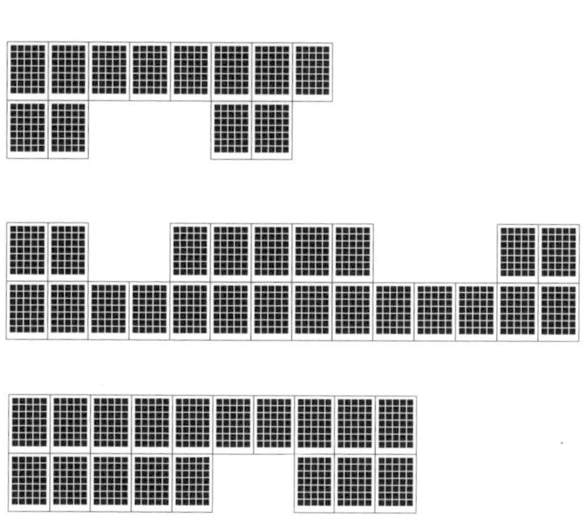

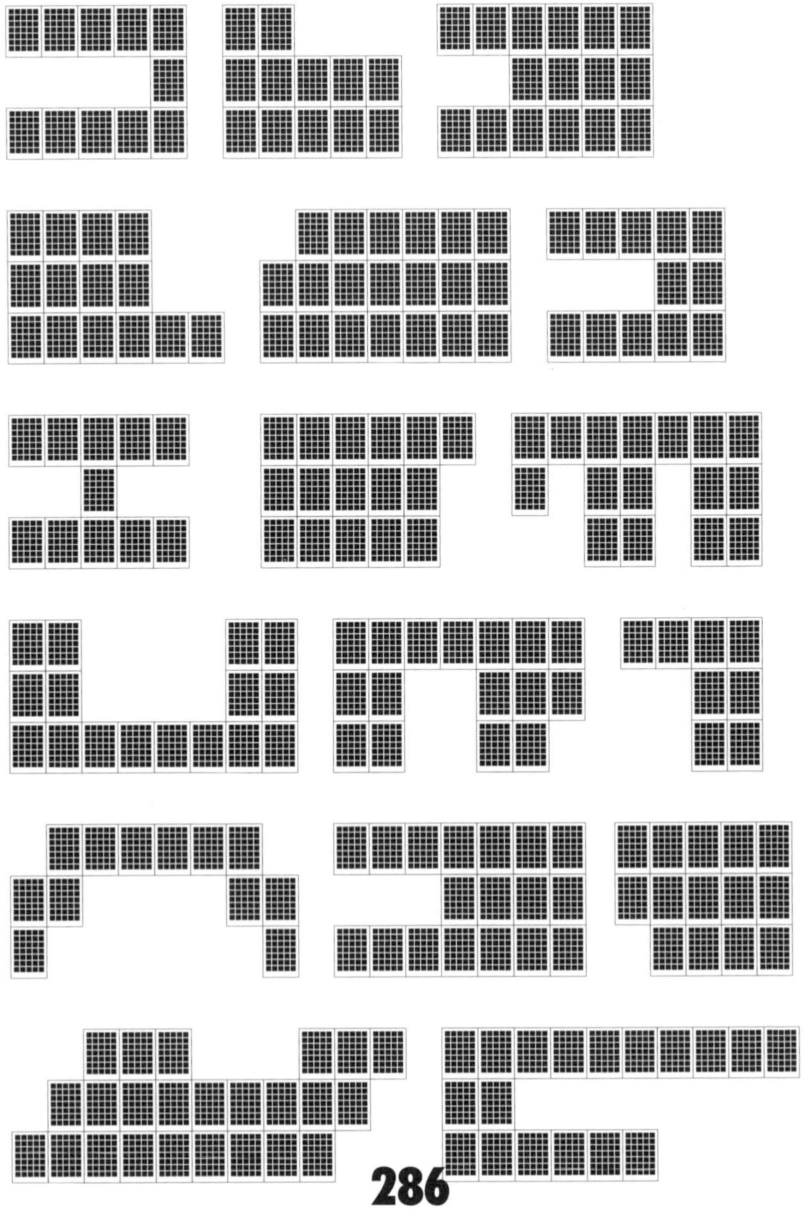

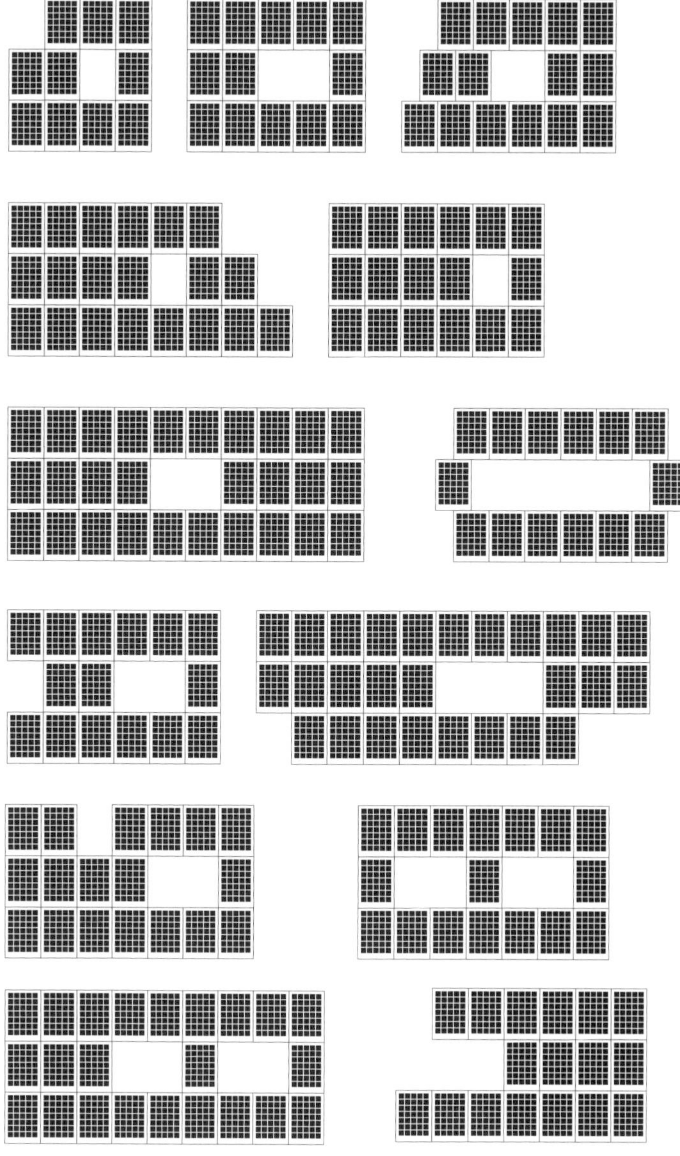

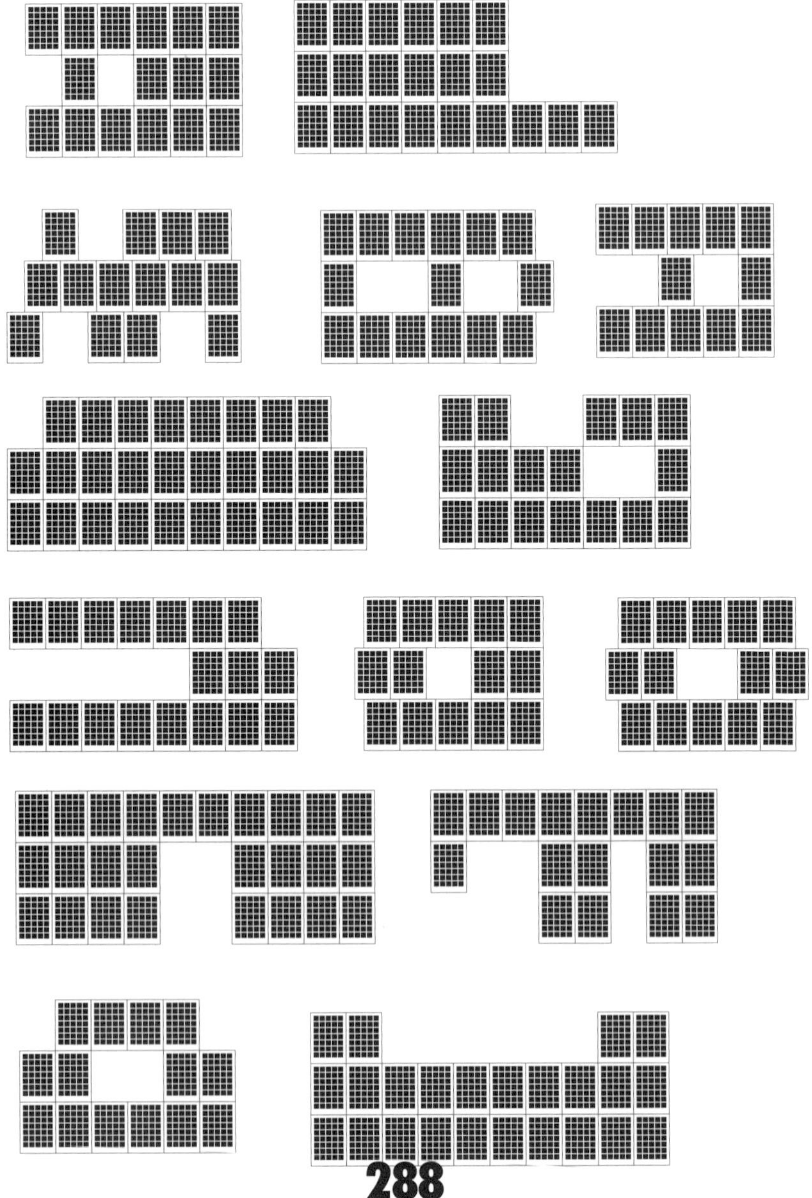

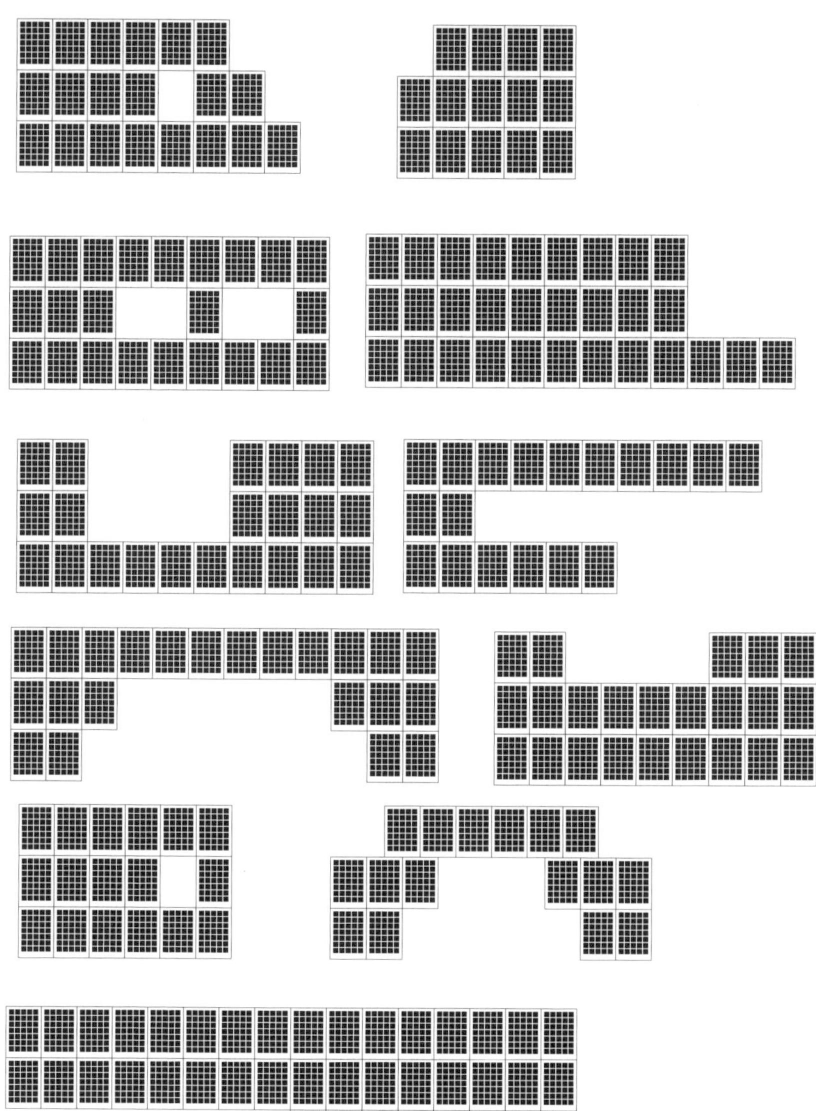

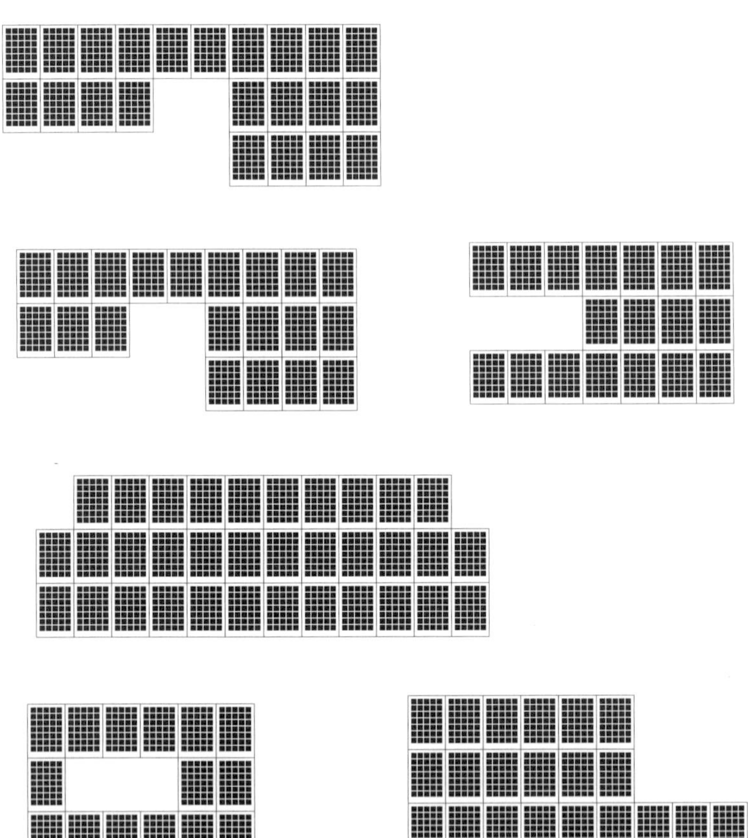

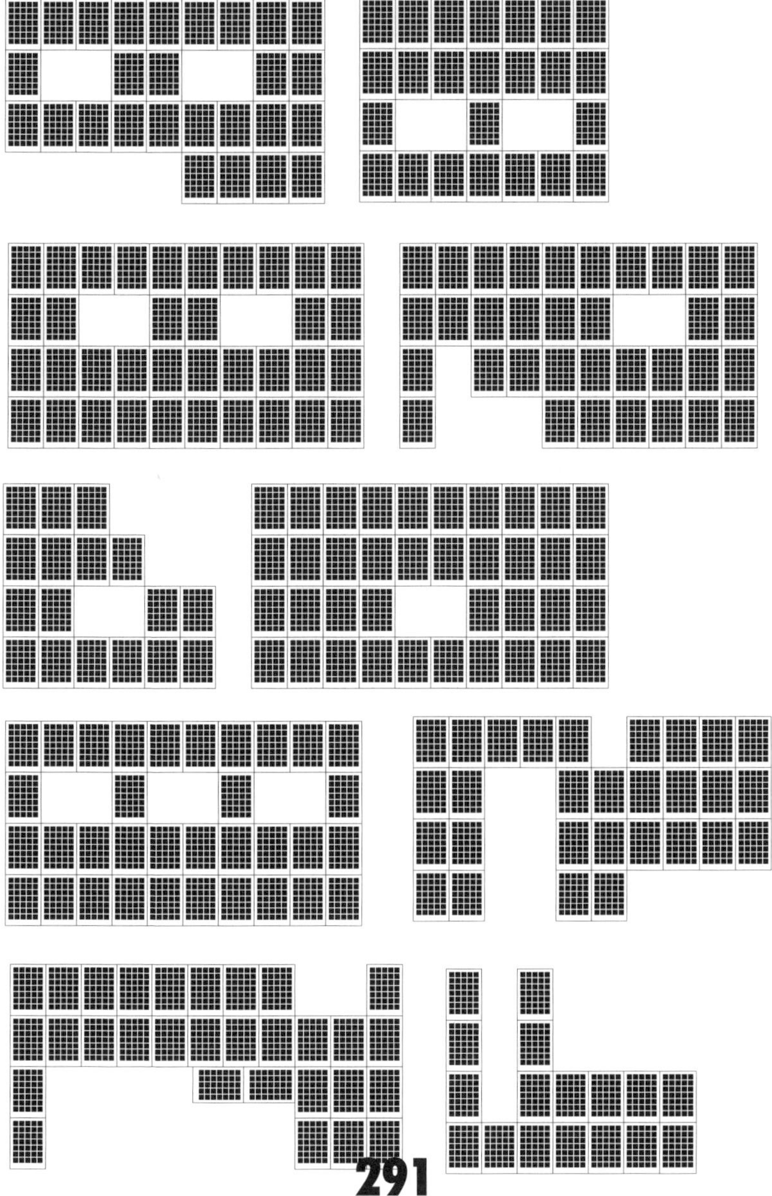

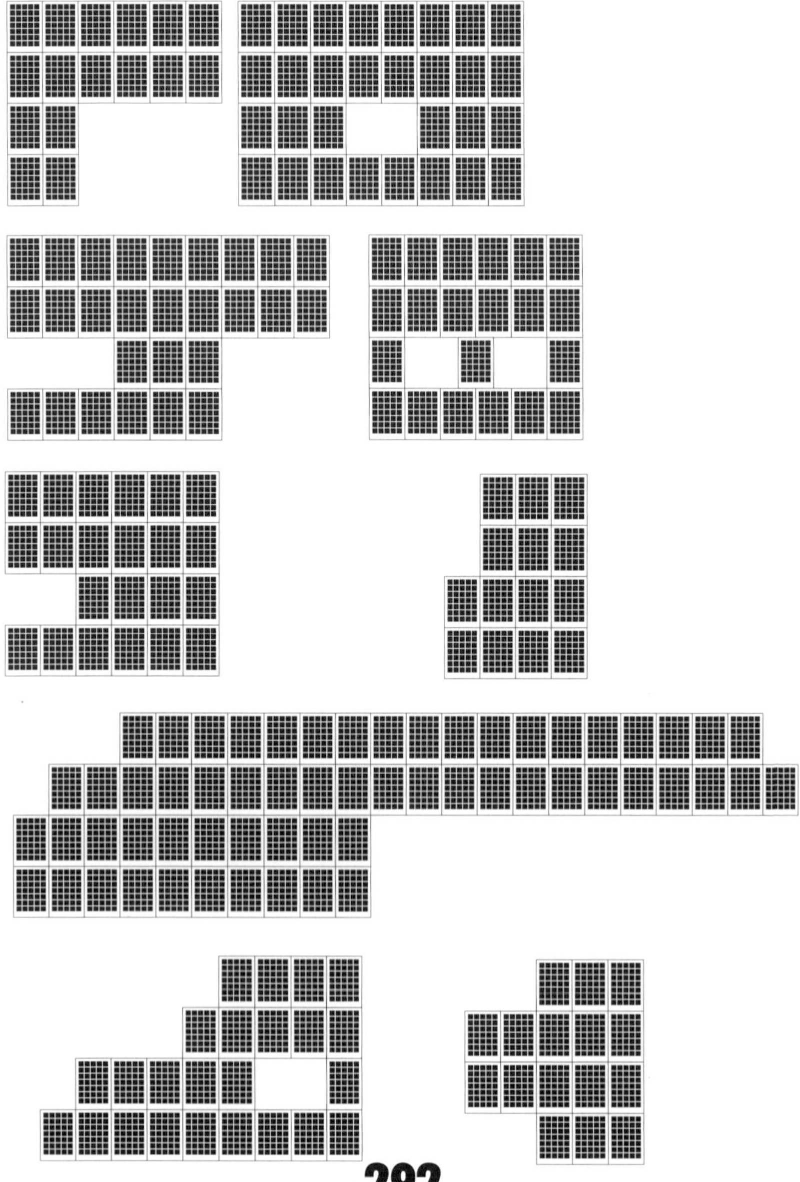

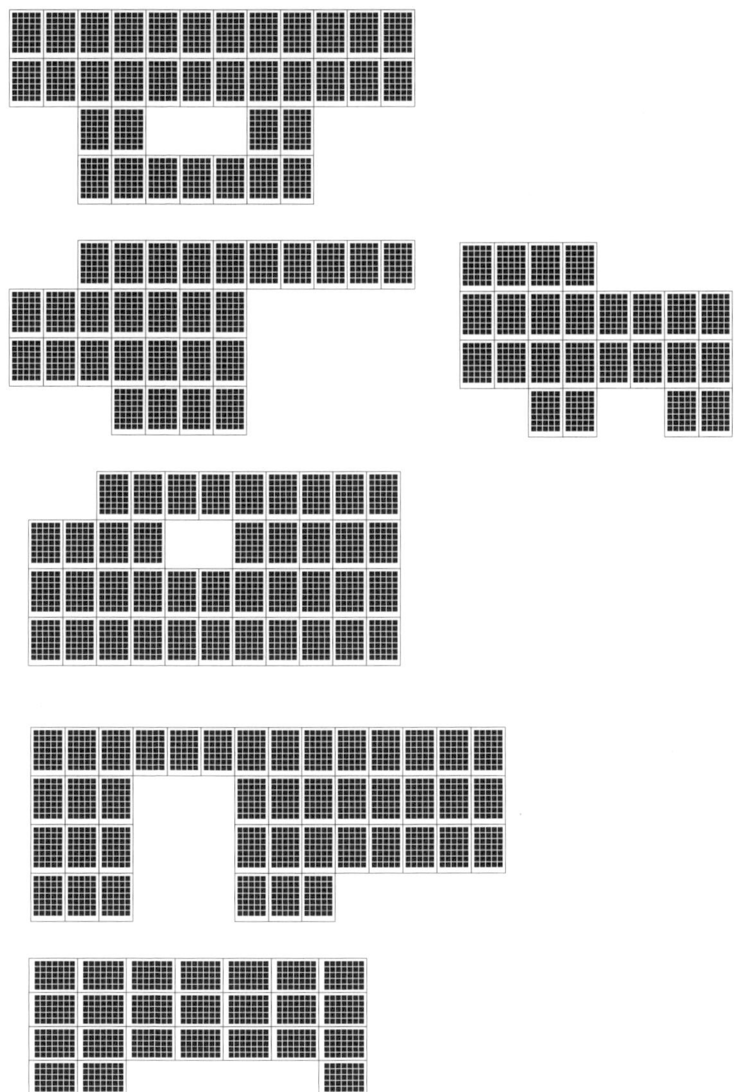

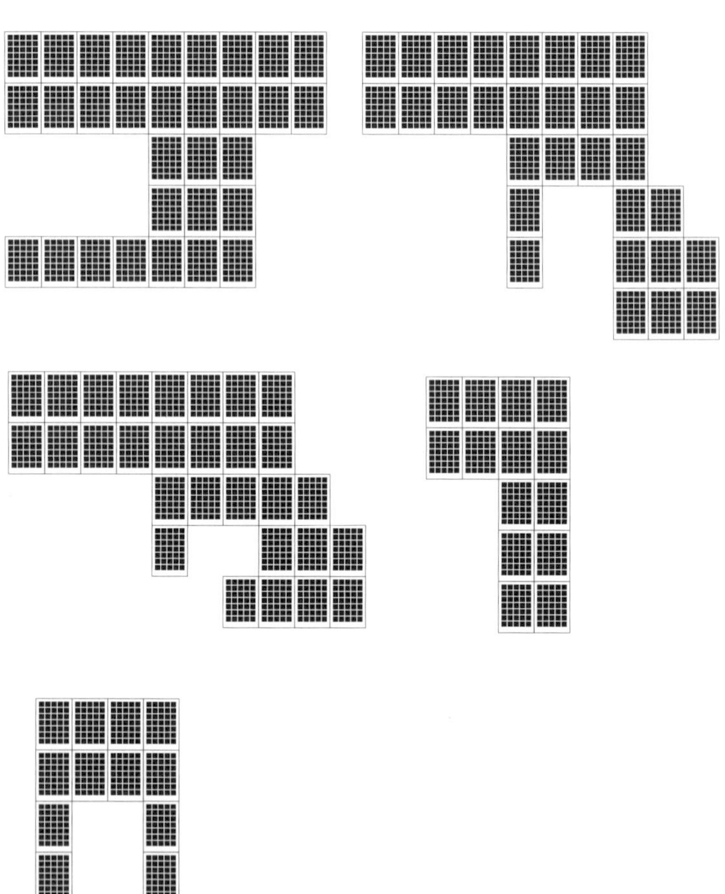

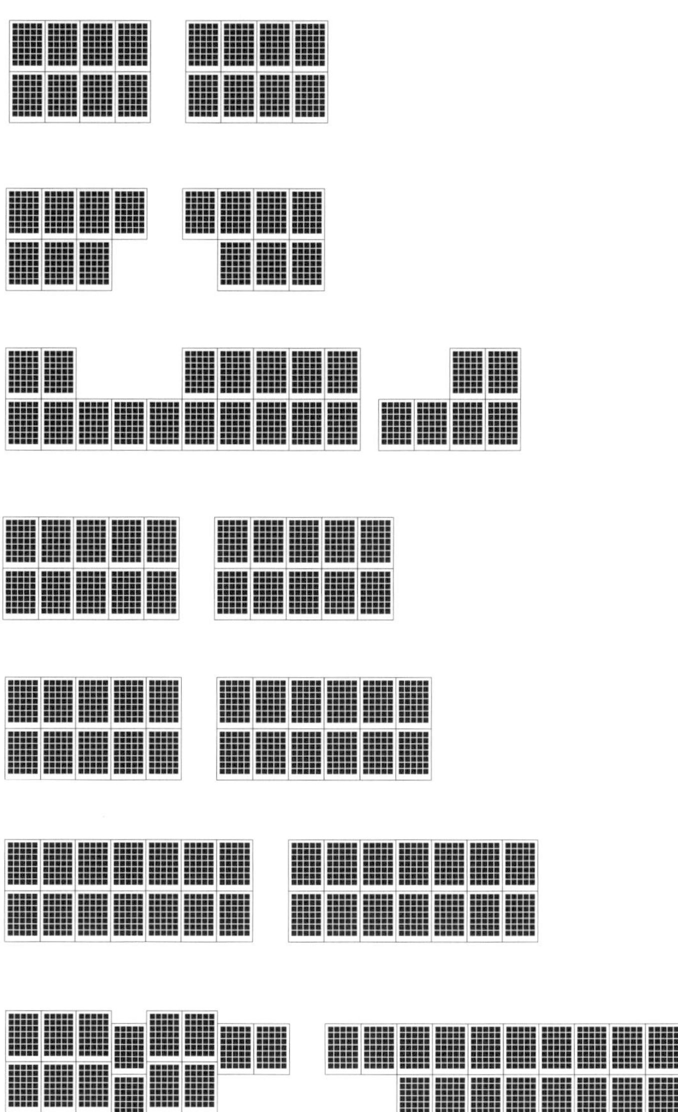

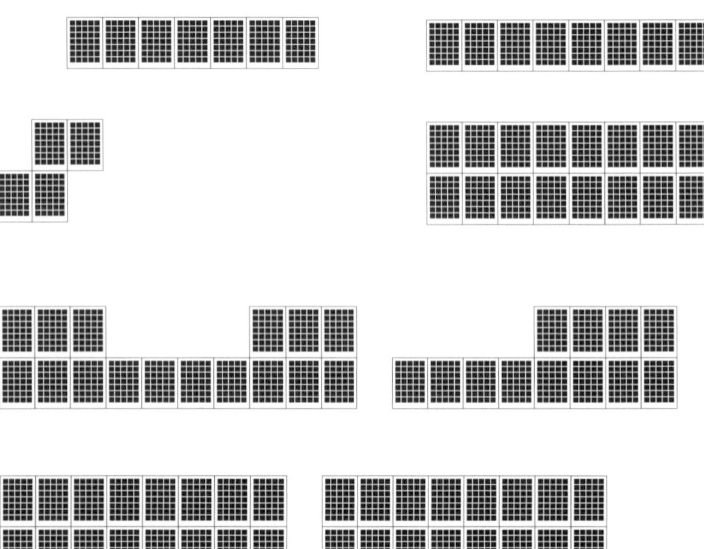

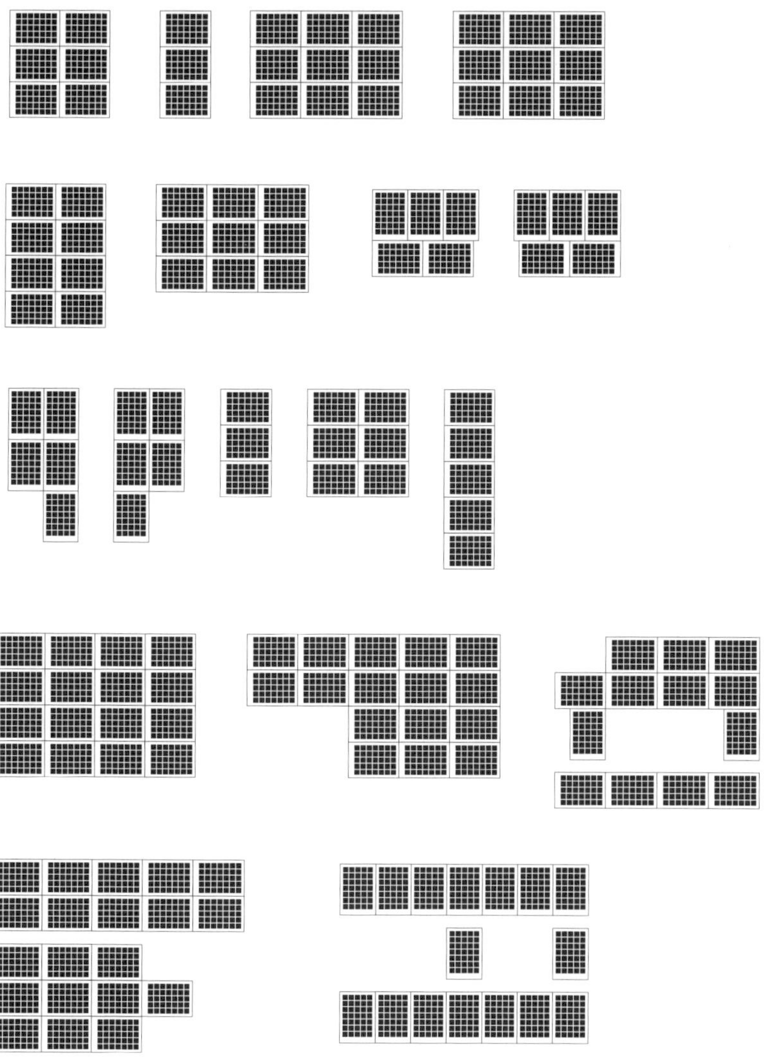

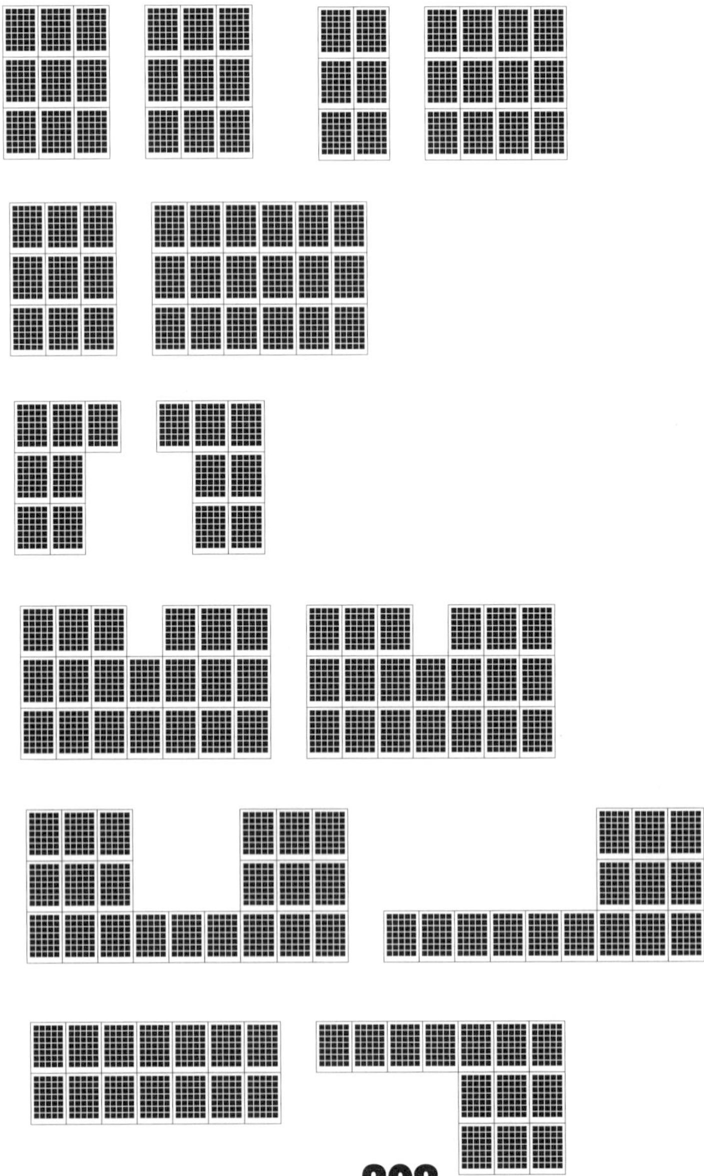

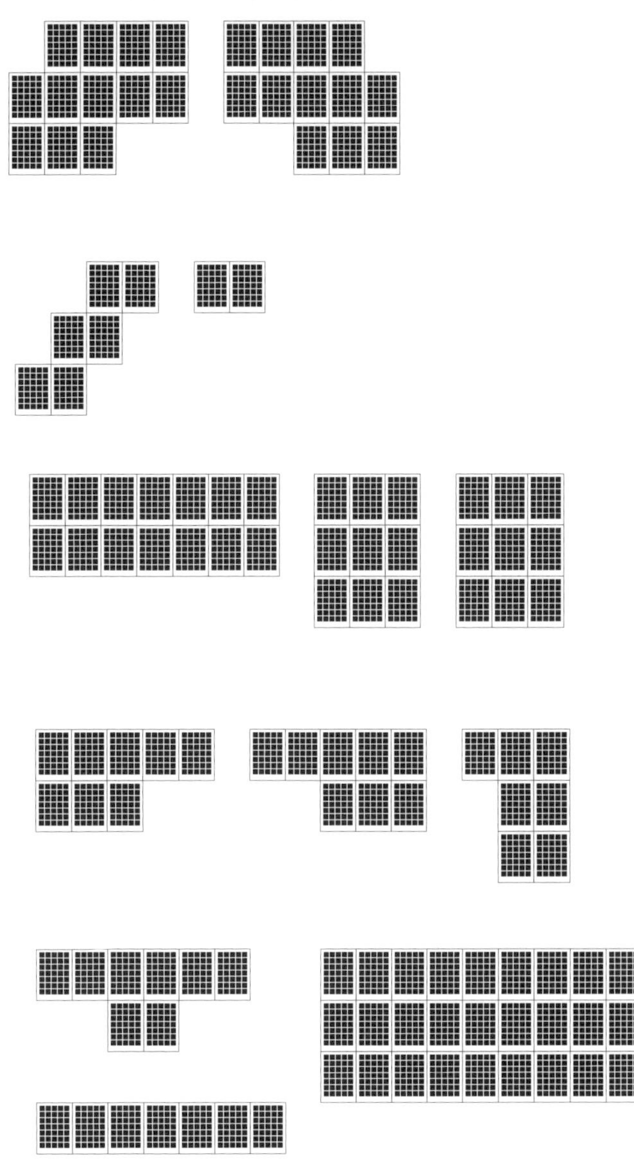

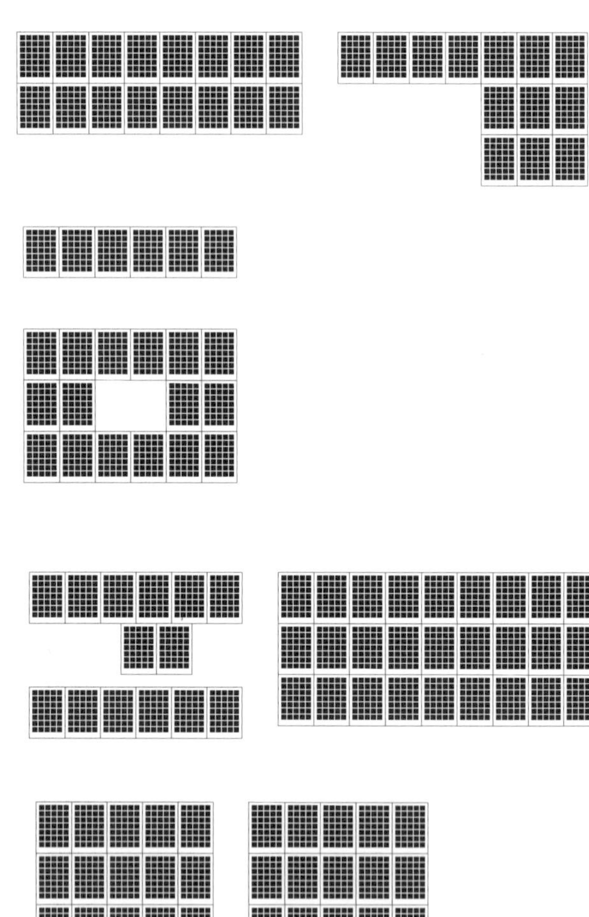

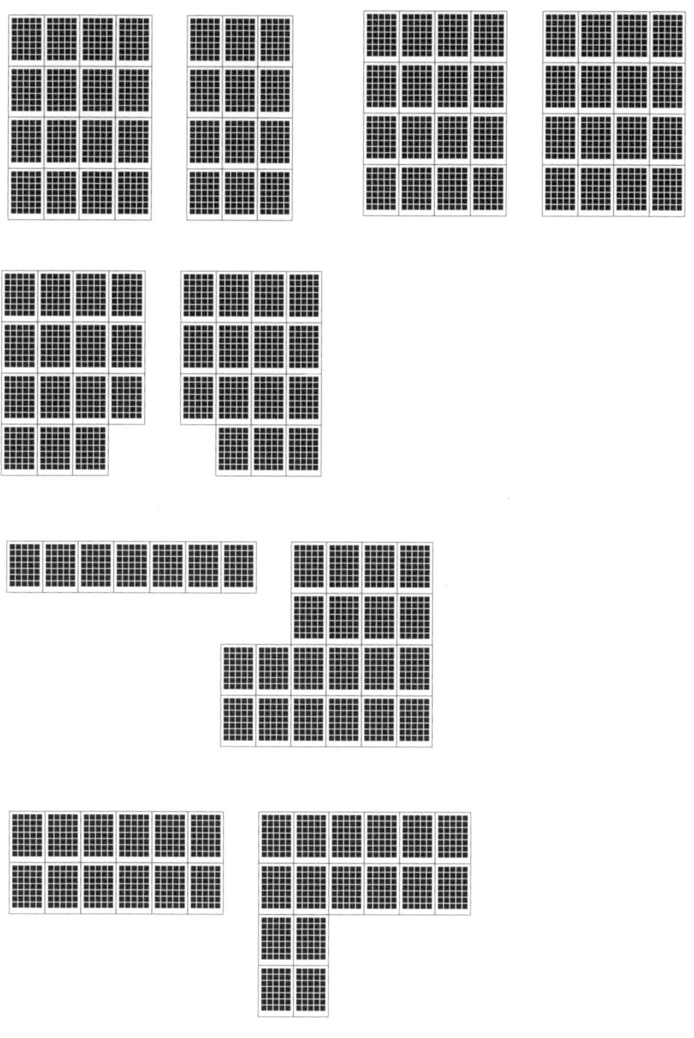

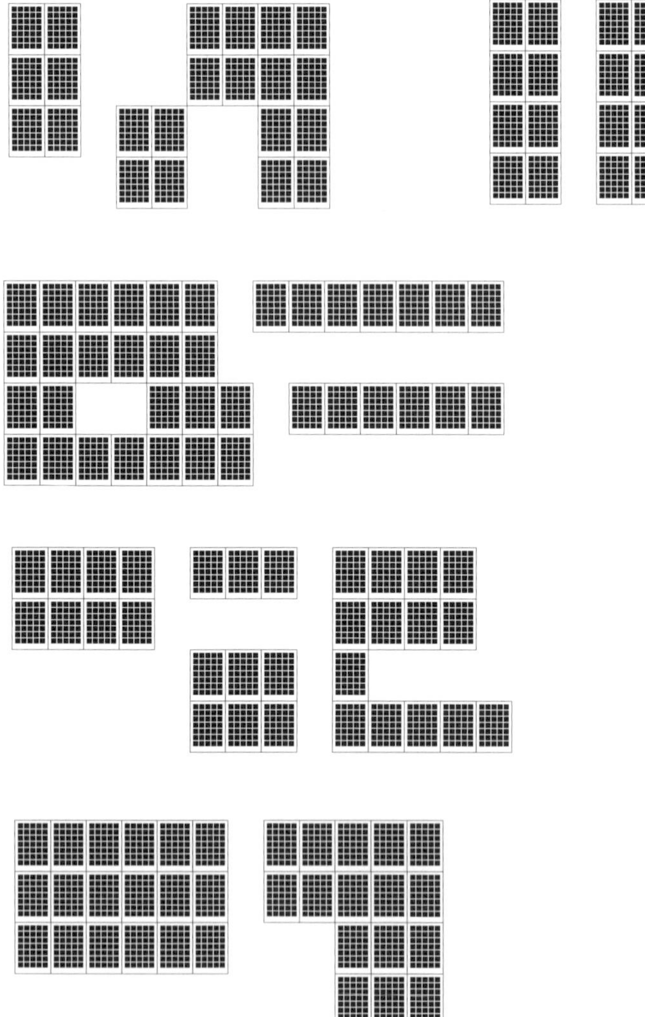

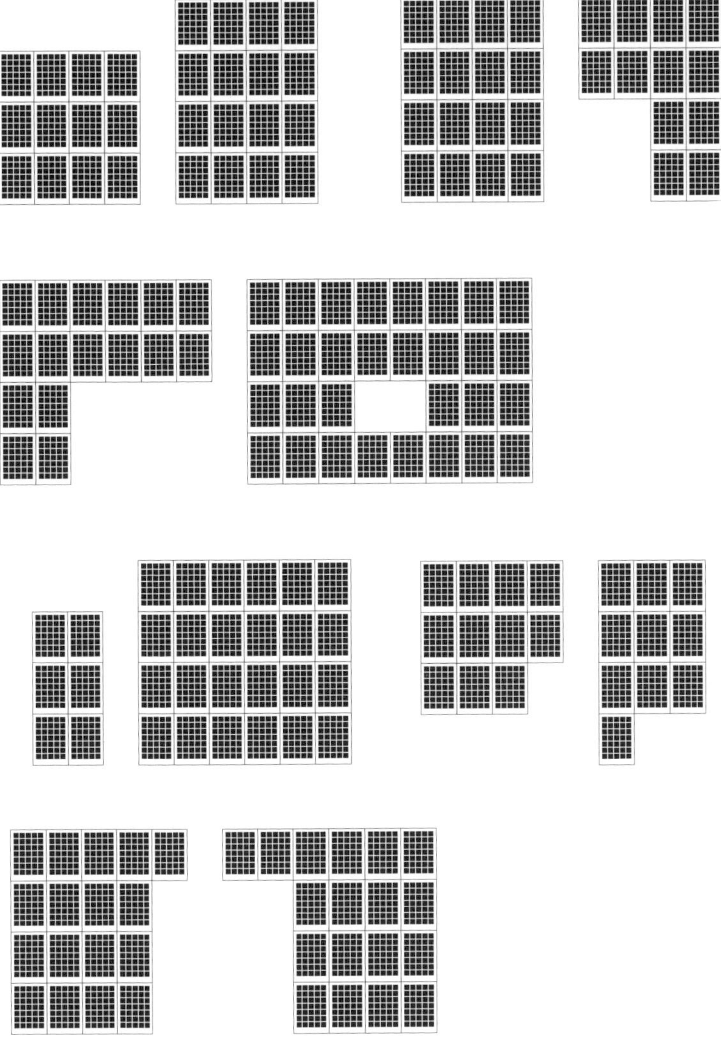

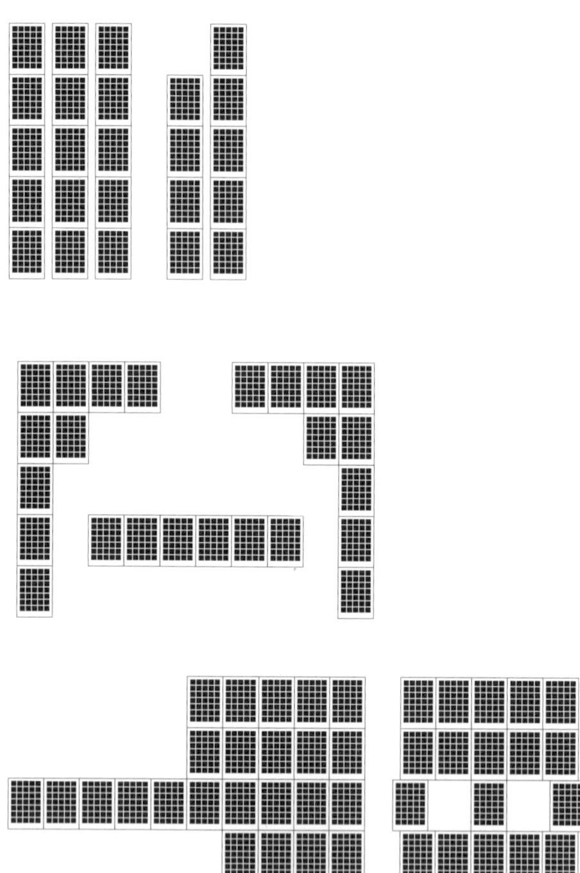

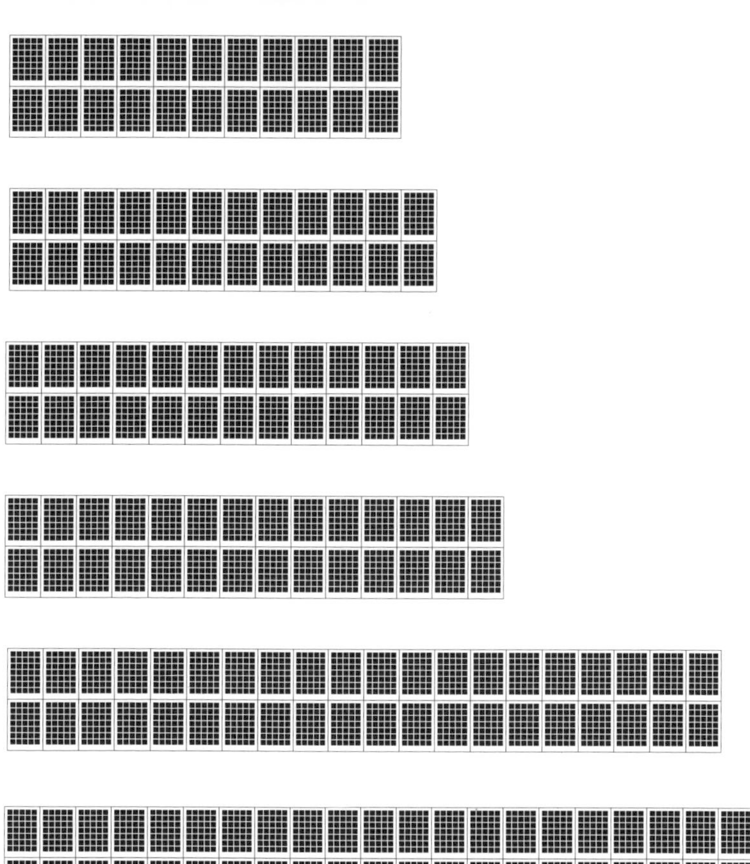

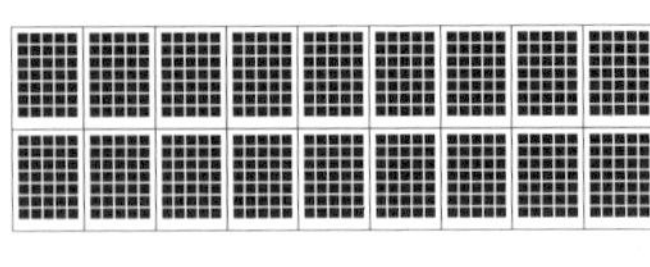

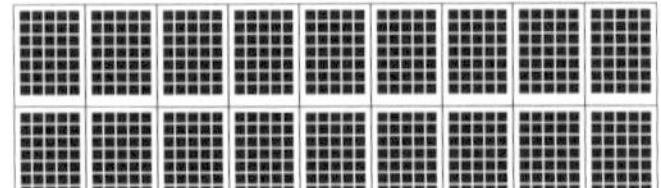

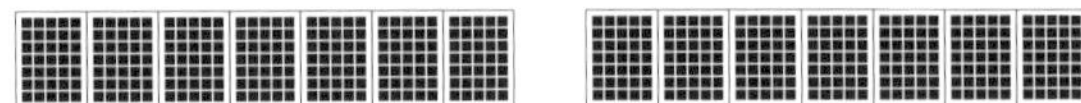

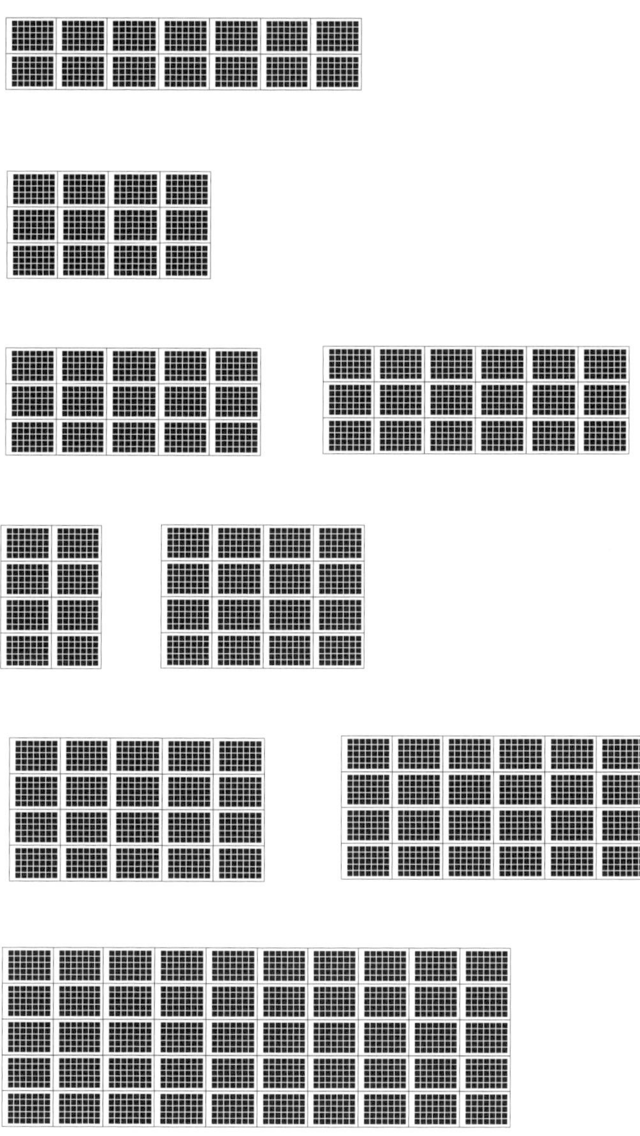

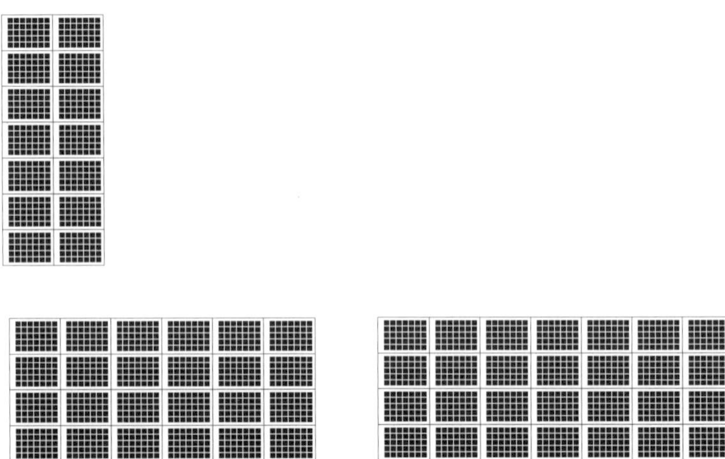

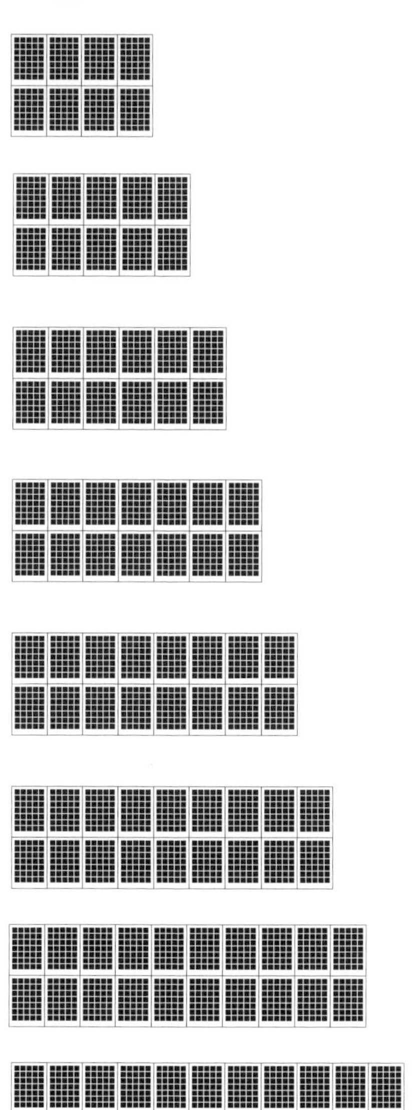

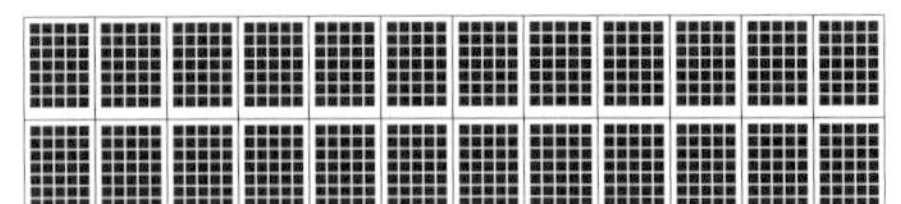

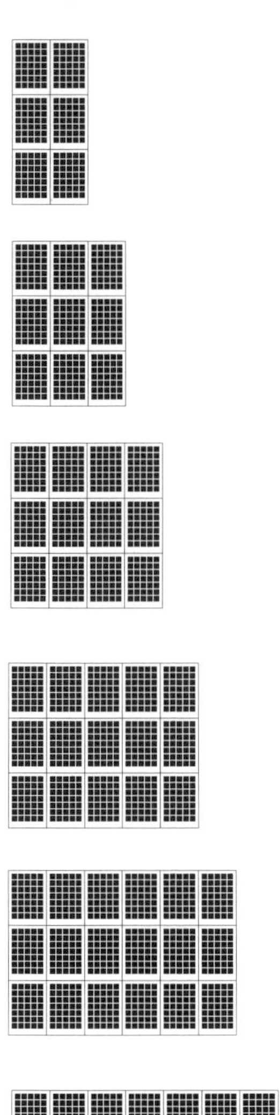

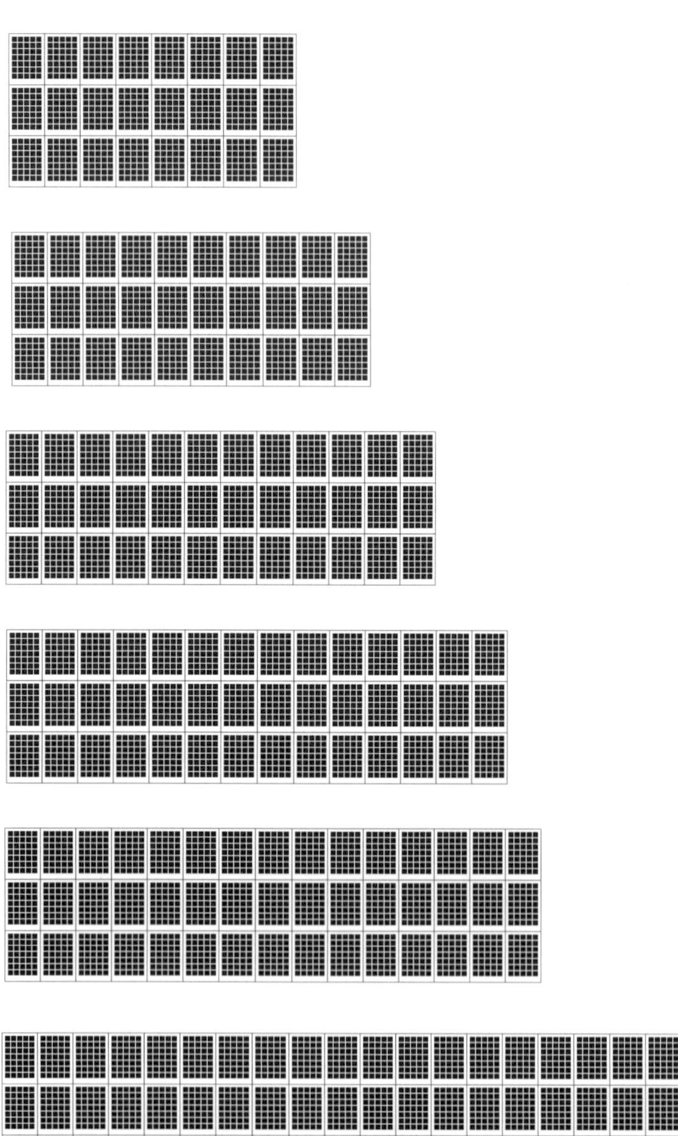

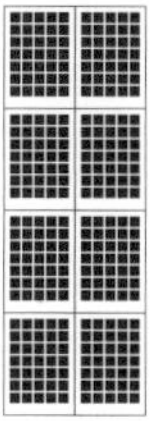

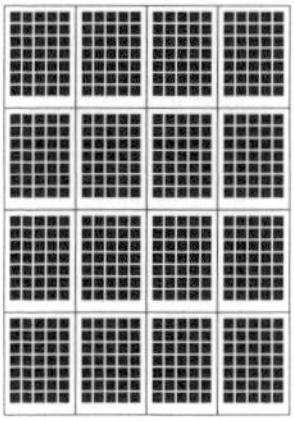

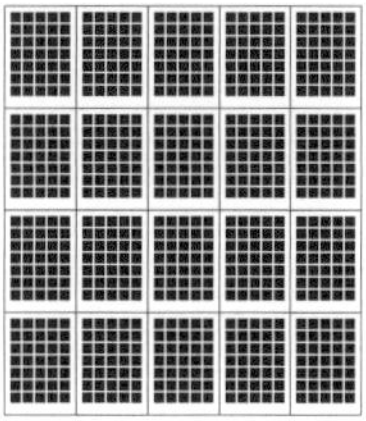

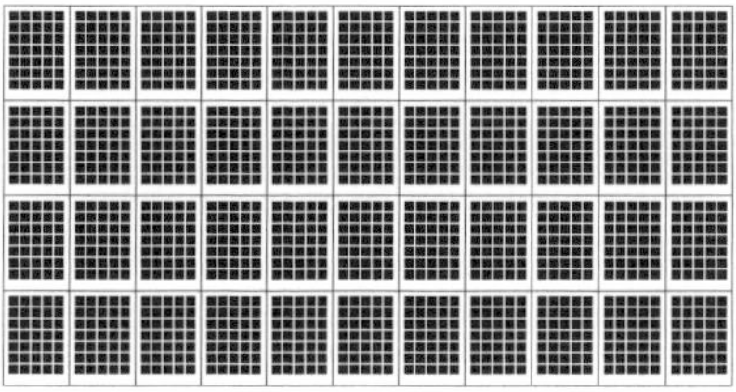

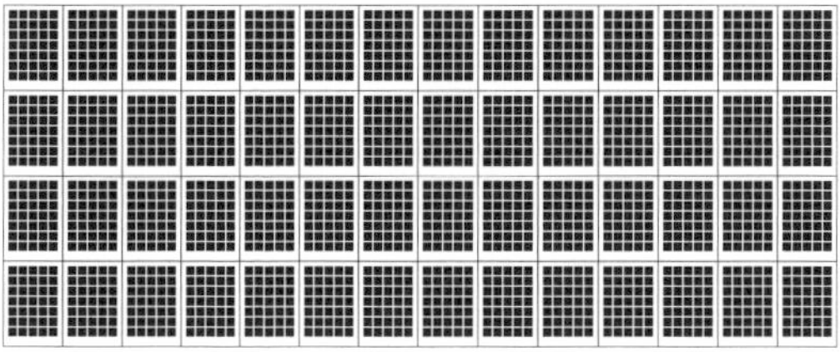

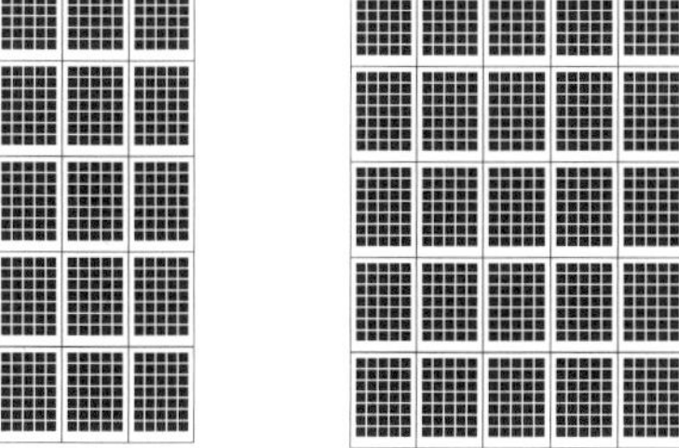

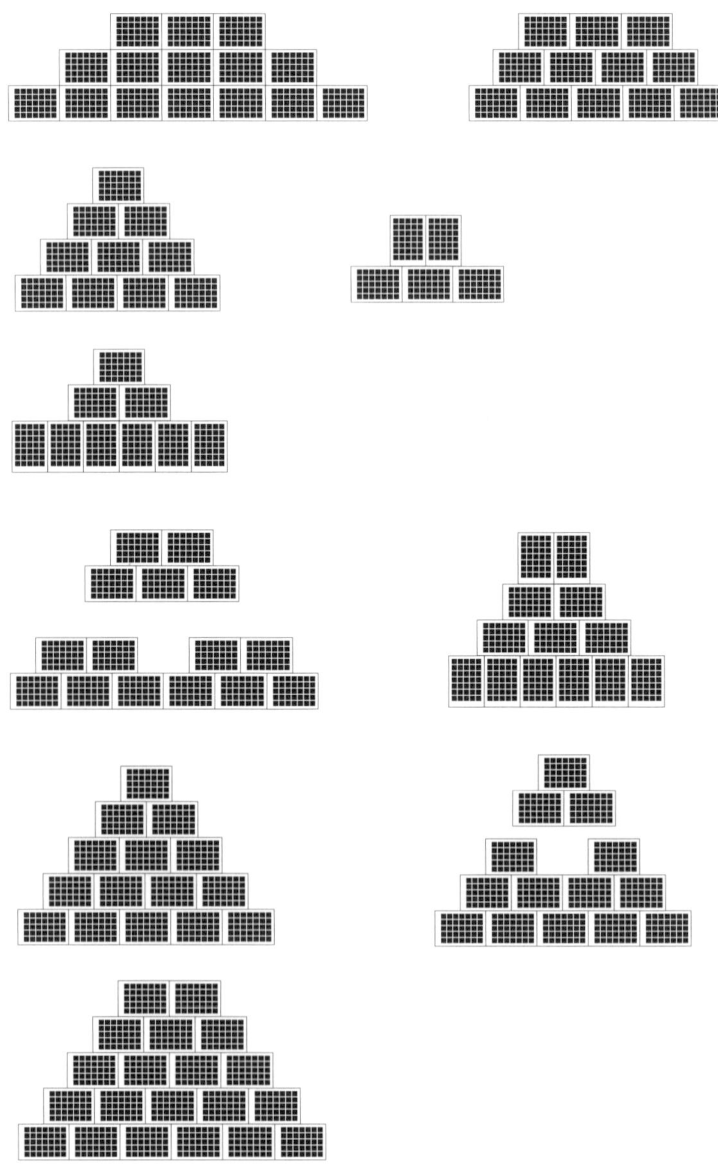

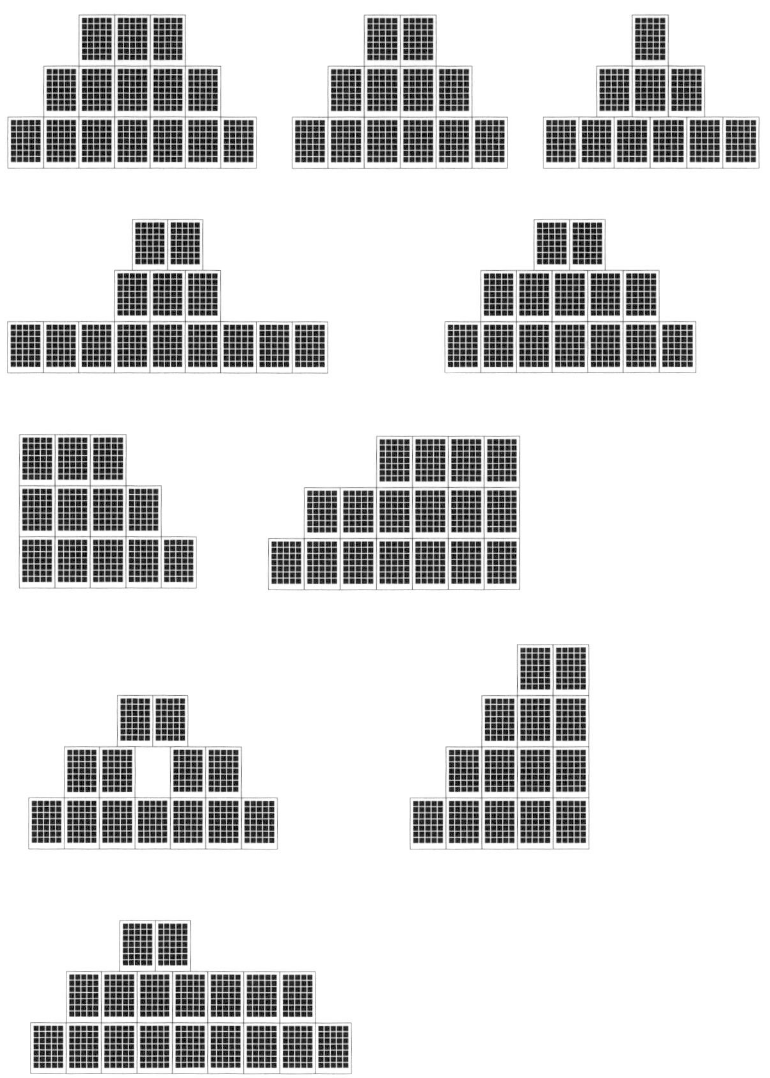

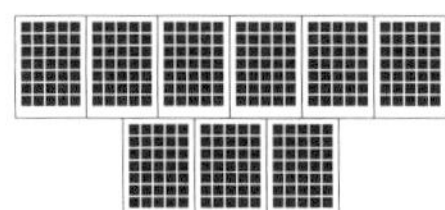

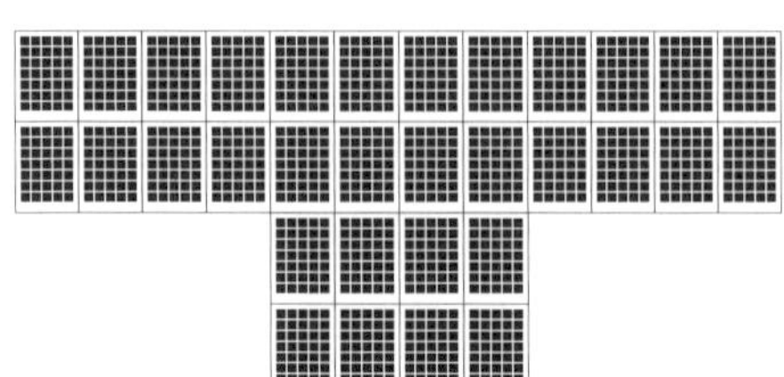

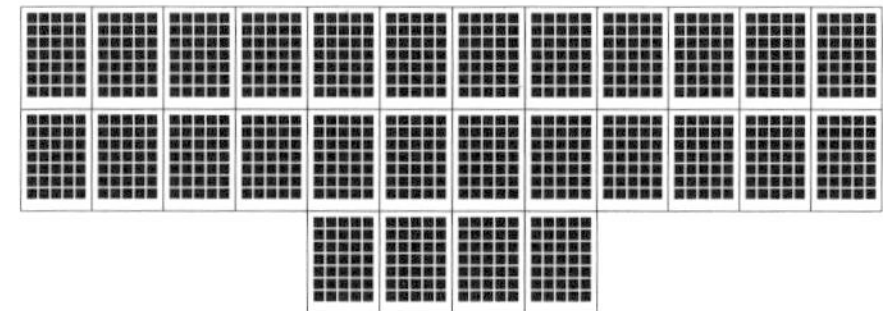

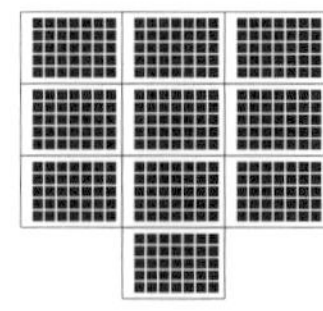

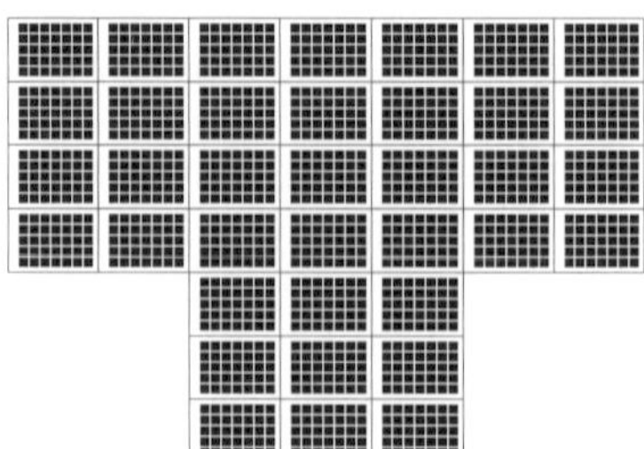

SPEED TRIP

0

#SURFACE
#BLOGOSPHERE
#FOMO
#DOOM
#HAPPYCONSENSUS
#LIFEWITHOUTOBJECTIONS

Our culture glides on the surface of things: light, fast, unnatural, superficial, conflictual. Our lives are hyperreal; they are themed, spectacular, illusionary. Concepts turn into alibis; idees-fixes mirror trends. Life without objections. We move in networks where relations between nodes have seemingly become unconditional, condition-less. This is a one-dimensional network, a cloud, in which all centers collide in a nucleus of individuality, the capsule's capsule, and inside everyone continuously pimps, remixes,

recollects and represents their own identity.

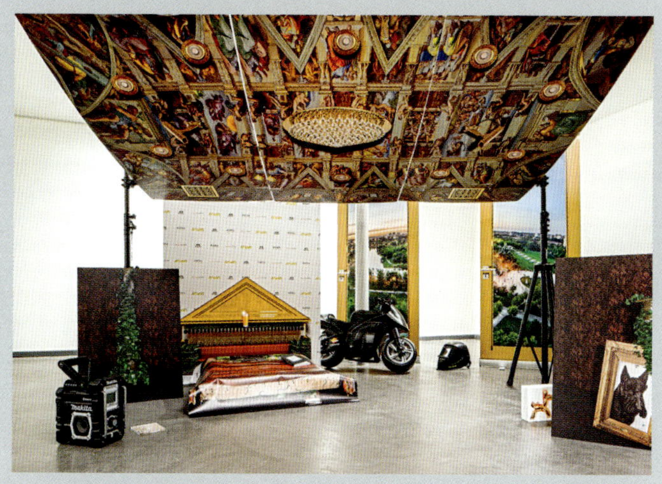

SPEEDISM started off from me looking at a real situation. In an accelerated world of pre-figuration and project realization, the relation between the render, as a visual translation of the imagined into the real, and the physical world blurs. I describe this contemporary state as one of Radical Saturation.

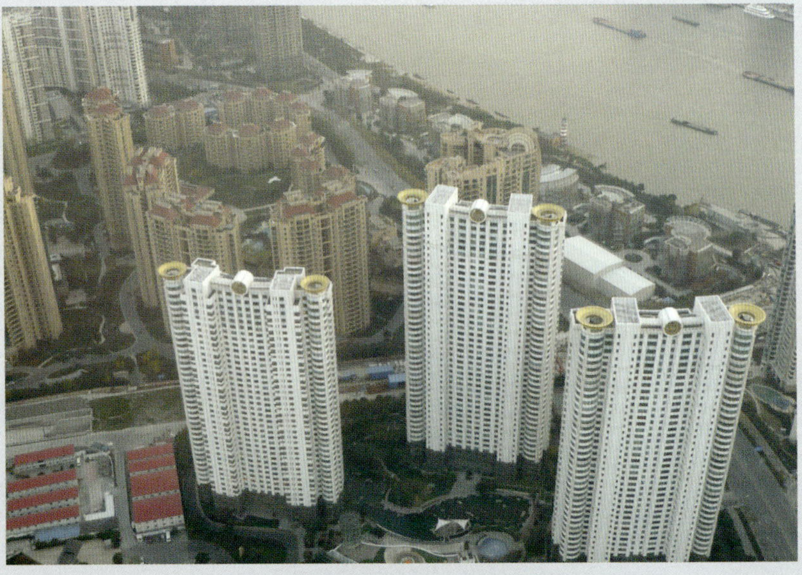

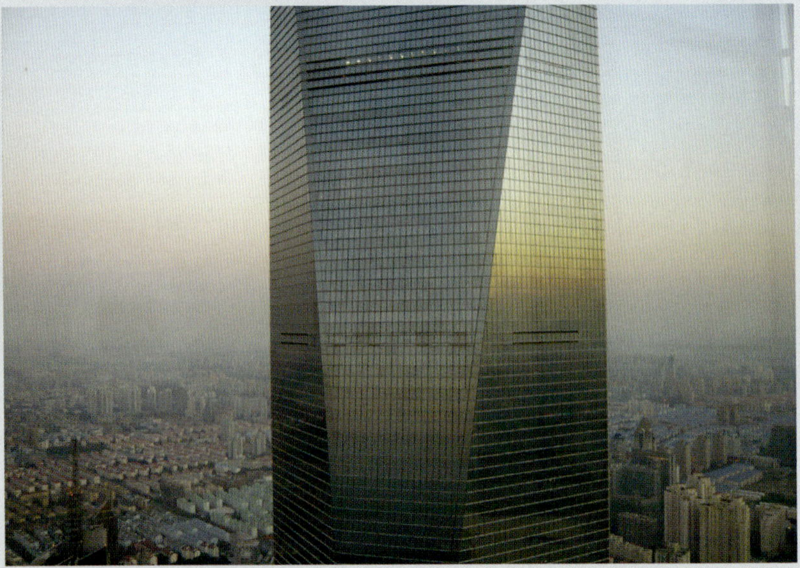

Social media reshape processes and discourse in architecture, as well as the general environment in which architects live and work.

Architects are surface makers. Images are our product, our mental universe, our theoretical landscape. The rendered image is architecture's bottom line product and the blog-o-sphere harbors its shipwrecks.[1] The rendering's sad, anticlimactic twin is its unrealizable promise.

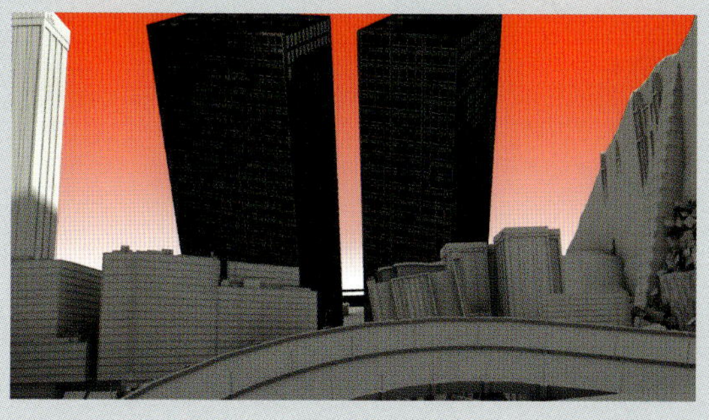

1 "When you invent the ship, you also invent the shipwreck; when you invent the plane you also invent the plane crash; and when you invent electricity, you invent electrocution... Every technology carries its own negativity, which is invented at the same time as technical progress." Paul Virilio, *Politics of the Very Worst*. New York: Semiotext(e), 1999, p. 89

To deal with this, Radical Saturation can strategically be coined both as a condition of surface culture and as a method for surface-making. In order to know Radical Saturation, you've got to become Radical Saturation. Fight fire with fire!

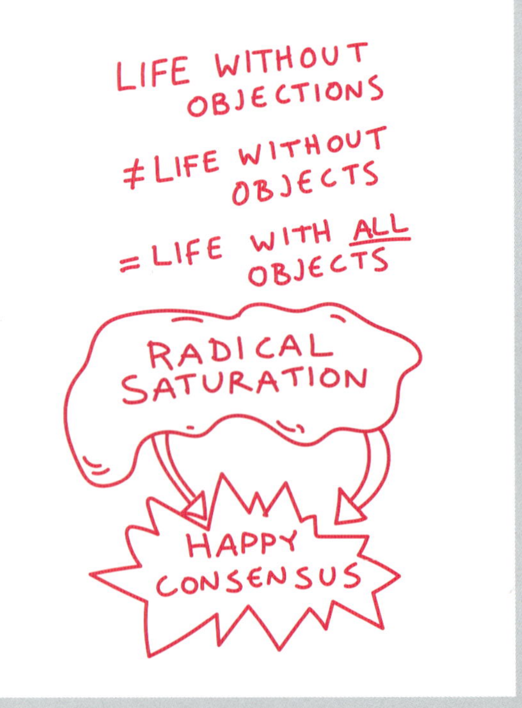

Surfing the surface, SPEEDISM image making is my desk research and SPEED TRIP is its deep probe. An immersive reality check of the state of the world, a Radical Saturation construction site visit.

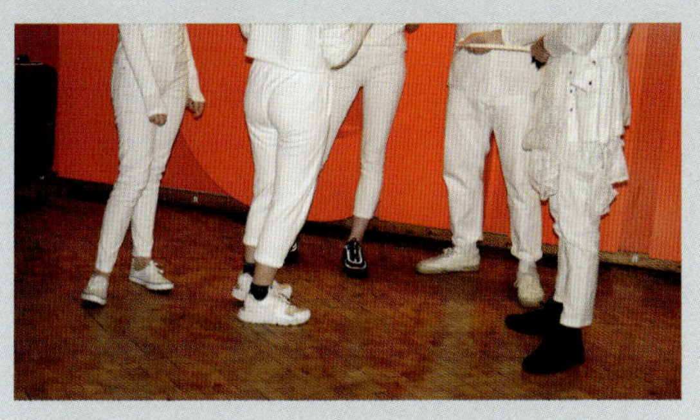

In order to understand the landscape as such, we approach it as the playground of Radical Saturation, and we must play its game. Furthermore, this mental position is shared through collective experiments with a participating audience of peers and students.

Both method actor and easy rider, the SPEED TRIPPER surrenders to its context and, equipped with necessary props, finds herself at the center of mediation.

Architecture as performance, performance as architecture. The accumulation of SPEED TRIP souvenirs would ideally shed a light on the cultural and physical landscape in terms of Radical Saturation, whilst also offer us guidance in developing our own, performative, positioning probes to move along and thrive at the surface.

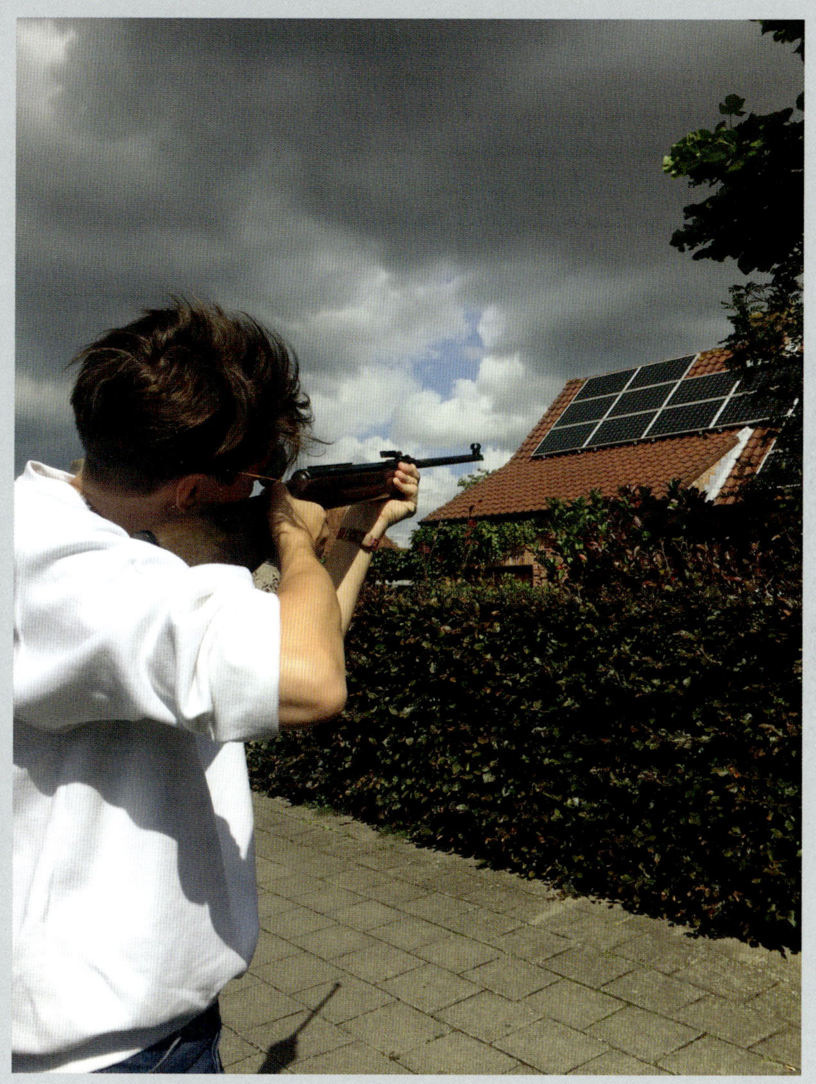

I took this picture in Las Vegas, 7am, on a Sunday morning in 2014. Radical Saturation. With SPEEDISM, we titled this image The Saddest Oldenburg in The World, and depending on how you cope with oversaturated scenes, you are able to spot a Claes Oldenburg sculpture in the center of the image. The Oldenburg is put in a corner of a rooftop walkway on a Daniel Libeskind designed building. The then brand new building is a shopping mall named Crystals. Its floor tiles slant sideways, as if to make way for the sculpture, although the piece looks rather well-constrained behind a circle of Libeskind style chrome-legged glass plates.

The sculpture is like a character, caught on the fly, as if it escaped original Las Vegas but could not get away in time before the Libeskind crew got to it. Presumably, a project architect Photoshopped an Oldenburg in a presentation drawing, and here we are.

The piece's rounded bottom is clearly visible but the blue flock of wires — hair? — seems to evaporate into the massive wall of blue glass, highrise background. The sculpture is a scaled up typewriter eraser and this is exactly what one needs in this context: an eraser to wipe out some of the impulses shooting at you. It is almost as if the developers play a sad joke and placed the eraser there as a real life version of the Photoshop eraser tool icon.

I cannot help but fantasize that the effects of the light reflection on the little glass fence are in fact the real design, as in a reverse trompe l'oeil: slanted, trapezoid glass panes, puzzled together in a loose, more hardcore Libeskind way.

In the background, Aria advertises a food bowl equally enlarged, printed on a banner. Is this a 1:1 scale Oldenburg? Is the background also a larger than life decor for Crystals, Vegas' catching up with proper downtown fashion? The rendering and reality merge. Agendas and fantasies are read into the same scene. Architecture as a hot-wired (ill-wired?) reality machine?

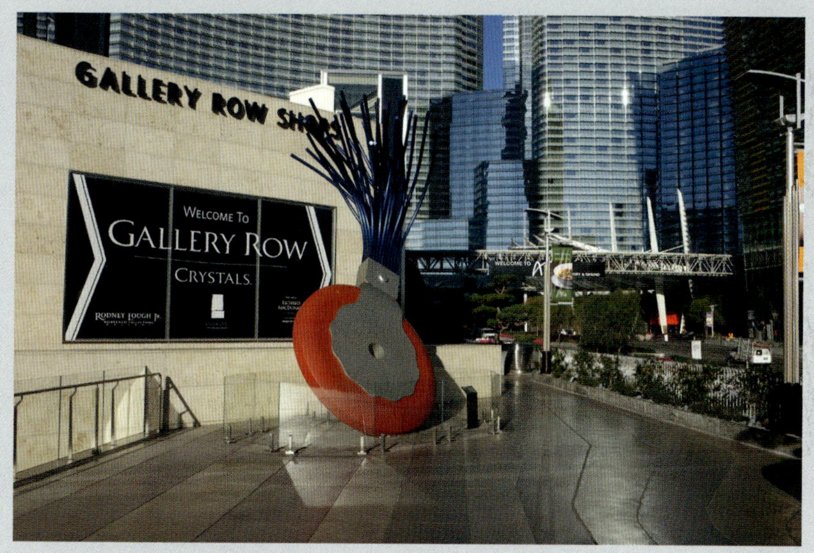

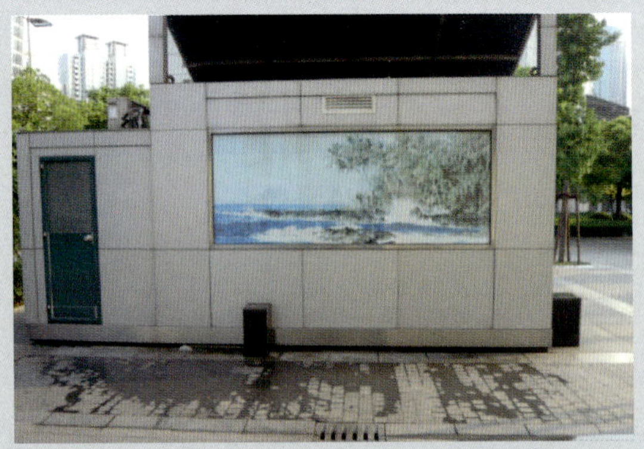

On a lighter note, this image, taken in 2008 on the Bund in Shanghai: I see a public toilet booth, which serves to frame a picture of a different reality. Whether painted, photographed rendered, it clearly makes me feel in two places simultaneously. The architecture as a projecting device. Very simple.

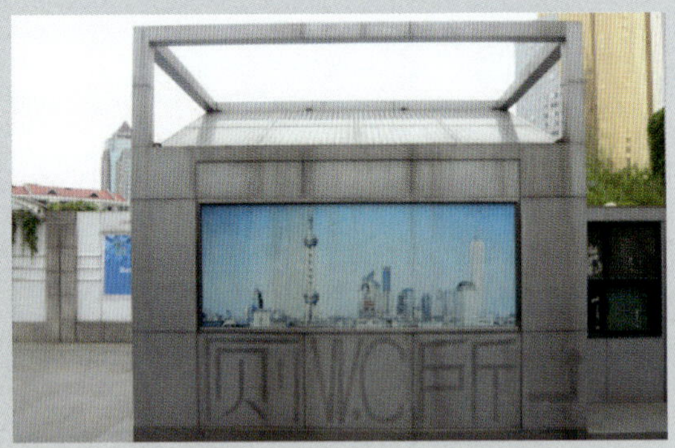

When I take a look at the backside of the booth, things become a little bit more complicated. I am not thrown back into a fantasy image of pure nature, but are offered a peek at what Shanghai's financial district, Pudong, should look like in the near future. So, a layer of time is added to the projection mix.

And then I find out the rendering was outdated! Reality caught up with the prefiguration! Moreover, reality is actively overtaking its own image, to which the permanent construction sites attest.

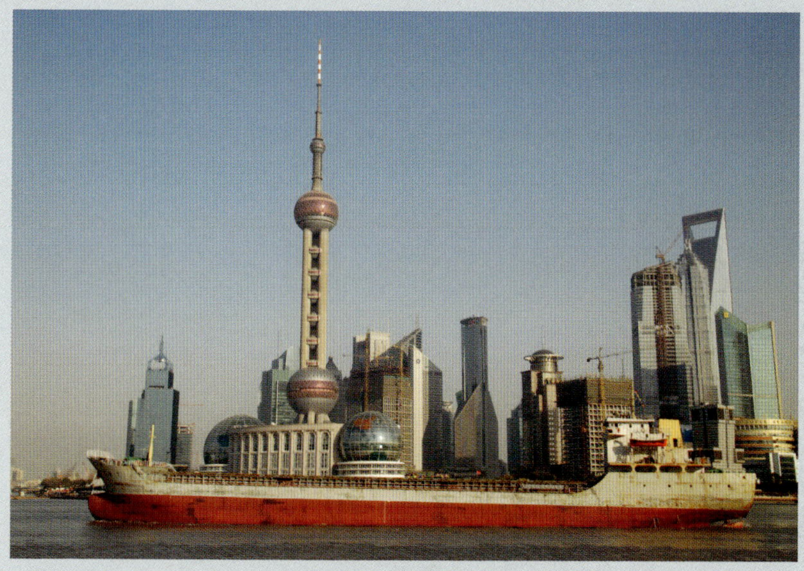

The speed of architecture, the speed of image making and the speed of reality making seemed to diverge. It felt as if architectural culture needed some catching up with the state of the world, and image making mediates between those two. I was most curious to experience the shifts and glitches this produced.

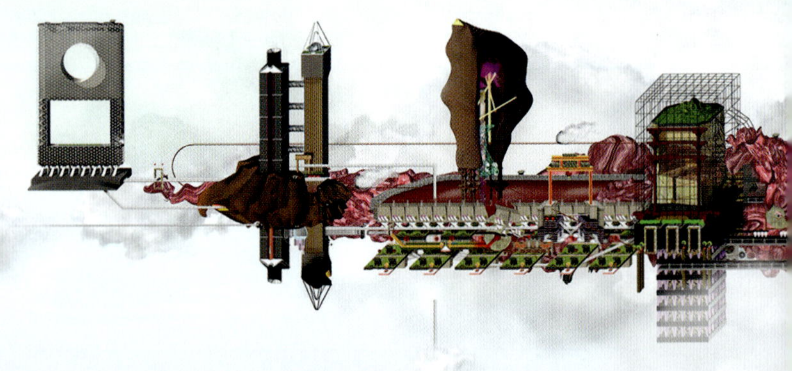

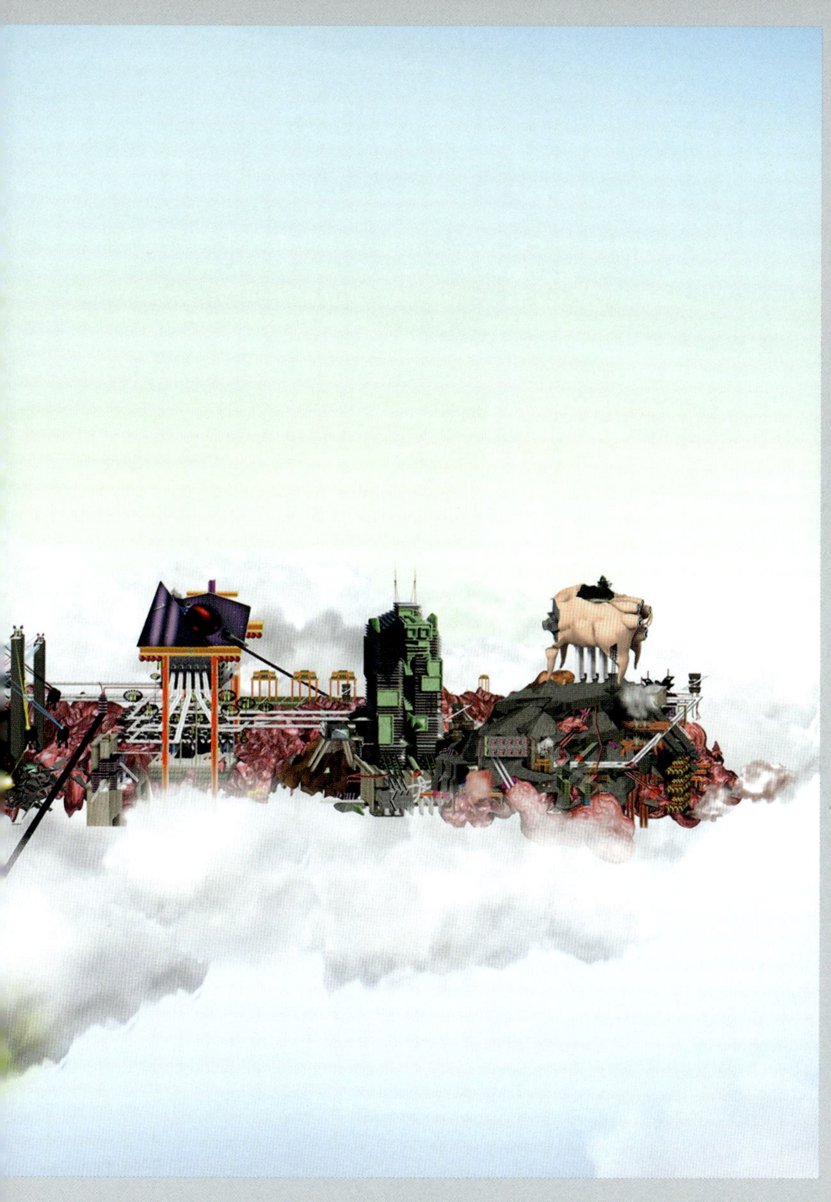

2 PIERCING THE RENDERING: I WAS THERE

And on that day its pure, bright colors and crisply etched outlines brought to my mind the Acropolis as it might have looked when they painted its marble. (...) I felt a shiver. Was it hate or love? I didn't know. It didn't matter. Something said, "This is key—it will be important to you."[2]

Denise Scott Brown

Denise Scott Brown's most famous photograph presents the young architect standing confidently in the desert just beyond the Las Vegas strip. "I was there!" the photo screams, and by looking us straight in the eyes, she makes us accomplice in what she is about to do; boldly piercing the rendering, trespassing the postcard! As much as Robert Venturi's famous punchline — You don't have to like something to learn from it[3] — authorizes us to look anywhere and actually learn from it, it is in this picture that we find real empowerment: Denise Scott Brown actually seems to like what she sees, and fully embraces whatever is necessary to uncover the stakes. The SPEED TRIPS are no less than a celebration of the spirit mediated through this picture, and attempt to produce collective experiences of the present, moments ". . . where everything makes sense, even the fragmented landscape of an anti-urbanism of rubble and billboards and ruins, that moment when the world opens up into kaleidoscopic possibility. "[4]

2 Denise Scott Brown, in: *Still Learning from Denise Scott Brown. 45 Years of learning from Las Vegas*. Stephanie Salomon and Steve Kroeter, January 7, 2014, retrieved October 6, 2015, from www.designersandbooks.com/blog/still-learning-from-denise-scott-brown

3 Robert Venturi, in: *Less is More – Mies Van der Rohe, Less is a Bore – Robert Venturi*. Paul Goldberger, The New York Times, 17 October 1971, p. 34

4 Sam Jacob: *Denise Scott Brown, Queen of the Desert*. Retrieved December 21, 2016, from www.strangeharvest.com

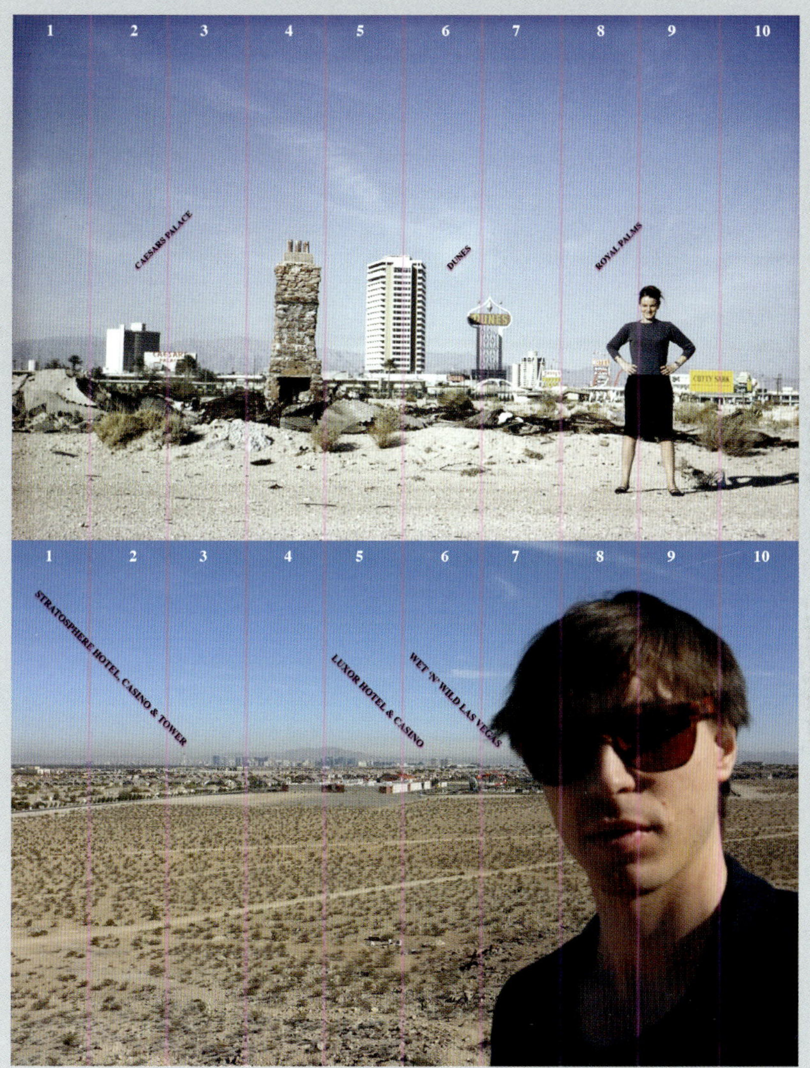
1
2
3
4
5
6
7
8
9
10
CAESARS PALACE
DUNES
ROYAL PALMS
DUNES
CUTTY SARK
1
2
3
4
5
6
7
8
9
10
STRATOSPHERE HOTEL, CASINO & TOWER
LUXOR HOTEL & CASINO
WET 'N' WILD LAS VEGAS

SPEED TRIPS are enactments running parallel to my image projects, sometimes re-enactments of ideas and places that were used in the images, sometimes preceding new image projects or stand-alone experiential performances.

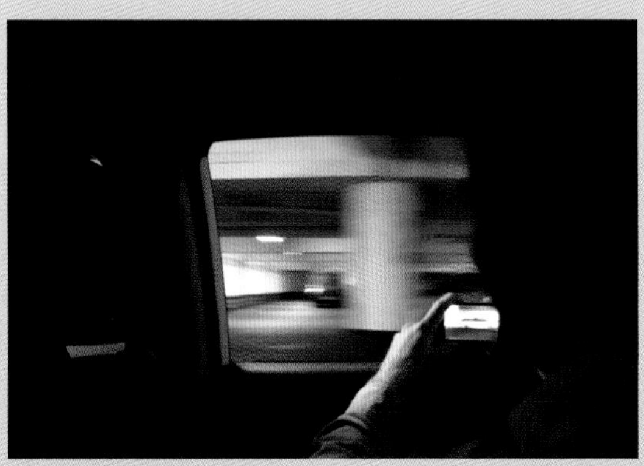

The idea of a SPEED TRIP grew out of a wish to deploy SPEEDISM working modes 'in real life': how do we stitch together existing physical realities in ways similar to the approach in Photoshopped projects? During SPEED TRIPS we document situations that by means of high speed reverberate between fantasy and reality, between constructed image and environment. Therefore participants use one mode of equally fast and superficial documentation (Instagram, Snapchat, Twitter, haiku's, Vine, Photostitch) and the total sum of all these constitutes a compiled portrait of the visited landscape: incomplete, speculative, superficial, disembodied and open to change.

The post-production of such events culminates in the SPEED TRIP SHRINE, which can be understood as the bibliography of field research[5], filled with souvenirs rather than references. Participants become performers that crash into the image-surface in order to be (in) the project.

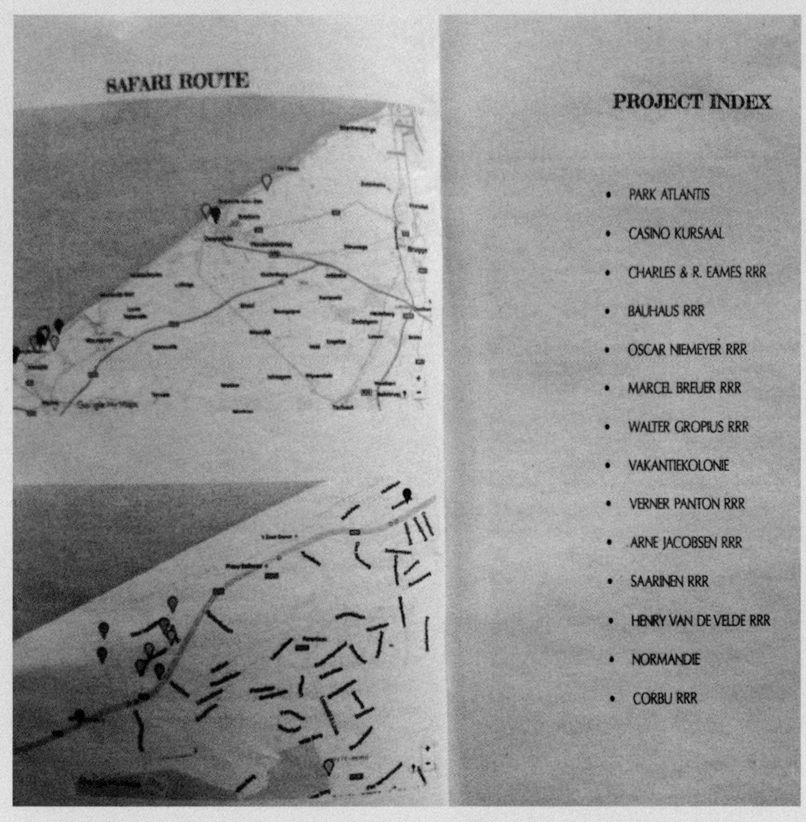

5 Intentional overlap of ambitions: SPEED TRIP, a malleable format to experiment with contemporary types of field research, simultaneously serves as an experiential testing ground for alternative referencing.

For every trip, a location is chosen, and hosts are invited to introduce an out of the ordinary place in this location, so-called too real to be true. These sites have been carefully selected because of their relationship with the issues at hand; themes and topics such as 'the hyperreal', 'acceleration', 'it architecture', 'remix' or 'constructed fiction'. Built realities that bear witness of accelerated transformations play an important role; they have at one point been touched by speed and possibly are already 'cooled down' again.

Speed can be understood on multiple levels at the same time, and may be qualified as a notably slower or faster speed of making, shifting, disrupting, experiencing, sharing and understanding image, architecture and context. A shortlist of sites is decided upon, and linked together along a route using Google Maps. The hosts share the ride with a varied group of participants, usually consisting of students, peers, partners and friends.

The self-proclaimed SPEED TRIPPERS travel from site to site and, in true tourist fashion, the group hops from one destination to another without expressing the wish to understand the environment in its totality. The working mode is fast, post-reflective and action based, not unlike the SPEEDISM design process, since these public SPEED TRIPS devour the scenes as a real-life SPEEDISM imagination. Much like architectural culture is trapped in a non-stop loop of prefigurations, the built effects of this reality-machine may be sensed at, speculated upon, or critically located by means of its residual postfigurations.

The SPEED SPECS, cardboard glasses designed for every SPEED TRIP, are a homage to Austrian architect Hans Hollein, who conceived a spectacle-making machine for his 1968 Milan Triennial installation. The Hollein-designed intervention at the Austrian pavilion consisted of a sequence of simulated environments, whose experience was aimed at the promotion of a technological architecture of effect.

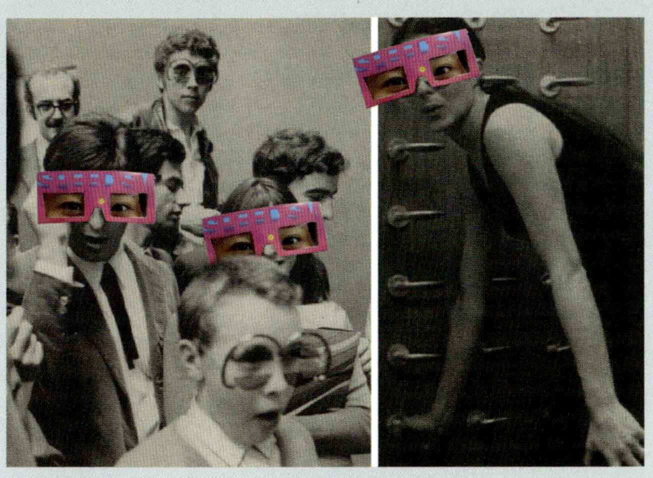

Besides the controlled atmospheres devised as a set of corridors, Hollein presented a machine that continuously fabricated and discarded sunglasses spectacles he intended for the audience to wear throughout the Triennale.[6] Not unlike his inflatable structures, these glasses expressed his point that one can augment reality by simple means as framing, coloration or conceptual isolation, and consequently count such tools into the architect's toolbox.

6 Hans Hollein, in: *Austriënnale*. The Architectural Forum, September 1968, pp. 40-43

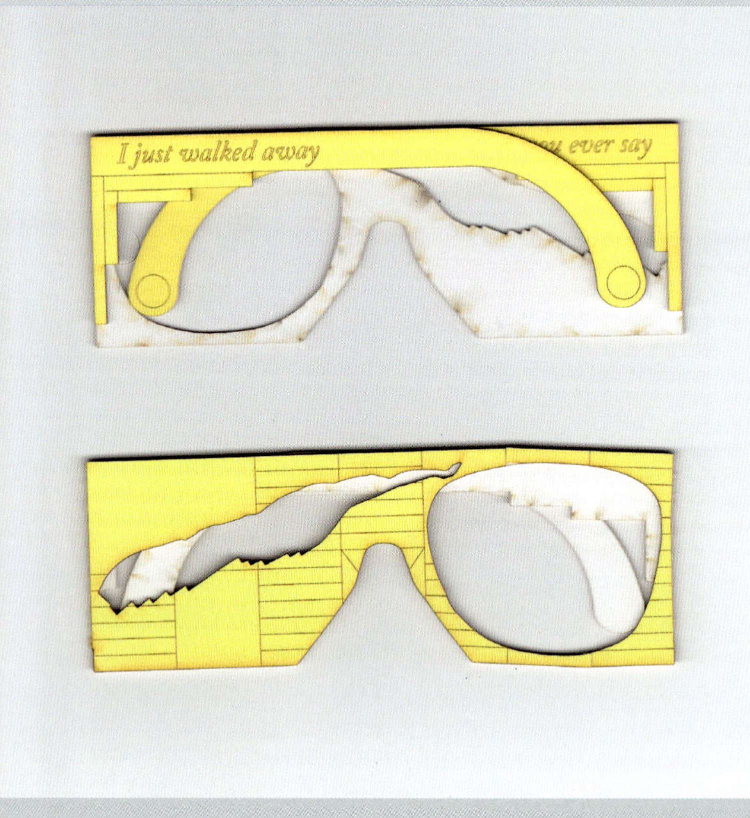
I just walked away
ever say

The spectacles designed for the LA SPEED DERIVE, Charles San Andreas and Ray Cyrus Wayfarer (or CSARCW), borrow from visible and invisible layers of the field trip's site:

- A subconscious geological lens cut-out outlines the San Andreas fault-line, where LA is positioned. As it is short sighted to build a metropolis on a virtually unbuildable site; LA is a time bomb.
- The layer of architectural history is represented by the facade drawing of the Charles and Ray Eames House. Their motto, LIFE=WORK=FUN=WORK=LIFE, applies to our trips. The Eames house, like their motto, symbolizes their sheer drive, focus and attitude. The geometrical rasterization on the CSARCW front is a gentle reminder that Charles and Ray travelled these same roads, stopped at the same sites and shopped at the same Sears department store[7].
- The 'regular' lens provides the aerial layer, bearing the shape of an archetypal Ray Ban pair of sunglasses, the Wayfarer. An associative pun on the Eames', Ray Ban also suggests flight, overview and heightened speed. This echoes the scales and perspectives deployed on the Speed Trip: walking and snapshotting the sites, highway-cruising between nodes, in traffic, and geo-locating on Google Maps. Wayfarer or Aviator?
- The poetic layer is engraved on the spectacles' temples. 'Don't you ever say' on the right temple, and 'I just walked away' on the left, sourced from

7 As third-generation disciplinary offspring of the Eames's or Denise Scott Brown, we can only attest to these visionaries' predictions about Radical Saturation: Denise proves decades onwards how the culture was shifting, and forefelt that architectural culture needed be disrupted to catch up; Charles and Ray – LIFE = WORK = FUN = WORK = LIFE ! – did not hint at a cramped cult of screen-tripping unpaid-but-liked-n-shared intern armadas, but searched for ways to get ahead of all-and-ever-conscious multidisciplinary convergence.

the Miley Cyrus 2013 summer hit 'Wrecking Ball', which symbolizes the Speed Trip mood. Moreover, participants are inattentive to what they are seeing as they are pre-occupied with self-publicizing their travel event.[8] Such a disconnected sightseeing investigation, produces a wrecking ball attitude, which is part of this experiment.

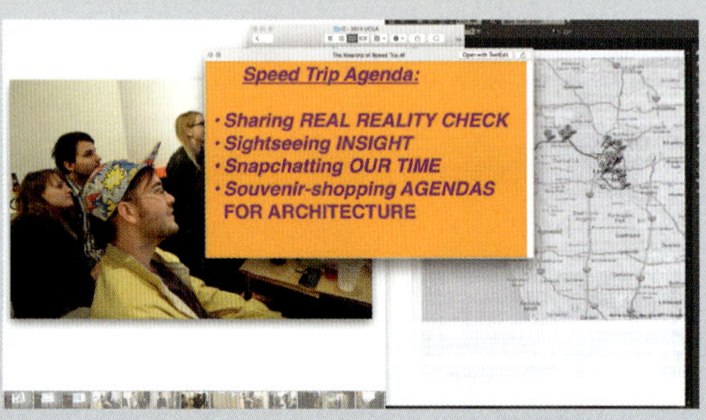

What obviously binds together the Triennale project of Hans Hollein, the field work projects of Venturi Scott Brown and my contextual experiments facing Radical Saturation, is the explicit design of an active involvement, turning participants into co-conspirators

8 Most SPEED TRIPS are executed by bus or by car. Between two stops, passenger participants take time to select, edit and add comments to their photos or videos, and post these on an online outlet to their liking. The virtual audience is served a string of framed snippets of the SPEED TRIP sites, not much different from their media host's real experience.

of a theoretical kind, altogether embodying a passion for the real world. SPEED TRIPS are also an explicit invitation to colleagues to partake in a real reality check. The ‘petit tour’ that is an after-noon’s worth of architectural projections on terrain, adorned with SPEEDISM specs that echo Hollein’s spectacles, generates excitement amongst participant-performers as in a feverish school trip. Just as Hollein’s rudimentary experiments with expanded architectural effects might have seemed ironic and detached from true disciplinary issues, especially given the silly ornaments on participants’ faces, a SPEEDISM-bespectacled joyride could wrongly be understood as mere entertainment.

The following documentation of SPEED TRIPS illustrates a collective sharing, sightseeing, Snapchatting and souvenir-shopping as a method for capturing agendas for architecture.

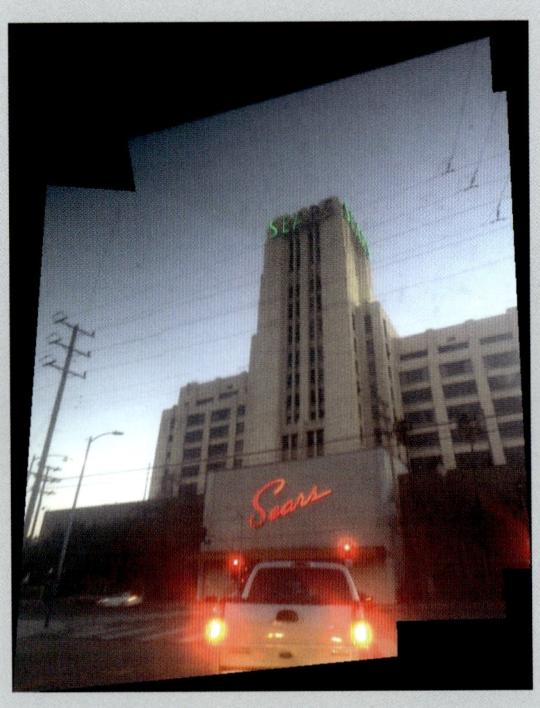

BEIJING'S HIDDEN SCIENCE FICTIONS

Location: PERIPHERAL BEIJING, CHINA. Date: 13 DECEMBER 2008. Partners: THEATRE IN MOTION (TIM/LAB) + ABITARE CHINA. Hosts: CHEN SHUYU (PLACE DESIGN), XU LI (ABITARE), NEVILLE MARS (DYNAMIC CITY FOUNDATION). Participants: SPEEDISM, THEATRE IN MOTION (TIM/LAB), A BUSLOAD OF BEIJING LOCALS. Props: SPEEDISM CARDBOARD "MADE IN CHINA" SPECTACLES; TOUR BUS.

Trip characteristics: Who builds the physical after-images of glossy rendered visions of this urban China? #PiercingTheRendering

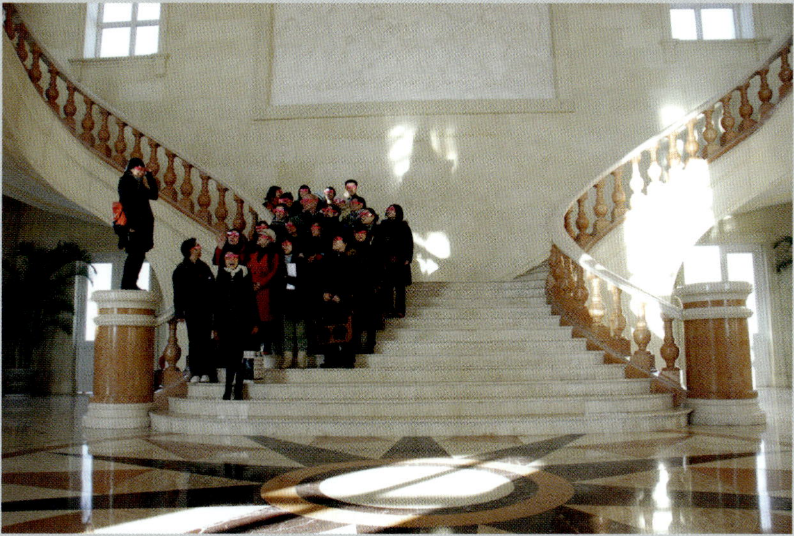

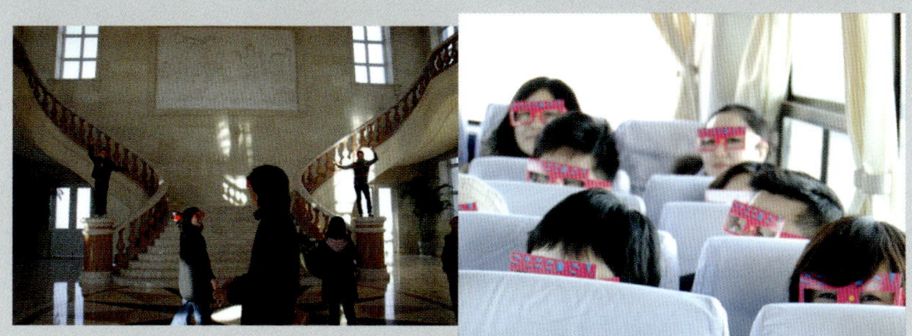

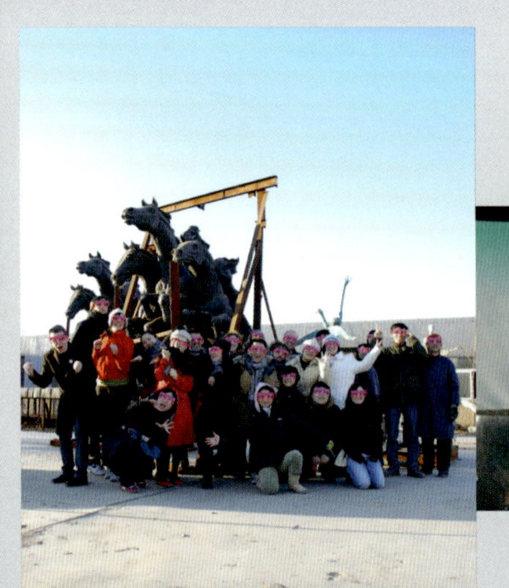

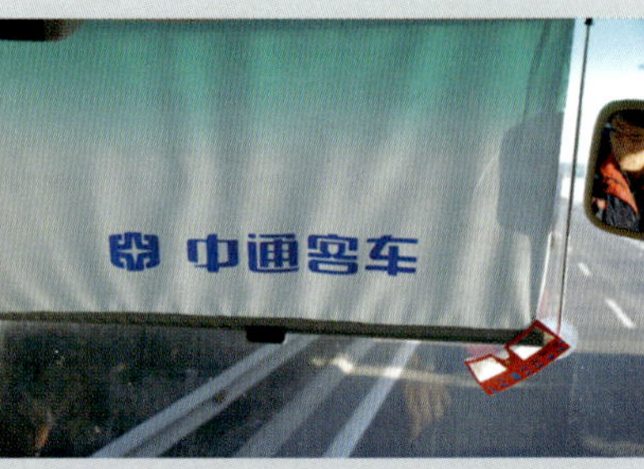
中通客车

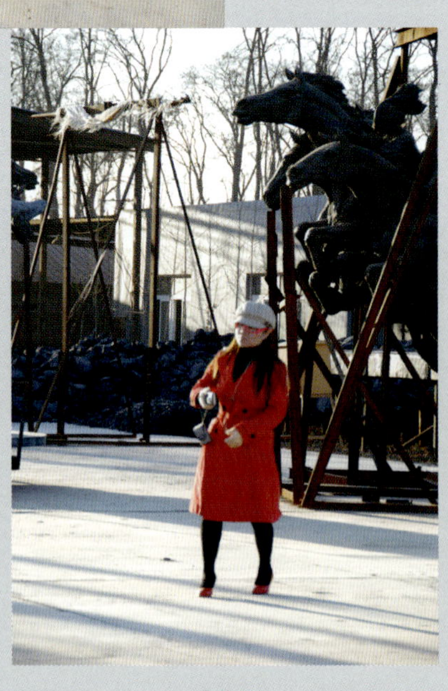

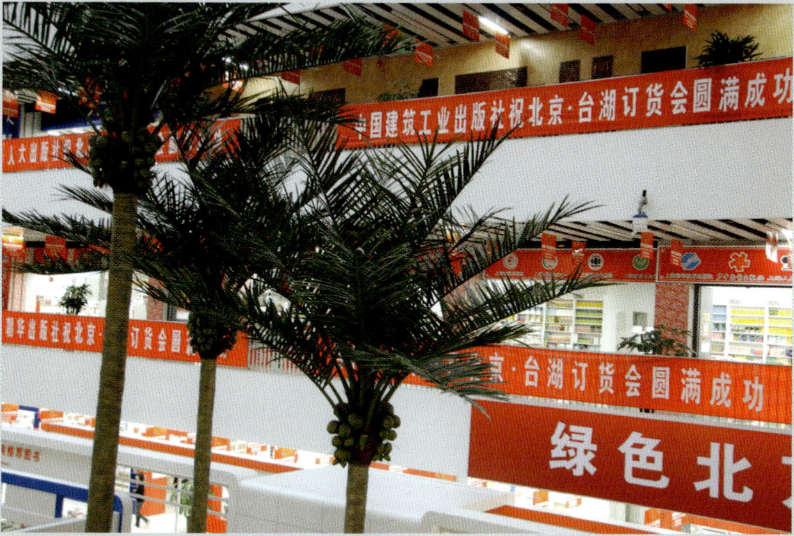

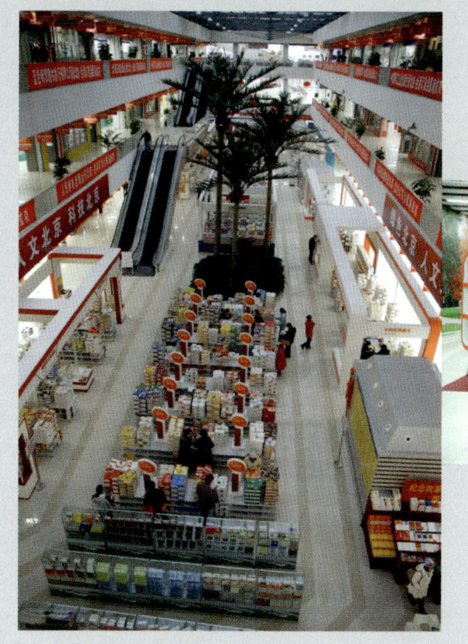

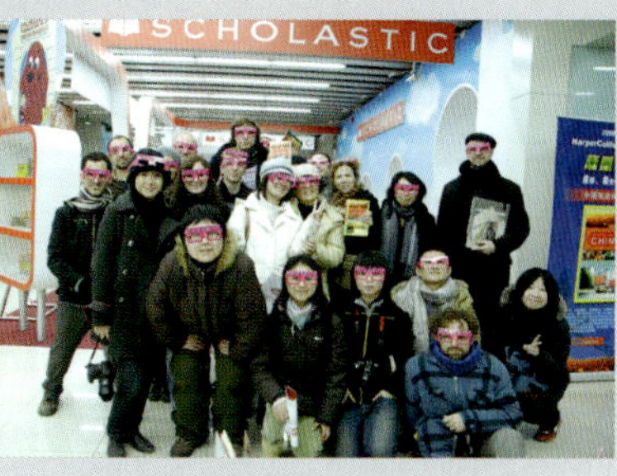
SCHOLASTIC

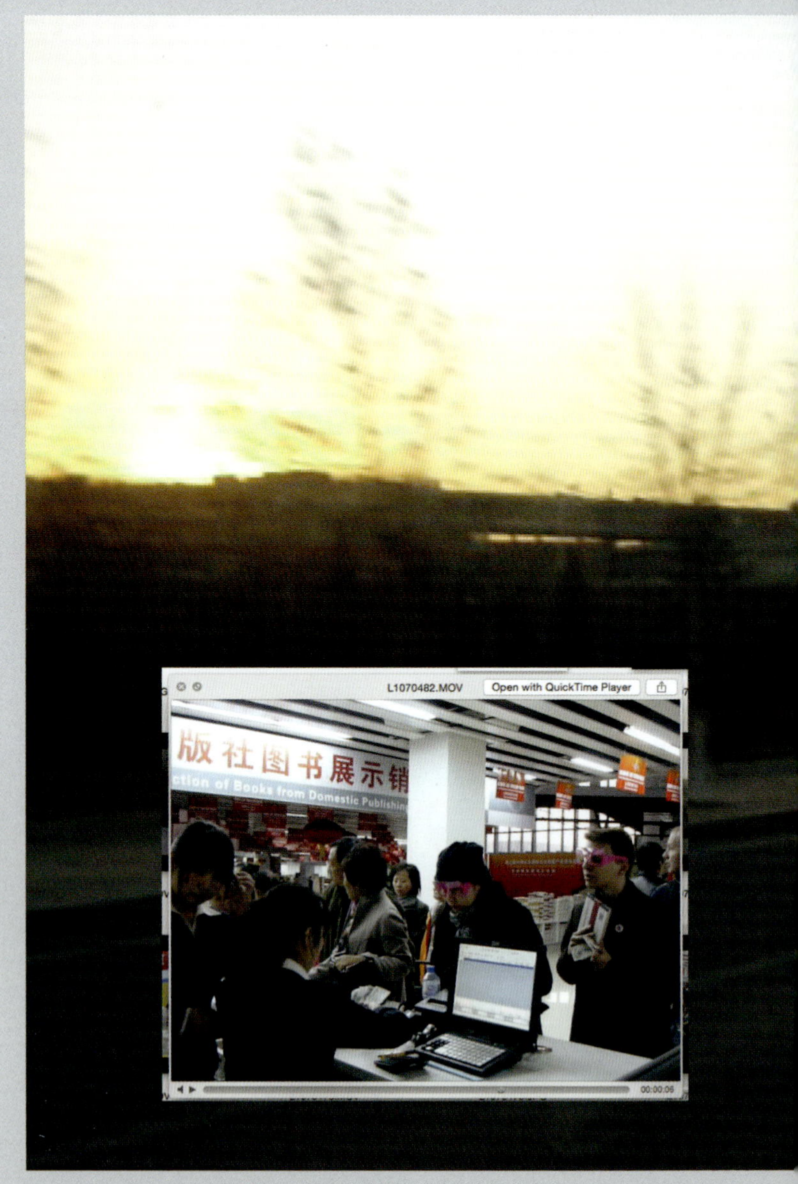
L1070482.MOV
Open with QuickTime Player
版社图书展示销
ction of Books from Domestic Publishin
00:00:06

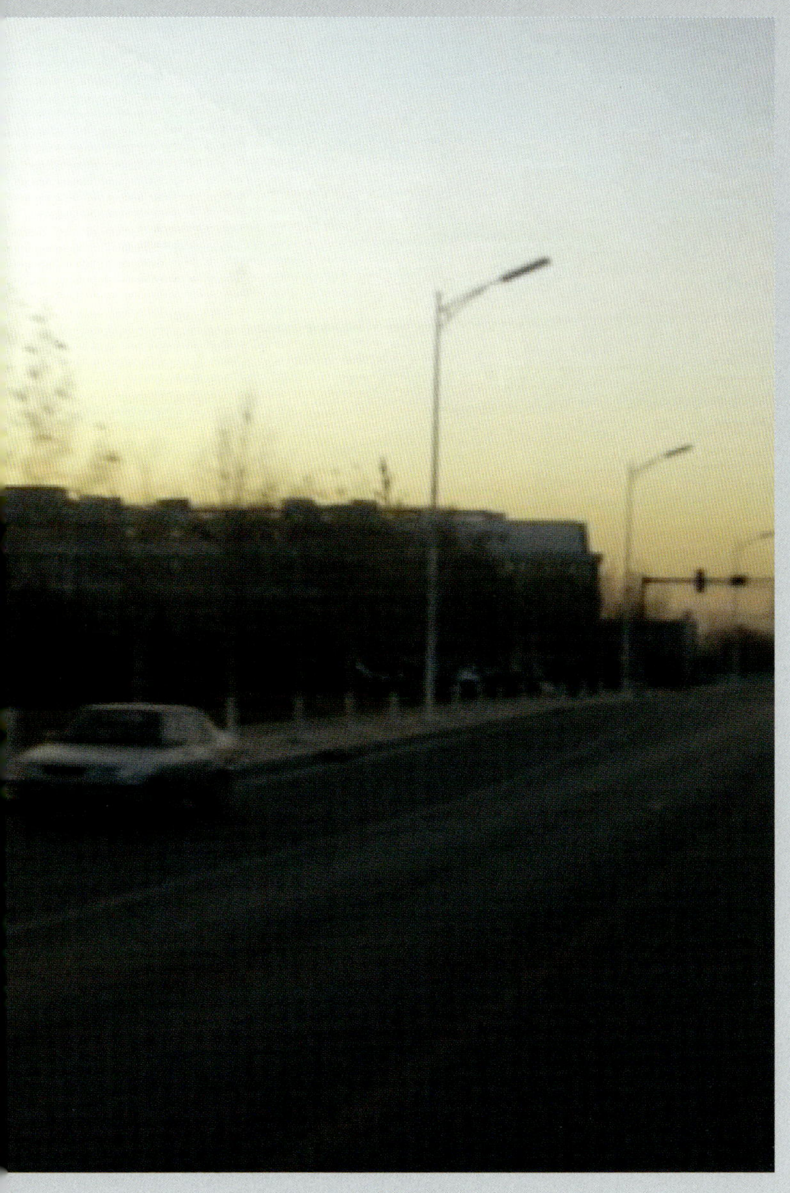

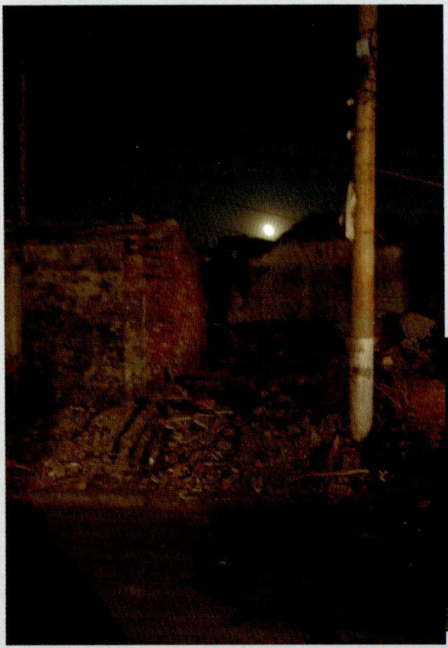

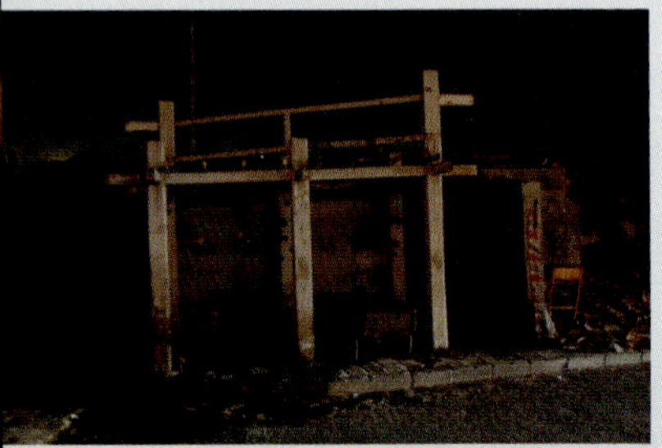

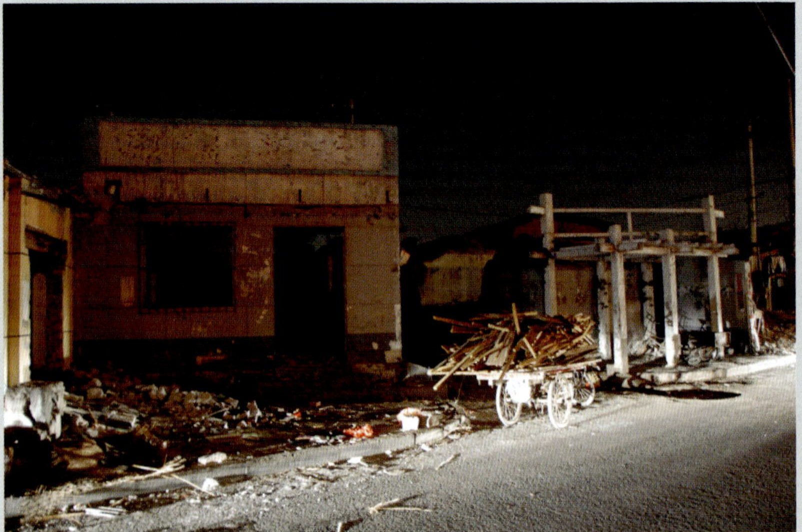

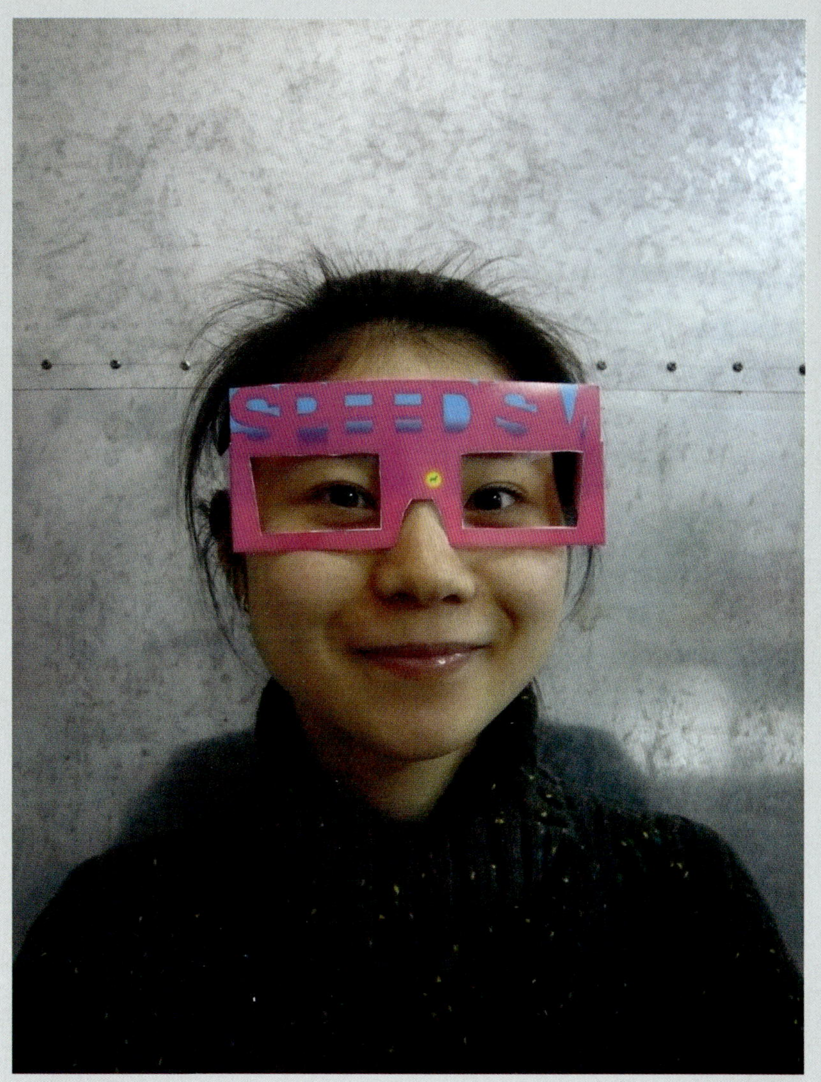
SPEEDS

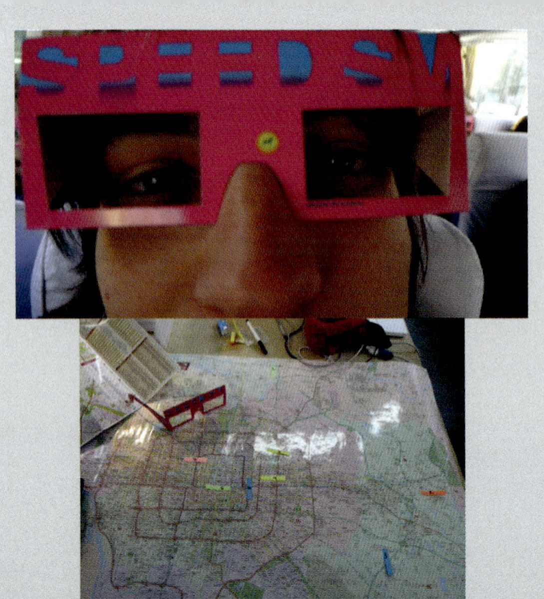

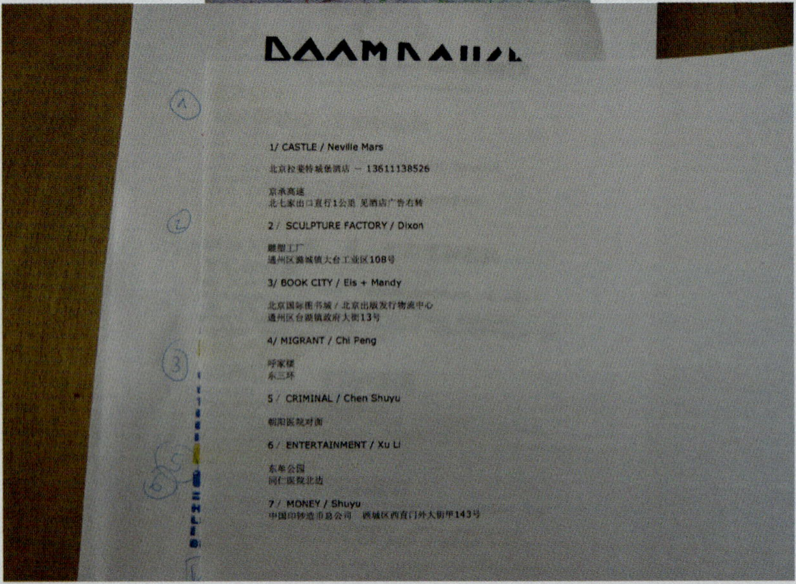

1/ CASTLE / Neville Mars

北京拉斐特城堡酒店 — 13611138526

京承高速
北七家出口直行1公里 见酒店广告右转

2 / SCULPTURE FACTORY / Dixon

雕塑工厂
通州区潞城镇大台工业区108号

3/ BOOK CITY / Els + Mandy

北京国际图书城 / 北京出版发行物流中心
通州区台湖镇政府大街13号

4/ MIGRANT / Chi Peng

呼家楼
东三环

5 / CRIMINAL / Chen Shuyu

朝阳医院对面

6 / ENTERTAINMENT / Xu Li

东单公园
同仁医院北边

7 / MONEY / Shuyu
中国印钞造币总公司 西城区西直门外大街甲143号

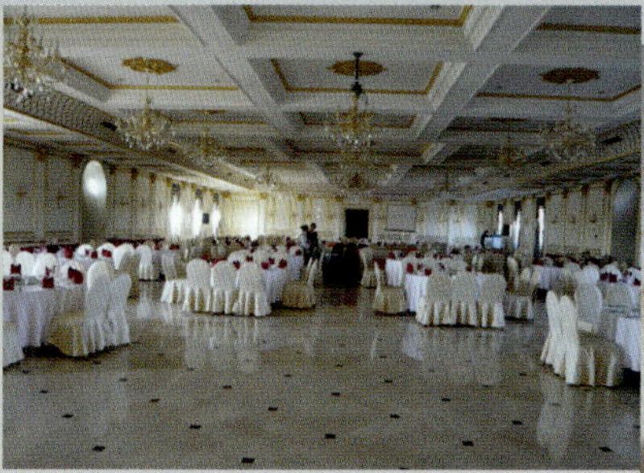

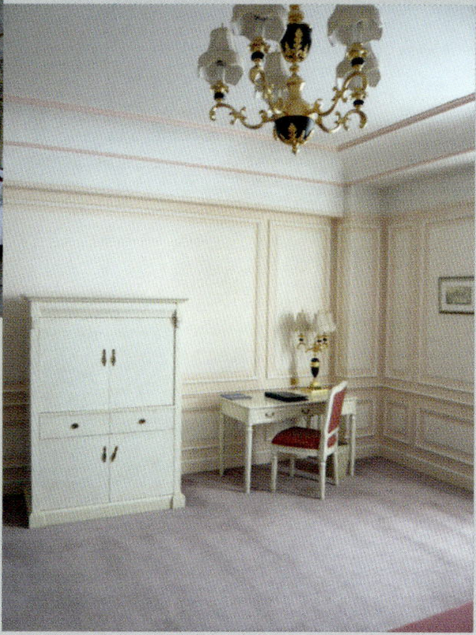

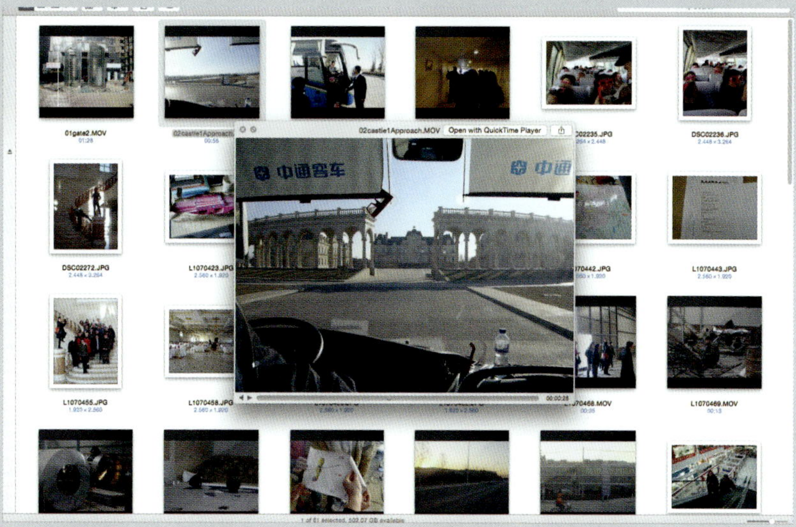

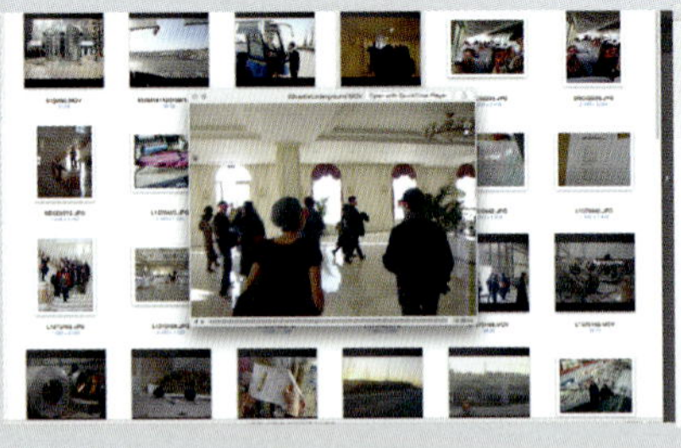

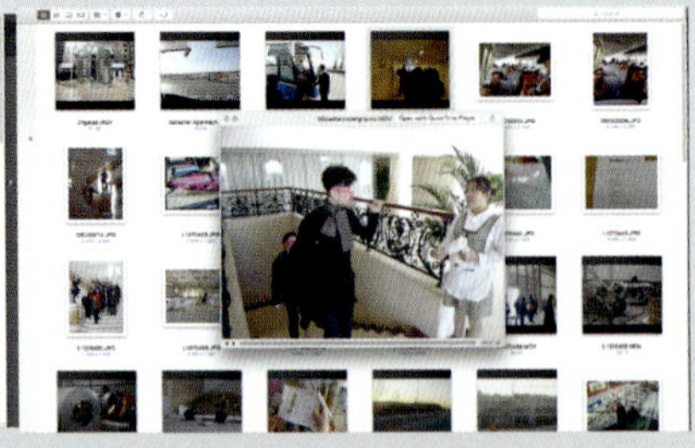

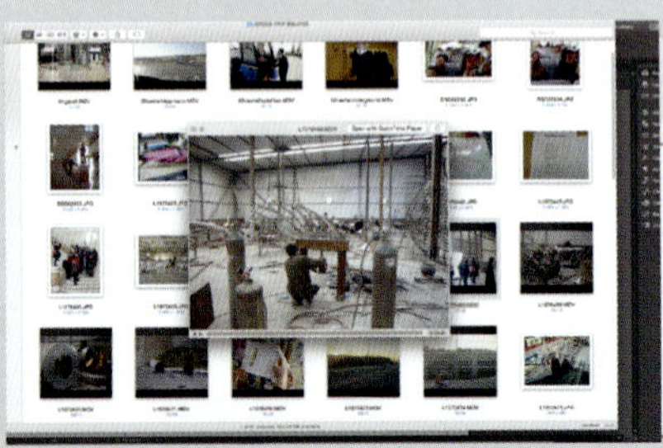

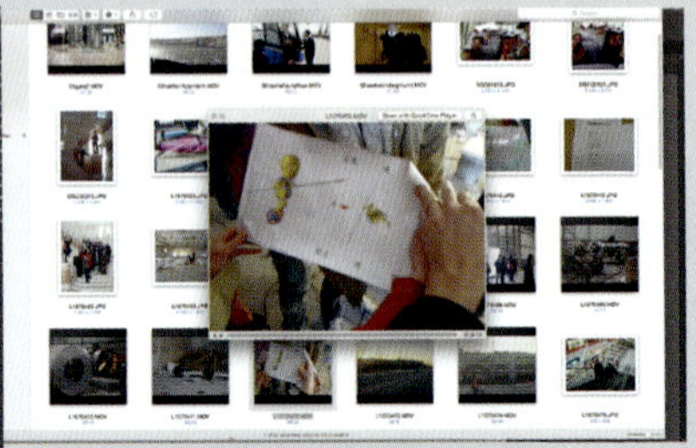

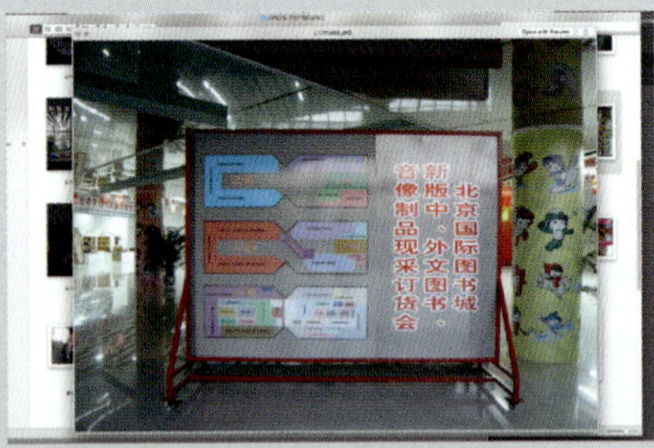
北京国际图书城
新版中、外文图书、
音像制品现采订货会

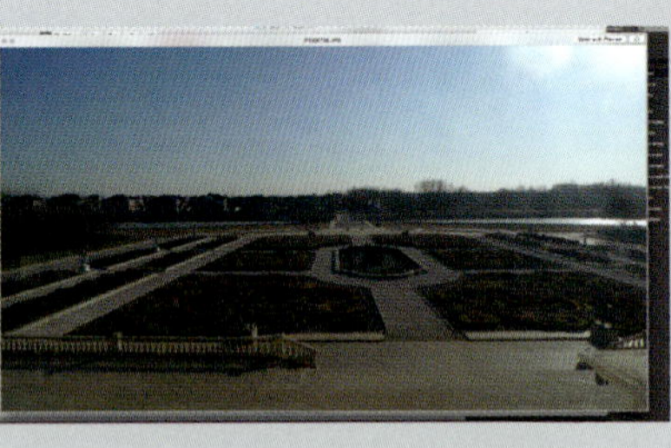

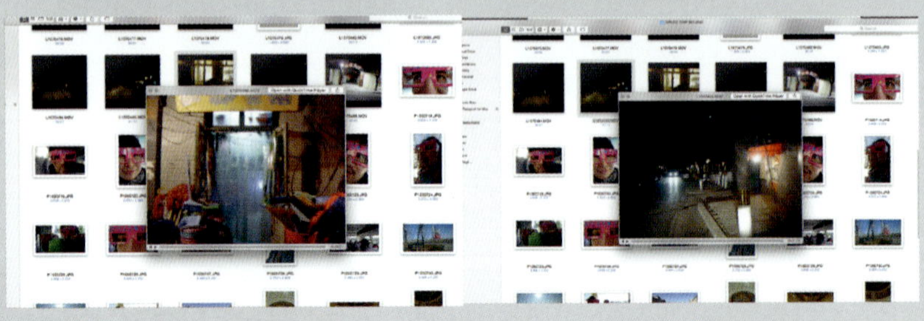

LOS ANGELES SPEED DERIVE

Location: LOS ANGELES, CA, USA. Date: 11 FEBRUARY 2014. Partners: UCLA SUPPER STUDIO + JAI & JAI GALLERY. Participants: PIETERJAN GINCKELS, JIA GU AND ANDREW KOVACS WITH kara.michelle.moore@[redacted], coco.coffman@[redacted], poster.jamie@[redacted], aidencarty@[redacted], melgeti@[redacted], msviri@[redacted], chrisgassaway@[redacted], steffioden@[redacted], hugo.ey.toro@[redacted], juliocesarperez@[redacted], andakins@[redacted], [redacted]@jiayigu.com. Props: SPEEDISM CARDBOARD "CHARLES SAN ANDREAS AND RAY CYRUS WAYFARER" SPECTACLES; FIVE-CAR CARPOOL.

Trip characteristics: Los Angeles Speed Derive starts at the Venice Canals. Different bridges serve different traffic flows. A biologist who joined the trip showed us around, and freaked on the real fiction's less perceptible mechanics: still water, no mosquitoes? Pacific fibre cables finally surface at One Wilshire Blvd., invisibly the fastest building on the West Coast, unnoticed. The group documents the scene in equally speedy fashion. After a full carpooling day of stitching together Los Angeles' areas of acceleration, the fabricated documentation was screened and discussed at a speculative dinner party at Jai & Jai Gallery in downtown LA.

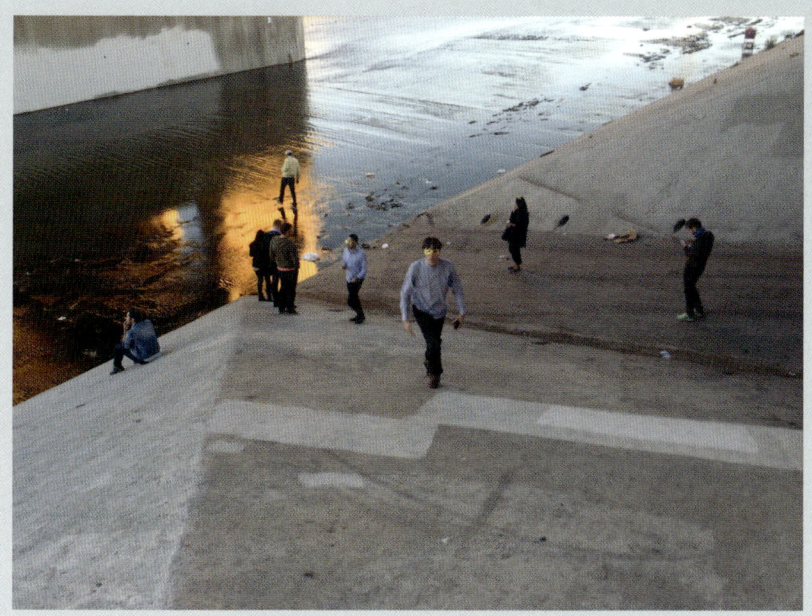

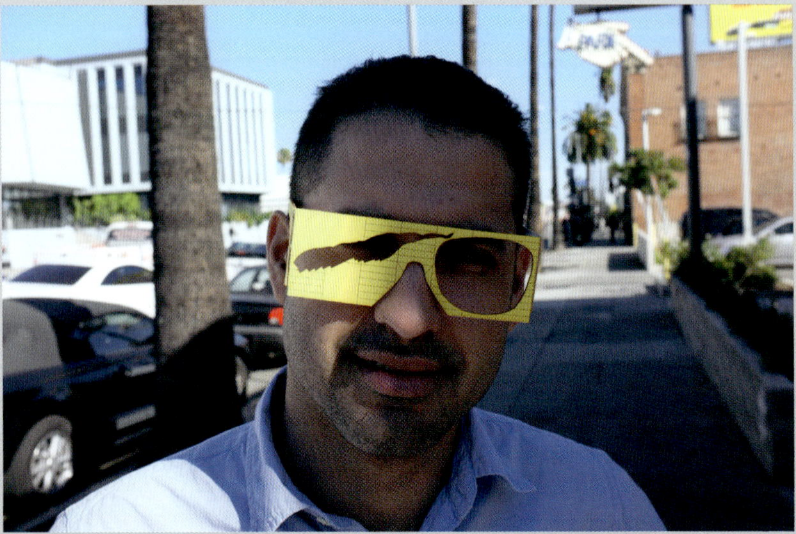

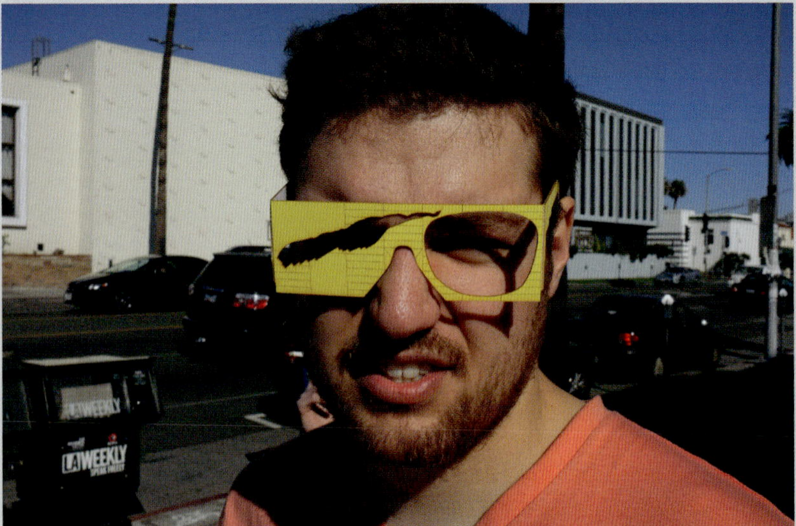

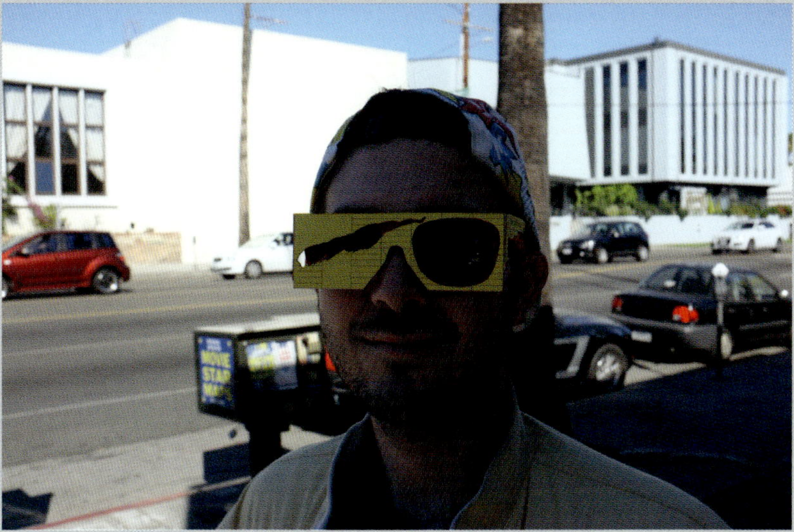

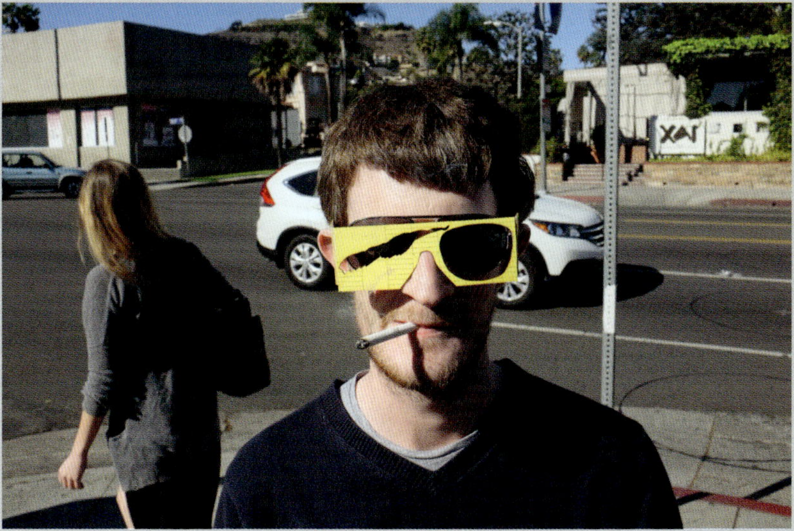

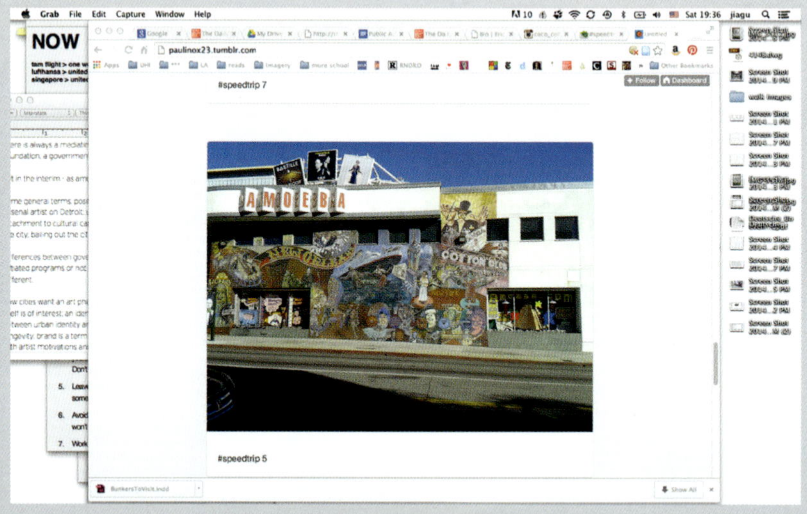
Grab File Edit Capture Window Help
Sat 19:36 jiagu
NOW
paulinox23.tumblr.com
#speedtrip 7
AMOEBA
#speedtrip 5

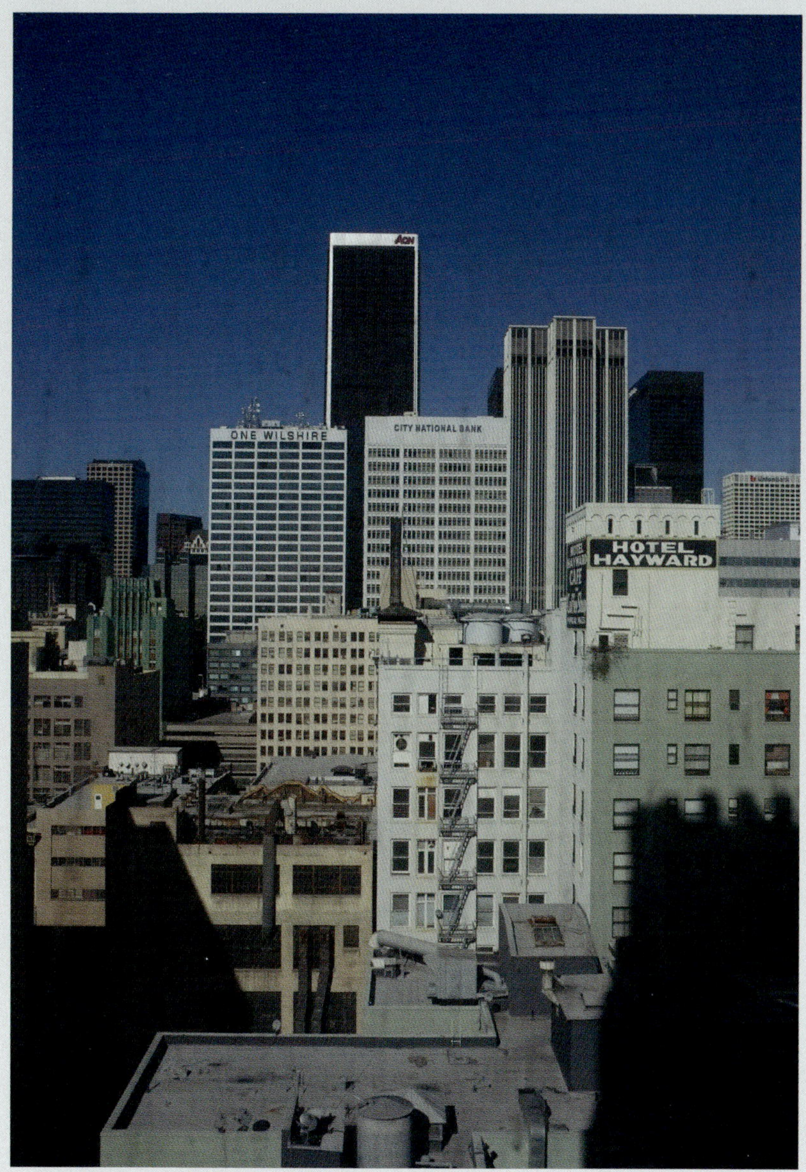
AON
ONE WILSHIRE
CITY NATIONAL BANK
HOTEL
HAYWARD

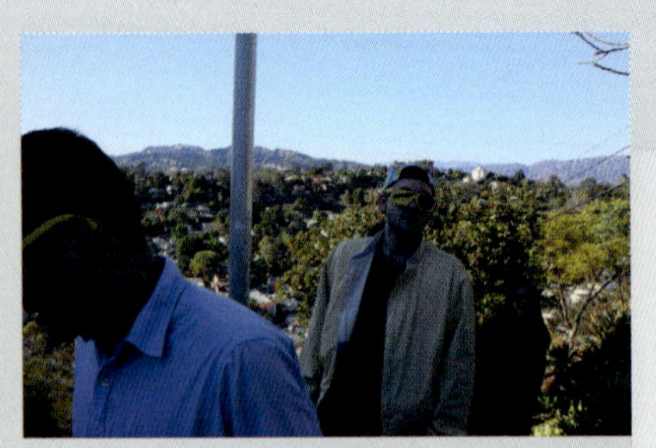

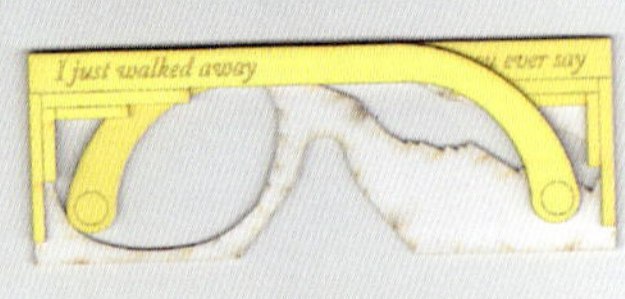

I just walked away
ever say

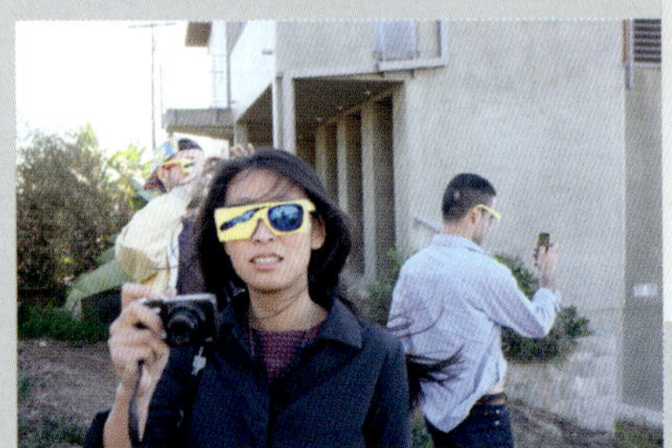

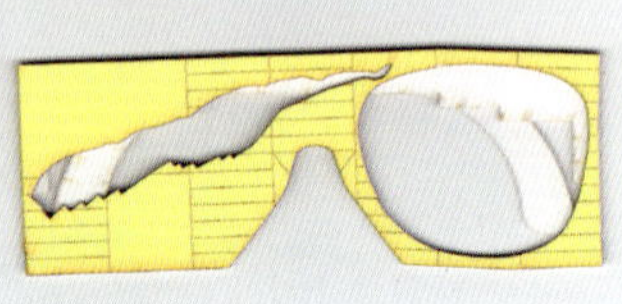

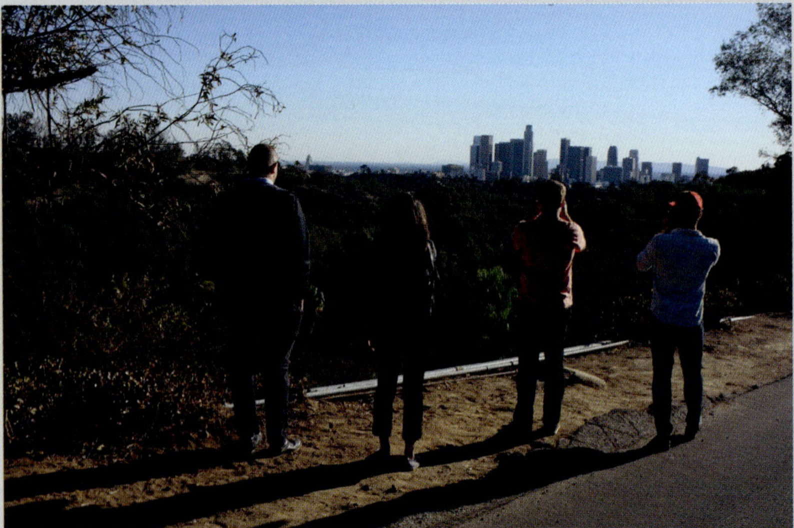

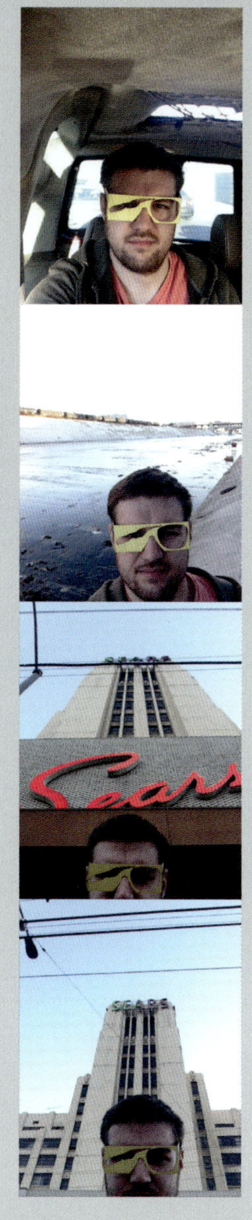
SEARS

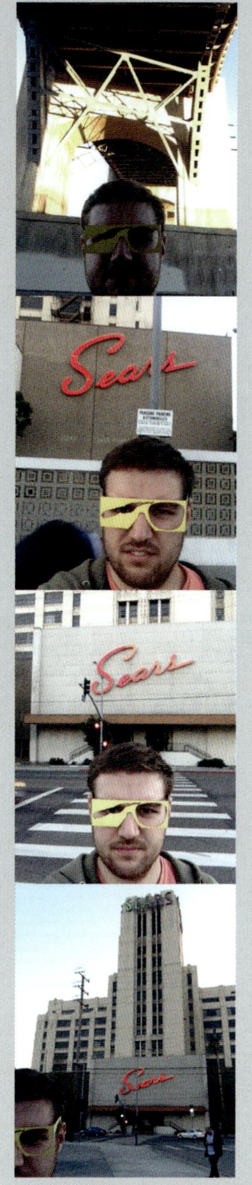
Sears
SEARS
Sears

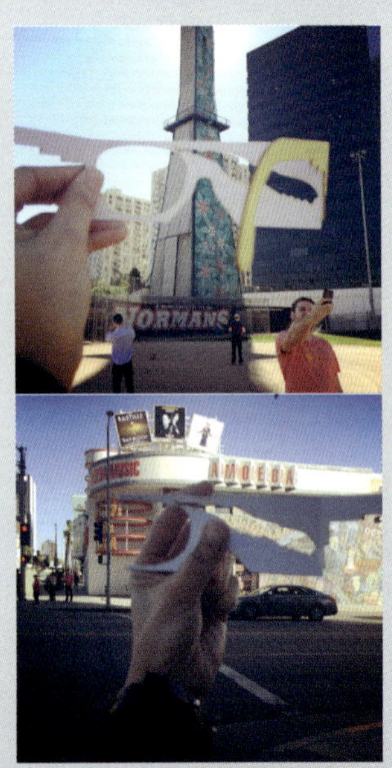
AMOEBA

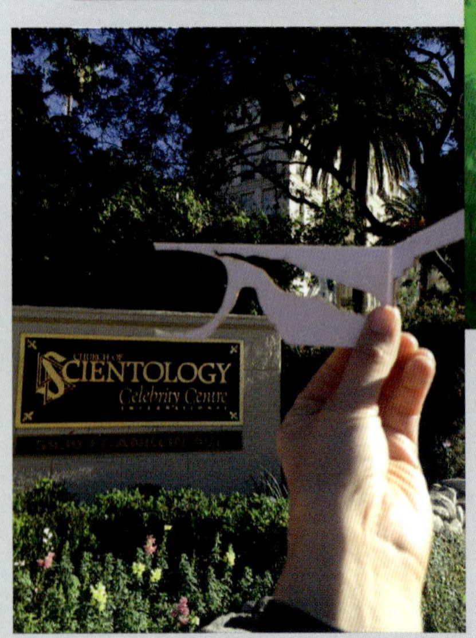
SCIENTOLOGY
Celebrity Centre

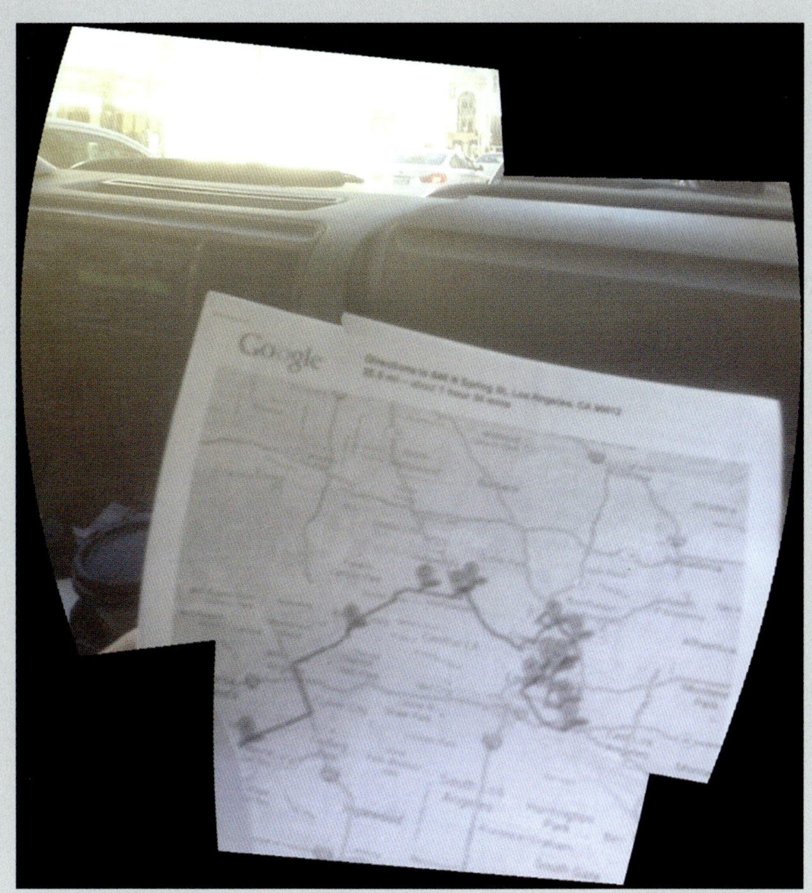
Google

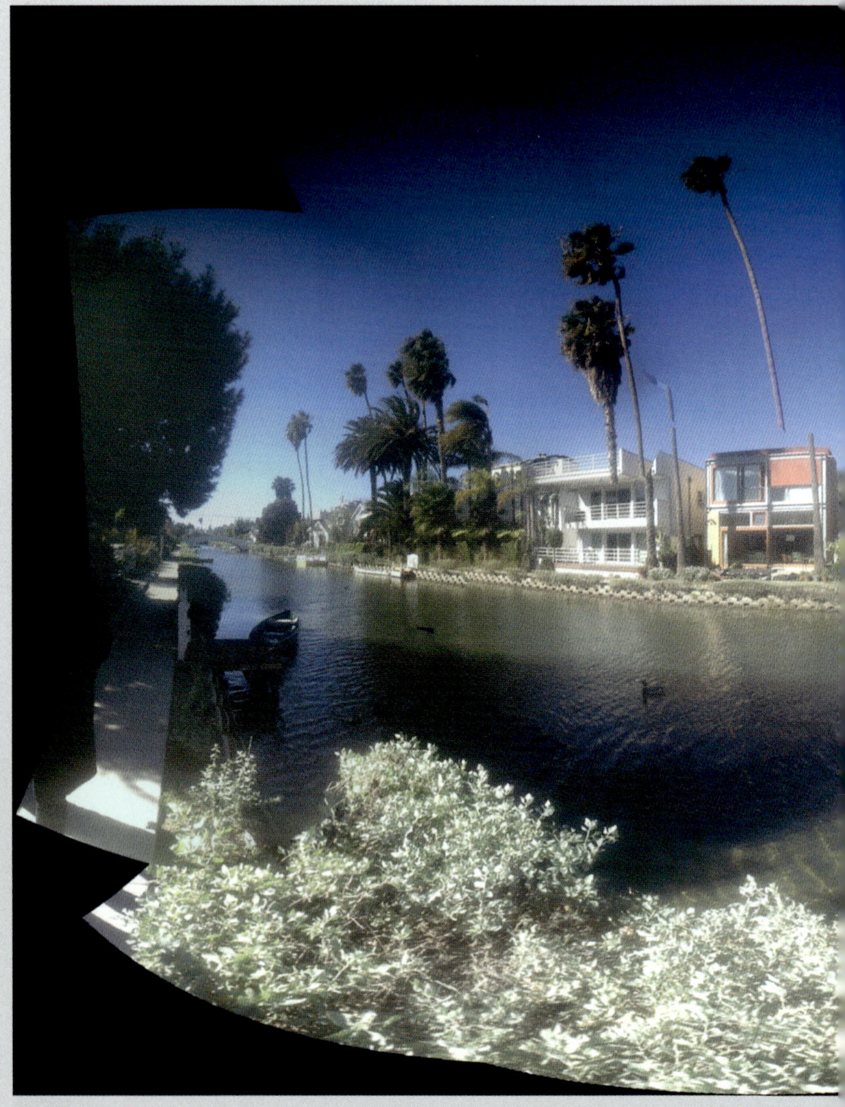

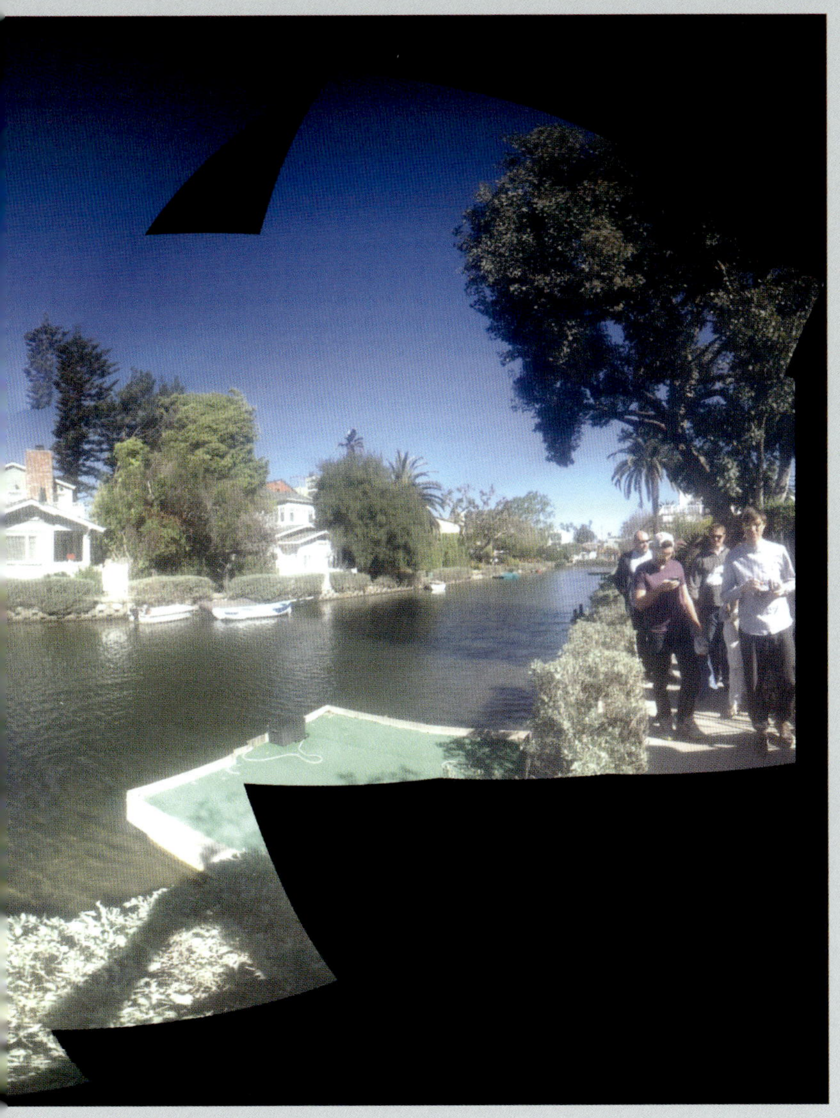

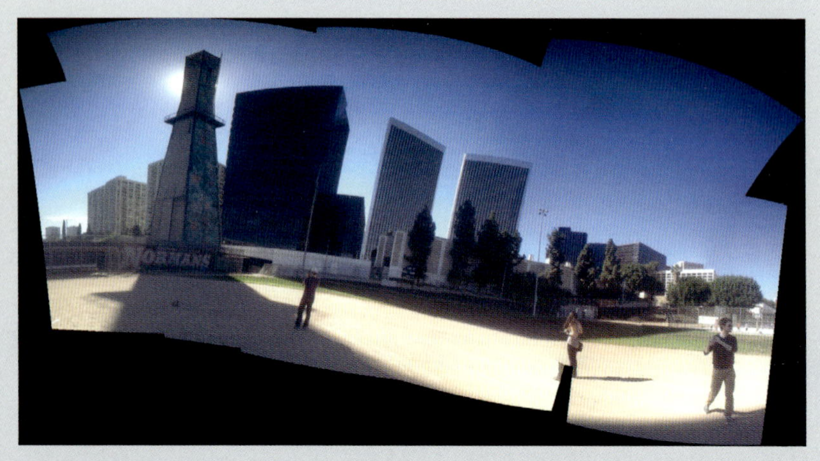
NORMANS

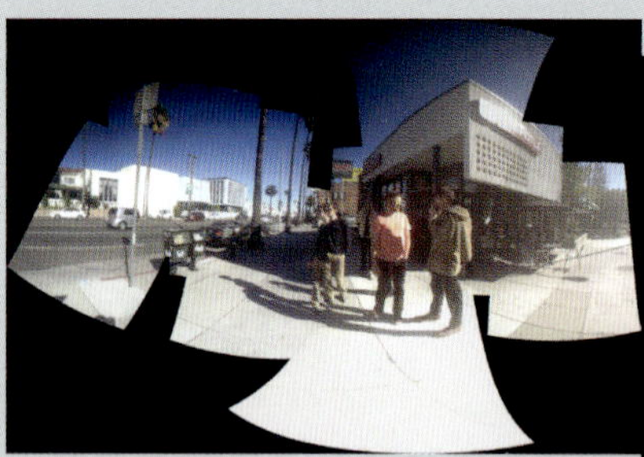

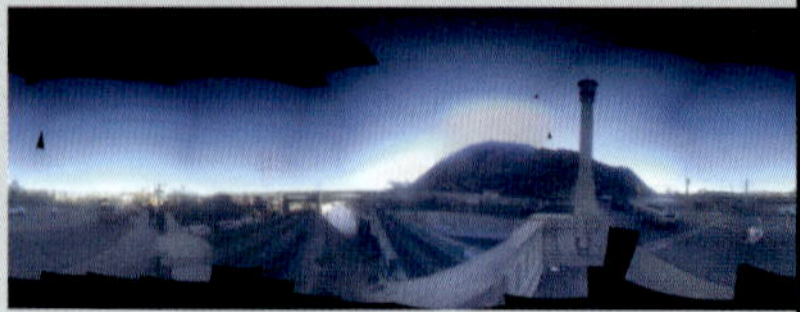

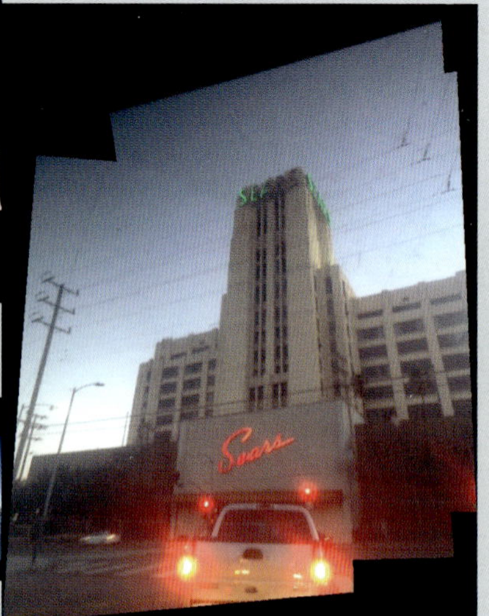

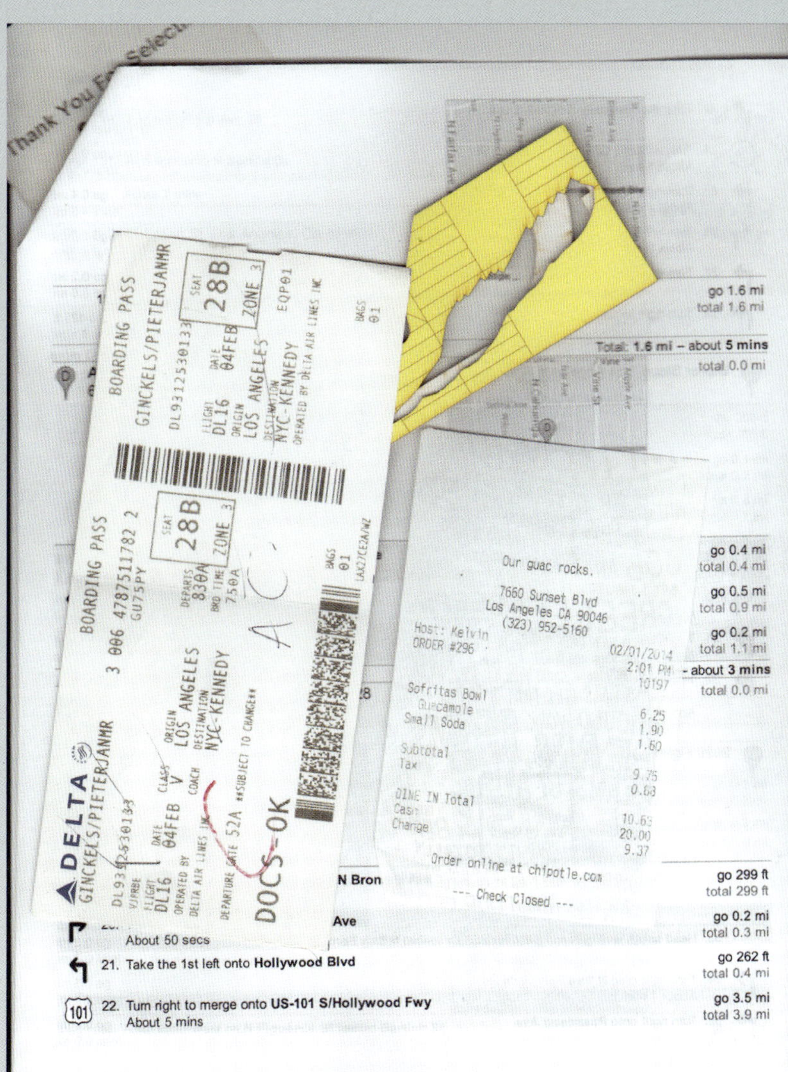

go 1.6 mi
total 1.6 mi
Total: 1.6 mi – about 5 mins
total 0.0 mi
BOARDING PASS
GINCKELS/PIETERJANMR
DL931253013
SEAT 28B
ZONE 3
FLIGHT DL16
DATE 04FEB
ORIGIN LOS ANGELES
DESTINATION NYC-KENNEDY
OPERATED BY DELTA AIR LINES INC
EQP01
BAGS 01
DELTA
BOARDING PASS
GINCKELS/PIETERJANMR
3 006 4787511782 2
GU75PY
SEAT 28B
ZONE 3
DEPARTS 830A
BRD TIME 750A
ORIGIN LOS ANGELES
DESTINATION NYC-KENNEDY
CLASS V
COACH
FLIGHT DL16
DATE 04FEB
OPERATED BY DELTA AIR LINES INC
DEPARTURE GATE 52A
SUBJECT TO CHANGE
BAGS 01
LAX27CE2A/WZ
DOCS-OK
Our guac rocks.
7660 Sunset Blvd
Los Angeles CA 90046
(323) 952-5160
Host: Kelvin
ORDER #296
02/01/2014
2:01 PM
10197
Sofritas Bowl
Guacamole
Small Soda
6.25
1.90
1.60
Subtotal
Tax
9.75
0.88
DINE IN Total
Cash
Change
10.63
20.00
9.37
Order online at chipotle.com
--- Check Closed ---
go 0.4 mi
total 0.4 mi
go 0.5 mi
total 0.9 mi
go 0.2 mi
total 1.1 mi
- about 3 mins
total 0.0 mi
N Bron
go 299 ft
total 299 ft
Ave
About 50 secs
go 0.2 mi
total 0.3 mi
21. Take the 1st left onto Hollywood Blvd
go 262 ft
total 0.4 mi
101
22. Turn right to merge onto US-101 S/Hollywood Fwy
About 5 mins
go 3.5 mi
total 3.9 mi

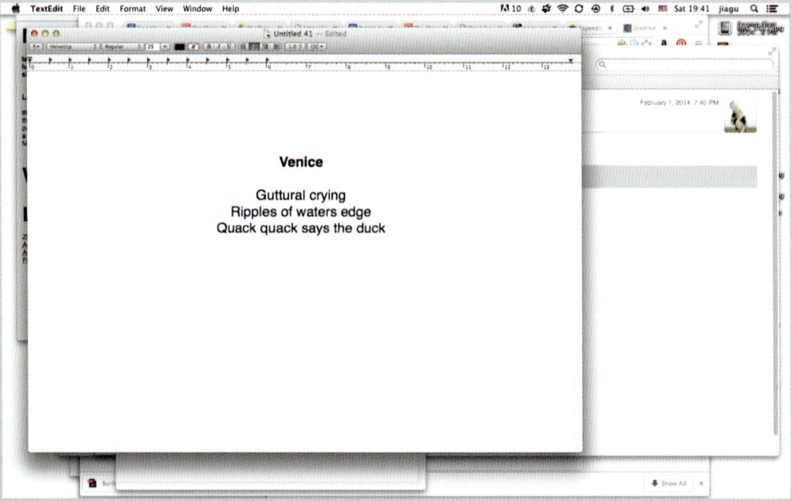

Venice

Guttural crying
Ripples of waters edge
Quack quack says the duck

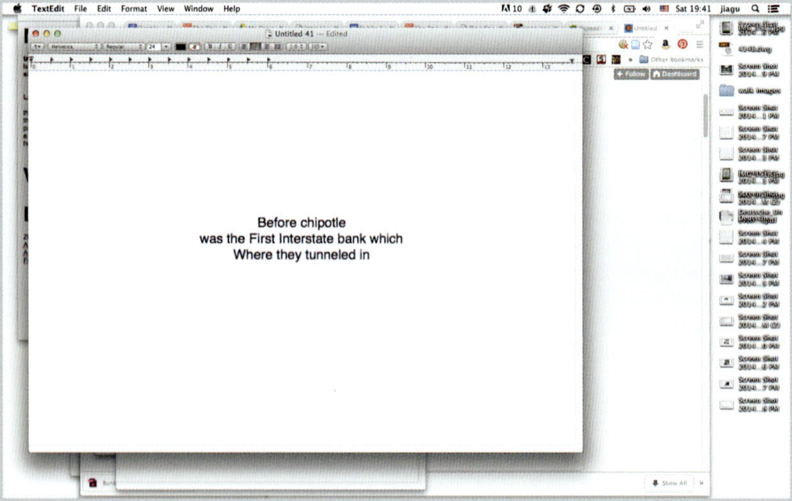

Before chipotle
was the First Interstate bank which
Where they tunneled in

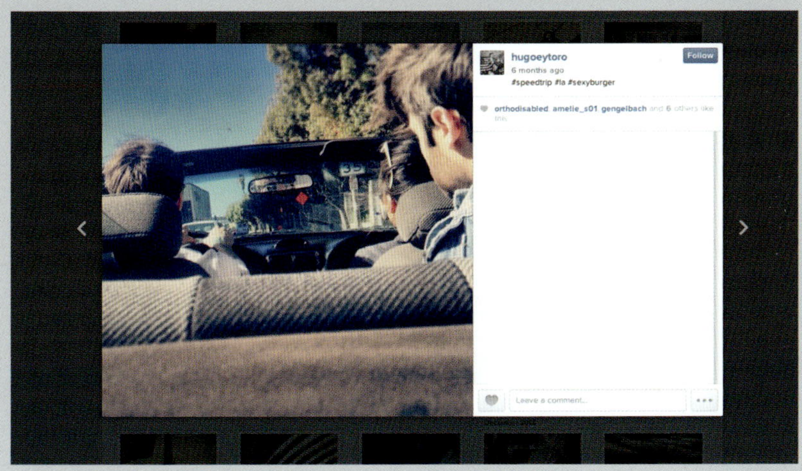
hugoeytoro
Follow
6 months ago
#speedtrip #la #sexyburger
orthodisabled, amelie_s01, gengelbach and 6 others like this.
Leave a comment...

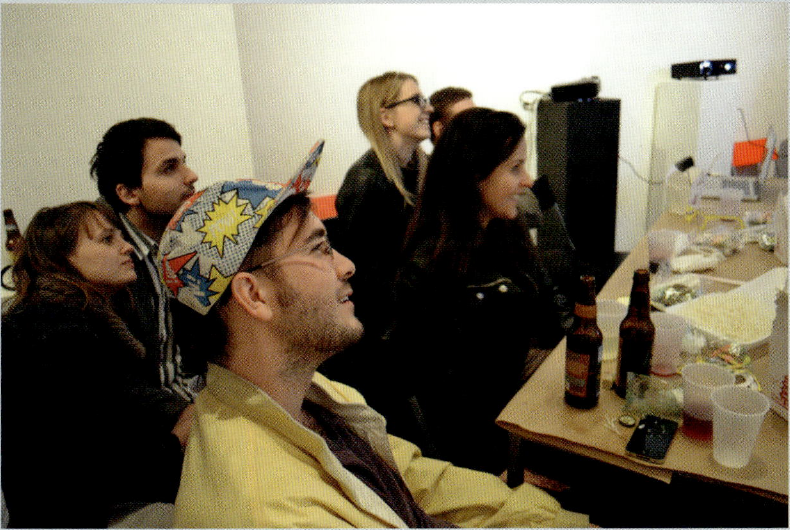

UNLEARNING FROM LAS VEGAS

Location: LAS VEGAS, NEVADA, USA. Date: 27 + 28 JANUARY 2014. Partners: ARCHIVE OF AFFINITIES. Participants: PIETERJAN GINCKELS WITH ANDREW KOVACS AND PATRICK TEIRNEY. Props: ROBERT VENTURI, DENISE SCOTT BROWN, STEVEN IZENOUR, LEARNING FROM LAS VEGAS, MIT PRESS, CAMBRIDGE MA, 1972; SUITE WITH JACUZZI AT THE NEW YORK-NEW YORK HOTEL.

Trip characteristics: To experience the reference, we undertake a pilgrimage to Las Vegas and re-enact Denise Scott Brown's famous photograph. Where did she pose? And where would she stand now, if Las Vegas were still the right grounds for a real reality check? The trip proved crucial in understanding the importance of being there, meditating and mediating such an experience.

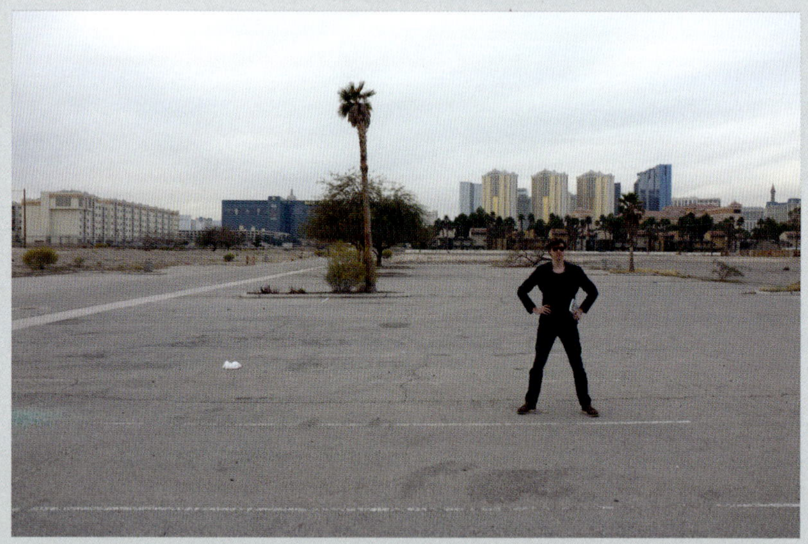

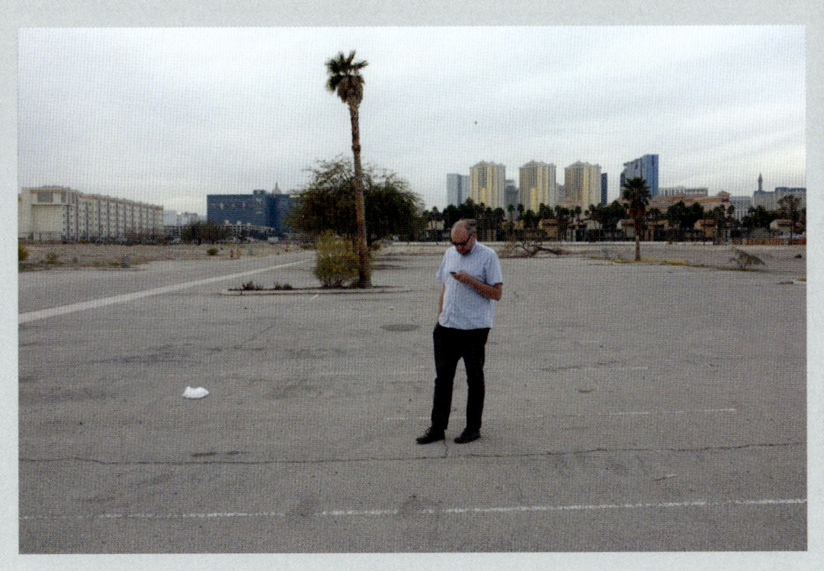

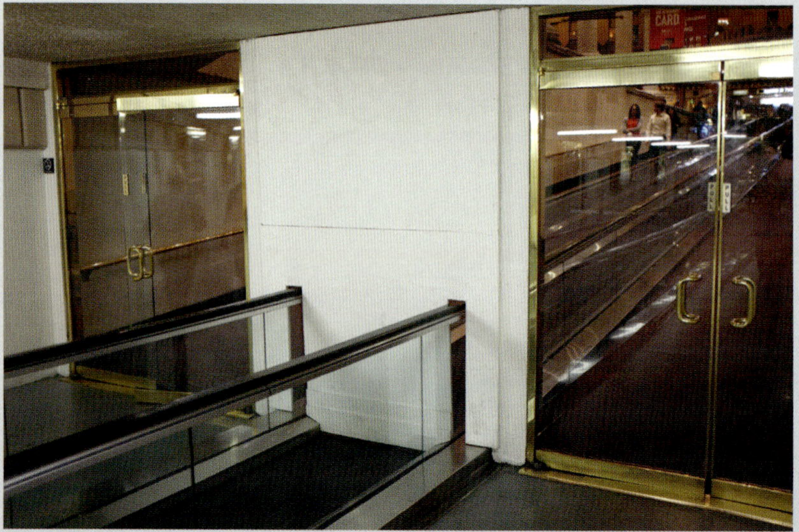

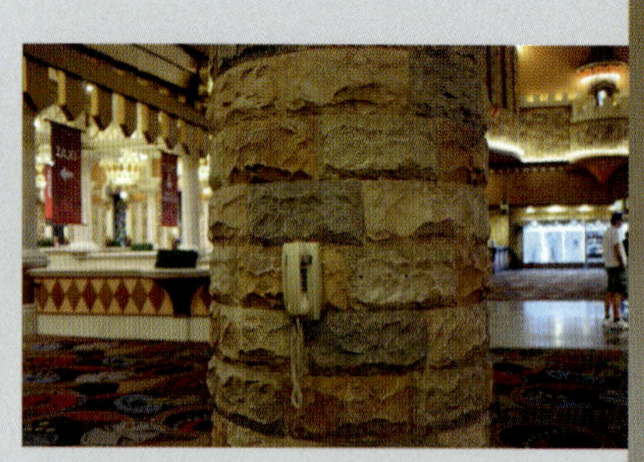
TAXI

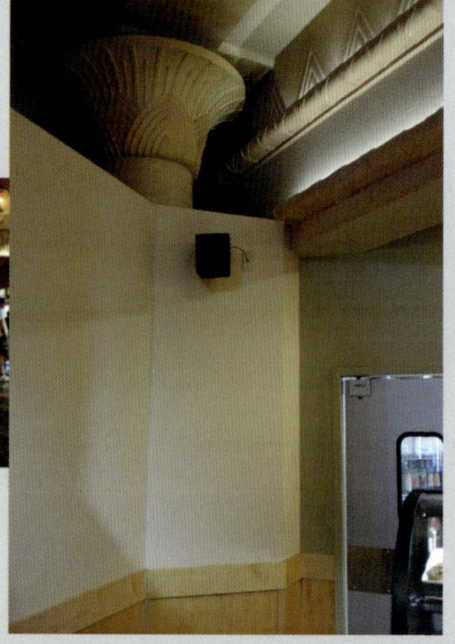

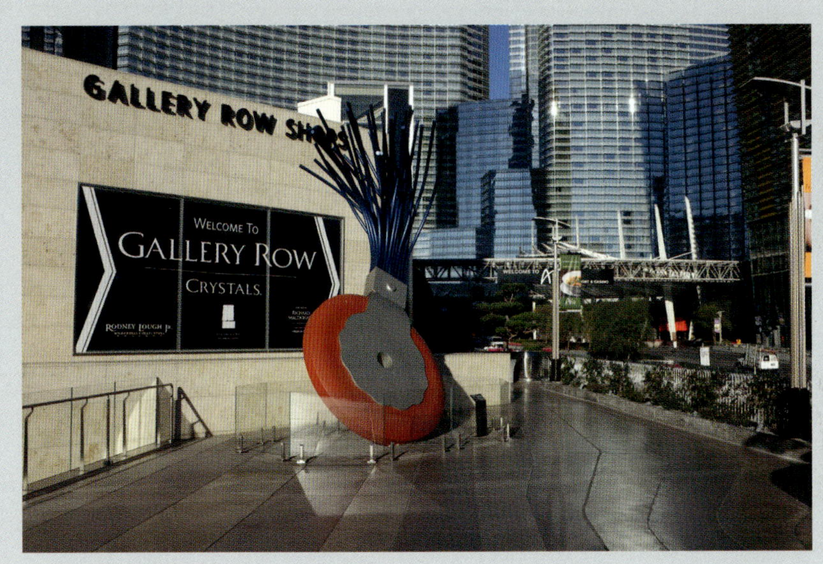
GALLERY ROW SHOPS
WELCOME TO
GALLERY ROW
CRYSTALS
RODNEY LOUGH JR.

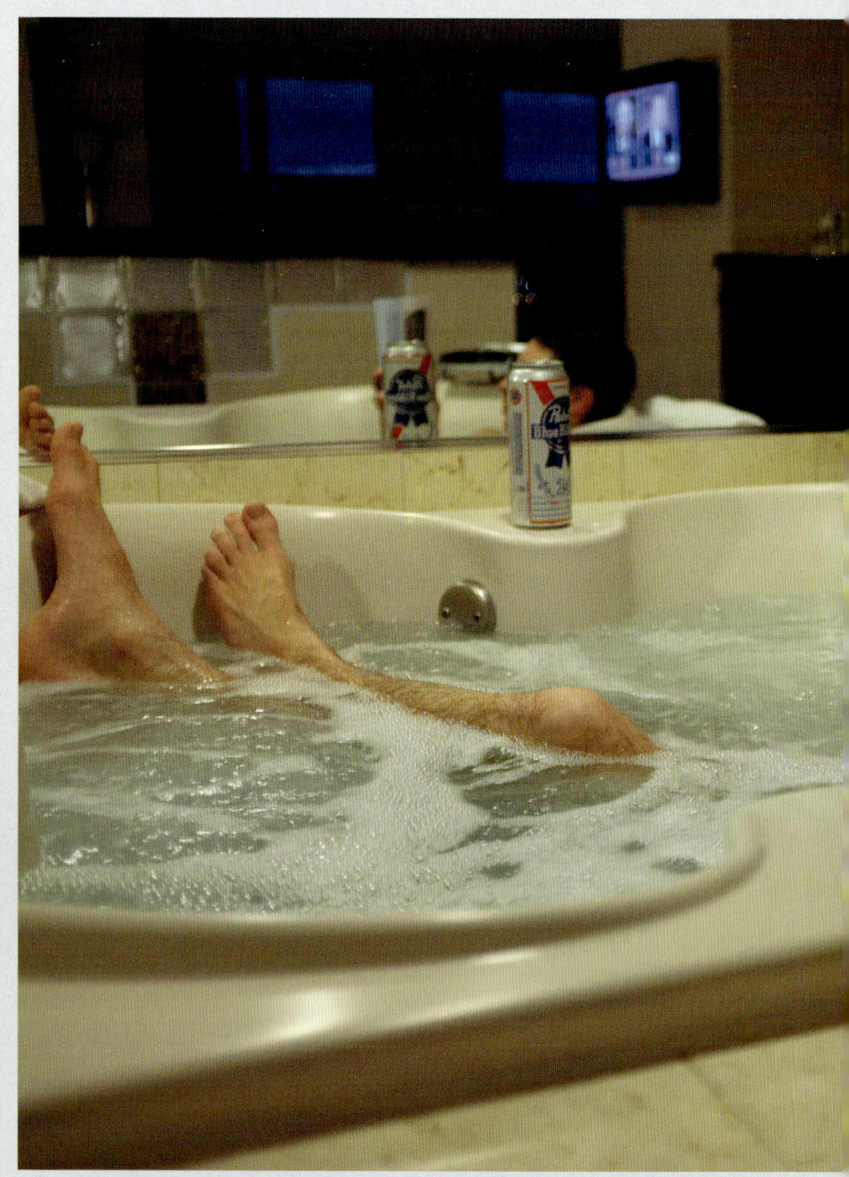

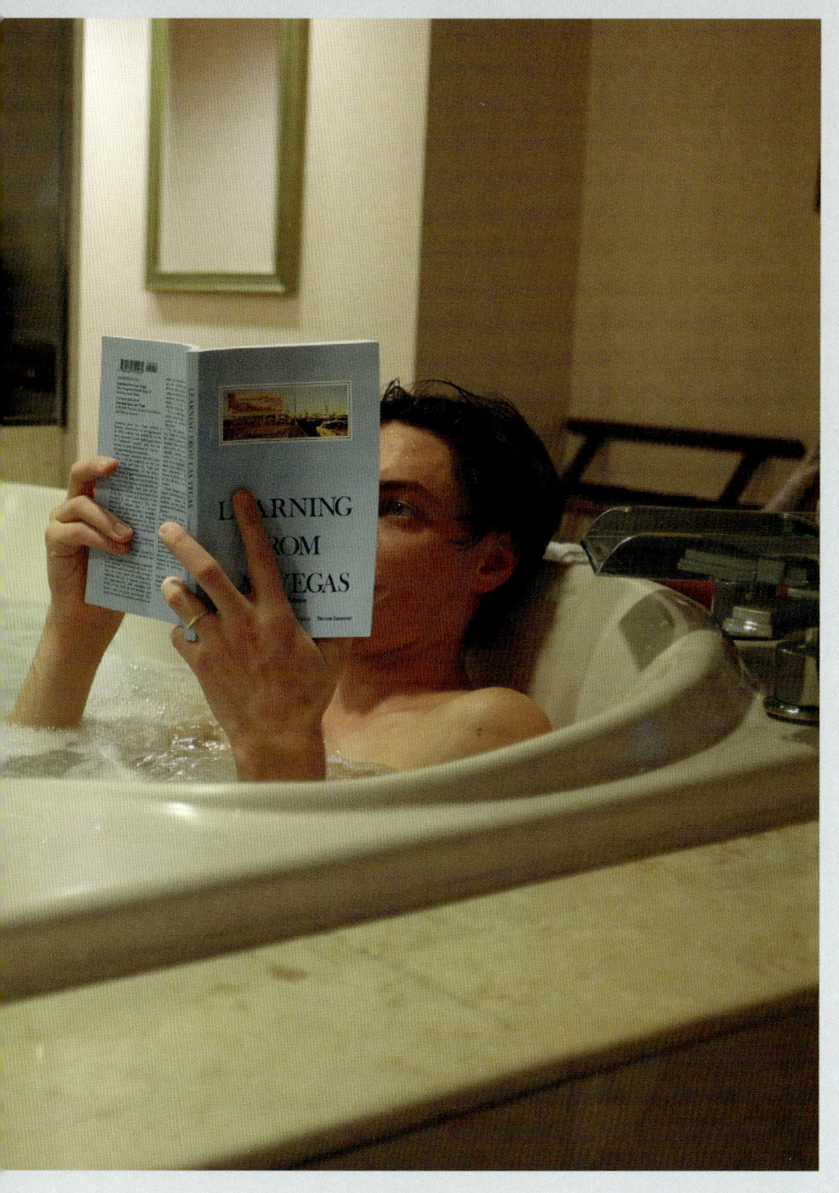
VEGAS

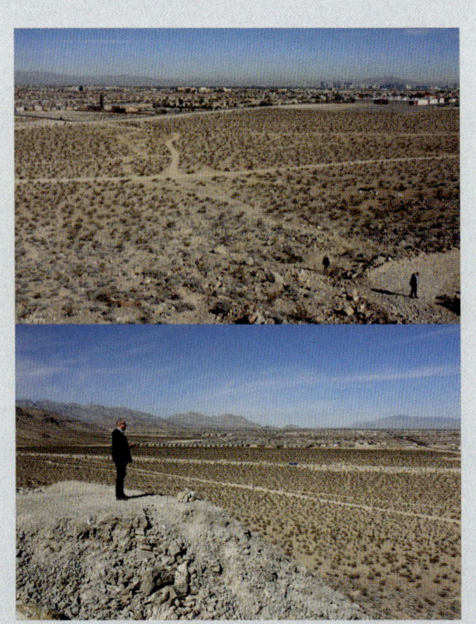

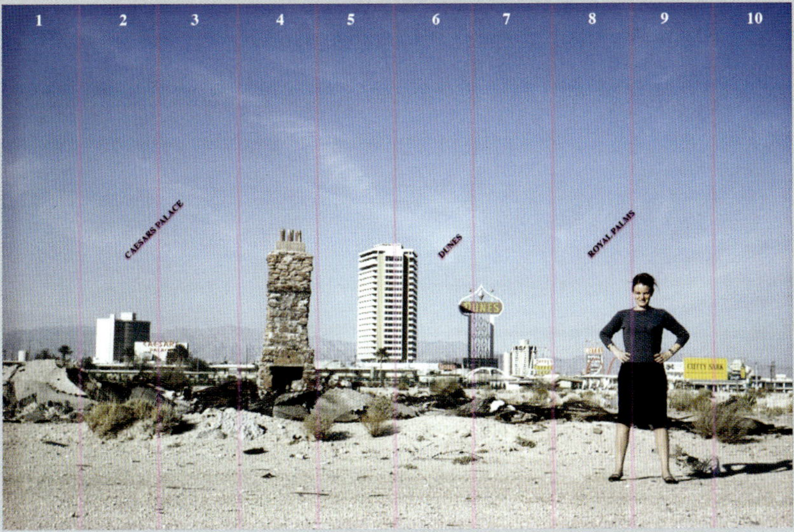

1 2 3 4 5 6 7 8 9 10
CAESARS PALACE
DUNES
ROYAL PALMS

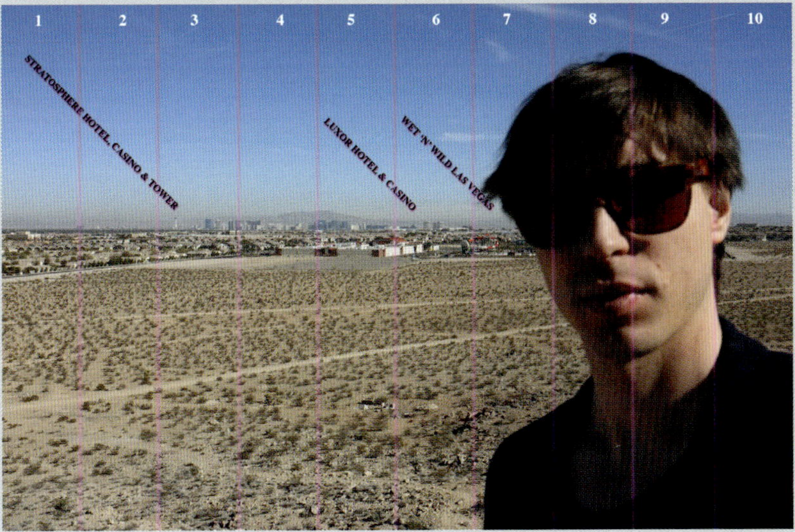

1 2 3 4 5 6 7 8 9 10
STRATOSPHERE HOTEL, CASINO & TOWER
LUXOR HOTEL & CASINO
WET 'N' WILD LAS VEGAS

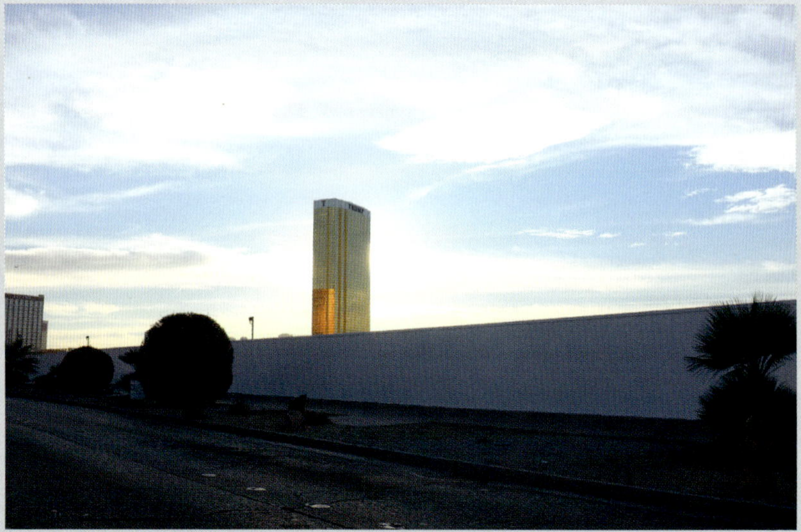

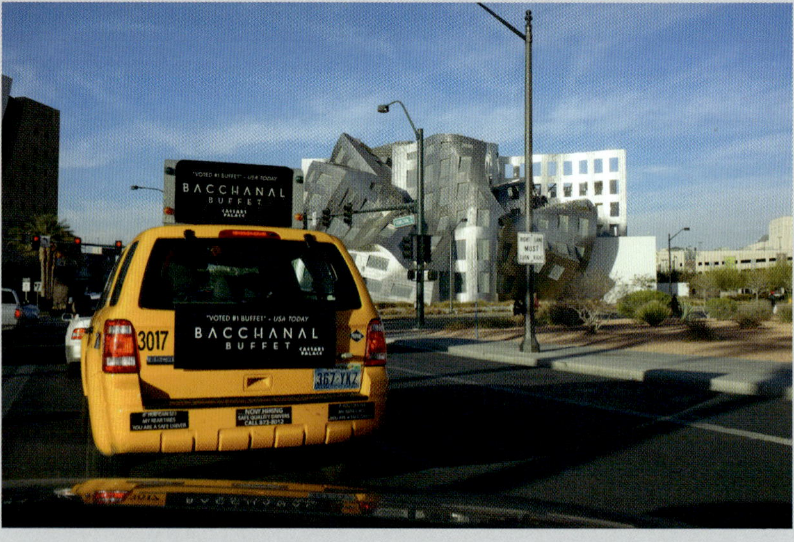
"VOTED #1 BUFFET" - USA TODAY
BACCHANAL
BUFFET
3017
"VOTED #1 BUFFET" - USA TODAY
BACCHANAL
BUFFET

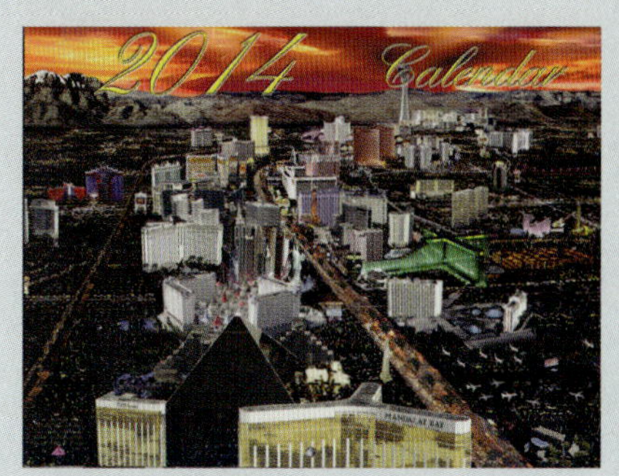
2014 Calendar

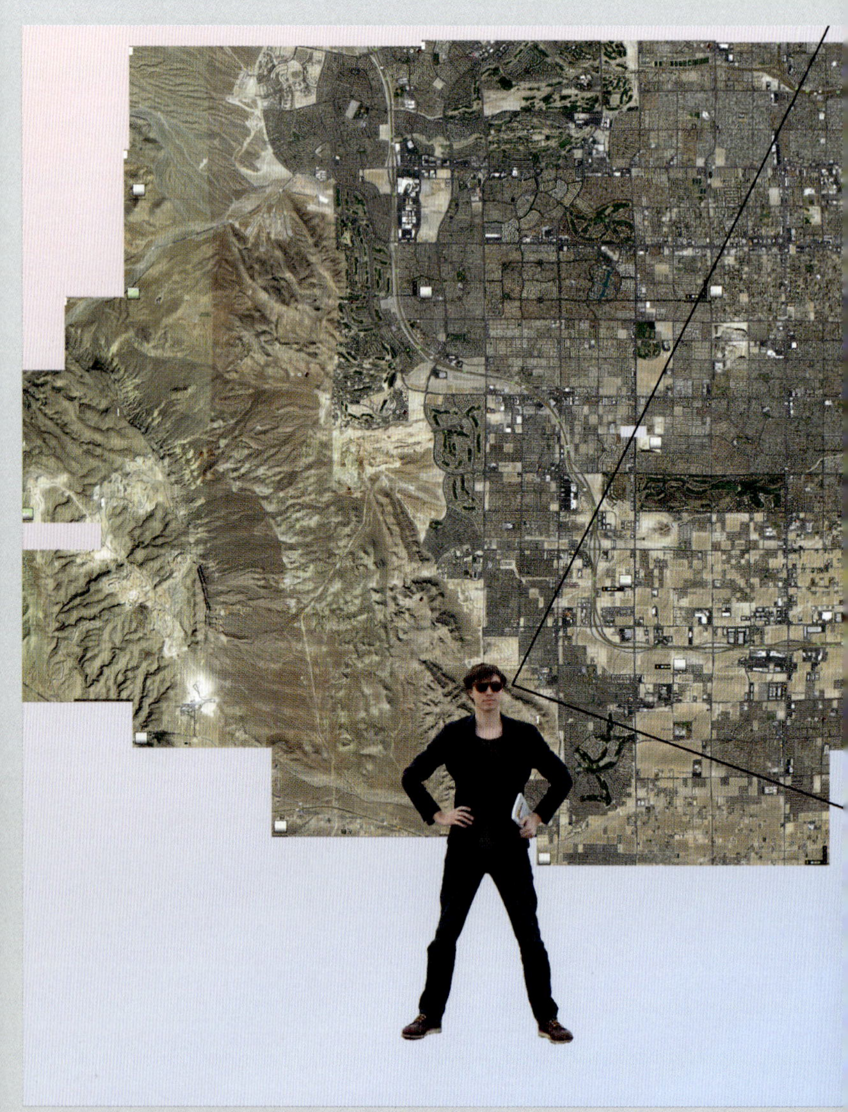

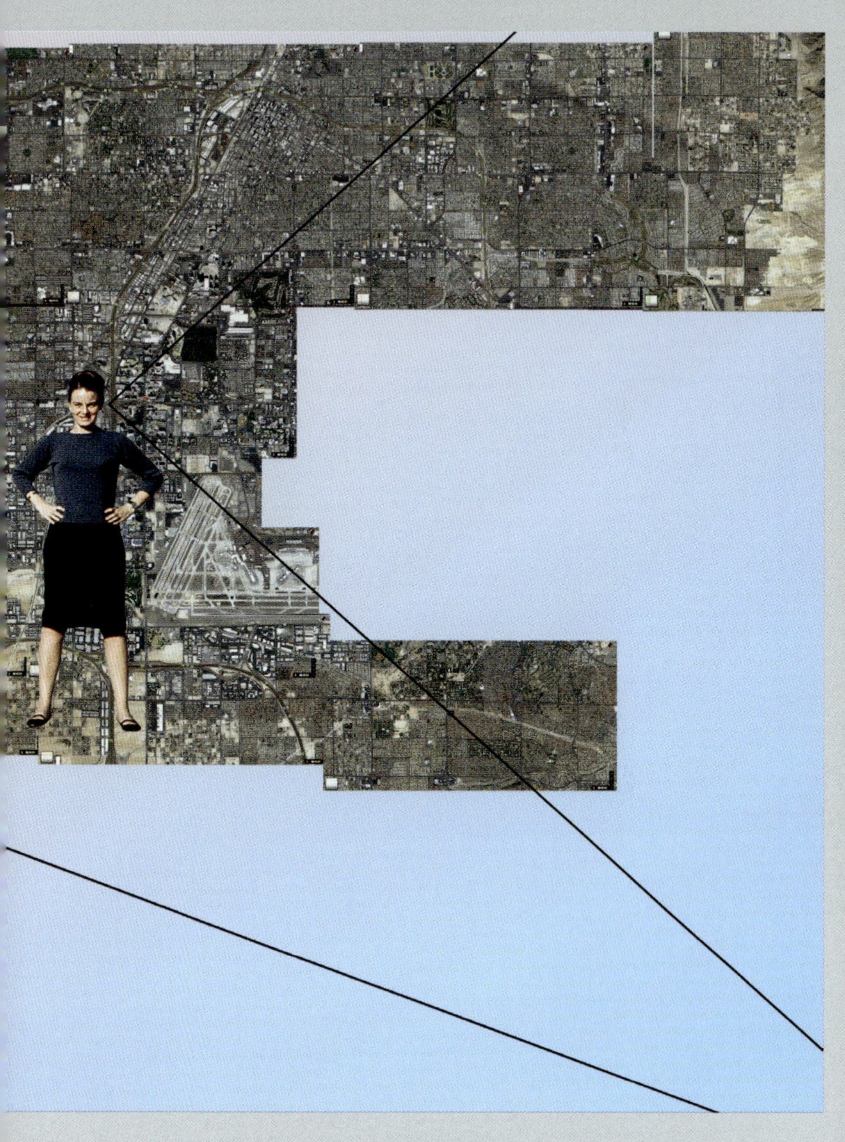

BRUSSELS UNDERGROUND PARKING DERIVE

Location: BRUSSELS CAPITAL REGION PARKING GARAGES, BELGIUM. Date: 9 DECEMBER 2014. Partners: PUBLIC SCHOOL FOR ARCHITECTURE BRUSSELS + Z33 HOUSE FOR CONTEMPORARY ART, HASSELT. Participants: PIETERJAN GINCKELS WITH JOEP GOSEN, HANS MAES, LARS FISCHER, TINE HOLVOET, ANNE VAN OPPEN, ELLEN EURLINGS, MAX ROYAKKERS, NINA JANSSEN. Props: COLLECTIVE ROAD TRIP MIXTAPES ON CD-R; THREE-CAR CARPOOL; IKEA MEATBALL LUNCH.

Trip characteristics: In our time, and especially in our city, parking garages are both hated and loved, booming and going extinct. Black holes, back rooms. Invisible monsters and aggressively inspiring architectural artefacts. Air pockets and sign systems. Panoramic in oblivion. SPEED TRIP: BRUSSELS PARKING GARAGE DERIVE proposes a carpool daytrip around town, in which we stitch together a route via both Brussels' well-known and its more exotic parking garages. Usually, an entry ticket to a garage grants you a fifteen minute timeframe in which you can drive off again – not having found a decent spot to park. These free moments – and the collective soundtrack – will decide the pace of the trip.

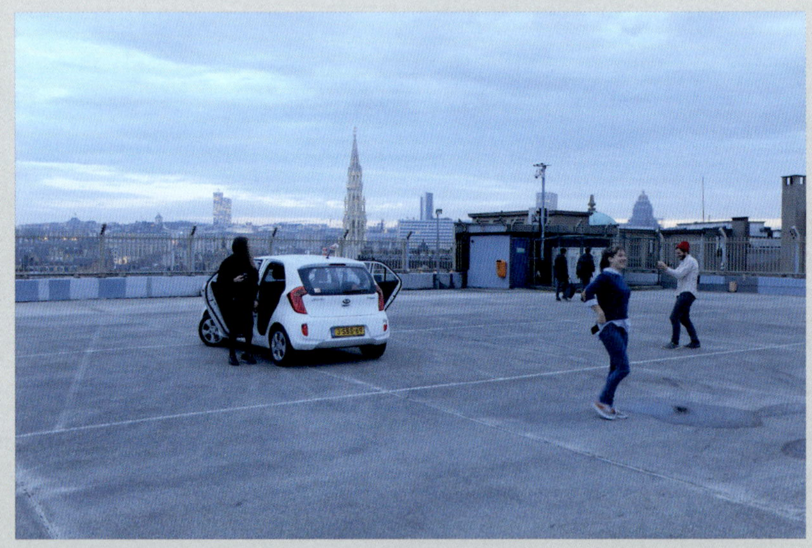

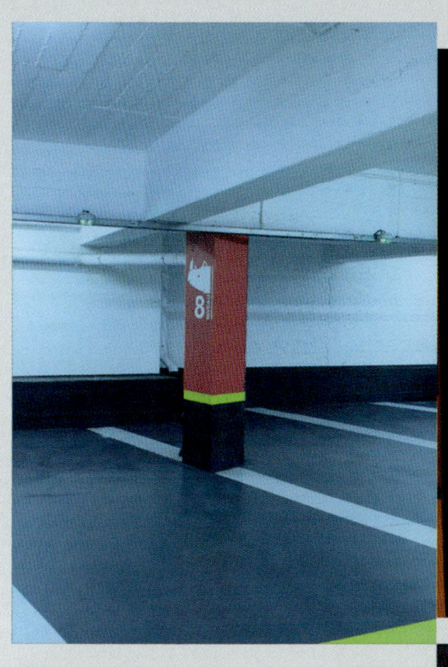

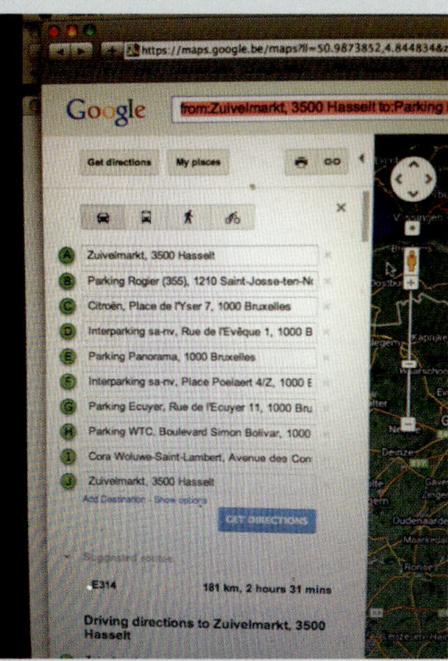
https://maps.google.be/maps?ll=50.9873852,4.844834&z
Google
from:Zuivelmarkt, 3500 Hasselt to:Parking
Get directions
My places
Zuivelmarkt, 3500 Hasselt
Parking Rogier (355), 1210 Saint-Josse-ten-N
Citroën, Place de l'Yser 7, 1000 Bruxelles
Interparking sa-nv, Rue de l'Evêque 1, 1000 B
Parking Panorama, 1000 Bruxelles
Interparking sa-nv, Place Poelaert 4/Z, 1000 E
Parking Ecuyer, Rue de l'Ecuyer 11, 1000 Bru
Parking WTC, Boulevard Simon Bolivar, 1000
Cora Woluwe-Saint-Lambert, Avenue des Con
Zuivelmarkt, 3500 Hasselt
GET DIRECTIONS
E314
181 km, 2 hours 31 mins
Driving directions to Zuivelmarkt, 3500 Hasselt

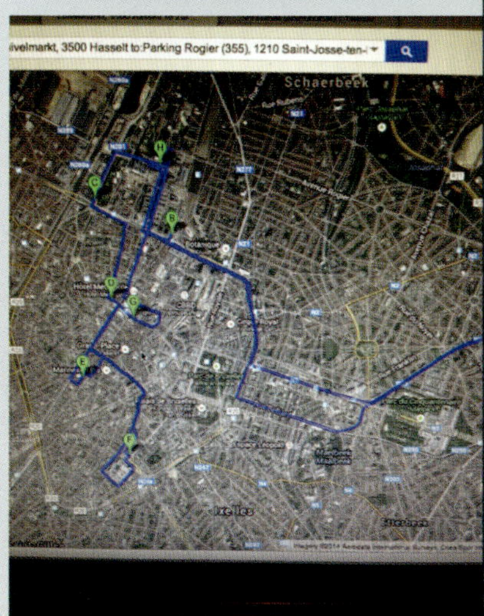
ivelmarkt, 3500 Hasselt to:Parking Rogier (355), 1210 Saint-Josse-ten-
Schaerbeek

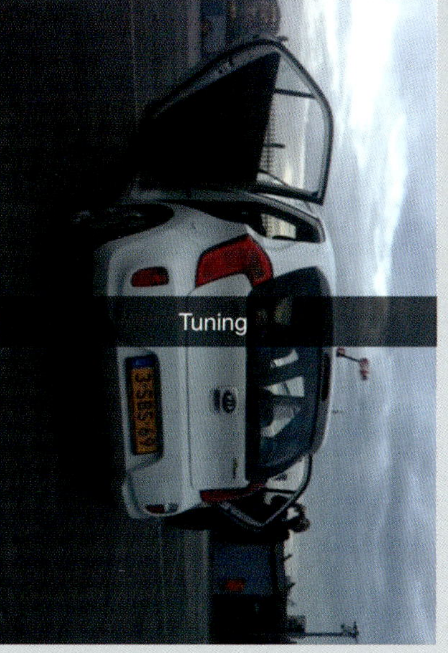
Tuning

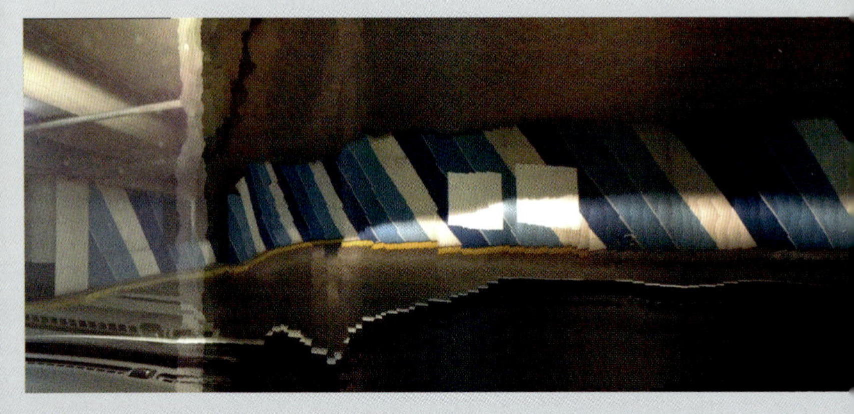

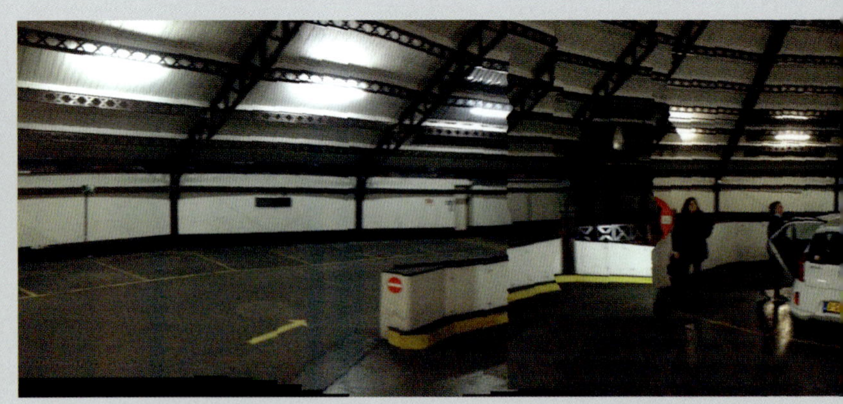

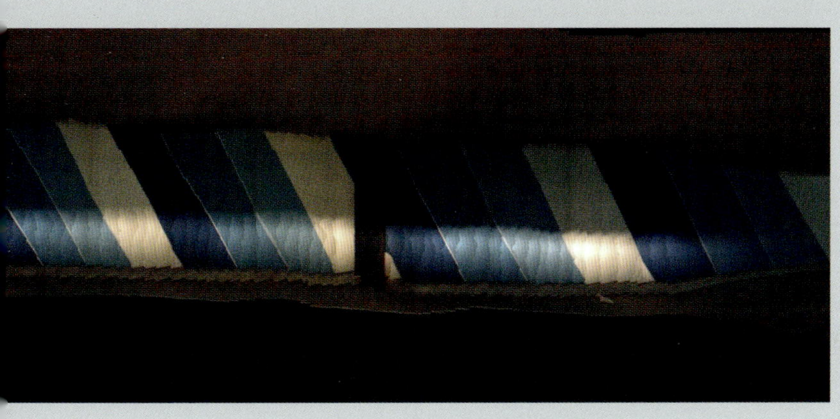

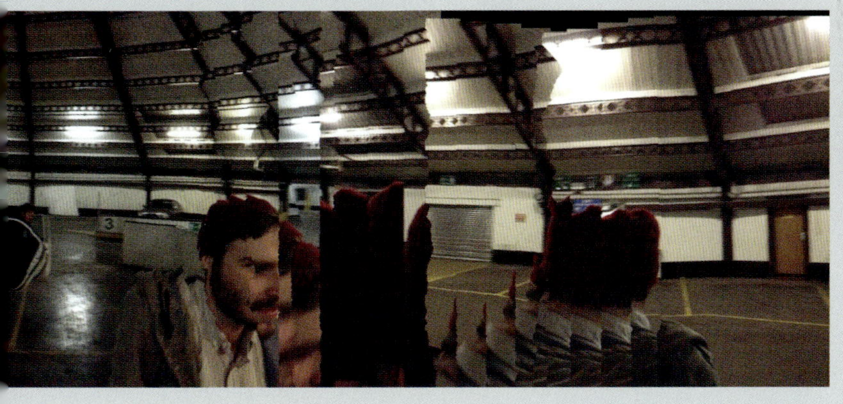

Safari File Edit View History Bookmarks Window Help

psfa-bxl.org

dec 10, 2014, architectuur en macht: de mach

gebruiker, herinnering, context. gebruiker—de bewoner is diegene die ruimte
de ruimte. deze ruimte, het gebouwde is bedacht door de architect, het zijn zijn ideeën die de ruimte
hebben vormgegeven. herinnering—nostalgie is iets persoonlijk. iets dat iets blijft zonder dat het
fysiek nog aanwezig is, juist de herinnering. context—de plaats heeft een macht op ons als
gebruiker van de ruimte. een context kan mensen opleggen om bepaalde acties te ondernemen.
maar kan het ons ons ook volledig vrij laten zonder aan ruimtelijke kwaliteit in te boeten. we starten
met drie introducties waarin we werken rondom deze thema's. om daarna deze resultaten in een
overkoepelend debat over architectuur en macht samen te brengen. om ons hierbij te ondersteunen
komen lieven de cauter, gideon boie en kristof uytterhoeven.

nov 28, 2014, speed trip—brussels parking garage derive

in our time, and especially in our city, parking garages are both hated and loved, booming and going extinct. speed trip: brussels parking garage dérive proposes a carpool daytrip around town. we'll stitch together a route via both brussels' well-known and its more exotic parking garages. participants will share cars and document the disconnected nodes along the way.

nov 16, 2014, [psfa-bxl—outpost charleroi] présentation du projet chemindesterrils

projet chemindesterrils, présentation du projet déposé à la ville et les avancées actuelles. présentation diapo par micheline dufert. passionnés de sentiers, de liaisons vicinales, de chemins au long cours, de sentiers de grande randonnée, d'architectures urbaines, de paysages de terre et de béton, du charbon à la métallurgie.

nov 16, 2014, [psfa-bxl—outpost charleroi] mapping charleroi

this class explores the role that maps can play in how we under
tool, the class aims to explore our vario
participants are invited to

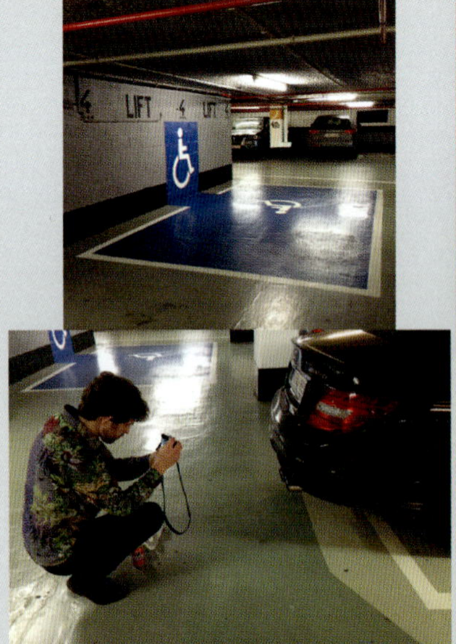

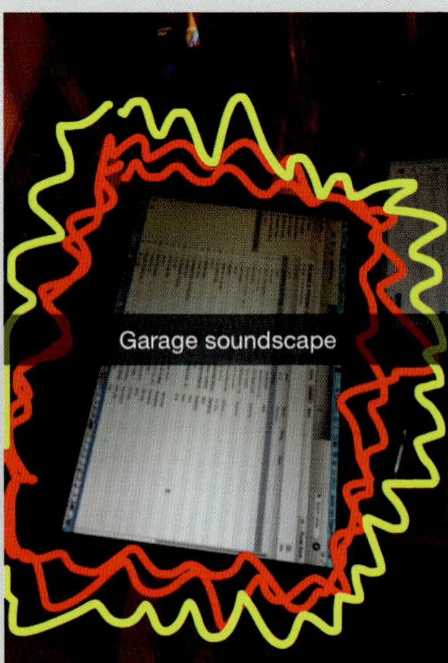

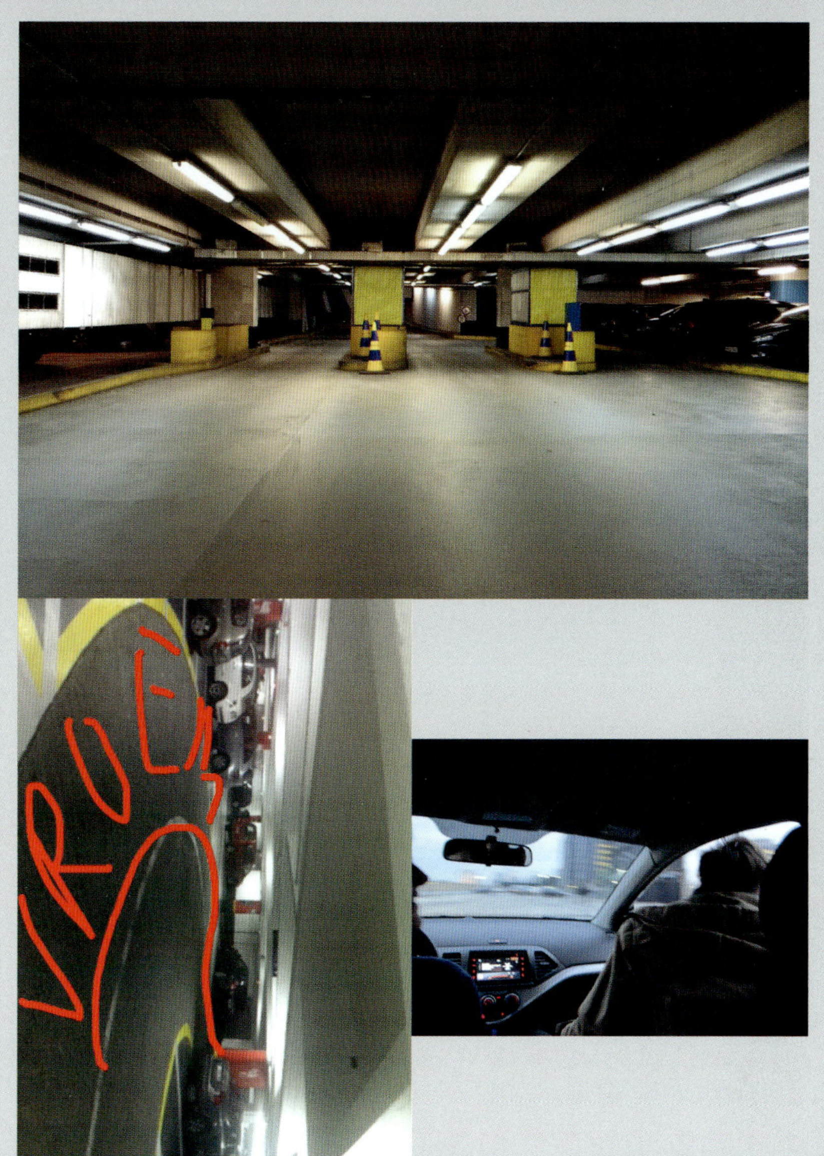

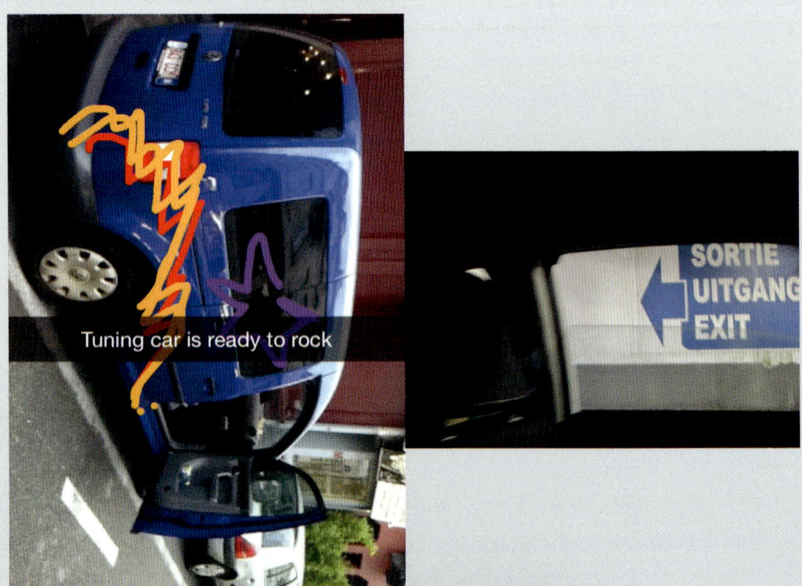
Tuning car is ready to rock
SORTIE
UITGANG
EXIT

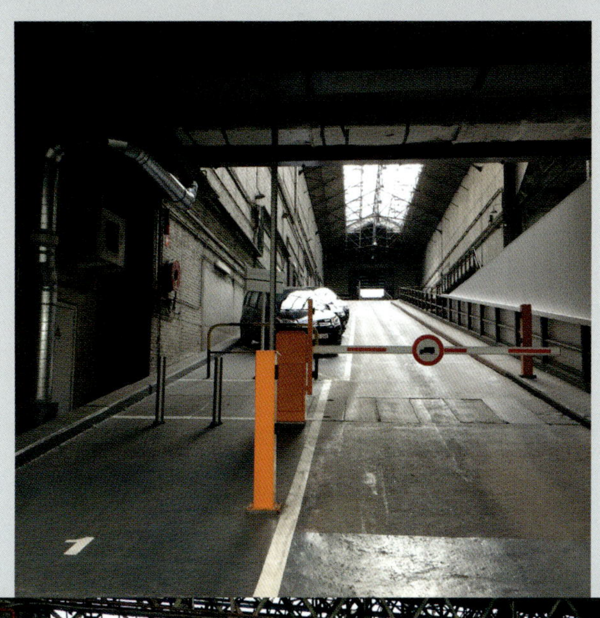

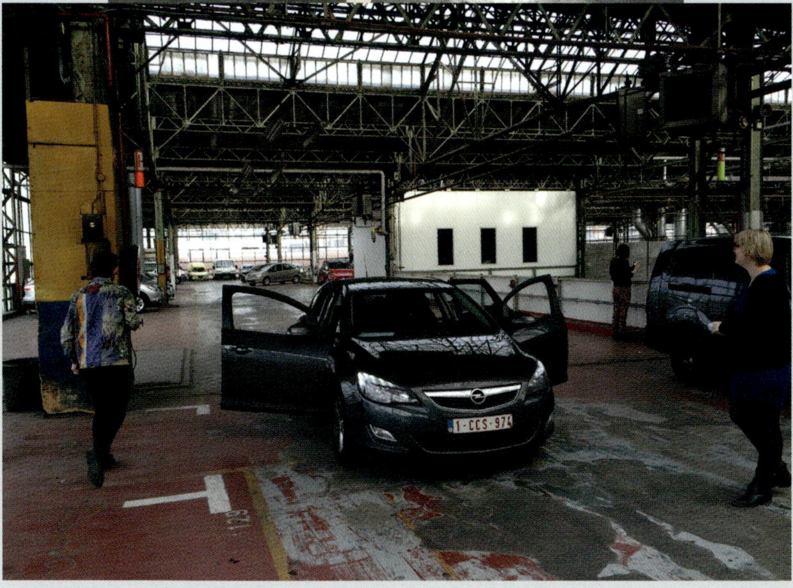

RIETVELD SAFARI

Location: BELGIAN COAST. Date: 19 FEBRUARY 2016. Partners: "PARADIGM WEEKLY: KANYE KABANON" MASTER ELECTIVE STUDIO AT KU LEUVEN FACULTY OF ARCHITECTURE, SINT-LUCAS CAMPUS. Participants: PIETERJAN GINCKELS, CORNEEL CANNAERTS, GILLES RETSIN AND PARADIGM WEEKLY: KANYE KABANON 2016 STUDENTS: KATRIEN COPPIETERS, FRANCESCA CREMONA, NIKOLAS DEBRAUWER, THIJS DE PAUW, ASTER DE VALCK, HENRI DEVLAMINCK, VAAGARD ERDAHL NYAAS, XIAOQI GUO, SAMUEL HERMANS, MATEUSZ JUCHIMOWICZ, BARBORA JURICKOVA, ALESSANDRO MARTINELLI, MILDA PACEVICIUTE, REBECCA SARA SILVA, NATHAN VAN DEN BOSSCHE, CAMILLE VINCK, YILING ZHOU. Props: PARADIGM WEEKLY DESIGNED, LASER-CUT CARDBOARD GLASSES; PORTABLE SPEAKERS AND PHONES PLAYING THE GREY ALBUM BY DANGER MOUSE; BLACK AND/OR CAMO OUTFIT.

Trip characteristics: Beyond imagination, we take international architecture students on a prospective career-tour along Rietveld real estate projects. Concentrated in prime locations along the Belgian coast, these neo-minimal condos rise and shine by means of their names, and their names only: Oscar Niemeyer RRR, Walter Gropius RRR, Charles & Ray Eames RRR, Henry Van De Velde RRR. Are we in a post-blogism theme park, where interior delight, rendered finesse and all-you-can-eat perfectly converge?

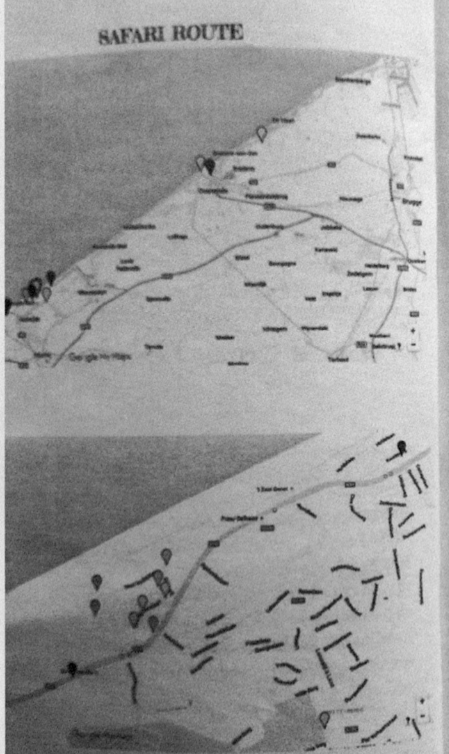

PROJECT INDEX

- PARK ATLANTIS
- CASINO KURSAAL
- CHARLES & R. EAMES RRR
- BAUHAUS RRR
- OSCAR NIEMEYER RRR
- MARCEL BREUER RRR
- WALTER GROPIUS RRR
- VAKANTIEKOLONIE
- VERNER PANTON RRR
- ARNE JACOBSEN RRR
- SAARINEN RRR
- HENRY VAN DE VELDE RRR
- NORMANDIE
- CORBU RRR

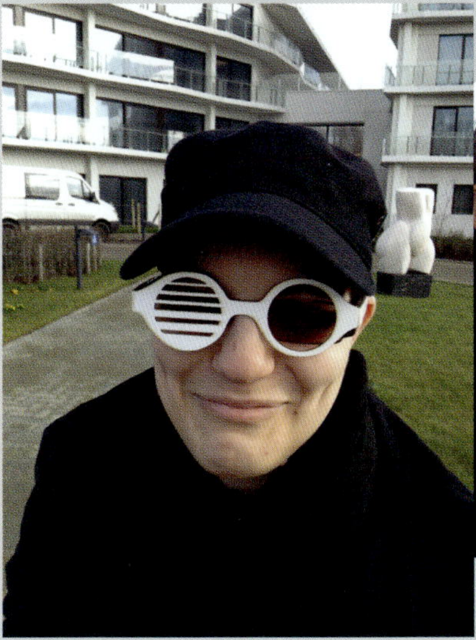

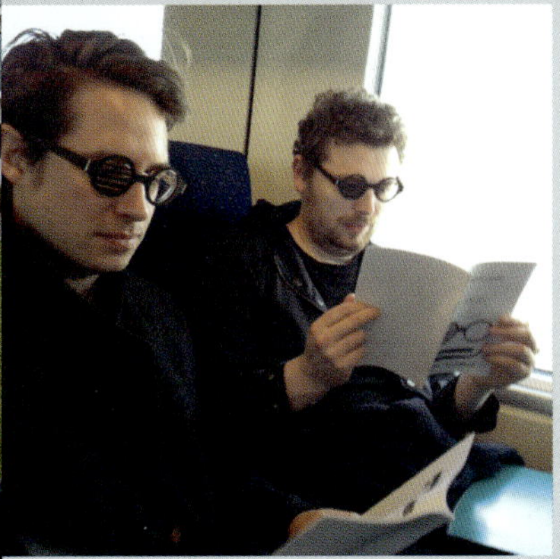

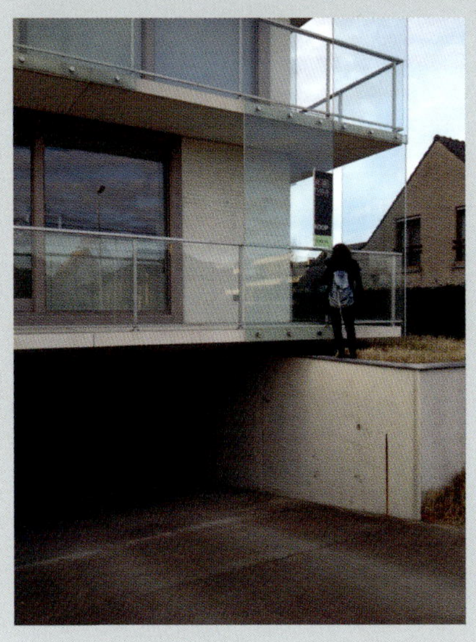

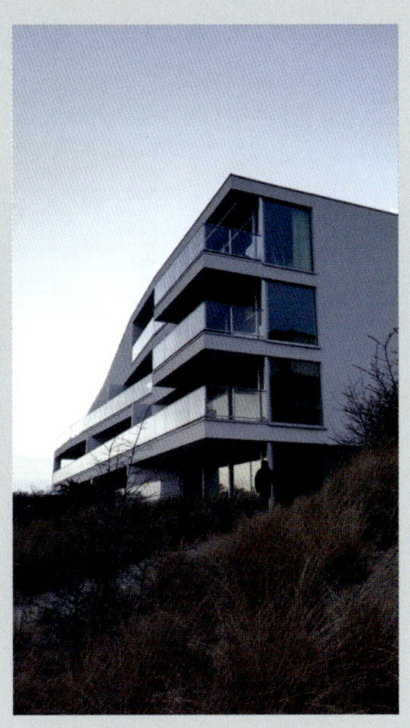

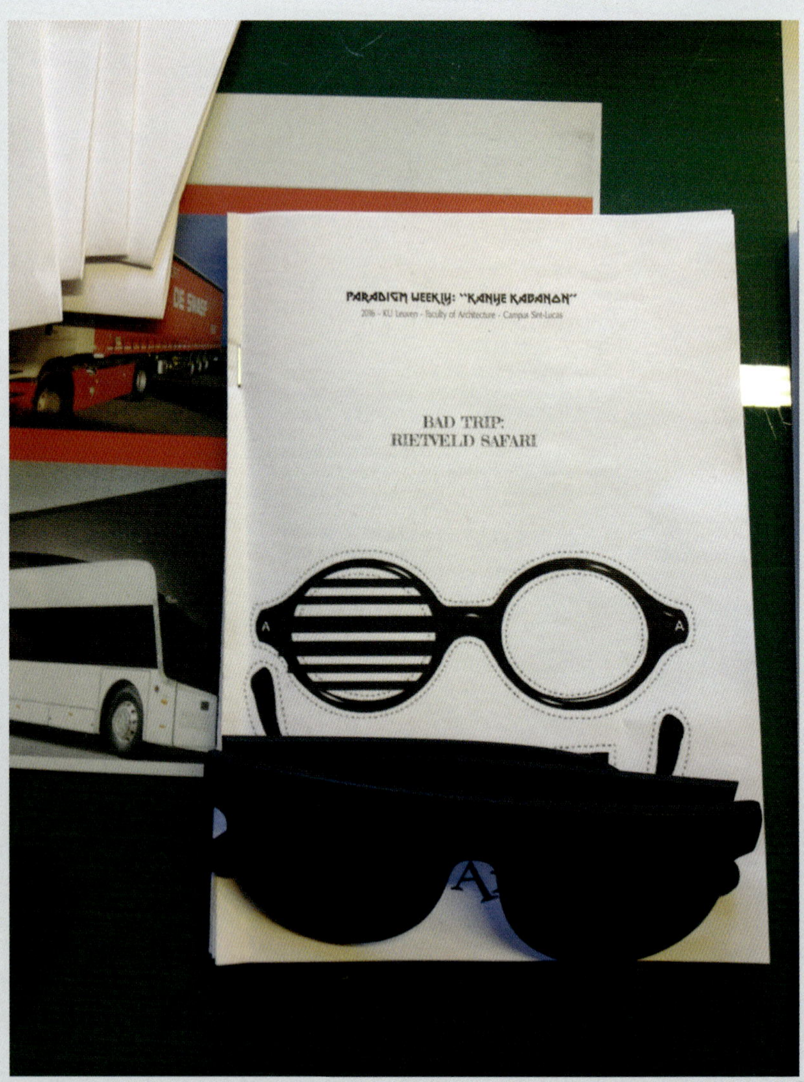
PARADIGM WEEKLY: "KANYE KABANON"
2016 - KU Leuven - Faculty of Architecture - Campus Sint-Lucas
BAD TRIP:
RIETVELD SAFARI

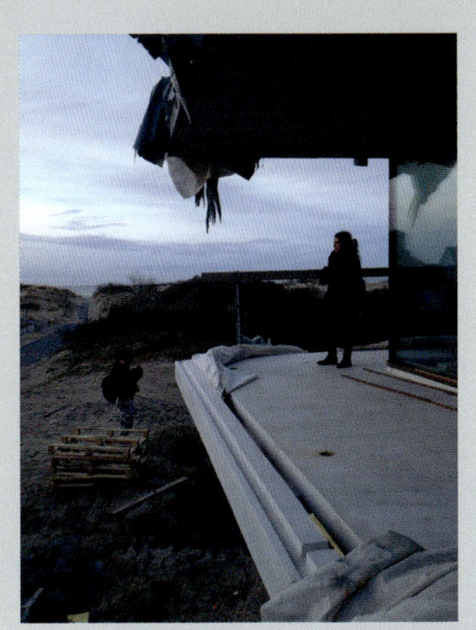

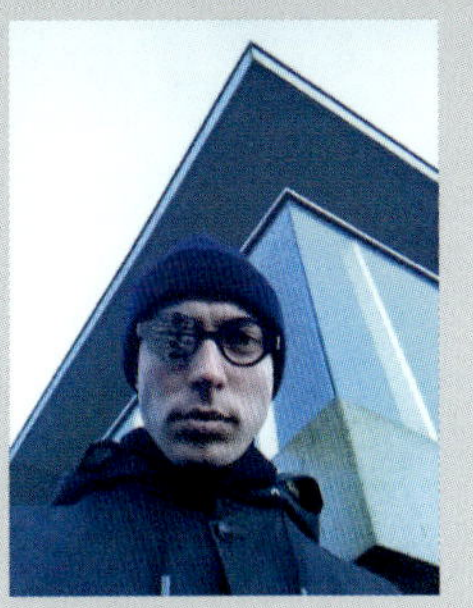

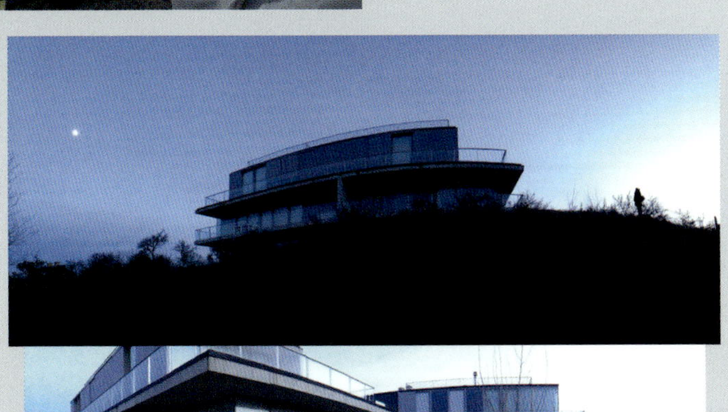

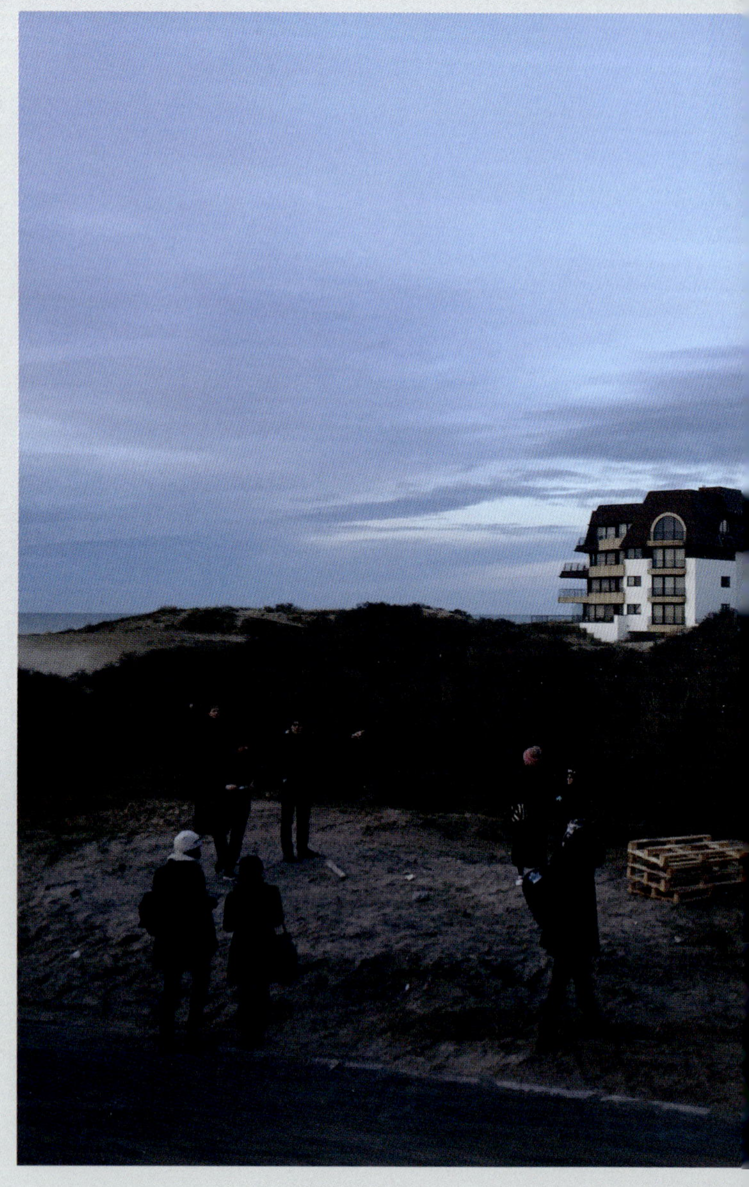

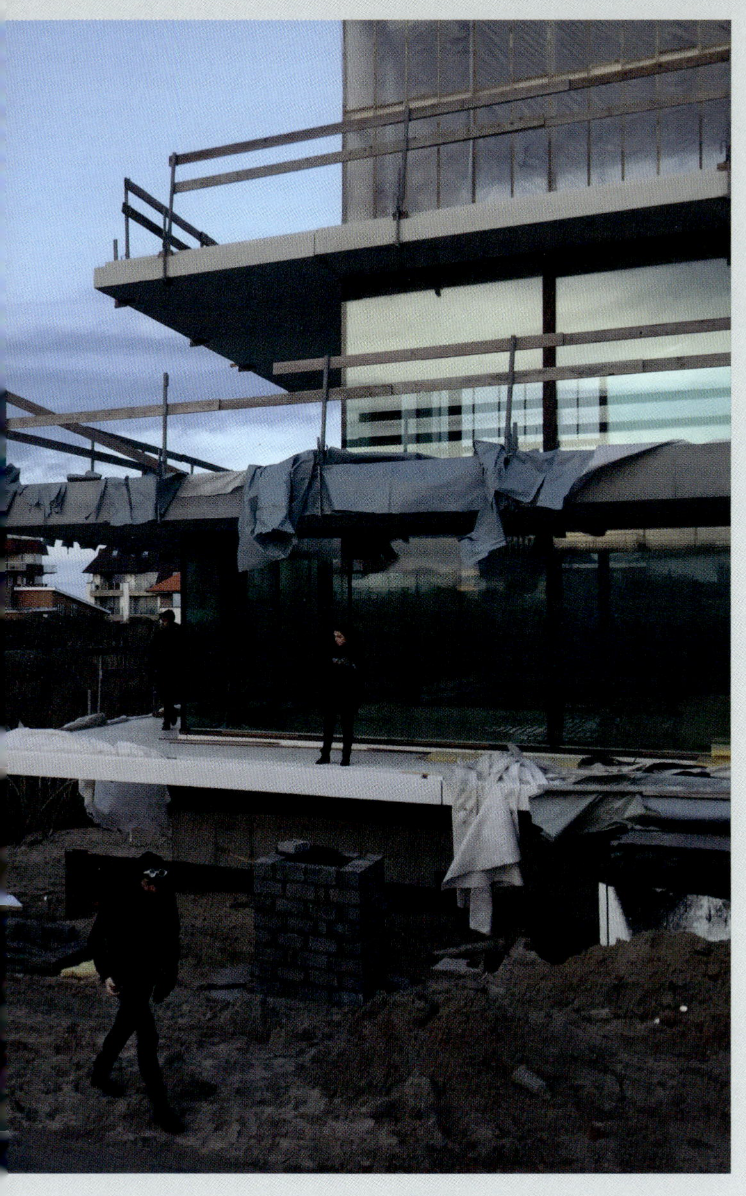

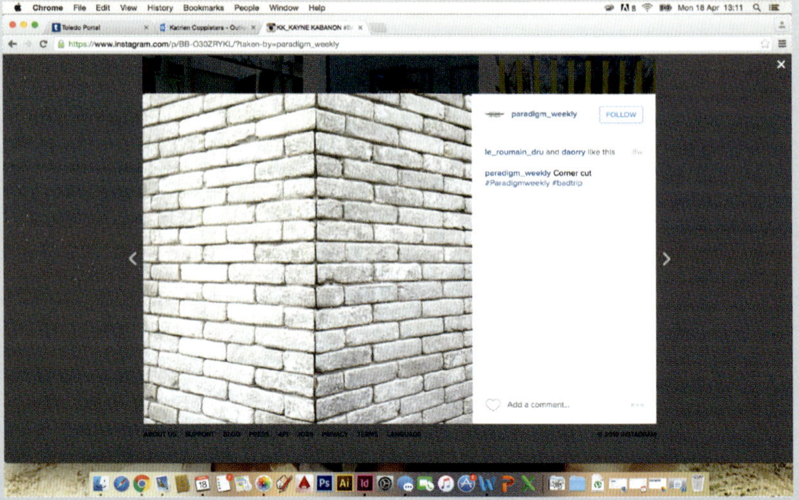

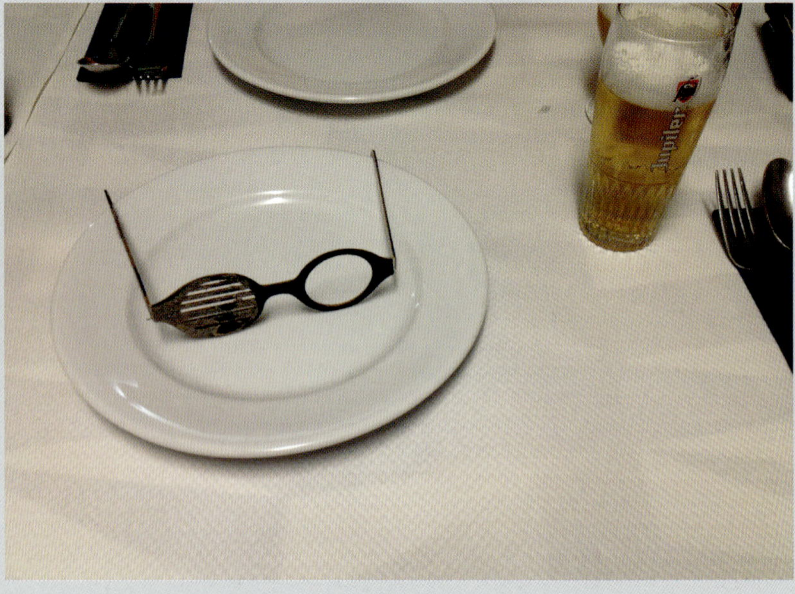

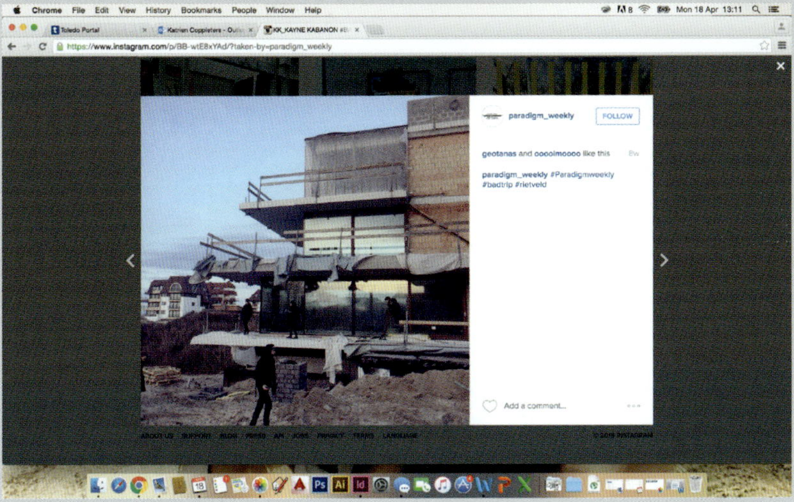

Chrome File Edit View History Bookmarks People Window Help
Mon 18 Apr 13:11
Toledo Portal
KK_KAYNE KABANON
https://www.instagram.com/p/BB-wtE8xYAd/?taken-by=paradigm_weekly
paradigm_weekly
FOLLOW
geotanas and oooolmoooo like this
paradigm_weekly #Paradigmweekly #badtrip #rietveld
Add a comment...

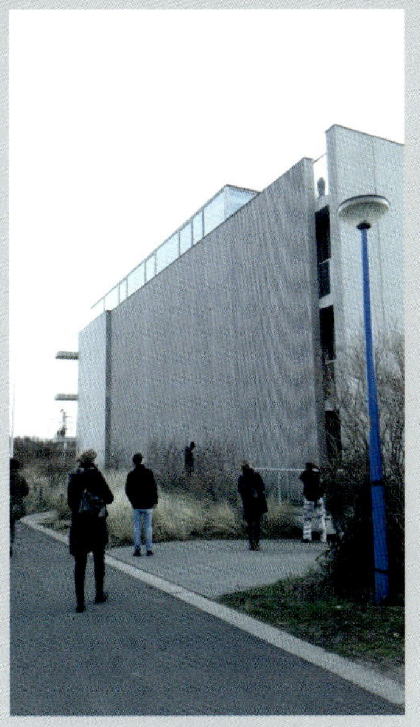

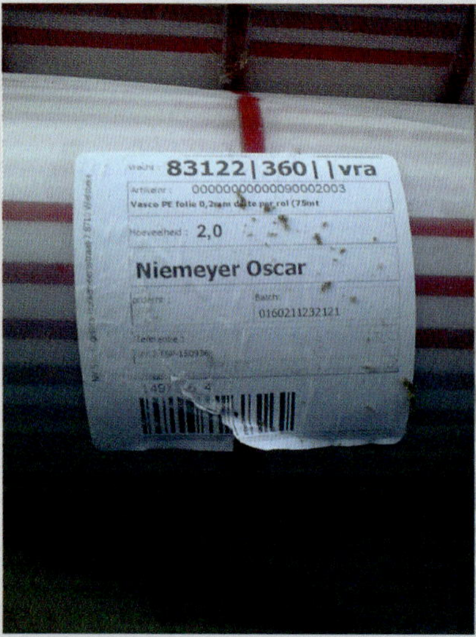

83122|360| |vra
0000000000090002003
Vasco PE folie 0,2mm
Hoeveelheid: 2,0
Niemeyer Oscar
Batch:
0160211232121

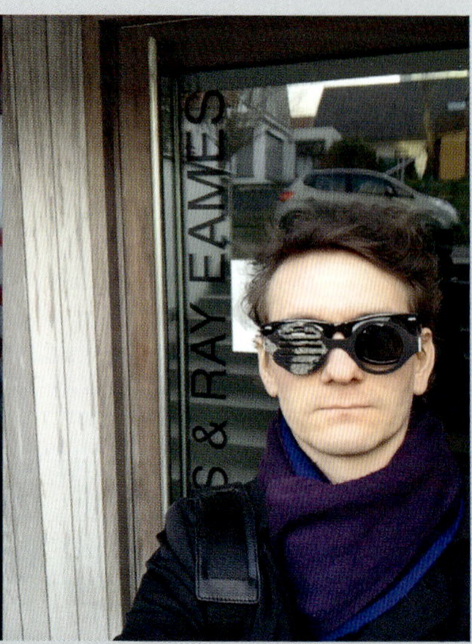

S & RAY EAMES

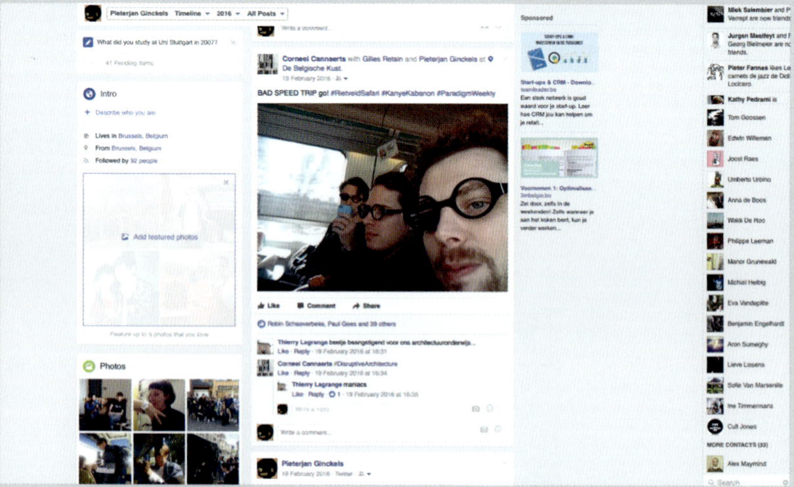

Pieterjan Ginckels Timeline 2016 All Posts
What did you study at Uni Stuttgart in 2007?
Intro
Lives in Brussels, Belgium
From Brussels, Belgium
Followed by 32 people
Add featured photos
Photos
Corneel Cannaerts with Gilles Retsin and Pieterjan Ginckels at De Belgische Kust.
19 February 2016
BAD SPEED TRIP go! #RietveldSafari #KanyeKabanon #ParadigmWeekly
Like Comment Share
Robin Schaeverbeke, Paul Gees and 39 others
Thierry Lagrange beetje beangstigend voor ons architectuuronderwijs...
Corneel Cannaerts #DisruptiveArchitecture
Thierry Lagrange maniacs
Pieterjan Ginckels
Sponsored
Start-ups & CRM - Downlo...
Een sterk netwerk is goud waard voor je start-up. Leer hoe CRM jou kan helpen om je relati...
Miek Salembier
Jurgen Maelfeyt
Pieter Fannes
Kathy Pedrami
Tom Goossen
Edwin Willemen
Joost Raes
Umberto Urbino
Anna de Boos
Waldi De Roo
Philippe Leeman
Manor Grunewald
Michiel Helbig
Eva Vandeplite
Benjamin Engelhardt
Aron Sumeghy
Lieve Lissens
Sofie Van Marsenille
Ine Timmermans
Cult Jones
MORE CONTACTS (33)
Alex Maymind

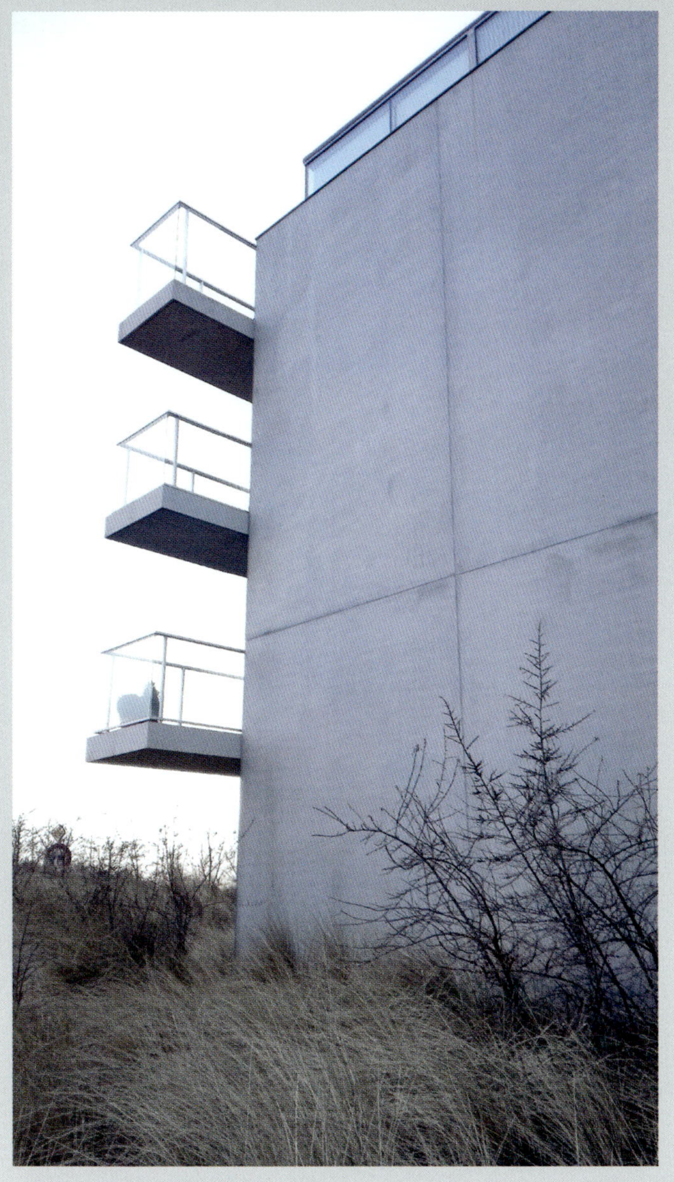

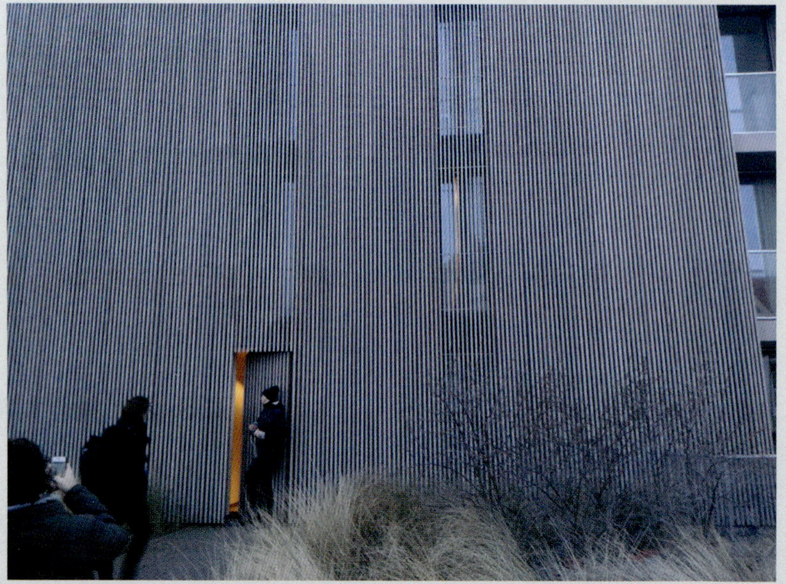

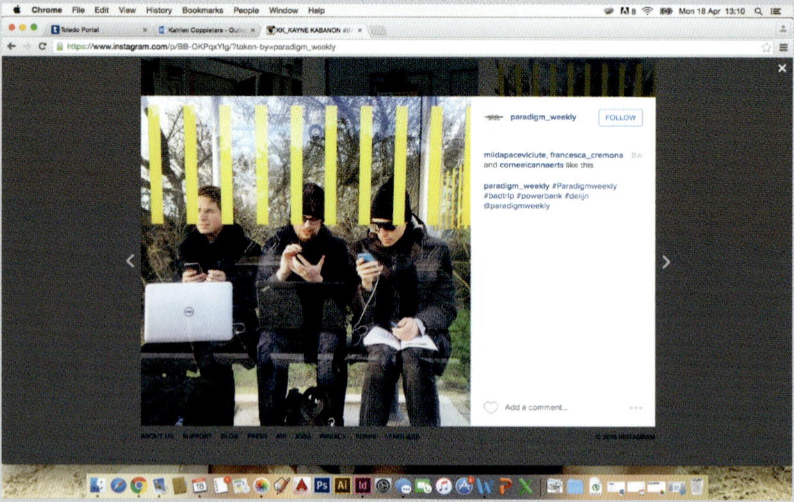

RETROMANIC DEPRESSION

Location: BELGIAN RAVE CULTURE MONUMENTS AND A MITSUBISHI GARAGE, BETWEEN ANTWERP AND BRUSSELS. Date: 6 AUGUST 2016. Partners: CONTEMPORARY ARTS HERITAGE FLANDERS (CAHF) + M HKA MUSEUM OF CONTEMPORARY ART ANTWERP. Participants: PIETERJAN GINCKELS, M HKA, CAHF, WITH A BUSLOAD OF NOSTALGIC RAVERS. Props: PJG SPRAY-PAINTED WIRE FRAME GLASSES; GIN + GINI CAMELBAK; HARD CANDY; 90'S RAVE MIXTAPE CD-R'S.

Pieterjan Ginckels and three protagonists of rave culture in Belgium – Geert Sermon, Tom Nys and Florence Atlas – take you on a SPEED TRIP around Belgium's rave monuments and ruins. At rapid pace, the SPEED TRIP takes us past the remnants of the Zillion and Cherry Moon, gas stations between Antwerp and Lille, empty industrial wastelands where legendary parties took place, tuning garages and waiting rooms of courthouses.

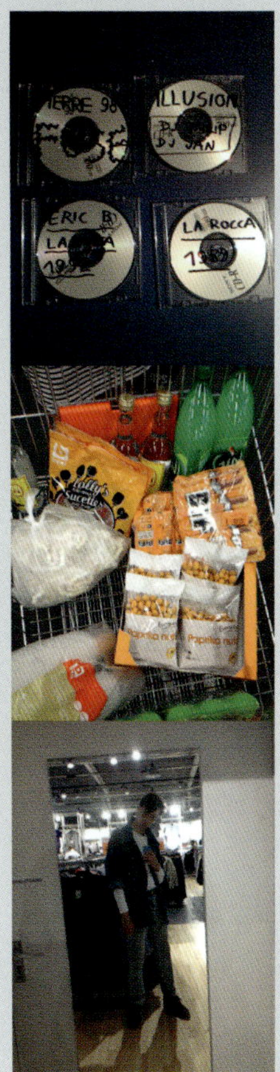

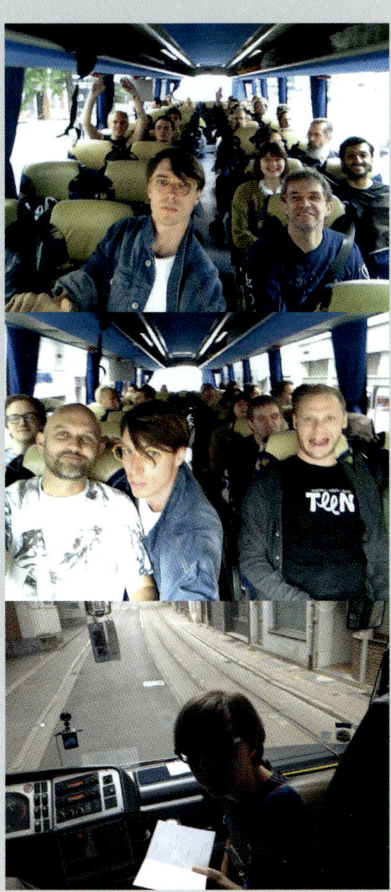

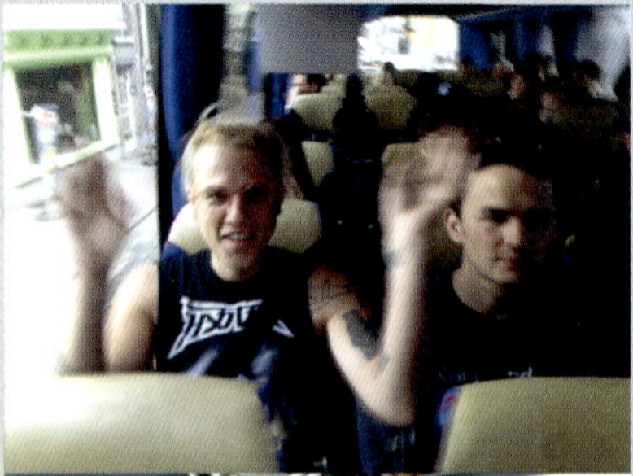
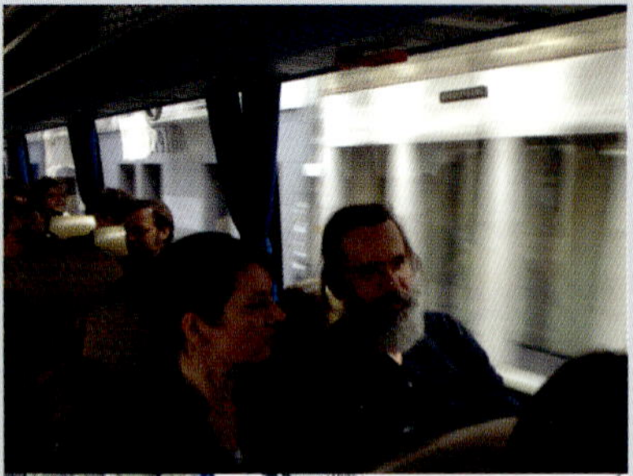
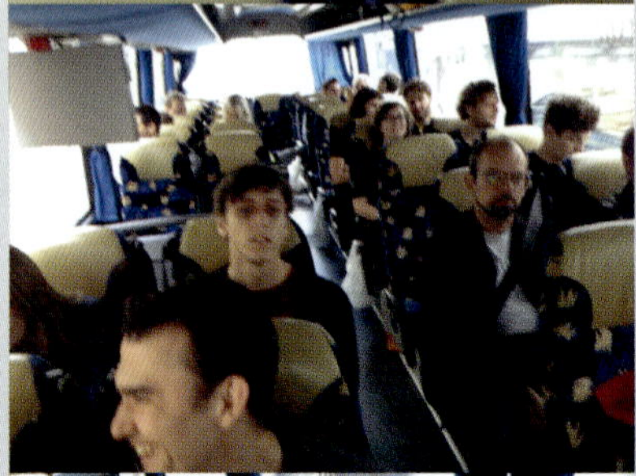
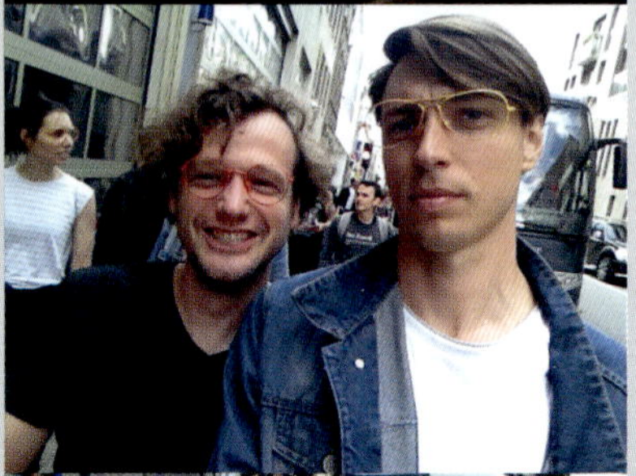
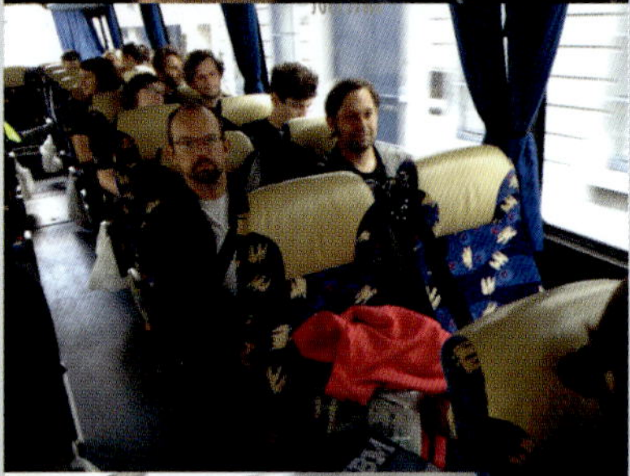
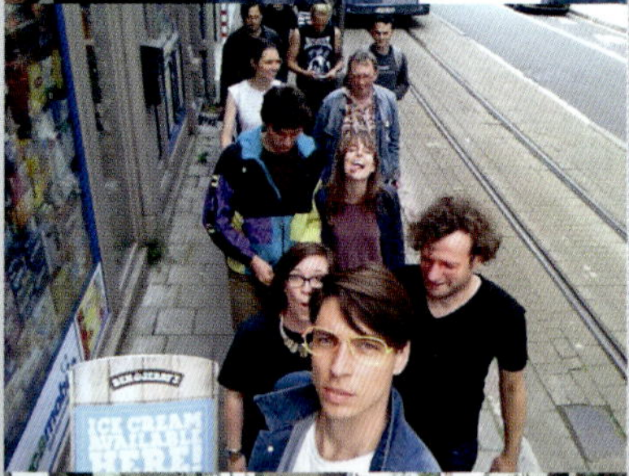
ICE CREAM
AVAILABLE
HERE!
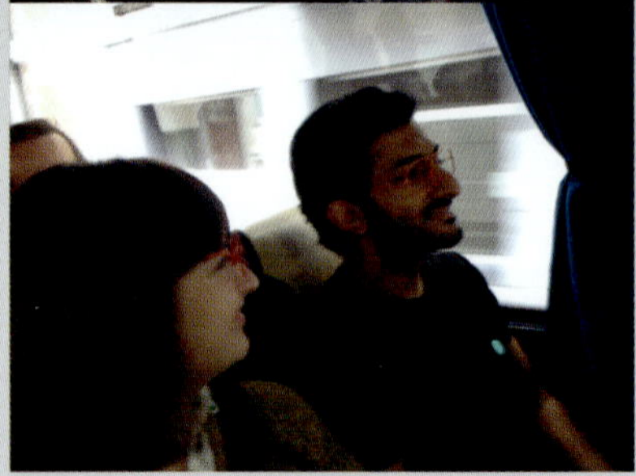
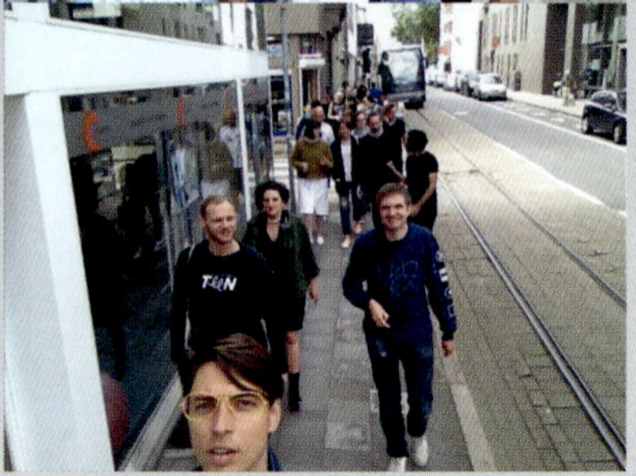

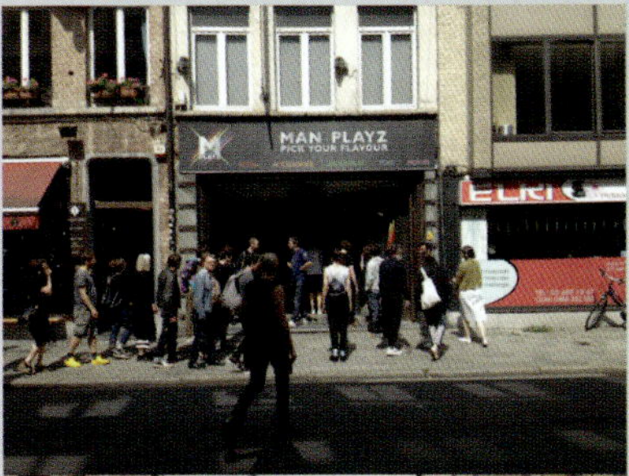

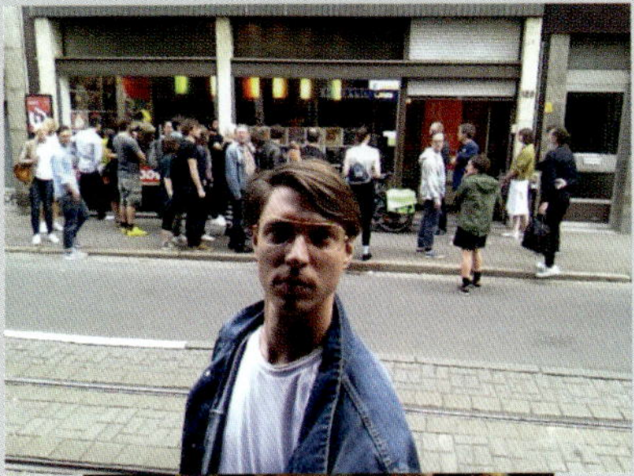

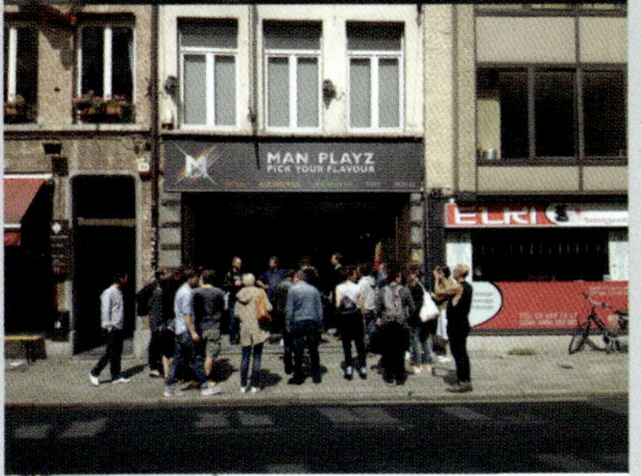

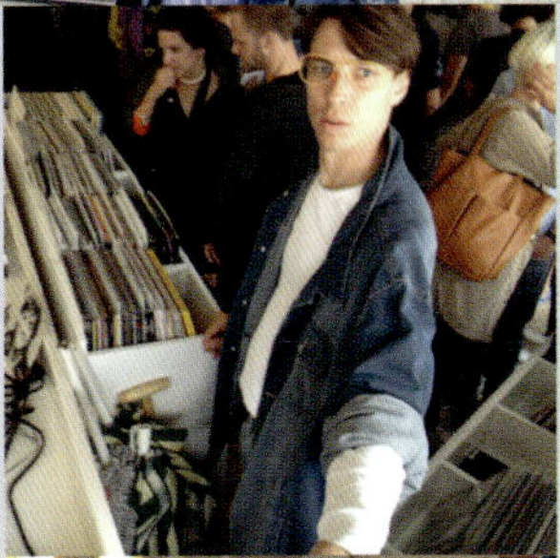

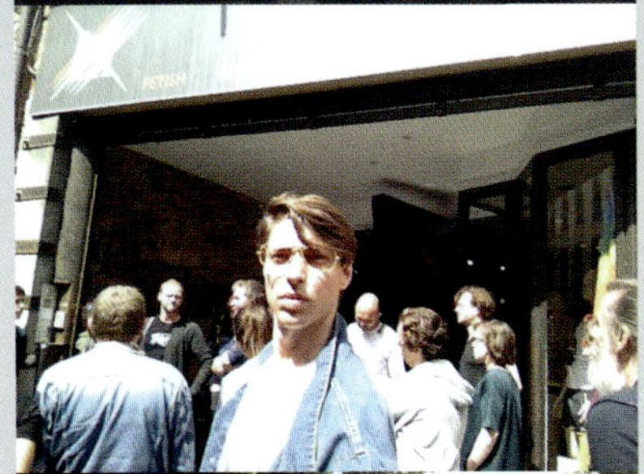

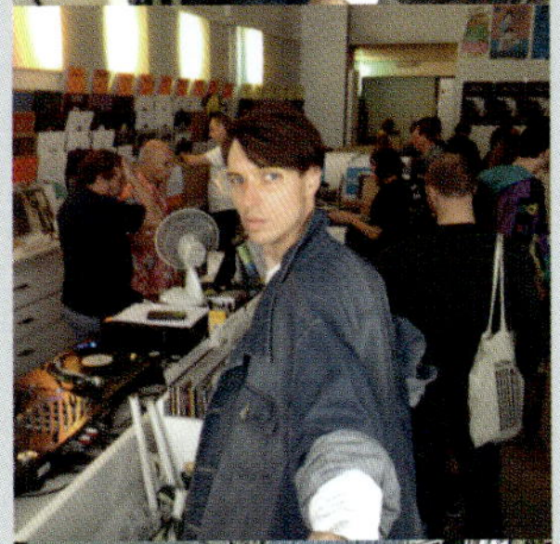

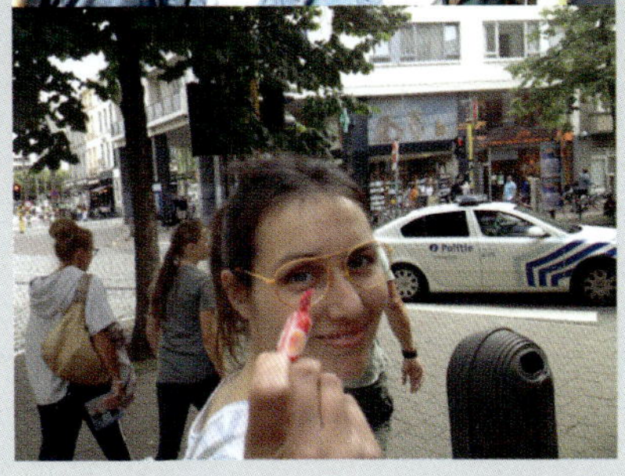

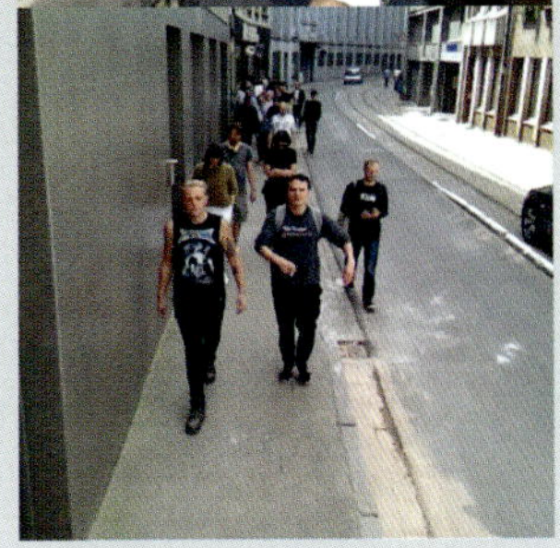

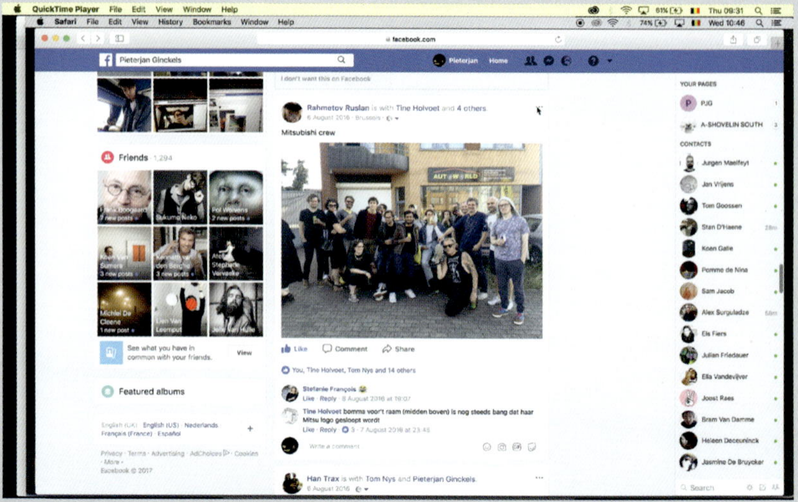

QuickTime Player File Edit View Window Help
Safari File Edit View History Bookmarks Window Help
facebook.com
Pieterjan Ginckels
Pieterjan Home
Rahmetov Ruslan is with Tine Holvoet and 4 others
Mitsubishi crew
Like Comment Share
You, Tine Holvoet, Tom Nys and 14 others
Stefanie François
Tine Holvoet bomma voor't raam (midden boven) is nog steeds bang dat haar Mitsu logo gesloopt wordt
Han Trax is with Tom Nys and Pieterjan Ginckels.
Friends
See what you have in common with your friends.
View
Featured albums
YOUR PAGES
PJG
A-SHOVELIN SOUTH
CONTACTS

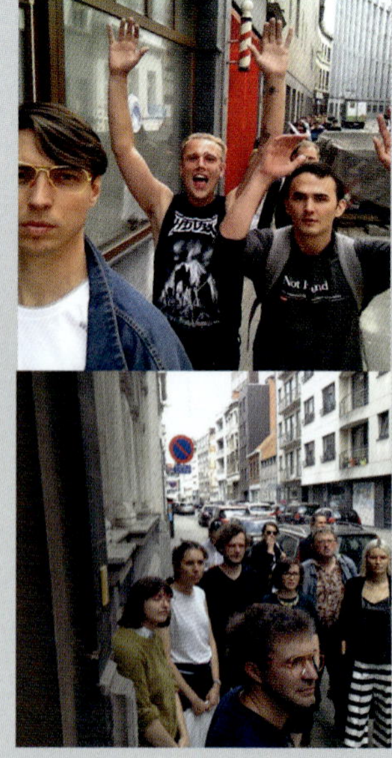

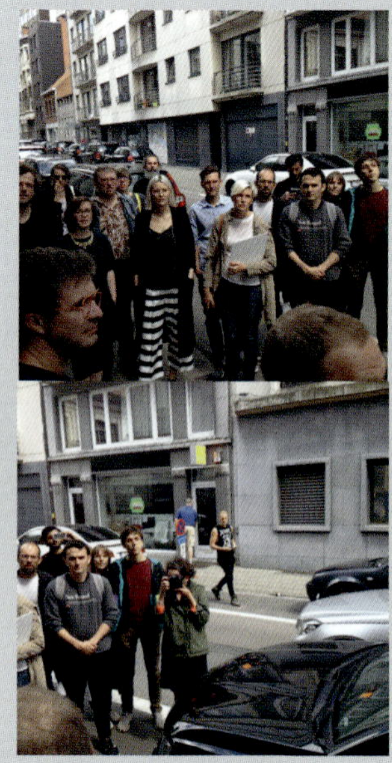

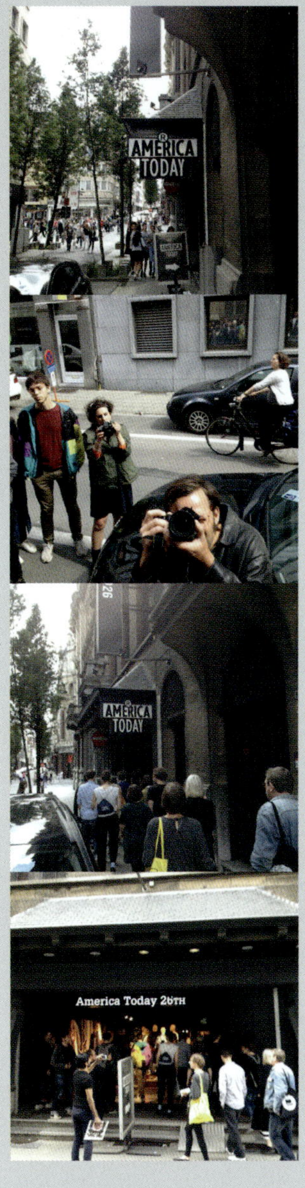
AMERICA
TODAY
AMERICA
TODAY
America Today 26TH

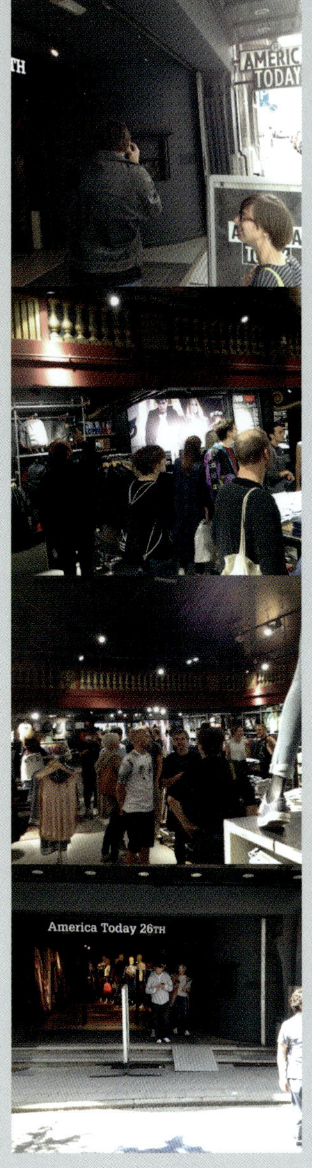
AMERIC
TODAY
America Today 26TH

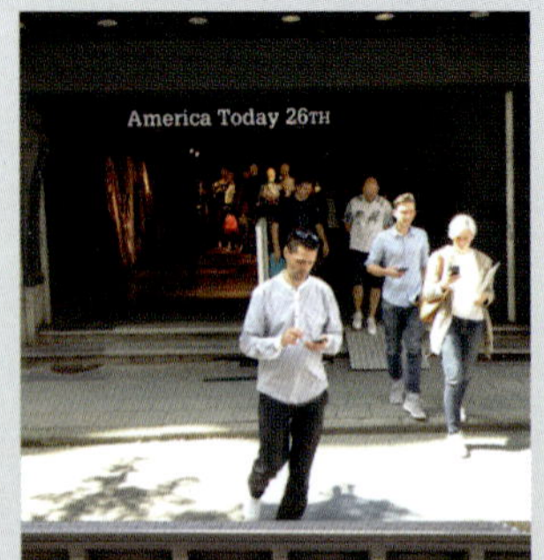
America Today 26TH

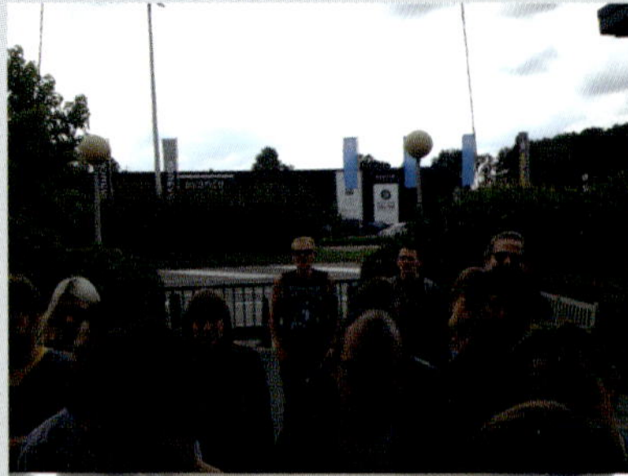

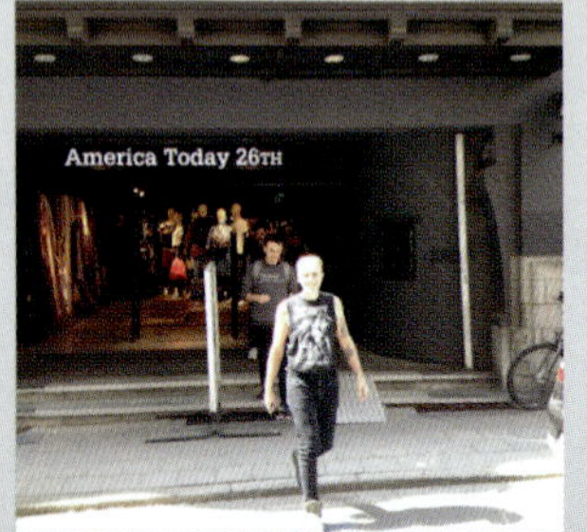
America Today 26TH

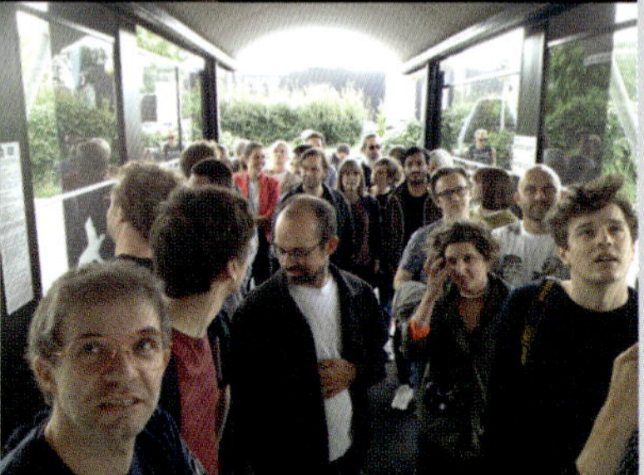

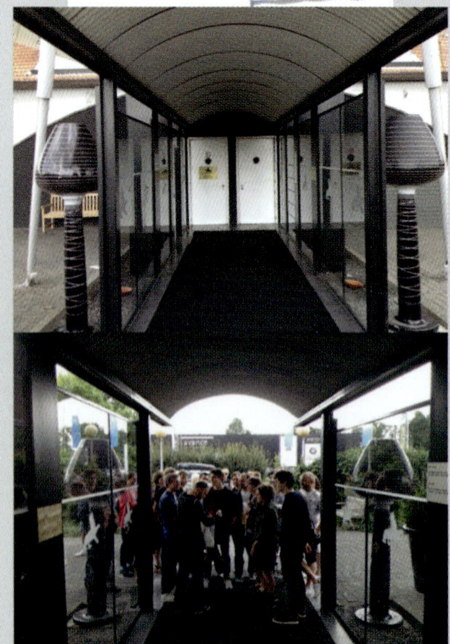

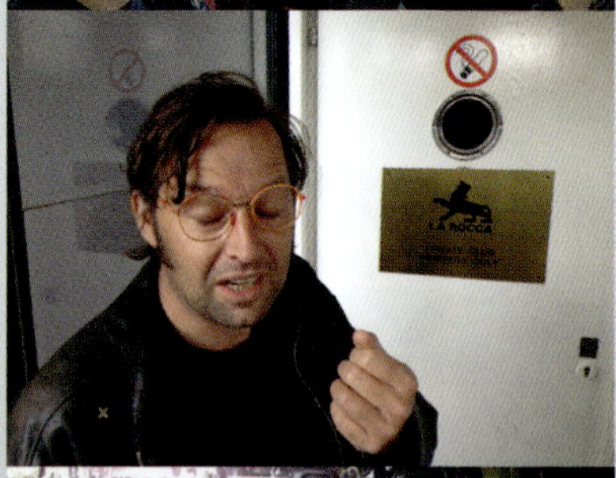
LA ROCCA

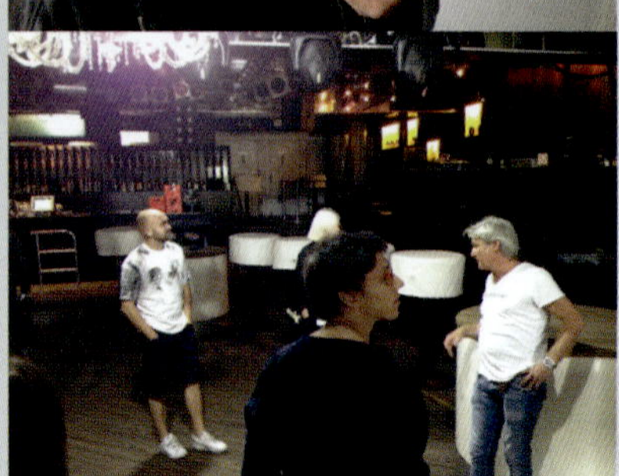

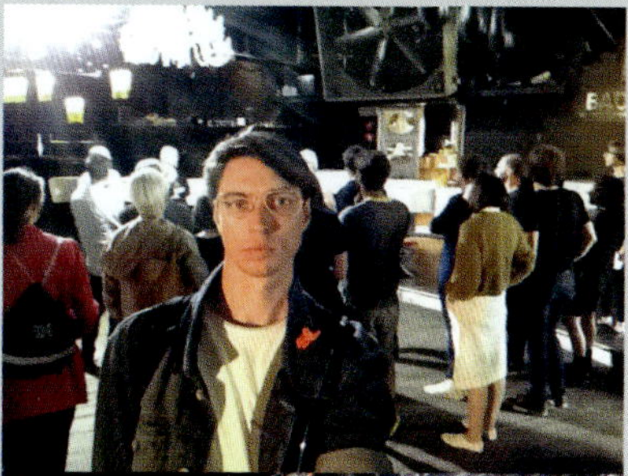

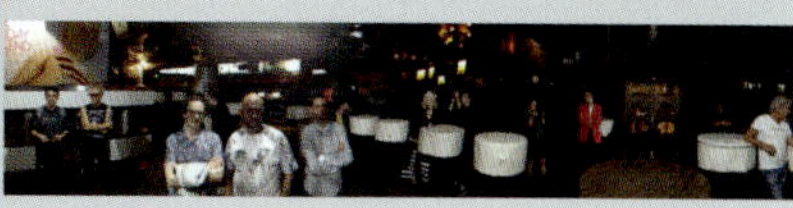

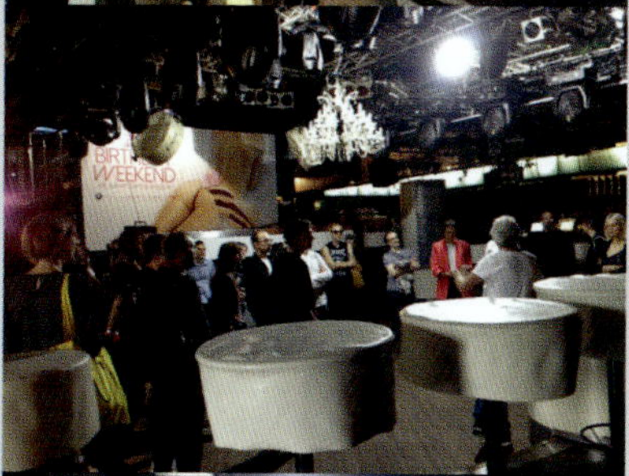

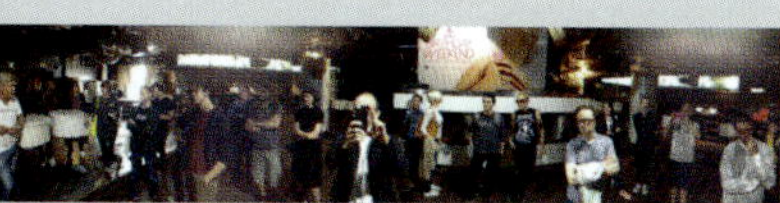

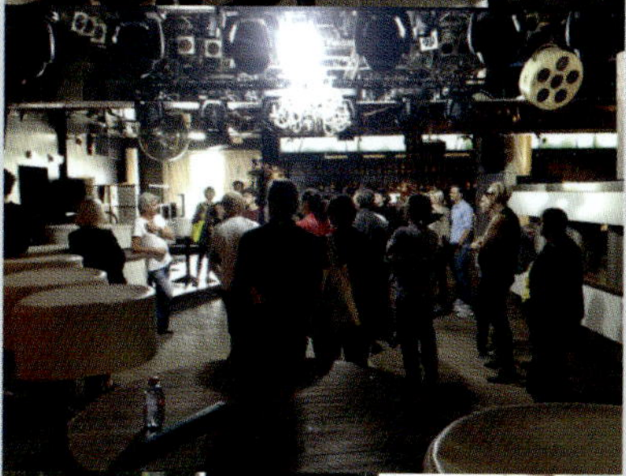

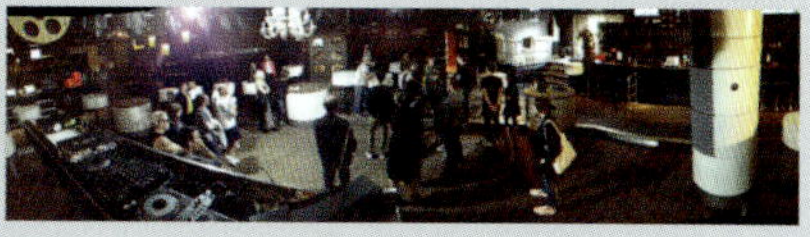

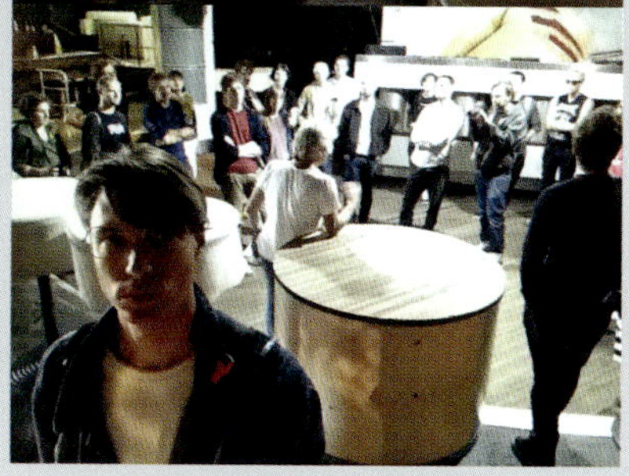

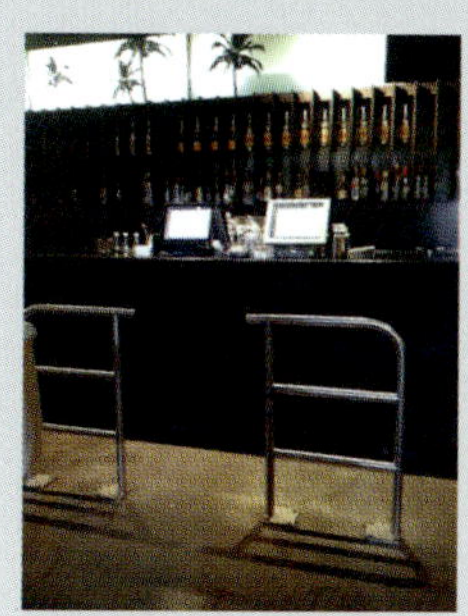

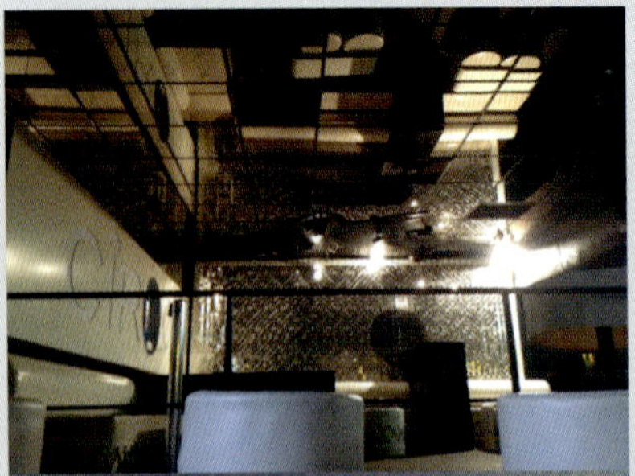

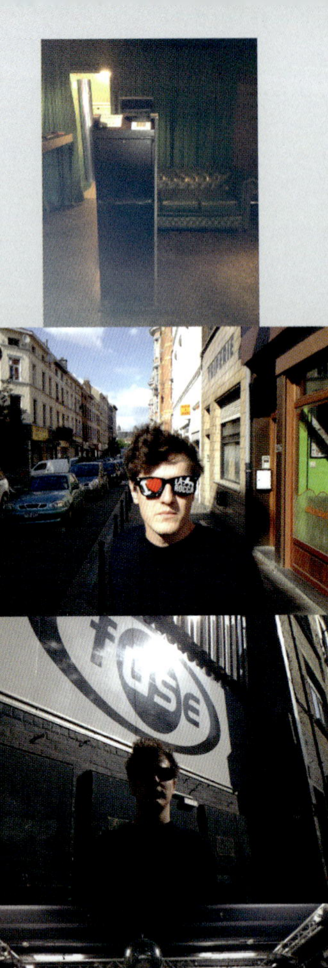

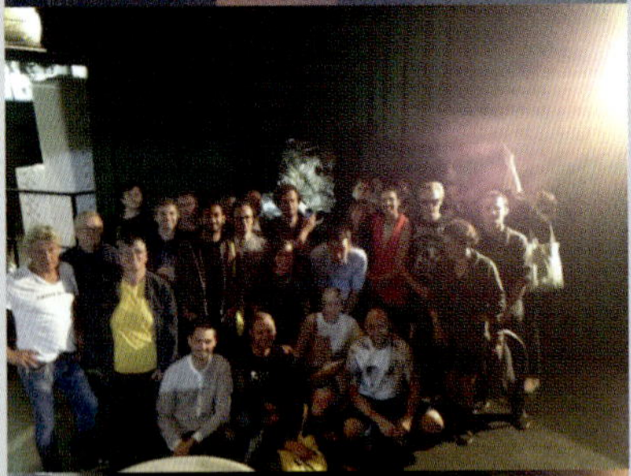

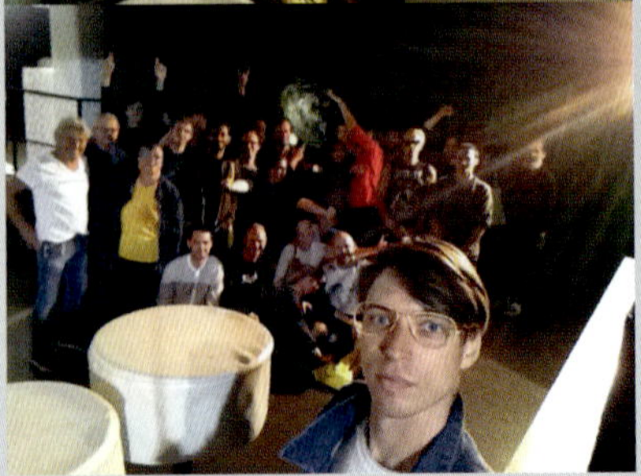

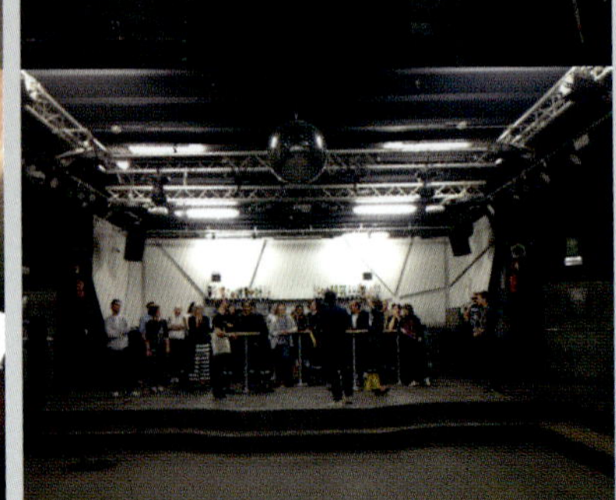

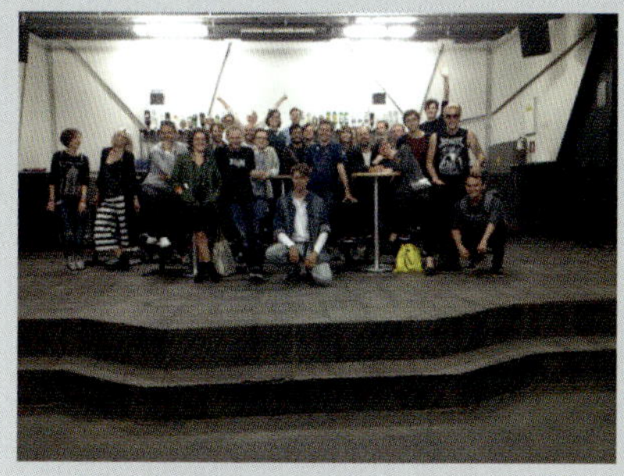

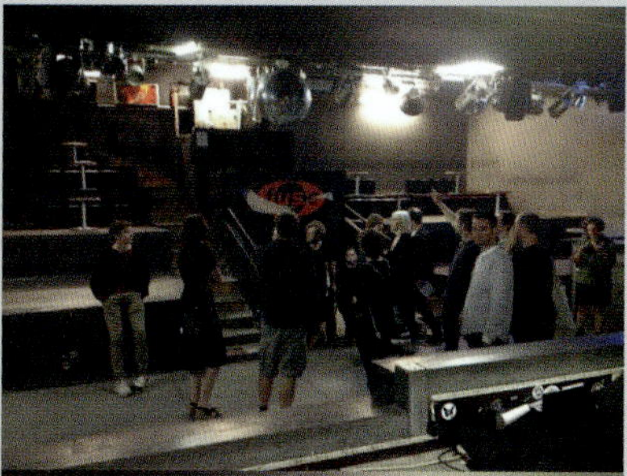

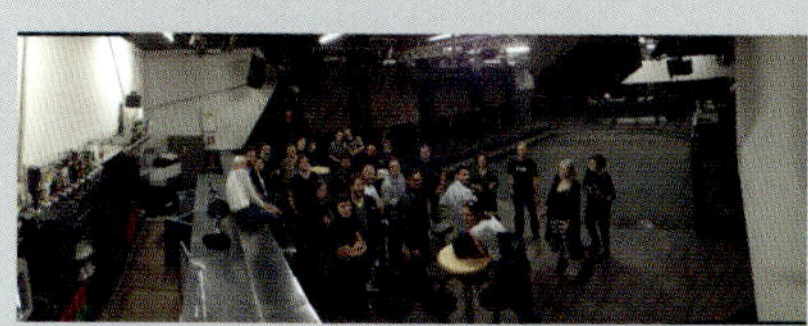

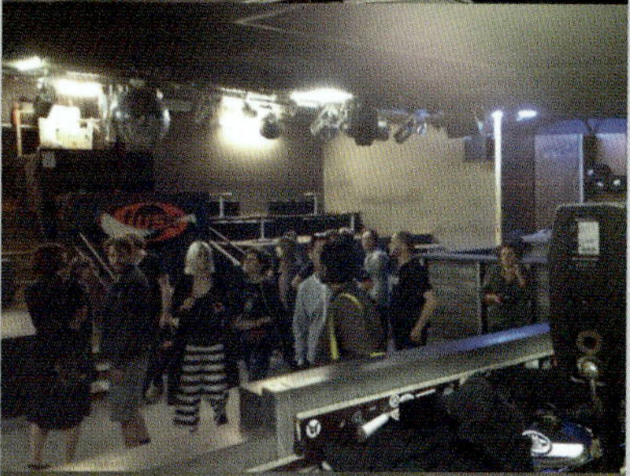

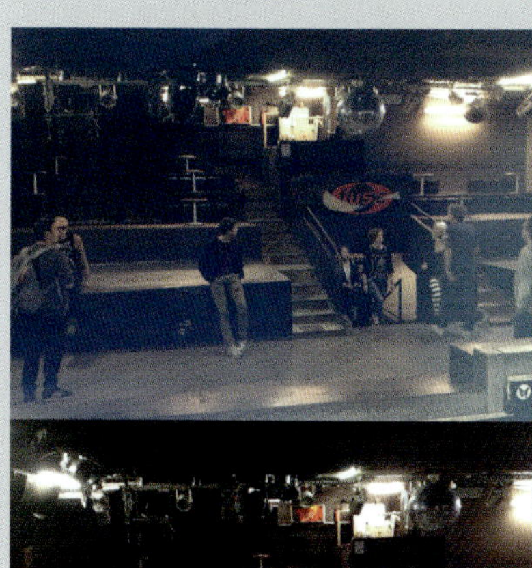

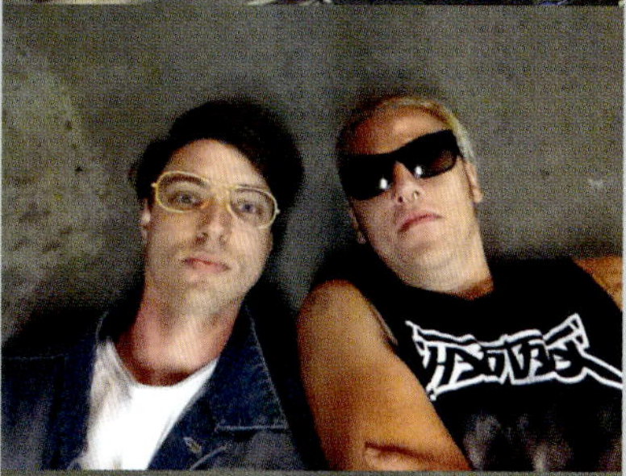

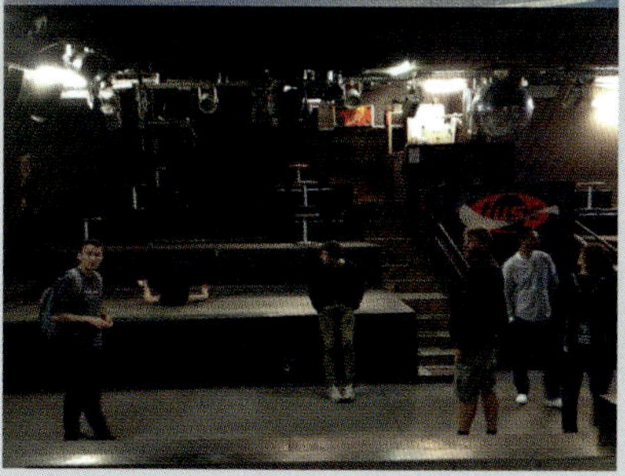

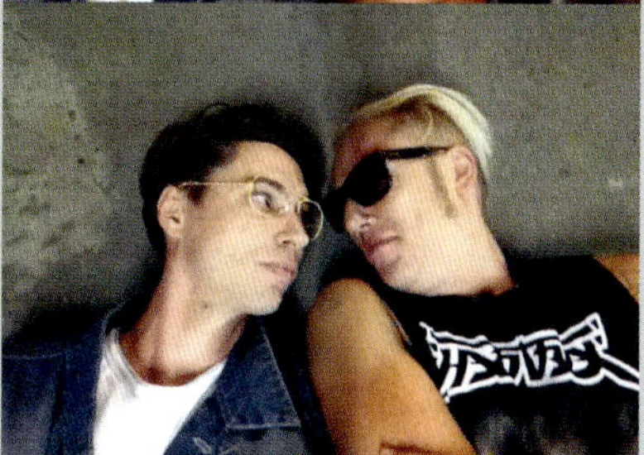

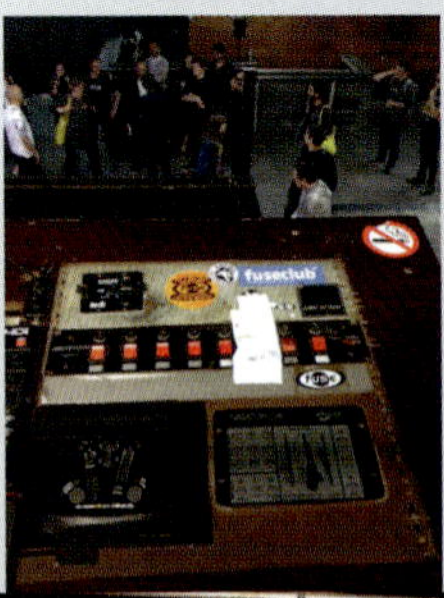

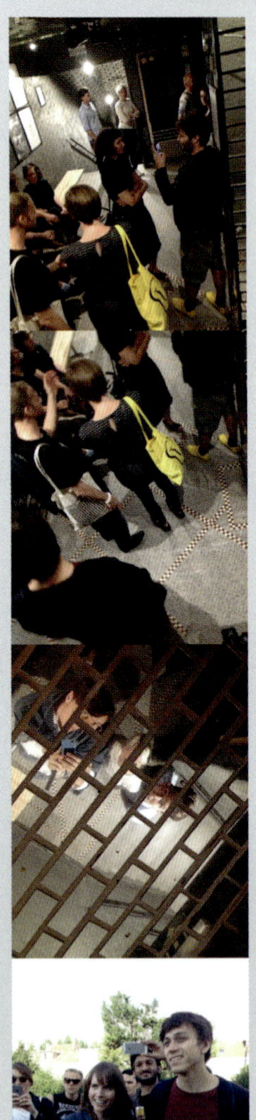

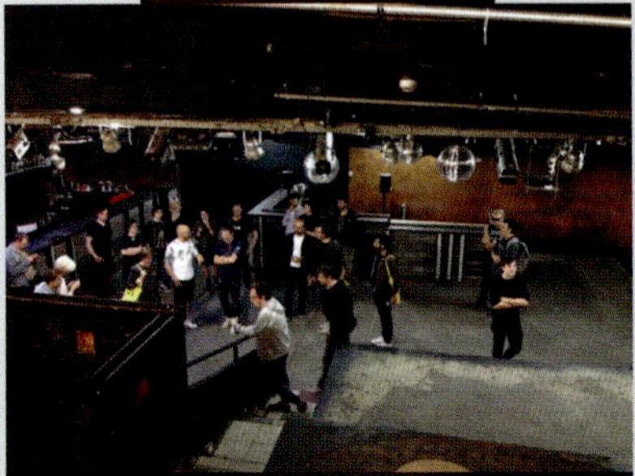

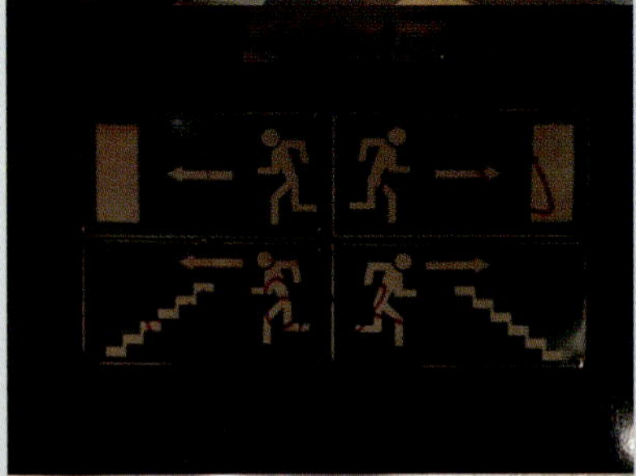

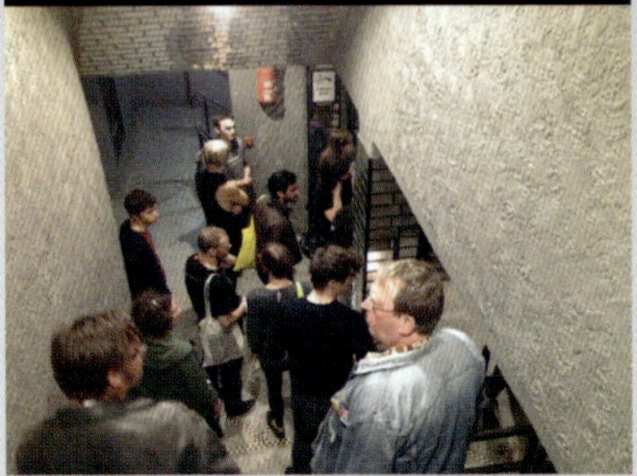

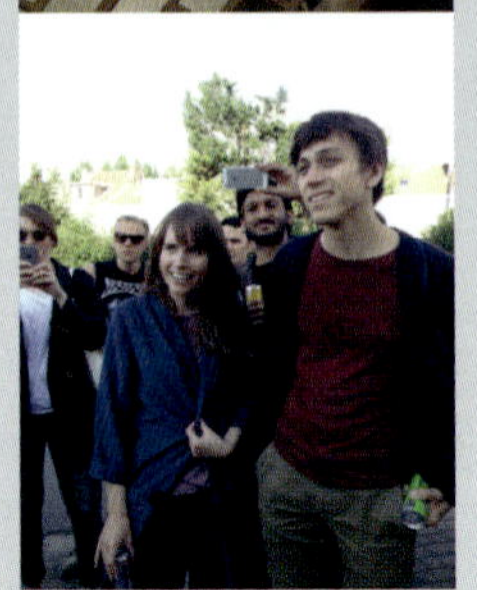

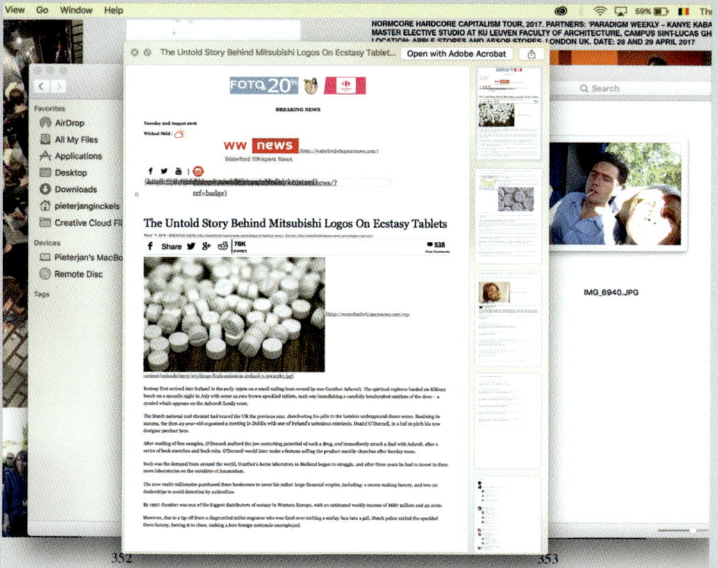

View Go Window Help

NORMCORE HARDCORE CAPITALISM TOUR, 2017. PARTNERS: 'PARADIGM WEEKLY – KANYE KABA
MASTER ELECTIVE STUDIO AT KU LEUVEN FACULTY OF ARCHITECTURE, CAMPUS SINT-LUCAS GH
LOCATION: APPLE STORES AND AESOP STORES, LONDON UK. DATE: 28 AND 29 APRIL 2017

The Untold Story Behind Mitsubishi Logos On Ecstasy Tablet... Open with Adobe Acrobat

Favorites
AirDrop
All My Files
Applications
Desktop
Downloads
pieterjanginckels
Creative Cloud Fi

Devices
Pieterjan's MacBo
Remote Disc

Tags

BREAKING NEWS

ww news

Waterford Whispers News

ref=badge)

The Untold Story Behind Mitsubishi Logos On Ecstasy Tablets

Share 76K 538

Search

IMG_6940.JPG

352 353

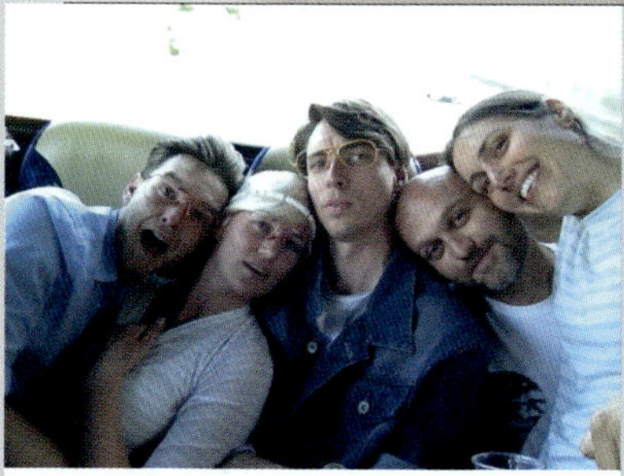

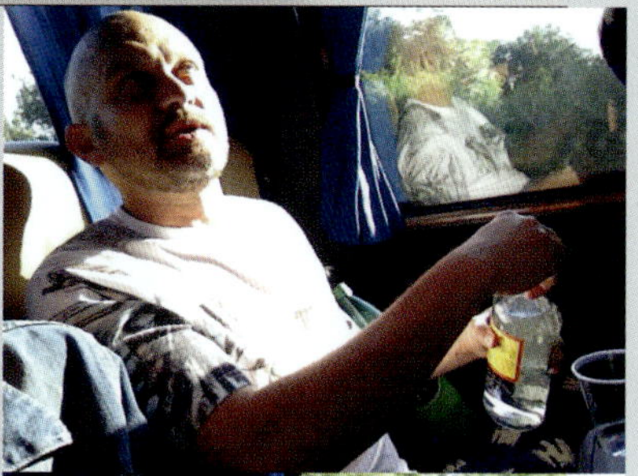

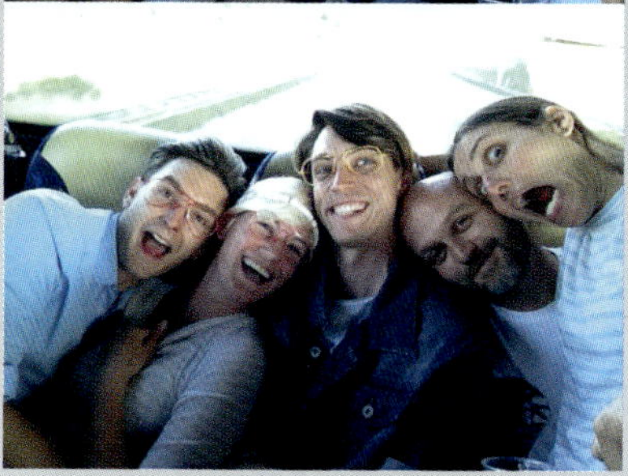

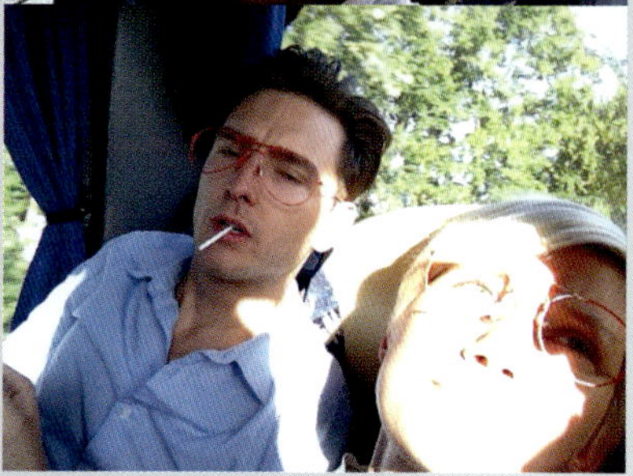

NORMCORE HARDCORE CAPITALISM TOUR

Location: APPLE STORES AND AESOP STORES, LONDON UK. Date: 28 AND 29 APRIL 2017. Partners: “PARADIGM WEEKLY: KANYE KABANON” MASTER ELECTIVE STUDIO AT KU LEUVEN FACULTY OF ARCHITECTURE, SINT-LUCAS CAMPUS. Participants: PIETERJAN GINCKELS AND PARADIGM WEEKLY: KANYE KABANON 2017 STUDENTS: VIT BURIAN, DARIA CHMIELEWSKA, STAN D’HAENE, PAUL FAURE, MARTA GUIN, NGOC MAI, MARIA MUSKOVA, GEORGE NAKANISHI, IWONA ANNA PAWLAK, URSZULA KATARZYNA PROKOP, NINA RAPP, ANNISSA RAUW, MICHAEL RAYMOND, ALEX SURGULADZE, JIRI VALA. Props: PARADIGM WEEKLY DESIGNED, LASER-CUT ACRYLIC THREE-PIECE RINGS; ALL-WHITE OUTFIT (AESOP DAY); ALL-BLACK OUTFIT (APPLE DAY).

Trip characteristics: NORMCORE HARDCORE CAPITALISM TOUR is the title of our mixed-agenda school trip: both performance and team building event, we prepare a getaway to London, hedonist center of the old universe, to roll out a Speed Trip. The premise instigating the trip’s production is: all Apple Store and Aesop Store interiors together constitute the Père Lachaise of Architecture: a graveyard of sexy tombs radiating bygone potential for a long-lost discipline, retromanically revisitable. These sites will be subjected to our fast-paced wandering eye, hungry for repetition, dirty realism, details, and points to charge our phones. The event was documented, published ’n’ posted, and its digital aftermath scoured for bits and bobs to raise discussions about capitalist minimalist style convergence.

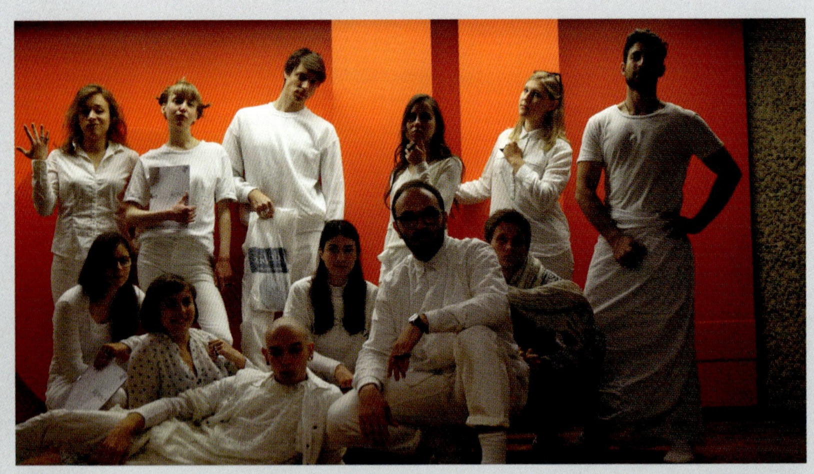

IMG_8485.PNG

SPEEDISM, Paradigm Weekly and the KU Leuven Faculty of Architecture organise another SPEED TRIP, named NORMCORE HARDCORE CAPITALISM TOUR, which will see participant performers hopping from every Aesop Store to every Apple Store all over London, on 28 and 29 April 2017.
The event is a documented performance, published 'n' posted, and its digital aftermath will be scoured for bits and bobs to raise discussions about capitalist minimalist style convergence.

The premise instigating the trip's production is: all Aesop Store interiors together constitute the Père Lachaise of Architecture: a graveyard of sexy tombs radiating bygone potential for a long-lost discipline, retromanically revisitable.

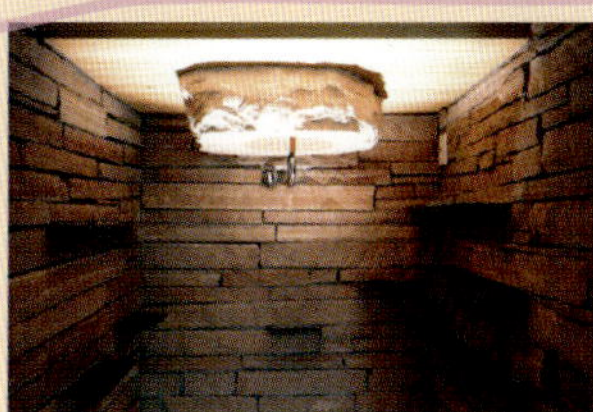

NORMCORE HARDCORE CAPITALISM TOUR is the title of our mixed-agenda school trip: both performance and team building event, we prepare a getaway to London, hedonist center of the old universe, to roll out a Speed Trip. Previous sightseeing-performances were held in Beijing, Los Angeles, Las Vegas, Brussels and along the Belgian coast, and submerged participants in a string of disconnected physical realities that precede and support our theory-in-development. The proof of the pudding is in the shopping. London boosts no less than a dozen Aesop stores, and a handful of official Apple stores. These sites will be subjected to our fast-paced wandering eye, hungry for repetition, dirty

366

IMG_8485.PNG

realism, details, and points to charge our phones. The compilation of all documentation, pushed into the cloud in the Apple stores, will shape a book. This book, NORMCORE HARDCORE GUNMETAL HANDS, will be launched at the end of the course, and will be published under pirated publishing houses' names.

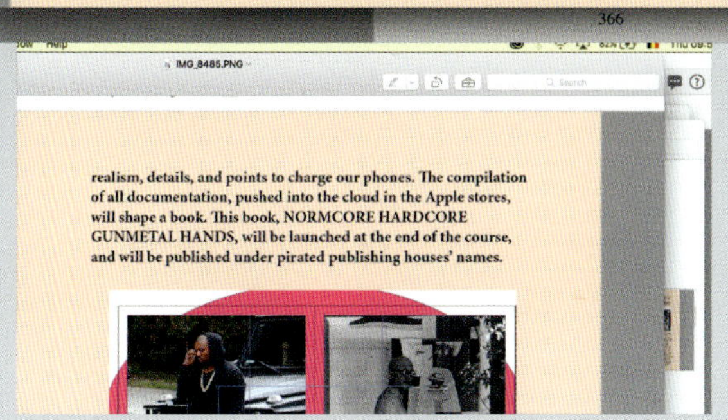

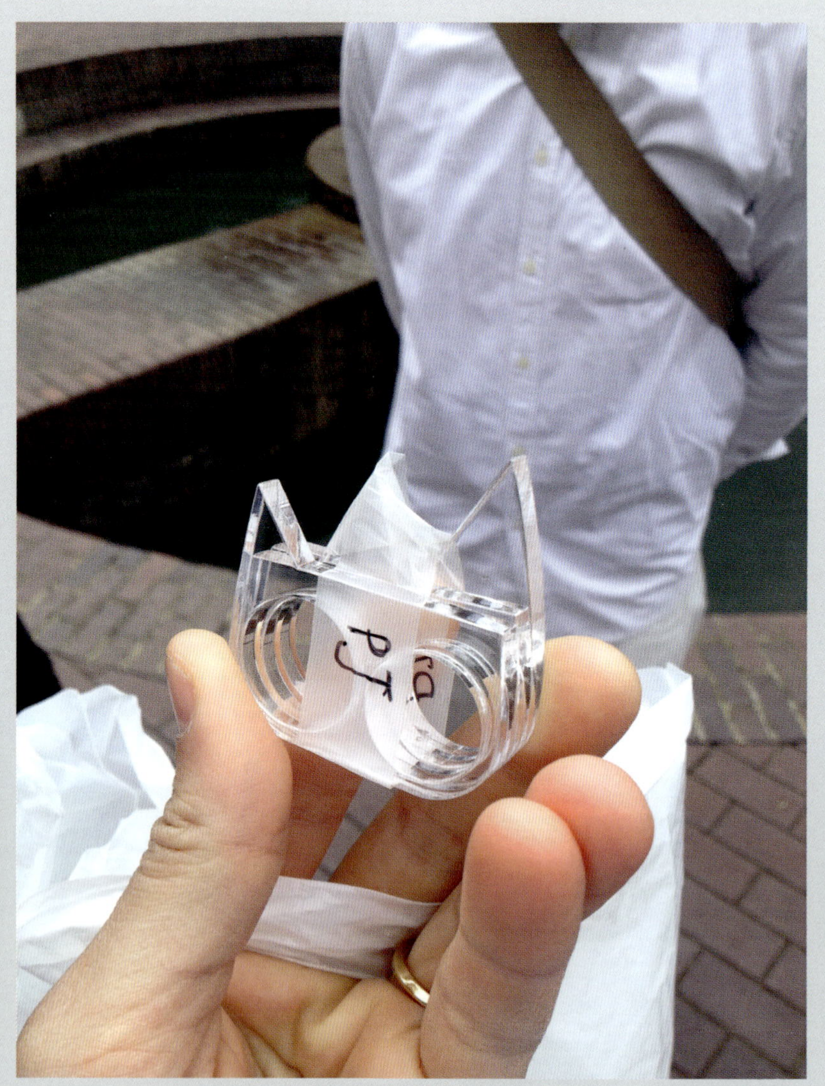
PJ

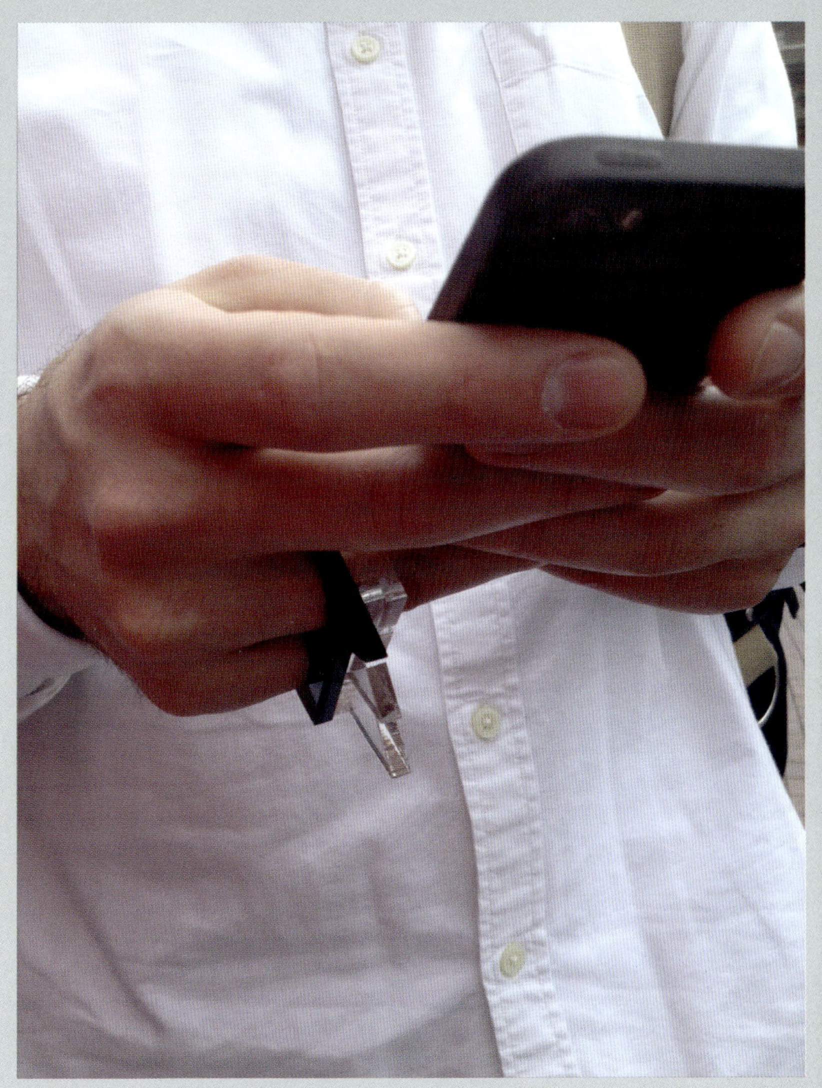

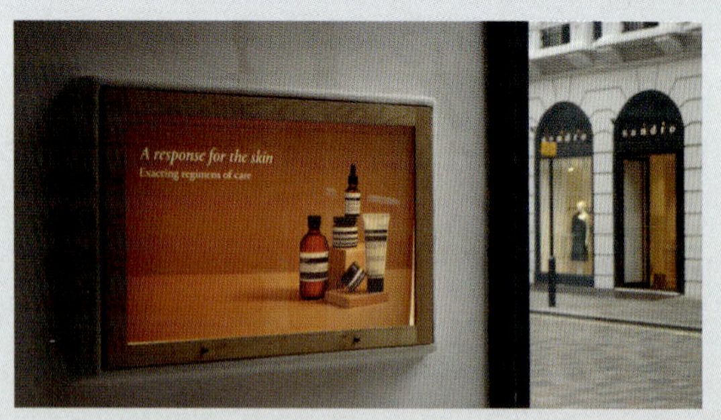
A response for the skin
Exacting regimens of care
sandro
sandro

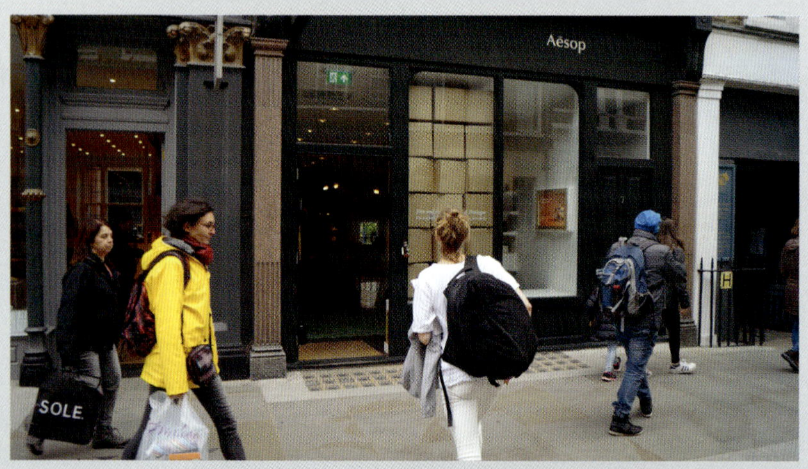
Aēsop
SOLE

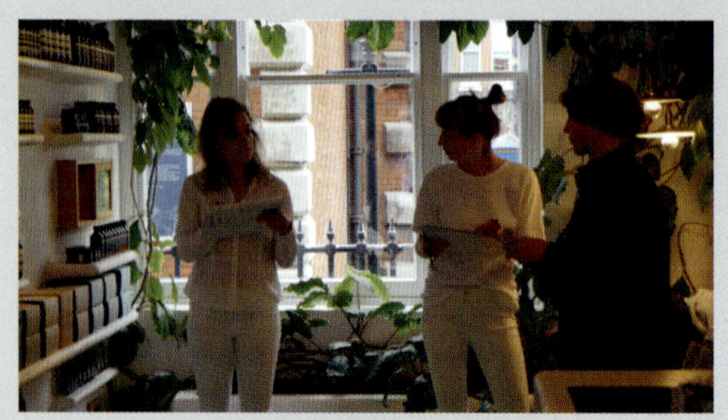

AESOP STORES

LONDON SPEEDTRIP
28-29.05/2017

I BOROUGH
II COVENT GARDEN
III SOHO
IV LIBERTY
V MARYLEBONE

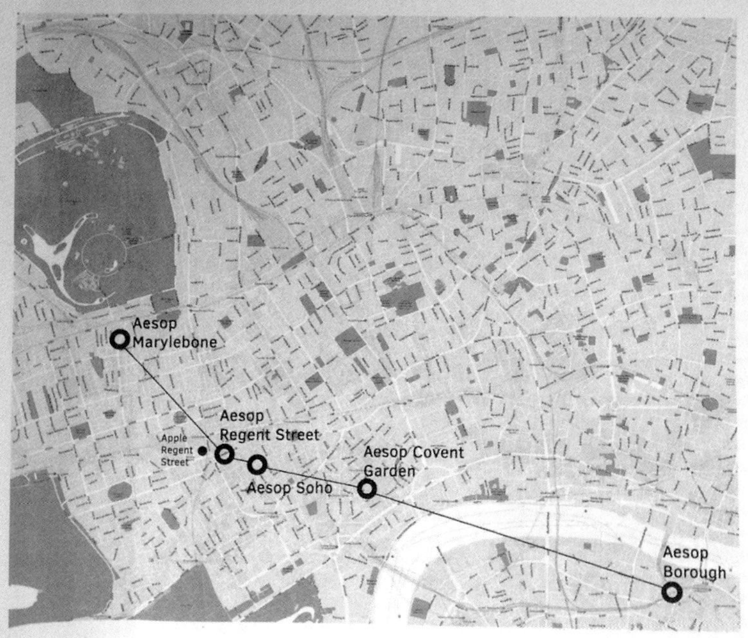

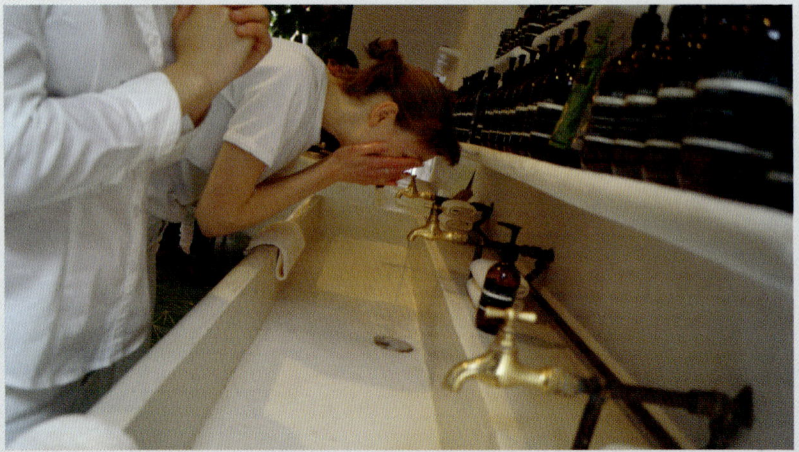

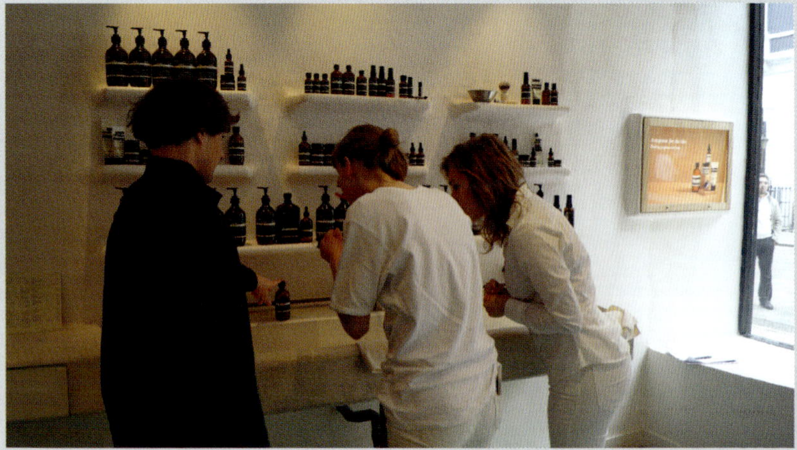

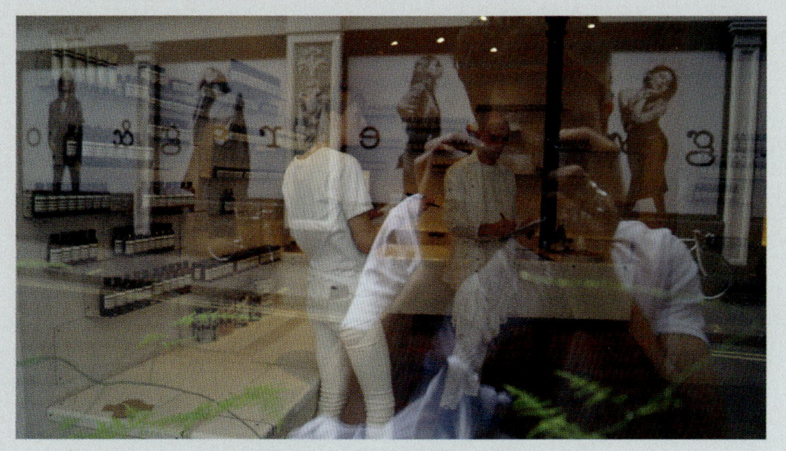

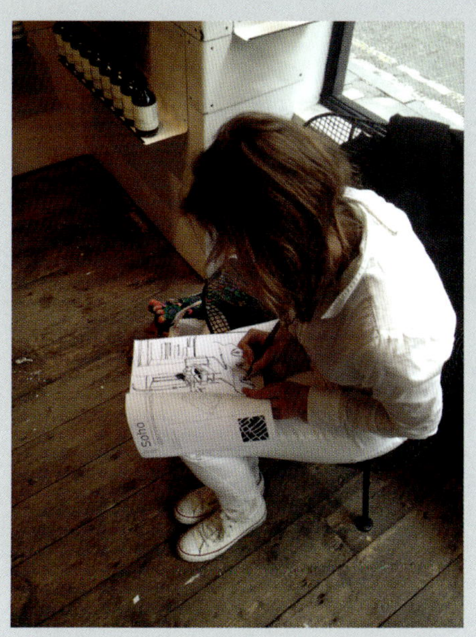
Soho

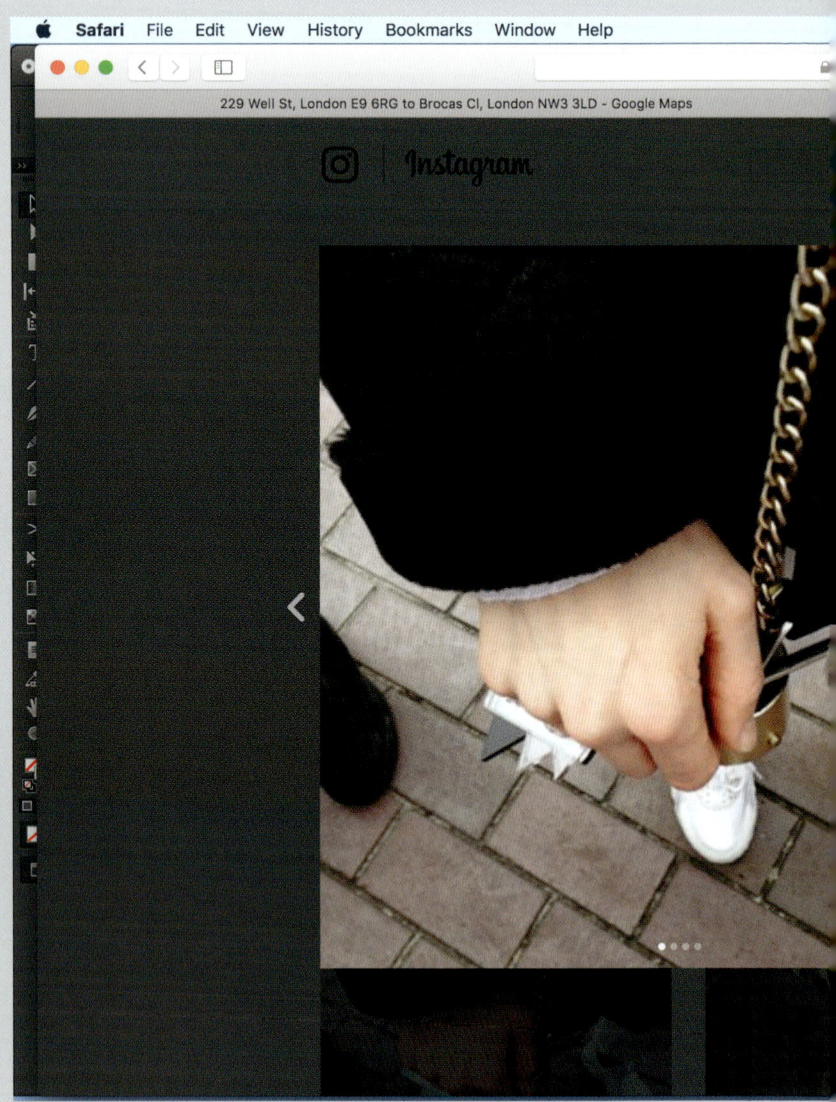
Safari
File
Edit
View
History
Bookmarks
Window
Help
229 Well St, London E9 6RG to Brocas Cl, London NW3 3LD - Google Maps
Instagram

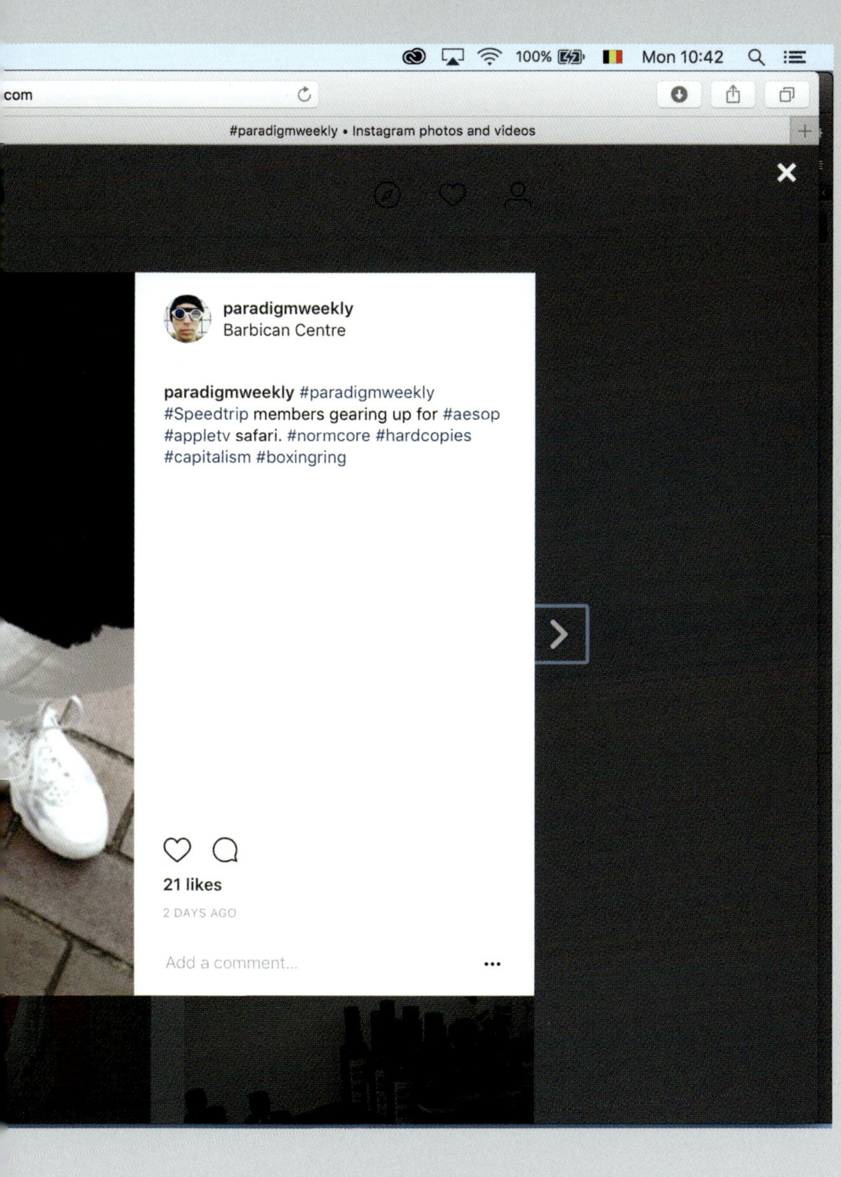
100% Mon 10:42
com
#paradigmweekly • Instagram photos and videos
paradigmweekly
Barbican Centre
paradigmweekly #paradigmweekly #Speedtrip members gearing up for #aesop #appletv safari. #normcore #hardcopies #capitalism #boxingring
21 likes
2 DAYS AGO
Add a comment...

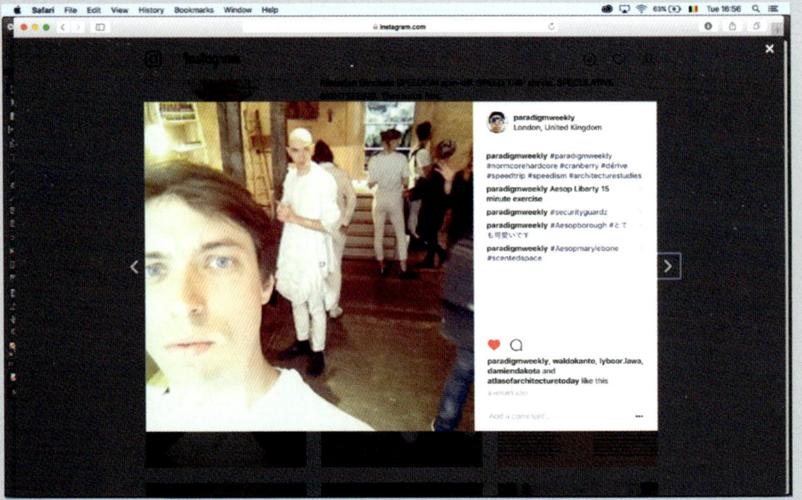

Safari File Edit View History Bookmarks Window Help

Tue 16:56

instagram.com

paradigmweekly
London, United Kingdom

paradigmweekly #paradigmweekly #normcorehardcore #cranberry #dérive #speedtrip #speedism #architecturestudies

paradigmweekly Aesop Liberty 15 minute exercise

paradigmweekly #securityguardz

paradigmweekly #Aesopborough #とても可愛いです

paradigmweekly #Aesopmarylebone #scentedspace

paradigmweekly, waldokanto, lyboor.lawa, damiendakota and atlasofarchitecturetoday like this

Add a comment...

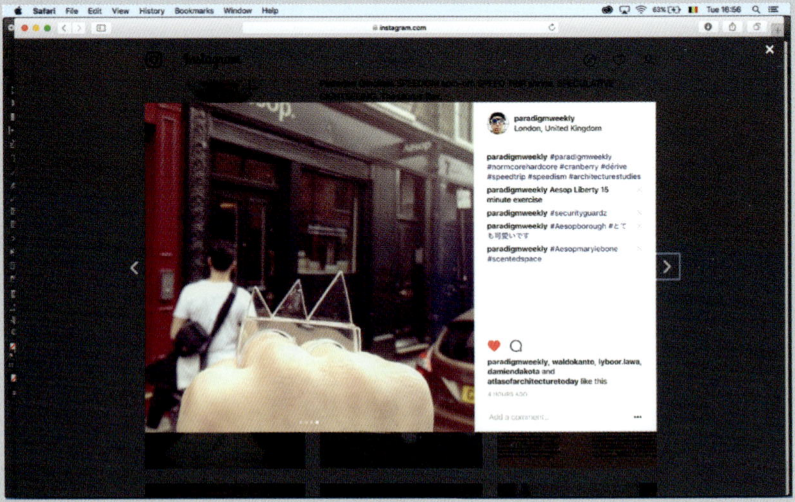

Safari File Edit View History Bookmarks Window Help

Tue 16:56

instagram.com

paradigmweekly
London, United Kingdom

paradigmweekly #paradigmweekly #normcorehardcore #cranberry #dérive #speedtrip #speedism #architecturestudies

paradigmweekly Aesop Liberty 15 minute exercise

paradigmweekly #securityguardz

paradigmweekly #Aesopborough #とても可愛いです

paradigmweekly #Aesopmarylebone #scentedspace

paradigmweekly, waldokanto, lyboor.lawa, damiendakota and atlasofarchitecturetoday like this

Add a comment...

APPLE STORES

I BRENT CROSS
II WHITE CITY

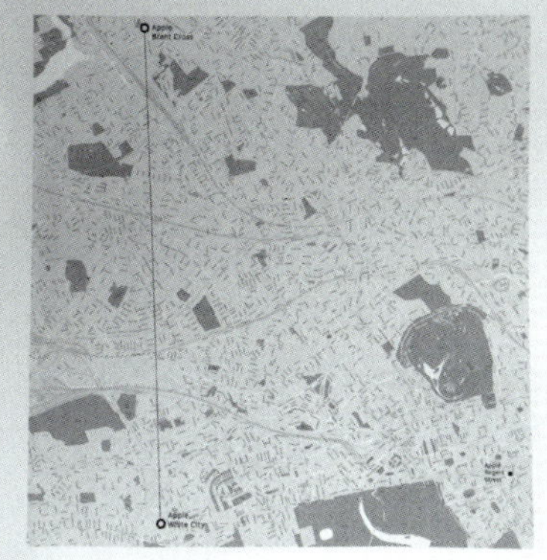

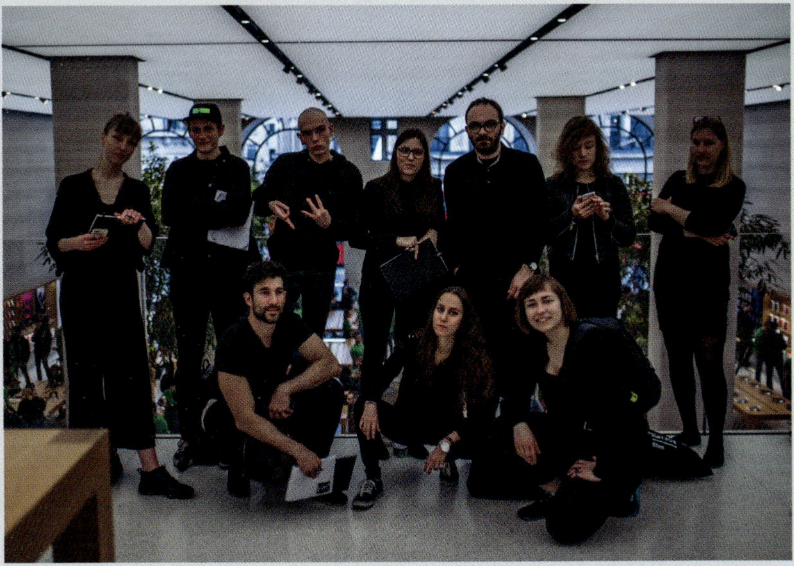

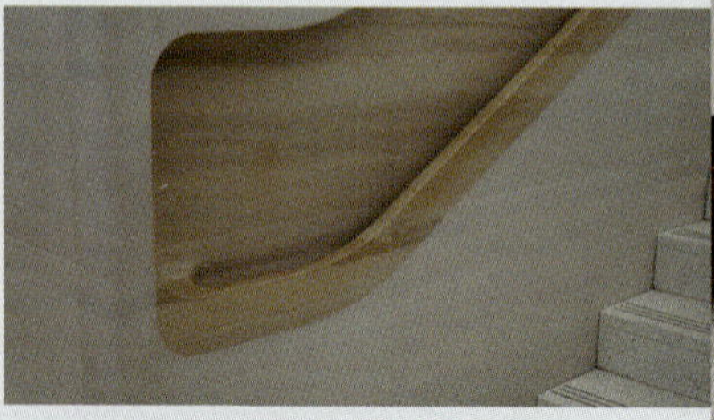

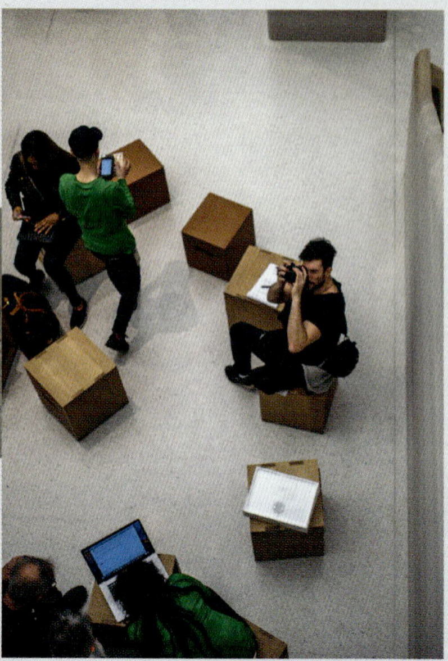

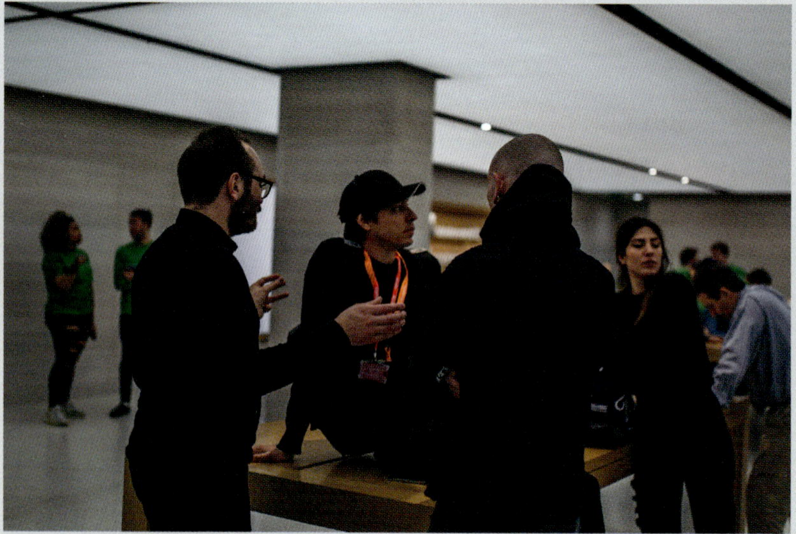

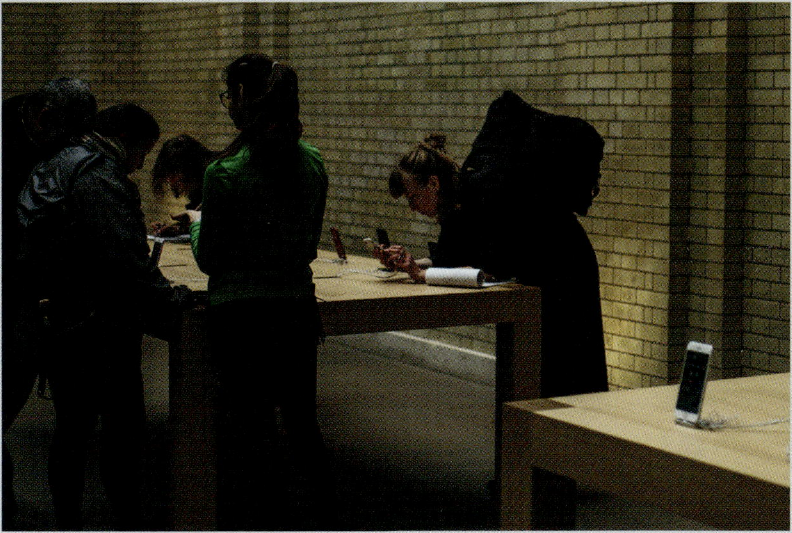

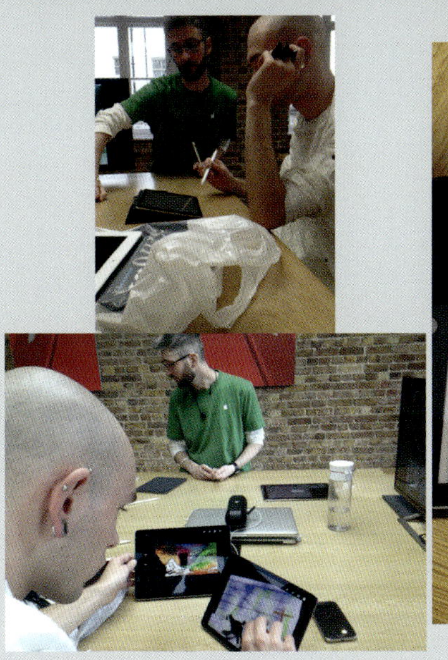

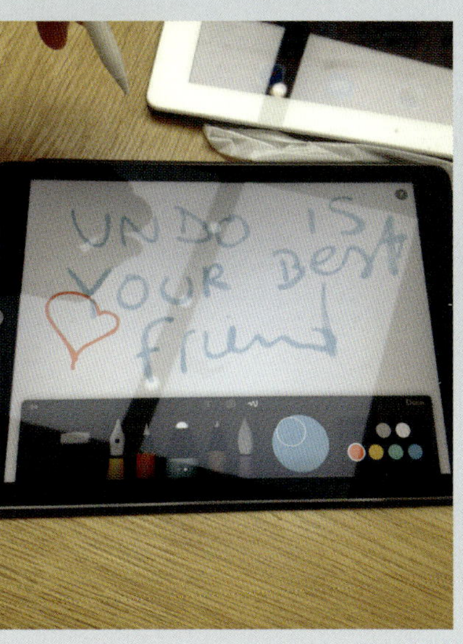
UNDO IS
YOUR BEST
friend

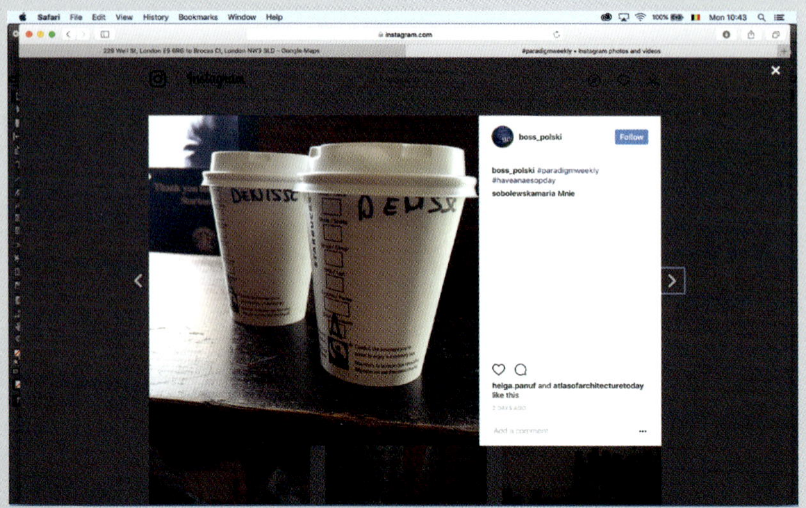
Safari File Edit View History Bookmarks Window Help
Mon 10:43
instagram.com
#paradigmweekly • Instagram photos and videos
boss_polski
Follow
boss_polski #paradigmweekly
#haveanaesopday
sobolewskamaria Mnie
helga.panuf and atlasofarchitecturetoday
like this

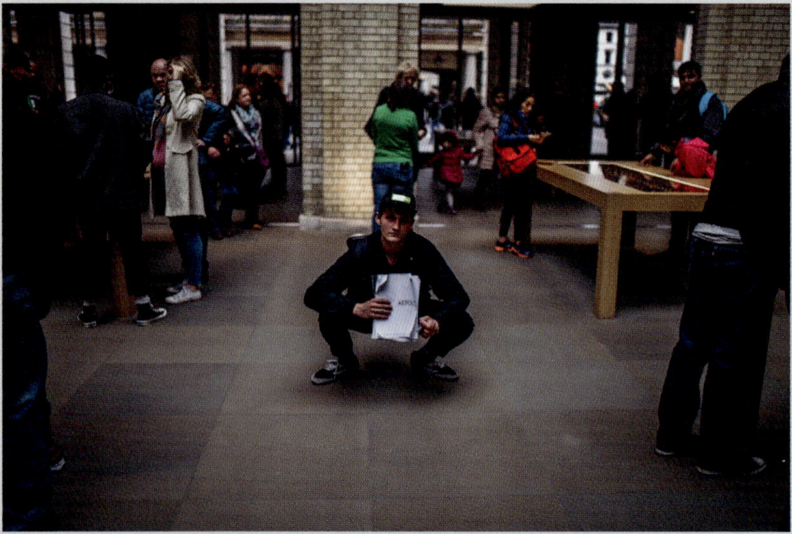

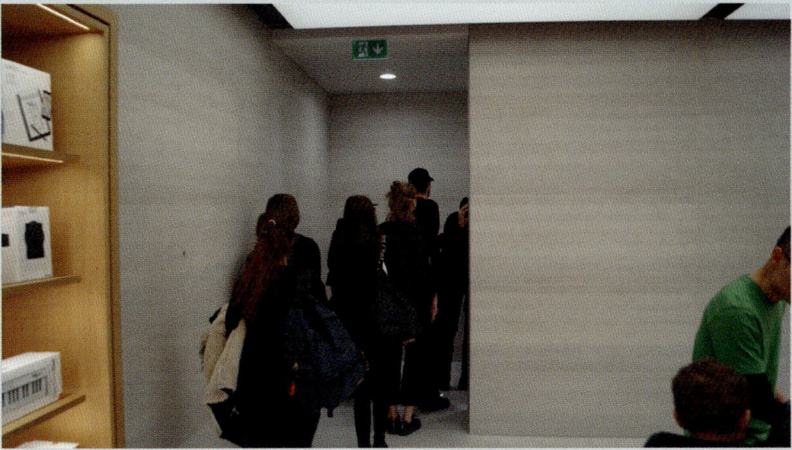

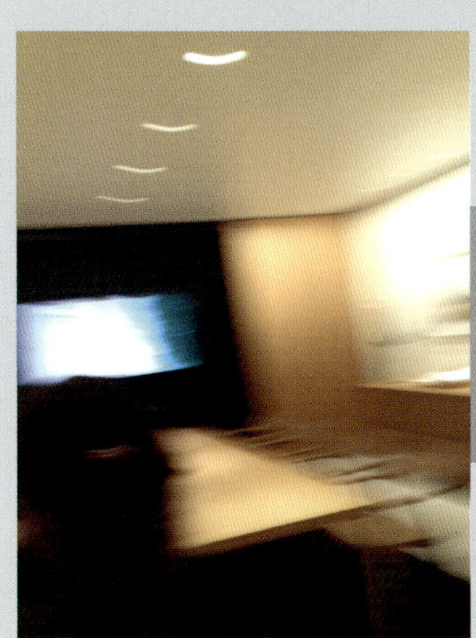

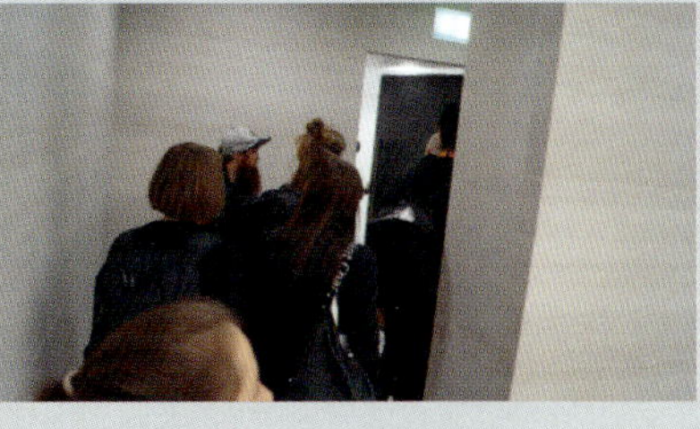

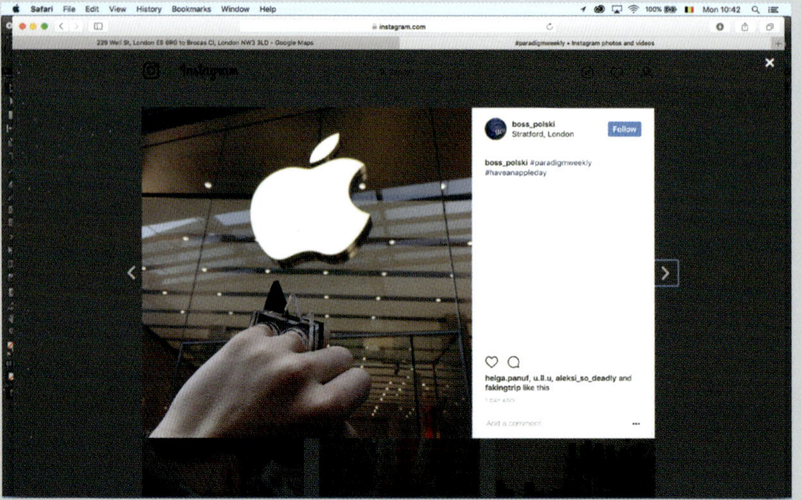
Safari File Edit View History Bookmarks Window Help
Mon 10:42
instagram.com
#paradigmweekly • Instagram photos and videos
boss_polski
Stratford, London
Follow
boss_polski #paradigmweekly
#haveanappleday
helga.panuf, u.ll.u, aleksi_so_deadly and
fakingtrip like this

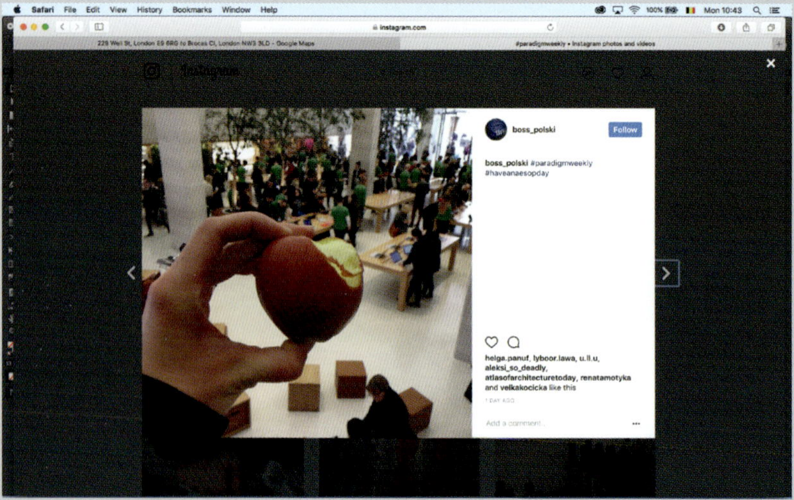
Safari File Edit View History Bookmarks Window Help
Mon 10:43
instagram.com
#paradigmweekly • Instagram photos and videos
boss_polski
Follow
boss_polski #paradigmweekly
#haveanaesopday
helga.panuf, lyboor.lawa, u.ll.u,
aleksi_so_deadly,
atlasofarchitecturetoday, renatamotyka
and velkakocicka like this

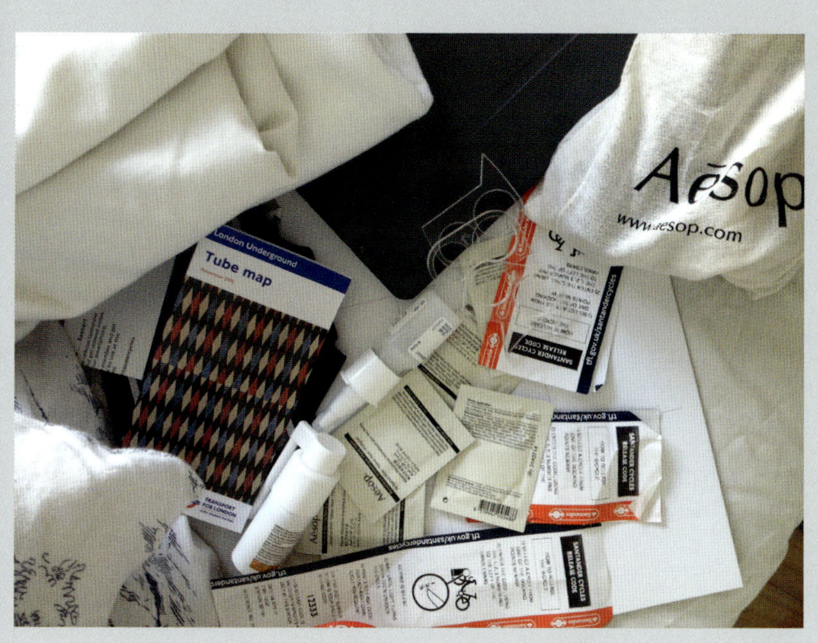
London Underground
Tube map
Aēsop
tfl.gov.uk/santandercycles

SOUVENIRS

(page)

319 SPEEDISM, TRUMP L'OEIL, 2016.

320 Blue and red workers' housing rooftops serve as the flat pedestal for Shanghai's high-rise personalities.

321 SPEEDISM, TWO-FACED MF EASY RIDE, 2015, film still.

323 What to wear at a theoretical construction site? Gameplay uniform = mask = flexibility.

325 Pieterjan Ginckels, SOLAR SAFARI, 2017.

330-331
SPEEDISM, Doomdough Royale, 2009.

333 Drawings mapping the locations of Denise Scott Brown and Pieterjan Ginckels just beyond the Las Vegas built fabric, 2017.

334 Drive-by underground sightseeing, Brussels Parking Garage Derive, 2014

335 Map and listings of the Rietveld Safari, illustrating the concentration of RRR projects, all looking similar, connected by a TOTP list of 20th Century architect's names.

337 The specs are distinct, but what it does to a group of convinced wearers is essential. Shared Gaze Empowerment! SPEEDISM on Hans Hollein, 2018

343 Centerpiece of Beijing's hotel and golf resort Chateau Laffitte (sic) is this staircase. Unconvincingly and sparingly furnished, a knock on the wall confirms our sheetrock suspicions.

A busload of Chinese enthusiasts participates in SPEEDISM's mania. Pink spectacles (made in China) unify hosts, guests, and a bus driver.

344 Mega open air sculpture factory caters to the international art scene's on-demand fantasies. Based off a sketch or a rendering, pieces are hand-fabricated and answer to a matrix of time, weight, and cost requirements.

345-347
More-or-less-pirated books cover a 57.000 square

meter sales area at the biggest bookstore in China. The Beijing International Book Mall is housed in a gigantic figure 8-shaped building. Amongst the books, Neville Mars, one of the trip's hosts, even discovered his own book (The Chinese Dream, A Society under Construction; DCF, Neville Mars, Adrian Hornsby; 010 Publishers) in a slightly better execution than the authorized edition.

348 Who builds the physical after-images of glossy rendered visions of this urban China? Where do the construction workers sleep, when not building? Invisible ghost-workers building ghost-towns.

350 How far is Château Lafite Rothschild from Saint Petersburg's Kazan cathedral? Why not stick 'em together?

356 Amoeba, largest collection of oldest music storage formats.

357 Probably the fastest building on the West Coast! Although SOM-designed, this inverted Beaubourg could easily be missed on an archi-tour.

358 Pre-car era Angelenos made use of stepped roads to cross Echo Park's hills. The Baxter stairway is probably the single tallest in the city and covers a vertical distance of 180 feet. Once pedestrian necessity, now workout / hangout. Vertical archaeology by performance.

359-360

Earnestness + consciousness. You see that I see?

362-363

Los Angeles Speed Derive starts at the Venice Canals. A biologist who joined the trip showed us around, and freaked on the real fiction's less perceptible mechanics: still water, no mosquitoes?

Mark Mack lives in one Californian house, but he wasn't home.

364 Is this a high school playground oil derrick, wrapped in flowery duvets? Performance archaeology by verticality.

That old Sears department store crowned

by first-gen neons, second-gen neons, 2000-and-late-gen neons.

The lunch at Chipotle fast food where once surfaced the slow tunnel of a fast Interstate Bank robbery.

366 Haiku ≠ Vine?

368-369

Finding the spot: where was a thrilled Denise Scott Brown photographed in the Las Vegas desert, just outside the urban fabric? For some, the hands-on-the-hips pose brings more effect than reading the actual book. For others, being stuck in geolocation technology, there are no hands free to rest on the hips.

370 Luxor vs Excalibur, Las Vegas, 2014.

Real magic: the décor that is the interior world of Las Vegas hotels and casinos reveals itself as a true construction most strikingly on the transition between spheres. These spheres are thematic (from knights to centurions to pyramids), but also technological and technical; network cables resurface, walkways halt at The Excalibur's subterranean entrance, service telephones adorn faux rocky columns.

371 The Saddest Oldenburg in The World, Las Vegas, 2014.

372-373

Unlearning From Las Vegas, New York-New York, Las Vegas, 2014. In Las Vegas, in New York-New York, one finds time to nostalgically read the venture into a proto-Vegas in the architectural sense: a report on a weird, alien, off-culture phenomenon that once fallen into the architectural sphere stood as an alternative island of subversion, a theme park of things to come maybe? Lying in the jacuzzi in 2014, letting the sweat wash off from a trip to the 'end' of Vegas, it's only the bubbling noise and a PBR that shake off the taints of time.

374-375

Looking For The Vegas Desert, Las Vegas, 2014. Expanding experience: finding the DSB photograph location proved difficult. At best, a derelict parking lot subsumed by the ever expanding urban fabric of Las Vegas – one of the fastest growing cities in the

USA – could be pinned as the former desert spot.

So we set out to drive towards the desert, out out out on the freeway, and while in the rearview mirror we saw all the spectacular fortresses, sphinxes and temples shrink, we eventually arrived at a turn in the road where suburban expansion froze; we parked the car near the last houses, a school and Wet 'n' Wild Las Vegas. This terrain seems characteristic of Las Vegas' expansion: the city now halts where the desert rises into hilly territory. Conveniently, the 'new spot' provided us a bit of elevation for a better perspective to look back on the fabric we traversed.

376 Trump In Vegas, Las Vegas, 2014. This building, though, embodies both the old and the new Vegas: it's simultaneously 100% original and 100% fake. A happy consensus flagship for architecture.

Gehry In Vegas, Las Vegas, 2014. At first on drive-by architecture safari, you can't help but believe this must be a fake, too! Better than the original, although placed somewhat out of the buzz of the strip, as if The Gehry is already on its way out.

378-379

Mapping (by) The Hips, 2017.

380-381

Would you like to join the Brussels Parking Garage Derive? Great! Send an email to futurefictions@z33.be, with the mention of 'Brussels Parking Dérive' in the subject line. Please also mention name, contact information (telephone, address, email), profession/training. Please also respond briefly to the following questions: Why are you interested in participating? Which songs are in your playlist for the SPEED TRIP? Which parking garage in Brussels would you like to visit? Will you drive your own car? How would you like to document the trip (video, photo – smartphone / (semi) professional, drawings, audio ...)?

388 Map and listings of the Rietveld Safari, illustrating the concentration of RRR projects, all looking similar, connected by a TOTP list of 20th Century architect's names.

389 Paradigm Weekly rules for the Rietveld Safari included: all black and/or camo outfits; laser-cut Corbu vs Ibiza trash specs, spray-painted black and rolled in the sand; soundtrack through phone speakers The Grey Album, Danger Mouse.

396 A special order of sheet plastic delivered for Oscar Niemeyer. Vaagard & Ray Eames. A live Facebook conversation with arch school colleagues.

399 We burned 4 exclusive and original 90's DJ sets for our bus driver! Gin+Gini stock for Camelback dispersion. Selfie stick's introduction to Speed Trips.

410 We meet inside the Barbican center for a little antidote to what's to come: a full day of Aesop store visits.

412-420

Rings not specs. All white. Face wash over authentic sinks-with-stories. 45 minute design briefs serve as deep probes.

421-424

Apple time: all black. Curves international. The Green Apple Crew vs the Black Denises!

425 Apple Store Regent Street. The Sir Jonathan Ive and Foster + Partners-designed store features an exclusive board room. When a SPEED TRIPPER set off the emergency exit alarm, another one quickly snapped some photos.

427 "You really should've been there!" < 3 FOMO

FOOD

FOOD PAIRING (2018) **PIETERJAN GINCKELS**
FOR **NO BULL** PREMIUM TAURINE

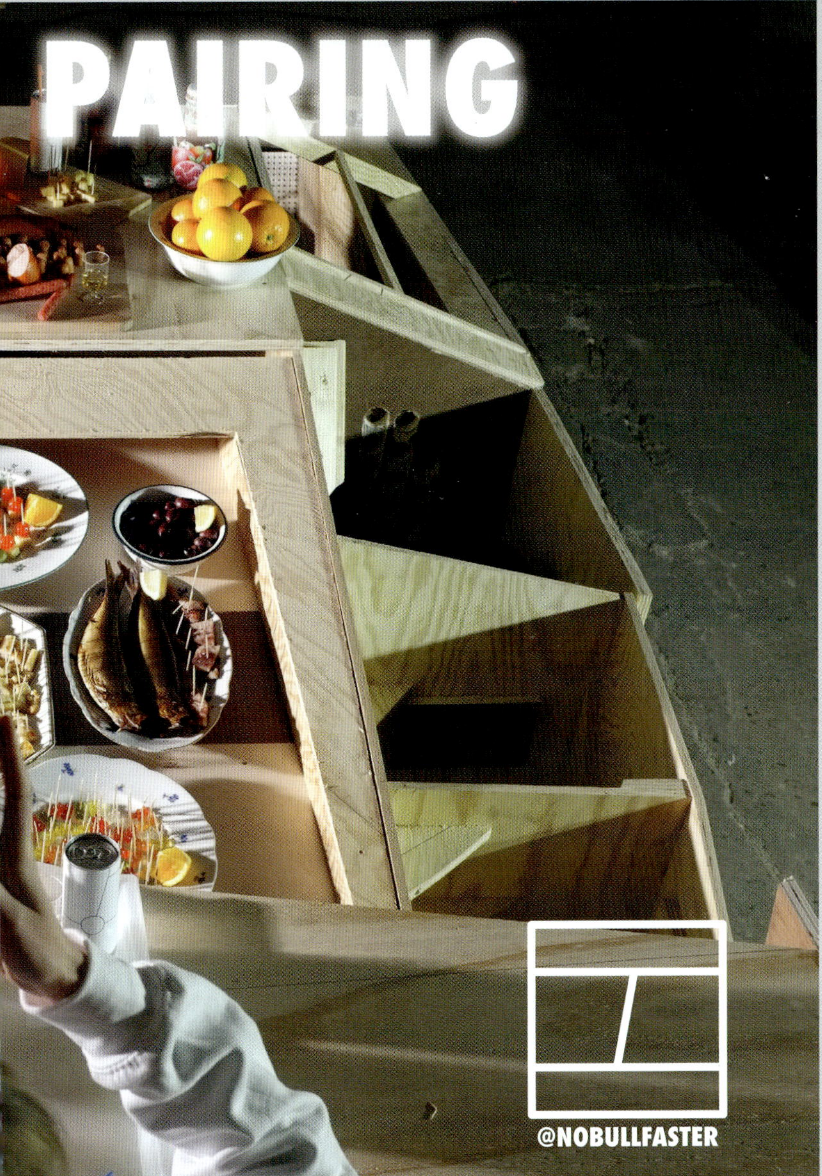
PAIRING
@NOBULLFASTER

APE#101
Pieterjan Ginckels
SOLAR SAFARI

ISBN 9789490800772
www.artpapereditions.org
www.pieterjanginckels.be

First edition of 300 copies
March 2018

Graphic design:
6'56" (Jurgen Maelfeyt,
Jonas Temmerman)

Printing: KOPA, Vilnius
(Lithuania)

International distribution:
ideabooks.nl

Distribution Belgium:
exhibitionsinternational.org

SOLAR SAFARI was
collected and engineered
by Pieterjan Ginckels with
Waldo De Roo, Stan D'Haene,
Tine Holvoet, Maria Muskova
and Elena Pankova.

Part of this artist book is
the result of the research
project 'Radical Saturation'
initiated by Pieterjan
Ginckels at KU Leuven,
Department of Architecture,
Sint-Lucas Campus.

With the support of

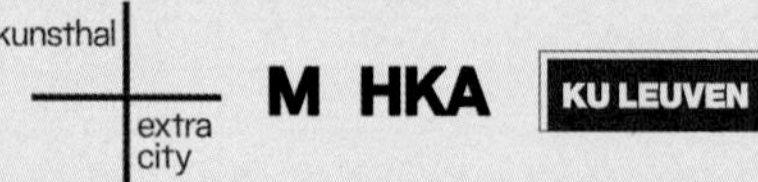